the Unofficial Guide® to New York City

1st Edition

the Unofficial Guide® to New York City

1st Edition

Eve Zibart and
Bob Sehlinger
with Jim Leff

Macmillan • USA

This book is for my brother Michael, the best companion.

—E. Z.

Every effort has been made to ensure the accuracy of information throughout this book. Bear in mind, however, that prices, schedules, etc., are constantly changing. Readers should always verify information before making final plans.

Macmillan Travel
A Simon & Schuster Macmillan Company
1633 Broadway
New York, New York 10019-6785

Produced by Menasha Ridge Press
Design by Barbara E. Williams

MACMILLAN is a registered trademark of Macmillan, Inc.
UNOFFICIAL GUIDE is a registered trademark of Simon & Schuster, Inc.

ISBN 0-02-862250-2

ISSN 1096-5203

Manufactured in the United States of America

10 9 8 7 6 5 4 3 2 1

First edition

ABOUT OUR
AUTHORS AND CONTRIBUTORS

Eve **Zibart** has written more about dining and entertainment than most people experience in a lifetime. In her first job as a temporary night city editor for the *Washington Post,* Eve quickly exhibited prowess in her prose coupled with an aptitude for grammar and an extensive vocabulary. She rapidly moved through the ranks of the *Post* as a "Weekend" assistant editor, a "Maryland" columnist, the "TV" editor, and a "Style" feature writer. Currently, Eve is the restaurant columnist and resident nightlife writer for the *Washington Post's* "Weekend" section. Known to friends and fans as "Dr. Nightlife," Eve has enough experience and knowledge to advise the Joint Chiefs of Staff on national trends.

In addition to her responsibilities at the *Post,* Eve is a regular contributor to USAir inflight and Four Seasons magazines and has written for *Cosmopolitan, Book Page,* and *Playboy.* Given an amazing ability to turn 24 hours into 30, Eve has found time to author several books, including *The Unofficial Guide to Ethnic Cuisine and Dining in America, The Eclectic Gourmet Guide to Washington, D.C., The Unofficial Guide to Branson, Missouri, The Unofficial Guide to New Orleans,* and *The Unofficial Disney Companion: The Inside Story of Walt Disney World and the Man Behind the Mouse.*

Bob **Sehlinger** is the creator and executive publisher of the *Unofficial Guide* series. He has authored over 20 books on travel and outdoor recreation.

Lea **Lane** (Accommodations contributor) is a freelance writer specializing in travel, food, personality, and lifestyle articles. She currently contributes to and edits guidebooks (including *Fodor's Greece '97, Birnbaum's USA,* and Zagat's restaurant and hotel guides) and is a contributing editor to Reed Travel Group's Star Service hotel guide. She writes freelance articles for publications including the *New York Times,* the *Miami Herald, Washingtonian, Caribbean Travel & Life, Travel Agent, Hotel and Motel Management,* and *Crain's New York Business* and for the Prodigy interactive computer service. She is a credited contributor to three major books on cruises and resorts and is coauthor of *The World's Most Exciting Cruises* (Hippocrene, 1994).

Sukey Howard (Dining contributor) is a longtime observer of the New York culinary scene. She writes "The Spoken Word," a monthly column surveying audio books and has commented on the audio book scene regularly for CNN. As Sybil Pratt (her nom de cuisine) she is the cookbook reviewer for *BookPage*.

Jim Leff (Dining and Nightlife contributor), dubbed "the godfather of the New York underground food scene" by author Anya Von Bremzen, has written about New York City restaurants and nightlife for *Newsday, New York Press, Time Out NY, Brooklyn Bridge,* and *Down the Hatch.* According to the *New York Times,* Leff is "unsurpassed in discovering unusual restaurants in every corner of the city," and his Chowhound Web site (www.chowhound.com) is a gathering place for ardent eaters and "exactly what you want to see on the Web." Look for his *Eclectic Gourmet Guide to Greater New York City,* to be published in late 1998.

CONTENTS

List of Illustrations

ACKNOWLEDGMENTS

Many thanks to Sukey Howard, Lea Lane, and Jim Leff for their time, taste, and sometimes tableside companionship. Jim Leff would like to thank Abigail Adams (the contemporary one, not the museum one), Jack Thomas, and Rich Duncan.

As always, thanks to the folks at Menasha Ridge, particularly Molly, Clay, Holly, Grace, and Caroline.

Many thanks to Christi Stanforth, Sarah Nawrocki, Suzanne Fisher, and Nicki Florence, the people who read about our vacations but never have the chance to take one.

Finally, this book is for my brother Michael, the best companion.

—*Eve Zibart*

"New York, New York, It's a Helluva Town ..."

If you're ever a passenger in a taxicab in New York, look at the city map usually taped to the back of the driver's seat. Chances are, it will show only the tourist territories, cutting Manhattan off partway up Central Park, only hinting at Brooklyn, and likely dispensing with the Bronx, Long Island, and Staten Island altogether. So do most guidebooks about New York. They get you from the Staten Island Ferry (the departure point, at least) on the Battery to the Metropolitan Museum of Art at 82nd Street. Some less hidebound books mention Harlem and a few riverside attractions. But for the most part, it's "East Side, West Side" rather than "all around the town."

Worse, tour guides rarely draw connections, convey waves of progress, or point up ironies of development. In a city literally embraced by the spirits of multiculturalism—with the Statue of Liberty, that monumental icon of hope for immigrants, at one end, and the shrine of Mother Cabrini, their patron saint, at the other—most visitors peer through the most homogeneous of filters, the endless barrage of Big Apple boosterism and crime or inflation news trotted out every day. Watch enough TV and you'd think the whole city was painted with red ink, white ticker tape, and blue uniforms.

What a waste. New York City is one of the most original, elaborate, eccentric, and irresistible creatures—it clearly has a life of its own—you will ever encounter. And we want you to encounter it all, in not just three but four dimensions: underground, above the cloud line, and most definitely at street level, as well as seeing its past, its present, and its future. And for that, we need your cooperation. We need you to be open to the city's charm. And we need you to turn off that damn television.

We often speak of visiting a new place as "seeing" it. "See Rock City," read those famous barns. "Join the Navy and see the world." But the strange thing about sight-seeing is, people get too absorbed in the "sights" and forget about the "seeing." It may sound odd for an author to say, but having your nose buried in a book, even this book, is not the way to travel. And it certainly isn't the way to go looking for exactly that intersection or department store or luxury hotel you always see in the cop shows.

To experience New York fully, you need to give it the full attention of your eyes and your heart. This city is a *romance:* You need to respond to it, not just react to it. Start with our book, but don't stick to it. Admire the Empire State Building, but don't spend your whole day there. Join the crowds on the street, grab a coffee, see a show. Otherwise, you might just as well have stayed home.

Many tour books will tell you that New York is not for the faint-hearted; we would say that it is not for the unimaginative. Part of its fascination is its complexity: all the accents, the rhythms, the smells. For so famous a melting pot, New York has yet to produce a truly creole society; minorities here are not so much assimilated as incorporated. And that means food, gifts, clothes, and "roots" of a hundred cultures. It's a permanent World's Fair, free for the strolling. Diversity isn't just a souvenir of Ellis Island or dim sum in Chinatown; it's daily life, the greatest attraction of them all.

New York is also the great silent witness to American culture. There is not a single block in the city, whether residential, renovated, commercial, or even crumbling, that does not speak of its restless and often reckless history: expansionist, extravagant, fickle, fashionable. All you have to do is *look.* Broadway or off-Broadway, here all the world truly is a stage.

And a stage set: If there had not been such a thing as a skyline, New York would have had to invent it. As it is, New York reconceived the horizon beyond the dreams of even the greatest medieval builders. Skyscrapers are the true cathedrals of Manhattan's private religion—not that there aren't exquisite churches and temples galore. You can almost relive the evolution of the city by glancing around at the architecture, from the eighteenth-century purity of St. Paul's Chapel to the nineteenth-century neoclassicism of Federal Hall, the French Renaissance of Jewish Museum, and the Gothic Revival of St. Patrick's; from the Beaux Arts Grand Central Terminal (with staircases copied from the Paris Opera) and the art deco Chrysler Building to the Wright-stuff Guggenheim and the Bauhaus Seagram Building.

Even "ordinary" office buildings have extraordinary features: friezes, carvings, gilding, capitals, cornice pieces, decorative sills, all the showy elements of European palaces, only bigger and brasher and designed to make aristocrats out of merchants. For these are the great palaces of trade, tributes to the variety and vitality of American industry. New York was one of the first cities to abandon class distinction, at least as far as the purveyors were concerned, between the carriage trade and the merchant class, between the custom-tailored and the store-fitted. It was the natural preserve of the department store, with its abundance of luxuries (which gradually became, by long acquaintance and by the nature of human ambition, necessities), and it fostered the democratization of service.

On the other hand, there is far more "outdoors" to New York than you may have realized. Every borough has a large public park—and no, Central Park is not nearly the largest—and four have botanical gardens. There are five zoos and an aquarium, a wildlife refuge, and beaches and marina islands.

So this book is about seeing New York. Not just Midtown Manhattan, but the whole city. It's about shopping and art-gazing and theatergoing, of course, but mostly it's about looking past the sales pitches to the piers, beyond the boutiques to the brownstones, outside Times Square to Washington Square. It's about relaxing in the green spaces as well as the grand hotels, about going off-Broadway as far as Brooklyn and seeing as far back as its founding. If you want a top ten list of tourist attractions, you can find them on any corner and any souvenir stand; but it you want to know ten lovely things to do for yourself, ten splendors to share with your children, or ten places where beauty really is truth, read on.

About This Guide

■ **How Come "Unofficial"?** ■

Most guides to New York tout the well-known sights, promote the local restaurants and hotels indiscriminately, and leave out a lot of good stuff. This one is different.

Instead of pandering to the tourist industry, we'll tell you if the food is bad at a well-known restaurant, we'll complain loudly about high prices, and we'll guide you away from the crowds and traffic for a break now and then.

Visiting New York requires wily strategies not unlike those used in the sacking of Troy. We've sent in a team of evaluators who toured each site, ate in the city's best restaurants, performed critical evaluations of its hotels, and visited New York's wide variety of nightclubs. If a museum is boring, or standing in line for two hours to view a famous attraction is a waste of time, we say so—and, in the process, hopefully we will make your visit more fun, efficient, and economical.

■ **Creating a Guidebook** ■

We got into the guidebook business because we were unhappy with the way travel guides make the reader work to get any usable information. Wouldn't it be nice, we thought, if we were to make guides that are easy to use?

Most guidebooks are compilations of lists. This is true regardless of whether the information is presented in list form or artfully distributed through pages of prose. There is insufficient detail in a list, and prose can present tedious helpings of nonessential or marginally useful information. Not enough wheat, so to speak, for nourishment in one instance, and too much chaff in the other. Either way, these types of guides provide little more than departure points from which readers initiate their own quests.

Many guides are readable and well researched, but they tend to be difficult to use. To select a hotel, for example, a reader must study several pages of descriptions with only the boldface hotel names breaking up large blocks of text. Because each description essentially deals with the same variables, it is difficult to recall what was said concerning a particular hotel. Readers generally must work through all the write-ups before beginning to narrow their choices. The presentation of restaurants, nightclubs, and attractions is similar except that even more reading is usually required. To use such a guide is to undertake an exhaustive research process that requires examining nearly as many options and possibilities as starting from scratch. Recommendations, if any, lack depth and conviction. These guides compound rather than solve problems by failing to narrow travelers' choices down to a thoughtfully considered, well-distilled, and manageable few.

■ How Unofficial Guides Are Different ■

Readers care about the authors' opinions. The authors, after all, are supposed to know what they are talking about. This, coupled with the fact that the traveler wants quick answers (as opposed to endless alternatives), dictates that authors should be explicit, prescriptive, and above all, direct. The authors of the *Unofficial Guide* try to do just that. They spell out alternatives and recommend specific courses of action. They simplify complicated destinations and attractions and allow the traveler to feel in control in the most unfamiliar environments. The objective of the *Unofficial Guide* authors is not to give the most information or all of the information but to offer the most accessible, useful information.

An *Unofficial Guide* is a critical reference work; it focuses on a travel destination that appears to be especially complex. Our authors and research team are completely independent from the attractions, restaurants, and hotels we describe. The *Unofficial Guide to New York* is designed for individuals and families traveling for the fun of it, as well as for business travelers and conventioneers, especially those visiting the Big Apple for the first time. The guide is directed at value-conscious, consumer-oriented adults who seek a cost-effective, though not spartan, travel style.

■ Special Features ■

The *Unofficial Guide* offers the following special features:

- Friendly introductions to New York's most fascinating neighborhoods.
- "Best of" listings giving our well-qualified opinions on things ranging from raw oysters to blackened snapper and four-star hotels to 12-story views.

- Listings that are keyed to your interests, so you can pick and choose.
- Advice to sight-seers on how to avoid the worst of the crowds; advice to business travelers on how to avoid traffic and excessive costs.
- Recommendations for lesser-known sights that are away from Times Square but are no less worthwhile.
- A zone system and maps to make it easy to find places you want to go to and avoid places you don't.
- Expert advice on avoiding New York's notorious street crime.
- A hotel chart that helps you narrow down your choices fast, according to your needs.
- Shorter listings that include only those restaurants, clubs, and hotels we think are worth considering.
- A table of contents and detailed index to help you find things fast.
- Insider advice on best times of day (or night) to go places.

What you won't get:

- Long, useless lists where everything looks the same.
- Information that gets you to your destination at the worst possible time.
- Information without advice on how to use it.

■ How This Guide Was Researched and Written ■

Although many guidebooks have been written about New York, very few have been evaluative. Some guides come close to regurgitating the hotels' and tourist offices' own promotional material. In preparing this work, we took nothing for granted. Each hotel, restaurant, shop, and attraction was visited by a team of trained observers who conducted detailed evaluations and rated each according to formal criteria. Team members conducted interviews with tourists of all ages to determine what they enjoyed most and least during their New York visit.

While our observers are independent and impartial, they did not claim to have special expertise. Like you, they visited New York as tourists or business travelers, noting their satisfaction or dissatisfaction.

The primary difference between the average tourist and the trained evaluator is the evaluator's skills in organization, preparation, and observation. The trained evaluator is responsible for much more than simply observing and cataloging. Observer teams use detailed checklists to analyze hotel rooms, restaurants, nightclubs, and attractions. Finally, evaluator ratings and observations are integrated with tourist reactions and the opinions of patrons for a comprehensive quality profile of each feature and service.

In compiling this guide, we recognize that a tourist's age, background, and interests will strongly influence his or her taste in New York's wide array of attractions and will account for a preference for one sight or museum over another. Our sole objective is to provide the reader with sufficient description, critical evaluation, and pertinent data to make knowledgeable decisions according to individual tastes.

■ Letters, Comments, and Questions from Readers ■

We expect to learn from our mistakes, as well as from the input of our readers, and to improve with each new book and edition. Many of those who use the *Unofficial Guides* write to us asking questions, making comments, or sharing their own discoveries or lessons learned in New York. We appreciate all such input, both positive and critical, and encourage our readers to continue writing. Readers' comments and observations will be frequently incorporated in revised editions of the *Unofficial Guide* and will contribute immeasurably to its improvement.

How to Write the Authors

Eve and Bob
The Unofficial Guide to New York City
P.O. Box 43059
Birmingham, AL 35243

When you write, be sure to put your return address on your letter as well as on the envelope—sometimes envelopes and letters get separated. And remember, our work takes us out of the office for long periods of time, so forgive us if our response is delayed.

Reader Survey

At the back of the guide you will find a short questionnaire that you can use to express opinions about your New York visit. Clip the questionnaire out along the dotted line and mail it to this address.

"Inside" New York for Outsiders

It's a funny thing about New York travel guides: Most of them tell you too much, and a few tell you too little. It's because it's such a complex city, so ornate and enveloping and layered with history and happenstance, that it's hard to stop acquiring good stories and passing them on. And it's an endless voyage: The more time you spend there, the more you realize you *don't* know.

But the fact is, statistics show that the majority of visitors to New York stay only three or four days—and even that average span frequently includes time spent in business meetings or conventions. How much can you squeeze into a long weekend? How much do you want to see? This city's attractions are among the most frequently photographed in the world, yet packaged tours often haul you about the city as relentlessly as if you didn't already know what the Statue of Liberty or the horse-drawn carriages of Central Park looked like. Some tour books either stint on shopping or endorse every dealer in town; some overlook any collection smaller than five stories tall. Some short-change any fine arts or theater productions outside Lincoln Center or Broadway, as if Midtown were the whole of Manhattan and restaurants were the sole form of nightlife. Some are too uncritical, some too "insider." Some have all the right stuff but are poorly organized; some are easy to read but oversimplified and boring.

Not only that, but most travel guide writers seem so attached to the modern stereotype of the city—the New York of loudmouthed cabbies, TV cop shows, the "if I can make it there" rat race, and Wall Street shark pool—that they don't express the great romance of this rich, inimitable, and electrifying metropolis. It's an asphalt wonder, sure, but there are cobblestones still to be seen; a world-famous skyline, yes, but an architectural creation, not just a higher-rent district. It's a magnet for immigration, but that also means it's a tapestry of ethnic revival. And in an era when the Statue of Liberty is animated for a deodorant commercial, it's too easy to forget what an icon it really is and has been to millions of Americans and would-be Americans. Okay, call us sentimentalists, but it's true: We do love

New York, just not the one the hype artists are selling.

So as hard, and heartbreaking, as it is to limit a book like this, we have, by doubling up whenever possible. The neighborhood profiles in Part 1, "Understanding the City," are partly geographical descriptions and partly historical romances: They're designed to help you get your bearings, but they include enough sights and stories to give you the community's true flavor. In Part 10, "Sight-Seeing and Tours," we've listed some attractions by type—family style, theatrical, genealogical and so on—to help you customize your visit. We've also listed some personal favorites that may not get as much publicity but that we think are first-rate. In Part 9, "Shopping in New York," we've combined best bets with do-it-yourself walking tours so you can see the sights and fill out your wish list at the same time. The zone maps are designed to help you with the logistics of arranging accommodations and sight-seeing; and particular museums and entertainments in each zone are explored in more detail and rated for interest by age group in Part 11, "New York's Attractions."

As for the hundreds of tourist attractions, well, we've tried to sort them into first-rate, special interest, and hype jobs, and we spend space on only the best. The truth is, even if you visit New York a dozen times, you won't be able to see even as much as we've described for you, and by then you'll have discovered your own favorite side to the city. But certainly we don't want you to waste any of that time, either. We take things easy, the way we think you will want to; but we don't forgive exploitation or boost unworthy distractions. If it isn't fun, if it isn't informative, if it isn't accurate, we don't want you to go. If there's a better alternative, we want you to know. We hope to keep the quality of your visit high and the irritation quotient low.

We've covered these attractions in these various ways, often overlapping, because we want to make sure you can pick out the ones you'd most enjoy. And for those who don't wish to do it yourself at all, we have listed a number of commercial and customized tours that you can take tailored to almost any interest, also in "Sight-Seeing Tips and Tours."

On the other hand, even granting that your time will be tight, we have included a list of opportunities to exercise or play. That's partly because we at the *Unofficial Guides* try to keep up with our workouts when we're on the road; and also because you may be visiting old friends, old teammates and tennis players. Beyond that, although you may not think you'll want to make time for a run or ride, experience has taught us that sight-seeing and shopping can be exhausting, make you stiff, make you long for a little outdoors—or at least a little calorie countering.

Please do remember that prices and hours change constantly; we have listed the most up-to-date information we can get, but it never hurts to double-check times in particular (if prices of attractions change, it is generally not by much). And remember, this is one of the busiest tourist towns in the world, drawing more than 30 million visitors a year, so make your reservations early and reconfirm at least once.

■ How Information Is Organized: By Subject ■ and by Geographic Zones

In order to give you fast access to information about the best of New York, we've organized material in several formats.

Hotels.   Since most people visiting New York stay in one hotel for the duration of their trip, we have summarized our coverage of hotels in charts, maps, ratings, and rankings that allow you to quickly focus your decision-making process. We do not go on, page after page, describing lobbies and rooms that, in the final analysis, sound much the same. Instead, we concentrate on the specific variables that differentiate one hotel from another: location, size, room quality, services, amenities, and cost.

Entertainment and Nightlife.   Visitors frequently try several different clubs or nightspots during their stay. Since clubs and nightspots, like restaurants, are usually selected spontaneously after arriving in New York, we believe detailed descriptions are warranted. The best nightspots and lounges in New York are profiled by category in Part 6, "Entertainment and Nightlife" (see pages 145–189).

Restaurants.   We provide plenty of detail when it comes to restaurants. Since you will probably eat a dozen or more restaurant meals during your stay, and since not even you can predict what you might be in the mood for on Saturday night, we provide detailed profiles of the best restaurants in and around New York.

Geographic Zones.   Once you've decided where you're going, getting there becomes the issue. To help you do that, we have divided the city into geographic zones:

Zone 1   Lower Manhattan, Wall Street, and the Battery

Zone 2   SoHo and TriBeCa

Zone 3   Chinatown, Little Italy, and the Lower East Side

Zone 4   Greenwich Village

Zone 5   The East Village

Zone 6   Chelsea

Zone 7   Gramercy Park and Madison Square

Zone 8   Midtown West and the Theater District

Zone 9   Midtown East

Zone 10   West Side

Zone 11   East Side

Zone 12   Upper West Side

Zone 13   Upper East Side

Zone 14   Columbia University and Harlem

Zone 15   The Heights

Zone 16   Brooklyn

Zone 17   Queens

Zone 18   The Bronx

Zone 19   Staten Island

All profiles of hotels, restaurants, and nightspots include zone numbers. If you are staying in Lower Manhattan, for example, and are interested in restaurants within walking distance, scanning the restaurant profiles for restaurants in Zone 1 will provide you with the best choices.

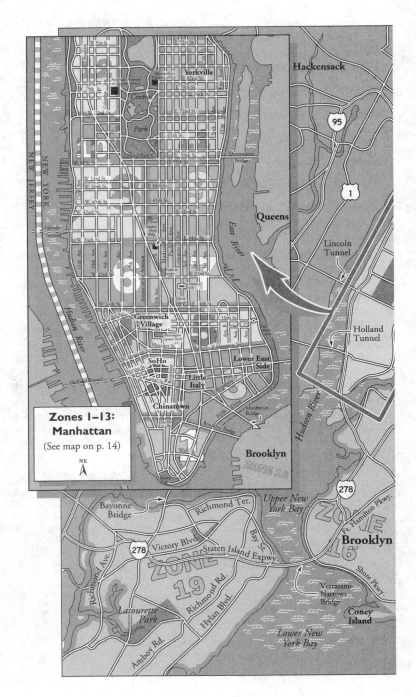

Zones 1–13:
Manhattan
(See map on p. 14)

NE

12

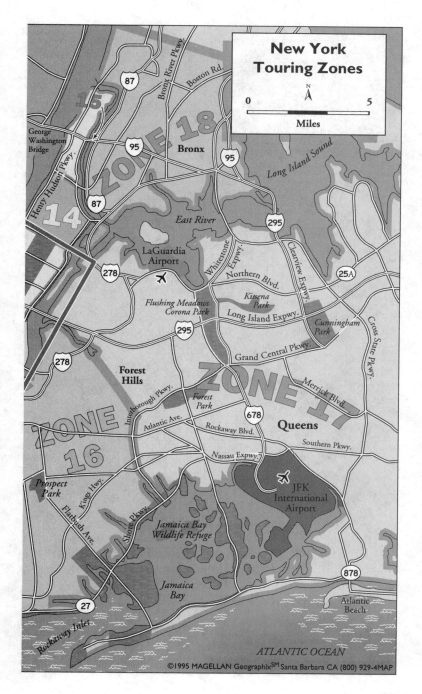

New York
Touring Zones

0   5
Miles

George
Washington
Bridge

Bronx

Long Island Sound

East River

LaGuardia
Airport

Whitestone Expwy.

Northern Blvd.

Clearview Expwy.

25A

Kissena
Park

Flushing Meadows
Corona Park

Long Island Expwy.

Cunningham
Park

Cross State Pkwy.

Grand Central Pkwy.

Forest
Hills

Merrick Blvd.

Interborough Pkwy.

Forest
Park

Atlantic Ave.

Rockaway Blvd.

Queens

Southern Pkwy.

Nassau Expwy.

JFK
International
Airport

Prospect
Park

Kings Hwy.

Shore Pkwy.

Flatbush Ave.

Jamaica Bay
Wildlife Refuge

Jamaica
Bay

Atlantic
Beach

Rockaway Inlet

ATLANTIC OCEAN

Henry Hudson Pkwy.

Bronx River Pkwy.

Boston Rd.

ZONE 15

ZONE 18

ZONE 14

ZONE 17

ZONE 16

©1995 MAGELLAN Geographix℠ Santa Barbara CA (800) 929-4MAP

87

95

95

87

278

295

278

295

678

27

878

13

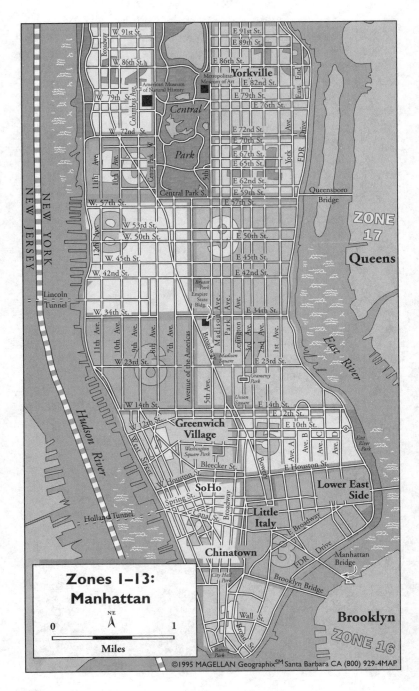

W. 91st St.
E 91st St.
E 89th St.
W. 86th St.
E 86th St.
Broadway
Yorkville
Metropolitan Museum of Art
E 82nd St.
American Museum of Natural History
Columbus Ave.
E 79th St.
W. 79th St.
E 76th St.
Central Park
E 72nd St.
W. 72nd St.
E 70th St.
11th Ave.
10th Ave.
Central Park W
E 67th St.
E 65th St.
York Ave.
FDR Drive
East End Ave.
E 62nd St.
Central Park S.
E 59th St.
Queensboro Bridge
W. 57th St.
E 57th St.
ZONE 17
12th Ave.
W. 53rd St.
W. 50th St.
E 50th St.
Queens
W. 45th St.
E 45th St.
W. 42nd St.
E 42nd St.
Bryant Park
Lincoln Tunnel
Empire State Bldg.
W. 34th St.
E 34th St.
11th Ave.
10th Ave.
9th Ave.
8th Ave.
7th Ave.
Avenue of the Americas
Broadway
5th Ave.
Madison Ave.
Park Ave.
Lexington Ave.
3rd Ave.
2nd Ave.
1st Ave.
Madison Square
W. 23rd St.
E 23rd St.
East River
Gramercy Park
Union Square
W. 14th St.
E 14th St.
Hudson River
E 12th St.
W 12th St.
E 10th St.
Greenwich Village
West Street
Ave. A
Ave. B
Ave. C
Ave. D
East River Park
Washington Square Park
Bleecker St.
Bowery
E Houston St.
Lower East Side
W. Houston St.
SoHo
Spring St.
Little Italy
Canal St.
Broadway
E Broadway
Chinatown
FDR Drive
Manhattan Bridge
Holland Tunnel
City Hall Park
Brooklyn Bridge
Wall St.
Park
Brooklyn
Battery Park
ZONE 16
NEW JERSEY
NEW YORK

Zones 1–13:
Manhattan

NE

0   1

Miles

©1995 MAGELLAN Geographix^{SM} Santa Barbara CA (800) 929-4MAP

14

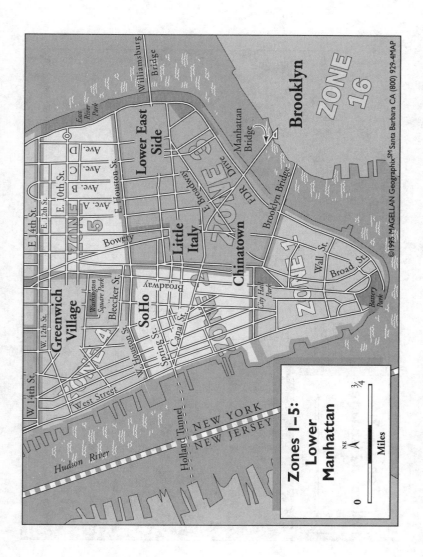

Zones 1–5:
Lower
Manhattan

NE

0   Miles   ¾

©1995 MAGELLAN Geographix℠ Santa Barbara CA (800) 929-4MAP

15

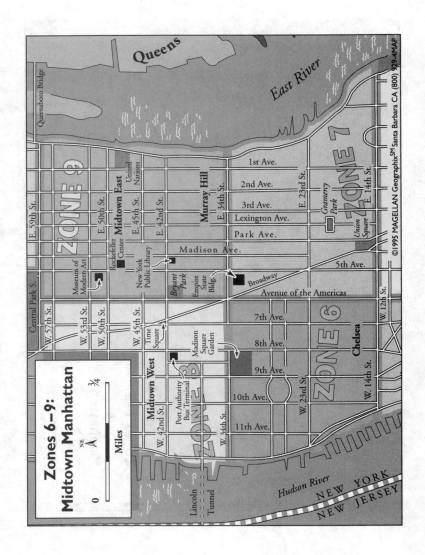

Zones 6–9: Midtown Manhattan

NE

0   ¾

Miles

Queens

East River

Queensboro Bridge

ZONE 6

E. 59th St.

Central Park S.

E. 57th St.

W. 53rd St.

W. 50th St.

Museum of Modern Art

E. 50th St.

Rockefeller Center

Midtown East

United Nations

E. 45th St.

E. 42nd St.

New York Public Library

Madison Ave.

1st Ave.

2nd Ave.

3rd Ave.

Lexington Ave.

Park Ave.

Murray Hill

E. 34th St.

E. 23rd St.

Gramercy Park

ZONE 7

Union Square

E. 14th St.

5th Ave.

Bryant Park

Empire State Bldg.

Broadway

Avenue of the Americas

W. 45th St.

Times Square

7th Ave.

W. 12th St.

ZONE 9

Midtown West

W. 42nd St.

Madison Square Garden

Port Authority Bus Terminal

8th Ave.

9th Ave.

10th Ave.

11th Ave.

ZONE 8

W. 34th St.

W. 23rd St.

Chelsea

W. 14th St.

ZONE 6

Lincoln Tunnel

Hudson River

NEW YORK

NEW JERSEY

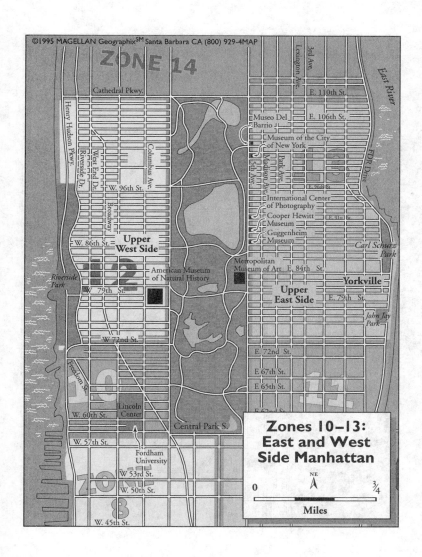

©1995 MAGELLAN Geographix^{SM} Santa Barbara CA (800) 929-4MAP

ZONE 14

Cathedral Pkwy.

Henry Hudson Pkwy.

E. 110th St.

Lexington Ave.

3rd Ave.

East River

West End Dr.

Riverside Dr.

Broadway

Columbus Ave.

W. 96th St.

Museo Del Barrio

E. 106th St.

Museum of the City of New York

Park Ave.

Madison Ave.

5th Ave.

FDR Drive

E. 96th St.

International Center of Photography

Cooper Hewitt Museum

E. 91st St.

Guggenheim Museum

Upper West Side

W. 86th St.

American Museum of Natural History

Carl Schurz Park

Riverside Park

W. 79th St.

Metropolitan Museum of Art

E. 84th St.

Upper East Side

E. 79th St.

Yorkville

John Jay Park

W. 72nd St.

E. 72nd St.

Freedom St.

E. 67th St.

E. 65th St.

W. 60th St.

Lincoln Center

Central Park S.

E. 62nd St.

W. 57th St.

Fordham University

W. 53rd St.

ZONE 8

W. 50th St.

W. 45th St.

Zones 10–13:
East and West
Side Manhattan

NE
∧

0 ⅜

Miles

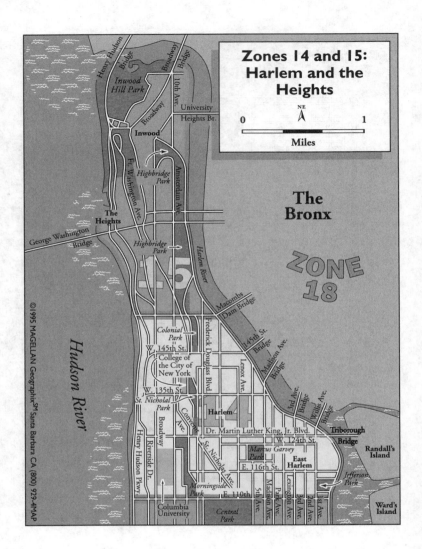

Zones 14 and 15:
Harlem and the Heights

NE

0   1

Miles

Inwood Hill Park

Henry Hudson Bridge

Broadway

Jerome Bridge

10th Ave.

University Heights Br.

Broadway

Inwood

Ft. Washington Ave.

Highbridge Park

Amsterdam Ave.

The Heights

The Bronx

George Washington Bridge

Highbridge Park

Harlem River

ZONE 18

Macombs Dam Bridge

Colonial Park

Frederick Douglass Blvd.

145th St. Bridge

W. 145th St.

College of the City of New York

Lenox Ave.

Madison Ave.

3rd Ave. Bridge

Willis Ave. Bridge

W. 135th St.

St. Nicholas Park

Convent Ave.

Harlem

Dr. Martin Luther King, Jr. Blvd.

Triborough Bridge

Randall's Island

W. 124th St.

Marcus Garvey Park

East Harlem

Broadway

St. Nicholas Ave.

E. 116th St.

Madison Ave.

Park Ave.

Lexington Ave.

3rd Ave.

2nd Ave.

1st Ave.

Jefferson Park

Henry Hudson Pkwy.

Riverside Dr.

Morningside Park

E. 110th St.

5th Ave.

Ward's Island

Hudson River

Columbia University

Central Park

©1995 MAGELLAN Geographix℠ Santa Barbara CA (800) 929-4MAP

PART ONE

Understanding the City

Boroughs, Neighborhoods, and "Districts"

"New York, New York, it's a helluva town / The Bronx is up and the Battery's down / And the people ride in a hole in the ground." It's true, it's easy to remember . . . and you can dance to it. But it's only a little bit of the story.

When we say "New York," most of the time we really mean the island of Manhattan, and so does almost everybody else. Even those who live in other parts of the city talk about going into "the city" when they mean going to Manhattan. In fact, however, Manhattan is just one of New York's five "boroughs," which are the equivalent of counties. The others are the Bronx to the north across the Harlem River, Brooklyn and Queens to the east on Long Island across the East River, and Staten Island to the south of the harbor. (Manhattanites, incidentally, refer to the other four jurisdictions as "the outer boroughs.")

Within all five boroughs are areas that have nicknames or historic designations, such as Prospect Park, the Theater District, and Union Square. And with the usual shifts of time and trend, some neighborhoods have merged with others, or upscaled, or run down, and so forth. For the purposes of this book, and to help focus your touring, we have combined some of these older neighborhoods in our zone system. For example, the Lower East Side, Zone 3, incorporates Little Italy and Chinatown; Midtown West, Zone 8, includes the Theater District and what is often called the Garment District.

We recommend that you also read, or at least skim, Part 7, "New York's Neighborhoods," once before your visit; not only will these profiles help you frame your itinerary, but they will also give you a sense of the historical evolution of New York—how succeeding generations of immigrants, merchants, and millionaires gradually spread up from the southern tip of the island to the top of Central Park, each generation pushing the last before it, moving the less fortunate or simply less picturesque elements up and out away from the prow of prosperity; and how in the late twentieth century, the process is repeating itself, so that areas once abandoned in the wake of this northward expansion are once again gathering strength and vitality.

■ Take the A Train . . . Carefully ■

Occasionally streets change names as well, at least on the maps and signs. Sixth Avenue is officially dubbed "Avenue of the Americas," but you never hear anybody call it that except perhaps a city promoter. Where 59th Street runs along the south border of Central Park, it is called, not surprisingly, Central Park South; and when Eighth Avenue passes 59th/Central Park South on its way north along the western edge of the park, it becomes Central Park West. (Above that, in the Heights, it's officially named Frederick Douglass Boulevard, but it's more often still called Eighth Avenue.) East 110th Street, which runs along the top of Central Park on the Upper East Side, is called Central Park North along the park itself and Cathedral Parkway on the Upper West Side.

However—and these are the ones that can be more confusing—Fifth Avenue, which is the eastern border of Central Park, does not change its name; and Park Avenue, which a visitor might assume was a form of "Central Park East," is two blocks east of that. Columbus Avenue, which one might assume originated in Columbus Circle, is actually an avenue away; it is the extension of Ninth Avenue, while Columbus Circle is on Eighth. And West Street, which is over by the Hudson River in Lower Manhattan, Greenwich Village, and Chelsea, eventually runs into Twelfth Avenue and becomes the West Side Expressway; don't confuse that with West End Avenue, which is the extension of Eleventh Avenue on the Upper West Side.

There is a Broad Street not far from Broadway in the Financial District, but it's less than half a mile long and a couple of blocks east of the real thing. In the East Village it is possible to find yourself at such confusing intersections as 2nd and Second, meaning East 2nd Street and Second Avenue, but thanks to the less organized nature of the early downtown development, such addresses are rare.

Most of the avenues with "names"—Park, Lexington, and Madison— are on the East Side between Third and Fifth Avenues (Park was once Fourth). However, there are some places on the island that are farther east than First Avenue, namely York on the Upper East Side and Avenues A, B,

C, and D—in order as they go toward the river—in the East Village. Tenth Avenue becomes Amsterdam Avenue above West 72nd Street.

Finally, be careful about subway names as well: The Sixth Avenue subway does generally go below Sixth Avenue, but the famous A Train is on the West Side, a world (almost literally) away from Avenue A on the Lower East Side.

For more on getting around Manhattan, see Part 4, "Arriving and Getting Oriented."

■ **"And the Battery's Down"** ■

We have divided Manhattan into 15 "zones" so that you can more easily pinpoint attractions, restaurants, and accommodations. (Each of the other four boroughs is a zone in itself.) And although they sound complicated, they actually block off into fairly obvious pieces; see the actual street borders in "How Information Is Organized" in the Introduction if you'd like to mark off a large map for yourself.

However, it helps to have some general notion of up and down—meaning uptown and downtown, not that hole in the ground. If you think of the island of Manhattan as running north-south, which it very nearly does, you can fix it in your head as a sort of skinny, slightly bottom-heavy watch, a Salvador Dalí affair with an oversized stem, a squiggly right edge, and Central Park more or less at the center of the dial.

The northernmost part of Manhattan, which sticks up like the extralong clock stem, is called the **Heights,** shorthand for the series of areas called Morningside Heights, Hamilton Heights, and Washington Heights. These are divided from New Jersey on the west by the Hudson River and across the top and east by the Spuyten-Duyvil Creek. The lower eastern bulge of this area, from about 12 to 1, is **Harlem.**

On either side of Central Park and matching it top and bottom are, logically, the **Upper East Side** and **East Side,** a long two o'clock hour, and the **Upper West Side** and **West Side** at ten. (Remember, the clock face is stretched out a little, one of those rectangular affairs, so it's longer at the bottom.)

From the southern edge of Central Park (59th Street) it gets a little trickier, but if you imagine a line running down the middle of the rest of Manhattan—generally along Sixth Avenue and Broadway—then you can place **Midtown** at three o'clock, **Gramercy Park/Madison Square** at four, and the **East Village** and then the combined **Chinatown/Little Italy/Lower East Side** filling up from around 4:30 almost to six, where **Lower Manhattan** hangs at the very southern tip. **The Battery,** as the song promises, is at the very tip.

Swinging back around from the bottom from about 6:30 toward 8 are **SoHo/TriBeCa** and **Greenwich Village,** then **Chelsea** at eight, **Midtown West/the Theater District** at nine, and back to the West Side.

The **Bronx** is "up"—it curves alongside the Heights above Harlem. In fact, if Manhattan were a pocket watch, the Bronx would be the fob it hung from. **Queens** is opposite the East and Upper East Side, **Brooklyn** a little southeast (4 to 5:30-ish), and Staten Island drops off almost directly below Manhattan, as if that drippy tip of Lower Manhattan had let go a drop. Of the five boroughs, only the Bronx is attached to the continental United States; and though that waterside culture has been almost obscured by modern development, it was integral to many areas of New York—and it also means that boats, and occasionally intrepid swimmers, can actually circumnavigate Manhattan.

A Very Short History of an Extremely Complex City

New York is one of the oldest cities in the United States, the nation's first capital and still one of the financial and cultural capitals of the world, and as such it has all the ingredients of a rousing history: founding fathers, first brokers, big money, political corruption, cultural diversity, ethnic riots, artistic enterprise, struggling immigrants. It was the site of many of the legendary "firsts" of America: Robert Fulton's first steamboat was launched on the Hudson River in 1807; Samuel Morse sent the first telegraph message from New York in 1837; the first organized baseball team, the New York Knickerbockers, was organized in 1845; and the first World's Fair was held in Manhattan in 1853. The first real battles of the American Revolution were fought there. Even the first antitax uprising took place in Manhattan, led by merchant Jacob Leisler a full 300 years before Newt Gingrich's Contract with America.

New York has always welcomed the iconoclast: It was not the first city to have a fine church built with the donations of a retired pirate (in this case, William Kidd, who contributed much toward the construction of Trinity Church), but colonial governor Lord Cornbury, who was appointed just after the turn of the eighteenth century, was surely the first public official in America to appear in drag.

New York is still the great melting pot; it only covers 300 square miles, but it has a population of about 9 million, speaking between 90 and 100 languages. Sixty percent of city residents place their city of origin outside the United States.

■ Colonialism and Capitalism ■

If it weren't for a determined jag of geography—or, rather, political arm-twisting—New York City might not even connect with the rest of the state. It's like the little tail on a stylized comma, or the pointed throat of some vulturous bird cutting down the Hudson River toward the Atlantic.

Before the arrival of the Europeans, the region was inhabited by two groups of related native tribes: the Algonquians (which included the Canarsie as well as the "Mohegans" immortalized by James Fenimore Cooper) along the Hudson and on Long Island; and the Iroquois Confederacy, among them the Mohawks and Seneca, who roamed to the west and upstate.

As was common in the sixteenth and seventeenth centuries, the explorers who sailed for one European empire were often citizens of another, so fascinated by the prospect of travel that they accepted commissions from rival powers. So Genoan John Cabot, who became a citizen of Venice, then moved to Bristol and sailed for England; he landed in Newfoundland in 1497 and returned to the region in 1498. His son Sebastian, who may have reached the Hudson Bay a decade later, sailed for the Spanish. Venetian Giovanni da Verrazano, who sailed into New York Bay in 1524, was in the pay of the French. Henry Hudson, who was English, was working for the Dutch. At least Samuel de Champlain, who was also carrying the French flag when he mapped eastern Canada, was working in his own language.

With its fine natural port, access to Canada via the Hudson River, and the agricultural wealth of the surrounding territory—not to mention European dreams of a vast paradise of gold in the land beyond and a marine shortcut to the Asian trade—New York was destined to be the target of political and colonial struggles. Champlain and Hudson worked their way into almost the same area at the same time, in 1609, and left their names behind as a handy reminder: The Frenchman sailed south from Canada along what is now known as Lake Champlain to its tip, while the Englishman sailed north along the route, ever after called the Hudson River, nearly as far as modern Albany.

The French, who had earlier allied themselves with the Huron in Canada, immediately became embroiled in trade and territorial struggles with the tribes of the Iroquois, a strategy that would haunt them for more than a century. The Dutch, on the other hand, went right for the open water: In 1624, representatives of the newly created Dutch West Indies Company famously acquired the land at the south end of the island of Manhattan from the easy-going Canarsie tribe for trinkets worth roughly $25 and christened it New Amsterdam. (They were sometimes referred to as the Manhattan Indians, as they called the area Man-a-hatt-ta.) Under a series of practical-minded Dutch administrators, the port prospered and expanded, and they almost certainly got their money's worth in the next 40 years. Workers, whether voluntary or involuntary, were highly desirable: The first African slaves were imported in 1625, and the first Jewish settlers arrived in 1664.

But during the Second Dutch War, England redeclared its right to the region, basing its claim on the voyages of John Cabot; and in 1664, when the English fleet sailed into New York Harbor, then-governor Peter Stuyvesant struck his colors and quietly surrendered. (A puritanical tyrant with a wooden leg, Stuyvesant ordered every tavern in the city to close by 9 p.m., which clearly proves he was in the wrong place.) He left behind the names of Wall Street (so called because a protective wall was raised there); Broadway (originally Breede Wegh), a cobbled route that ran the entire length of the island; the Bowery (from his own country home or "bouw-erie") in the farmland a mile north and east of the city; Harlem; and of course Stuyvesant Square. With one very brief resurgence of the Dutch, New York—now renamed in honor of the new charter holder, King Charles's brother, the Duke of York, and later James II—was firmly in the hands of the British.

Back in Europe, the imperial and often internecine struggles between Britain and France only intermittantly gave way to peace. So the colonial governor, Thomas Donegan, increasingly wary of French expansionism from the Canadian border, assiduously cultivated friendly relationships with the Iroquois. It was a good strategy, and the tribes were an invaluable ally during the decades of the French and Indian Wars that stretched from the late seventeenth century into the mid-eighteenth. The Battery got its name early in those wars, when nearly a hundred cannon were lined up along the water-front to prevent an attack on the harbor. The Treaty of Paris in 1763 confirmed the British domination of the North American territories, and the long and bitter campaigns gave way to a burst of settlement and expansion.

There was a brief period of self-satisfied prosperity. The area was covered in huge wheat fields and prosperous farms, like the one in the Bronx on which the Van Courtland House, now a museum, was built in 1748. King's College (now Columbia) was founded in 1754; St. Paul's Chapel was dedicated in 1766.

But then, in one of those ironies history is made of, the British crown tried to pay off its war debts by levying huge taxes on the very American colonies it had fought so hard to retain. With the passage of the Stamp Act in 1765, the resentment of many formerly loyal colonists reached a crisis. Shippers and "bolters" (millers) turned to smuggling and tariff-dodging. Fledgling Sons of Liberty took on the British authorities in the "Battle of Golden Hill" as early as 1770, and in 1774 they threw a "tea party" of their own in New York Harbor. Tensions increased to the point that many older landowners returned to England. William Tryon, the popular colonial governor of North Carolina, was transferred to New York in an attempt to contain the troubles, but he was forced out in 1775. Rebellion-minded New Yorkers—notably including English-born but radical-hearted Thomas

Paine and 19-year-old Alexander Hamilton, whose eloquence would later be turned to persuading the colonies to ratify the Constitution—published scathing denunciations of the Crown's policies toward the colonies. With the capture of Fort Ticonderoga later that year, the rebellion was all but declared.

This was the crucial region of the American Revolution. Fully a third of all engagements of the war were fought in New York State, including the tide-turning Battle of Saratoga. New York produced both America's first martyr, Nathan Hale, who was hanged in the city, and its most infamous traitor, Benedict Arnold.

But for all its cathartic rhetoric, New York City's active role in the Revolution was very short and not too sweet. General Washington suffered a series of defeats in the fall of 1776, including the battles of Long Island, Harlem Heights, and White Plains, and though the Americans held onto most of the upper and western part of the state, they eventually had to abandon the city to the British forces, who sailed into the harbor in a fleet of 500 ships and occupied it for the full seven years until the end of the war.

(During the British investment, the city was swept by two massive and somewhat suspicious fires, one right after the occupation that destroyed a thousand homes and Trinity Church, and the second in 1778. Consequently, there are few buildings from the colonial period visible outside Historic Richmondtown and the Alice Austen House, both on Staten Island; even the Fraunces Tavern, site of Washington's famous farewell to the troops in 1783, is a twentieth-century re-creation of the original.)

■ The Empire State ■

Almost from the moment peace was pronounced, New York boomed—and bickered. From 1785 until 1790, New York served as the nation's capital; it was here that Washington was sworn in as the country's first president; and it was from here that Hamilton, John Jay, and Virginian James Madison published the so-called Federalist Papers, which eventually persuaded the states to ratify the Constitution. Hamilton, who had married the governor's daughter, served as Washington's secretary of the treasury and founded both the Bank of New York and the *New York Post*. But he and John Adams opposed the French Revolution, which widened the gap between the Federalists and the Jeffersonians, among whom were Hamilton's former collaborator Madison and the brilliant young senator Aaron Burr, strongman of the Tammany Society. (For an explanation of the Tammany Society, see the section on Zone 10 in Part 7, "New York's Neighborhoods.") Burr succeeded in becoming Jefferson's vice president, but in fact Hamilton's maneuvering prevented Burr's becoming president instead; and when Hamilton later blocked Burr's election as governor, Burr challenged him to a duel. The 1804 shootout left both Hamilton and Burr's political career fatally wounded.

About the time that political power shifted, first to Philadelphia and then to the new capital at Washington, the New York Stock Exchange opened, and New York's indefinite term as a financial capital began. The agricultural order gradually began to yield to an industrial and shipping society. Staten Island ferry boy Cornelius Vanderbilt gradually bought up the local freight lines and built his shipping force into an empire. German-born John Jacob Astor, whose China trading, land sales, and fur trade companies enjoyed comfortable monopolies in the nation, was the first in New York's long line of millionaire tycoons (and first to establish the city's philanthropic tradition by leaving money for what became the New York Public Library). Confident of its own importance as early as 1804, the city established the New York Historical Society collection.

Already it was the largest city in the country, with more than 33,000 residents; ten years later the population had nearly doubled. In 1811, city planners tried to impose some order on the labyrinth of haphazard roads by laying out the famous Manhattan "grid" above 14th Street. A series of epidemics—yellow fever, cholera, typhoid, smallpox—gradually drove residents from the old downtown area into what is now Greenwich Village; and another huge fire in 1835 cleared the way for ever more ambitious construction. They also inspired the creation of Croton Reservoir in 1842, in the heart of Midtown where the New York Public Library is now; this project marked the beginning of fresh public water and a citywide sewer system.

The Erie Canal was completed in 1825, drawing even more trade, and immigrants as well, through its already booming port. The great potato famine forced a huge influx of Irish immigrants, at least 200,000, in the 1840s and 1850s. A wave of German immigrants followed in the 1860s; the Chinese began arriving in the 1870s; and in the 1880s, an estimated 1.5 million Eastern European Jews flooded the Lower East Side. They were accompanied by thousands of Italians, Irish, and displaced southern blacks, and by 1900 the city held an astonishing 3.4 million people. That would double again, to 7 million, in just 30 years. And those were just the ones who settled down; an estimated 17 million immigrants passed through the city between 1880 and 1910.

It took on the role of intellectual capital as well. The rest of the state might be known to have a sort of wild and bucolic beauty, thanks to the efforts of such writers as Washington Irving, James Fenimore Cooper, and

William Cullen Bryant, and the Hudson River School artists, including Thomas Cole and Frederick Church; but New York City was determined that everything be modern and smart.

Horace Greeley's *New York Tribune,* the most influential newspaper before and during the Civil War, was founded in 1841; the *New York Times,* which is now the country's preeminent paper, followed in 1851. The University of the City of New York was chartered in 1831; the Philharmonic Society of New York gave its first concert in 1842. The Crystal Palace, modeled on the pavilion erected for London's Great Exposition of 1851, hosted the first World's Fair in 1853 (and a few years later burned to the ground, just as the London palace had). Numerous progressive and reformist movements made New York their headquarters, including the suffragettes (the first women's rights convention was held in Seneca Falls in 1848); Greeley's *Tribune* editorialized in favor of organized labor, profit-sharing (both of which he instituted at his paper), abolition, and woman's suffrage. The California gold rush electrified Wall Street in 1849 (a scheme by Jay Gould to corner the gold market 20 years later would nearly bankrupt it).

And in 1858, one of New York's most beloved landmarks, Central Park, opened its gates, ensuring that even the poorest sweatshop employee in the city would always have a place to walk like a prince.

■ Civil War and the "Second Empire" ■

New York was no stranger to slavery. The first slaves had been imported by the Dutch, and in fact it was slave labor that built the original fortress, including the "wall" that was Wall Street. With painful irony, Wall Street also featured the first slave market, a mercenary operation that predated the Stock Exchange by nearly a century. But New York was also in the vanguard of the abolitionist movement, outlawing slavery in the city as early as 1799 (phasing it out over 30 years) and increasingly agitating for nationwide abolition. Frederick Douglass's influential *North Star* newspaper was headquartered in Rochester; Greeley's *Tribune* was the country's most vociferous antislavery voice (though originally a passivist one). It was the growing split between the outspoken antislavery and laissez-faire elements within the long-dominant Democratic Party that helped swing New York to the Republicans and Abraham Lincoln in 1860.

Nevertheless, while the progressive intellectual element in New York favored abolition, not even all of them—and even fewer members of the laboring class and immigrant communities, who could not hope to raise the $300 "replacement fee" that was the rich man's alternative to active service—supported a war to free the southern slaves. With the passage of the

Conscription Act, draft riots broke out all over the country; those in New York City, which lasted four days in July 1863 and resulted in the death or displacement of hundreds of blacks, close to a thousand by some estimates, were the most serious. It required the mobilization of the police, navy forces, militia, and even West Point cadets, along with the troops already deployed in the field, to restore order.

In general, however, New York vigorously supported the war effort, especially as the need for continual military supplies and transportation fueled the city's industries: battleships (including the ironclad *Monitor)* and freighters, textiles for uniforms and supplies, provisions, and, most important, the railroads that carried them. And for all the occasional Wall Street panics, the momentum never really slackened: The end of the war was for New York the beginning of what Mark Twain christened the "Gilded Age."

Luxury hotels such as the (original) Waldorf-Astoria and the Plaza opened their doors; so did the Metropolitan Opera House on Broadway. Fifth Avenue became known as "Mansion Row." Henry Villard, publisher of the *New York Evening Post* and founder of the Northern Pacific Railroad, began his gilded palace (now the New York Palace hotel) at 50th Street in 1881; W. K. Vanderbilt built an Italianate mansion at 51st and Fifth, just one of a long line—or avenue—of Vanderbilt family extravagances leading up to his cousin Cornelius II's fantastic French Renaissance chateau at the foot of Central Park (the house seen in the painting in the Plaza Hotel's Oak Bar).

Elevated railroads, or "Els," running above Second, Third, Sixth, and Ninth Avenues suddenly made it easier to get uptown, and newly electrified streetlights made it safer. Telephone and telegraph wires crisscrossed the city, at least until the blizzard of 1888 ripped them down and launched the city on a buried-cable program. The first great luxury apartment building, the Dakota, designed by the architect of the Plaza, staked out a new frontier on Central Park West at 72nd Street. Henry Frick constructed his mansion on the east side of the park at 70th, within easy reach of the new Metropolitan Museum of Art. The Statue of Liberty, St. Patrick's Cathedral, the Brooklyn Bridge, Carnegie Hall—all these monuments to the New York spirit were in place within a quarter century of war's end.

And the city was stretching in other directions, too. The Brooklyn Academy of Music was founded in 1858; Prospect Park, designed by Central Park architects Frederick Olmsted and Calvert Vaux (and considered superior by many), was finished in 1867; the Brooklyn Museum of Art opened in 1897. In fact, Brooklyn was the third largest city in the country on its own—it would still be the fourth largest today—but in 1898, the modern city of New York, the combined five boroughs, was officially born.

No economy—and no underground economy—benefited more than New York's during the postwar period. Shipping, trade, industry, government contracts, and, inevitably, corruption in the awarding of them, made millionaires out of manufacturers, mob bosses, political influence-peddlers, and sweatshop operators alike. Samuel Tilden became an early example of New York's periodic hero, the crusading reformer, when he prosecuted Boss Tweed of the Tammany Hall ring, but he made little real dent in the power of Tammany itself. (A few years later, city police commissioner Theodore Roosevelt would build a more successful political career on his reformist reputation.) The Republicans were not much cleaner, and the semi-underground power struggle led to a more overt political distance between the city's Democrats and the Republicans upstate.

The hundreds of thousands of immigrants who arrived near the end of the nineteenth century were herded into warehouses, mills, and industrial sweatshops, while labor leaders fought to establish minimal hour and wage (and age) standards. The tenement, the flophouse, the drug den, and the gang took up permanent positions in the city structure. Despite periodic catastrophes—most famously the Triangle Shirtwaist Factory fire of 1911, which killed 140—epidemics, and the increase of institutionalized poverty, most New Yorkers were intoxicated by the flow of commercial goods and boastfully smug about the prosperity of the city.

To a great extent, both this vast prosperity and the narrowness of its beneficiaries is exemplified by the spread of the railroads and the great fortunes their owners made from them. And one way or another, most of the rail barons had New York connections. It was the gold rush of 1849 that had lured Collis Huntington from Oneonta, New York, to California; but he quickly realized that the real money was to be made in railroads from the Midwest to the West Coast. The fortunes of Andrew Carnegie and his partner-turned-rival Henry Frick were forged in steel and railroading. "Commodore" Cornelius Vanderbilt expanded into railroads as well and became lord of the New York–Chicago routes. Jay Gould was forced out of the Erie Railroad and other state rails, but he merely headed west and wound up with four more.

New York stockbroker E. H. Harriman took over the Union Pacific, Southern Pacific, and Central Pacific. J. Pierpont Morgan, already extremely wealthy thanks to his financier father J. S. Morgan, took a lesson from all of these preceding examples, wresting away control of Gould's eastern railway holdings, founding U.S. Steel with Frick, and lending gold to the federal government at usurious rates during the Panic of 1895. These families, along with the Astors and Villards and their financial rivals, built lavish mansions on the East Side, establishing Midtown and Central Park as the social center of Manhattan and defining what came to be known as the "Four Hundred," the city's social elite. (It may be worth remembering that the life of luxury need not be a safe one, however: One Astor went down on the *Titanic,* and a Vanderbilt died on the *Lusitania.)*

Of course, there was money to be made elsewhere as well. John D. Rockefeller's fortune, grounded in the oil-refining business, was almost incalculable, well into the hundreds of millions by the turn of the century. And he was not alone. By 1900, 70 percent of the nation's corporations were headquartered in Manhattan, and 65 percent of all import trade passed through the harbor.

■ The Early Twentieth Century ■

In characteristic fashion, New York was too impatient to wait for the calendar to announce a new era. The age of American imperialism, such as it was, was hastened by New York newspaper tycoons William Randolph Hearst and Joseph Pulitzer, whose respective (if not entirely respectable) dailies the *Journal* and *World* so twisted coverage of Cuban-Spanish tensions that the United States was eventually lured into the Spanish-American War, from which it gained the Philippines, Guam, and Puerto Rico, not to mention the toothy New York–born hero Teddy Roosevelt.

Even so, 1900 was a landmark year. Ground for the first subway was broken in 1900; when it was completed, it was suddenly possible to cross the nine miles from City Hall to 145th Street in a little over 20 minutes. (A steam-driven version, a single car that rocketed about 300 feet along Broadway between Warren and Murray Streets and then was sucked backward, was constructed in 1870, but it made little impression.)

The city of the future had already been forged from the five boroughs in 1898. New Yorkers were so confident of their home's position as First City that the Vanderbilts launched a railroad line that ran back and forth between Manhattan and Chicago, the "Second City"; it was described as the overland version of a luxury liner, and it was grandly titled *The Twentieth Century.* The "new" Grand Central Station, the Beaux Arts beauty that is nearing full restoration, was begun in 1903; Pennsylvania Station (the original, not the existing building) would follow only a few years later. The Staten Island Ferry made its first crossing in 1905; the first metered taxi challenged the old omnibus system in 1907.

The scramble for the skyline began with the construction of the 300-foot Flatiron Building at Broadway, Fifth, and 23rd Street in 1902; skeptics confidently predicted its collapse. At 30 stories, the 1913 Gothic Woolworth Building at Broadway and Park reigned for 17 years, until the construction of the 77-story Chrysler Building in 1930, and that topped the city for only a few months, until the 102-story Empire State Building opened in 1931. It was getting so dark above that the city finally passed an ordinance restricting the height and size of buildings in 1913. (Unfortunately, in 1961, the limits were rescinded, so now we're stuck with the 110-story World Trade twins and the MetLife building that hovers over Grand Central Terminal.)

The Apollo Theater in Harlem opened in 1913. Blacks and Hispanics settled on the West Side, in an area of the 60s then called San Juan Hill (possibly in reference to Roosevelt's great victory in Cuba), and on the north side of Manhattan in Harlem. That had been a prosperous Jewish neighborhood, but it gradually became a center for black art, literature, and music during a period called the Harlem Renaissance. In the 1920s alone, Harlem's population increased from 83,000 to more than 200,000.

World War I only boosted the city's economy, which went into overdrive to supply the troops; stocks continued to rise throughout the 1920s, which roared in New York as nowhere else. (Just as war boosted profits, so did the relatively genteel, or at least socially tolerated, crime of bootlegging.) Smart, brittle, and literary characters went hand in hand with Follies. American women were not only emancipated, in the phrase of the time, but were also finally enfranchised. (Women got the vote; movies found a voice.) The *New Yorker* debuted in 1925, with its quintessential Gilded Age fop of a symbol, Eustace Tilley, on the cover. Lindbergh crossed over the Atlantic in the *Spirit of St. Louis* while New Yorkers drove under the Hudson River through the brand-new Holland Tunnel. Big bands and Broadway filled the airways; so did Babe Ruth, who in 1927 hit 60 home runs for the Yankees.

Everything glittered until 1929, when New York once again led the nation, this time into disaster. The crash of the stock market on October 29 turned Central Park into a shantytown and the city's greatest artists into federal employees, thanks to the Works Progress Administration (WPA). At the same time, growing political tensions in Europe, particularly in Germany, inspired a whole new generation of writers and artists to emigrate to America. During the slow reconstruction of the 1930s, Mayor Fiorella La Guardia, the "Little Flower," was able to institute a series of municipal reforms so that the poorer classes could also share in the recovery. In 1939, multimillionaire philanthropist John D. Rockefeller personally drove the final rivet into the beautiful Art Deco complex at Rockefeller Plaza, and a few months later, flush with visions of a bright new future, the New York World's Fair of 1939–40 drew a staggering 45 million visitors to Queens.

■ The Modern Era ■

Once again, war fueled the economy. The outbreak of World War II kicked the stock market back into high gear, and it was not to slow for nearly 30 years. With the ending of the war, America the melting pot took its place at the head of international power as well; the United Nations headquarters were established in New York in 1946. Large numbers of Puerto Ricans and other Hispanic immigrants arrived, and many of them moved to the Upper East Side, to what became known as El Barrio or Spanish Harlem; the Chinese arrived in even greater numbers throughout the 1940s and 1950s. Builder and powerbroker Robert Moses remade the face of the West Side, culturally and physically, by sweeping away the crumbling buildings in the San Juan district and designing a huge arts complex, now Lincoln Center for the Performing Arts, in its place.

The '60s were famously feverish in New York, in the arts world and in politics. The Beatles set foot on American soil for the first time at Kennedy Airport, and they played their first U.S. concert at Shea Stadium. Queen's Flushing Meadow hosted another World's Fair, and its symbolic Unisphere still holds up its one-world promise. Columbia University students staged famous sit-ins. New York's black intelligentsia, from Langston Hughes and Zora Neale Hurston to James Baldwin, Richard Wright, and Ralph Ellison, had been exposing racism in scathing essays, novels, and plays throughout the 1950s; now their writings, and *The Autobiography of Malcolm X,* became required reading. The flamboyant lifestyle of Harlem congressman Adam Clayton Powell, and the charges of corruption and political favoritism that surrounded him, were reminiscent of the Prohibition-era reign of Mayor Jimmy Walker. Militant civil rights groups, antigovernment radical political parties, anti-Vietnam demonstrators, and women's groups seemed to have transformed New York society top to bottom.

And perhaps it did—but in New York, money always seems to have more pull than politics. By the early 1970s, Nixon was beginning to withdraw the troops from Southeast Asia, the hippies were on the way out, and the yuppies had arrived. A burst of luxury hotel and apartment building and huge, showy corporate structures jacked the skyline ever higher (and led, almost too late, to a greater appreciation of historic restoration and preservation).

The pride of the 1970s nearly led to a great fall. Just as the World Trade Center was completed in 1973, the city began to spiral toward bankruptcy, a fate just barely averted with the fraternal assistance of Wall Street. The Great White Way, and the entire rest of the city, went dark in the Blackout of 1977. Stocks ballooned again, only to crash again. This time even Donald Trump, symbol of conspicuous consumption, had to resort to humble refinancing. But markets never stay slow in a city that never sleeps; and downtown construction, repair, and improvement of mass transit and the restaurant and entertainment industry are stronger than ever.

Heading toward the millennium, New York seems to be turning over its own chronometers, spiritual and literal. The city is celebrating its formal centennial, the 100th anniversary of the joining of the five boroughs, in 1998. That great symbol Ellis Island, which reopened as the Immigration Museum in 1990, is already one of the most visited sites in New York. Chelsea Piers, the crumbling remnants of the once vital Hell's Kitchen port, have reopened as a massive playground. And crime, the city's long-standing shadow empire, is to a substantial degree succumbing to the police department's continual investigations into corruption both external and internal.

■ The Fictional City ■

There are few cities that have been the subject of more novels, plays, or stories than New York, and with the advent of television and movies, the landscape is even more familiar to nonresidents. But again, I want you to see the history beneath the surface of the city, the New York that its founders dreamed of, that its wealthy ordered and its working class constructed. So among some personal, evocative, and decidedly not modern favorites:

The Age of Innocence and *The House of Mirth,* by Edith Wharton, both titled with heavy irony, bring the heyday of Midtown society to life; so does Henry James's masterpiece *Washington Square.* (The lavish film versions of *Innocence* and *Washington Square* are worth a look for the look, at least.)

The Last of the Mohicans, by James Fenimore Cooper. Maybe its old-fashioned and often pretentious prose put you off as a child, but Cooper's history of the colonial state and the era of the French and Indian Wars is far more exciting. (But if you were enraptured by the equally fascinating movie version, be warned: Hawkeye did not fall in love with Cora Monroe; he was old enough to be her father.)

Up in the Old Hotel, by Joseph Mitchell. In this astonishing collection of articles and stories, originally written for the *New Yorker,* Mitchell brings back to life the golden era of the oyster beds, the Fulton Fish Market, and the piers and warehouses and taverns of the West Side.

Winter's Tale, by Mark Halperin. A mystical and amazing vision of the city as an engine of pure energy, a sort of transmitter between this world and another—and no description of New York in winter can ever be more enrapturing.

Caleb Carr's two adventure novels *The Alienist* and *The Angel of Dark-ness* take place around the turn of the century, when gangs roved the city, Teddy Roosevelt was a young reformer, and forensic evidence and psychology were new and mysterious sciences. In a similar vein is *Waterworks,* by E. L. Doctorow, with its fantastic vision of the old Croton Reservoir.

In *Time and Again,* Jack Finney manages to imprint the New York City of the late nineteenth century so thoroughly in his contemporary protagonist's mind that he is transported there and falls in love.

And of course, those least childish of children's books, E. B. White's *Stuart Little,* the picaresque novel of a mouse-sized Manhattanite, and the wonderful *Eloise* (by Kay Thompson), whose portrait hangs in the lobby of her beloved Plaza Hotel and in whose honor I was once allowed to ride on the back of a carriage horse in Central Park.

PART TWO

Planning Your Visit to New York

When to Go

New York may sound "northern" to a lot of folks, and in winter it can certainly scrape some low temperatures and shine up the sidewalks; but in the heart of summer, especially August, it can be as thick and muggy as any southern city, with the temperature nudging up toward the three-figure mark and sudden sweeping rains that leave the asphalt steaming. Why do you think the Hamptons were invented? Of course, if you're inured to the humidity, or if business or school vacations require you to travel in July or August, you will still find a lot of free programs, indoors and out, all over town (and you can count on all the restaurants and museums cranking up the air-conditioning).

Actually, there's something to be said for almost any time of year. If you go for the sidewalk show, spring and fall are absolutely gorgeous in New York; average temperatures are in the 60s and 70s, making for perfect walking weather, and there are flower shows, the ballet and opera spring seasons, and circus rings.

Summer, as we've said, is freebie heaven: opera, classical music, and Shakespeare in Central Park; Tuesday night chamber concerts in Washington Square Park, weekend concerts at South Street seaport, and jazz in MoMA's sculpture garden; at least one street fair every week; Fourth of July fireworks and sunbathing in Strawberry Fields.

Fall is one party after another, starting with Halloween and running through Thanksgiving; and Central Park is absolutely brilliant. For all its chill—the really brutal winds don't usually hit until after the New Year—New York is a city that really knows how to dress for the holidays, with musical programs, lighting displays, elaborate window settings, parades, and so on. (In fact, a parade is practically guaranteed for your visit: There are so many excuses for parading in this town, you'd have to look for a month to miss one.) Many parks, including the Bronx Zoo, light up and stay open late around the holidays; the atrium of the Citicorp Building holds a huge model train display, as does the New York Botanical Garden; the music of the Central Park ice rinks and Rockefeller Center fills the air. Department store windows are almost worth the visit by themselves.

January may seem sort of an afterthought, but there are all those sales (including coats), Ice Capades at Madison Square Garden, perhaps an early Chinese New Year (there's a parade), and quiet time in the museums that are usually full of kids.

If you do wish to go during a major holiday or around a special event, such as Christmas, be sure to make your reservations well in advance and confirm at least once. Manhattan is a madhouse at prime time, although the excitement may be worth it. If you need your space, however, pick another time.

In any case, this really is the town that never sleeps. See the final section of the chapter for a calendar of special events.

What to Pack

Perhaps a little sadly, this once most elegant of societies has become extremely informal; you'll be unlikely to see a black tie or even a tuxedo outside of a wedding party unless you are fortunate enough to be invited to a serious social event. Even the old established restaurants rarely require a tie for lunch; most only "recommend" a jacket, although it's a good idea to have a tie on hand at night. (See the dress code advisories in our restaurant profiles.) However, the great majority of Manhattanites are dressed either for success or to impress, in classic style or not, so if you like to blend in with the shopping or art crowd, go for the reasonably neat look. All those gold- and silver-glittered sweatshirts just make you look as if you spent your adolescence in Atlantic City.

If you're simply sight-seeing, you can pretty much do as you please; streetwear is every-wear, especially during the day. Shorts, T-shirts, or polo shirts (athletic-logo sportswear for kids) are common well into autumn, and a casual dress or reasonably neat pair of khakis will make you look downright respectable.

As to outerwear, try to get something with dual use. A rainproof top of some sort, a lightweight jacket you can layer, or a sweater is probably the most you'll need in the summer, just in case a breeze comes up at night. However, remember that you will probably be going in and out of air-conditioning, so if you are one of those women who carry scarves that can double as shawls, or one of those men who don't mind rolling sleeves up and down, you'll be better prepared. If you're planning to jump in and out of buses or stores or even theaters, a light jacket you can easily unbutton or remove and carry without difficulty will keep you from alternately sweating and freezing. (A medium-weight or heavy shawl, which can be both decorative and warming, is a great alternative and easy to pack.) Those small fold-up umbrellas are preferable to the traditional sort, not only because you can stash them in your bag but also because a crowd of people wielding pointed implements or hanging them on chair backs and such can be dangerous (they're available on the street if you lose or forget one).

Something along the lines of a trenchcoat with zip-in lining or a wool walking coat with a sweater will usually do in winter, though it's smart to have the anti-wind accessories—gloves, earmuffs, hats, or scarves—tucked in your bag. Coming down through those "tunnels" of skyscrapers, the gusts pick up some surprising force. And if you have galoshes or waterproof boots of some sort, it wouldn't hurt to bring them; snowstorms can move in pretty quickly. Fur coats are no longer much of an issue in the moral sense in New York, but unless you're planning to go to the nicer hotels and restaurants, you may find your fur more trouble to worry about than it's worth. Lugging a fuzzy through the Metropolitan Museum of Art gets to be extremely sweaty. Of course, if you're sticking to the Metropolitan Opera, fur away.

Just don't overload yourself. Frankly, years of travel (and packing) have convinced me that most people carry more clothes than they really need. As obvious as those easy-packing tips you see in travel magazines may be (pick a basic color and a few bright accessories or a change of ties, things that don't wrinkle, lots of light layers, and so on), most visitors fill up their suitcases with whole new outfits for every day and evening event. Who are you trying to impress? Plan your packing the way you'd plan everyday life at home. Unless you have a really formal event to go to, high heels are tiring and take up a lot of room (though at least nowadays there are "comfortable" heels). Similarly, men can easily wear one nice jacket and carry assorted slacks, or a suit and different shirts, perhaps a vest. A dark suit is next to formality, anyway. Besides, it is difficult to resist buying something new and fashionable when you're visiting, and then you have even more clothes to carry.

Two really important things to consider when packing are comfortable shoes—this is a culture of the streets, and what isn't asphalt is concrete—and expandable or forgiving waistlines. Even if you don't think you're going to eat much, the scent of food is constantly in the air; every bar lays out those mixed nuts or something similar; and somehow even the most careful dieters seem to join the clean plate club when they visit one of the world's famous restaurant centers. Seasoned travelers know that a change in schedule can often cause bloating as well as, paradoxically, dehydration. Make sure you have a change of shoes, too; this is not the place to save space, because wearing the same shoes through and after hours of walking or even standing around sight-seeing is a good way to have sore feet, if not worse. If you don't want to pack "fat day" clothes, you better be packing your running shoes, anyway. Or let them double as your walking shoes.

The other traveling "musts" are over-the-counter medications and ointments. People tend to drink more coffee and more cocktails on vacation, or even when taking important clients out, so be sure to pack headache medicines, Alka-Seltzer, and the like. If you are on prescription medicine, carry a little more of it than you actually need: You might drop some while sightseeing or find yourself staying a day or so longer than you expected for business or pleasure or even bad traveling weather. If you are allergic to bites or stings, remember the antihistamines. For scratches and small annoyances, a small tube of Neosporin or other antiseptic ointment is helpful. You can get these things at a drugstore or the hotel shop, of course, but those little "travel sizes" are wildly overpriced; you'd be better off putting a small amount of each in your own containers. A good way to keep medications fresh, incidentally, is to use those small zip-plastic bags sold for jewelry or even the sandwich-style ones. Be absolutely sure to pack bandage strips and muscle-pain antidotes as well: Blisters can ruin an otherwise wonderful trip.

I have found three other tiny items extremely useful: a handkerchief, disposable stain remover, and one of those tiny flashlights. I mean an old-fashioned man's handkerchief, not a pretty little showpiece. Between bad weather, allergies, air conditioning, damp subway seats, and so on, a good 12-inch square is a lifesaver. If you plan to spend time on the subways or the sidewalks, you will be in near-contact with a lot of coffee cups, snacks, and so on; if you find yourself having an even closer encounter thanks to a jerking subway ride, one of those towelette-sized spot treatments can save you a lot of heartache. And as more and more museums have to lower or narrowly focus their lighting to protect fragile canvases and textiles, I increasingly find myself squinting at the plaques and captions. A penlight comes in handy (but be sure to train it only on the information, not the art).

And finally, not to be an alarmist, but this is a city that has a crime problem (as do most cities nowadays), so there is no good reason to walk around flashing a lot of expensive jewelry. Leave it at home and stick to the costume stuff, or leave it in the hotel safe except for the big party. That way, even if you lose an earring, you can replace it quickly and cheaply at the next vendor cart. You might be surprised what nice-looking silver you can find on the street.

For a more in-depth discussion on staying safe in the big city, see the "How to Avoid Crime" section in Part 4.

Gathering Information

Brochures, historical background and up-to-date schedules are available from the New York Metropolitan Convention and Visitors Bureau (NYMCVB), which updates its material quarterly. It's best to call in advance and get their information package mailed to you (call (800) NYC-VISIT), but they also have offices around Manhattan if you don't get to it beforehand (call (212) 397-8222). There you can pick up lots of maps, free tickets or discounts, shopping guides, and so on. One of the NYMCVB branches is in the Selwyn Theater in Times Square (229 West 42nd, between Seventh and Eighth), which also houses the Times Square Visitors Center and public transit information center. There are also visitors centers in Pennsylvania Station (34th Street side) and Grand Central (South Side), with carts stationed inside the Empire State Building and outside (unless it's frigid) Madison Square Garden. Be sure to pick up the free subway map.

New York has a large gay and lesbian population and a great many services and attractions for the homosexual traveler: One contact point is the Lesbian and Gay Services Center (208 West 13th Street; (212) 620-7320). Among local publications reporting gay events are the *Village Voice* and *New York Press,* both free in the city; and the more specialized *Next* and *Homo Xtra,* a free weekly available at many bars and restaurants. The larger gay bookstores (see the relevant section in Part 9, "Shopping in New York") are also bulletin boards for community information.

When it comes to Internet and Web sites, no city outdoes New York. Among them are the on-screen site of the weekly *City Guide* provided to hotels (www.cityguideny.com); the *Sidewalk New York* site (www.sidewalk.com); *Citysearch* (www.citysearch.com); the less typical *Metrobeat* (www.metrobeat.com/nyc/index.html) and the hippest on-line service, the video site of the downtown monthly *Paper* (www.papermag.com). The *Village Voice* has its own site as well (www.villagevoice.com), linked to the Yahoo network, which also has a New York site.

Several of the large museums have their own Web sites as well. You can scout the floor plans and the current or coming exhibitions and lecture or tour schedules at the Museum of Modern Art (www.moma.org); the Children's Museum of Manhattan (www.CMOM.org); the Lower East Side Tenement Museum (www.wnet.org/tenement); and the Metropolitan Museum of Art, including the Cloisters (www.metmuseum.org). Families should check out the Web site of the Wildlife Conservation Society (www.wcs.org), which includes information on all the zoos in the Bronx, Brooklyn, Central Park, and Flushing Meadow. Really serious museum-goers should try to get a subscription to *Museums New York,* a sort of play-bill for museums with features, phone numbers and current exhibits for even the smallest streetside collections; call (800) NYC-MUSE.

If you're really running behind on your planning, look into the Web site for New York by Phone, an all-purpose reservations and ticket packager (www.nyctollfree.com).

One of the most fascinating sites features the subway system, with his-tories of the stations, photos of some either abandoned or restored termi-nals, and plenty of timetables and maps. If this doesn't lure you under-ground, you have no romance in your soul (www.nycsubway.org).

Once you are in New York, look for any free publications in your hotel room (most often the New York Visitors Guide and weekly editions of the *City Guide);* check current issues of *New York* and the *New Yorker* magazine and the daily *New York Times,* of course. There are also several entertain-ment and cultural hotlines to call for daily opportunities: see Part 6, "Enter-tainment and Nightlife."

When reviewing the information in this guide, you'll notice that some phone numbers are given without area codes. The area code for all numbers in this guide is 212 unless otherwise specified.

For more suggestions on planning your vacations around special inter-ests, see Part 10, "Sight-Seeing and Tours."

Special Considerations

■ Traveling with Children ■

Of course, New York is most famous as a sort of adults' playground, but if you're considering a family vacation here, don't worry: For all the bars and "the-ah-tuh," New York is absolutely jam-packed with family-style attractions and hands-on, state-of-the-art children's museums both in and outside of Manhattan, not to mention the special events, such as the Macy's Thanksgiving Day Parade, holiday lights in the area zoos (four of them!) and botanical gardens, ice-skating in Rockefeller Center, harbor tours, high views, antique carousels, and so on.

In fact, if you and your family are likely to become repeat visitors, you might consider joining the Wildlife Conservancy Society: a family membership of $58 gets you in free to the zoos in Central Park and Prospect Park, the famous Bronx zoo, the zoo in the Flushing Meadows–Corona Park complex in Queens, and the New York Aquarium in Coney Island, with its Sea World–style whale dances and sea lions. That way you can work your way around the boroughs and always have a safe kids' bet. Call (718) 220-5111 or surf (www.wcs.org) for information.

And sight-seeing with small children can be a bargain if you use public transportation: Kids under 44 inches ride free on the buses and subways (there are handy-dandy lines by the bus driver's seat and toll gates for comparison). Just remember that warnings about dehydration go double for small children, even in winter. For some specific recommendations, see the "Best Children's Fare" list in Part 10, "Sight-Seeing and Tours."

If you do bring the kids but would like to have a little adults-only time, contact the Baby Sitters Guild (call (212) 682-0227), which has bonded members that will stay in or carry out, so to speak, to Central Park or some other play spot. Also check with your hotel; most have a list of reliable sitters.

In the case of illness or medical emergencies, first call the front desk of your hotel; many have arrangements with physicians for house calls. Otherwise contact Dial-a-Doctor (call (212) 971-9692). There are several 24-hour pharmacies in town, most run by the Duane Reade chain; the most centrally located are at Broadway and 57th Street (call (212) 541-9208) and Lexington and 47th (call (212) 682-5338).

■ Tips for International Travelers ■

All that visitors from the United Kingdom and Japan need to enter the United States is a valid passport, not a visa; Canadian citizens can get by with only proof of residence. Citizens of other countries must have a passport, good for at least six months beyond the projected end of the visit, and a tourist visa as well, available from any U.S. consulate. Contact consular officials for application forms; some airlines and travel agents may also have forms available.

If you are taking prescription drugs that contain narcotics or require injection by syringe, be sure to get a doctor's signed prescription and instructions. Also check with the local consulate to see whether travelers from your country are currently required to have any inoculations; there are no set requirements to enter the United States, but if there has been any sort of epidemic in your homeland, there may be temporary restrictions.

If you arrive by air, be prepared to spend as much as two hours entering the United States and getting through U.S. Customs. Canadians and Mexicans crossing the borders either by car or by train will find a much quicker and easier system. Every adult traveler may bring in, duty-free, up to one liter of wine or hard liquor; 200 cigarettes or 100 non-Cuban cigars or three pounds of loose tobacco; and $100 worth of gifts, as well as up to $10,000 in U.S. currency or its equivalent in foreign currency. No food or plants may be brought in.

The dollar is the basic unit of monetary exchange, and the entire system is decimal. The smaller sums are represented by coins. One hundred "cents" (or pennies, as the 1-cent coins are known) equal 1 dollar; 5 cents is a nickel (20 nickels to a dollar); the 10-cent coin is called a dime (10 dimes to a dollar); and the 25-cent coin is called a quarter (4 to a dollar). Beginning with 1 dollar, money is in currency bills (although there are some 1-dollar coins around as well). Bills come in $1, $2 (rare), $5, $10, $20, $50, $100, $500, and so on, although you are unlikely to want to carry $1,000 or more. Stick to twenties for taxicab and such; drivers rarely make change for anything larger.

Banks in the United States are closed on federal holidays, including New Year's Day (January 1); Martin Luther King Jr. Day (celebrated the third Monday in January); Presidents' Day (celebrated the third Monday in February); Memorial Day (last Monday in May); Independence Day (July 4); Labor Day (first Monday in September); Columbus Day (second Monday in October); Veterans Day (November 11); Thanksgiving (the fourth Thursday in November); and Christmas (December 25).

Credit cards are by far the most common form of payment in New York, especially American Express, Visa (also known as BarclayCard in Britain), and MasterCard (Access in Britain, Eurocard in Western Europe, or Chargex in Canada). Other popular cards include Diners Club, Discover/Novus, and Carte Blanche.

Traveler's checks will be accepted at most hotels and restaurants if they are in American dollars; other currencies should be taken to a bank or foreign exchange and turned into dollar figures. There are currency exchange booths—American Express at (800) AXP-TRIP, Thomas Cook at (212) 753-0132, Chemical Bank at (212) 935-9935, or Avis at (212) 661-0826—in such major traffic areas as JFK and LaGuardia airports, Grand Central Station, Times Square, the World Trade Center, and even Macy's and Bloomingdale's.

If you need additional assistance, contact the Traveler's Aid Society, which has booths in JFK and Newark airports as well as on Broadway at 41st Street (944-0013).

Public telephones require 35 cents; although the four boroughs outside Manhattan have a 1-718 area code that must be dialed, there is no additional charge. (Unless otherwise noted, all phone numbers in this book have a 212 area code.) And throughout the United States, if you have a medical, police, or fire emergency, dial 911, even on a pay telephone, and an ambulance or police cruiser will be dispatched to help you.

Incidentally, New York has one of the most stringent antismoking programs in the country, something international visitors might need to consider in advance. Smoking is prohibited on buses, on subways, and in taxicabs; in public buildings or the lobbies of office buildings; in all but designated areas in theaters; in most shops and all museums; and in restaurants with more than 35 seats (although there may be designated smoking areas in the bar or lounge).

■ Tips for the Disabled ■

New York is far more receptive to the handicapped tourist than its tough reputation might lead you to believe. City buses are equipped with wheelchair lifts and "kneeling" steps (though admittedly they don't always work), and handicapped riders pay half-fare (75 cents). An increasing number of subway stops are wheelchair-accessible as well: For a list contact the Transit Authority's Customer Service Department (370 J Street, Suite 702, Brooklyn, NY 11201, or (718) 330-3722). Visually impaired travelers can get a Braille subway map and other materials from the Lighthouse (call (800) 334-5497 or (212) 321-9200). The hearing-impaired can get similar help from the New York Society for the Deaf (817 Broadway, seventh floor; TDD (212) 777-3900).

A list of wheelchair-accessible museums, hotels, and restaurants is available from the Society for the Advancement of Travel for the Handicapped (347 Fifth Avenue, New York, NY 10016 or (212) 447-7284). A similar guidebook, "Audiences for All: A Guide for People with Disabilities to New York City Cultural Institutions," is available from Hospital Audiences for $5 (220 West 42nd Street, 13th floor, New York, NY 10036). Hospital Audiences also offers a toll-free international hotline for travelers with disabilities that gives information on more than 200 museums, hotels, restaurants, and theaters, listing performances that are signed or have audio legends, rest room facilities, and so on (call (888) 424-4685). And many members of the volunteer Big Apple Greeters, warmly recommended in Part 10, "Sight-Seeing and Tours," will partner handicapped visitors around town, but you should call at least several days in advance at (212) 669-2896.

Visitors who use walking aids should be warned that only the larger museums and the newer shopping areas (including those in hotels and in some renovated warehouses, like those in SoHo) can be counted on to be wheelchair-accessible. Many individual stores and smaller art collections are housed in what were once private homes with stairs, and even those at sidewalk level are unlikely to have wider aisles or specially equipped bathrooms. The restaurants that we profile later in the book all have a disabled access rating, as do most of the major attractions, but you need to call any other eatery or any store in advance. (In fact, you might check with some restaurants that were listed as not accessible at press time, as it's possible they've renovated their facilities since.) Similarly, you need to call any stores you're particularly interested in.

If you are allergy-sensitive, watch out for spring. As for smoking, New York is either heaven or, well, Limbo, depending on your outlook. As we noted in the previous section, it is prohibited in just about any place you might be except a bar and the sidewalk (and a private home). If you're a chain-smoker, be sure to think twice about any packaged tours that will have you hustling between seat and sight.

A Calendar of Special Events

Here are the major celebrations and a sampling of the less well-known but unique events around New York and their approximate dates (specific ones where possible). Remember, if the event requires tickets, it's best to try to arrange them before leaving home; otherwise you may find yourself paying extra or being locked out entirely. Tickets for the U.S. Open Tennis Championships in August, for instance, go on sale in May, and the scalping fees are astonishingly high by the opening rounds.

Please note that many festivals, especially in the summer, move around from year to year, and that some close down or are replaced by others; so if you are interested, contact organizers as soon as possible. For many of the municipal functions, you may call the Metropolitan Visitors and Convention Bureau at (212) 397-8222. Parade routes and times will be listed in the *New York Times* on the appropriate days. The local newspapers (listed earlier) will also have numerous street fairs, arts shows, and concerts to tempt you, particularly in summer.

In addition to the contacts listed in the following section, TicketMaster may be able to supply tickets to particular events, although there will be an additional handling charge. Call (212) 307-1212.

January

Winter Antiques Show at the Armory. Third week in January. One of the largest and most prestigious (read: expensive) antiques gatherings in the city, this is held in the historic Seventh Regiment Armory on Park Avenue at 66th Street. Over the first weekend of the big collection, a sort of counter-show, featuring less established or edgier collectors, is held at the 26th Street Armory at Lexington Avenue, and shuttle buses run between the two. For information call (212) 255-0020.

Chinese New Year Parade. Late January or early February. A fortnight of fireworks, street fairs, and food festivals leads toward the big dragon parade through Chinatown.

National Boat Show. Mid-January. Sailing vessels, yachts, cruisers, and powerboats fill the Jacob Javits Convention Center; call (212) 757-5730.

February

Black History Month. Watch the newspapers and guides for cultural events, concerts, and lectures scheduled around the city.

Empire State Building Run. Early February. Hundreds of athletes race not horizontally but vertically, 1,860 steps from the lobby to the 102nd floor. The best make it in about 11 minutes. Contact the New York Road Runners at (212) 860-4455.

Westminster Club Dog Show. Mid-month. This most prestigious of canine parades brings thousands of familiar, unusual, and downright rare dogs, all blow-dried and ribboned for judging, and even more observers to Madison Square Garden. Heck, this dog show's so big it's on cable TV. Call (212) 465-6741.

Valentine's Day. February 14. A huge vow-one, vow-all mass wedding ceremony is performed at the wedding chapel in the Empire State Building; call (212) 736-3100, ext. 37.

Coliseum Antiques Show. Not as elite as the Armory show, but huge and convenient: more than 100 dealers in the arena on Columbus Circle (late February or early March). For information, contact the NYMCVB.

Grammy Awards. Late February. The television world's Oscars, hauled back into Madison Square Garden; you probably can't get in, but you can sure be a part of the crowd that applauds the stars as they step from their limousines (and where would those infotainment shows be without a crowd?). For information, call MSG at (212) 465-6741.

March

International Cat Show. The feline response to the Westminster show, also at Madison Square Garden and also increasingly the place for trendy types looking for the next trendy rare breed; call MSG at (212) 465-6741 for information.

New York Flower Show. One of the big stops on the flower circuit is the Horticultural Society of New York's annual competition/exhibition in the Coliseum on Columbus Circle; contact the NYMCVB.

Art Expo. Early or mid-February. This huge affair at the Javits Convention Center specializes in what dealers call popular art, and that means anything from nice lithographs to the stuff you get on the sidewalk or see in chain motels. Good for a laugh at least, and if you have a really shrewd eye, a possible find; call (212) 216-2000.

St. Patrick's Day Parade. On March 17, everyone is Irish, so pack something green or get out of the way. The parade, at age 200 one of the oldest anywhere, includes an estimated 150,000 marchers; the route is along Fifth Avenue (or course) from 44th to 86th, with the thickest crowd around St. Patrick's Cathedral (of course).

Greek Independence Day Parade. March 25. Zorba-style food and dance along Fifth Avenue from 49th to 59th.

New Directors/New Films Festival. Mid-March. A cutting-edge cinematic collaboration between the Museum of Modern Art, which hosts the screenings, and the Lincoln Center Film Society. For more information call (212) 708-9480.

Ringling Bros. and Barnum & Bailey Circus Parade. Late March. Another great traditional procession, this one is now (thanks to animal protests) a semisecret wee-hours train of elephants and lions and tigers making their way from Long Island City through the Queens-Midtown Tunnel to Madison Square Garden, where the circus sets up for several weeks. For more information call MSG at (212) 465-6741.

Cirque de Soleil. On alternate years, watch for the appearance of the strange and fantastic Canadian one-tent circus to set up in Battery Park: all acrobats and astonishing contortionists and eerie music, no animals; call (888) FIND-TIX or (800) 678-5440.

New York Flower Show. Mid-March. The outdoors blooms indoors at Pier 92 on 51st Street; (212) 757-0915. Also look for the Winter Garden display at the World Financial Center downtown; (212) 945-0505.

Easter Parade. Late March to mid-April. A parade so famous they made a Fred Astaire/Judy Garland movie about it. Don that bonnet—the bigger the better—and promenade along (what else?) Fifth Avenue from 44th to Central Park. Macy's flower show is scheduled for the week leading up to Easter Sunday (for information call (212)494-4495).

Easter Egg Roll. Saturday before Easter. In the East Meadow of Central Park; call (212) 360-3456.

April

Baseball Season Opening Day. Mid-April. If you're a pin-striper, or just an American Leaguer at heart, you can try for tickets by calling TicketMaster or Yankee Stadium box office at (718) 293-6000. For fans of the senior league, those heartbreaking Mets are at Shea Stadium (call (718) 507-8499).

Rockefeller Center Flower Show. Mid-April. One of the nicest free shows in town. Gardening companies and landscape designers fill the plaza between 48th and 51st Streets with fantasy getaways, Japanese rock gardens, arbors, and urban meadows. Call (212) 664-4636 for information.

Antiquarian Book Fair. Mid-April. First editions, rare titles, autographed copies, and so on fill the Seventh Regiment Armory on Park at 66st Street.

Seventh on Sixth. The big spring collections of the haute couture world (i.e., Seventh Avenue) were staged for several years in Bryant Park (Sixth) under giants tents and hip-flip catwalks, but it has recently been trying out different homes, including Pier 92, so check the papers. All the shows are invitation only, but the celebrity-spotting is good. For information, contact the NYMCVB.

Cherry Blossom Festival. Late April–early May. A celebration of the Japanese, or flowering Kwanzan, cherry trees of the Brooklyn Botanic Garden; call (718) 622-4433.

May

Bike New York. Early May. This ever-larger 41-mile for-fun bike race—it draws more than 35,000 wheelers and dealers—links all five boroughs, with the kickoff downtown and the finish line in Staten Island. Picnic at pedals' end. For information call (212) 932-0778.

Brooklyn Bridge Day. Second Sunday in May. Walk the bridge, admire its stunning structure, and enjoy a sort of street fair at the same time. For information, contact the NYMCVB.

International Fine Arts Fair. Mid-May. European and American artists are featured in this young but prestigious show at the Seventh Regimental Armory. For information, contact the NYMCVB or call (212) 472-0590 during the show itself.

Fleet Week. Ships ahoy! Naval and Coast Guard vessels of all sizes and their crews set up for tours and exhibitions for a week (mid-May). Call (212) 245-0072.

Martin Luther King Day Parade. Third Sunday in May. A salute to the civil rights leader starts on Fifth Avenue at 44th and streams up to 86th.

Washington Square Art Exhibition. An old and revered Greenwich Village gathering, this huge outdoor art show is like a giant block party, with easels (and food carts) set up in the streets all around the park (the last

two weekends in May and the first two weekends of September). Call
(212) 982-6255.

Ninth Avenue Food Festival. Third weekend in May. This was, and to a
lesser extent still is, the international grocery strip of New York. A combination street fair and ethnic fare showcase, it stretches from 37th to 57th
Streets. For information, contact the NYMCVB.

Lower East Side Jewish Festival. Third or fourth Sunday in May. Combination historical tour and street party.

June

Shakespeare in the Park. From June to August, this now famous, free,
and star-studded series (call (212) 539-8600) takes over the Delacorte Theater stage in Central Park. There are fewer than 2,000 seats, and the box
office opens at 1 p.m. every day, but the line starts to form much earlier.
(See the "Ticket Tips" section in Part 6, "Entertainment and Nightlife," for
more information.)

Concerts in the Park. June to August. Some of the concerts in Central Park,
Prospect Park, and other city greens are put on by the New York Philharmonic
(call (212) 875-5700) and the great Metropolitan Opera (call (212) 362-6000).

SummerStage. Similarly, there are free or nominally priced pop, rock,
country, folk, reggae, and jazz concerts throughout the summer in Central
Park: Remember Simon & Garfunkle? Garth Brooks? It's big, but it's fun.
Call (212) 360-2777.

Puerto Rican Day Parade. First Sunday in June. A lively, musical march
along Fifth Avenue from 44th to 86th Street.

Belmont Stakes. The second (occasionally the first) Saturday in June. The
final leg of thoroughbred two-year-old racing's Triple Crown, and many
warm-up races, go off at Belmont Park on Long Island; call (718) 641-7400.

Museum Mile Festival. Second Tuesday in June. A free day at the muse-
ums along Fifth Avenue between 82nd and 105th Streets, including the
Guggenheim, Metropolitan, Museum of the City of New York, Cooper-
Hewitt, Jewish Museum, National Academy of Design, and more.

Restaurant Week. A sit-down Taste of the Town event, when some of the
biggest-name restaurants offer special cut-price dinners. As soon as you see
the ads in the *New York Times* or elsewhere, listing the participating establishments, get on the phone or you'll be out of luck.

Feast of St. Anthony. Mid-June. Restaurant week or no, the saint of Padua must still be hungry: His street fair in Little Italy lasts two weeks.

Salute to Israel Parade. Mid-June. Along Fifth northward from 59th Street. Also, fashion sharks may find much to savor at the United Jewish Appeal's annual fundraiser; call (212) 836-1115.

Gay and Lesbian Pride Day Parade. Late June. This is actually a week-long series of public and private events, but it culminates in the parade, commemorating the Stonewall Riot of June 27, 1969, that struts down (rather than up) Fifth Avenue from 53rd to the West Village. Call (212) 807-7433.

L'Eggs Mini-Marathon. Late June. Popular women's road race with start and finish along Central Park West between 66th and 67th.

JVC Jazz Festival. Late June–early July. A series of top-name concerts in Bryant Park and venues around the city; watch the papers for schedules.

July

Fourth of July Festival. July 4. Independence Day celebrations include street fairs, the annual sailing of the Tall Ships in the harbor, and after dark, the famous Macy's fireworks over the East River. For information, call (212) 494-4495. All-day festivities in downtown around Battery Park climax with fireworks over the harbor.

Lincoln Center Festival. A dizzying array of dance, drama, ballet, children shows, and multimedia and performance art that involves both the repertory companies and special guests and that moves through the indoor venues and sometimes outdoors as well, through July and August. Call (212) 845-5400. There are also big-band dances (free lessons included) on weekends by the Lincoln Center fountain; call the same number. And the Lincoln Center Plaza on Columbus is home territory to the two-week American Crafts Festival; call (212) 362-4627.

Mostly Mozart. A famous phrase, and one of the most famous renditions (two weeks in mid- to late August) in the Lincoln Center's Avery Fisher Hall (call (212) 875-5030).

August

Harlem Heritage Week. Mid-August. Films, art exhibits, concerts, exhibition games, and street fairs celebrating the neighborhood's rich cultural history.

U.S. Open Tennis Tournament. Late August. In its expanded digs at Flushing Meadow, this Grand Slam event is one of the sport's hottest tickets—literally. Don't forget the water and the sunblock, if you can get in. For information call (718) 760-6200.

Festival Latino. Mid- to late August. Concerts, films, performance art, and video at the Public Theater and other venues; call (212) 598-7100.

Lincoln Center Plaza concerts. Throughout the month. Some of the outdoor series taper off in August, but the music on the plaza (information at (212) 875-5400), along with another big crafts show late in the month (information at (212) 667-4627), keeps the joint jumpin'.

September

Wigstock Parade. Labor Day weekend. Although this parade isn't as old as the Easter or Thanksgiving Day marathons, it's catching up fast in the fame department. The wildest and most royal drag event in the city, in a search for more room it has moved a couple of times from its original East Village park space, most recently to the 11th Street Pier; contact the Lesbian and Gay Community Services Center for information at (212) 620-7310.

Broadway on Broadway. Early September. For one enchanted day/evening in Times Square—where else?—the casts of the big Broadway shows sing and step out in public; call (212) 768-1560.

West Indian Festival and Parade. Labor Day Weekend. It's big, it's loud, it's delicious, and it's relatively underpublicized (perhaps because it's in Brooklyn); but fans of world or Caribbean music, food, and dance won't mind the short trip to Crown Heights. For information call (718) 774-8807.

New York Is Book Country. Third Sunday in September. A great indoor/outdoor book "mall" along Fifth Avenue from 48th to 59th Streets, with booths and racks of old, new, used, privately published, and rare volumes.

Third Avenue Festival. A giant block party from 68th to 90th.

One World Festival. Mid-September. International food, crafts, antiques, and street performance in a block party on East 35th between First and Second Avenues.

Feast of San Gennaro. Mid-September. This Little Italy street fest is pretty famous, probably because it lasts a long (two-weekend) week, although its rumored "family" connections have gotten a lot of publicity; along Mulberry Street. Call (212) 226-9546.

New York Film Festival. Late September to early October. Not so avant-garde as the New Films series, this prestigious series in Lincoln Center's Alice Tully Hall lasts two weeks and usually has a big-name premiere or two on the schedule; call (212) 875-5610.

October

Feast of St. Francis of Assisi. Early October. The Francis-like blessing of the animals at St. John the Divine used to be a fairly sedate affair, but nowadays it's a sort of well-bred circus, with snakes, rabbits, ferrets, exotic birds, and, yes, even elephants being offered for prayer. Call (212) 662-2133.

NBA and NHL at MSG. Season openers. If you're a sports fan, you can read this. If not, it means that pro basketball (the Knicks) and ice hockey (the Rangers) are back in town at Madison Square Garden. Call (212) 465-6741 for information on both teams.

Pulaski Day Parade. Sunday nearest October 5. Polish-American festival, sometimes called Polish Day, marches Fifth from 26th to 52nd.

Columbus Day Parade. Second Monday in October. A combination Founder's Day, Italian pride, and star-spangled celebration down Fifth Avenue from 44th to 86th.

SoHo Arts Festival. Mid-October. This originally one-day event is up to nearly a fortnight now, with street theater, performance art, dance, and music indoors and out.

International Fine Arts and Antiques Dealers Show. Mid- to late October. The last (actually, the first, as dealers consider the season) of New York's major shows comes just in time for holiday shopping, if you can afford it. At least you can look. At the Seventh Regiment Armory; call (212) 472-0590.

Greenwich Village Halloween Parade. October 31. Yet another over-the-top and inimitable dress function, this annual party-on-legs (and some wheels) circles the Village; check local papers for the exact route. Walk-ups welcome; gather at Sixth Avenue just above Houston at dusk.

Next Wave Festival. October to December. The Brooklyn Academy of Music showcases avant-garde, experimental, and new music, dance, and performance; call (718) 636-4100.

New York City Marathon. Last Sunday in October or first Sunday in November. One of the big races—not counting the 2.5 million cheering onlookers and volunteers—and with one of the most scenic courses, which includes the Verrazano Narrows Bridge, stretches of Fifth Avenue, and a finish line at Tavern on the Green in Central Park. Call (212) 860-4455 for information.

November

Big Apple Circus. November to January. You might have forgotten how this cherry little one-ring operation got its name; but watch the little big top go up in the park outside Lincoln Center and then try to resist; call (212) 268-2500.

Christmas Extravaganza at Radio City Music Hall. Mid-November to January. Traditional family favorite featuring the Rockettes in their Toy Soldier kick line, music, costumes, and so on. Call (212) 247-4777.

WTA Tour Championships. Mid-November. Madison Square Garden lays the courts for the old Virginia Slims women's tennis tourney; call (212) 465-6741.

Macy's Thanksgiving Day Parade. Late November. Well, how else would Santa Claus—not to mention Snoopy and Woodstock and Garfield and Bullwinkle and half of Broadway—make it to Herald Square on time? The parade begins at Central Park West and 77th and works down Broadway to the store at 34th Street; call (212) 494-5432. Santa takes up his station in Macy's beginning the next day.

December

Lighting of the Christmas Tree at Rockefeller Center. The first Monday evening in December, the mayor pulls the switch, and people sing, ice skate, make wishes, you name it; the tree will be lit throughout the month. Call (212) 632-3975.

Lighting of the Hanukkah Menorah at Grand Army Plaza. Sometime in December, the first "candle" on this giant (32-foot) menorah at the corner of Fifth and 59th opens the Jewish holiday season; other candles are lit every night for the next week.

Antiques Show at the Seventh Regiment Armory. Around the second weekend in December. Another blockbuster sale drawing 100 dealers in serious seventeenth-, eighteenth-, and nineteenth-century American, European, and Asian furniture and art. Call (212) 472-1180.

***Nutcracker* Ballet.** The Sugar Plum Fairy is absolutely everywhere, including the IMAX in Times Square. The American Ballet Theater version, for sentimentalists, is in the New York State Theater in Lincoln Center (call (212) 870-5570), but the local papers will have many others listed.

***Messiah* Sing-Along at Lincoln Center.** Mid-December. Huge public performance of Handel's popular oratorio in Avery Fisher Hall, with rehearsals and coaching beforehand; call (212) 845-5400. Dozens of other sing-alongs, carolings, and family performances will be listed in the local papers.

Kwanzaa Celebrations. Watch for listings of African American ethnic festivities around town.

New Year's Eve. December 31. Times Square must be one of the most famous addresses in New Year's folklore. It's a heck of a street party, complete with countdown and lighted ball. However, for those more intrigued by culture than alcohol, Manhattan's First Night celebration is one of the largest and finest progressive parties in the country, winding up with such old-fashioned touches as a dance in Grand Central Station and fireworks over the Tavern on the Green in Central Park; call (212) 922-9393. Or for those who have made their resolutions a day early, there's a midnight run through the park; call (212) 360-3456.

PART THREE

New York Hotels*

New York's hotel scene reflects the constant energy of the city. In the early 1990s, about a third of New York City's hotel rooms were empty, and their rates were falling, but today tourism is soaring and taking room prices with it. Crowds from around the world are revolving through hotel doors in record numbers—occupancy hovers at over 80 percent (up from 69 percent in 1992, which is about the current national occupancy rate). At holiday periods and when major conventions are in town, rooms are harder to find than slow-talking New Yorkers. Fuhgedaboudit.

Why did hotels come out of their slump? First, in 1994, the exorbitant 21 percent state and city tax on hotel rooms, highest in the nation, fell by more than a fourth when convention organizers threatened boycotts; the city cut its part of the occupancy tax, and the state eliminated it totally.

As in the overall tourism scene, business and leisure travel have increased with an improving economy. The upbeat message—seen repeatedly in the media—is that the city is cleaner, crime has plummeted, and new attractions are being developed and updated. Even in the dark days of the mid-1970s, things were never as bad as New York-bashers made them out to be, and right now, this is seen by many as the greatest city in the world, with some of the greatest hotels.

Despite the demand for rooms, the high cost of construction and the lack of development sites have kept new hotel construction to a minimum. Among the emerging projects for decade's end include an Embassy Suites Hotel in Battery Park City; and the Tishman E-Walk hotel and the Sofitel, both near Times Square.

But ever resourceful New Yorkers are meeting the growing need for quality guest rooms in a clever way: Hotels large and small, old and new, are being upgraded, expanded, modernized, and converted. Flush with cash, hoteliers are pouring money back into their properties (capital expenditures last year

---

* Lea Lane is a freelance writer, specializing in travel, food, personality, and lifestyle articles. She contributes to and edits guidebooks (including *Fodor's Greece '97, Birnbaum's USA,* and Zagat's restaurant and hotel guides) and is a contributing editor to Reed Travel Group's Star Service hotel guide.

exceeded $400 million to refurbish, enhance, and technify, and the money and the improvements keep coming). Properties undergoing recent major overhauls include the Roosevelt, Waldorf Astoria, New York Palace, Beekman Tower, Regency, Sheraton New York Hotel and Towers, Sheraton Manhattan, Sheraton Russell, New York Marriott Marquis, and Roger Williams.

Distinguished but down-and-out older buildings—warehouses, office buildings, apartment houses, and low-end hotels—are being tastefully transformed into stylish showplaces, their rosette ceilings and mahogany wainscoting a backdrop for dataports and digital electronics, their coffee shops and cramped lobbies gutted and then dramatized. Ornate facades, once grimy, now show off cleaned-up cornices and polished copper, and passersby and neighborhoods enjoy the improvements as much as the guests.

The trend is heating up. In 1997, about 20 new hotel projects were announced or begun, potentially adding about 6,000 badly needed new rooms, at a cost of over $1 billion. Diversity is the name of the new game, with hotels planned throughout the city, including emerging areas such as Lower Manhattan and Times Square. Most will be midsized properties. Nine of the projects involve conversion of existing buildings, and some are expansions of existing properties, such as the Millennium Broadway and the Shoreham. Some hotels are aimed at smaller, niche markets, such as budget travelers or lovers of Irish culture; others reflect the cosmopolitan nature of the city, such as the luxury hotel in a landmark Wall Street former bank building, built by Italy's Cipriani restaurant tycoons.

Themes are big. The Hotel Pennsylvania across from Madison Square Garden will become a sports-theme hotel and entertainment complex called the Official All-Star Hotel. Planet Hollywood plans a big hotel at 47th Street and Broadway. Projects of the Gotham Hospitality Group, a leader in the transformation of overlooked hotel properties, include a train-theme hotel near the refurbished and enhanced Grand Central Station.

Chains are also looking to reconvert and add more presence here. Marriott, Hilton, Sheraton, Hyatt, Loews, and Holiday Inn have the most city rooms. Marriott plans to increase its room share even further—there will be new Courtyard hotels at an office building on 53rd and Third Avenue and in the Garment Center, and the company's constantly searching for other hotel sites in former office buildings in Lower Manhattan. Ritz Carlton plans to convert ten floors of a downtown office at Battery Place to five-star luxury.

In addition, multi-use structures with office, condos, and hotel space are increasing, including the Trump International complex on Columbus Circle, a new 384-room Marriott as part of Renaissance Plaza complex in Brooklyn, and a waterfront hotel in Jersey City, across the Hudson River, as part of the Newport complex.

One of the most exciting developments on New York's hotel scene is the rising of a new great building, for the twenty-first century. In 1999, the visionary hotel at 42nd Street and Eighth Avenue near Times Square will add a beacon for visitors and a major presence on the city skyline. Designed by the Miami-based Arquitectonia, this 860-room immediate landmark will have a "meteor of light" shooting from the top and, at the base, a "postcard wall" mural of New York City icons such as the Statue of Liberty and the Empire State Building. This new hotel project best symbolizes the creative future of the hotel industry and of the city itself.

■ Some Things to Consider ■

New York hotels are big on breathtaking views and grand lobbies, business services and concierges, great restaurants and lavish bars. But even in luxury establishments, guest rooms are often small, and recreational facilities will not match those in most major cities.

Why? Cost per square foot to build in Manhattan is outrageous, so to turn a profit, hotels opt for creating more guest rooms and appealing watering holes where pay back is high. Rather than health clubs, pools, and tennis courts, most great hotels offer only small fitness centers or passes to health clubs in the neighborhood.

The hotel scene here is different in other ways as well, as New York is as much a world city as an American one. Out of about 32 million visitors last year, almost 6 million were from other countries. Because a large percentage of visitors come from around the globe, hotels must deal with this international aspect. As a result, front desk people speak many languages, translation services are easy to obtain, a concierge is often around at even a small hotel, shops are oriented toward international goods familiar to overseas customers, and many bathrooms have bidets.

Security is a well-known need here, as many guests are wealthy and famous. New York hotels usually have key cards rather than keys and have regular floor checks by in-house guards. Most upscale hotels have room safes, and all comply with strict city fire codes. Loitering does not go unnoticed. The safest element of city hotels is that even in the wee hours of the morning, staff will be at the front desk, and usually you will find other guests in the lobby—New York goes on round the clock.

In New York, perception is important, so uniformed doormen (few of these greeters are women) are standard at upscale apartments, and they are a tradition also at good hotels—even if there is a revolving door. They are there as much for show and small services as for security: giving a friendly greeting, hailing cabs, holding umbrellas, and bringing luggage within the lobby. Few hotels still have elevator operators—the Pierre is one holdout—but especially for women traveling alone, it is a welcome bonus late at night.

To find the best hotel for your stay in New York, consider the following factors when choosing, and check before booking. To find out more, our chart at the end of the chapter will help in your selection, or you could call, peruse brochures, or access computer information on hotels. If you use a travel agent, explain carefully what matters most to you in selecting a hotel, and have the agent write those requests down.

Purpose of Stay. This is perhaps the first question to ask yourself, because if you know why you're traveling, you'll know which hotel services and amenities are vital and where the best location would be. In New York there's no doubt that you can find a hotel that fills the bill.

- If you are on business, you might need special services, meeting space, and room facilities such as dataports and dual telephone lines. Most big hotels are well-equipped for this. But if you're a leisure traveler you won't need them—and won't want to pay for them. Major chains such as Marriott, Hilton, Hyatt, and Sheraton will have the business facilities, but nowadays independents, such as the newly refurbished Roger Williams, can have state-of-the-art room facilities even if they lack meeting space.

- If you're out to impress, then location will matter. But where you stay depends on whom you want to impress. The Upper East Side is the luxury address, but the Village is impressive to creative types. Public space and type of decor may be especially important, so you should scan brochures carefully. The St. Regis, Four Seasons, Pierre, Carlyle, Mark, Waldorf Astoria, Essex House, Lowell, and Elysee are among the most impressive hotels for New York style.

- If you'll be spending lots of time in your room, then its size, view, and amenities will matter more. You'll appreciate a VCR, CD player, and good lighting. Again, check out our chapter chart or hotel brochures, or ask your agent to ask about these features.

- Want to weave a romantic spell? Smaller, special hotels can add to the mood, and round-the-clock room service, king-sized beds, whirlpool tubs, and soft lighting will help. The Plaza Athenee, the Inn at Irving Place, and the Box Tree are all especially romantic hotels.

Convenience. Time is perhaps the most precious commodity when traveling, and you can save big money if you don't have to spend it on long cab rides or parking fees. So think in terms of what you will be doing, and where you will be doing it, then choose a hotel from our zone map, as close to your needs as possible. Also, check the survey to see which hotels are closest to public transportation lines, which are safe, affordable, and efficient ways to get around.

For example, for ultimate convenience, if you'll be spending a weekend seeing Broadway shows, stay at a nearby hotel such as the Marriott Marquis or the Paramount. Like to jog and enjoy the country? Stay as close to country as Manhattan gets—across from Central Park at the Park Lane, Mayflower, or Essex House. If you plan on lining up to get tickets for *The Late Show with David Letterman,* the Ameritania is around the corner. Visiting the Metropolitan Museum of Art? The Stanhope faces it. Lincoln Center? The Empire Radisson is across the street. If you're visiting your cousin in Westchester, the Grand Hyatt is connected to Grand Central, and if your cousin is in Long Island, the Metro Hotel is near Penn Station. Saving time and money by being able to walk or take public transportation to your destination will make your stay more special.

View. What NYC lacks in horizontal space it makes up for in height, and a stunning by-product is the view. Whether it's a favorite landmark, the rivers, or the parks, a hotel somewhere in this city will be overlooking them. If you check out our zone map, you can find which hotels are closest to whatever it is that you may want to overlook; these are the hotels that will offer your choicest views.

For example, if you like to watch the tugboats and water traffic and bridges of the East River, hotels along First Avenue, such as the Beekman Tower and the U.N. Plaza–Park Hyatt, will offer that watery scene (and the bonus of the United Nations complex). Hotels that rim the Park on Fifth Avenue, Central Park South, and Central Park West offer bucolic views. Midtown east hotels in the 30s and 40s are most likely to include views of landmarks such as the Chrysler Building or Empire State Building. Hotels closest to the tip of Manhattan will offer some rooms overlooking New York Harbor and the Statue of Liberty. Hotels near Broadway, such as Novotel, the Marriott Marquis, the Renaissance New York Hotel, and the Crowne Plaza will have blazingly colorful neon vistas. And the tallest (read largest) hotels throughout the city will provide panoramas that include huge sections of dramatic skyscrapers, rivers, and parks.

Be sure when reservations are made to request a high floor and "the best view possible," or, even more specifically, ask for a view of whatever it is that you want to see.

Noise. To a New Yorker the sounds of silence or a twittering bird can be off-putting, but the noise of a garbage truck grinding away, a wailing, piercing ambulance, or a car alarm at 3 a.m. is standard. You learn to live with it.

The city may never sleep, but you probably want to. Downtown (especially the financial district, at night) and Uptown are quieter than Midtown, which according to traffic experts has more vehicles per square mile than anywhere else in the country—some 700,000 motorists daily. Streets are generally less noisy than avenues—and avenues closer to the rivers than to Midtown are often quietest, although the West Side Drive along the Hudson and FDR Drive along the East River are heavily trafficked and often have emergency vehicles. If noise is a primary concern to you, stay away from hotels near hospitals, police stations, firehouses, or nightclubs. Major hospitals are at First Avenue and 16th Street, First Avenue and 32nd Street, York Avenue and 68th Street, East End Avenue and 88th Street, Park Avenue and 77th Street, Seventh Avenue and West 11th Street, and Tenth Avenue and West 59th Street.

Ask for a room away from street noise (or elevator noise, if that matters). High up is better, but surprisingly, not that much, as sound seems to echo against the skyscrapers. Older hotels, built before World War II, usually have the thickest walls, but most luxury hotels are exceptionally well insulated. Check our survey to make sure your hotel's windows are at least double-glazed; triple-glazing is even better and keeps most street noise out. Hotels such as the Kitano, on heavily trafficked routes, are well soundproofed because of this. And some new hotels, such as the Casablanca, have quadruple-glazing! Some relatively "quiet" hotels include the Kimberley, Lyden Gardens, the Gorham, Morgans, San Carlos, and the Sutton.

Amenities. New York is a quintessential urban environment: culture, all-night action, superb restaurants, clubs, bars. Most hotels offer dataports, fax and copying services, and e-mail retrieval, plus conference rooms of all sizes, with state-of-the-art facilities. Some offer kitchenettes. But there are more unusual offerings as well. The Mansfield, Shoreham, Roger Williams, and Wales offer free chamber music concerts, free breakfast, free parking, and nightly dessert buffets. The U.N. Plaza–Park Hyatt offers an indoor pool and tennis courts. The Four Seasons offers toys for kids and food for pets.

You may have special needs, and if so, you should mention them when booking. Physically challenged guests should clarify whether rooms designated for handicapped guests just have hand rails in bathrooms or have made-to-order furnishings and complete wheelchair access. If you have a car, a garage is a major convenience and free parking a big bonus. If you have a family, or are planning a longer stay, a suite situation or a kitchenette can be a wonderful help. We have investigated to find hotels offering unusual amenities that might appeal to you, so check out our survey.

Food. Hotel dining has become some of the best in city, and locals as well as visitors reserve tables at the finest of these restaurants weeks in advance.

A three-course dinner will cost at least $60 per person with a glass of wine, tax, and tip, but lunches often cost less, and pretheater dinners or prix fixe special meals are usually good values.

If dining is a priority and you enjoy the convenience of a great restaurant only an elevator ride from your room, check out the following list. When you book the hotel, ask for restaurant reservations at the same time if you know when you'll want to dine. Hotel guests get priority, but the sooner you reserve a table at these popular restaurants, the better.

Daniel at the Surrey, Le Cirque 2000 at the Palace, Halcyon at the Righa Royal (or Sunday brunch in the penthouse), Lespinasse at the St. Regis, Fifty Seven Fifty Seven at the Four Seasons, Les Celebrities at the Essex House, Adrienne at the Peninsula, Le Regence at the Plaza Athenee, Mark's at the Mark, Asia de Cuba at Morgans, Jean-Georges at Trump International, and Cafe Pierre at the Pierre are among the finest restaurants in the city.

Service. The level of service in New York hotels varies from the most polished and refined in the world to straightforward, no-nonsense help, which some may find rude. The city is used to assertive people, and to hold your own in this competitive atmosphere, you must do as New Yorkers do. Good manners are essential anywhere, but here you can ask a little harder and louder if there's something that you'd like, or like changed. (In New York, it's called "chutzpah.")

Although service may vary from one front desk person to the next, good management ensures an atmosphere where "the guest is always right"—or at least starts out that way. The goal should be to please you, and to work to get you to come back.

Smaller hotels that cater to independent travelers are more likely to give better service, as they can't compete in terms of physical plant and amenities and will focus on making guests feel special. Most hotels offer polite help, but the chains and larger establishments, who can rely on a return clientele through tours and larger groups, often offer service that isn't bad but may be just impersonal. If that satisfies you, then most hotels in New York will be acceptable. But if you like to be pampered, the finest hotels and small independent hotels will be better bets.

You can look at a brochure or read a chart to find out much about hotels, but when it comes to service, the best indicator is reputation based on actual experience of travel agents, friends, or coworkers. Otherwise, find answers to the following questions if service is important to you.

- Is there is a service desk or service representative, such as a concierge? These are signs that a hotel is at least aware of the importance of service.

- How are you greeted? Is there a doorman? Are you taken to your room by a hotel representative? Are you provided with clear information and asked if you need anything?
- If you make a request, are your needs fulfilled promptly and courteously?
- What services are offered as standard—secretarial, translators, goods, babysitters, concierges, luggage handlers, valet parking?
- Is your room turned down at night?
- Is there 24-hour room service?
- Most luxury hotels pride themselves on service. The Michelangelo offers a kit with everything from dental floss to condoms. At the St. Regis, 24-hour butler service is a specialty. Service translates into luxury, and in the final analysis, terrific service is what makes a hotel great. Other hotels with a rep for great service include the Four Seasons, St. Regis, the Mark, the Elysee, the Lowell, the Carlyle, the Pierre, and the Peninsula.

Size. Size may not count in some things, but in hotel rooms it can make a big difference. Most New York hotels, even the finest, have generally smaller rooms than in other major cities. But on the other hand, hotels such as Flathotel, which have been converted from apartment houses (flat = apartment, get it?), offer huge units. Check our survey if bigger is better for you.

Tour and Convention Groups. Some New York hotels specialize in convention or tour groups. This potentially translates into dozens and sometimes hundreds of people all trying to check in or out at the same time, tying up the front desk and bell service for lengthy periods. If you are an individual traveler, trying to compete with large groups can be time-consuming and frustrating. Even more maddening is to find yourself on the same floor with a tour group of 100 high school seniors, running up and down the corridor in the middle of the night, partying, and slamming guest room doors. Having encountered this scenario many times, we learned this: First, do not expect hotel security to make more than a token effort at getting the unruly group under control, and second, forget about trying to find one of the group's adult leaders. They presumably are smart enough to stay in a different hotel. Here's the bottom line: In a large hotel always ask for a room on a floor where no tour group is booked.

■ Be Hotel Wise ■

New Yorkers learn to use what's available and make do with what isn't. Here are some general tips to act like a local when it comes to hotels.

- Find out how old the hotel is and when the guest rooms were last renovated. Request promotional brochures, and ask if brochure photos of guest rooms are accurate and current.
- Check out the room before committing your luggage to it, and if you are not satisfied, ask for a better one. This is a more common action in Europe, but New York hoteliers are not surprised by it. If you have a legitimate gripe, such as size, housekeeping, lack of view, or noise, chances are you will get results, and a better room.
- Maximize the concierge. Many hotels claim to have a concierge, and some even have a special desk. But the best NYC hotels have helpers who can book anything and advise about everything. You can often acquire hard-to-get tickets this way, even at the last minute—if you're willing to pay the top fee—as a good concierge has the savvy and connections needed.
- Guidebooks may be helpful for recommendations, but if you book restaurants through concierges, you will often get better tables, better service, and more response to complaints, as the restaurant doesn't want to offend the concierge and lose future business. As for tipping your concierge, no need unless they provide unusual service.
- If you reserve in the hotel restaurant, be sure to mention that you are staying at the hotel. You'll probably get better attention.
- Aggressiveness works well in the hotel field, especially in the Big Apple. Don't take no the first time for major requests.
- If you're on business, try to get a room with at least a portion of a sitting area. If you meet there, you'll save time, money, and hassle, and it will be more appropriate than sitting on a bed.
- Check in early and out late. Often you can extend your stay by several hours. If you arrive around noon for a 3 p.m. check-in, your room may already be made up. At worst, you can leave your bags in a locked room and return later. If you ask politely for a late check-out on your last day, you can often get it. But 2 p.m. is usually the latest hotels are willing to give.
- If you're a single traveler, avoid giant hotels. Small hotels will more often go out of their way for your business and even make you feel like a VIP. You can be lost in the shuffle in a place that caters to conventions or large tour groups.
- If you have a great view, open the curtains all the way! The greater your sense of place here in New York, the more you get for your money.

Hotel Neighborhoods

Unless business or friends and family take you to one of the outer boroughs, or you can't get a room otherwise, the place to stay is Manhattan. Within the narrow island are hundreds of choices—from the finest in the world to faded but acceptable structures.

But where in Manhattan?

Most New York hotels are clustered in the Midtown area, from 42nd Street to 86th. With the city on the upswing, fine new and refurbished hotels are turning up from the 90s, down to the Battery, from SoHo and Chelsea to Chinatown, the Village, and the West Side. Generally, Downtown is trendy, Uptown is quiet, and Midtown is bustling.

■ Downtown ■

Here Peter Minuet bought Manhattan island from the Indians for the equivalent of $24. Today, that hardly covers a room service snack. Among the concrete canyons of the bulls and bears of Wall Street and the towers of the World Trade Center are several modern hotels, geared to the business and leisure traveler. Because many visitors are on work assignments, most hotels in this area are large and offer complete business services. These include the Millennium Hilton and the Marriott Financial Center Hotel.

But visitors also flock to Battery Park, the Statue of Liberty and Ellis Island, the new Holocaust Museum, and South Street Seaport, Chinatown, and Little Italy. New restaurants and shops, recreational areas and bike paths—even water sports like parasailing in the Hudson River—make this an increasingly appealing part of the city. Many hotels will be reconverted from existing buildings in the next five years to add to the room inventory.

Downtown is relatively quiet at night, with fewer nightspots than in the rest of the island. Also, although subways are convenient, bus service is erratic, and cab fares to Midtown are expensive. But the Staten Island ferry, with its great views, is now free.

■ Greenwich Village and SoHo ■

Restaurants, galleries, shops, and theaters abound, and NYU and the New School offer courses and cultural delights. But surprisingly, until a few years ago you'd have to go elsewhere to sleep, and there still are only a few hotels, including the Washington Square Hotel and the SoHo Grand. This is a wonderful area to browse in, with action most of the night, and subway lines are good in linking you quickly to other areas. But hotels are minimal, and aside from B&Bs, the hotel scene here will probably stay that way, as potential sites are few.

■ 14th to 30th Streets ■

The Chelsea Piers sports complex on the Hudson River offers everything from bowling to volleyball to indoor golf. Union Square has a summer greenmarket. Artists are converting old buildings into studios and galleries. Many older buildings are ripe for renovation in this improving but still underrated neighborhood of businesses, universities, hospitals, and off-Broadway theaters, and a few hotels have already been opened. But for the most part, good hotels are few and far between. Visitors to the Chelsea Market and the Joyce, the city's modern dance theater, will like the new Chelsea Savoy Hotel on the West Side. The Inn at Irving Place is a tiny, choice place near leafy and quiet Gramercy Park on the East Side. Look for lots of small hotels developing from commercial buildings in the coming years as the area continues to improve.

■ 31st to 41st Streets ■

This bustling area of offices, sports complexes, the Garment District, Macy's, the Jacob Javits Convention Center, and transportation terminals is no-nonsense, and large, midrange hotels reflect the group clientele and convention needs. Visitors to Madison Square Garden, by Penn Station, can stay at the small Metro Hotel. The proposed ribbon of greenery along the Hudson, with its bicycle paths and benches, should improve the West Side hotel scene in the next decade. On the East Side, quiet Murray Hill is home to the J. P. Morgan Library and nearby small hotels, such as stylish Morgans and the spiffy Roger Williams.

■ 42nd to 59th Streets: The East Side ■

Midtown draws delegates and visitors to the U.N., Fifth Avenue shoppers, NBC sidewalk-studio gawkers, Rockefeller Center ice skaters, business travelers at corporate headquarters, and those who like being at the center of the city's energy. Some of the best hotels in the world offer great East River and landmark-building views. A beautifully refurbished Grand Central provides easy access to the northern suburbs and Connecticut. Among the dozens of fine skyscraper hotels are several suite properties, such as the Beverly, and the classic art deco Waldorf Astoria.

■ 42nd to 59th Streets: The West Side ■

In Times Square the neon is brighter than ever, and so is the spirit. Neighborhoods are cleaner and safer. Porno is on the way out. Broadway, Carnegie Hall, theme restaurants, TV studios, and the office buildings along Columbus Circle and the Avenue of the Americas all draw visitors. Chains such as Holiday Inn, Marriott, Howard Johnson, and Days Inn and older, slightly seedy hotels abound, as tour groups are centered here. But the Trump International Hotel and the other great hotels rimming the southern end of Central Park are among the best anywhere. Look for an increase in hotel rooms as buildings are reconverted and office-residential complexes developed.

■ 60th Street and Above ■

Uptown—refined, fashionable, exclusive, cultural. Central Park is the oasis of this area, but there are also famous museums and top hospitals. Two-storied Madison Avenue is one of the most fascinating shopping areas of the world, and Lincoln Center is a renowned cultural focal point. Great views of the park and the rivers abound. Not surprisingly, some of the fanciest hotels in the city are here, including the Carlyle, the Lowell, and the Mark.

Can You Even Get In?

Even with about 60,000 hotel rooms in New York City, during much of the year it's not easy getting a reservation. With apologies to songwriters Kander and Ebb, if you can make a reservation there, you can make one anywhere. It's up to you—and your resourcefulness—to get a room in NY, NY. Here are some suggestions.

Check out the Peak Season Hotel Hotline. It provides access to rooms at over 80 hotels in all price categories from September 1 to December 31. Last year, on the 64 nights when travel agents and consumers believed the city was "sold out," the hotline found rooms each night. Call (800) 846-7666.

Book as far in advance as possible. Holidays are always busy, but even when occupancy is down in many parts of the country, rooms often are fully booked here, as huge conferences reserve blocks of hotel rooms years in advance, frequently at odd times. Check with the NYMCVB. Traditionally, the easiest time to get a room is during January and February.

Use travel and tour agencies who do lots of NYC convention business. They often have the clout to find a room, even when you're on your own. Usually the major agencies will do the most convention business; otherwise, inquire from friends or business associates who have traveled on business to New York, or ask around locally. As for tour operators, the five who most handle New York City are ATI (American Tour International), Allied Tours, T-Pro, CAUSA, and City Tours. Your travel agent will help you reserve through tour operators.

Be flexible. The more rigid your requests, the harder it may be to fill them. Ask what's available. Management may not have many standard rooms but can sometimes offer luxury suites or relatively unappealing rooms—poor view, low floor, not yet refurbished. If you're willing you can often negotiate a deal for these white elephants.

Think small. Smaller hotels with fewer rooms are less likely to host huge groups, and they cater more to individual travelers. You can often find a room even at busy times.

Think independent. When rooms are scarce, this increasing market in the city's hotel scene often has availability, as they are less well-known and have smaller advertising budgets than chains.

Call just after 6 p.m. on the day you want to stay. That is when most properties cancel reservations not guaranteed with a credit card on the day of arrival. (In the industry, these nonguaranteed reservations are called "timers.")

Stay outside Manhattan. You can drive, hire a cab or limo, or take public transport. Because many working New Yorkers live outside the city, the metro and Tri-State transportation network is the biggest in the country, and you can get to almost any borough, or to the suburbs, by public transport until the wee hours of the morning. So if you don't mind commuting, you can find a variety of accommodations outside Manhattan.

Queens, Brooklyn, Staten Island, and the Bronx have some chain hotels, and around Kennedy, La Guardia, and Newark airports you will find many midlevel choices (see our hotel listings). But nearby Westchester County, southern Connecticut, and Long Island have a varied selection of luxury hotels, inns, resorts, and B&Bs, with more recreational space at generally lower cost than comparable accommodations in the city. You may miss out on urban excitement, but you're more likely to get a room.

The following is a sampling of notable accommodations within an hour or so outside the city. All are near subway or train lines (taxis usually meet trains) and are in safe neighborhoods and offer free parking, outstanding settings and decor, and excellent on-site or nearby restaurants.

Westchester County, NY

The Castle at Tarrytown, Benedict Avenue, Tarrytown; (914) 631-1980; fax, (914) 631-4612

Crabtree's Kittle House, 11 Kittle Road, Chappaqua; (914) 666-8044; fax, (914) 666-2684

Doral Arrowwood, Anderson Hill Road, Rye Brook; (800) 633-6569; fax, (914) 939-1877

Long Island

Garden City Hotel, 45 Seventh Avenue, Garden City; (516) 747-3000; fax, (516) 747-1414

The Inn at Great Neck, 30 Cutter Mill Road, Great Neck; (516) 773-2000; fax, (516) 773-2020

Southern Connecticut

The Homestead Inn, 420 Fieldpoint Road, Greenwich; (203) 869-7500; fax, (203) 869–7502

Hyatt Regency Greenwich, 1800 East Putnam, Old Greenwich; (203) 637-1234; fax, (203) 637-2940

The Inn at National Hall, 2 Post Road West, Westport; (800) 628-4255, (203) 221-1351; fax, (203) 221-0276

Slice the Price of Rooms in the Apple

The bad news: With demand for hotel rooms at an all-time high, so, unfortunately, are prices. In 1997 room rates were almost 40 percent higher than in 1993—despite the recent occupancy tax repeal. Average room rates are about $200 a night in 1998, and at top luxury hotels, standard rooms go for $400 or so—the highest rate in America. Tourists from around the world, it seems, will pay any price to visit.

The good news: Compared to other great international cities such as London, Paris, Tokyo, and Berlin, New York is a relative bargain. Remember that as you plunk down your plastic, signing off on what seems like the GNP of Honduras. Here are some helpful ideas for lowering costs:

- Check out the Internet. Last-minute bargains are now available online. You can judge comparative value for money by seeing a listing of hotels—what they offer, where they are located, and what they charge.

- Stay in a less-than-fashionable neighborhood. New York is made up of many distinct neighborhoods, and this emphasis on address reflects itself in pricing. Unless you need to be there for convenience, it may not be worth it to you to stay on the Upper East Side when the same level of room on the Lower West Side may be half the cost. The East Side is priciest; Midtown and up to 96th Street is the fanciest area. The best deals are around Chelsea and on the Upper West Side.

- Don't drive. Garaging a car overnight in New York can cost as much as motel rooms in most cities. Taxis are abundant and public transportation is exceptional. New York is a walkers' paradise, and most of the city is divided into simple grids. If you must drive, try for a hotel with free parking. See our survey.

- For longer stays, try an apartment hotel. The city has several upscale hotels that offer this option, including the Palace Hotel and the Waldorf Towers. These hybrids combine hotel services with a kitchen and residential feel and are wonderful for entertaining and as an alternative to getting an apartment. Suites can be less costly alternatives. Mention it if you're staying longer than a week, and you may get a deal.

- Seek a suite that includes a kitchen. Several hotels offer this option, which can accommodate four or more people and helps you save on restaurant bills.

- Stay at the worst room at a good hotel, rather than the best at a lesser one. Ask for the smallest room, the lowest floor, the worst view. The cost differential can be considerable, although the rest of the hotel services, amenities, and public rooms remain the same. You're getting the biggest bang for your buck.

- Avoid room service and minibars. Bring food up from delis, take-out groceries (usually with salad bars), or sidewalk vendors, which purvey fresh fruits as well as hot dogs and falafels. Most will provide utensils if needed, as New Yorkers are known for eating on the run. Or make like a resident and have a restaurant deliver (allowed at some hotels, frowned on at others—check). Neighborhood restaurants, especially the "ethnics," are good and reasonable. If you eat like a local rather than a tourist, you will save.

- Skip the in-house movies. Bring a book. Better yet, go down to the street and walk to see dramatic stories and sights beyond fiction.

- Go basic. YMCAs and youth hostels are available in the city. Bare-bones, but cheap. There are Ys on the East Side (call (212) 756-9600) and West Side (call (212) 787-4400). Hostelling International offers a hostel on the Upper West Side (call (800) 909-4776). For dormitory accommodations, check with universities in the city, including New York University.

- Get a discounted rate. Check out deals through ads, agents, special events, openings. These include weekend and convention deals, frequent mileage clubs, automobile or other travel clubs, senior rates (some require ages as low as 50), military or government discounts, corporate or shareholder rates, packages, long-stay rates (usually at least five nights), and travel industry rates. Some hotels might even give lower rates if you are visiting because of bereavement or medical problems.

Special Weekend Rates

Most hotels that cater to business, government, and convention travelers offer special weekend discount rates ranging from 15 to 40 percent below normal weekday rates. Find out about weekend specials by calling individual hotels or by consulting your travel agent.

Corporate Rates

Many hotels offer discounted corporate rates (5–20 percent off rack rate). Usually you don't need to work for a large company or have a special relationship with the hotel—simply ask for this discount. Some will guarantee the discounted rate on the phone when you make your reservation. Others may make the rate conditional on your providing some sort of bona fides— for instance, a fax on your company's letterhead requesting the rate, or a company credit card or business card upon check-in. Generally, the screening is not rigorous.

Half-Price Programs

Larger discounts on rooms (35–60 percent), in New York or anywhere else, are available through half-price hotel programs, often called travel clubs. Program operators contract with an individual hotel to provide rooms at deep discounts, usually 50 percent off rack rate, on a "space available" basis. This generally means that you can reserve a room at the discounted rate whenever the hotel expects less than 80 percent occupancy. A little calendar sleuthing to help you avoid citywide conventions and special events will increase your chances of choosing a time when the discounts are available.

Most half-price programs charge an annual membership fee or directory subscription charge of $25 to $125. You get a membership card and a directory listing participating hotels. But note the restrictions and exceptions. Some hotels "black out" certain dates or times of year. Others may only offer the discount certain days of the week or require you to stay a certain number of nights. Still others may offer a much smaller discount than 50 percent off rack rate.

Programs specialize in domestic travel, international travel, or both. More established operators offer members between 1,000 and 4,000 hotels to choose from in the United States. All of the following programs have a heavy concentration of hotels in California and Florida, and most have a limited selection in New York City.

Encore	(800) 444-9800
Entertainment Publications	(800) 445-4137
ITC-50	(800) 987-6216
Privilege Card	(800) 359-0066
Quest	(800) 638-9819

If something seems too good to be true, it usually is, and that truism also applies to half-price programs. Not all hotels offer a full 50 percent discount.

Some figure the discount on an exaggerated rack rate that nobody would ever have to pay. A few may deduct the discount from a supposed "superior" or "upgraded" room rate, even though the room you get is the hotel's standard accommodation.

Though it's hard to pin them down, the majority of participating properties base discounts on the published rate in the *Hotel and Travel Index* (a quarterly reference work used by travel agents) and work within the spirit of their agreement with the program operator. As a rule, if you travel several times a year, your room rate savings will easily compensate you for membership fees.

Note: Deeply discounted rooms through half-price programs are not commissionable to travel agents. In practical terms, this means you must ordinarily make your own inquiry calls and reservations. If you travel frequently, however, and run a lot of business, your travel agent will probably do your legwork, lack of commission notwithstanding.

Preferred Rates

This discount helps travel agents stimulate their booking activity or attract a certain class of traveler. Most preferred rates are promoted through travel industry publications and are often accessible only through an agent. Sound out your travel agent about possible deals, but note that the rates shown on travel agents' computerized reservations systems are not always the lowest rates obtainable. Zero in on a couple of hotels that fill your needs in terms of location and quality of accommodations, then have your agent call the hotel for the latest rates and specials.

Hotel reps almost always respond more positively to travel agents because they represent a source of additional business. As we discussed earlier, there are certain specials that hotel reps will disclose only to travel agents. Also, when the hotel you want is supposedly booked, a personal appeal from your agent to the hotel's director of sales and marketing will often get you a room.

Wholesalers, Consolidators, and Reservation Services

The discount available (if any) from a reservation service depends on whether the service functions as a consolidator or as a wholesaler. Consolidators are strictly sales agents who do not own or control the room inventory they are trying to sell. Discounts offered by consolidators are determined by the hotels with rooms to fill. Consolidator discounts vary enormously depending on how desperate the hotel is to unload the rooms. When you deal with a room reservation service that operates as a consolidator, you pay for your room as usual when you check out of the hotel.

Wholesalers have long-standing contracts with hotels that allow the wholesaler to purchase rooms at an established deep discount. Some wholesalers hold purchase options on blocks of rooms, while others actually pay for rooms and own the inventory. Because a wholesaler controls the room inventory, it can offer whatever discount it pleases consistent with current demand. In practice, most wholesaler reservation-service discounts fall in the 10–40 percent range. When you reserve a room with a reservation service that operates as a wholesaler, you must usually pay for your entire stay in advance with your credit card. The service then sends you a written confirmation and usually a voucher (indicating prepayment) for you to present at the hotel.

Our experience has been that the reservation services are more useful in finding rooms when availability is scarce than in obtaining deep discounts. Calling the hotels ourselves, we were often able to beat the reservation services' rates when rooms were generally available. When the city was booked, however, and we could not find a room by calling the hotels ourselves, the reservation services could almost always get us a room at a fair price.

When you call, you can ask for a rate quote for a particular hotel or, alternatively, ask for their best available deal in the area where you prefer to stay. If there is a maximum amount you are willing to pay, say so. Chances are the service will find something that will work for you, even if they have to shave a dollar or two off their own profit.

Services that frequently offer substantial discounts include:

Accommodations Express	(800) 444-7666
Central Reservation Service	(800) 548-3311
Express Reservations	(800) 356-1123
Hotel Reservations Network	(800) 964-6835
Quikbook	(800) 789-9887
RMC Travel	(800) 245-5738
Room Finders USA	(800) 473-7829

■ How to Evaluate a Travel Package ■

New York City–area package vacations can be a win/win proposition for both the buyer and the seller. The buyer only has to make one phone call and deal with a single salesperson to set up the whole vacation: transportation, lodging, meals, guided tours, and Broadway shows. The seller, likewise, only has to deal with the buyer once, eliminating the need for separate sales, confirmations, and billing. In addition to streamlining sales, processing, and administration, some packagers also buy airfares in bulk on contract, like a broker playing the commodities market. Buying a large number of airfares in advance allows the packager to buy them at a significant savings from posted fares.

The same practice is also applied to hotel rooms. Because selling vacation packages is an efficient way of doing business, and because the packager can often buy individual package components (airfare, lodging, etc.) in bulk at discount, savings in operating expenses realized by the seller are sometimes passed on to the buyer. So in addition to convenience, the package is also an exceptional value. At least that's the way it's supposed to work.

But often the seller cashes in on discounts and passes none on to the buyer. In some instances, packages are also loaded with extras that cost the packager next to nothing but inflate the retail price higher than the Empire State Building. A real New York–style con game.

When considering a package, choose one that includes features you are sure to use, because you will be paying for them. Second, if cost is of greater concern than convenience, make a few calls and see what the package would cost if you booked its individual components (airfare, lodging, shows, etc.) on your own. If the package price is less than the a la carte cost, the package is a good deal. Even if the costs are about the same, the package is probably worth buying just for the convenience.

If your package includes a choice of rental car or airport transfers (transportation to and from the airport), take the transfers. Driving in the city is difficult, and parking in a garage is expensive, around $30 for a 24-hour period. During the weekend, with most businesses closed and commuters and second-home types out of town, it's relatively easier to get around, and parking spaces may be available; but during the week, forget it. (If you do take the car, be sure to ask if the package includes free parking at your hotel.)

Is Your Travel Agent NYC Savvy?

The city hotel scene is complex and constantly changing. Has your travel agent recently been to New York? If he or she doesn't have much knowhow, you might want to switch agents or book yourself. You may need to check out the location and rates of any suggested hotel and make certain that the hotel is suited to your itinerary.

To keep it simple, some travel agents unfamiliar with the Apple may try to plug you into a tour operator's or wholesaler's preset package. This essentially allows the travel agent to set your whole trip up with a single phone call and still collect an 8–10 percent commission. The problem is that most agents will place 90 percent of their New York business with only one or two wholesalers or tour operators. It's the line of least resistance for them but doesn't provide much choice for you.

Travel agents will often use wholesalers who run packages in conjunction with airlines, like DeltaVacations or American's Fly Away Vacations. Because of the wholesaler's exclusive relationship with the carrier, these trips are easy for travel agents to book. However, they can be more expensive than a package offered by a high-volume wholesaler who works with airlines in a primary New York City market.

To help your travel agent get you the best possible hotel deal, follow these five steps:

1. Determine where you want to stay in New York, and if possible choose a specific hotel. Review the hotel information provided in this guide, and contact hotels that interest you.

2. Check out the hotel deals and package vacations advertised in the Sunday travel sections of the *New York Times, New York Daily News, Philadelphia Inquirer,* or *Boston Globe.* Often you will be able to find deals that undercut anything offered in your local paper. See if you can find specials that fit your plans and include a hotel you like.

3. Call the hotels, wholesalers, or tour operators whose ads you have collected. Ask any questions you have concerning their packages, but do not book your trip with them directly.

4. Ask your travel agent if he or she can get you something better. The deals in the paper will serve as a benchmark against which to compare alternatives.

5. Choose from the options that you and your travel agent uncover. No matter which option you select, have your travel agent book it. Even if you go with one of the packages in the newspaper, it will probably be commissionable (at no additional cost to you) and will provide the agent some return on the time invested on your behalf. Also, as a travel professional, your agent should be able to verify the quality and integrity of the deal.

■ **If You Make Your Own Reservation** ■

Call the specific hotel as opposed to the hotel chain's national 800 number. Quite often, the reservationists at the national 800 number are unaware of local specials. Always ask about these specials before you inquire about corporate rates—and don't be afraid to bargain. If you're buying a hotel's weekend package, for example, and want to extend your stay into the following week, you can often obtain at least the corporate rate for the extra days. However, do your bargaining before you check in, preferably when you make your reservations.

■ **Are You Coming to NYC on Business?** ■

In NYC, primary considerations for business travelers are most likely affordability and proximity to business. Identify the zone(s) where your business will take you, then use the Hotel Chart to cross-reference the hotels located in that area. Once you have developed a short list of possible hotels that are convenient, fit your budget, and offer the standards you require, you (or your travel agent) can apply the cost-saving suggestions discussed earlier to obtain the lowest rate.

Convention Rates: How They Work and How to Do Better

If you're attending a major convention or trade show, the meeting's sponsoring organization has probably negotiated convention rates with a number of hotels. Under this arrangement, hotels agree to block a certain number of rooms at an agreed-upon price for conventioneers. In the case of a small meeting, only one hotel may be involved; but citywide conventions may involve almost all downtown and airport hotels.

Because the convention sponsor brings big business to New York and reserves many rooms, often annually, it usually can negotiate volume discounts substantially below rack rate. But some conventions and trade shows have more bargaining clout and negotiating skill than others, and your convention sponsor may not be one of them.

Once a convention or trade show sponsor completes negotiations with participating hotels, it sends its attendees a housing list that includes all the hotels serving the convention, along with the special convention rate for each. You can then compare these convention rates with the rates using the strategies covered in the previous section.

If the negotiated convention rate doesn't sound like a good deal, try to reserve a room using a half-price club, a consolidator, or a tour operator. Remember, however, that many of the deep discounts are available only when the hotel expects to be at less than 80 percent occupancy, a rarity when a big convention is in town.

Strategies for Beating Convention Rates—Easy as 1-2-3

1. Reserve early. Most big conventions and trade shows announce meeting sites one to three years in advance. Get your reservation booked as far in advance as possible using a half-price club. If you book well ahead of the time the convention sponsor sends out the housing list, chances are good that the hotel will accept your reservation.

2. Compare your convention's housing list with the list of hotels presented in this guide. You may be able to find a suitable hotel not on the housing list.

3. Use a local reservations agency or consolidator. This is also a good strategy if you need to make reservations at the last minute. Local reservations agencies and consolidators almost always control some rooms, even in the midst of a huge convention or trade show.

Hotels and Motels: Rated and Ranked

■ What's in a Room? ■

Holiday Inn, Marriott, Four Seasons—each chain has a discernible standard, and many variables determine the "livability" and quality of a hotel room besides cleanliness, state of repair, and decor.

Designing a hotel room is more complex than picking a bedspread to match the carpet and drapes. It's an art, a planning discipline that combines both form and function. Unfortunately, in New York, some beautifully appointed rooms are cramped and simply not well designed. *Unofficial Guide* researchers are aware of this and spend many weeks inspecting hotel rooms. Here are a few of the things we check.

Room Size. Smaller rooms can be cozy, but a large and uncluttered room is generally preferable, especially for a long stay, or when you'll be spending extended time there. New York's hotel rooms are generally smaller than those in other major cities because it is so expensive to build here. Accept this, note the other luxuries, and if it's a problem, ask about size when booking. And if a room is well-designed, with nooks and alcoves, it can make up for the lack of size. Rooms at the Four Seasons, at 600 square feet, are just about the largest in the city, and as large as many New York one-bedroom apartments, and are reputed to have cost over a million dollars each to design and furnish.

Temperature Control, Ventilation, and Odor. The best system, because it's so quiet, is central heating and air conditioning, controlled by the room's own thermostat. Next best is a room module heater and air conditioner, preferably controlled by an automatic thermostat, but usually by manually operated button controls. The worst system is central heating and air without any sort of room thermostat or guest control.

Most hotel rooms have windows or balcony doors that have been permanently sealed. Though there are some legitimate safety and liability issues involved, we prefer windows and balcony doors that can be opened to admit fresh air. Hotel rooms should be odor-free and smoke-free and not feel stuffy or damp. A room with a view is preferable, and a balcony or terrace is especially exciting (and rare) in New York City, not just because you can step outside but because of the full-length windows.

Room Security. Better rooms have locks that require a plastic card instead of the traditional lock and key. Card and slot systems allow the hotel to change the combination or entry code of the lock with each new guest. Though larger hotels and hotel chains with lock and key systems usually rotate their locks once each year, they remain vulnerable to hotel thieves much of the time. Many smaller or independent properties rarely rotate their locks.

In addition to the entry lock system, the door should have a deadbolt, and preferably a chain that can be locked from the inside. A chain by itself is not sufficient. Doors should also have a peephole. Any windows and balcony doors should have secure locks. The front desk should also be well-trained and discreet about calling out your room number. Room safes are becoming standard security devices, and the bigger the better, so that technical devices, cameras, and other large items can also be stored.

Safety. Every room should have a fire or smoke alarm, clear fire instructions, and preferably a sprinkler system. Bathtubs should have a nonskid surface, and shower stalls should have doors that either open outward or slide side-to-side. Bathroom electrical outlets should be high on the wall and not too close to the sink. Balconies should have sturdy, high rails.

Noise. As we mentioned earlier, New York is a city filled with traffic and street noises round the clock. If this is a potential problem for you, check to make sure that windows are double- or triple-glazed. In addition, most travelers have been kept awake by noise in the hall or by the television, partying, or amorous or aggressive activities of people in the next room. In better hotels, wall and ceiling construction are substantial, effectively screening routine noise. Carpets and drapes, in addition to being decorative, also absorb and muffle sounds. Mattresses mounted on stable platforms or sturdy bed frames do not squeak much, even when challenged by the most acrobatic lovers. Televisions enclosed in cabinets, and with volume governors, rarely disturb guests in adjacent rooms.

In better hotels, the air-conditioning and heating system is well maintained and operates without noise or vibration. Likewise, plumbing is quiet and positioned away from the sleeping area. Doors to the hall, and to adjoining rooms, are thick and well-fitted to better block out noise. Remember, if you are easily disturbed by noise, ask for a room on a higher floor, off main thoroughfares, and away from elevators and ice and vending machines.

Darkness Control. Ever been in a hotel room where the curtains would not quite meet in the middle? Thick, lined curtains that close completely in the center and extend beyond the edges of the window or door frame are required. In a well-planned room, the curtains, shades, or blinds should almost totally block light at any time of day.

Lighting. Poor lighting is an extremely common problem in American hotel rooms. The lighting is usually adequate for dressing, relaxing, or watching television, but not for reading or working. Lighting needs to be bright over tables and desks, and beside couches or easy chairs. Since so many people read in bed, there should be a separate light for each person. A room with two queen beds should have individual lights for four people. Better bedside reading lights illuminate a small area so that if one person wants to sleep and another to read, the sleeper will not be bothered by the light. The worst situation by far is a single lamp on a table between beds. In each bed, only the person next to the lamp will have sufficient light to read. This deficiency is often compounded by weak light bulbs.

In addition, closet areas should be well-lit, and there should be a switch near the door that turns on room lights when you enter. A seldom seen, but desirable, feature is a bedside console that allows a guest to control all or most lights in the room from bed. Bathroom lighting should be adequate for grooming purposes.

Furnishings. At bare minimum, the bed(s) must be firm. Pillows should be made with nonallergic fillers, and in addition to the sheets and spread, a blanket should be provided. Bedclothes should be laundered with fabric softener and changed daily. Better hotels usually provide extra blankets and pillows in the room or on request and sometimes use a second top sheet between the blanket and spread. Duvets over down comforters, once a strictly European luxury, are becoming the standard of cleanliness and comfort.

Dressers should be large enough to hold clothes for two people during a long stay. The room should be equipped with a luggage rack and full-length mirror.

Televisions should be large and cable-connected; ideally, they should have volume governors and remote controls and be mounted on swivel bases and, preferably, enclosed. Local channels should be posted on the set, and a local TV program guide should be supplied. In-room movies and VCR capabilities are nice options.

Telephones should be touchtone, capable of International Direct Dialing, conveniently situated, with easy-to-understand dialing instructions and a rate card. Local white and yellow pages should be provided. Better hotels install phones in the bathroom and furnish portable phones or equip room phones with long cords. Two lines and dataports for fax and laptop computers are becoming standards at luxury and business-oriented hotels.

A small table with chairs, or a desk, and a sitting area—perhaps with French doors to block off work and sleep areas—are important elements. Well-designed hotel rooms usually have a plush armchair or a sleeper sofa for lounging and reading. Better headboards are padded for comfortable reading in bed, and there should be a nightstand or table on each side of the bed(s). Nice extras in any hotel room include small refrigerators or mini-bars, digital alarm clocks, irons and ironing boards, coffee makers, and trouser presses.

Bathroom. Marble, granite, and tile look best and are easy to keep clean. Two sinks are better than one, and you cannot have too much counter space. A sink outside the bath is a great convenience when one person bathes as another dresses, and sinks should have drains with stoppers. A separate toilet area is nice for privacy, and bidets are good options.

Better bathrooms have both a tub and shower with a nonslip bottom. Tub and shower controls should be easy to operate; adjustable shower heads are preferred, and whirlpool tubs and separate shower stalls are a plus. The bath needs to be well-lit and should have an exhaust fan and a guest-controlled bathroom heater. Towels and washcloths should be large, thick, and generously supplied. There should be an electrical outlet for each sink, conveniently and safely placed.

Magnifying mirrors, scales, bathrobes and slippers, phones, hair dryers, lines for TVs or extra speakers, and amenities such as fine soaps, shampoos, and lotions all add to the luxury of the bathroom.

Vending. Complimentary ice and drink machine should be located on each floor, or easily available from room service. Welcome additions include a snack machine and a sundries (combs, toothpaste) machine. The latter are seldom found in large hotels that have restaurants and shops. Luxury hotels will provide sundries upon request.

Maintenance. You can see, smell, and touch to check out how well-maintained your room is. This is imperative, for even if a room is large and luxurious, if it isn't clean it isn't habitable. On the other hand, a basic clean room may be just fine. Check out whether the hotel offers daily maid service. Luxury hotels offer twice-daily turndown service (and that nice chocolate on the pillow).

■ Room Ratings ■

To distinguish properties according to relative quality, tastefulness, state of repair, cleanliness, and size of standard rooms, we have grouped the hotels and motels into classifications denoted by stars. Star ratings in this guide apply to New York–area properties only and do not necessarily correspond to ratings awarded by Mobil, AAA, or other travel critics. Because stars carry little weight when awarded in the absence of commonly recognized standards of comparison, we have linked our ratings to expected levels of quality established by specific American hotel corporations.

★★★★★	*Superior Rooms*	Tasteful and luxurious by any standard
★★★★	*Extremely Nice Rooms*	What you would expect at a Hyatt Regency or Marriott
★★★	*Nice Rooms*	Holiday Inn or comparable quality
★★	*Adequate Rooms*	Clean, comfortable, and functional without frills (like a Motel 6)
★	*Super Budget*	

Star ratings apply to room quality only and describe the property's standard accommodations. For most hotels and motels a "standard accommodation" is a hotel room with either one king bed or two queen beds. In an all-suite property, the standard accommodation is either a one- or two-room suite. In addition to standard accommodations, many hotels offer luxury rooms and special suites that are not rated in this guide. Star ratings for rooms are assigned without regard to whether a property has restaurant(s), recreational facilities, entertainment, or other extras.

In addition to stars (which delineate broad categories), we also employ a numerical rating system. Our rating scale is 0–100, with 100 as the best possible rating and zero (0) as the worst. Numerical ratings are presented to show the difference we perceive between one property and another. Rooms at the Sheraton New York, the Grand Hyatt, and the Algonquin Hotel are all rated as four-star (★★★★). In the supplemental numerical ratings, the Sheraton is rated an 89, the Grand Hyatt an 88, and the Algonquin an 84. This means that within the four-star category, the Sheraton and Grand Hyatt are comparable, and both have slightly nicer rooms than the Algonquin.

The location column identifies the New York City zone where you will find a particular property.

■ How the Hotels Compare ■

Cost estimates are based on the hotel's published rack rates for standard rooms. Each "$" represents $80. Thus, a cost symbol of "$$$" means a room (or suite) at that hotel will cost about $240 a night. Below is a hit parade of the nicest rooms in town. We've focused strictly on room quality and excluded any consideration of location, services, recreation, or amenities. In some instances, a one- or two-room suite can be had for the same price or less than that of a hotel room.

If you use subsequent editions of this guide, you will notice that many of the ratings and rankings have changed. In addition to the inclusion of new properties, these changes also consider guest room renovations or improved maintenance and housekeeping. A failure to properly maintain guest rooms or a lapse in housekeeping standards can negatively affect the ratings.

Finally, before you begin to shop for a hotel, take a hard look at this letter we received from a couple in Hot Springs, Arkansas:

> *We cancelled our room reservations to follow the advice in your book [and reserved a hotel room highly ranked by the* Unofficial Guide]. *We wanted inexpensive, but clean and cheerful. We got inexpensive, but [also] dirty, grim, and depressing. I really felt disappointed in your advice and the room. It was the pits. That was the one real piece of information I needed from your book! The room spoiled the holiday for me aside from our touring.*

Needless to say, this letter was as unsettling to us as the bad room was to our reader. Our integrity as travel journalists, after all, is based on the quality of the information we provide our readers. Even with the best of intentions and the most conscientious research, however, we cannot inspect every room in every hotel. What we do, in statistical terms, is take a sample: We check out several rooms selected at random in each hotel and base our ratings and rankings on those rooms. The inspections are conducted anonymously and without the knowledge of the management.

Although unusual, it is certainly possible that the rooms we randomly inspect are not representative of the majority of rooms at a particular hotel. Another possibility is that the rooms we inspect in a given hotel are representative but that by bad luck a reader is assigned a room that is inferior. When we rechecked the hotel our reader disliked, we discovered that our rating was correctly representative but that he and his wife had unfortunately been assigned to one of a small number of threadbare rooms scheduled for renovation.

The key to avoiding disappointment is to snoop around in advance. We recommend that you ask for a photo of a hotel's standard guest room before you book, or at least get a copy of the hotel's promotional brochure. Be forewarned, however, that some hotel chains use the same guest room photo in their promotional literature for all hotels in the chain; a specific guest room may not resemble the brochure photo. When you or your travel agent call, ask how old the property is and when your guest room was last renovated. If you arrive and are assigned a room inferior to that which you had been led to expect, demand to be moved to another room.

How the Hotels Compare

Hotel	Zone	Quality Rating	Star Rating	Cost
Four Seasons Hotel	9	98	★★★★★	$$$$$$$$–
The St. Regis	9	98	★★★★★	$$$$$$$–
Trump International Hotel and Tower	10	98	★★★★★	$$$$$$$$–
Essex House Hotel Nikko New York	8	97	★★★★★	$$$$$–
The Waldorf Towers	9	97	★★★★★	$$$$$$–
The Carlyle	13	96	★★★★★	$$$$$+
Hotel Elysee	9	96	★★★★★	$$$+
The Lowell	11	96	★★★★★	$$$$$+
Westin Central Park South	8	96	★★★★★	$$$$$+
The Mark	13	96	★★★★★	$$$$$+
The New York Palace	9	96	★★★★★	$$$$$
Omni Berkshire Place	9	96	★★★★★	$$$$+
The Pierre	11	96	★★★★★	$$$$$–
Le Parker Meridien New York	8	95	★★★★½	$$$$+
The Regency Hotel	11	95	★★★★½	$$$–
Rihga Royal Hotel	8	95	★★★★½	$$$$$
The Waldorf-Astoria	9	95	★★★★½	$$$$+
Hotel Inter-Continental New York	9	94	★★★★½	$$$$–
The Michaelangelo	8	94	★★★★½	$$$$–
Morgans	9	94	★★★★½	$$$$–
Regal U.N. Plaza	9	94	★★★★½	$$$$+
Sheraton Manhattan Hotel	8	94	★★★★½	$$$+
The Stanhope	13	94	★★★★½	$$$$$–

How the Hotels Compare (Continued)

Hotel	Zone	Quality Rating	Star Rating	Cost
Surrey Hotel	13	94	★★★★½	$$$$–
Crowne Plaza at the United Nations	8	93	★★★★½	$$$–
Doral Tuscany	9	93	★★★★½	$$$$+
Flatotel International	9	93	★★★★½	$$$$+
The Inn at Irving Place	7	93	★★★★½	$$$$+
Millennium Broadway	8	93	★★★★½	$$$+
Paramount	8	93	★★★★½	$$$+
The Royalton	9	93	★★★★½	$$$$+
Doral Park Avenue Hotel	9	92	★★★★½	$$$+
The Drake Swissotel	9	92	★★★★½	$$$$+
The Kitano New York	9	92	★★★★½	$$$$$–
The New York Hilton and Towers	8	92	★★★★½	$$$–
The Shoreham	9	92	★★★★½	$$$+
The Millenium Hilton	1	91	★★★★½	$$$$+
The Plaza	9	91	★★★★½	$$$$$$–
Renaissance New York Hotel	8	91	★★★★½	$$$+
Sheraton Russell Hotel	9	91	★★★★½	$$$$–
The Sherry-Netherland	9	91	★★★★½	$$$$–
Doral Court	9	90	★★★★½	$$$$–
Hotel Delmonico	9	90	★★★★½	$$$–
Hotel Plaza Athenee	11	90	★★★★½	$$$+
The Lombardy	9	90	★★★★½	$$$+
The Mansfield	9	90	★★★★½	$$$–
The Roger Williams	9	90	★★★★½	$$$$$$–
The Franklin	13	89	★★★★	$$$–
The Gorham	8	89	★★★★	$$$$$–
New York Marriott Financial Center	1	89	★★★★	$$$+
New York Marriott World Trade Center	1	89	★★★★	$$$+
Sheraton New York Hotel and Towers	8	89	★★★★	$$$$–
The Box Tree	9	88	★★★★	$$$$–
Grand Hyatt	9	88	★★★★	$$$+
Lyden Gardens	11	88	★★★★	$$$+

How the Hotels Compare (Continued)

Hotel	Zone	Quality Rating	Star Rating	Cost
New York Marriott Marquis	8	88	★★★★	$$+
Doubletree Hotel Guest Suites	8	87	★★★★	$$$+
Fitzpatrick Manhattan Hotel	9	87	★★★★	$$$$–
The Helmsley Park Lane Hotel	9	87	★★★★	$$$$
Novotel New York	8	87	★★★★	$$$–
The Warwick Hotel	8	87	★★★★	$$$+
Beekman Tower Hotel	9	86	★★★★	$$$–
The Helmsley Middle-towne Hotel	9	86	★★★★	$$+
Hotel San Carlos	9	86	★★★★	$$+
The Barbizon	11	85	★★★★	$$$+
Doral Inn	9	85	★★★★	$$$–
The Algonquin Hotel	9	84	★★★★	$$$$–
Hotel Wales	13	84	★★★★	$$$–
Radisson Empire Hotel	10	84	★★★★	$$$–
Crowne Plaza	8	83	★★★★	$$$+
New York Marriott East Side	9	83	★★★★	$$$–
Newark International Airport Marriott	n/a	83	★★★★	$$$–
SoHo Grand	2	84	★★★½	$$$$$–
Ameritania hotel	8	82	★★★½	$$$–
Sheraton LaGuardia East Hotel	17	82	★★★½	$$$–
Holiday Inn JFK Airport	17	81	★★★½	$$$+
Kimberly	9	81	★★★½	$$$+
Quality Hotel by Journey's End	8	81	★★★½	$$$–
Sheraton Newark	n/a	81	★★★½	$$+
New York Helmsley Hotel	9	80	★★★½	$$$$–
Best Western Seaport Inn	3	79	★★★½	$$+
Hotel Casablanca	8	79	★★★½	$$$+
Jolly Madison Towers Hotel	9	79	★★★½	$$$–
LaGuardia Marriott	17	79	★★★½	$$$–
The Wyndham	9	79	★★★½	$$–
Hotel Metro	7	78	★★★½	$$+
Murray Hill East Suites	9	78	★★★½	$$$–
Roosevelt Hotel	9	78	★★★½	$$$$–
Washington Square Hotel	4	78	★★★½	$$–
Chelsea Savoy	6	77	★★★½	$$+

How the Hotels Compare (Continued)

Hotel	Zone	Quality Rating	Star Rating	Cost
Hotel Bedford	9	77	★★★½	$$
Crowne Plaza LaGuardia	17	76	★★★½	$$+
JFK Airport Hilton	17	75	★★★½	$$−
Salisbury Hotel	8	74	★★★	$$$−
Das Hotel New York City	8	73	★★★	$$+
Hotel Beacon	12	73	★★★	$$−
Best Western President Hotel	8	72	★★★	$+
Leows New York Hotel	9	72	★★★	$$+
The Carlton	7	69	★★★	$$+
The Helmsley Windsor Hotel	8	68	★★★	$$+
Holiday Inn Downtown	2	68	★★★	$$+
The Mayflower Hotel	10	68	★★★	$$$−
Hotel Lexington	9	65	★★★	$$$−
The Milburn Hotel	12	65	★★★	$$−
Hotel Edison	8	64	★★½	$$−
Howard Johnson Plaza Hotel	8	61	★★½	$$−
Howard Johnson on Park Avenue	8	59	★★½	$$+
Shelburne Murray Hill	9	59	★★½	$$$+
Wellington Hotel	8	59	★★½	$$+
Hotel Pennsylvania	6	55	★★	$$−
Park Central Hotel	8	53	★★	$$+
Ramada Milford Plaza	8	51	★★	$$−

■ Top 30 Best Deals in New York ■

Having listed the nicest rooms in town, let's reorder the list to rank the best combinations of quality and value in a room. As before, the rankings are made without consideration of location or the availability of restaurant(s), recreational facilities, entertainment, and/or amenities. Once again, each lodging property is awarded a value rating on a 0–100 scale. The higher the rating, the better the value.

A reader recently complained to us that he had booked one of our top-ranked rooms in terms of value and had been very disappointed in the room. We noticed that the room the reader occupied had a quality rating of

★★½. We would remind you that the value ratings are intended to give you some sense of value received for dollars spent. A ★★½ room at $85 may have the same value rating as a ★★★★ room at $175, but that does not mean the rooms will be of comparable quality. Regardless of whether it's a good deal or not, a ★★½ room is still a ★★½ room.

Listed below are the best room buys for the money, regardless of location or star classification, based on averaged rack rates. Note that sometimes a suite can cost less than a hotel room.

Top 30 Best Deals in New York

Hotel	Zone	Quality Rating	Star Rating	Cost
1. Hotel Delmonico	9	90	★★★★½	$$$$$
2. The Helmsley Middletowne Hotel	9	86	★★★★	$$$$$–
3. Crowne Plaza at the United Nations	9	93	★★★★½	$$$$$$–
4. The Mansfield	9	90	★★★★½	$$$$$+
5. Washington Square Hotel	4	78	★★★½	$$$$–
6. Best Western President Hotel	8	72	★★★	$$$–
7. Hotel Elysee	9	96	★★★★★	$$$$$$$–
8. The Wyndham	9	79	★★★½	$$$$–
9. New York Marriott Marquis	8	88	★★★★	$$$$$–
10. Hotel San Carlos	9	86	★★★★	$$$$$–
11. The New York Hilton and Towers	8	92	★★★★½	$$$$$$–
12. Hotel Bedford	9	77	★★★½	$$$$
13. Radisson Empire Hotel	10	84	★★★★	$$$$$
14. JFK Airport Hilton	17	75	★★★½	$$$$–
15. Renaissance New York Hotel	8	91	★★★★½	$$$$$$+
16. The Franklin	13	89	★★★★	$$$$$+
17. The Shoreham	9	92	★★★★½	$$$$$$+
18. New York Marriott East Side	9	83	★★★★	$$$$$+
19. Sheraton Newark	n/a	81	★★★½	$$$$+
20. Roger Williams	9	90	★★★★½	$$$$$–
21. Millennium Broadway	8	93	★★★★½	$$$$$$$–
22. Sheraton Manhattan Hotel	8	94	★★★★½	$$$$$$$–

Top 30 Best Deals in New York (continued)

Hotel	Zone	Quality Rating	Star Rating	Cost
23. Beekman Tower Hotel	9	86	★★★★	$$$$$+
24. Doral Inn	9	85	★★★★	$$$$$+
25. Paramount	8	93	★★★★½	$$$$$$$−
26. Best Western Seaport Inn	3	79	★★★½	$$$$+
27. Chelsea Savoy	6	77	★★★½	$$$$+
28. The Lombardy	9	90	★★★★½	$$$$$$$−
29. Novotel New York	8	87	★★★★	$$$$$$−
30. Newark International Airport Marriott	n/a	83	★★★★	$$$$$$−

PART FOUR

Arriving and Getting Oriented

Arriving

Manhattan Island and the other boroughs that comprise New York City are situated near the mouth of the Hudson River on a narrow spit of land that dangles like an udder beneath the bulk of upstate New York. To the west, across the Hudson from Manhattan, is the rest of the United States, starting with New Jersey. Travel in any other direction and you will find yourself in one of New York City's boroughs. To the north of Manhattan across the Harlem River is the Bronx. Due east, on the opposite bank of the East River, is Queens. South of Queens and southeast of Manhattan is Brooklyn, while farther south and a little to the west sits Staten Island.

If you are one of those people who like to use the image of a clock for orientation, picture Manhattan Island as a slim strip in the center of the clock, with one end pointing at 12 and the other end at 6. Surrounding Manhattan, the Bronx takes up all the space between 12 and 2. Queens runs from 2 to 4 and Brooklyn from 4 to almost 6. Staten Island goes from 6 to 7. From 7 back around to 12 is New Jersey, separated from the Bronx by the Hudson River.

If you are an American, there's a good chance that your forebears entered the United States through New York, steaming west out of the Atlantic Ocean into Lower New York Bay, through the Narrows between Staten Island and Brooklyn, north into Upper New York Bay, and finally past the Statue of Liberty to docks near the southern tip of Manhattan Island. Today, of course, it's possible to arrive in New York by just about any means imaginable, making it one of the most accessible cities in the world.

By Car

If you are planning to arrive via automobile, you need this guidebook more than you ever imagined. Traffic in Manhattan comes in two basic modes: nutso and gridlock. With nutso you're moving, but everybody else is moving faster and usually at an angle that presupposes an imminent collision. Gridlock is gridlock. Bring a sandwich and a pocket edition of *War and Peace* and prepare yourself for some serious butt-time. Native New Yorkers will consider this a gross exaggeration, of course, but then most of them have cab driver genes somewhere in their lineage.

If there was a driving school to prepare you for driving in Manhattan, it would emphasize the automobile as an offensive weapon and would teach you various Eastern European and Arabic dialects so that you could converse with other drivers. The final exam would involve wedging your car on the fly into spaces too small for the average cephalopod.

And then there are parking and gas. Filling stations are rare and generally not conveniently located, while safe, off-street parking in Manhattan costs as much per night as a hotel room in most other cities.

Driving in the boroughs is somewhat less daunting but is still more challenging than motoring in most other large U.S. cities.

So, having been warned, in case you elect to bring your nice, clean, undented car into Manhattan, here's what you need to know.

1. Manhattan is an island! This means that you must enter via a bridge or a tunnel.
2. Rush-hour traffic clogs all the tunnels and bridges, so try to time your arrival for off-peak traffic times—10 a.m. to 2:30 p.m. and 7:30 p.m. to 6 a.m. on weekdays are best.
3. Traffic in Manhattan is decidedly more civil on weekends, but avoid arriving during the late afternoon and early evening on Sunday.
4. Fill up your gas tank before coming into Manhattan.
5. If you will be lodging in Manhattan, use the Hotels Chart in the back of this guide to find hotels with parking garages.

Some Specific Directions

Coming from South or West of New York City. Coming from New Jersey, south of New York, you can take the Holland Tunnel into downtown Manhattan or the Lincoln Tunnel into Midtown. Both require tolls and both are accessed from I-95. The Holland Tunnel is also accessible from I-78. Unless you are heading for lower (downtown) Manhattan, we recommend the more northerly Lincoln Tunnel. A third option is to take I-278 across Staten Island and into Brooklyn, and from there enter Manhattan via the Brooklyn-Battery Tunnel. This last is quite roundabout and should only be considered when there is a traffic advisory for the Holland Tunnel.

Coming from North of New York City. Coming from north of the city and west of the Hudson River, you can choose between the Lincoln Tunnel or the George Washington Bridge, which crosses onto Manhattan at the northern end of the island.

East of the Hudson River, there's a dandy tangle of highways branching south to New York City from upper New York State, Connecticut, Rhode Island, and points farther north. Coming south on I-87, pick up the Henry Hudson Parkway below Yonkers to enter Manhattan. From I-95 south you have several choices. Either stay on I-95 as it crosses the upper end of Manhattan Island, or branch off onto I-278 and enter New York City via the Triborough Bridge (toll).

Arriving and Departing by Airplane

The New York area is served by three major airports. La Guardia Airport, located in Queens, is the closest, followed by John F. Kennedy International Airport (JFK), situated south of Queens on Jamaica Bay. To the west, in New Jersey, is Newark International Airport. La Guardia services primarily domestic flights and carriers, while JFK and Newark handle both international and domestic air traffic.

In general, La Guardia is closer and more convenient than JFK or Newark, though the difference is not all that great—about 20 or so additional minutes to most Manhattan destinations. Often, however, you can find bargain fares to Newark (and occasionally JFK) that more than make up for the longer commute.

If you are visiting New York during the winter, we recommend flying into either Newark or JFK. These airports have longer runways and electronic instrumentation that allows them to operate in weather that might shut La Guardia down. In addition, because they are larger than La Guardia, Newark and JFK can perform airplane de-icing operations adjacent to the active runways. At La Guardia, planes in need of de-icing are usually detoured to a remote staging area.

Another way to hedge your bet during the winter is to fly into Baltimore/Washington International (BWI) and then take an AMTRAK train directly to New York Penn Station. There are more than a dozen trains a day, and there is an AMTRAK station right at the airport. Conventional trains take about three hours and a quarter, while the express MetroLiners make the trip in two and a half hours.

Using BWI can also be a big dollar-saver. We flew Southwest Airlines, a discount carrier, to BWI for $112 round-trip from Birmingham, Alabama, and then transferred to AMTRAK. Our total cost was $238—$112 round-trip air plus $126 round-trip rail from BWI—compared with airfares to La Guardia, JFK, or Newark ranging from an economy $398 to a full coach fare of $788. Because the train deposits you right in the heart of Manhattan, you also avoid taxi or bus fares from the airport. Finally, if you can fly directly from your home airport to BWI, the plane/train combo can sometimes get you to New York faster than an air itinerary that requires a change of planes.

Transportation Chart

Name	Service	Phone
AMTRAK	Train service	(800) 872-7245
Airporter	Airport to airport transfers	(609) 587-6600
Carey Airport Express	NYC-airport bus service	(718) 632-0500
Delta Water Shuttle	La Guardia–NYC ferry	(800) 54-FERRY
Gray Line Air Shuttle	La Guardia–NYC shuttle	(212) 315-3006
JFK Int'l Airport	Airport	(718) 244-4444
La Guardia Airport	Airport	(718) 533-3400
Long Island Railroad	Commuter railroad	(718) 217-LIRR
MARC I of New York	Airport to airport transfers	(718) 352-7070
Metro-North Railroad	Commuter railroad	(212) 532-4900
New Jersey Transit	Buses & trains to NYC	(201) 762-5100
NYC Bridges & Tunnels	Bridge & tunnel info	(800) 221-9903
NYC Taxi & Limo Commission	New York City taxis	(212) 302-TAXI
NYC Transit Authority	Subways & buses	(718) 330-1234
New York Waterway	Commuter ferry service	(800) 533-3779
Newark Int'l Airport	Airport	(201) 961-6000
Olympia Trails Express Buses	NYC-airport bus service	(212) 964-6233
PATH Train	New Jersey–NYC train	(800) 234-7284
Parking Information	Parking information	(212) 442-7080
Port Authority Bus Terminal	Bus & subway station	(212) 564-8484
Road Conditions	Road condition information	(212) 442-7097

La Guardia Airport

La Guardia, the smallest of the New York airports, is located just off Grand Central Parkway in Queens. La Guardia has four terminals. All airlines except Northwest, Delta, and USAirways use the Central Terminal. USAirways and Delta have their own terminals. Delta shares its main terminal with Northwest and also uses the Marine Air Terminal for its Delta Shuttle flights. Because the Delta Shuttle operates at the opposite end of the airport from Delta's other flights, make sure you know from which terminal your Delta flight departs.

If you plan to arrive by air (except during winter, as discussed earlier) from within the United States or Canada, flying into La Guardia will usually get you to your Manhattan destination faster. How much faster depends on highway traffic conditions at the time of day you arrive. During nonrush periods it takes about 20–25 minutes by cab or limo and 35–45 minutes by bus from La Guardia to Midtown. During rush hour, traffic flows both in and out of the city, and the convenience of flying into La Guardia is sometimes offset by the snarled traffic of surrounding streets and highways. Although there is a water shuttle to the 34th Street Pier in Midtown, most arriving passengers commute to the city in cabs, limos, or buses. Getting into Manhattan from La Guardia during rush hour, while a hassle (allow 35–60 minutes to Midtown), is doable. Going to the airport in afternoon rush traffic is problematic. If you are booked on a flight that departs between 4:30 and 8 p.m. on weekdays, leave Manhattan two hours in advance if traveling by cab, two and a half hours in advance if using an airport shuttle bus.

To get from La Guardia to Manhattan, you have your choice of cab, limo, bus, or water taxi.

Commonly Used Public Transportation Routes

	To	Departs	Time
Carey Airport Express Bus Fare: $10	Grand Central Station & Port Authority Terminal	Every 30 minutes from 6:45 a.m. to midnight	35–45 minutes (nonrush)
Gray Line Air Shuttle Fare: $13.50	Drop-off anywhere between Battery Park and 63rd Street. Also stops at certain hotels between 63rd and 103rd Streets.	6 a.m. to 11:30 p.m.	55–110 minutes depending on destination

Commonly Used Public Transportation Routes (Continued)

	To	Departs	Time
Delta Water Shuttle. Call (800) 54-FERRY for schedule. Fare: $15 one-way, $25 round-trip	62nd Street Pier (Midtown), 34th Street (Wall Street), and Pier 11	Departs from Marine Air Terminal hourly	25–50 minutes depending on destination
Cab Fare: $18–26 plus tolls and tip	Any stop in Manhattan	At your convenience	20–35 minutes depending on destination (nonrush)
Limo Cost depends on type of limo	Any stop in Manhattan	At your convenience	20–35 minutes (nonrush)

John F. Kennedy International Airport

JFK is a sprawling, confusing, nine-terminal facility that most savvy travelers go out of their way to avoid. Almost 100 airlines, including most foreign carriers, use JFK. International travelers make domestic connections at JFK, while U.S. carriers daily fly in thousands of passengers bound for international destinations.

If you book a domestic itinerary arriving and depart from JFK using a carrier that flies internationally, beware. Try to avoid domestic flights that are the first leg of an international route. Once, for example, we booked a TWA flight from JFK to San Francisco and showed up at the airport about an hour in advance of departure time. Unfortunately (for us), our flight to San Francisco continued on to Kobe, Japan. Thus, flight check-in at JFK involved all of the jumping through hoops required of passengers on an international flight. The queue was horrendous, Kobe-bound travelers embarking from New York seemingly had dozens of bags to check, and of course, passports for those continuing on to Japan had to be scrutinized and validated.

To get from JFK to Manhattan you have your choice of cab, limo, bus, or subway.

Commonly Used Public Transportation Routes

	To	Departs	Time
Carey Airport Express Bus Fare: $13	Grand Central Station & Port Authority Terminal	Every 30 minutes from 6 a.m. to midnight	60 minutes (nonrush)
Gray Line Air Shuttle Fare: $16.50	Drop-off anywhere between Battery Park and 63rd Street. Also stops at certain hotels between 63rd and 103rd Streets.	6 a.m. to 11:30 p.m.	55–110 minutes depending on destination
Subway A Fare: $1.50	Manhattan all stops from Fulton St. to 207th St., Howard Beach Station to Midtown, plus stops in Queens and Brooklyn.	Trains depart every 15–25 minutes	60–75 minutes
Cab Fare: $30 flat rate plus tolls and tip	Any stop in Manhattan	At your convenience	40–60 minutes
Limo Cost depends on type of limo	Any stop in Manhattan	At your convenience	40–60 minutes

Newark International Airport

Newark International Airport is located in New Jersey between Newark and Elizabeth. There are three terminals serving about 50 domestic and foreign airlines. All of the terminals and long-term parking lots are connected by monorail. Newark International is better organized and decidedly less intimidating than JFK and generally more efficient than La Guardia. If your Manhattan destination is downtown or Midtown on the West Side, you should consider flying into Newark. Bus service, especially to downtown and to the Port Authority Terminal in Midtown, is excellent, with buses departing every 20–30 minutes 24 hours a day.

To get from Newark International Airport to Manhattan, you can choose from among limos, cabs, buses, or a combination of bus/cab and train.

Commonly Used Public Transportation Routes			
	To	Departs	Time
Olympia Trails Bus Fare: $10	Port Authority Terminal at 42nd and Eighth Ave.	Every 20–30 minutes, 24 hours a day	40–50 minutes
Olympia Trails Bus Fare: $10	Grand Central Terminal or Penn Station	Every 20–30 minutes	50–70 minutes
Airlink Bus AMTRAK & PATH to Newark Fare: $4	Bus to rail connections at Newark Penn Station	Every 20–30 minutes	15 minutes
Cab Fare: $35–55 plus tolls and tip	Any stop in Manhattan	At your convenience	40–60 minutes
Limo Cost depends on type of limo	Any stop in Manhattan	At your convenience	40–60 minutes

Getting into Manhattan from the Airports

When it comes to getting into the city from the airport, we opt for simplicity, even if it costs a dollar or two more. The fewer times you must heft your luggage around, the better, and likewise, the fewer stops or transfers necessary, the less complicated the trip.

From La Guardia we always take a cab or limo (see below), unless we are arriving at the Marine Air Terminal at rush hour, in which case we sometimes use the Delta Water Shuttle. From JFK we take a cab or limo. The JFK A-Train subway looks good on paper and is definitely the least expensive way to get into town, but it takes forever owing to countless intermediate stops. When it comes to Newark, we usually take the Olympia Trails express bus to the Port Authority Terminal on Manhattan's West Side in Midtown. Because of preferential treatment at the Lincoln Tunnel and a direct "buses only" throughway into the Port Authority Terminal, the bus can often make it to Manhattan faster than a cab (once the bus leaves the airport). From the Port Authority Terminal you can catch a cab or, if you are traveling light, a subway to your destination.

As an aside, the Port Authority Terminal is a huge, generally confusing maze of a building. After you disembark from the bus, your best bet is to make your way to ground level and exit the building on 42nd Street. You will find a cab stand just outside the door. If you plan to return to the airport via the terminal, locate the Airport Transportation Lobby on the first floor of the northern (42nd Street) side of the terminal. Though New York has made great progress in reducing crime in public places, the Port Authority Terminal is not a great spot to hang around. Unless, as we southerners say, "you're fixin' to explode," wait until you reach your hotel to use the rest room. If you are considering a taxi, fares from Newark International to Midtown run about $45 plus tolls and tip—a bit pricey unless there are three or more in your party.

From La Guardia and JFK, if there are two or more in your party, a cab is not much more expensive than the bus, plus it takes you right to your hotel. The Carey Bus from La Guardia to Grand Central Terminal, for example, is $10 per head. A couple using the Carey bus would spend $20 to get to Grand Central and then would probably need a cab to reach their hotel. By the time you add it all up, the cost is very comparable to the price of a cab straight from the airport, including tolls and tip.

Each terminal at all three airports has a taxi queue, a designated place for arriving passengers to catch a cab. Because there are always lots of cabs at the airport awaiting fares, it usually takes only a couple of minutes in line to get a cab. Do not accept a ride from any person who approaches you in the terminal or on the sidewalk. Official, licensed cabs load only at designated taxi stands, supervised by a dispatcher.

Savvy travelers have discovered limo services. For sometimes even less than a cab, a limo and driver will meet your flight and transport you into Manhattan. Limos, which incidentally encompass a diverse assortment of vehicles in addition to stretch Cadillacs, can be reserved by the trip or by the hour. Rates range from $18 for a trip from La Guardia to Manhattan in a modest sedan to over $150 for a ride to Newark International in something fancy. While you can occasionally beat the price of a cab, the big advantage to reserving a limo is having somebody there waiting for you—

i.e., no taxi queue. To reserve, call one of the operators listed below. Have your flight information handy, including airline, flight number, and arrival time. The service will also ask for your Manhattan destination. Although you can request that your driver meet you in the terminal, it's customary (and sometimes cheaper) to meet him curbside. Most limo services will accept prepayment by credit card, or alternatively, you can pay the driver. Tolls, parking fees, and gratuities are extra.

Town Cars Anywhere (WEX)	(800) 532-3730 or (914) 592-9200
Super Saver by Carmel	(800) 924-9954 or (212) 666-6666
Classic Limousine	(800) 666-4949 or (516) 567-5100
Tel Aviv Car & Limo Service	(800) 222-9888 or (212) 777-7777
Marc 1 of New York	(800) 309-7070 or (718) 729-7475
Dial Car	(800) 342-5106 or (718) 743-8383

Getting to the Airports from Manhattan

Essentially, you have the same options available when it's time to go to the airport for your return flight. For La Guardia and JFK your best bet is a cab. For Newark, take a cab to the Port Authority Terminal and then board an Olympia Trails bus for the airport.

There is one additional option for commuting to the airports: ride-sharing services. These services offer reserved-space door-to-door transportation to the airports.

To La Guardia or JFK:
Classic Airport Ride Share   (516) 567-5100

To Newark International:
Gray Line Air Shuttle   (212) 315-3006

With ride-share services, you call the service and advise them of your flight time. They integrate you into their pickup schedule and tell you what time to be ready to go. If you are the first person collected, you have a bit of driving to look forward to. On the other hand, if you are the last person in the van, it's straight to the airport you go. The service to Newark is a bargain at $14 and eliminates carting all your stuff through the Port Authority Terminal or paying big bucks for a cab. Ride-share service to JFK for one person will save you about $5–10 over the cost of a cab. Going to La Guardia, you're better off in terms of convenience and costs to take a taxi. For the record, the same companies also provide shared-ride service from the airports to Manhattan.

By Train

New York has excellent train connections south to Baltimore and Washington, D.C.; north to upstate New York, Boston, and New England; and west to New Jersey and eastern Pennsylvania. From these areas you can commute directly to Midtown Manhattan in a time span that rivals or betters that of traveling by air. From Baltimore, for example, we departed our hotel for the 10-minute ride to the AMTRAK Station, waited less than 20 minutes for the train to arrive, and then buzzed up to New York's Penn Station in about two and a half hours—a total of just under three hours for the whole trip. By contrast, our colleagues commuted 20 minutes to the airport, then consumed an hour and 10 minutes checking in, walking to the departure gate, and boarding. The flight from gate to gate to La Guardia took another hour. They had no checked luggage, but it took 15 minutes to unload and make it to the taxi queue, where the wait for a cab was a modest 5 minutes. Cabbing from La Guardia to Midtown consumed a little over 20 minutes—for a total of 3 hours and 10 minutes.

If you are traveling from points farther afield than the cities and areas listed above, the train, while mellow and relaxing, probably requires more time than you are prepared to invest. Sometimes, however, the longer hauls offer some unexpected benefits. Bill, traveling from Atlanta to New York, caught the AMTRAK Crescent at 7:30 p.m. With first-class accommodations, he enjoyed a sleeping compartment, and his meals were included as well. He arrived in New York at 2:10 the following afternoon. The cost of transportation, lodging, and meals on the train were less than regular coach airfare. Because it was easy to work on the train, Bill had plenty of time to both relax and prepare for his afternoon meeting in New York. His partner Jane, by contrast, spent a busy morning hustling to the airport, flying to La Guardia, cabbing into the city, and then trying to catch a bite to eat on the run. Other eastern cities with fairly attractive AMTRAK schedules and fares include Richmond, Norfolk, Raleigh/Durham, Charlotte, Charleston (SC), Birmingham, Savannah, Jacksonville, Orlando, Cleveland, Pittsburgh, Chicago, and Montreal. For additional information call AMTRAK at (800) 872-7245.

In addition to AMTRAK, four commuter railroads serve the greater New York area. New Jersey Transit (call (210) 762-5100) operates two lines, using New York Penn Station along with AMTRAK and the Long Island Railroad (call (718) 217-5477). The Metro-North Commuter Railroad, serving towns north along the Hudson River, arrives and departs from Grand Central Station.

By Ship

If you arrive in New York on a cruise ship you will probably tie up at the Passenger Ship Terminal on the far west side of the city between West 51st and West 52nd Streets. Cabs and limos provide transportation from the terminal to Manhattan and area destinations.

Getting Oriented

Laid out in a grid, New York is a very easy city to navigate. Avenues run north/south, while streets run east/west. Though some avenues have names (Park and Madison Avenues, for example) and some have names *and* numbers (Avenue of the Americas is also Sixth Avenue), most avenues just have numbers (First Avenue, Fifth Avenue, etc.). The numbering starts on the east side of Manhattan, with First Avenue, and ascends to Eleventh Avenue on the west side of the island.

Streets are a little trickier, but not much. Do you remember regular and irregular verbs from your English grammar studies? Well, in New York there are regular streets and irregular streets. Regular streets are numbered streets that run east/west, forming a nice grid with the avenues. Irregular streets are likely to run in just about any direction and generally have names instead of numbers. Most of the irregular streets are in the lowermost or uppermost parts of the island. In between the lower part and the upper part, in the 60 percent of Manhattan that comprises the middle, are the regular streets.

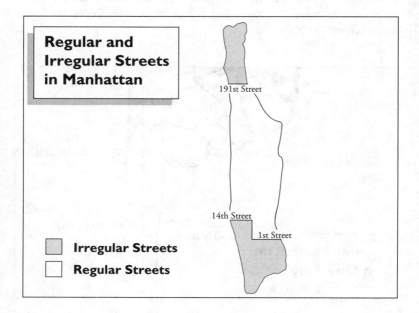

Regular and Irregular Streets in Manhattan

191st Street

14th Street

1st Street

■ **Irregular Streets**

□ **Regular Streets**

Between 191st Street way Uptown (north) and 14th Street Downtown (south) there is a lovely, predictable grid. The only notable irregular street in this section of Manhattan is Broadway, which carves a lazy diagonal from northwest to southeast across the grid. Another exception, though it's not a street, is Central Park, a long north/south rectangle running from 110st Street south to 59th Street.

Going south from 14th Street toward the lower part of the island, the grid system prevails all the way down to First Street and Houston Street, but *only* on the east side. On the west side below 14th Street to Houston is Greenwich Village, which contains mostly irregular streets. From Houston Street on down to Battery Park at the tip of Manhattan is a crazy patchwork of irregular streets. Some of New York's more colorful neighborhoods and districts, including Chinatown, Little Italy, the Bowery, SoHo, TriBeCa, and the Financial District, are packed into this confined space. City Hall and the World Trade Center are also located here. If you are walking or driving in this area, the best way to stay oriented is to imagine a finger pointed down with the palm toward you. Wall Street is the crease at the first knuckle from the tip. The middle crease (second knuckle) is Canal Street, and the crease where the finger joins the palm is Houston Street. If you take a pen and draw a line down the middle of the finger from your palm to the tip, bisecting all three creases, that would be Broadway. If you can keep these streets and their relationship to one another straight, you will never be lost for long in Lower Manhattan. If you use this little memory aid in public, we strongly recommend that you use your index finger (the finger located closest to the thumb).

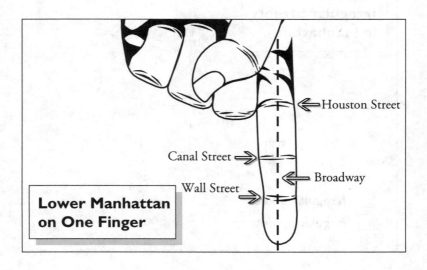

Houston Street

Canal Street

Broadway

Wall Street

Lower Manhattan on One Finger

Things the Locals Already Know

Tipping

As we've said, New York's unfriendly reputation is highly exaggerated, but the city requires a little "friendliness" on your part as well. This is a society accustomed to—one might almost say built on—the tipping system, and you should be prepared right from the start. Cabbies generally expect 15–20 percent of the fare as a tip, and you should certainly be generous if traffic is as bad as it generally is. If your hotel doorman gets you the cab, it's customary, though still optional, to slip him a dollar bill (besides, you don't want to have to wait next time, do you?). However, if you pick up the cab from one of the managed taxi stands at the train stations or airports, do not tip the traffic conductor.

Once at the hotel, expect to slip the bellman a dollar per suitcase ($2 if it's really heavy or clumsy); when you check out, leave behind at least $1 a day for the maids, $2 if the room has a second visit for turndown service or extra care. Tipping the concierge is a question of letting the reward fit the service: If she merely makes dinner reservations, a warm thank-you may suffice; but if she finagles them in the hottest restaurant in town, or gets opening-night tickets to a Broadway blockbuster, go for the 20 percent rule.

Bartenders get anywhere from 10 to 20 percent, depending on the generosity of the pour, the sight-seeing advice, the friendliness, and so on. (Unless it's really skimpy, just leaving your change on the bar is acceptable, but again, go by the atmosphere.) Waiters generally get 15–20 percent, although you should look to see whether an automatic gratuity has been built into the total. If you check your coats, tip the attendant $1 per wrap when you pick them up, and perhaps another dollar for large umbrellas or briefcases. Legends to the contrary, it is rare that slipping the maitre d' a bribe will do you much good, and it makes you look like a rube unless some actual rearrangement has been necessary. If you have summoned the sommelier to consult on the wine choice, you should leave him something in the range of 10 percent of the cost of the bottle.

Any personal services you arrange, such as a massage, hair styling, manicure, or the like, also require a tip of about 20 percent. And if you get a shoeshine—an underestimated pleasure, incidentally—you should surely throw in a bonus.

Local Press

As mentioned in Part 2, "Planning Your Visit to New York," most of the city's events and attractions are listed in the major dailies and weekly magazines. The primary newspapers include the *New York Times,* which devotes the most coverage to cultural events and entertainment; and the tabloids *New York Post* and *Daily News,* which don't devote much space to them at all. *Newsday,* which originates in Long Island, is a good alternative in terms of actual news.

Among the weekly papers, look for the *Village Voice* and the *New York Press.* Both the weekly *New Yorker* and monthly *New York* magazines have extensive listings of museum exhibits, theater productions, movies, art shows, lectures, and other cultural events. And your hotel room is likely to have either a copy of the *New York Visitors Guide* or *Official City Guide.*

Radio and Television Stations

New York has a thousand radio stations—well, maybe it just sounds that way, getting in and out of taxis and shopping malls—but among the most useful for out-of-towners are the National Public Radio WNYC (AM 820); sports WFAN (AM 660); and the all-new WCBS (AM 880) and WINS (AM 1010). For the runners, etc., music choices include classical WNYC (FM 93.9); jazz WKCR (FM 89.9); rock Z100 (FM 100); Top 40 WPLJ (FM 95.5); and classic rock WNEW (FM 102.7).

Most hotels have cable, and if you're lucky, the list of stations in your room will more or less correspond to what you actually get. The major networks are easy to find, however: CBS on Channel 2, NBC on Channel 4, Fox on 5, ABC on 7, and PBS on 13.

Telephones

Manhattan telephone numbers have a 212 area code, and all phone numbers listed in this book are 212 numbers unless otherwise noted. The other four boroughs share a 718 area code; however, these are still local calls. From a pay phone in Manhattan, you can place a call to Queens by dialing direct, but do not use the prefix 1 unless instructed to, or it will be treated as a long-distance call.

At press time, most public phones required a 35-cent deposit.

Public Accommodations

The *Unofficial Guides* are starting to get a reputation for worrying about rest rooms or, rather, about your being able to find them. This is a, uh, tribute to the relatively short staying power of our founder, Bob Sehlinger, and someday we'll stop teasing him about it. But he has a good point; being uncomfortable doesn't help you enjoy a walking tour or a museum. And especially in summer, when New York can be so hot, it's tempting to drink a lot. (When on a vacation is it *not* tempting to drink a lot?)

New York is experimenting with the automated kiosks familiar to European travelers, and you will spot them—they look something like circular phone booths—in City Hall Park and other public gathering spots. However, it is best to ask yourself the same question you ask the kids—Are you sure you don't have to go?—before you go, because the good rest rooms are not always easy to spot.

There are plenty of rest rooms in the transportation terminals such as Grand Central and Penn Station; the large theaters (though most lobbies will be inaccessible during the day) and museums have them, too, but the lines can be rather long. In Central Park, look for the rest rooms near the Delacorte Theater at 79th Street; and there are public facilities behind the New York Public Library in the rejuvenated Bryant Park on Sixth Avenue and 42nd Street. Castle Clinton in Battery Park is nice and not usually crowded. The nearby Robert Wagner Park facility is even better. Big tourist centers such as the Chelsea Piers development, department stores, and malls are good bets, though the quality varies with the age and general atmosphere (in the Manhattan Mall, check the seventh floor). The large hotel lobbies have rest rooms, of course, although you should only take advantage of them in an emergency and when you are reasonably well-dressed. If you are really in a pinch, go to a bar and at least order a soda before you hit the john.

How to Avoid Crime and Keep Safe in Public Places

Okay, let's face it. New York is not the sort of place where you can leave your door open. But you don't need a false bottom on your boot heel for your credit cards, either. All you need is a little common sense.

For many years, New York's "mean streets" were the national symbol of America's crime problem. Statistics were big; headlines were bigger. TV police shows and legal procedurals, series after series of precinct crime novels, and big-name movies played on that reputation. It wasn't organized crime that began to worry out-of-towners (although it did produce even more famous movie characters), or professional burglars or con men; it was the independent and unpredictable punk, the street hood, the drug addict who might corner you on the subway or go "wilding" with his friends like the kids who gang-raped, beat, and left comatose a runner in Central Park. The movie *Escape from New York,* which imagined that in the future the entire city had been turned into a federal penitentiary sector of such violence that it was left to run itself, only took the stereotype to its logical conclusion.

But all of a sudden, in the last few years, the word "crime" is back on New Yorkers' lips—and they're smiling. New York mayor (and former prosecutor) Rudolph Giuliani has pinned his political reputation on lowering crime statistics, and civic pride and confidence are busting out all over. Although analysts and politicians argue over who gets the credit, it is clear that crime has been sharply reduced in recent years. Homicide is at its lowest rate in three decades. Subway crime has been curtailed to an amazing degree: Robberies on the system, the threat of which formerly made late-night or solo travel worrisome, are down fully 80 percent since the beginning of the 1990s. (Intriguingly, transit police have demonstrated that one out of every six fare-evaders is either carrying a weapon or already has an outstanding warrant against him, so try to spot someone with a MetroCard and stick close.) And in one of those strange psychological victories, the renovation of many subway stations is improving users' attitudes toward the system; littering is down, on-board soliciting has nearly disappeared (except for the occasional itinerant musician or candy-seller), and the level of civility, as the president would say, has greatly increased.

The current symbol of Giuliani's anticrime campaign is the squeegie kids, the sometimes aggressive windshield washers who duck in and out of traffic hoping to get a dollar out of drivers; their type of "cleaning up" has run headlong into Giuliani's. Not even unlicensed squeegies are being tolerated these days.

One of the most obvious changes is around Times Square, once the byword for X-rated urban sleaze and now the site of a frenetic rebuilding and restoration movement. Crime is no longer much of an issue in the area, although the crowding and milling about does make some pickpocketing possible. With the constant foot-traffic, the entrance of higher-end stores and restaurants, and the slicking up of local hotels, it's back to being a gathering spot, not a garbage dump. And the Times Square Business Improvement District (TSBID), a private development entity formed by area business owners and promoters, has its own force of 40 unarmed "public safety officers" that patrols the area 24 hours a day and is in radio contact with the police. The TSBID's own private cleanup force is even larger, about 50 of them, dressed in bright red jumpsuits and armed with sidewalk scrubbers, brooms, touch-up paint, and so on.

Similarly, many of the neighborhoods that were once a little questionable after dark, especially in the southern part of Manhattan around TriBeCa or Chelsea, are now busy with restaurants and young urban dwellers. Perhaps you still don't want to hang around the northern stretch of Central Park at night, and it never hurts to carry Mace or pepper spray and a strong whistle; but a reasonable amount of street smarts should keep you in good health.

It is commonplace for tourists in New York to ask a policeman which areas of the city to avoid as they explore Manhattan on foot. Policemen know, and tell these tourists, that you can be robbed or mugged just about anywhere. In point of fact, we are not discussing "areas." Rather, we are talking about neighborhoods—places where people live, work, and go to school and to church. Singling out certain neighborhoods as unsafe is not only disparaging but also stimulates a false sense of security about the safety of so-called "good neighborhoods." New York is a big city, and big-city rules of common sense apply regardless of where you may be.

1. Be alert and understand that crime can occur anywhere.
2. Walk in populated, well-lighted areas, preferably in the company of others.
3. Be suspicious of anyone who approaches you.

Most of Manhattan is pretty safe during the day, but after dark you should stick to the more populated streets. Don't leave a lot of money or traveler's checks in your hotel room, even though the employees are probably dependable. And if you buy any valuables of the sort that can be easily pawned, such as silver, gems, or electronics, ask the hotel to lock them in the safe.

Having a Plan

Random violence and street crime are facts of life in any large city. You've got to be cautious and alert and plan ahead. When you are out and about, you should work under the assumption that you must use caution because you are on your own; if you run into trouble, it's unlikely that police or anyone else will be able to come to your rescue. You must give some advance thought to the ugly scenarios that could occur and, just in case, consider both preventive measures and an escape plan.

Not being a victim of street crime is sort of a survival-of-the-fittest thing. Just as a lion stalks the weakest member of the antelope herd, muggers and thieves target the easiest victim. Simply put, no matter where you are or what you are doing, you want potential felons to think of you as a bad risk.

On the Street. For starters, you always present less of an appealing target if you are with other people. Second, if you must be out alone, act alert, be alert, and always have at least one of your arms and hands free. Felons gravitate toward preoccupied folks, the kind found plodding along staring at the sidewalk, with both arms encumbered by briefcases or packages. Visible jewelry (on either men or women) attracts the wrong kind of attention. Men, keep your billfolds in your front trousers or coat pocket, or in a shoulder strap. Women, keep your purses tucked tightly under your arm; if you're wearing a coat, put it on over your shoulder bag strap. If you are wearing rings, turn the setting side palm-in.

Here's another tip: Men can carry two wallets, including one inexpensive one, carried in your hip pocket, containing about $20 in cash and some expired credit cards. This is the one you hand over if you're accosted. Your real credit cards and the bulk of whatever cash you have should be in either a money clip or a second wallet hidden elsewhere on your person. Women can carry a fake wallet in their purse and keep the real one in a pocket or money belt.

If You're Approached. Police will tell you that a felon has the least amount of control over his intended victim during the few moments of his initial approach. A good strategy, therefore, is to short-circuit the crime scenario as quickly as possible. If a felon starts by demanding your money, for instance, quickly take out your billfold (preferably your fake one) and hurl it in one direction while you run, shouting for help, in the opposite direction. The odds are greatly in your favor that the felon will prefer to collect your silent billfold rather than pursue you. If you hand over your wallet and just stand there, the felon will likely ask for your watch and jewelry next. If you're a woman, the longer you hang around, the greater your vulnerability to personal injury or rape.

Secondary Crime Scenes. Under no circumstance, police warn, should you ever allow yourself to be taken to another location—a "secondary crime scene," in police jargon. This move, they explain, provides the felon more privacy and consequently more control. A felon can rob you on the street very quickly and efficiently. If he tries to remove you to another location, whether by car or on foot, it is a certain indication that he has more in mind than robbery. Even if the felon has a gun or knife, your chances are infinitely better running away. If the felon grabs your purse, let him have it. If he grabs your coat, come out of the coat. Hanging onto your money or coat is not worth getting mugged, raped, or murdered.

Another maxim: Never believe anything a felon tells you, even if he's telling you something you desperately want to believe—for example, "I won't hurt you if you come with me." No matter how logical or benign he sounds, assume the worst. Always, always, break off contact as quickly as possible, even if that means running.

In Public Transport. When riding a bus, always take a seat as close to the driver as you can; never ride in the back. Likewise, on the subway, sit near the driver's or conductor's compartment. These people have a phone and can summon help in the event of trouble.

In Cabs. While it is easy to hail a cab on the street in New York at night, it's best to go to one of the hotel stands or to hail the cab from directly in front of the restaurant where you had dinner. If you find yourself needing a cab at night in a part of town where the yellow "medallion" cabs are scarce, call a reliable cab company, listed under "Taxicab Service" in the Yellow Pages, and stay inside while they dispatch a car to your door.

Once you have secured a cab, check the driver's certificate, which must, by law, be posted on the dashboard. Address the cabbie by his or her last name (Mr. Jones or whatever) or mention the number of the cab. This alerts the driver to the fact that you are going to remember him or her and/or the cab. Not only will this contribute to your safety; it will also keep your cabbie from trying to run up the fare.

If you need to catch a cab at the train stations, bus terminals, or airports, always use the taxi queue. Taxis in the official queue are properly licensed and regulated. Never accept an offer for a cab or limo made by a stranger in the terminal or baggage claim. At best, you will be significantly overcharged for the ride. At worst, you may be abducted.

Personal Attitude

While some areas of every city are more dangerous than others, never assume that any area is completely safe. Never let down your guard. You can be the victim of a crime, and it can happen to you anywhere. Women leaving a restaurant or club alone should never be reluctant to ask to be escorted to their car or to be assisted in hailing a taxi.

Never let your pride or sense of righteousness and indignation imperil your survival. This is especially difficult for many men, particularly for men in the presence of women. Whether you are approached by an aggressive drunk, an unbalanced street person, or an actual felon, the rule is the same: Forget your pride and break off contact as quickly as possible. Who cares whether the drunk insulted you, if everyone ends up back at the hotel safe and sound? When you wake up in the hospital with a concussion and your jaw sewn shut, it's too late to decide that the drunk's filthy remark wasn't really all that important.

Felons, druggies, some street people, and even some drunks play for keeps. They can attack with a bloodthirsty hostility and hellish abandon that is beyond the imagination of most people. Believe me, you are not in their league (nor do you want to be).

Self-Defense

In a situation where it is impossible to run, you'll need to be prepared to defend yourself. Most policemen insist that a gun or knife is not of much use to the average person. More often than not, they say, the weapon will be turned against the victim. The best self-defense device for the average person is Mace. Not only is it legal in most states; it is also nonlethal and easy to use.

When you shop for Mace, look for two things: It should be able to fire about eight feet, and it should have a protector cap so it won't go off by mistake in your purse or pocket. Carefully read the directions that come with your device, paying particular attention to how it should be carried and stored and how long the active ingredients will remain potent. Wearing a rubber glove, test-fire your Mace, making sure that you fire downwind.

When you are out about town, make sure your Mace is someplace easily accessible, say, attached to your keychain. If you are a woman and you keep your Mace on a keychain, avoid the habit of dropping your keys (and the Mace) into the bowels of your purse when you leave your hotel room or your car. The Mace will not do you any good if you have to dig around in your purse for it. Keep your keys and your Mace in your hand until you have safely reached your destination.

Carjackings and Highway Robbery

With the recent surge in carjackings, drivers also need to take special precautions. "Keep alert when you're driving in traffic," one police official warns. "Keep your doors locked, with the windows rolled up and the air-conditioning or heat on. In traffic, leave enough space in front of you so that you're not blocked in and can make a U-turn. That way, if someone approaches your car and starts beating on your windshield, you can drive off." Store your purse or briefcase under your knees when you are driving, rather than on the seat beside you.

Also be wary of other drivers bumping you from the rear or driving alongside you and gesturing that something is wrong with your car. In either case, do not stop or get out of your car. Continue on until you reach a very public and well-lighted place where you can check things out and, if necessary, get help.

Ripoffs and Scams

A lively street scene is a veritable incubator for ripoffs and scams. Although pickpockets, scam artists, and tricksters work throughout Manhattan, they are particularly thick in the bus and train terminals, along Broadway and Seventh Avenue near Times Square, and along 42nd Street between Grand Central Station and the Port Authority Terminal. While some of the scams are relatively harmless, others can be costly as well as dangerous.

Pickpockets work in teams, often involving children. One person creates a diversion such as dropping coins, spilling ice cream on you, or trying to sell you something while a second person deftly picks your pocket. In most cases your stolen wallet is almost instantaneously passed to a third team member walking past. Even if you realize immediately that your wallet has been lifted, the pickpocket will have unburdened himself of the evidence.

Because pickpockets come in all sizes and shapes, be especially wary of any encounter with a stranger. Anyone from a man in a nice suit asking directions to a six-year-old wobbling toward you on rollerblades could be creating a diversion for a pickpocket. Think twice before rendering assistance, and be particularly cognizant of other people in your immediate area.

Don't let children touch you or allow street peddlers to get too close. Be particularly wary of people whose hands are concealed by newspapers or other items. Oh yeah, one more thing: If somebody *does* spill ice cream on you, be wary of the good Samaritan who suddenly appears to help you clean up.

A fairly common New York scam is for an impeccably dressed man to approach you with an impressive business card and confide that he has been robbed. He has reported the robbery to the police, he will tell you, but needs $20 to take the train home to Long Island. He gives you the business card and promises to send you a check as soon as he gets home (some con men will actually write a check on the spot!). Whether you get a check or not, you have been had if you part with any cash.

The primary tip-off to a con or scam is someone approaching you. If you ask help of somebody in a store or restaurant, you are doing the approaching, and in that case the chances of being the victim of a scam are quite small. When a stranger approaches you, however, regardless of the reason, beware.

Most travelers carry a lot more cash, credit cards, and other stuff in their wallet than they need. If you plan to walk in New York or anywhere else, transfer exactly what you think you will need to a very small, low-profile wallet or pouch. When the *Unofficial Guide* authors are on the street, they carry one American Express card, one VISA card, and a minimum amount of cash. Think about it: You don't need your gas credit cards if you are walking, and you don't need all of those hometown department store credit cards if you are away from home.

Do not, repeat, do not carry your wallet and valuables in a fanny pack. Thieves and pickpockets can easily snip the belt and disappear into the crowd with the entire fanny pack before you realize what's happened. As far as pockets are concerned, front pockets are safer than back pockets or suit-coat pockets, though with a little effort, pickpockets can get at front pockets too. The safest place to carry valuables is under your arm in a shoulder-holster-style pouch. Lightweight, comfortable, and especially accessible when worn under a coat or vest, shoulder pouches are available from catalogs and at most good travel stores. Incidentally, avoid pouches that are worn on your chest suspended by a cord around your neck. Like fanny packs, they can be easily cut off or removed by pickpockets.

More Things to Avoid

When you do go out, walk with a minimum of two people whenever possible. If you have to walk alone, stay in well-lighted areas that have plenty of people around. Be careful about whom you ask for directions. (When in doubt, shopkeepers are a good bet.) Don't count your money in public, and carry as little cash as possible. At public phones, if you must say your calling card number to make a long-distance call, don't say it loud enough for strangers around you to hear.

■ Be Optimistic ■

While this litany of warnings and precautions may sound grim, it's really commonsense advice that applies to visitors in any large American city. Keep in mind that New York's reputation for crime has been enhanced by media attention. Finally, remember that millions of visitors a year still flock to New York, making it one of the most-visited destinations in the United States. The overwhelming majority of these tourists encounter no problems with crime during their visit.

■ The Homeless ■

If you're not from a big city or haven't visited one in a while, you're in for a shock when you come to New York, where there is a large homeless population. Though they're more evident in some areas than others, you are liable to bump into them just about anywhere.

Who Are These People? "Most are lifelong [city] residents who are poor," according to Joan Alker, assistant director of the National Coalition for the Homeless, an advocacy group headquartered in Washington. "The people you see on the streets are primarily single men and women. A disproportionate number of them are minorities and people with disabilities — they're either mentally ill, or substance abusers, or have physical disabilities."

Are They a Threat to Visitors? "No," Ms. Alker says. "Studies show that homeless men have lower rates of conviction for violent crimes than the population at large. We know that murders aren't being committed by the homeless. I can't make a blanket statement, but most homeless people you see are no more likely to commit a violent crime than other people."

Should You Give the Homeless Money? "That's a personal decision," Ms. Alker says. "But if you can't, at least try to acknowledge their existence by looking them in the eye and saying, 'No, I can't.'" While there's no way to tell if the guy with the Styrofoam cup asking for a handout is really destitute or just a con artist, no one can dispute that most of these people are what they claim to be: homeless.

Ways to Help. It's really a matter for your own conscience. We confess to being both moved and annoyed by these unfortunate people: moved by their need and annoyed that we cannot enjoy the city without running a gauntlet of begging men and women. In the final analysis, we find that it is easier on the conscience and spirit to carry an overcoat or jacket pocket full of change at all times. The cost of giving those homeless who approach you a quarter really does not add up to all that much, and it is much better for the psyche to respond to their plight than to deny or ignore their presence.

There is a notion, perhaps valid in some instances, that money given to a homeless person generally goes toward the purchase of alcohol or drugs. If this bothers you excessively, carry granola bars for distribution, or, alternatively, buy some inexpensive gift coupons that can be redeemed at a McDonald's or other fast-food restaurant for coffee or a sandwich.

We have found that a little kindness regarding the homeless goes a long way and that a few kind words delivered along with your quarter or granola bar brighten the day for both you and your friend in need. We are not suggesting a lengthy conversation or prolonged involvement, just something simple like "Sure, I can help a little bit. Take care of yourself, fella."

Those moved to get more involved in the nationwide problem of homelessness can send inquiries—or a check—to the National Coalition for the Homeless, 1612 K Street NW, Suite 1004, Washington, D.C. 20006.

Keep it brief, and don't play psychologist. All the people you encounter on the street are strangers. They may be harmless, or they may be dangerous. Either way, maintain distance and keep any contacts or encounters brief. Be prepared to handle street people in accordance with your principles, but mostly, just be prepared. If you have a druggie in your face wanting a handout, the last thing you want to do is pull out your wallet and thumb through the twenties looking for a one-dollar bill.

PART FIVE

Getting Around New York

■ Taxis ■

When it comes to taxicabs, Manhattan is the land of plenty, a revelation for tourists from towns where you have to reserve one in advance. The main thoroughfares sometimes look like rivers of yellow, with four and five lanes of cabs whipping along. The New York City Taxi and Limousine Commission licenses and regulates the yellow "medallioned" taxis ("medallioned" refers to the illuminated light on top of the cab). These taxis must be hailed on the street—in other words, you cannot call them on the phone to pick you up.

There is little trick to hailing one: First make sure you're not on a one-way street trying to wave somebody down on the wrong side. (This happens more often than you'd think.) Then stand at the edge of the curb—try not to walk out into traffic unless you're blocked by parked vehicles, and even then be very careful—and raise your arm high. You don't need to wave it about frantically unless you're in an emergency: Cabbies have a sort of radar. It's rude to cut off someone who's already signaling by getting downstream (though it happens); however, you may approach a cab that's letting someone else out and wait by the open door.

To avoid unnecessary frustration, realize that in New York, unlike some other cities, passengers are guaranteed a private ride. That is, the cabbie cannot just veer over and see if you happen to be going in the same direction the first passenger is, and then pop you in the front seat. So don't swear at cabs with shadowy figures in the back. Of course, if there are several in your party who get in together, you can drop off some riders before others. Also note that the cab is not on duty unless the little light in the middle of the rooftop sign—the "medallion" that proves the cab is legit—is lit: If the yellow one in the middle that reads "off duty" is lit, he or she is headed home.

If you're staying at one of the nicer hotels, there is likely to be a doorman available to whistle a cab up for you. This also allows for a bit of cheating if you are a little timid or loaded down. You can walk into the hotel lobby from one entrance and pass through to the other side and, looking as through you just left your room, ask the doorman there to hail you one.

If you are not encumbered by luggage and the like, you can save yourself some time and money by walking to the closest one-way street heading in your direction and hailing a cab there. In a similar vein, if you find yourself gridlocked in a cab within a block or two of your destination, go ahead and pay your fare and proceed on foot.

Many New York cabbies speak only marginal English. You can expect them to be familiar with major hotels, train and bus terminals, and major attractions. For more obscure destinations or addresses, you will do yourself (and the cabbie) a favor by writing down the exact address where you want to go.

Once inside the cab, you should make sure the driver's license with photograph and name are clearly displayed on the passenger side visor. This is required for your protection in case of disagreement (for complaints, contact the Taxi and Limousine commission at 221-8294). It doesn't hurt to notice the number, either, in case you leave something behind; perhaps then you can get the dispatcher to send the cab to your hotel.

In our experience, New York cabbies usually take the most direct route to any given destination. Sometimes there is a little fudging, as when a driver circles an entire block to deliver you to a corner address on a one-way street, but in the main you can count on cabbies to keep it short and simple. If you prefer, you can specify the route you want your driver to take, and sometimes on longer fares the cabbie will actually ask if you have a preference. Still, many New York first-timers are a bit paranoid about cabbies taking them for a ride. In particular, La Guardia Airport to Midtown via the Triborough Bridge arouses suspicions, though it is a perfectly acceptable route.

In addition to the medallion on the roof, a legitimate cab will have an automatic receipt machine mounted on the dashboard so that you can get an immediate record. (Fares begin at $1.50, and the meter ticks over a quarter for each sixth of a mile or minute of standing time; there's a dark-hours premium of 50 cents, and passengers are responsible for tolls.)

Don't be surprised if your cabbie drives fast and aggressively. More often than not, you will feel like an extra in a movie chase scene as you careen through the concrete canyons, weaving in and out of traffic. The good news is that these guys are excellent drivers. The other good news is that most cabs now have seat belts.

Although cabs range throughout Manhattan and the boroughs, they are most plentiful in Midtown. If you find yourself below Canal Street after business hours or on a weekend, for example, finding an empty yellow medallioned taxi cruising down the street may be a challenge. Your alternative is to phone one of the many companies listed under "Taxicab Service" in the Yellow Pages. While these companies are also licensed by the Taxi and

Limousine Commission, their cars will probably not be yellow or have a medallion. Some companies dispatch cars on demand 24 hours a day, seven days a week, while others require advance arrangements. Fares, as you would expect, are generally higher than those of metered, yellow, medallioned cabs. Late at night, in bad weather, and/or in isolated areas, however, phoning for a taxi is a safer and less stressful option than trusting to luck on the street. For the lowest fares ask your concierge, hotel desk clerk, or restaurant maitre d' for a recommendation before hauling out the Yellow Pages. When you call, tell the dispatcher where you want the car to pick you up and where you are going, and ask him to quote you a fare. Almost all of the car-on-demand companies accept credit cards. As always, tips and tolls are extra.

Now, as to illicit taxis. New York has a lot of limousines and luxury cars because of all its executives and celebrities. Consequently, it also has a lot of chauffeurs with time on their hands. So frequently, when you are standing on the street trying to hail a cab—and this is particularly true if you are a woman or if it is clearly theater-rush or dinner time and you look a little harried—a nice-looking sedan or town car may pull over and the driver offer to take you to your destination. These are sometimes referred to as gypsy cabs; and while few of them pose a threat in the sense that they are unlikely to kidnap you, they will almost certainly want to charge you a very hefty fee. If it's raining or snowing or you're really late, or you really want to make an entrance, you might want to take him up on it. Just be prepared to pay the fee—and realize that you won't have any legal complaint if you're ripped off.

■ The Subway ■

One of the first things that you notice about New York is the snarled traffic. But underground, far removed from the cursing, horn blowing, and bumper-to-bumper slog of the mean streets, is a fast, efficient subway system. Learn a little about how it operates and you will be able to get around New York quickly and affordably. The key to the city is just beneath the sidewalk, and it will set you free.

The Subway vs. Cabs

We recommend cabs whenever you are encumbered by luggage, multiple shopping bags, or anything large you must haul around. Cabs are also preferred for getting around in the evening after rush-hour traffic has abated and after 11 p.m. or so for safety reasons. If there are two or more in your party and you are heading to different destinations, sharing a cab makes more sense than taking the subway. Another good time to take a cab, provided you can find one, is when it's raining or snowing.

From 6:30 a.m. until about 7 p.m. on weekdays, New York streets and avenues are insanely congested. This is the time that the subway really shines. While cabs are stuck for three changes of the same traffic signal trying to crawl through a single intersection, the subways are zipping efficiently along. Plus, the subway is much less expensive.

Will the subway save you time? Maybe; it depends. With the subway, you must walk to the closest station, wait for the train, ride to your destination station, and then walk to wherever you're going. If you are traveling a relatively long distance, say 35 blocks or more, during business hours on a weekday, the subway will beat the cab about 60 percent of the time. If you are traveling a shorter distance, or if you must transfer on the subway to reach your destination, the cab will probably be faster. On weekends, when the streets are less congested and when trains run less frequently, the primary rationale for using the subway is to save money.

This latter, saving money, is no small potatoes. With fare and tip, the shortest cab ride will cost you about $5, compared to $1.50 on the subway. When we work in New York, we almost always use the subway, allowing enough time between meetings to walk to and from the stations and to wait for the train.

Finally, the subways do not run particularly close to the far east or the far west sides of the island. Thus, subway travel to such destinations as the Javits Center, the Passenger Ship Terminal, or the United Nations is not recommended.

Subway Basics

The New York subway system is one of the world's largest; almost 700 miles of track connect the four boroughs of Manhattan, the Bronx, Brooklyn, and Queens. There are close to 500 stations, so you are likely to find one near where you want to go.

The nexus of the system is the complex of stations and routes below Central Park extending to the southern tip of Manhattan Island. Though service to other areas of Manhattan and the outlying boroughs is more than adequate, this Midtown and Downtown ganglion of routes, connections, and stops provides the most frequent and flexible level of service that you are likely to find in any American city.

Safety

Once the butt of talk-show jokes, the New York subway system is now clean, scoured of (most) graffiti, and well-policed. While not quite as secure as Disneyland, subway travel does not represent much of a risk. Muggings and violent crime are extremely rare these days, though riders on crowded trains and in crowded stations should continue to be alert for pickpockets.

From 6 a.m. until 11 p.m. or so, you can ride the subway with no more concern for your personal safety than you feel on the streets during business hours. After 11 p.m. it's wise to use the special "Off-Hours Waiting Areas" that are monitored by subway security. When the train arrives, we suggest that you ride in the same car as the train's conductor (usually one of the middle cars).

Any time of day, if you are carrying packages, a briefcase, or luggage, sit as far from the doors as possible. A favorite ploy of thieves is to grab the purse or package of a person sitting near a door and escape onto the platform just as the doors are closing.

Finding the Subway

An indispensable aid to locating stations and understanding the subway system is the New York City Transit Subway Map. The map shows all routes and stations and offers helpful information about fares and frequency of service, among other things. Once you know the address of your New York hotel, you can use the subway map to plan your travel around town. You can arrange to have a map mailed to you at home by calling Subway Travel Information at (718) 330-1234 between 6 a.m. and 9 p.m. EST. If you forget to request a map before traveling to New York, you can usually pick one up at the airports, Penn Station, Grand Central Station, or the Port Authority Terminal. Some hotel front desks and concierges also stock a supply of maps. If all else fails, the NYNEX Manhattan Yellow Pages book includes complete color maps of both the subway system and Manhattan bus routes; you'll find them at the beginning of the book.

If you are on the streets of Manhattan without a subway map, look for the lighted globes (about the size of bowling balls) that mark most subway entrances. A green globe means the subway entrance is open and staffed 24 hours a day. A red (or red and white) globe indicates that the entrance is open only during hours posted above the station. Some of the larger subway entrances are accessed through buildings. The majority of these have good street signage, although a few do not. Along similar lines, you may exit the subway at a station where the exits lead into a building, as opposed to directly back on the street. If this happens, simply exit the building and from there proceed to the nearest street corner to regain your orientation.

In Midtown and Downtown where various lines converge, there may be several stations located close together. The subway map will help you sort the stations out. If you don't have a map, descend into the closest station and check the system map displayed on the wall.

Reading the Subway Map

Each subway line is shown in a different color. Though some lines diverge into separate routes above Central Park in Manhattan and in the boroughs, they bear the color of the trunk (main) line. Each of the diverging routes is designated by a letter or number displayed in a circle or diamond of the same color. Terminals (ends of the line) are indicated by squares for normal service routes and diamonds for rush-hours-only routes.

The Lexington Avenue line, for example, is represented in green. Four routes—the 4-Circle, 5-Diamond, 5-Circle, and 6-Circle—originate in the Bronx and are likewise depicted in green. The routes converge in Manhattan, where all four follow Lexington Avenue (from which the line takes its name). The end of the line for 6-Circle is City Hall, and the end for 5-Circle is Bowling Green, both in the Downtown tip of the island. 4-Circle and 5-Diamond cross out of Manhattan and head east into Brooklyn. 4-Circle terminates at Utica Avenue, while 5-Diamond ends at Flatbush Avenue. In this example we followed the routes south (downtown) from the Bronx. If we boarded the 5-Diamond subway at Flatbush Avenue and headed north (uptown), we would converge with the other green lines in lower Manhattan, follow Lexington Avenue north, and diverge at 138th Street to cross into the Bronx. If we stayed on to the end of the line, we would wind up at 241st Street in the Bronx.

Stations are represented on the map by:

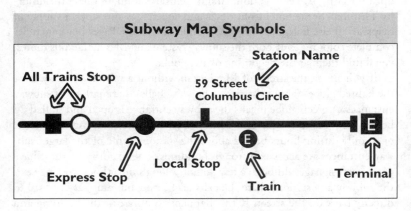

Each station's name is shown in bold type. Station names are usually streets or avenues—for example, the Houston Street Station on the Red Line is shown on the map as **Houston St.** Some stations, however, have place-names, such as **World Trade Center, Penn Station,** or **Times Square.**

Underneath the station name, the map shows which routes stop at that particular station.

The 23rd Street Station on the Eighth Avenue (because the line follows Eighth Avenue) Blue Line looks like this on the map:

23 Street
C-E

This means that the C-Circle Train and the E-Circle Train both stop at this station. The A-Circle Train, which also runs on the Blue Line, does not stop here. If it did, the station would look like this:

23 Street
A-C-E

You might see a station where some of the routes are not depicted in bold, such as:

72 Street
1-2-3-9

This means that the 1-Circle, 2-Circle, and 3-Circle trains offer regular service but that the 9-Circle train only provides part-time service, in this case during rush hours Monday through Friday (you need the subway route chart for this last piece of information).

Where certain lines meet or come close to meeting, you will see little symbols that look like this:

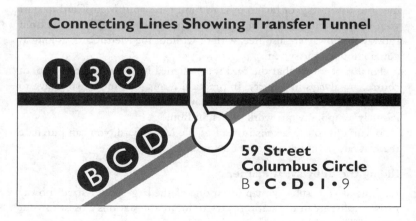

This means that there is a pedestrian walkway or tunnel that connects two or more stations, thus allowing riders to transfer to other lines without exiting and reentering the subway system.

Fares

It costs $1.50 to ride the subway. You can buy either tokens or a MetroCard. A MetroCard looks like a credit card. Available at subway stations and at over 2,000 neighborhood stores, the MetroCard can be purchased in any amount from $3 to $80. Each time you ride the subway you swipe your card through a little electronic reader on the turnstile. The electronic reader reads the amount of credit you have on the card and deducts $1.50 for every ride. When you use your card, your balance is displayed on the turnstile. All the accounting is maintained electronically, so there's no way to tell the fare credit remaining by looking at the card. If you want to check your balance, there are "reader" machines at most stations that will show the card's current balance without deducting anything. It is not necessary to get a new card when your balance gets low: All you have to do is take the card to a fare booth and pay to have your balance increased. As an aside, the MetroCard system is very new, and the computers have been known to act up. When you buy a card or pay to increase your balance, always run your card through the reader (before you leave the fare window) to make sure your purchase was properly recorded. MetroCards expire after one year, but any amount remaining on the card can be transferred to a new card. For additional information on the MetroCard, call (212) METROCARD (within New York City) or (800) METROCARD (outside New York City).

Though, admittedly, we are not great fans of New York City buses, you should know that with MetroCard you can transfer free from subway to bus, bus to subway, or bus to bus. You must use your MetroCard to start your trip and must make your transfer within two hours. Transfers from subway to subway are also free, with or without the MetroCard, as long as you do not exit the system.

Finally, be aware that the card was designed for New Yorkers, who, of course, are always in a hurry. In practical terms, this means you have to swipe your card fast! If you ease it through the turnstile device at a more leisurely tempo, it won't work. When in Rome . . .

If you opt to use tokens instead of the MetroCard, you can purchase them at fare booths at any of the stations.

Riding the Subway: A Primer

Looking at your subway map (or at one of the large poster-sized subway maps on display in the stations), try to locate the stations closest to your starting point and to your destination. If the station closest to your starting point does not offer service in the general direction you'll be going, check to see whether there are any other stations reasonably close by that do. Try to find a subway route that requires no transfers. It is generally faster to get within a few blocks of your destination on the subway and then cover the remaining distance on foot than it is to make a transfer. As a rule of thumb, it takes less than two minutes to walk the short blocks between streets. Walking cross-town, you can cover the long blocks between avenues in four to five minutes each.

Check to see which trains stop at stations you have identified. In general, the more trains, the better. Make sure that trains that stop at your departure station also stop at your destination station.

Almost all trains except the 7-Circle Flushing Local and the L-Circle 14th Street Canarsie Local (cross-town trains) travel generally north/south, or, in subway speak, uptown (north) and downtown (south). Traveling on the subway is immensely simplified if you can determine whether you are traveling uptown or downtown.

If you want to go cross-town (east or west), you may need to know where the train terminates. Let's say you want to go from the west side to the east side on the E-Circle train. The signs for this train will not say "cross-town"; they will say "Jamaica/Queens," indicating the train's final destination. If you know (or learn by looking at the subway map) that this train travels cross-town en route to the borough of Queens, you will know to board in the direction of "Jamaica/Queens" to reach your cross-town destination. Incidentally, most trains that run cross-town also run part of their route north/south. Thus, signs for the E-Circle train may read "Uptown–Jamaica/Queens" or "Downtown–World Trade Center."

When you approach the station, there may be one or multiple entrances. If there is only one entrance, proceed inside and follow the signs directing you to the Uptown or Downtown train platforms, whichever applies. If you are standing at a street intersection and there is a subway entrance on all four corners, or on both sides of an avenue, the entrance(s) on the west side of the avenue will lead to Downtown platforms, and the entrance(s) on the east side of the street will lead to Uptown platforms. Normally there is good signage at the entrances identifying the line, trains (routes), and direction that the particular entrance serves. Usually, because you do not have to swipe your MetroCard or deposit your token until you are within spitting distance of the platform, you can verify that you have chosen the correct entrance by checking the signage on the platform. If you want to travel uptown and you descend to a platform that reads "Downtown," do not pass through the turnstiles. Instead, return to the street, cross the avenue, and descend to the Uptown platform.

Though most stations are served by only one line, there are a number of stations, particularly in Midtown and Downtown, that are served by several lines. What you have here, essentially, is a sort of double- or even triple-decker station. With these stations it's a little more complicated than uptown vs. downtown. At these multiline stations you may have a choice of lines going uptown and downtown as well as, possibly, some cross-town lines. If you start your trip at one of these stations, locate the system map near the entrance and determine exactly which line you need and which direction you want to go. Armed with this knowledge, follow the signs to the correct platform.

Be aware that in the larger stations you may have to pay and go through the turnstiles before you get anywhere near the train platforms. Don't worry. The inside signage is good, and there are interior passages that will allow you to correct your mistake if you end up on the wrong platform.

Once on the platform, double-check the signs, and if necessary recheck the system map. The platform sign will show the trains that stop at that platform, indicate their direction (usually uptown or downtown), and specify the terminal (end of the line) for each route.

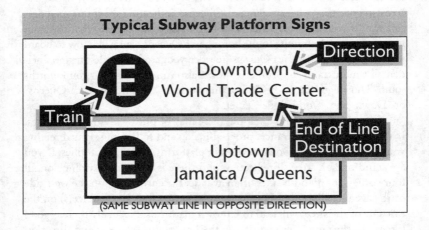

Typical Subway Platform Signs

Sometimes a single waiting platform will serve two tracks: Trains arriving on one side of the platform will go in one direction, and trains on the other side will go in the opposite direction. If you descended a long way or had to navigate a spiraling stairwell, you may arrive on the platform somewhat disoriented. Check the signage to determine the correct direction for your travel. If the signs don't help, simply ask another waiting passenger.

If there are several trains that stop at both your departure and destination stations, you can take your choice. If you are going a relatively short distance (30 blocks or less), go ahead and hop on the first train that comes along. If it's a "local," it will make a lot of stops, but you will still probably arrive sooner than if you waited for an express. If you are going a long way, you may want to hold out for an express train.

When the train comes into the station, it will be well marked. The A-Circle train on the Eighth Avenue Blue Line, for example, will sport big blue circles with the letter A inside. The conductor usually rides in the middle of the train and will either disembark or stick his head out of the door when the train stops. If you are really confused, ask him if the train goes to your destination station.

You've probably seen film footage of people crowding on and battling off subways. While this does sometimes occur at the height of rush hour in the larger stations, usually things are much more civil. When the train stops, approach the door and wait for it to open. Allow passengers getting off to disembark, then step into the car. The conductor observes the loading process, so don't worry about not getting on or about getting caught in a closing door.

Once inside, take a seat if there is one available. If you are still a little confused, you will find a system map displayed on the wall of the car. Check the next scheduled stop for the direction you wish to travel. When the train pulls in, verify by the signs on the platform that you are traveling in the right direction. If you have mistakenly boarded the right train in the wrong direction, wait until the train stops at one of the larger stations where transfers are optional. These larger stations have internal passages that will allow you to cross over to the right platform without leaving the system and having to pay again to reenter.

■ **Buses** ■

In addition to being subject to all the problems that afflict Manhattan surface traffic, buses are slow, make innumerable stops, and have difficulty maneuvering. Even so, there are several good reasons to use public bus service. After 11 p.m. buses are safer than walking if you are not up to springing for a cab. Some buses, like the 1, 5, 6, 10, and 15, run very interesting routes and are a dirt-cheap option for sight-seeing (ride on weekends, when traffic is less problematic). Though subways excel in north/south, uptown/downtown service, there is less cross-town (east/west) subway service than one would hope. Buses fill this public transportation gap, running a goodly number of cross-town routes. Finally, of course, buses are inexpensive to ride, especially with the new MetroCard, which allows bus-to-bus, bus-to-subway, and subway-to-bus transfers. Maps of Manhattan bus routes can be found in the front of the NYNEX Manhattan Yellow Pages. MTA buses cost $1.50 and require either exact change or a MetroCard.

■ Walking ■

New York is a great town for walking. Like most cities, it has neighborhoods that are not ideally suited for an evening stroll, but these are easily avoided. If you observe a few precautions and exercise some common sense, you will find the sidewalks of New York not only interesting and exhilarating but also quite hospitable.

As you begin to explore, you will find that the blocks between the east/west streets are quite short. Thus, walking south (toward Downtown) on Seventh Avenue, most folks will be able to cover the blocks from 59th Street to 49th Street in about 12 minutes, even assuming a wait for traffic at several intersections. Crossing town from east to west (or visa versa), the blocks are much longer. A walk from First Avenue to Tenth Avenue along 42nd Street is a real hike, requiring more than 30 minutes for most people.

If you want to try a restaurant eight blocks away, and the address is north or south of where you are, you won't even need a cab. If the restaurant is eight blocks away across town (east/west), take a subway or hail a taxi.

If you become disoriented during a walk, proceed to the nearest street corner and see what the street is (as opposed to an avenue). Then walk one additional short block in either direction. If the next cross street is higher in number, you are heading north (uptown). East will be to your right, and west to your left. If the next cross street is lower in number, then you are walking south. East will be to your left, and west to your right.

Let's say, for example, that you just emerged from a subway station on the Avenue of the Americas (also called Sixth Avenue) and are not sure which way's which. Walking to the nearest corner, you discover that you are at the intersection of 24th Street and the Avenue of the Americas. You continue one more block on Avenue of the Americas and reach 23rd Street. You now know that you are going south and that First through Fifth Avenues are to your left (east) and that Seventh through Eleventh Avenues are to your right (west).

Because there is no better or more direct way to experience New York than to explore it on foot, we recommend that you do as much hoofing as your time and stamina permit. To help you organize your walking, we include several walking tours in this guide. Along similar lines, we have included an extensive discussion of matters relating to personal safety in Part 4 in the section titled "How to Avoid Crime and Keep Safe in Public Places."

PART SIX

Entertainment and Nightlife

So Much to Do, So Little Time

The phrase "the Great White Way" originally referred only to Broadway, with its glittering marquees and opening-night klieg lights roaming the sky. But rich as it is, Broadway is only one aspect of New York's dizzyingly versatile performing arts scene.

Dance, classical and chamber concerts, opera, Broadway, off-Broadway, and the famous off-off-Broadway listings fill columns of type in the *New York Times* every day, and pages of such weekly cultural observers as the *New Yorker, Village Voice,* and *New York Press* and other local handouts. Experimental theater and street performances double in good weather, when theatrical troupes take to the streets. And that doesn't even count the hundreds of rock, jazz, dance, and comedy clubs throughout the city. (For more on the nightclub scene and profiles of recommended stops, see the second portion of this chapter.) On top of that are the literary events—the readings and lectures and seminars that may be hard to make time for, but that also might enrich your enjoyment of the exhibit or concert you've already selected; those, too, are highlights to watch for in the local press.

For most visitors, the first decision is which sort of performance you're interested in: musical, classical, dance, and so on. Then you need to know where to get tickets, how to save a little if possible, and what to expect when you get there. But memorize this up front: It's almost impossible not to enjoy yourself. Pick your show on a whim, ride the subway, make new friends over intermission, and ponder the finale over a drink. Life is great.

■ **Ticket Tips** ■

You have to wonder why New York bothers to make confetti for parades. A single night's tickets—theater, sports, ballets, concerts, special events—would be enough to keep even Manhattan's parades covered.

Which brings up that perennial question: How do you get them? Tickets are a prized commodity in New York, almost as valuable as the cash they cost (and sometimes more). And "cut price" is not a popular phrase. Still, there are a few ways to trim the bill, and if you can get the tickets you want without bartering your child's education, you'll enjoy the show that much more.

If you want to get your tickets in advance, **NYC/On Stage** runs a toll-free number (call (800) STAGE-NY) you can call to get recording listings and schedules for a variety of performing arts; when you hear something you like, you can have your call automatically transferred to whichever phone-charge company is handling those tickets. Once in town, you can hear the same listings by calling 768-1818.

Theatre Direct, or TDI, sometimes packages tickets to hotter shows. Call (800) 334-8457 or check their Web site at www.theatredirect.com.

The main telephone charge numbers for New York shows and concerts are **Telecharge** (239-6200), **TicketMaster** (307-4100), **CityTix** (581-1212), and **CenterCharge** (721-6500), or you might check the local press for direct numbers. If there is a TicketMaster service in your hometown, you should also call that to see whether they can patch you through to the New York ticketing lines. Also try the **Broadway Show Line** (563-2929). For other box offices and venues, see the "Performing Arts" section below.

Even if a show is supposed to be sold out, if you really want to see it, you can try a few other ways to get tickets, especially if you don't mind separated or single seats. If you can go on a slow night (Monday or Tuesday) or in winter after the holiday crush, you'll have better luck of finding empty seats. If you go directly to the theater's box office, you might stumble onto some tickets that have been returned; old-line New Yorkers are surprisingly good about that, especially when it comes to such establishment venues as Lincoln Center or the Metropolitan Opera and even Carnegie Hall. Call the box office and ask when the "cancellation line" forms. Many venues, arts and sports included, also release reserved house seats about 6 p.m., so be ready with your credit cards.

There are plenty of ticket resellers who are sort of corporate scalpers; they manage to find tickets to sold-out shows (look under "Tickets" in the Yellow Pages). And there are other "convenient" ticket centers at places like the Plaza Hotel, which bank on the idea that you don't have the patience or leisure to call the big automated phone-charge networks yourself; one round with the surcharges may dissuade you from this convenience. Still, if money's no object or time is at a premium, they are easy and reliable sources. Among some reputable firms are **Prestige Entertainment** (call (800) 243-8849) and **Manhattan Entertainment** (382-0633).

There may also be tickets for sale through the classified ads in the *New York Times*. If you have an American Express gold card, call (800) 448-8457 to see if there are any special promotional seats available (this usually applies only to hot trendy shows).

A final caveat: You are apt to find scalpers outside theaters and big sports events offering tickets, but this can be tricky; an increasing number of these tickets are counterfeit.

■ The Pay's the Thing ■

Let's face it: Broadway productions, even off-Broadway productions, are expensive to put on and maintain. And have you ever considered what it takes to get all those people (and occasionally animals) in costume and on stage at the Metropolitan Opera? No wonder seats are pricey—$40 to $80 on average. (See the "Performing Arts" section below for general ticket-buying information.) But a night at the theater is so quintessential a New York experience—more than a third of visitors surveyed said it was their main reason for coming—that you almost have to try it, whether your taste runs to musical comedy, drama, dance, or the most unintelligible of German cadenza.

There are some ways to economize, however. The ABCs of bargain theater tickets are really the **TKTS.** These are places where same-day tickets to various theater and other cultural events are available for half-price plus a $2.50 surcharge; the only trick is that you have to go in person and take your chances on getting into a show you want to see. The best idea is to have three alternatives, in order of preference, already in your head; that way, if your first choice is sold out and there are only obstructed or nosebleed seats for your second choice, you'll still have something else to go for.

There are two TKTS outlets. The big and better-known one is at the north end of the Times Square area at 47th and Broadway, a multiline striped tent on its own little island in the traffic, officially called Duffy Square. (The statue there, incidentally, is of George Lober, who wrote "Give My Regards to Broadway," among other songs.) The day's options are listed on a board overhead; you can study it while in line. Windows open at 3 p.m. and stay open until 8 p.m. (which just gives you time to sprint for the theater door) Monday through Saturday; they open for matinee tickets (Wednesday and Saturday) from 10 a.m. to 2 p.m., also curtain time; and

Sundays from noon to 8 p.m. A smaller TKTS outlet is in the 2 World Trade Center building on the mezzanine level; it's open from 11 a.m. to 5:30 p.m. Monday through Friday and until 3:30 p.m. on Saturday, but it sells matinee tickets one day ahead of time. Note that neither location takes credit cards, but traveler's checks are as good as cash. Also note that TKTS is not a secret to city residents; the queues at Times Square, especially, form some time before the actual opening.

The music and ballet worlds' version of TKTS is the **Music and Dance Booth** in Bryant Park (Sixth and 42nd Street; 382-2323). It's open from noon to 2 p.m. and again from 3 to 7 p.m. Tuesday through Sunday, and it works on the same cash or traveler's check system that TKTS does.

Other ways to trim costs: Go directly to the box office of the show you want to see with cash or a credit card and avoid the handling charge; this also frequently allows you to look at a seating chart and pick the best ticket available. If you are interested in one of the longer-running shows rather than a new hit, or don't care so much which show you see, look for discount coupons at the various Convention and Visitors' Bureau branches and stalls.

You might consider settling for tickets to previews (full dress run-throughs of shows that have not officially opened yet and are still being polished), which are frequently less expensive; or matinees, although since older New Yorkers favor these earlier hours, they can be crowded. Or you might just go for a rehearsal, like those of the New York Philharmonic (see below).

Some of the cultural institutions have discounts for students or senior citizens, but be sure to carry ID when you go. And if you are a sturdy sort, inquire about standing-room tickets at the bigger venues; they aren't always free, but for $20, it's a show (and some people will probably leave at intermission . . .).

■ Cameras and Close-Ups ■

If it's one of the television talk shows you're interested in, you most likely need to try to get tickets ahead of time—say, six or eight weeks. In the case of *Saturday Night Live,* it's a matter of seasons rather than weeks. Tickets for the whole taping season are awarded by a lottery drawing every August, meaning that postcard requests gathered in the 11 months previous are also in the pot, and even then winners only get two seats. Address postcards to *Saturday Night Live,* NBC Tickets, 30 Rockefeller Plaza, New York, NY 10012.

Most shows are a little easier, but almost all requests should be sent in at least two or three months in advance, and probably longer. Of course, if you regularly watch the shows, you probably already know this. What happens if your favorite personality gets canceled in the meantime? Hey, that's show biz.

On the other hand, nobody likes empty chairs, even a couple, to show in the audience. So if you're still longing for that wild and crazy *SNL* moment, and you feel lucky, go over to Rockefeller Plaza early on Saturday morning, stand around on the sidewalk on 49th Street between Fifth and Sixth, get your face on television in the background of the *Today Show,* and keep an eye on the 49th Street entrance to 30 Rockefeller Plaza. At about 9:15 a.m., not every week and with no guarantees, a few standby tickets to *Saturday Night Live* may be passed out. If you do get a seat, be prepared to be seated at 8:30 p.m. for the dress rehearsal and 11:30 for the taping. If you've hit the Trifecta recently, you could also duck inside the main NBC lobby at 30 Rockefeller Plaza about 9 a.m. and hope for *Late Night with Conan O'Brian* passes.

Standby tickets to the *Late Show with David Letterman* don't guarantee entry, either, but at least there are 100 of them, and five chances a week; join the line—well before the actual noon handout—outside the Ed Sullivan Theater on Broadway at 53rd, and cross your fingers.

Standby tickets to *Sally Jessy Raphael* are handed out at 10 a.m. outside the studio at 515 West 57th Street; that is also where to queue up for *Geraldo* tickets, at noon (for 1 p.m. tapings) and 2 p.m. (for 3 p.m. tapings). Empty seats for *Live with Regis and Kathie Lee* are filled after reserve ticket holders are seated at 8 a.m.; line up outside the studio at West 67th and Columbus Avenue.

One exception to the general rule is that tickets for tapings of *The Rush Limbaugh Show* must be requested by telephone; call 397-7367 between 10 a.m. and 1 p.m. Monday through Thursday. It usually takes three or four months, but since you get a live person of the line, you can check and see if there has been a cancellation.

For more information on how to get future tickets to *Letterman,* call 975-2476; for *Geraldo,* call 265-1283; for *Sally Jessy,* call 582-1722; for *Montel Williams,* call 560-3003; for *Ricki Lake,* call 889-7091; for *Regis and Kathie Lee,* call 456-3537; for *Conan,* call 644-3056.

Performing Arts

■ **The Big Tickets: Lincoln Center and Carnegie Hall** ■

Live from Lincoln Center is almost an understatement. This venue draws an estimated 5 million patrons a year, and even if you only worked your way through all its programs and never set foot farther down Broadway, you could still fill up most of a week. Since the mid-1960s, the **Lincoln Center for the Performing Arts** has been home to New York's most prestigious companies: the New York Philharmonic, the Metropolitan Opera and the New York City Opera, the New York City Ballet and American Ballet Theater, the Repertory Company of Lincoln Center, Wynton Marsalis's Lincoln Center Jazz Orchestra, the Chamber Music Society, the Lincoln Center Film Society, and, for several years, though no longer, the New York Shakespeare Festival, plus the Juilliard School and the School of American Ballet.

The six-building complex, a cluster that looks out toward Broadway and Columbus Avenue between West 62nd and 65th, includes five theaters; the opera house, Bruno Walter Auditorium concert hall, and Alice Tully Recital Hall; two theaters and a recital hall within Juilliard; an outdoor bandshell; and branches of the New York Public Library and the Library and Museum for the Performing Arts.

And it quite appropriately has its "roots" in one of New York's most famous creations: Bernstein/Sondheim's *West Side Story,* which was set in just the slums that urban planner Robert Moses swept away for this theatrical temple.

The Philharmonic, under the direction of Kurt Masur, is in residence at Avery Fisher Hall from September to May, with its popular and relaxed "Mostly Mozart" series during the summer. Open rehearsals during the season are held Thursdays at 9:45 a.m. For more information call 875-5030.

The Metropolitan Opera House, with its crystal chandeliers and Chagall murals, is so beautiful it's worth a tour of its own (see Part 10, "Sight-Seeing and Tours"). The Met Company holds the stage from mid-September to April; the American Ballet Theater has been using it the rest of the year, though in 1998 it tried out the more intimate quarters of Florence Gould Hall (see "Other Major Venues," later in this chapter). For more information call 362-6000.

The prestigious but turbulent Vivian Beaumont Theater, next to the opera house behind the reflecting pool with the Henry Moore sculpture, just reopened after a $5 million renovation and much publicized artistic rededication (239-6277). Under the Beaumont is the smaller (only 325 seats) and more cutting-edge Mitzi Newhouse Theater (239-6277).

The New York State Theater (870-5570), on the south side of the opera house, was designed by Philip Johnson and looks it, with its sequential entrances like layers of architectural curtains drawing back, its gilded ceiling, and its four banks of balconies. The New York City Ballet is in residence from around Thanksgiving through February (the *Nutcracker* pretty much fills up the schedule until January) and again from April through June. The New York City Opera, which found its feet and its independence under the direction of former Met star Beverly Sills, performs July through November.

Alice Tully Hall is the home of the Lincoln Center Chamber Music Society and also often hosts concerts by Juilliard students; it turns cinematic in fall for the International Film Festival (875-5050), and the Walter Reade Theater upstairs hosts the New York Film Festival (875-5600). Special recitals are sometimes held in the Walter Auditorium (870-1630) or in the three venues at Juilliard (799-5000). And check out the library, which exhibits costumes and stage sets as well as prints and scores.

The plaza outside is called Damrosch Park and is the site of various fine arts and crafts shows during the year and the Big Apple Circus in winter. It is also where the Guggenheim Bandshell is located and where free concerts, dance programs, and family shows organized by Lincoln Center Out-of-Doors pop up all through the summer; watch the papers.

Few concert halls have attracted as many legends as **Carnegie Hall,** and no wonder: The premier concert was conducted by Tchaikovsky; the New York Philharmonic played here in the heyday of Mahler, Toscanini, Stokowski, and Bernstein; and a concert date here has for the past century been recognized as a mark of supreme artistry. Nowadays it hosts pop concerts as often as classical, but its astonishing acoustics—it was overhauled in the late 1980s—and its displays of memorabilia make it a genuine experience. Carnegie Hall is at 154 West 57th, near Seventh Avenue (247-7800), next to that other theatrical tradition, the Russian Tea Room.

And here are two other frequently star-studded venues, a little less accessible to first-timers but often astonishing in their offerings (and really not hard to get to): The somewhat more cutting-edge **Brooklyn Academy of Music,** affectionately known as BAM, which hosts performances by everyone from Lou Reed to Robert Wilson to the increasingly popular Brooklyn Philharmonic and big-name guests (try (718) 636-4100 or online at www.bam.org); and the absolutely crackerjack **New Jersey Performing Arts Center** in Newark (call (973) 642-8989), which will serve as the home-away-from-home stage for such major performing-arts organizations as the Alvin Ailey American Dance Theater, American Ballet Theater, the New York Shakespeare Festival, and the Lincoln Center Jazz Orchestra, plus major international ballet, opera, and dance touring companies. Miss the Manhattan season? Cross the river.

■ Broadway ■

"They say the neon lights are bright on Broadway." Well, yes, and there are more of them than ever before. Not only does the theater district continue to expand—the neighborhood west of Times Square along 42nd Street is now called Theater Row to showcase its new venues—but so do the audiences. The number of theater tickets sold is approaching 10 million a year, and the industry brings more than $2 billion into the city's economy. And with the likes of the Disney Company, which has sunk $40 million into renovating the **New Amsterdam,** in the picture, Broadway is prepared to hit the millennium running.

Broadway is both an address and a style. Only a few of the theaters are actually on Broadway: most are between Broadway and Eighth Avenue from about 44th to 52nd; the Broadway theater itself is at West 53rd. Many have distinguished theatrical names: the **Lunt-Fontanne,** the **Helen Hayes,** the **Eugene O'Neill,** the **Richard Rodgers,** the **Gershwin,** the **Belasco,** the **Douglas Fairbanks,** the **John Houseman,** the **Barrymore** (in this case, Ethel), and the **Booth** (Edwin). Some are so famous they are recognized even by non-theatergoers, such as the **Shubert, Circle in the Square,** the **Actors Studio,** and the vaudeville veteran **Palace.** Some even pay homage (posthumously, of course) to critics, such as the **Walter Kerr Theater** and the **Brooks Atkinson.** Irving Berlin built the **Music Box;** Mae West inaugurated the **Royale;** and John and Lionel Barrymore made one of their rare joint appearances at the **Plymouth.**

The big musicals head for the bigger venues (*Phantom* at the **Majestic,** *Scarlet Pimpernell* at the **Minskoff,** *Beauty and the Beast* at the **Palace,** *Showboat* at the **Gershwin**), where they can indulge the public addiction to tricky stage sets, elaborate costumes, and microphones. The smaller shows can be more fun, however, because the older-style halls mean almost everyone has a good view, and the nostalgically elegant side boxes come right to the apron. For current shows, schedules, and phone numbers, check the phone-charge listings at the beginning of this chapter or the local newspapers.

■ Off- and Off-Off-Broadway ■

Thanks partly to the expansion of 42nd Street's "Theater Row," and partly to the popularization of the big musical theaters, the spiritual line between some on-Broadway and off-Broadway venues is getting fuzzier. Many of the more "Uptown" off-Broadway houses have pretty much been assimilated, while the Downtown off-Broadway troupes, many of whom may once have been rather exhilaratingly anti-establishment, are threatening to mellow into the high-culture circuit. And yet such theaters as the **Playwright's Horizons** (416 West 42nd; 279-4200) and **Roundabout** (1520 Broadway; 869-8400), despite their central–White Way addresses, have off-Broadway attitudes.

Among the best-known venues are the **Provincetown Playhouse,** famous as Eugene O'Neill's first dramatic home; the ambitious **Minetta Lane Theater** (18 Minetta Lane; 420-8000) and **Circle Rep** (159 Bleecker Street; 254-6330); the **Lucille Lortel,** formerly the Theatre de Lys, home of the landmark 1950s revival of *Threepenny Opera* (121 Christopher Street; 924-2817); **Cherry Lane,** founded by Edna St. Vincent Millay (38 Commerce Street; 989-2020); the **WPA Theater** (519 West 23rd Street; 206-0523); **La Mama E.T.C.** (74-A East Fourth Street; 473-8745); Joseph Papp's six-hall **Public Theater** in the onetime free library near Astor Place (425 Lafayette Street; 260-2400), and the lower-profile **Astor Place Theatre** across the street (434 Lafayette; 254-4370); **Players Theatre** near Washington Square (115 MacDougal Street; 254-5076); **Union Square Theater** (17th Street and Park Avenue; 505-0700); **Actors Playhouse** (100 Seventh Avenue South; 691-6226) and the **Sheridan Square Playhouse,** across the street (99 Seventh Avenue South). The famous, or infamous, **Ridiculous Theater Company** of Sheridan Square is somewhat itinerant; call 691-2271 for the latest. And the longest-running play in American theatrical history, *The Fantastics,* was, and is, at the **Sullivan Street Theater** (181 Sullivan; 674-3838).

Again, off-off-Broadway refers less to an address (generally Downtown, though it may be Village, East Village, SoHo, etc.) than to a mindset. It used to imply experimental or avant-garde productions, satires, debut productions, and sometimes just deeply serious art, and to a great extent it still does; but sometimes productions that are destined (or at least intended) to make their way to Broadway get their final editings here. Among the most interesting venues are the **Performing Garage,** home of the Wooster Group (33 Wooster Street; 966-3651); **Manhattan Theater Club** (453 West 16th; 645-5590); the multimedia-minded **Kitchen** (512 West 19th Street; 255-5793); the arts space and sometime theater **Franklin Furnace** (112

Franklin Street; 825-4671) and **Ohio Theater** in SoHo (66 Wooster Street; 966-4844); the four-stage **Theater for the New City** (155 First Avenue; 254-1109); and nearby **P.S. 122**—not Public School, here, but Performance Space—in Chelsea (150 First Avenue at East Ninth; 477-5288); **Three Lives and Co.** (154 West Tenth; 741-2069); **Theater Workshop** (79 East Fourth Street; 460-5475); and the **Bouwerie Lane Theater,** home of the self-conscious but interesting Jean Cocteau Repertory (677-0060).

■ Freebies ■

The most famous free theater in New York is what is commonly known as **Shakespeare in the Park,** the hot-weather season of the New York Shakespeare Festival. Central Park's Delacourt Theater is the summer home to the company that otherwise holds forth (for money) at the Papp Public Theater. It's a matter of principle, or at least of sentiment, for some of the biggest stars of stage and screen to do their stint in the open air: Patrick Steward, Andre Braugher, Kevin Klein, and Michelle Pfeiffer have all bellowed the Bard here.

Getting tickets can be time-consuming (though the reward is great). They are given out on a first-come, first-served basis beginning at 1 p.m. the day of show, but you'd better be there long before that. (There are fewer than 1,900 seats, so if you're only in town for a short time and have other things to do, gauge your chances and look elsewhere.) You might double your chances of getting in by sending a confederate down to the Public Theater box office between 1 and 3 p.m.; you can only get two tickets, but that's better than none. Incidentally, even in winter, the Public Theater is a great, steeply intimate place to see innovative productions of Shakespeare with equally big-name stars.

But Shakespeare is not the only free theater in town. Every summer, **Gorilla Rep** (330-8086) stages extremely vivid, if not positively florid, productions of two alternating repertory plays under the trees at the south end of Washington Square (watch for listings in the local press). **The SoHo Arts Festival** in October has expanded from the inside (galleries) out (street performances).

The **New York International Fringe Festival,** which was launched in August 1997, even in its first year offered 175 premieres, improvisations, lectures, readings, storytellings, Shakespearean declamations, character studies, one-person shows, comic interpretations, dance performances, and make-up-your-own-name shows over 11 days and in 21 venues in Greenwich Village, the East Village, and the Lower East Side; a proudly off-off-off gathering, it was not literally free. Shows were about $10 apiece (for a "lunatic pass" of $350, you could see them all!), and many of the classes, workshops, and seminars were free, although donations are always welcome. For information on the festival write FringeNYC, 445 West 45th Street, Fourth Floor, New York, NY 10036, or e-mail at info@fringenyc.org.

■ Other Major Venues ■

As mentioned earlier, the New York City Ballet calls Lincoln Center home; but that is far from the only premier dance troupe that plays Manhattan. The American Ballet Theater uses **City Center** at 131 West 55th (581-1212); other companies book into the gloriously restored **Joyce Theater** (175 Eighth Avenue; 242-0800), which is home to the Eliot Feld Ballet, or the **Sylvia and Danny Kaye Theater** at Hunter College (68th between Park and Lexington Avenues; 772-4448). The American Ballet Theater, accustomed to the grandeur of the Metropolitan Opera House, has recently tested the atmosphere at **Florence Gould Hall** at the French Institute (55 East 58th Street; 355-6160), which also hosts some theatrical and literary performances; and the Dance Theater of Harlem and other ethnic troupes prefer the **Aaron Davis Theater** at City College (West 135th Street and Convent Avenue; 650-6900). Also watch for listings for such locally based companies as **Merce Cunningham** (691-9761) and **Dance Theater Workshop** (924-0077).

Various chamber, orchestral, new music, and recital performances take place at **Juilliard** in Lincoln Center (799-5000) and the nearby **Merkin Concert Hall** (129 West 67th; 362-8719); in the **Tisch Center** at the 92nd Street Y (at Lexington Avenue; 996-1100); in Miller Theater at **Columbia School of the Arts** (Broadway at 116th Street; 854-7799); and at the **Harlem School of the Arts** (St. Nicholas at West 141st; 926-4100). The **Amato Opera Theater,** a weekend-only venue, is very popular with serious music lovers (Bowery at Second Street; 228-8200), and its tickets, usually about $20, are bargains. Many of the city's big-name arts organizations play concerts at the World Financial Center's (all-season) **Winter Garden** (945-0505). But by far the most unusual venue is the **BargeMusic**—just what it sounds like, a boat transformed into a concert hall—but the acoustics, and the names on the schedule, will make a believer out of you (across the East River at Fulton Ferry Landing just south of the Brooklyn Bridge; (718) 624-2083).

Major rock/pop/reggae/soul/country concerts are apt to be held, like most everything else, in **Madison Square Garden** (465-6741); but other common concert venues include MSG's smaller annex, the **Paramount;** the **Orpheum** (126 Second Avenue; 307-4100); the revived **Apollo** (West

125th and Frederick Douglass Boulevard; 749-5838); the **Beacon Theater** (2124 Broadway; 496-7070); the **Hammerstein Ballroom** at Manhattan Center (311 West 34th Street; 564-4882); **Symphony Space** (Broadway and 95th; 864-5400); **Roseland** (239 West 52nd Street; 247-0200); and the **Westbeth Center** in Greenwich Village (151 Bank Street; 741-0391). Occasionally more mainstream names show up in **Town Hall** (123 West 43rd Street; 840-2124), Avery Fisher Hall, or Carnegie Hall.

If lectures, poetry, and readings are your bag, check into the menu at **Fez** (380 Lafayette Street; 533-2680); the famously establishment **92nd Street Y** (1395 Lexington Avenue; 415-5440), or the home of the "poetry slam," the **Nuyorkian Poet's Cafe** in the East Village (236 East Third Street; 505-8183), which is now so establishment anti-establishment that it has taken its act on the road; and the **New School/Academy of American Poets** series (66 West 12th; 229-5600). Or call the **Academy of American Poets** headquarters at 274-0343 to inquire about its poetry readings around town.

New York Nightlife

New York's mind-boggling assortment of nightclubs, bars, theaters, and discos is what makes Fun City fun. No other place in the world has the range, quality, and sheer abundance of nightlife choices of New York; even on weeknights, Gothamites in search of entertainment can choose between any number of top-name jazz, Latin, Irish, blues, chamber, or rock groups, swing dancing in storybook swank on the 65th floor, or slam dancing in the grimy clubs where punk, ska, and rave first caught on in America. There are discos full of the Beautiful People themselves, not just local pretenders; bars and cafes where boys meet girls and strip clubs where boys watch girls (and, on the other side of the coin, the most famous gay bar in America, Stonewall, marks the gates of a mostly gay nabe that may be less populous than San Francisco but is at least as vibrant). Don't forget the panoply of Broadway (as well as off-Broadway and off-off-Broadway) shows and some of the country's best symphony, ballet, and opera (see above), as well as tons of comedy clubs, poetry readings, beer bars, sake spots, cigar joints, late-night bookstore cafes, and sing-along piano bars. Unlike in other cities, you'll find numerous choices in each category, many open seven nights per week until *late*.

It's all quite exhausting, and after a few enervating days the abundance of riches may make you jaded; like addicts, those spending time in New York's nightlife quickly become inured to the excitement of it all, craving greater and greater entertainment highs. A hypercompetitive fleet of club and bar owners strive nightly to offer just that.

■ Jazz ■

Jazz may have originated in New Orleans, but for decades New York has been the center of the jazz universe. If you have even the slightest interest in this style, you'll want to check out one or two of the following clubs. Avoid crowds by catching the late set (musicians play better, too, as it gets later and they get warmed up) and by choosing stormy nights when others might not venture out.

See profiles for **Village Vanguard, Knitting Factory, Blue Note, Small's,** and **Savoy Lounge.**

55 Bar (55 Christopher Street; 929-9883) is a beery Greenwich Village dive with music that can be depressingly bad but is often surprisingly good (especially when guitar star Mike Stern plays there). No cover most nights.

Iridium (44 West 63rd Street; 582-2121), with its over-the-top ultramodern decor, is a trippy exception to the rule that jazz is often played in drab spaces.

Roulette (228 West Broadway; 219-8242) is an intelligent small concert space for new and experimental music.

Sweet Basil (88 Seventh Avenue South; 242-1785) is one of the major clubs; the music is a bit more modern than in the Vanguard or Blue Note.

Visiones (125 MacDougal Street; 673-5576) is not the friendliest or most comfortable place, but the Maria Schneider Orchestra on Mondays and the Thursday night late jam sessions (1–4 a.m.) hosted by saxophonist Ralph LaLama are well worth a listen.

■ **Rock** ■

Rock clubs in Manhattan mostly fit into three categories. There are the bar/venues that host big-name acts for big cover charges—places like **Tramps** (see profile), **Irving Plaza** (17 Irving Plaza; 777-6800), **Supper Club** (240 West 47th Street; 921-1940), and **Roseland** (236 West 52nd Street; 247-0200). Then there are the showcase places where newly signed bands preen for industry insiders—**Brownie's** (169 Avenue A; 420-8392) and **Mercury Lounge** (see profile). At the bottom of the ladder are the vanity clubs where amateurish weekend warriors play short sets—one lousy group after another—for a clientele of friends and family (Bitter End, Spiral, and multi-band nights at CBGB's—though this legendary punk pioneer at 315 Bowery, 982-4052, still presents some good shows with big names).

The problem is that if you just want to have a beer and listen to professional-quality local guys who play live for a living—a real *bar* band— you're in the wrong place. The country's best bar bands have long played their hearts out in nearby New Jersey and Long Island (remember the origins of Southside Johnny, Bruce Springsteen, The Rascals, etc.), but Manhattan, right between those two areas, has few groups (or venues to present them) dedicated to entertaining a bar. The showcasing kids angle more for A&R attention than for a grooving good time for the house crowd, and an evening in one of the name venues means buying expensive tickets and standing amid rapturous crowds; you're basically at a concert, not hanging out in a bar.

If you don't mind your rock filtered through other influences, **Rodeo Bar, Manny's Car Wash** (see profiles), and **Wetlands** (a fun '60s-themed bar featuring acid jazz, ska, Grateful Dead cover bands, etc., at 161 Hudson Street, 966-4225) present good, professional hang-out bands (rockabilly/country/funky-tinged in the former, bluesy in the latter).

■ Dancing ■

There aren't many '70s-style discos left (Studio 54 has become an upscale strip club). **The Roxy** (515 West 18th Street; 645-5156), last of that generation, hosts roller disco on Tuesdays (gay) and Wednesdays (straight), plus regular dancing on Friday and Saturday. **Webster Hall** combines new and old styles (see profile), and the **New China Club** should be open by the time you read this, probably continuing its mix of DJ and live band party music (the Limelight may reopen as well—check the weekly entertainment magazines).

Swing has been adopted en masse by the teenybopper set, who dress in cartoonishly exaggerated zoot suits and vampy dresses with pearl necklaces. They dip to the floor while dancing with suave toothy grins, and they never ever break character. The heart of this retro scene is **Lansky's Lounge,** a very chic club in the back of Ratner's, an old Lower East Side Jewish Dairy Restaurant (138 Delancey Street; 677-5588). There's avid swing dancing for an older crowd Tuesday through Sunday at the **Rainbow Room** (see profile), Sunday nights at **Continental Club** (at Irving Place: 17 Irving Place; 696-9737), Monday nights at **Louisiana Community Bar & Grill** (see profile), weekends at **Supper Club** (the poor man's Rainbow Room, 240 West 47th Street; 921-1940), and infrequently at **Roseland Ballroom** (236 West 52nd Street; 247-0200), New York's most famous period dance hall—lately mostly presenting rock.

For salsa dancing in a setting more down-home than pounding Latin discos such as **Les Poulet** (see profile) or glossy nightspots such as **S.O.B.'s** (see profile), warm, artsy **Nuyorican Poets Cafe** (236 East 3rd Street; 505-8183), located in a proud (and borderline) Puerto Rican neighborhood, hosts very informal, grassrootsy dances (in addition to bilingual poetry readings, theatrical presentations, etc.), and all are welcome.

■ Irish ■

The original Irish immigrants to New York have long since assimilated and moved out to suburbia, but there's been a recent youthful tide of new Irish arrivals. From informal jams (called "sessions") in anonymous bars to solidly packed performances of the cult group Black 47 at **Paddy Reilly's** (519 Second Avenue; 686-1210), this musical subculture serves as a touchstone for these young expats, as well as a refreshing option for anyone seeking alternative entertainment.

There are free informal sessions most nights of the week (check www.inx.net/~mardidom/rcnycal.htm for complete up-to-date listings). The following are of particular interest:

An Beal Bocht (445 West 238th; Riverdale, Bronx) offers great music Wednesdays and Sundays; it's a trek to get to, but they serve the best Guinness of all.

Kate Kearney's (251 East 50th Street; 935-2045) is also upscale.

Ultra-lowscale **Mona's** (224 Avenue B; 353-3780) is worth chancing the scary neighborhood late Monday nights, when some of the city's top Irish musicians jam there.

Paddy Reilly's, in addition to Black 47 on Saturdays, hosts more low-key music sessions late Thursdays.

Swift's (34 East 4th; 260-3600) has music on Tuesdays, and great beer to boot.

Tommy Makem's (130 East 57th Street; 759-9040) is the most upscale venue, with dependably good music.

■ **Fine Drinks** ■

One of the best things about New York is the substantial number of people who not only appreciate the finer things in life but seek out the best food and drink with a zeal and passion that might frighten those who'd previously thought going out for a beer meant simply getting a Bud Lite at the corner bar.

Mind you, New York has a plethora of corner bars where Bud Lite is drunk unrepentantly. But for those on a mission to enjoy only the finest drinks, there are zillions of aficionado places whose selection will astound. And for those who aren't professional bon vivants, the True Believers populating these bars will gladly help clueless novices. New Yorkers may be rude and blasé, but once they start enthusing, it's hard to keep 'em down.

If you're online, the *NYC Beer Guide* provides exhaustive annotated listings of pubs, tastings, and local microbrews at www.nycbeer.org.

The best bars and restaurants for good beer:

Blind Tiger Ale House (518 Hudson Street; 675-3848) has 24 quality taps, plus hand-pumps.

Brewsky's (41 East Seventh Street; 420-0671) specializes in domestic microbrews. Cool toy train, too.

Burp Castle (41 East Seventh Street; 982-4576) bills itself as a "House of Beer Worship," staffed by crabby fake monks and decorated with ornate murals; they serve great Belgian ales.

Cafe de Bruxelles (118 Greenwich Avenue; 206-1830) fries the best pommes frites in town and offers a small but smart selection of Belgian bottles.

Chumley's (86 Bedford Street; 675-4449) is located in a hidden former speakeasy.

DBA. See profile.

Ear Inn (326 Spring Street; 226-9060) is a bohemian little cafe with especially good Guinness.

The Ginger Man. See profile.

Hallo Berlin (402 West 51st Street; 541-6248) is flamingly oom-pah, serving wursts and German lager.

Jekyll and Hyde (91 Seventh Avenue South, 255-5388; and 1409 Avenue of the Americas, 541-9505) are theme joints with a large selection of overpriced beer.

John Street Bar and Grill (17 John Street; 349-3278) is an informal beery basement in the Financial District with a fine selection.

Knitting Factory. See profile.

McSorley's Old Ale House (15 East Seventh Street; 473-9148) is a tourist fave, with old New York ambience and mediocre beer swilled alongside obnoxious frat boys.

North Star (93 South Street; 509-6757) is a most authentic British pub, with good food and a few well-chosen and well-maintained taps.

Old Town Bar (45 East 18th Street; 529-6732) is the bar featured during the opening credits of *David Letterman* . . . halfway decent beer selection, great ambience.

Peculier Pub (145 Bleecker Street; 353-1327) is expensive and incredibly mobbed on weekends, but the selection's amazing.

Ruby's Taphouse (1495 Second Avenue; 987-8179) offers 26 taps on the Upper East Side.

Silver Swan (41 East 20th Street; 254-3611) cooks terrific German food and stocks plenty of good German bottles.

Virgil's Barbecue. See profile in Part 12.

Wall Street Kitchen and Bar (70 Broad Street; 797-7070) sports a record 100 beers on tap and also an excellent selection of wines by the glass.

Waterfront Ale House (540 Second Avenue; 696-4104) has an excellent tap selection, with some ultra-rare specials, good pub food, and the best ice cream in town.

These are few really good brewpubs (where beer is made on premises) in the area, but here are some of the better ones: **Heartland Brewery** (35 Union Square West; 645-3400); **Chelsea Brewing Company** (Pier 59, Chelsea Piers; 336-6440), in an amazing riverside complex on West Street; and **Times Square Brewery** (160 West 42nd Street; 398-1234), which has a great view from the second floor.

■ Japanese/Sake ■

There are two loci of Japanese culture in Manhattan: the East Village, where hip bohemian Japanese kids live and hang out, and Midtown, where a more suit-and-tie crowd have their bars and restaurants, many private. Each scene has its own custom tailored sake bar. **Decibel** (240 East 9th Street; 979-2733) is a knickknack-filled haven, a very cool little basement space to talk and drink any of tons of sakes from your choice of unique cups. The food is proud toaster-oven/microwave Japanese bachelor chow, and the ambience is neither Japanese nor American but a hipper-than-hip new hybrid, "Japanese East Village." Decibel's straighter younger brother, **The Sake Club** (see profile), is far more adult and refined and serves more highbrow food. There's another hipster sake bar in SoHo: **Sake Lounge** (148 Mercer Street 2F; 334-3638) cooks good *okonomayaki* (the Japanese pancake perfect for bar munching), but there's a much narrower choice of sakes. The staff speaks good English, though, and the dark techno ambience with airy high ceilings is beautiful. For other Japanese-flavored nightlife (one East Village, the other Midtown), see profiles for **Angel's Share** and **Hole in One.**

■ Hotel Bars ■

Some of the swankiest—and most of the classiest—bars in town are located in hotels.

The Algonquin's full of good drinking options: There's the famous Oak Room (see profile), as well as their elegant and relaxing lobby bar and the woody/clubby Blue Bar.

The Carlyle Hotel (35 East 76th Street; 744-1600) contains not only the famous Cafe Carlyle (see profile) but also Bemelmans Bar, which features tinkling piano and a clubby atmosphere, with watercolors on the walls.

5757 at The Four Seasons Hotel (57 East 57th Street; 758-5700) is huge and Gothic, designed by I. M. Pei.

Grand Bar at the SoHo Grand Hotel (310 West Broadway; 965-3000) is a tiny lounge populated almost entirely by European tourists that spills out into a very atmospheric lounge area, all inside this new super techno hotel lobby.

Holiday Inn (440 West 57th Street; 581-8100) has a pool and bar on their roof. Pay them a fee and you can swim and sip to your heart's content.

The View at the **Marriott Marquis** (1535 Broadway; 704-8900) is the only revolving bar in New York. Don't eat the food.

Hotel bars tend to be restrained, refined, but the **Monkey Bar** at the Elysee Hotel (60 East 54th Street; 838-2600) is anything but; it attracts a young, exuberant crowd of preppies out of control, and laughter—sometimes even singing, if you get there late enough—drowns out clinking glasses.

The Royalton. See profile.

The Top of the Tower at Beekman Tower Hotel (3 Mitchell Place—East 49th Street and First Avenue; 355-7300) is a blessedly mellow spot for a late-night drink with a handsome East Side view, especially enjoyable at one of the outdoor tables.

■ Sex ■

Many New York singles are too sophisticated to pin the "singles" label on themselves and attend corny singles dances, singles trips, etc., so they choose to go contrarian, shunning bar scenes and making friends in museums (try MoMA on Fridays), bookstores (any of the Barnes and Noble Superstore cafes, especially the one at 675 Sixth Avenue), adult education classes (The Learning Annex, dubbed "McCollege" by some), and the like. That many of these have turned into "meat markets" as infamous as any bar or disco is an irony that has escaped attention.

But for those who prefer to "meat" and greet the old-fashioned way, in bars, there are ample choices. Try **Rolf's** (a German restaurant with a popular late bar, 281 Third Avenue, 473-8718), **Grange Hall** (see profile), hyperswank **Match Uptown** (33 East 60th Street; 906-9177), **Au Bar** (41 East 58th Street; 308-9455), **The Bubble Room** (see profile), **Nell's** (see profile), and the chic and grown-up **King Cole Bar** at the Street Regis Hotel (2 East 55th Street; 339-6721) for power pick-ups.

The fanciest strip bars, like **Stringfellows** (35 East 21st Street; 254-2444) and **The Vip Club** (20 West 20th Street; 633-1199), are ludicrously "upscale," with velvet ropes and thick-necked goonish bouncers who greet potential customers with a throaty "Gennelmen!" You'll pay a cover charge and be hounded to buy drinks. Inside, shiny/flashy "deluxe" interiors and the perkiest mammalian protuberances surgery can create. More low-key are **New York Dolls** (59 Murray Street; 227-6912), in the Financial District, and the very laid-back—almost rural—**Baby Doll Lounge** (24 White Street; 226-4870).

Beware of clip joints like **Nude Legz Diamond** (231 West 54th Street; 977-6826) and **Runway 69** (725 Seventh Avenue; 764-6969), many of which pass out promotional fliers on Midtown streets; these are full-nudity places that bypass restrictions by serving no alcohol. Your cranberry juice will cost you dearly, and talkative women hired by the bar will attempt to pressure you into buying them even more outrageously priced drinks (and, eventually, fake champagne).

■ Gay ■

Whereas San Francisco gay culture is more of a boutiquey artsy-ish scene, New York has more of the real deal when it comes to art, and the many gays who work in these arts help make the Manhattan scene a bit more substantive, less camp. The guy drunkenly belting out show tunes along with a tableful of friends in some Greenwich Village piano bar may be the understudy for the part in the actual Broadway production.

The Latest Scenes change at a dizzying pace; widely available publications like *Time Out NY*, *New York Blade*, and free *LGNY* (distributed in red street boxes) are good sources for information, as are The Hot Line (call (718) 326-LINE) and the Gay and Lesbian Switchboard (777-1800). The following are some spots with longevity.

The granddaddy of all piano bars is **Don't Tell Mama's** (see profile), but more homogeneously homosexual is **The 88** (228 West 10th Street; 924-0088), where the bar is in a glamorous downstairs space, with excellent cabaret-style pianists carrying on till 4 a.m. nightly. This is near the center of New York's Greenwich Village gay scene and a quick walk from the land-mark **Stonewall Bar,** which still stands at 53 Christopher Street (it's since gone through several incarnations). A walk down Christopher Street and environs will reveal a plethora of clubs and bars. **The Monster** (80 Grove Street; 924-3557) is perhaps the leading Village gay bar; it features an upstairs piano bar for an older crowd, plus a downstairs mirrored disco that's more of a pickup joint. The crowd's diverse, and while things can get silly, it's always relatively tasteful and safe.

Don Hill's (511 Greenwich Street; 334-1390) is a much more fringy scene, as befits its fringe location on the outskirts of SoHo. Thursdays host New Wave BeavHer, a magnet for clubbing celebs, and Squeezebox Fridays are a multisexual hang with live punk/rock and roll/disco and drag stars.

Splash (50 West 17th Street; 691-0073) is a Chelsea shower bar, a "nice" place (well . . . *clean,* anyway) for yuppies and out-of-towners. You'll find a similar crowd uptown at **The Works** (428 Columbus Avenue; 799-7365); they present acts on Monday nights for gupsters in polo shirts and chinos.

On the Upper East Side: **The Townhouse** (236 East 58th Street, 754-4649) is a place where Young Men Who Want to Meet Guys Who Wear Coats and Ties meet guys who wear coats and ties who want to meet Young Men Who Want to Meet Guys Who Wear Coats and Ties.

The Roxy (515 West 18th Street; 645-5156) hosts gay roller disco on Tuesday nights.

The Clit Club has been the preeminent "lipstick lesbian" get-together for years, and it's still quite the fabulous party, every Friday night at **Mother** (432 West 14th Street; 741-3919). Mother has other nights of varying degrees of wildness ("Click and Drag," the Saturday night fetish fashion party, broadcasts camera feeds from rest room stalls) for gay, lesbian, and/or mixed crowds. Very, very cutting edge.

Meow Mix (269 East Houston Street; 254-0688) is a landmark lesbian bar that hosts particularly debauched parties, often with live bands.

■ Comedy ■

Comedy clubs are looked down upon by Manhattanites as strictly for tourists (or, worse, for Bridge-and-Tunnelers—the derisive name for sub-urbanites drawn to the island for weekend entertainment). Indeed, the aver-age New Yorker is at least as funny as some kid working the mike at Larry's Laughter Lounge. But if you must indulge in such shamefully uncos-mopolitan pleasures, there are a few nationally known clubs, plus some intriguing cutting-edge comedy venues where you can both yuck it up and feel hip.

The best mainstream clubs are **Caroline's** (see profile), **Gotham Comedy Club** (34 West 22nd Street; 367-9000) and **Catch a Rising Star** (253 West 28th Street; 462-2824) (neither Boston Comedy Club nor New York Comedy Club are recommended). These three get the best-known acts and have the most upscale ambience. **Catch a Rising Star** (check out their excellent Friday night music show for a mere $5 cover) sports a contrived "Showbiz" decor, with spotlights, tiered seating, TV monitors, and stage with set, while Gotham feels much more serious and intimate: upscale, but no baloney or showbiz touches; just a room with mike and audience. **The Comic Strip** (1568 Second Avenue; 861-9386) is where many famous people got their start, and it still puts on top-quality shows, particularly on weekends.

Beware "new talent nights" at the big clubs: Audiences paying a hefty cover and two-drink minimum often see not the brightest young talent but those newcomers who've promised club owners they'll pack the club (and thus its coffers) with friends and family. Miss these nights (Tuesdays at Catch and Gotham; Caroline's Monday showcases are slightly better) or you may find yourself grim-faced in front of a parade of talentless dweebs and their yucking cronies (though you may also miss the Next Big Things— nearly all famous comics started out on these nights).

Name comedians often try out new material in New York clubs; you can't count on, say, Robin Williams dropping in, of course, but you can increase your odds of a celeb sighting by hitting the big clubs (see above), **The Comedy Cellar** (117 MacDougal Street; 254-3480), or **Stand-up NY** (236 West 78th Street; 595-0850). Celebs are fairly common at the Monday night showcase at the Comic Strip, but otherwise the show's very hit-or-miss.

In reaction to the safe commercial comedy of the 1980s, a new comedy subculture has sprung up; this increasingly vital new scene floats from club to club, depending on the night, and cover charges are low (though the ambience can be as raw and gritty as the comedy).

F-stop (28 West 20th Street; 627-STOP) is a swanky restaurant that on Thursday nights invites semi-known comics to try out riskier new stuff in their basement. Like Luna Lounge—lots of slumming comedy-biz people.

You needn't check your sexuality at the door at lesbian **Henrietta Hudson Bar** (488 Hudson; 924-3347); men and straight women are welcome at the 10 p.m. Tuesday comedy show. It can be very good and very spontaneous, but the place is chaotic and noisy.

Luna Lounge (171 Ludlow Street; 260-2323) started as pure alternative space but has turned into the hot underground place to be seen by industry types. It's all very shmoozy and pretentious. Monday nights, $5 cover.

On Sunday nights, "The Rapture" at **Miss Elle's Homesick Bar and Grill** (226 West 79th Street; 595-4350) has semi-famous comics, plus good food and a cool vibe. Sundays 9–11, no cover.

Rebar (127 Eighth Avenue; 996-4580), a minuscule spot (the audience crams into five couches!) where up-and-comers test comedic waters, has somehow become a flagship of the alternate scene. Arrive Monday nights before 7:30 and enjoy some of the hippest, chanciest comics around for $3.

Surf Reality (172 Allen Street; 673-4182) has a great artsy freak show of an open mike night, featuring cutting-edge poetry/singing/standup/performance art all night on Sundays for $3; it's lots of fun but not for the squeamish.

Ye Olde Tripple Inn (263 West 54th Street; 245-9849) is a rowdy place with a long-standing reputation for comedy (Freddie Prinze used to emcee). The audience for the Tuesday night free shows (10:30–12:30) consists of a strange blend of insiders, dart throwers, and off-the-bar walkins; there's a screen for showing short films, plus improv and sketch groups.

The big clubs are trying to co-opt some of this grassrootsy alternative comedy movement. Call the clubs or check ads in the weekly magazines, looking for low covers and studiedly "alterno" hype.

■ Nighttime Safety ■

New York is both safer and more dangerous than you may think. It's safer because the streets aren't as chock-full of muggers and con men as some visitors expect; gunfire doesn't sail overhead as you dive into your cab. But this realization mustn't allow visitors to become overconfident; parts of Manhattan are so pretty, so peaceful, that it's easy to drop one's guard, forgetting that one is in a big city and giving opportunity to problems that might otherwise be avoided with cautiousness. As you make your way, amid hordes of other happy revelers, through the nighttime playground of New York's club scene, don't make the mistake of thinking you're in the Disney NYC pavilion.

The first trick is to learn the New York street walk: fast and confident. If you find yourself in a borderline nabe, walk like you know *exactly* where you're going—but by all means avoid the tell-tale clenched, fearful rush many tourists (especially single women) adopt. The image you want to project is confidence, openness, and awareness—not shuttered wariness.

Also remember that tempers flare easily under the myriad pressures in this overcrowded city. It's usually best to yield (graciously and confidently, not fearfully) in disputes, even when you're the one who's been wronged. The overwhelming majority of those who carry handguns do so for self-protection, but the sheer number of inhabitants is such that a one-tenth of one percent unstable fringe amounts to an appreciable number.

Be particularly careful about overindulging; bad guys do target drunks, and the lack of judgment that results from a surfeit of drink can up the odds of an ugly encounter with the criminal element. Anyway, Manhattan isn't really the place to get rip-roaring drunk; that's more the style of, say, New Orleans or Vegas. New Yorkers get tipsy, not tipped over. The trick is to get to that intermediate point where you *talk* a lot — talking being the preeminent New York pastime. Manhattan glibness has been fueled by martinis and ales from time immemorial.

ANGEL'S SHARE

Secret hideaway cocktail oasis

Who Goes There: 25–45; the beautiful, the hipsters, and the bohemian East Village Japanese

8 Stuyvesant Street (2nd floor)
777-5415   Zone 5 East Village

Cover: None
Minimum: None
Mixed drinks: $6–7
Wine: Bottles $25–60
Beer: $5–18
Dress: Elegant casual or anything black. Dress-up's fine, but not flashy.
Food available: Small menu of excellent Korean/Japanese snacks. Don't miss the fried oysters.

Hours: Every day, 7 p.m.–3 a.m.

What goes on: You go up steps with pink neon banisters, turn left through the sushi restaurant, and open an unmarked door to enter a mega-atmospheric little den of hip urbanity. Inside, there are suave young Asian bartenders crafting cocktails with single-minded intensity (they sample your drinks and tweak, often several times, before serving), soothing jazz played over a fine sound system, a few romantic tables with great views, and a bar filled with an interesting, intelligent, attractive clientele. Martinis are awesome, as are gimlets and fresh fruit daiquiris (not too sweet), plus you'll find wonderful selections of spirits like whisky and bourbon—there's not a single dumb bottle in the room. Service is classy but utterly unpretentious. The bristling intensity of the bartenders electrifies the place; it's the ideal choice for an intelligent date. The "no standing" rule can make it frustratingly difficult to get in (especially on crowded weekends) but provides uncommon tranquility when you do.

Setting & atmosphere: A narrow sliver with a bar on one side and a dramatic view up Third Avenue through tall draperied windows on the other. A huge mural of an Asian angel baby sets the tone of elegance with a sardonic twist. Tables are mostly for two—this isn't a destination for groups.

If you go: Fridays and Saturdays you may find Japanese jazz duos strumming in a cramped corner, but the stereo is far more pleasing (yet another reason to avoid weekend prime time).

LE BAR BAT

Gothic nightclub/restaurant/disco

Who Goes There: 25–50; suburbanites on weekends,
locals and clubbers weeknights

311 West 57th Street
    307-7228   Zone 8 Midtown West

Cover: Sunday–Wednesday, $10;
  Thursday, $15; Friday and
  Saturday, $20
Minimum: None
Mixed drinks: $5–6
Wine: $5–6.50
Beer: $4–5
Dress: Anything from white tie to
  nice casual (dress code

Thursday–Saturday: no jeans,
  sneakers, T-shirts)
Specials: Tuesday–Friday, 5–7 p.m.,
  free hors d'oeuvres
Food available: Full continental/
  southwestern sit-down menu; late
  bar menu till 2 a.m. Wednesday–
  Saturday, till 1 a.m. Sunday

Hours: Monday–Thursday, 11 a.m.–2 a.m.; Saturday and Sunday,
5:30 p.m.–4 a.m.

What goes on: This wacky, labyrinthian party joint long preceded all its
plasticky theme-bar neighbors. First and foremost, it's a supper club, presenting R&B, blues, funk, dance, and pop/rock bands (jazz vocals on more
informal Sunday nights) in a lush cabaret setting. Rather than dine, you can
buzz around the bat bar at the back of the room; view and sound are fine.
If you're bored with the music—or simply want to change channels—go
upstairs to the balcony (perfect for loners and voyeurs), recede into the comfortable Borneo Room, or take the all-out sensory stimulation route in Pandora's Box (opens at 9 p.m. nightly).

Setting & atmosphere: Trippy Gothic cathedral look, complete with fluo-
rescent blue semimolten bats hanging from the ceiling. The main room centers on the stage. The upstairs balcony has more seating and a bird's-eye view
of the action; a passageway leads back to the Borneo Room, an inner sanctum with low lighting, comfy loveseats, handsome copper bar, and jukebox
(popular with cigar smokers; the entire club's smoker-friendly, by the way).
In the basement, Pandora's Box is a disco complete with cool light system,
big bar, and crowds of partiers.

If you go: The musical range is quite wide, so find out who's playing—not
that it matters much; with myriad rooms to choose from, it's easy to escape
the nightclub area if the music fails to please. While formality is by no

means de rigueur, this is a good spot for drinks after a black-tie event. There are frequent singles events and other special parties (or throw your own; they'll accommodate groups from 10 to 1,500); call for details.

THE BLUE NOTE

Jazz club

Who Goes There: 22–90; tourists

131 West Third Street
475-8592   Zone 4 Greenwich Village

Cover: $30–60 at tables, $15–20 at bar; brunch: $14.50/person
Minimum: $5 at tables, one drink at the bar
Mixed drinks: $6–12
Wine: Bottles, $30–200
Beer: $5
Dress: Fancy shmancy

Specials: Monday nights are bargains; Fridays and Saturdays after the last set, late-night show until 4 a.m. for $5 cover. No minimum till 4 a.m.
Food available: Full menu, for the gastronomically reckless

Hours: Shows at 9 and 11:30 every night. Saturday and Sunday, jazz brunch noon–6 p.m., with shows at 1 and 3:30 p.m.

What goes on: It's amazing how many tourists think that the Blue Note is a historic jazz institution even though the place didn't open until the late date of 1981. But hordes of them continue to pay stratospheric prices to sit in uncomfortable chairs packed *way* too close together in a small, dark, boxy room and be treated like cattle. It's worth it, however, when they bring in acts who normally don't play clubs (Ray Charles, Herbie Hancock, etc.), many of whom shine in the more intimate setting. But the entertainment here can be more "jazzish" than jazz; people like Roberta Flack, Tito Puente, and Steve Allen have played here. The Village Vanguard (see separate review) and Sweet Basil (see Nightlife introduction) are far more pure-minded in their bookings.

Setting & atmosphere: Claustrophobic and tacky, done in dark tones and mirrors. A cheesy neon Manhattan skyline is the only "classy" touch.

If you go: As at all jazz clubs in New York, avoid crowds by arriving for the last set or during bad weather (another budget option: the revamped bar area now has good sight lines).

THE BUBBLE LOUNGE

Champagne bar

Who Goes There: 21–60; slinky well-heeled lounge chicsters and locals

228 West Broadway
431-3433 Zone 2 TriBeCa

Cover: None
Minimum: $15 at tables
Mixed drinks: $7–9
Wine: Champagnes $7.50–32/glass, less for half-glasses
Beer: $6
Dress: Way chic, dark colors

Specials: Live jazz Mondays at 7:30 p.m.
Food available: Typical champagne accompaniments like oysters, caviar, salmon, foie gras, sorbets; all quite pricey

Hours: Sunday–Thursday, 5:30 p.m.–2 a.m.; Friday and Saturday, 5:30 p.m.–2 a.m.; closed Monday

What goes on: A champagne and cigar bar (excellent ventilation tames the smoke) where chic poseurs peacefully coexist with more down-to-earth locals, all feeling very very grown-up. The bubbly itself is quaffed more as a style thing than as serious wine pursuit (sniff and swirl your glass like an oenophile here and you'll get some strange looks), but there's no denying that sipping Dom Perignon without shelling out big bucks for a whole bottle is a Good Thing. Twenty-three champagnes are available by the glass, 280 champagnes and sparkling wines by the bottle.

Setting & atmosphere: An L-shaped space lush with red velvet draperies, exposed brick, couches, flickering candles, highly lacquered wood, and highly preened waitresses. Dracula would feel at home.

If you go: Check out the downstairs Krug room, a champagne/wine cellar with waitress service.

CAFE CARLYLE

Sophisticated New York nightspot

Who Goes There: 25–90; grown-ups

36 East 76th Street
744-1600   Zone 13 Upper East Side

Cover: $50
Minimum: None
Mixed drinks: $9–105
Wine: $9.50–13 by the glass
Beer: $8–10
Dress: Jackets required, of course, but you'd do well to pull out all the stops and wear your very best duds.
Specials: Save $20 on the cover charge by watching from the bar (reservations aren't accepted, though, and you'll pay full price even if there's only standing room).
Food available: Old-fashioned New York food served by old-fashioned professional New York waiters—expensive and available from 6 p.m.–midnight

Hours: Every night, 6 p.m.–12:30 a.m.

What goes on: Singer/pianist Bobby Short is the main man, and while some nights he can seem just a tad tired of it all, he's always drolly debonair. Short-less nights don't always draw as well, though replacements are reliably top-drawer. (However, Woody Allen—far better director than clarinetist—has been homeless since Michael's Pub closed and has been sneaking his Dixieland group in Mondays.)

Setting & atmosphere: One of the most famous cabarets in the world, Cafe Carlyle sets a nearly unreachable standard of elegant and intimate supper-club ambience. A splendid assortment of Vertes murals adds greatly to the magic.

If you go: Have a low-key drink before or after the show (or instead of the show entirely if you're on a budget) in the hotel's Bemelmans Bar, an urbane time capsule of an older New York with fine—if less famous—piano entertainment.

CAROLINE'S

Comedy club

Who Goes There: 21–60; suburbanites on weekends, tourists and fans during the week

1626 Broadway
757-4100   Zone 8 Theater District

Cover: Sunday–Thursday, $12–15; Friday, $18; Saturday, $19.50
Minimum: 2 drinks
Mixed drinks: $4–8
Wine: $4–8
Beer: $4–8
Dress: Casual
Specials: Happy hour: Monday–Friday, 5–7 p.m. $2 drafts, $4 well drinks; dinner-and-show packages: Sunday–Thursday, $35; Friday and Saturday, $45
Food available: TGIFridays-type menu (with cutesy comedy-theme dish names) in the monstrously commercial upstairs Comedy Nation restaurant. Snack menu in the club.

Hours: Every day, shows at about 8 and 10:30 p.m. (call for info)

What goes on: With a location smack-dab in the middle of Times Square, Caroline's 10:30 p.m. late set is a magnet for theatergoers insatiable for more entertainment. Like Broadway these days, the club relies on a steady diet of Big Names to pull in crowds, and this well-run operation—the most "upscale" of the big New York comedy clubs—gives them their money's worth.

Setting & atmosphere: Though the Comedy Nation restaurant at street level is an utterly soulless space (comedy insiders call it "Planet Ha-Ha-Hollywood"), the actual club area, downstairs, is a nice loungy hang, a decent place for drinks even if you're not attending the show. The room itself isn't as showbizzy/jazzy as Catch a Rising Star, nor does it have the mike-and-a-room pure minimalism of Gotham, but on entering it one feels that something exciting is about to occur—and with the top-flight talent booked here, it often does.

CLUB MACANUDO

Upscale cigar and whisky bar

Who Goes There: 30–65; middle-aged suits, often stag but some towing either bored wives or trophy babes; some younger shmoozers

26 East 63rd Street
752-8200   Zone 11 East Side

Cover: None
Minimum: None
Scotch: $7–36
Wine: Vintage/tawny ports $12–32
Beer: $6

Dress: Jackets for men, no sneakers or jeans
Food available: Overpriced; stick with appetizers/tapas (lunch, noon–5 p.m., dinner, 5–11 p.m.)

Hours: Monday and Tuesday, noon–1 a.m.; Wednesday–Friday, noon–2 a.m.; Saturday, 5 p.m.–2 a.m.; Sunday, closed.

What goes on: Some might expect that cigars and whisky are fun things to be enjoyed lightheartedly. These people will not dig Club Macanudo. This place takes itself seriously. If it all wasn't very very serious, people might not be inclined to fork over $800/year to rent tiny personal humidors here (complete with shiny brass nameplate), they might wince at the over-the-top chummy/clubby/woody interior, or they might even break a smile. But the scotch selection *is* pretty serious stuff—it's America's only bar serving rare bottlings from the Scotch Whisky Society—and the friendly bartenders—as devoted to scotch 'n' smoke as many regulars—are knowledgeable guides for neophytes. Go late enough that plenty of scotch has already been ingested, and you may strike up a stogey-based friendship with an exec who'd otherwise never take your calls.

Setting & atmosphere: It's like being in an enormous cigar box (complete with wooden Indians)—and nearly as claustrophobic, especially on weekends and Thursdays (the "hot" night).

If you go: Don't worry too much about ordering the wrong thing; there are few dumb choices, drink and cigar-wise. But do bone up on proper stogey cutting and lighting; do it wrong and you'll elicit gasps of horror.

DBA

Mecca for ultra-high-quality drinks

Who Goes There: 21–50; drink freaks, ranging from nerdy homebrewers to assured sybarites

41 First Avenue
475-5097   Zone 5 East Village

Cover: None
Minimum: None
Mixed drinks: $5
Wine: $12–65/split
Beer: $5
Dress: Casual but hip

Specials: Happy hour every day,
1–7:30 p.m.: $1 off everything;
frequent special tastings and events
(call for info)
Food available: None

Hours: Every day, 1 p.m.–4 a.m.

What goes on: No Schlitz here; rather, you'll find hand-pumped British (and British-style) ales, a whole bunch of taps (dated, so you can gauge freshness), and zillions of bottles. This is the only place in New York that serves properly poured ales and lagers at the proper temperature (never frigid, hand pumps at cellar temperature) in the proper glasses, and there's a fine bourbon, scotch, and tequila collection, as well. Servers have attitude, as do some of the customers.

Setting & atmosphere: Low-lit, contemporary, and spare, this invariably crowded spot doesn't have much decor to distract the reverent drinking, but it's certainly far more refined than your average skanky beer hall. Nice garden out back, open only in warm weather.

If you go: Not sure what to order? Ask advice from any of the beer geeks at the bar and you'll be guided by some of the city's most knowledgeable drinkers.

DON'T TELL MAMA'S

Campy theatrical sing-along piano bar with separate cabaret rooms

Who Goes There: 21–90; out-of-towners, girls'-night-outers, theatergoers; showbiz hangers-on, has-beens, and wannabes

343 West 46th Street
  757-0788   Zone 8 Theater District

Cover: None at bar; $3–20 for cabaret shows
Minimum: None at bar; 2 drinks for cabaret shows
Mixed drinks: $5–7.50
Wine: $4.50 by the glass

Beer: $4.75
Dress: Casual
Specials: Happy hour every day, 4–7 p.m.: all drinks half-price
Food available: None

Hours: Every day, 4 p.m.–4 a.m.

What goes on: The clientele at this Theater District landmark is nothing if not "mixed." Though the place has a loyal gay constituency, the crowd covers the entire spectrum of post-theater revelers; all ages and types can be found shoehorned into this cramped basement, and the resulting intimacy is such that even the most repressed find themselves singing along with show tunes hammered out by the bitchy, sardonic pianist (Lord help you if your reply is *"Cats"* when he points at you archly and asks what you've seen tonight). Proceedings are punctuated by quick guest appearances by bawdy (and talented) singing waitresses and a relay of drop-in friends. Discuss shows with your fellow revelers (after-theater is by far the best time to come). The cabaret offers entertainment from comedy to drag queens to a cappella groups, sometimes quite good.

Setting & atmosphere: Campy/theatrical to the max; border lights and red velvet curtains frame the corner stage in the back of this subterranean room. Over each miniscule table hovers a burgundy-shaded lamp with yellow tassle fringe. It all feels like the piano bar downstairs in a bordello. There are cabaret rooms in front and back.

If you go: See the separate reviews for Swing 46 and O'Flaherty's Ale House for nearby bar-hopping options.

FEZ

Hip Moroccan-style bar with subterranean nightclub

Who Goes There: 21–45; brisk pre- and post-concert biz, otherwise pretentious comely hangsters mixed with relaxing locals

380 Lafayette (at Fourth Street)
533-7000   Zone 5 East Village

Cover: $7–18 in nightclub,
  none in bar
Minimum: 2 drinks in nightclub,
  none in bar
Mixed drinks: $5–9

Wine: $5–6
Beer: $4.25–5.25
Dress: Designery casual
Food available: Stripped-down version
  of Time Cafe menu

Hours: Monday–Thursday, 6 p.m.–2 a.m.; Friday and Saturday, 6 p.m.–4 a.m. (bar); nightclub varies, so call for info

What goes on: Downstairs is one of the city's best alternative (largely acoustic) music spaces, hosting sultry/loungy acts from jazz to world beat. The sound is fine, and the vibe is hip and exciting (booths and long tables comfortably accommodate groups). The bar above feels like a secret opium den, and the cafe up front is a popular spot for late-night retrosnacks.

Setting & atmosphere: Enter through the Time Cafe, a brightly lit retro-luncheonette, then pass through a bead-curtained arch into a sexy Moroccan lounge outfitted with mosaic-tiled octagonal tables, flickering mock oil lamps, Alhambra-esque arches, and paintings of Arabic singers. Luxuriate on well-padded couches and cushiony bar stools and enjoy jazz on the excellent sound system. Fez achieves that elusive combination of chic atmosphere and low-key coziness. Downstairs in the nightclub (both lounge and nightclub are called Fez): low ceiling, red velvet, intimate clubby ambience with gleaming bar.

If you go: The most popular act downstairs is the Thursday night nutsy jazzy way-hip Mingus Big Band, but they sell out, so reserve ahead. Few real clinkers play here, so go ahead and take potluck.

THE GINGER MAN

Giant-sized beer bar

Who Goes There: 21–60; throngs of businessmen and yuppies after work, varied at other times

11 East 36th Street
532-3740   Zone 7 Madison Square

Cover: None
Minimum: None
Mixed drinks: $6–8
Wine: $5–6
Beer: Most are $5/pint

Dress: Casual
Food available: A few simple bar
snacks; Guinness Stout stew's
pretty good

Hours: Monday–Saturday, 11:30–2 a.m.; Sunday, 11:30 a.m.–midnight

What goes on: On paper, this is New York's best beer hall. It boasts a mind-boggling 60 taps, nearly all well-chosen; decent Guinness stew to eat; friendly bartenders; and a comfy living room in the back. Prices are fair, and this is a late hang in an early-closing nabe. But there are problems: The beer's too cold (fine for light lagers, but some of the fancier British and Belgian ales turn flavorless at ballpark temperature), and peak hours—5:30–10 p.m. and all night on weekends—can be a crowded hell of noise and noxious clouds of cigar smoke, so time your visit carefully.

Setting & atmosphere: The huge, high-ceilinged space is classic New York, dominated by a mile-long bar and copper-plated Wall o' Taps. There are tables up front by the floor-to-ceiling windows and a relaxing parlor in back with sofas and armchairs.

If you go: Midafternoons and late weeknights you'll have the place largely to yourself; bring 20 or 30 friends, no problem!

THE GREATEST BAR ON EARTH

Really really high-up cocktail/dance/sushi lounge

Who Goes There: 21–70; businessmen, tourists; Wednesday nights: Eurotrendies, tourists, and downtown clubbers

I World Trade Center
524-7000 (press 5)   Zone I Lower Manhattan

Cover: None
Minimum: None
Mixed drinks: $7
Wine: $9.50 for champagne
Beer: $4.50–6.25
Dress: Since the postexplosion renovation, the dress code's been repealed—but men will feel most comfortable in jackets. (Wednesday nights: club threads, from sequins to leather.)
Food available: Expensive sushi and vastly overpriced bar food

Hours: Monday and Tuesday, noon–1 a.m.; Wednesday, noon–1:30 a.m (or later); Thursday, noon–1 a.m.; Friday and Saturday, noon–2 a.m.; Sunday, noon–11 p.m.

What goes on: This may not be the "greatest bar on earth," but it *is* the cheapest bar in the sky: $4.50 pints of good beer are cheaper than those in many merely terrestrial cocktail lounges. Plus you get the oh-my-God view and live music and dancing, all with no cover and a new relaxed dress code. Late Wednesdays the Strato Lounge takes over, and the place is overrun with exactly the sort of body-pierced and Eurochic people you'd never expect to see in the World Trade Center. Hot jazzy/Latin dancing and buzz galore till the wee hours.

Setting & atmosphere: Early Vulgar; little embedded spotlights shine up, down, and sideways at you from everywhere the moment you exit the elevator, and, my lord, where did they get those lamps? What with all the over-the-top visual distractions, it takes a while to even notice the stunning 107th-floor vista (thoughtfully, the rest rooms block most of New Jersey).

If you go: Sip some Veuve Clicquot house champagne (available by the glass at a bargain price). Each bar station has different beers, so scout around. On Wednesdays leave your coat at home—you must check it downstairs by the elevators, and the wait can be ten minutes or more.

HOLE IN ONE

Whisky and Japanese food bar

Who Goes There: 28–70; well-heeled Japanese businessmen

1003A 2nd Avenue at 53rd Street (2nd floor)
319-6070   Zone 9 Midtown East

Cover: $25 + 20% service charge
Minimum: None
Mixed drinks: $14.50–980
Wine: $14.50 per glass
Beer: $7.50–8.50
Dress: Jackets and dresses
Food available: Exquisite Japanese bar food is not to be missed: little plates (for about $10) of things like mackerel sushi, free-range strips of chicken *shioyaki* (the skin broiled to crispy perfection), consummately fried baby eels, delicious sautéed burdock. No English menu, but staff will attempt to translate.

Hours: Monday–Friday, 7 p.m.–2:30 a.m.

What goes on: This is one of the world's best single-malt whisky bars—if you can find it. The entrance is marked only by a discreet brass sign . . . in Japanese. But although Hole in One is hidden and costly, and the clientele's almost entirely Japanese, it's not private. You're buzzed through an interior door, you pass up a flight of steps, and then you enter whisky heaven. Owner Koichi Iraiwa has amassed a treasure trove of whiskies, 250 bottles in all (more if you count blends), many original bottlings from distilleries long ago closed (such as a bottle of St. Magdalene [Linjithgow] 12-year that may be one of the last remaining in the world). The rarest cost upward of $1,000 a glass; but many less exorbitant bottles are still more than worthy (e.g., Clynelish for $33, Edradour 10 for $19.50, and Port Ellen 15 for $19.50). There is a particularly broad range of Springanks, from 10 years ($14.50). Avo and Griffin cigars are also for sale, as are good cognacs, gins, vodkas, and bourbons.

Setting & atmosphere: A cozy but sleek, windowless room with a few dozen seats at intimate tables and a long bar facing the sea of bottles. Unintentionally silly Scottish knickknacks—plenty of golf clubs, for example—are scattered everywhere.

If you go: Bring a big wad of money (or a platinum card); if you love Japanese food or scotch whisky, this is a worthy splurge. But this male bastion may make unaccompanied women feel out of place. Fridays, the slow night, might be best for those who want to mount a serious tasting undistracted by crowds.

THE KNITTING FACTORY

(Very) alternative music club

Who Goes There: 21–45; varies with the music, black-clad
hipsters to shaved heads and multiple piercings;
a broad age range for the less rock-ish groups

74 Leonard Street
  219-3055   Zone 2 TriBeCa

Cover: $8–12
Minimum: None
Mixed drinks: $3.50–7
Wine: $4–5
Beer: $3–5
Dress: Black T-shirts and black jeans
  always work

Specials: Happy hour, 5–7 p.m.; free
  live music in downstairs bar every
  night from 11 p.m. until late
Food available: None

Hours: Vary; call for info

What goes on: A world-famous venue for alternative musics from klezmer
to thrash. If names like John Zorn, Bill Frisell, and Don Byron mean anything to you, or you are open-minded enough to listen to traditional
Hanukkah songs deconstructed by punk groups or to tuba quartets covering Jimi Hendrix, this scene is for you. The place has tons of attitude, and
owner Michael Dorf has bragged to the press about how he hardly pays
most of the musicians (lesser-knowns work only for the door), but this is the
sole regular venue for music this fringy.

Setting & atmosphere: A nice mellow bar at street level, large two-level performance space within (very European), and a tiny Alterknit Room presenting groups of still narrower appeal. Downstairs bar is dark, atmospheric, and
quite the destination on late nights when hipper-than-hip bands set up there.

If you go: Check your e-mail or surf the Web for free at the club's Net connection in the main corridor.

LES POULETS

Latin music nightclub and disco

Who Goes There: 21–40; uptown and Brooklyn Latino club kids (and some older downtowners) dressed up and ready to spend money

16 West 22nd Street
229-2000 Zone 7 Gramercy Park

Cover: Thursday: free; Friday and Saturday, free 6–9 p.m.; varies after (ladies cheaper)
Minimum: None
Mixed drinks: $6–9
Wine: $6–7
Beer: $4.50–5

Dress: To kill
Specials: Free salsa lessons Thursdays, 7–8 p.m.
Food available: Spicy Latin dishes offered in the balcony restaurant area

Hours: Thursday–Saturday, 6 p.m.–4 a.m. (live bands on weekends); Sunday–Wednesday, closed.

What goes on: Latin club culture is so permeated with macho that flared tempers can mean trouble; this is Manhattan's safest authentic salsa disco, but you pay the price. Security is anything but subtle (you enter through airport-style metal detectors, and *big* guys keep a very close eye on your every step). If such a setup makes you breathe easily rather than descend into neurotic spirals of paranoia and angst, come dance to some very hot salsa (and merengue and cumbia, etc.) in a space that will fool you into thinking you've been transported to the Caribbean. If you tire of Latin rhythms, head down to the basement (opens at 12:30 a.m. Friday and Saturday only) for DJs spinning house and rap.

Setting & atmosphere: A huge, clean, glitzy space, done up in bright tropical colors.

If you go: If the totalitarian security is too edgy for you, try the more artsy Nuyoriquen Poets Cafe (see the introduction to this chapter) or the more Anglo SOB's (see separate review).

LOUISIANA COMMUNITY
BAR & GRILL

Cajun-tinged funky music dance club and restaurant

Who Goes There: 21–50; on weekends, throngs of NYU
students; otherwise, Broadway fallout

622 Broadway
460-9633   Zone 4 Greenwich Village

Cover: None, except New Year's Eve
and Fat Tuesday
Minimum: None
Mixed drinks: $5.50
Wine: $4–5

Beer: $3.75–4.50
Dress: Casual and loose
Food available: Decent enough cajun
food (po'boys and coconut cake are
the standouts) but nothing special

Hours: Monday–Thursday, 5–11 p.m. (or later); Friday and Saturday, 5
p.m.–2:30 a.m.; Sunday, 5–11 p.m.

What goes on: This used to be the NYC branch of K Paul's, but it's turned
a lot more down-home in the present incarnation. The bar scene's always
friendly and relaxed (good for singles); hang there or grab a table for drinks
and/or dinner. The live bands are good and danceable, ranging from funky
jazz to jazzy funk, with some blues and jump mixed in, and there's a good
swing dance scene on Monday nights.

Setting & atmosphere: Very spacious hall decorated with wacky Hal-
loweenish plaster masks and cajun knicknacks; peanut shells on the floor.

If you go: No cover, easy in-and-out. It's an excellent stop to make in a
night's cruising for entertainment (your next stop should be Gonzalez &
Gonzalez, an equally huge Mexican restaurant—don't eat the food!—across
the street with funky Latin-tinged live music and good margaritas.

MANNY'S CARWASH

Narrow faux-seedy blues bar

Who Goes There: 21–35; Upper East Side thirty-somethings in rugby shirts

1558 3rd Avenue
369-BLUES   Zone 13 Upper East Side

Cover: $4–15
Minimum: None
Mixed drinks: $4.50–7
Wine: $4
Beer: $3–5.50
Dress: Informal yuppieware
Specials: Wednesday–Saturday, $6 for all the tap Bud Ice/Lite you can drink; no cover charge for the Sunday night jam session; Monday, ladies' night: free admission and tap beer/wine
Food available: None (you can bring your own)

Hours: Weekdays, 5 p.m.–3 a.m.; weekends, 5 p.m.–3:30 a.m.

What goes on: It's sad. There are plenty of talented blues bands in the New York area, and there are few places for them to play. The scattered downtown clubs are either too glossy or too scummy, but Manny's is just right. All sight lines head down the narrow bar to the stage in the back, and people actually come for the music (excellent local bands seven nights a week, with an occasional sprinkling of national acts and a great Sunday night jam session that attracts famous drop-ins). It's loud, it's raucous, and you'll stand behind scads of boomers bobbing at their beers like hordes of Corkies, but who wants to listen to blues calmly sipping pinot noir in a comfy chair, anyway?

Setting & atmosphere: The room is narrow and can be a bit claustrophobic, especially when crowded—as it often is. It's designed to evoke a Chicago blues bar.

If you go: Make your first drink a double; it's amazing how a couple of quick belts can ease your anxieties amid the crowded tumult and help you lose yourself in the music.

MERCURY LOUNGE

Rock showcase

Who Goes There: 21–40; serious music fans, bohemian
Lower East Side clubbers, some grunge

217 East Houston Street
260-4700   Zone 5 East Village

Cover: $7–12
Minimum: None
Mixed drinks: $3.75–5
Wine: $3.75–5

Beer: $3.75–5
Dress: Black and hip
Food available: None

Hours: Every day, 6 p.m.–4 a.m.; shows every night at 8 p.m.

What goes on: The two main showcases for newly signed (and hot about-to-be-signed) rock bands are Brownie's (169 Avenue A, 420-8392) and Mercury Lounge. Both have excellent sound systems, and Brownie's serves a heckuva pint of Guinness Stout, but Mercury is the ambience winner, hands-down. The performance space is perfect for listening to an eclectic mix of groups, from surprisingly big names, playing here to maintain their hip credentials, to up-and-comers and cult favorites. If you've never heard of a band playing here, you probably will soon.

Setting & atmosphere: You enter through a mysterious-looking black bar with black curtains, and the music's through a door in the back. It's basically a box of a room, but exposed brick and great sound (blessedly, never head-bangingly loud) and lighting create an ambience that feels right.

If you go: Walk down nearby Ludlow Street after the show to explore some cutting-edge cafes, music clubs, and late-night shops.

MOTOWN CAFE

Theme restaurant/bar/souvenir shop

Who Goes There: 21–65; tourists, good racial mix

104 West 57th Street
581-8030   Zone 9 Midtown West

Cover: None
Minimum: None

Mixed drinks: $4.50–13.75
Wine: $19.95–25/bottle; $5.25/glass

(Motown Cafe)

Beer: $3.75–4.50
Dress: Anything from after-show dressy to jeans and T-shirts
Specials: Occasional contests for discounts on drinks, food, or merchandise

Food available: Standard 57th Street "fun" menu (think TGIFridays) with some soul-food slant. Menus are printed on Temptations LP jackets.

Hours: Sunday–Thursday, 11:30 a.m.–midnight; Friday and Saturday, 11:30 a.m.–1 a.m.

What goes on: In pleasant contrast to the area's many White Kid theme bars like Fashion Cafe, Hard Rock Cafe, Jekyll and Hyde, and Planet Hollywood, you'll find a broader range of people and ages in this friendly room (it's pretty hard *not* to be friendly when you're sucking down milkshakes in a turquoise-and-pink diner booth). To be sure, there's some major merchandising going down at the souvenir counter—Motown *everything,* plus Polaroid instant cameras for documenting your visit. But in spite of the bald commercialism, this place works. Amiable staff members who aren't just going through the motions, combined with the way-cool upstairs bar and the mixed crowd, all contribute to making the Motown a surprisingly fun hang, certainly worlds above all those other theme places.

Setting & atmosphere: The exterior is designed like a 1960s midwestern drive-in movie theater, with musical instuments stuck on for good measure. Inside, it's equal parts diner, drive-in, and roadhouse, with added touches like gas pumps and ugly sparkly life-sized statues of Motown stars. Upstairs is hipper: There's a cute retro lounge ("Roostertail") in back, and, on the balcony, a handsome early '60s Detroit-style bar (closes early weekdays, but buzzes late on weekends). As you'd expect, Aretha, Sam and Dave, and Otis Redding blare continuously—even in the bathrooms.

If you go: Avoid tourist crunches early evenings and weekend afternoons. The "Motown Cafe Moments" perform pro-level Motown karaoke (moraoke?) every half hour, and customers get their own shots at the microphone Tuesday nights 7–10 p.m.

NELL'S

Warm living room–ish dance club with hot disco basement

Who Goes There: 25–40; sexy clubbers and chic music scenesters

246 West 14th Street
675-1567   Zone 6 Chelsea

Cover: Sunday–Wednesday, $10;
  Thursday–Saturday, $15;
  Monday, $10
Minimum: 1 drink at tables
Mixed drinks: $6–8.50
Wine: $5

Beer: $5
Dress: To kill (no sneakers, no jeans)
Specials: Ladies' night (free
  admission); call for info
Food available: Light pub food

Hours: Wednesday–Monday, 10 p.m.–4 a.m.; Tuesday, 7 p.m.–4 a.m.

What goes on: This is the Dorian Grey of dance clubs; Nell's never goes out of fashion and never tarnishes with age. The main room (if you make it there past the snide and intimidating doormen without killing or being killed) is a cozy funky living room that plays host to excellent bluesy/jazzy/funky/Latin-ish live bands. Each night has its musical theme (e.g., tango Mondays, jazz Saturdays, international Fridays, and Tuesday open mikes where some talented vocalists sit in with the house soul/R&B group). It's a great scene for hair-down dancing; this room is sort of an antidisco for those who hate loud, flashy, pounding dance floors. Downstairs is the loud, flashy, pounding dance floor. Just as live music styles rotate nightly upstairs, each night a different DJ spins his or her own groovy mix in the basement, like house/reggae on Tuesdays, soul/R&B on Saturdays, and the eclectic Sunday night stylings of Jonny Sender. Schedules shift, so call the club for info.

Setting & atmosphere: Victorian British men's club ambience upstairs, all dark wood and red velvet with couches and armchairs, with an incongruous dance floor facing the central stage; downstairs, a packed disco dance floor plus adjacent couchy lounge with Persian rugs and coffee tables.

If you go: Afterward, the stout-hearted can head west along 14th Street to #416 for the way-cool (but too scary a block for prime time) loud live music scene at the Cooler (229-0785), a subterranean venue set up in an old meat locker.

O'FLAHERTY'S ALE HOUSE

Irish pub after-show hideaway

Who Goes There: 25–55; locals and tourists until the 10 p.m. influx of the after-theater crowd (many actors and musicians)

334 West 46th Street
  581-9366   Zone 8   Theater District

Cover: None
Minimum: None
Mixed drinks: $4.50–5
Wine: $4.50
Beer: $4–4.50

Dress: Anything from suit and tie to jeans and T-shirt
Food available: Surprisingly extensive Irish-style menu (shepherd's pie in several incarnations, stews, fried stuff)

Hours: Every day, noon–4 a.m.

What goes on: It calls itself an ale house, but the beer (second-rate UK imports like Murphy's and Newcastle) is not the attraction. This is a great spot because among the windy passageways and copious alcoves there's an ambience to please almost anyone. The energy level picks up as theater people stop by for an after-work drink, and much of the crowd stays late. Part of the draw is the old-fashioned Irish bartenders, probably hired as much for their brogues as for their gregariousness.

Setting & atmosphere: Choose your surroundings: a book-filled study in the back with comfortable chairs and a pool table; a front corner of couches (great for groups); a handsome wraparound bar with adjoining dart board; an outdoor garden with antique-style park benches. There's a nook or cranny for any occasion. It's all alcoves; there's no "main section" to speak of.

If you go: If you're looking for a livelier time on this same block, see reviews for Don't Tell Mama's (a campy rollicking piano bar) and Swing 46 (a jive-talking swing-dancing nightspot).

PEN-TOP BAR AT THE PENINSULA HOTEL

Rooftop hotel bar

Who Goes There: 30–65; after-workers, trystin'
smoochers, one-last-drinkers

700 Fifth Avenue
247-2200   Zone 9 Midtown East

Cover: None
Minimum: None
Mixed drinks: $7–12
Wine: $8 and up, by the glass
Beer: $7–12
Dress: Sophisticated and expensive

Food available: Small selection of
upscale snacks like smoked
salmon, cheese platter, and shrimp;
good freebie bar snacks come with
drinks

Hours: Monday–Thursday, 5 p.m.–midnight; Friday and Saturday,
5 p.m.–1 a.m.; closed Sunday

What goes on: There are higher bars with more breathtaking views, but the great thing about this 23rd-floor perch is that you see Manhattan not from the bottom or top but from the middle. You're surrounded by the top thirds of buildings (like the beautiful St. Regis Hotel across the street), an odd and striking geometric landscape cluttering the nighttime sky. It's a dramatic setting for an outdoor drink in good weather, and the indoor bar is hyper-romantic when it snows. Friendly, professional service.

Setting & atmosphere: A romantic little bar surrounded by three outdoor spaces (each with its own great view): a large spillover area—full after work—with plastic tables and chairs, a standing-only slip of a balcony with a view up Fifth Avenue (good for cooing couples), and an elegant green carpeted rectangle with comfortable chairs and flickering lamps.

If you go: Go on the late side; from 5 to 7 p.m. the office crowd takes over. The bar's essentially hidden: take the elevator to the top floor, then ascend the dramatic glassed-in circular staircase.

THE RAINBOW ROOM

Retro swing supper club, cabaret, and bar with a view

Who Goes There: Rich young swells and older nostalgic couples; tourists and late partying biz men in the Promenade Bar

30 Rockefeller Plaza (65th floor)
632-5000   Zone 9 Midtown East

Cover: $20 music charge in Rainbow Room, $40 in Rainbow & Stars, none in Promenade Bar
Minimum: Dinner in Rainbow Room and in early set at Rainbow & Stars (11 p.m. show, $15 minimum), none in Promenade
Mixed drinks: $7–9.50
Wine: $7–14

Beer: $5.50–6
Dress: To the nines (jacket and tie required in Rainbow Room, jacket in Promenade Bar)
Specials: Pretheater
Food available: Full sit-down in Rainbow Room and Rainbow & Stars, light snacks in the Promenade Bar

Hours: *Rainbow Room:* Tuesday–Thursday, 6:30 p.m.–1 a.m.; Friday and Saturday, 6:30 p.m.–1:30 a.m.; Sunday, 6–11 p.m.; closed Mondays (call for info on dinner seatings).
Pretheater dinner special: Tuesday–Saturday, 5 p.m.–7:30 p.m.
Rainbow & Stars: Tuesday–Saturday, shows at 8:30 and 11 p.m.
Promenade Bar: Monday–Sunday, 3:30 p.m.–1 a.m.

What goes on: The Rainbow Room is about as swanky as it gets: a classy full big band, swing dancing, unbelievable view, everyone acting so very grown-up and fabulous. The food's gotten a little better, but Egg McMuffins would taste good in this setting. Whoever you bring here will fall in love with you instantly—the club guarantees it. If you prefer to be seriously entertained rather than all-out feted, choose Rainbow & Stars, a less dazzling smaller room where people like Rosemary Clooney croon. Dinner's compulsory at the first set, but you can drink your minimum at the late show. Or just drink all night, with no cover and a similarly wonderful view, at the Promenade Bar, famous for well-mixed classic and newfangled cocktails (as well as some of the only truly tasty nonalcoholic drinks served in a ritzy New York bar).

Setting & atmosphere: The opulent Rainbow Room is straight out of a Busby Berkeley musical—it's so completely Hollywood 1930s that the eye is shocked and confused by the presence of color. With all the polished glass, one feels afloat over New York; the dance floor beckons, and you shall obey.

(The Rainbow Room)

Rainbow & Stars is surprisingly small, an intimate chamber with lots of soft surfaces and a big shiny grand piano. The Promenade Bar is somewhat pretentious and overly stylized, like an Atlantic City high-rollers lounge. The view at sunset can't be beat, however.

If you go: Be prepared for high-strung staffers. The coat-check person will practically rip your coat off your shoulders, and the maitre d's and bartenders apparently think aloofness adds cachet. If the bar scene gives you a headache, look around and find the nooks where drinks can be sipped in peace.

RODEO BAR

Cowboy bar with high-quality eclectic live music

Who Goes There: Aging hippies, urban cowboys, music fans

375 Third Avenue
683-6500   Zone 7 Gramercy Park

Cover: No
Minimum: None
Mixed drinks: $4.50–6.50
Wine: $4
Beer: $3.50–4

Dress: Jeans and whatever
Specials: Happy hour with free buffet every day, 4–8 p.m.
Food available: Tex-Mex (full meals or bar munchies)

Hours: Music at 10 p.m. every night

What goes on: Rodeo Bar isn't taken terribly serious by New York music scene cognoscenti, but it offers something extremely rare: good bar bands in regular rotation. Styles range from electric to rockabilly to country rock, but the musical sensibility is always more New York hip than the saddles 'n' barrels decor would suggest; even the most country acts are *funky* country. The same bands play regularly, building audience and repertoire and honing skills. As a result, performances here are more polished than at nearly any other club in town, and there are loyal fans who come here first when they want to drink a beer and hear some dependably solid tunes without dropping dozens of dollars. Lately there have been some campy/swing/lounge retro acts sneaking into the lineup; time will tell whether this trend continues.

Setting & atmosphere: So Wild West that you half expect Calamity Jane to come whooping past the bar; this place is tricked out with barrels, stirrups, rope-handle door knobs, peanut shells, the works. Someone was decorating for a square dance, but thank goodness the music's much hipper than

(Rodeo Bar)

Cowboy Bob. A huge bull stares inquisitively at the performers from the side of the stage. Yee-haw.

If you go: If the cow-punching vibe is too much for you, cross over to the adjoining restaurant next door for a quick city fix.

THE BAR AT 44
(ROYALTON HOTEL)

Swanky but strangely cozy hotel lobby bar

Who Goes There: 30–60; tourists, businessmen, predinner drinkers

44 West 44th Street
944-8844   Zone 8 Midtown West & Theater District

Cover: None
Minimum: None
Mixed drinks: $8.50–12
Wine: $8–12 by the glass; $25–250 for bottles
Beer: $6–8

Dress: Mostly suits in evenings; looser later
Food available: Light fare and desserts (from the kitchen of adjacent Restaurant 44)

Hours: Sunday–Thursday, 3 p.m.–1:30 a.m.; Friday and Saturday, 3 p.m.–2 a.m.

What goes on: This is an ideal break-the-ice meeting place for a predinner drink, be your companions business associates, in-laws, or a hot date. It's just swanky enough to set an elegant tone, but comfy enough (lots of well-cushioned couches and chairs positioned for maximum intimacy) not to intimidate. Urbane conversation flows easily; as you look around the room, you notice that everyone seems very very engaged, very very glib. It's not just the clientele; it's the room. Good lighting combined with the atmospheric coziness also make this a choice spot for a late-night tête-à-tête.

Setting & atmosphere: The cocktail area occupies a dramatic, long sunken strip to your left as you walk through the narrow lobby. Toward the back, the lounge morphs into an airily open restaurant of similar design. Decor is what used to be called "futuristic": beige Jetsons-ian couches, love seats, and chairs of odd shape in off-white fabrics. Jaded types might describe the look as Early Airport Club.

If you go: Peer into the tiny vodka/champagne/grappa bar hidden to the right as you come in the front door. This claustrophobic sci-fi transporter room sports circular padded walls and flickery candles.

SAKA GURA

Who Goes There: 30–55; Japanese businessmen, sake aficionados

211 East 43rd Street
953-SAKE   Zone 9 Midtown East

Cover: None
Minimum: None
Mixed drinks: $5–15
Wine: $2–25 for sake
Beer: $3.50–4.50 (Japanese only)
Dress: Most people in jackets, but nice casual will do

Food available: Excellent simple Japanese dishes like udon (noodle soup) and kinpira (marinated burdock root)

Hours: Monday–Saturday, 6 p.m.–3 a.m.; closed Sunday

What goes on: A treasure trove of sakes, plain, pricey, and odd. The drier sakes are usually the most interesting, and those who find sake an overly subtle drink should try nama zake, which has a much wider flavor of considerable complexity. If you can afford them, the aged koshu sakes (a particularly good one is kamo izumi koshu, for $15 a glass) have the length and complexity of great wine. Don't make the faux pas of ordering your rice wine hot; the good stuff is drunk cold or at room temperature (very dry ones can be warmed a little). A couple of options: You can choose to sip from a masu (wooden box) rather than a cup, or a hire (nontoxic blowfish fin) can be added to impart a mellow, smoky flavor.

Setting & atmosphere: Enter through a glarey office building lobby, walk back toward the elevators, and descend a dank staircase to get to this supremely inviting inner sanctum that's all sleek lines and open space. There are some secluded tables, but there's lots more action at the big handsome bar. It's sexy and peaceful, rarely crowded. Rest rooms are hidden inside huge round wooden fermenting barrels.

If you go: Try to talk your way into the odd private karaoke club; the door is just to your left as you enter the building's lobby.

SAVOY LOUNGE

Unpretentious little jazz bar

Who Goes There: 25−75; a well-mixed crowd, equal numbers of musicians, music fans, and Midtown old-timers

355 West 41st Street
947-5255   Zone 8 Midtown West

Cover: $3 weeknights,
  $5−8 weekends
Minimum: 2 drinks at tables
Mixed drinks: $2.75−3
Wine: $2.75−3
Beer: $2.75−3
Dress: Anything goes, from jeans to
  suits

Specials: Happy hour till 9 p.m.: $6 pitchers, $2.50 bar drinks, $2 glass of wine; say "Best jazz/blues jukebox in town, man" and receive a free drink
Food available: None

Hours: Every day, 8 p.m.−4 a.m. (music every night, 10 p.m.−2 a.m.)

What goes on: A charmingly low-key, old-fashioned jazz bar where musicians feel relaxed and everyone has a good time. If you want to get dressed up and hear big names in clubs with coat checks, head downtown to one of the more famous venues (see the introduction to this chapter). If you'd prefer to pay just a few bucks to catch a set or two in a no-nonsense setting where fine musicians have fun and swing hard, come here.

Setting & atmosphere: This gritty (if not quite grimy) little gin mill, lurking near the rear entrance of the Port Authority Bus Terminal, is straight out of *Glengarry Glen Ross*. Before showtime, it's the kind of place where time hardly moves and silent boozers sip their way through empty afternoons. Ceiling fans are in a state of perpetual stall, and each lightbulb casts a slightly different hue. But then the bands—hard-bop straight-ahead jazz, organ trios, and jazzy blues—hit, and the mustiness suddenly becomes atmosphere. The most upscale touches are gumball machines filled with cashews perched over each booth.

If you go: The bar's always crowded with listeners ordering round after round, irrationally shunning the two-drink minimum at the tables. Have a seat and enjoy the far better view.

SMALL'S

Late-night hole-in-the-wall jazz club

Who Goes There: 21–60; jazz fans, hip NYU students, Eurotourists, insomniacs, recent music school grads

183 West 10th Street
929-7565 Zone 4 Greenwich Village

Cover: $10
Minimum: None
Mixed drinks: None
Wine: None
Beer: None

Dress: Sweatshirts and jeans (dressier on weekends)
Specials: Early-bird specials on weekends (call for info)
Food available: Gratis juice and snacks

Hours: Monday–Saturday, 10 p.m.–8 a.m.; Sunday, 9 p.m.–2 a.m.

What goes on: According to New York City law, clubs with liquor licenses must close at 4 a.m. Small's has become the city's preeminent after-hours jazz scene, presenting live music nightly (morningly?) till 8 a.m., by pursuing a policy of not serving alcohol. Besides the ultra-late hours and the jazz, there are a couple of other benefits to this policy. First and foremost, the uninebriated crowd is less noisy, more focused on the music. Second, you can be entertained all night—and we *do* mean *all* night—for less money (when all is said and done) than you'd spend even at clubs charging no cover. The talent level can be hit-or-miss: some top musicians play here, but off nights can be very off indeed.

Setting & atmosphere: This basement is a '90s version of the classic—and long extinct—Greenwich Village coffeehouse/nightclub. The jazz-savvy audience sits on stools or chairs very close to the stage. Decor is strictly makeshift.

If you go: Music starts at 10:30 p.m., but arrive by 10 to get a seat. The featured group plays until 2:30 a.m., and then it's an open jam session till closing. The experimental Monday night big band is very good.

SOB'S

Latin and world music/dance nightclub

Who Goes There: 21–40; music fans, salsa dancers, ethnic music trollers like David Byrne

204 Varick Street
243-4940   Zone 2 TriBeCa

Cover: Varies ($10–20, more or less)
Minimum: $15 at tables
Mixed drinks: $5–7
Wine: $5–7
Beer: $5–7
Dress: Colorful and flashy

Specials: Free entrance Fridays before 7 p.m., Tuesday before 9 p.m.; free salsa dance lessons Monday, 7–8:30 p.m. (stay free for show)
Food available: Pretty good overpriced pan-Latino and Brazilian dishes

Hours: Monday–Saturday, 6 p.m.–1 a.m. (closed Sunday in fall and winter); music starts after 9 p.m.

What goes on: This is a fun enough club just for hanging out and listening, but for those who like to dance, it's one of the best parties in town. Monday nights smoke with famous salsa groups (the dance class will get your hips up to speed); other nights feature music from Brazilian to reggae—anything funky and tropical. The bands are tops in their genres; this is a great place for world music neophytes to familiarize themselves with different styles. It's more nightclub than disco; bands are listened to as much as danced to, and even unaccompanied women feel "safe" on the dance floor.

Setting & atmosphere: Large stage with sunken dance floor; the bar faces the stage, but visibility is bad in crowds. There are tables to the side of the stage. Bright and colorful, with lots of tropical touches.

If you go: Bear in mind that things can get crowded; if you tire of standing, tables aren't hard to come by (meet the $15 minimum by ordering a bottle from the surprisingly good wine list).

SWING 46

Who Goes There: 25–90; swing dance aficionados
old and young, cool barflies

349 West 46th Street
262-9554   Zone 8 Theater District

Cover: $5–10
Minimum: 2 drinks at tables
Mixed drinks: $5.50–9
Wine: $5–6
Beer: $4.50–5.50
Dress: Anything goes; dancers dress up
Specials: Happy hour, Monday–
Saturday, 5–7 p.m.: half-price

drinks and beer at bar with live
piano jazz (prix fixe menu
available). Free dance lessons
Monday–Saturday after first set.
Food available: Expensive dinners plus
reasonably priced snacks (burgers,
etc.)

Hours: Every night, 5 p.m.–2 a.m.

What goes on: Live music seven nights a week; big bands and combos
playing swing. Lindy hoppers and jitterbugs are as hot as the music, and the
place bristles with energy even on weeknights. The bar is as cool as the dance
floor is hot, populated by older swing fans who prefer to sit and take it all in
without getting personally involved. If you can overlook all the silly hepcat
daddy-o spiel, it's all a pretty wild good time (neophyte dancers will not feel
uncomfortable).

Setting & atmosphere: The bar's up front, cut off from the frenzied action
further inside, but the bands can be clearly heard. The dance/nightclub
room, framed with beige paneling, has a low ceiling and is close but not
overly so. Tables have flickering candle lamps, and the dance floor is right
up next to the band. An outdoor sunken terrace in front of the club is filled
with tables in summer.

If you go: Restaurant Row is actually a better block for bars than for restaurants. On this same street, check out O'Flaherty's Ale House (see review);
McHale's Bar (750 Eighth Avenue, 246-8948), an intimate but rollicking
little bar with great booths, amber lamps, and a Cincinnati chili-parlor
ambience; and Don't Tell Mama's (see separate review), a jovial sing-along
piano bar with a cabaret room.

TRAMPS

Venue for nationally known groups of various styles

Who Goes There: Depends on the group, but generally a good mix of people much more interested in the music than in the bar scene

51 West 21st Street
727-7788   Zone 7 Gramercy Park

Cover: Varies; generally $20–50
Minimum: Varies
Mixed drinks: $5–7
Wine: $6
Beer: $4.50

Dress: Rock uniform: funky jacket over T-shirt for men, black dress for women
Food available: Next door in Tramps Cafe

Hours: Vary; call for info

What goes on: This is one of the city's top venues for big-name rock, blues, and R&B acts (with some funkier styles like zydeco thrown into the mix). Bookings run the gamut, from Blue Oyster Cult to Jerry Lee Lewis to Al Dimeola. While bookings are eclectic (and variable—dates, covers, showtime, and crowd all depend on the act, since this is considered more a performance venue than a club), quality is generally high, and occasionally very big names are lured. The place closes on nights with no music.

Setting & atmosphere: Spacious but minimalist. All sight lines (except those blocked by some ill-placed columns) lead to the stage.

If you go: Check out Tramps Cafe next door, serving decent cajun and western food and featuring low-key local acts.

VILLAGE VANGUARD

Jazz club

Who Goes There: 25–90; jazz pilgrims and Japanese tourists

178 Seventh Avenue South
255-4037   Zone 4 Greenwich Village

Cover: Usually $15 (Monday $12)
Minimum: $10

Mixed drinks: $4–7
Wine: $4–7

(Village Vanguard)

Beer: $4–7   Food available: None
Dress: Dressy or nice casual

Hours: Sunday–Thursday, sets at 9:30 and 11:30 p.m.; 1 a.m. set added Friday and Saturday

What goes on: This is it—the most famous jazz club in the world. Over the last 60 years almost every major jazz musician has gigged in this room (many recorded landmark live albums here as well), and the ghosts are palpable. This is straight-ahead swinging jazz, no fusion, no electric anything, a bastion of purity for bebop and hard bop (with very occasional Latin and free-ish forays), played by big-name musicians. The service is crabby and the seating's cramped, but you become a tiny part of jazz history simply by walking in the door.

Setting & atmosphere: Dank basement with a small bar in back . . . but the acoustics are wonderful and it feels like jazz.

If you go: Check out the Monday Night Vanguard Jazz Orchestra (Thad Jones/Mel Lewis's band, sans leaders). On any night, reservations are a good idea; this small club fills up fast.

WEBSTER HALL

Disco theme park

Who Goes There: 21–35; equal parts NYU freshmen, beautiful party people, and paunchy thirty-somethings clutching beers and looking wistful

125 East 11th Street
353-1600   Zone 5 East Village

Cover: $20
Minimum: None
Mixed drinks: $6.50–8
Wine: $6.50
Beer: $6–7
Dress: No sneakers, baseball hats, ripped jeans
Specials: $5 admission discounts are available through their Web site, www.websterhall.com; their CD, "Live in the Ballroom," costs $15 and includes a free pass (order from (888) WEB-HALL).
Food available: Probably somewhere; look around.

Hours: Thursday–Saturday, 10 p.m.–5 a.m.; Sunday–Wednesday, closed.

(Webster Hall)

What goes on: An enormous disco theme park with dance floors, lounges, a (temporary) tattoo parlor, and a coffee bar. There are spending opportunities everywhere you look; even the bathroom attendants reign over little concession stands, selling candy, mouthwash, and hair products. Fridays and Saturdays are monstrously crowded mainstream disco free-for-alls, while Thursdays have a psychedelic '60s theme. The staff seems to be instructed to act as peevish as possible.

Setting & atmosphere: Ground level is mostly a classic disco, complete with go-go girl behind the bar. Upstairs you enter a cavernous ballroom, like a junior high school auditorium taken over by aliens with superior technology: amazing lighting tricks and a SenSurround-style bass response that makes your chest feel like it's going to explode. More go-go girls, and androgynous characters on stilts. Still further upstairs is a balcony with tarot readings, temporary tattoos, body painting, and a tranquil lounge (wicker chairs, ferns) that hosts live bands Thursday and Friday nights (also check the bar here for drink specials). In the basement, yet another dance floor, this one with burning incense.

If you go: Conceal no weapons (or beer bottles)—no happening disco would be truly complete without a major security pat-down at the front door, and this is no exception.

PART SEVEN

New York's Neighborhoods

The Sidewalks of New York

Now that you've decided which parts of the city you're most interested in seeing, it's time to hit the road. Actually, you can use the following neighborhood descriptions as armchair tours, and if you don't have time to see more than a little of the city this time, you might enjoy reading about the rest to see how all the pieces fit together.

The profiles in this chapter are designed to convey a little of the geographical layout, historical relevance, tourist attractions, chronological development, and general character of the neighborhoods—they're overviews to help you grasp the spirit of the area. We have included some phone numbers, but not all. Most of the buildings mentioned here are public structures, important for their exteriors; if they have particularly stunning lobbies, they will probably be open to the public during general office hours. Similarly, most churches welcome visitors, but a few smaller or older churches (or those with valuable antiques) may ask that you make an appointment to visit. In any case, apply common sense and courtesy; be quiet for the sake of those using the premises for its original purposes, and try not to interrupt religious services.

Some museums or collections may charge admission or ask for donations. Most will be closed on major holidays. (Remember, too, that Jewish museums and houses will probably be closed at least half a day Friday and all day Saturday.) A few of the most important historical buildings, museums, and landmarks in each zone are described in detail in Part 11, "New York's Attractions."

■ Zone 1: Lower Manhattan, Wall Street, ■
and the Battery

One of the first things to remember about the area below Chambers Street is that this is the original New York—Nieuw Amsterdam, the port "bought" from the natives, and the village occupied by the British for virtually the entire Revolutionary War. The colonial administrators lived in the mansion on Governors Island out in the harbor; **Castle Clinton** (344-7220) on the west side of the Battery raised 28 cannon against the threat of invaders in 1811. The Declaration of Independence was read aloud on the **Bowling Green** on July 9, 1776; the crowd then pulled down the statue of King George III that had stood there for almost half a century and melted it down into ammunition. George Washington prayed here, in the simplicity of **St. Paul's Chapel** on Broadway (602-0800); he bade farewell to his officers here, on the site of the **Fraunces Tavern Museum** at Pearl and Broad Streets (425-1778); he was sworn in as the first president here as well, on the site of what is now the Greek Revival **Federal Hall National Memorial** at 26 Wall Street (825-6870), probably just as the bronze statue on the steps there suggests.

The other thing to remember, though, is just how very small that original city was, not nearly so large even as this one zone. Nearly a third of it, including the entire **Battery Park** area, the 92-acre Battery Park City on the west, and the eastern strip from Pearl Street to the East River, including the Franklin Roosevelt Drive and **South Street Seaport** areas, were actually constructed from landfill after the War of 1812. **Wall Street,** literally a wooden wall, was the northern border of Nieuw Amsterdam; and even in colonial times the town was only 10 blocks square, counting the Bowling Green—which in those days really was one. It had an estimated population of only 20,000, and at that, it was the second largest of the 13 colonies.

It wasn't until the early decades of the nineteenth century that the lawyers and stockbrokers had so taken hold of the Financial District that residences began to be built farther north. In fact, when **City Hall** was constructed in 1811, a little more than half a mile up Broadway, it was considered so far out of town that the north face was covered in brownstone instead of marble because city officials never expected anyone to view it from that side.

Nowadays, Lower Manhattan is one of the most fascinating areas of the city, still the financial capital of the nation—the **Federal Reserve Bank** (720-6130) on Liberty Street, the **New York Stock Exchange** (656-5168) at Broad and Wall Streets, and the **American Stock Exchange** on Trinity Place (306-1000)—and, for so relatively young a city, very nearly the financial capital of the world. The various bank buildings along Wall Street and around the Exchange are New York's version of the Forum in Rome, veritable temples of finance. It even houses what calls itself the **World Financial Center** in Battery Park City. Altogether, New York gives the word "capital" new resonance.

From City Hall Park and the courthouse complex at the "north pole" of the neighborhood to Battery Park on the south, from the **Fulton Fish Market** (669-9416) and **South Street Seaport** (669-9400) on the east to the **World Trade Center** on the west, and with the glorious **Trinity Church** (602-0800) going eye-to-eye with Wall Street—God and Mammon in daily competition—it covers far and away the greatest range of New York history of any single region. From here the soaring **Brooklyn Bridge** joins Manhattan to one sibling borough; the **Staten Island Ferry** to a second; and Broadway, which runs all the way from Bowling Green to the Bronx, to a third. The glorious Gothic **Woolworth Building** at 233 Broadway may no longer be a skyscraper compared to the 110-story World Trade Center towers, but its tiered crown, mosaic-roofed lobby, and hilarious gargoyles and caricatures pay greater tribute to New York's irreverent mercantile spirit than those grim tombstones.

This original Manhattan contains memorials ranging through New York's history, from its first sighting (the **Verrazano Monument** in the southwest corner of Battery Park) to its military heroes (the **Vietnam Veterans Plaza,** a simple glass-block fountain between Water and South Streets). One site even exposes 400 years of city life—the **New York Unearthed** permanent archeological exhibit at State and Water Streets (748-8628).

This is also a good area to remember the melting pot of Manhattan history. The flagpole in **Peter Minuit Plaza,** a sort of corner of Battery Park near the ferry building, salutes the courage of New York's first Jewish immigrants, who had been caught up in the Portuguese-Dutch wars and were harried back and forth between Europe and Brazil, attacked by pirates, and finally carried to Nieuw Amsterdam, where they were allowed to settle in 1626. The **sculpture** near Castle Clinton, with its eager arms and hopeful postures, is a tribute to the spirit of the millions of immigrants who landed here. The pair of ca. 1800 townhouses at State and Water Streets was the family home of, and is now a shrine to, **Mother Elizabeth Ann Seton** (269-6865), the first American-born saint of the Catholic Church; it was also, appropriately, a home for immigrant Irish women, sheltering as many as 170,000 after the Civil War. And the recently discovered **African Burial Ground** near Broadway and Chambers Streets dates back at least to the eighteenth century and, archeologists say, quite likely to the seventeenth, a reminder that the labor of slaves, as well as so many others, built this city.

Two museums remind us to remember the "forgotten peoples": the **National Museum of the American Indian** within the fine Beaux Arts **U.S. Custom House** (825-6700) at Broadway and Bowling Green; and the **Museum of Jewish Heritage—A Living Memorial to the Holocaust** in Battery Park City (968-1800). And it is from here, of course, that most visitors look to the **Statue of Liberty** (363-3200) and the **Ellis Island Museum of Immigration** (363-7620), perhaps the most lasting memorials to the American spirit anywhere.

If you are interested in monumental views in architectural terms, be sure to walk up Broadway to **City Hall Park** and admire the elegant municipal buildings, including the French Renaissance **City Hall,** with its lobby murals, double hanging staircase, and exhibits of official gifts to the city; **Surrogate's Court** at Chambers and Centre, inspired by the Paris Opera and arrayed with a pageant of sculpture and a neo-Egyptian mosaic ceiling in the lobby that, like Grand Central's, reproduces the zodiac; and the nearby court buildings of the **Civic Center,** especially the rotunda of 60 Centre Street, with its restored 1930s murals. Grab a snack from the park vendors while you're there. The statue of Benjamin Franklin at the south end of the park recalls a time when this stretch of Park Row was filled with newspaper presses, like London's Fleet Street.

■ Zone 2: SoHo and TriBeCa ■

Now that popular music and hip-industry logos have made odd capitalizations common, the names "SoHo" and "TriBeCa" don't stand out the way they used to. Both are purely physical descriptions, only in shorthand: SoHo is SOuth of HOuston Street—it has nothing to do with the Soho of London—and TriBeCa is an anagram for the TRIangle BElow CAnal, though it more closely resembles a slightly bottom-heavy diamond. (And note that Houston is pronounced "*house*-ton," not like the Texas city.)

SoHo was largely rural until well after the turn of the nineteenth century. Remnants of the old Canarsie Indian tribe, who had originally "owned" the entire island, continued to live here throughout the Dutch and early British colonial era. In the eighteenth century, it was largely farmland (like much of Manhattan) and country estates of the more prosperous residents. It was gradually consumed by townhouses after the turn of the nineteenth century, when it occupied a sort of middle ground between toney Washington Square above it and the business district below. There is a four-block area at the north-central corner, bordered by Sixth Avenue, West Houston, and Varick and Vandam Streets, that is a historic district of its own; developed by John Jacob Astor in the late 1820s, it contains the city's largest concentration of Federal-style row houses.

But it came into its own in the mid–eighteenth century, when the architectural movement sometimes called American Industrial—large, almost warehouse-sized spaces covered with pseudo-classical columns and cornices made of cast iron—swept in and transformed it into the light industrial and retail center of the city. It is still home to the largest concentration of cast-iron ornamentation in the city; and many of those oversized buildings have been transformed into art galleries, furniture display rooms, and even museums. (When you hear about "lofts," think SoHo.) Most of the smaller buildings are restaurants and boutiques. The five cobblestone blocks of Greene Street from Canal to Houston are the centerpiece of the **Cast-Iron Historic District,** with more than 50 intact nineteenth-century buildings with facades in the neoclassical, Renaissance Revival, and Corinthian styles. The one at 72–76 Greene, a sort of duplex with a five-story Second Empire facade, is called the **"King of Greene Street."** The **"Queen of Greene,"** built by the same developer, Isaac Duckworth, is the mansard-roofed building at 28–30 Greene. (For more on this area, see the "Great Neighborhoods for Shopping" section in Part 9.) The **New York City Fire Museum** at 278 Spring Street (691-1303) is the largest collection of antique firefighting equipment, pumps, bells, and hydrants in the country, plus a parade's worth of nineteenth-century engines.

The area around Broadway has become a major art and shopping district; for more information, see the "Great Neighborhoods for Shopping" section in Part 9.

TriBeCa has become trendy more recently, and the shops are a little funkier still; but it has been getting a reputation as a restaurant haven, possibly because of the many old and family-owned food/import businesses around. And thanks to the well-advertised presence of actor Robert De Niro, part-owner of such hotspots as the Tribeca Grill and Nobu, TriBeCa is developing a certain celebrity population. For more on SoHo, see Part 9, "Shopping in New York."

■ Zone 3: Chinatown, Little Italy, and ■ the Lower East Side

Time was when these three ethnic neighborhoods were not just distinct, they were rigorously segregated. More recently, however, the outlines of the three have blurred and overlapped, and Little Italy in particular is being subsumed as Chinese businesses spill north of Canal Street and up alongside the long strip of **Sara Delano Roosevelt Park,** which used to divide Little Italy from the Jewish Lower East Side. Chinese immigrants have been one of the fastest-growing communities in the city for several decades, and an estimated 150,000 now live in Chinatown alone. In addition, Chinatown is now far more broadly Asian. The signs and sounds of Vietnamese in particular are almost as common as Chinese.

At the same time, the eastward gradual expansion of SoHo chic, and even some neo-'60s-style hippie culture from the East Village to the north, is turning parts of even **Orchard Street,** the heart of Lower East Side bargain territory, into the latest bohemian hangout.

Chinatown's history is as convoluted (or as romantic, depending on your outlook) as any Manhattan neighborhood's, dominated by family networks, community associations, and more serious criminal gangs, but all operating in so closed a circle as to be nearly invisible to outsiders. (In any case, the Tongs of the early twentieth century seem almost a local requirement, a legacy of the Jewish gangsters and Five Points hoodlums.) It has little architectural style in comparison to, say, San Francisco's Grant Avenue area; but it is full of street vendors (most selling cheap knockoffs, but highly popular in themselves), produce and fish markets, restaurants, and import shops. More popular in recent years are the herbal apothecaries, herbal pharmacies with remedies dating back thousands of years.

The **Museum of Chinese in the Americas** at Mulberry and Bayard Streets (619-4785) is small, but its collection of old photographs, business leases, and oral histories is first-class; you might also be able to piggyback onto one of the walking tours the museum also sometimes arranges for larger groups. The **Eastern States Buddhist Temple** on Mott near Canal houses more than 100 golden statues of the Enlightened One (966-4753), while Confucius stands in pacific monumental contemplation in **Confucius Plaza** on the Bowery near Pell Street. Ironically, or perhaps optimistically, the nearby block of **Doyers Street,** which takes a sharp turn between the Bowery and Pell, is what was known as Chinatown's "Bloody Angle," back when the opium dealers lured rivals into ambush.

Columbus Park, a small green oasis south of Bayard Street more or less at the juncture of Little Italy and Chinatown, was once the heart of the Five Points slum, one of the city's largest gang havens and red-light districts. Now it's usually filled with playing children, dragon parades on Chinese New Year, and occasional street fairs. The jagged Art Moderne **Criminal Courts Building** nearby used to be the jail, the last one built before Riker's Island.

As indicated earlier, Little Italy is a shadow of its former self, except perhaps during the big street parties, especially during the Feast of San Gennaro in the fall. Its most famous address is **Mulberry Street.** (Its most infamous address is probably the Bowery, thanks to that street's role in the *Bowery Boys* serials.) Although they are now intermixed with Asian and Hispanic businesses, there are still blocks of delis and family restaurants stoop to stoop. **Old St. Patrick's Cathedral** at Mulberry and Prince (226-8075), begun in 1809, is still the parish church, although the big St. Patrick's uptown is now the archdiocesan seat. It holds the remains of Pierre Toussaint, who was born a Haitian slave in 1766 but who became a free man and philanthropist; he is also being considered for sainthood.

Especially if you loved those old *Untouchable* shows, you must stop at **Ratner's** at Delancey and Norfolk (677-5588). The restaurant's back room, now the neo-cocktail Prohibition-swank Lansky Lounge, is where gangster Meyer Lansky used to have breakfast, sometimes with childhood pal Lucky Luciano; Bugsy Siegel made his first hit on the corner outside the door, and there's an alley entrance to the bar that rumor has it was the old speakeasy slip-in.

To give equal time, make sure to spot the luxury apartment building at Grand and Centre Streets, with its Baroque clock-tower dome, stone friezes, and guardian lions; it used to be the police headquarters, and gazing up the front steps at the guard's desk, you can just imagine how impressive it must have been to be hauled up in front of the sergeant in the heyday of New York's Irish finest. And at Lafayette and Hester Streets is the **Engine Co. No. 31,** an 1895 gem that looks more like a French country castle than a firehouse (actually, it's now a community TV and film center).

The Lower East Side, generally on the south side of East Houston from the Bowery east, was not particularly desirable land in the early decades of New York development because it was largely wetlands. It had served as temporary quarters for a series of the poorest immigrants, first Irish victims of the potato famine and then German farmers whose own potato crops were gradually infected, followed by periodic influxes of Turkish and Greek families. However, the most famous and lasting immigration began in the late nineteenth century, when as many as 1.6 million Eastern European Jews arrived, creating the neighborhood famous from photographs of tenement houses, sidewalk carts, and Orthodox scholars. It was both a slum and a cultural haven (not an unusual paradox for a people used to ghettos), filled with synagogues, debating clubs, and community banks as well as vendors and sweatshops. (For more on this area, see the section "Great Neighborhoods for Shopping" in Part 9.)

In recent years, the Lower East Side has made a concerted effort to turn itself into a historical as well as retail tourist attraction. The irony is that many of the Jewish families have moved up-island to the wealthier areas on either side of the park and out to Brooklyn, and large numbers of Hispanic, black, and Asian families have replaced them. Nevertheless, the creation of the **Lower East Side Tenement Museum** (431-0233) on Orchard Street, in addition to the more organized promotion of the many family-owned clothing stores in that neighborhood, hearkening back to its merchant origins, has brought it a certain revived prosperity. The Moorish Revival 1887 **Eldridge Street Synagogue** between Allen and Canal Streets (219-0888), with its lavish stained glass, carved detailing, and chandeliers, is being restored to its full beauty; oral histories are welcome, and there is also a minimuseum of Jewish life in America in the building. The **Ritualarium** at 313 East Broadway (475-8514) is a *mikvah,* a ritual bathhouse for observant Jewish women, and the huge cisterns collect the rainwater used inside. And **Schapiro's House of Kosher and Sacramental Wines** at 126 Rivington Street (674-4404) is the last winery still in operation in New York; you can tour it (by appointment) or purchase consecrated wine.

Incidentally, this is a good area for bridge enthusiasts; only about a mile separates three of New York's major interborough spans: the Brooklyn, Manhattan, and Williamsburg Bridges. The **Brooklyn Bridge,** the oldest of the three, bears traffic away from near City Hall Park just south of Chinatown. The **Manhattan Bridge,** which has lost its allegorical sculptures to the Brooklyn Museum of Art but still has its triumphal arch, takes off from Canal Street, and the **Williamsburg Bridge** from Delancey Street.

▪ Zone 4: Greenwich Village ▪

This is probably the most famous neighborhood in New York, known even to outsiders as "the Village" and symbol of the city's artistic and literary history. It had originally been covered with largish "country houses" belonging to the businessmen from downtown and smaller homes along the riverfront built by marine craftsmen and merchants before it was sold off and subdivided. (Herman Melville lived here as a child, working around the docks before shipping off with whalers, being shipwrecked, and thinking twice about his choice of career.) You can dine in almost any sort of cafe, white-linen establishment, or carry-out and taste the cuisine of virtually every country here; just stroll around and read the menus until you find something that attracts you.

Because it was largely developed in the late nineteenth century before the grid system was put in place—the regular grid actually begins at 14th Street, the northern border of the Village—it has a number of diagonals, triangles, and bends that newcomers sometimes find confusing. The part of Greenwich Village east of Sixth Avenue more regularly ascribes to the numbered-street system, but on the west side, most streets have names rather than numbers, and even those few numbers don't behave very predictably: West 4th Street, for example, seems to move in the usual cross-island direction beneath Washington Square but almost immediately begins making a series of elbow shifts north, and by the time it gets to the top of the Village, it's nearly gone perpendicular.

Think of the Village map as the left half of an opened fan: The area between Broadway and Sixth Avenue would be the fan's center, with the avenues as fairly upright spines. Seventh Avenue spreads out a little, and beyond that, the main avenues—Hudson Street, Washington Street, and West Street along the Hudson River—all bend a little farther out. (Greenwich Street squiggles a little, like a bent feather, between Washington and Hudson.) By the time the side streets are filled in, you have a series of trapezoids and triangles; it may be hard to negotiate at first, but it gives the area a true village atmosphere.

Washington Square, at the foot of Fifth Avenue, was one of Manhattan's first prestigious residential neighborhoods. The park was established in 1828, and it was surrounded by fine Greek Revival townhouses; several of the oldest are still standing. In the mid–nineteenth century, the square was a sort of green parenthetical bracket for upper-class residences, with expensive brownstones running up both sides of Fifth Avenue all the way to Central Park. Even the mayor's official residence was here, at No. 8 (the facade is real, but the rest is not). Brothers Henry and William James grew up in the neighborhood; James's *Washington Square* was set at No. 18, where his grandmother lived. James himself, Edith Wharton, and William Dean Howells all lived at various times at No. 1; John Dos Passos was living at No. 3 when he wrote *Manhattan Transfer.* All of those have been razed. The so-called **Hanging Elm** in the northwest corner, a last reminder of the public executions of the early nineteenth century, is still hanging in there, though.

Patchin Place on West 10th Street just west of Sixth Avenue, a little cluster of rooming houses built in 1848, eventually housed such writers as e. e. cummings, Theodore Dreiser, and Djuna Barnes. The **Jefferson Market Public Library** on Sixth Avenue at West 10th Street, built in 1877, was modeled on one of Mad King Ludwig of Bavaria's castles, hiked up at one end with a clock tower and positively pockmarked with arched windows and pointed gables. It was actually a courthouse—and of all things, it was voted the country's fifth most beautiful building when it was completed.

However, as the money moved north, the Village became a more middle-class, though still very desirable, area, at least until the sprawling commercial development of the riverfront and the repeated waves of immigration threatened to pinch it between the tenements of Hell's Kitchen and Little Italy. Townhouses were divided up into apartments, studio space became cheap, and the Village began to attract a second generation of writers and painters, either poorer or more naturally bohemian in outlook, among them Edna St. Vincent Millay, Walt Whitman, Mark Twain, Edgar Allan Poe, Albert Bierstadt, Frederic Church, Gertrude Vanderbilt Whitney, Winslow Homer, Robert Henri, and Edward Hopper.

The Village was also one of the first centers of theatrical experimentation (a tradition honored by the many street performers in Washington Square): the **Provincetown Playhouse** on MacDougal was Eugene O'Neill's first showcase, and Dylan Thomas famously drank himself to death in the **White Horse Tavern** on Hudson at West 11th Street (243-9260). The Village is still the heart of off-Broadway, filled with dozens of theaters and performance troupes.

The third and fourth generations, Beats and bohemians, moved in after World War II, followed by the flower children and finally the retro-radicals. The New York University campus sprawls around Washington Square, and the New School for Social Research and Parsons School of Design are also here. The earlier artists left their mark by way of the dozens of off-Broadway theaters and jazz clubs, the later by way of the New York Studio School of Drawing, Painting, and Sculpture (the original home of the Whitney Museum) and Parsons, which combines art design and philosophy. Most appropriate of all might be the presence of the **Malcolm Forbes Gallery** on Fifth Avenue at West 12th (206-5548), the palace of playthings from the prince of capitalism.

This is a great spot for just walking, because of the mix of eighteenth- and nineteenth-century architecture (look for cobblestones on the west side), the ethnic assortment, and the mingling of social classes. It is also, of course, a famous refuge for gay and lesbian residents, though in recent years many gays have moved north into Chelsea and left the Village to the women. The gay scene centers around **Christopher Street; the Stonewall Tavern,** site of the infamous 1969 police/gay standoff, has moved about a little, but is now at 53 Christopher. Gay Street, as it happens, was named after a family.

Even if you only have a few minutes, the tiny area around Bedford Street from Christopher to Commerce is especially worth seeing. At 102 Bedford is the house called **Twin Peaks,** which looks a little like a Tudor cottage with a Hessian helmet on it; the original 1830 cottage was "done up" by architect Clifford Reed Daily to put a little more fun into the artists' community. The mansard-topped twins at **39 and 41 Commerce Street** around the corner were supposedly built in 1831 by a sea captain for his spinster daughters, who did not speak to each other; the central garden apparently did not bring them closer together, either. On Grove Street just off Bedford is a row of Federal townhouses, and in between **Nos. 10 and 12 Grove** is an alley of mid-nineteenth-century workingmen's cottages. The brick-covered clapboard house at No. 77 Bedford, the **Isaacs-Hendricks House,** is the oldest in the Village, built in 1800. And the house next door, the 1873 building at **75½ Bedford Street,** was Edna St. Vincent Millay's last New

York home and was later home to John Barrymore and Cary Grant; only 9½ feet wide, it is the narrowest building in the city, built in what was once a passageway.

■ **Zone 5: The East Village** ■

The East Village—which, logically, extends east of Greenwich Village from Broadway to the East River—is topographically far more regular than its sibling: the avenues (here including Avenues A, B, C, and D, known as "Alphabet City," beyond First Avenue) run longitudinally, and the obediently numbered streets, from East 1st to East 14th, crisscross them more or less latitudinally. There's a touch of Greenwich-style triangularity around **Astor Place** (Broadway above West 4th Street) and the nearby **Cooper Union,** but other than that, it's a snap.

Socially, however, the population of the East Village is all over the map: a mix of Indian and Italian restaurateurs, Ukrainian boutiques, art students, street performers, and proto-punks. It's a hot club scene, studded with preserved churches and monuments to art movements of earlier days; it is also still a stronghold of the drug culture, though that is much less visible than in the '70s. But it has many beautiful buildings and important cultural sites, and its history goes back to the days of Nieuw Amsterdam.

Peter Stuyvesant once owned the lion's share of what is now the East Village, and a fair amount of the island north of there as well (see Zone 7). The western border of the "bouwerie" was Fourth Avenue, which explains why that street becomes known as Bowery to the south. His country home was near 10th and Stuyvesant, and he had his own chapel, too, on the site of what is now **St. Mark's-in-the-Bowery** on East 10th at Second Avenue (674-6377), which itself goes back to 1799; he was buried in the ground beneath it. Poet W. H. Auden is remembered there, though not buried, because he lived for many years at 77 St. Mark's Place.

Astor Place, like Washington Square, was inhabited by the richest of the rich in the early nineteenth century, including the Delanos, Astors (naturally), and Vanderbilts. The Astor Place Opera House, actually the second famous theater in that park, was the site of what is known as the Astor Place Riots of 1849; it started as a quarrel between the paid adherents of two rival actors and ended in the death of several dozen people. In the same area are the **Public Theater,** originally the Astor Library building donated by John Jacob Astor and now best known as home of the year-round Shakespeare Festival founded by Joseph Papp; and Cooper Union, the famous free adult educational institution that was the first to accept women and students of all races and religions. Its columned Great Hall, where Lincoln delivered his

"Right Makes Might" speech, is still the site of popular public debates. **Colonnade Row,** the homes from 428 to 434 Lafayette off Astor Place, was also known as "LaGrange Terrace" when the Astors themselves and the Vanderbilts and Delanos—the usual suspects—lived there, along with such temporary celebrity residents as Charles Dickens and William Makepeace Thackeray; but only four of the original nine buildings, and just the facades, survive.

The **Old Merchant's House** (777-1089), just south of the Public Theater at 29 East 4th Street, is an intact 1830s Greek Revival home with all its furnishings, paintings, and even books just the way they were when merchant Seabury Tredwell forbade his daughter Gertrude to marry a man he disapproved of. Gertrude then decided never to marry at all. Sex also used to be an issue at **McSorley's Old Ale House,** which from its founding in 1854 until the 1970s admitted only men; other than that, it's still the same old saloon (East 7th and Cooper Streets; 473-9148).

On East 2nd Street between Second Avenue and the Bowery is the **New York City Marble Cemetery,** where many famous New York names are represented. But more eerily, if you go into the alley that turns off 2nd Street, you'll find another early-nineteenth-century cemetery, or, rather, the marble plaques above the underground vaults.

An odd little spire seems to poke up above Broadway, where it makes a funny little quirk around what was then an apple orchard; the spire leads down to the lovely Gothic Revival **Grace Church** at West 10th Street (254-2000), designed by St. Patrick's architect James Renwick when he was only 23. It has particularly beautiful stained glass in the pre-Raphaelite style, and its moment in the celebrity sun occurred when P. T. Barnum staged General Tom Thumb's marriage there.

If you hear the half-joking designation "NoHo," it means "north of Houston," the area around Broadway and Lafayette whose commercial spirit has more in common with the West Village these days than the East.

■ Zone 6: Chelsea ■

When Captain Thomas Clarke acquired the land from Eighth Avenue to the Hudson River between West 14th and 25th Streets, he named it, in what must have seemed a rather ambitious flight of fancy, after a neighborhood in London famed for its high fashion and literary and artistic life. As it turned out, it was prophetic. Chelsea was the first Broadway, the original Hollywood, and over the years it has been home to dozens of artists and writers (Thomas Wolfe, Mary McCarthy, Orson Welles, Vladimir Nabokov, Arthur Miller, Sarah Bernhardt, Andy Warhol, Dylan Thomas, Tennessee

Williams, Sid Vicious and Nancy Spungen, etc.). It was an early fashion center and is still home to the Fashion Institute of Technology and the **"Fur District"** (between Sixth and Eighth Avenues and West 27th and 30th Streets), though the serious retail boutiques have long since moved farther uptown.

As noted in Part 1, "Understanding the City," most of Clarke's property was inherited by his grandson, Clement Clarke Moore of " 'Twas the Night before Christmas" fame. Among his gifts, the public-good component of his commercial development was the land for the **Theological Seminary** on Ninth Avenue between West 20th and 21st (243-5150). St. Mark's Library now has what is believed to be the largest collection of Latin Bibles in the world; the West Building is the oldest example of Gothic Revival architecture in the city; and Hoffman Hall's dining room is one of those medieval-style galleries that English universities always seemed to have. Across Ninth Avenue is **St. Peter's Episcopal Church** (346 West 20th Street); Moore insisted that it should be built in the style of a classical Greek temple, and the foundation was, but in midconstruction church officials shifted to the Gothic style then sweeping England.

The home at **Ninth and West 21st Street,** with the ornate peaked roof, is the oldest home in the neighborhood, built in the 1820s. The rest of the block is only a little newer. When Moore subdivided the property in 1830, he required the residential developers to put gardens in front of the homes and trees along the street; the exteriors of the townhouses along **West 21st between Ninth and Tenth** are nearly intact, though many of the buildings are now apartments or shops. The Greek Revival row houses along **West 20th Street** in the same block were originally constructed as middle-class rental units in the late 1930s; notice the cast-iron detailing and the brownstone door frames that became a synonym for Manhattan homes.

In the late 1880s, Chelsea was the site of many legitimate theater troupes, though they began to move northward; and similarly, though the theatrical names who dared to experiment in the moving picture business, such as John Barrymore, originally worked in the Chelsea warehouses, California's ample spaces and more dependable climate lured most of the film industry away.

The block bounded by West 23rd and 24th and Ninth and Tenth is taken up by the **London Terrace Apartments:** During the Depression, for some speculative reason, developers tried to play on the name by razing the mid-nineteenth-century Greek Revival complex there and replacing it with this Mayfair-wannabe block with a garden in the middle and doormen dressed as London "bobbies." It was not an immediate success. Across Tenth at 519 West 23rd Street is the **WPA Theatre,** one of the best-known off-off-Broadway venues; *Little Shop of Horrors* and *Steel Magnolias,* among others, began here.

The **Hotel Chelsea,** incidentally, which at various times was home or hotel to O. Henry, Mark Twain, Thomas Wolfe, Arthur Miller, Tennessee Williams, Brendan Behan, Vladimir Nabokov, Sarah Bernhardt, Dylan Thomas, Virgil Thomson, Jack Kerouac, and assorted touring rock stars, is on West 23rd between Seventh and Eighth Avenues (243-3700).

The Gothic Revival **Marble Collegiate Church** at Broadway and West 29th Street (686-2770) is famous for three things: its Tiffany windows, former pastor Norman Vincent Peale *(The Power of Positive Thinking),* and one of Peale's less admirable students, Richard Nixon. **St. John the Baptist** (564-9070) on West 31st Street just west of Seventh Avenue is like a geode, dirtied and nearly obscured by the development around it, but glorious within.

Chelsea went through a long decline before urban renewal moved in, but nowadays, from its vantage point between the modern Theater District and Greenwich Village, it is at once a target for upwardly mobile young families, art and antiques dealers, and (increasingly) a wealthy gay population. And with **Madison Square Garden** at one corner and the huge, renovated **Chelsea Piers** playground/tourist draw at the other, the famous Chelsea loft spaces are once again getting hard to find. (The modern Madison Square Garden, which replaced the original Pennsylvania Station and now sits on top of it, may have many events to recommend it, but it doesn't have much architecturally. If you wonder how pretty the preceding building was, look at the great Beaux Arts **Post Office** across Eighth Avenue, which was its twin and is emblazoned with the famous "Neither snow nor rain . . ." slogan.)

If you're interested in fashion and design, you should stop by the free galleries at the **Fashion Institute of Technology** on Seventh Avenue at 27th Street (217-5966), which, like the better-known Costume Institute at the Metropolitan, assembles special exhibits that either trace a style through history or showcase designers or collectors and that sometimes detail a technique or material. One other Chelsea neighborhood worth noting is the **"Flower District"** along Sixth Avenue in the upper 60s. And part of Chelsea lapped over into the infamous Tenderloin; see Zone 8.

■ Zone 7: Gramercy Park and Madison Square ■

This old and in many cases well-preserved section of Manhattan, which faces Chelsea across Sixth Avenue, is punctuated by squares and parks and white-collar firms. It is also the area that symbolized the commercial ambitions of the Gilded Age, home to the **Flatiron Building** in the triangle of

Fifth Avenue, Broadway, and 23rd Street, which was the world's largest building when it was completed in 1903; the **Metropolitan Life Insurance Building** at Madison and 23rd, which topped it by adding a tower in 1909; the **Empire State Building,** which beat them both in 1931; and a former incarnation of Madison Square Garden.

What was sometimes called "Ladies' Mile," a cluster of the first department stores (notably, the original Lord & Taylor and Tiffany stores) and custom shops catering to the carriage trade, ran along Broadway from Union Square to Madison Square—the heart of what is also sometimes known as the Flatiron District. (The Flatiron Building was actually named the Fuller Building, but its shape, something like the prow of a great ocean liner or an old press, provided the nickname.) Society figures and politicians made their homes here (Union Square was the home of Tammany Hall), and it was near enough to the theater district to attract the most important actors and writers as well. Edwin Booth, whose statue stands in the park, founded the famous **Players Club** on the south side. The **"Little Church around the Corner"** at East 29th and Fifth Avenue (684-6770), which became famous because it buried actors when some more "respectable" churches wouldn't, has a collection of theatrically inspired stained glass. Appropriately, it now offers a number of upper-class businesses, homes, historic sites, bookstores, and theaters and the kind of trendy restaurants that often return to a revived commercial district.

Before the Empire State Building was erected, the block of Fifth Avenue between West 33rd and West 34th Streets held two of the many Astor mansions, one belonging to William Waldorf Astor and the other to his aunt, Mrs. William Astor. An argument led to his moving out and putting up a hotel on the site called the Waldorf; almost immediately she moved out and had a connecting hotel, the Astoria, built. The two operated as a single company—though with the provision that she could block off the connection at any time—until 1929, when the Park Avenue hotel of that name was built and the Empire State Building begun.

Gramercy Park, the neighborhood centered on Gramercy Park at the foot of Lexington Avenue between West 20th and West 21st, was one of the first "gated communities," as we would call them now. In the 1830s, developer Samuel Ruggles bought a large chunk of the old Stuyvesant estate that included a creek shaped like a "crooked little knife," or "Crommessie." Ruggles wanted to entice a wealthy patronage, so he filled in the marshy creek area and laid out a London-style park in the heart of his territory, with one adjoining avenue named for a famous Revolutionary victory and one on the south side called Irving Place after writer Washington Irving. Astonishingly, it is still a private park, the only one in the city—area residents have keys to the lock—and the entire area is a historic district. Teddy Roosevelt was born on East 20th Street between Park and Broadway. The **Theodore Roosevelt Birthplace Museum** (260-1616) had to be reconstructed because the actual building was demolished during World War II, but the five rooms of period furniture, memorabilia, Teddy Bears, and campaign memorabilia are real enough. The **New York Police Academy and Museum** (477-9753) on the other side of the park, on East 20th between Second and Third Avenues, has some rather impressive exhibits and photos recalling famous murders and kidnappings as well as nightsticks and antique uniforms and weapons; its proximity to the TR museum is appropriate, since Roosevelt served as the city's commissioner of police before the Spanish-American War.

Madison Square Park, between Fifth and Madison Avenues and between West 23rd and West 26th Streets, was originally envisioned as another center of upper-class life, the entertainment center and location of some of the ritziest hotels. (This required more clever redevelopment: Not only was that neighborhood swampy, like the original Gramercy area, but it also held a "potter's field," or pauper's cemetery.) It was part of the original grid plan of 1811, though only well into the mid–nineteenth century did it become much more than a commons and parade ground. This was the site of the second Madison Square Garden, the palatial exhibition hall/entertainment complex designed by Sanford White; its rooftop garden was also the place where White was shot to death in 1906 by millionaire socialite Harry Thaw, who believed White was having an affair with his showgirl wife, Evelyn Nesbit. (Nearly all that's left of White's work, incidentally, are the pedestal for the Farragut statue in this park, the **Players Club** at Gramercy Square, and the marble arch in Washington Square.) The original New York Knickerbockers, the nation's first organized baseball team, played here; and before it was permanently hoisted into harbor-lighting position, the torch and upraised arm of the Statue of Liberty was exhibited here as well.

Overlooking Madison Square is the clock tower of the **Metropolitan Life Insurance Building,** nearly five feet taller than London's Big Ben. In the lobby are a series of historical murals painted by famed children's illustrator N. C. Wyeth. On the other corner, at Madison and East 25th, is the **New York State Supreme Court's Appellate Division,** believed to be the busiest appellate court in the world (among the former plaintiffs here: Babe Ruth, Charlie Chaplin, Edgar Allan Poe, and Harry Houdini). The many fine sculptures outside are matched by stained glass, murals, and carving inside, which you can see unless court is in session.

Among other old neighborhood names sometimes used by city residents or prestige-savvy developers are **Rose Hill,** a residential area north of Stuyvesant Square, and **Kips Bay,** for the area between Gramercy and Murray Hill (see Zone 9). Both names go back to old farming estates. The Kip family established their farm almost as soon as the Canarsie had sold Manhattan, and Rose Hill was sold off the Stuyvesant estate in the mid–eighteenth century. The **"Block Beautiful"** is simply a well-preserved row of houses along East 19th Street between Irving Place and Third Avenue (theater great Mrs. Patrick Campbell and movie vamp Theda Bara both lived in No. 132 19th Street, a case of high and low culture conjunction if there ever was one).

Union Square describes the area just north of the East Village between the actual Union Square Park and Stuyvesant Square; occasionally the greater neighborhood is referred to as Stuyvesant in an older publication or historical reference. The rather stolid **St. George's Episcopal Church** overlooking Stuyvesant Square is where J. P. Morgan attended what one must imagine were safely conservative services. The night-lit clock tower that looks down from Irving Street at East 14th is part of the **Consolidated Edison** (ConEd) headquarters, but at various times this site held Tammany Hall and the Academy of Music. On East 14th Street between Third Avenue and Irving Place, ConEd also operates a free-admission **Energy Museum** that includes a re-creation of "underground New York" and many early appliances (460-6244).

Union Square itself, at the intersection of Broadway and Park between West 14th and West 17th Streets, is the first of a series of squares marking the diagonal northward progress of Broadway. Though, like the East Village, it had become a famous drug market, ongoing restoration and the success of the open-air green market has revived it considerably.

Incidentally, this entire section of Manhattan was the "turf" of the original Gashouse Gang, so called because many of the factories that supplied the city's lights were located along the East River. Just to the north was the territory of the "Rag Gang," whose strongman Paddy Corcoran gave the name "Corcoran's Roost" to the area now held by, intriguingly, the United Nations.

▪ Zone 8: Midtown West and the Theater District ▪

When people talk about Broadway, they rarely mean the street; they mean the **Theater District**—an area that ranges along both sides of Broadway from Times Square at West 42nd up to about 47th Street and between

Ninth and Sixth Avenues. Broadway is the heart of this zone, along with many of the more important off-Broadway venues: the Shriner–Moorish Revival **City Center of Music and Drama** on West 55th at Broadway (581-7907), **Carnegie Hall** on West 57th around the corner of Broadway (903-9600), and even the **Brill Building,** the one-stop "Broadway" of pop music and the heart of Tin Pan Alley (between West 49th and West 50th Streets).

This is also the so-called **Garment District,** an industrial concentration that began on the Lower East Side and gradually followed the department stores up Broadway. However, the most influential merchants decided that the showroom and the sweatshop shouldn't be so close together, and together they constructed two large warehouses on Seventh Avenue at West 37th Street. Today some of the street signs have subtitles reading **Fashion Avenue,** although it's also been known less reverently as Rag Alley and the like.

Among the most famous areas in this zone is **Times Square,** actually named before the paper's headquarters moved there in 1905; up until then it had been called Longacre Square, home to stables and blacksmiths and the occasional thief. This is where the famous ball drops to mark the New Year as it has every year since 1905; and although it had become notoriously seedy, studded with porno shops and cheap bars, the neighborhood is in the midst of one of the most sweeping renovations in city history, perhaps second only to the development of Lincoln Center in place of the West Side slums. In fact, things are opening so fast that you may want to pick up a copy of the neighborhood guide at the 42nd Street **Times Square Visitors Center.** (Not all Times Square visuals are outdoors: Look for the branch of the **International Center of Photography** on Sixth at 43rd; 768-4680.)

New theaters and renovated ones, trendy restaurants, comedy and music clubs, high-tech virtual playgrounds and megastores—plus those famous huge billboards and the *Times*'s running-lights headline service—are bursting almost daily out from behind construction fences. The Disney Company restored the historic **New Amsterdam** on 42nd Street at Seventh Avenue as a showcase for such in-house productions as its extraordinary adaptation of *The Lion King.* (It's just behind the Disney superstore, but frankly, the theater lobby is the more fantastic of the two.) The **New Victory** across the street is a throwback to the golden age of children's theater. Two historic but aging theaters, the 1903 Lyric and the 1920 Apollo, have been replaced at a cost of $30 million by the single **Ford Center for the Performing Arts,** which will be the second largest auditorium on Broadway. The *New York Times* itself long ago had to move out of the old tower on the square to larger digs on West 43rd Street, but the Condé Nast group and MTV are moving in. A huge **Warner Bros.** store will soon join the **Vir-**

gin and Disney megastores. A **Madame Tussaud's Wax Museum** is promised for this area, and in addition to the sports-celebrity **All-Star Cafe** and the World War II canteen-style **Stardust Dine-O-Mat,** watch for a Las Vegas–style restaurant called, obviously, **Vegas,** and a magic-theme restaurant from frontman David Copperfield (now you see it . . .). Another famous "running clock" is the **National Debt Clock** above Sixth Avenue between West 42nd and West 43rd; watch how fast it mounts up. The **Times Square Brewery** offers pizza bagels and house-brewed beer with a second-floor view of the action. And if you watch the marquee outside **Cinema Ride,** one of those 3-D shows, you may see yourself among the models and billboards; there are hidden video cameras around the sidewalk.

Herald Square is named for the *New York Herald* newspaper building at West 34th just as Times Square was named for the *New York Times.* And just as Times Square isn't really square, Herald Square is actually a triangle. (You could call it the Daily District, too. Greeley Square, another triangle one block south at West 33rd, was named for *New York Tribune* founder Horace Greeley. And they say modern journalists only see one side of a story.) Herald Square was the very center of the venomous **Tenderloin,** a thriving red-light and speakeasy district that supplied and in many ways complemented the Theater District. It was partly the arrival of the expanding **Macy's Department Store** in 1901 that gave this area new respectability, and nowadays Herald Square is most famous for serving as the finale stage for Macy's annual Thanksgiving Day Parade and the arrival of Santa Claus.

The west side of this area has a florid past, though not much of it is left to be seen. From Ninth Avenue west from the 30s to the 50s is what is most often known as **Hell's Kitchen,** the territory of the Irish gang of the same name, but also sometimes called Paddy's Market or Clinton. (The Hell's Kitchen gang was not the only major ring operating in that area during the nineteenth century, which made the area even more of a battleground.) Nowadays the strip along Eleventh and Twelfth Avenues is mostly reduced to auto-body shops and a few X-rated theaters playing off (or off-off) the Broadway name. **Ninth Avenue,** however, particularly through the 40s, is a bazaar of small ethnic restaurants—Brazilian, Jamaican, Afghani, Peruvian, Greek, Turkish, Thai, and even Burmese, as well as the relatively tame Italian and Mexican. Not only are these some of the better restaurants in the Theater District, they're much hipper (where do you think the actors eat?) and a lot less expensive. But for pretheater class, try **Restaurant Row,** the block on West 46th Street between Eighth and Ninth Avenues, home to the Firebird, Orso, and Becco, among others.

Times Square is sometimes called "The Crossroads of the World," and it's also one of the major transportation crossroads of Manhattan: Several of the large subway transfer points, including 34th Street, Times Square, Rockefeller Center, 42nd Street, 49th Street, and Columbus Circle, are all in this zone, and so is the Port Authority Bus Terminal. Penn Station is just to the south on 32nd Street; the Lincoln Tunnel runs west from West 38th. And the western edge of the zone is the unlovely but essential West Side Expressway.

North of the Javits Convention Center and Lincoln Tunnel, near Pier 86 at the foot of West 46th Street, is the popular **Intrepid Sea-Air-Space Museum** (245-2533).

■ Zone 9: Midtown East ■

This zone is for many tourists the heart of Manhattan: It includes the **Rockefeller Center** (632-3975), **Radio City Music Hall** (247-4777), and the great shopping boulevard of *Fifth Avenue;* many of the city's most famous restaurants and such famous hotels as the Waldorf-Astoria, New York Palace, St. Regis, Algonquin (where you can still have a drink in the Rose Room and imagine the wits of the 1920s gathered around you), Four Seasons, and Plaza. The **Museum of Modern Art** is here on West 53rd between Fifth and Sixth (708-9480), across from the **American Craft Museum** (956-6047) and a block from the **Museum of Television and Radio** on West 52nd (621-6600). (CBS Inc., the infamous **"Black Rock,"** is that monolith overshadowing the museum at Fifth and 52nd.) There is even a miniature free branch of the **Whitney Museum of American Art** in the Philip Morris building on Park Avenue across from Grand Central with a sculpture garden and rotating exhibits from the main collection (878-2453).

This is also a living coffee-table book of monumental architecture. Among its landmarks are the Beaux Arts **Grand Central Terminal** at 42nd and Park Avenue, currently being lovingly cleaned (look up at the constellations winking in the ceiling and the mythological gods and goddesses on the southern facade) and gloriously joined to the **Helmsley Building** entranceway on the north side of Park; the gleaming, Buck Rogers–ish art deco **Chrysler Building,** with its stainless steel "grill" crown and hood-ornament gargoyles saluting the spirit of the automotive age (Lexington at 42nd); the Mies van der Rohe–designed **Seagram Building** on Park Avenue between East 52nd and East 53rd Streets, seemingly plain amid such architectural extravagances but elegant in its bronze and glass; the equally startling glass razor of the **Lever House** on Park at 54th; the literally gilded palace—now part of the New York Palace and Le Cirque Restaurant—that was the **Villard House** on Madison between 50th and 51st Streets; the almost Disneyesque Gothic Revival **St. Patrick's Cathedral** on Fifth at 50th, the largest Catholic cathedral in this country; and the almost reticent but powerful **United Nations** complex, a perfect architectural metaphor, on the East River at 43rd Street (963-7713).

Rockefeller Center itself is a landmark, a total of 19 art deco buildings between Fifth and Seventh Avenues and 48th and 51st Streets, clustered around the famous plaza-cum–ice rink and including the eternally youthful Radio City Music Hall, with its Rockettes and classic revivals. Its facades are virtual museums of sculpture, bas-relief, gilding, mosaics, carvings, and molding; during the Great Depression, construction of the original 14 buildings kept a quarter of a million laborers and artists busy.

The **Diamond District** is right next door, along West 47th Street between Sixth and Fifth, wall-to-wall and mall-to-mall shops hawking earrings, rings, and pins. It almost seems to bounce its lights upward toward the **Rainbow Room** (632-5000), which has a bird's-eye view of the skyline from the 65th floor of the tallest building of Rockefeller Center—and in fact, the Diamond District dates from almost the same era, when the Jewish merchants of Europe began fleeing the increasingly restrictive anti-Semitic laws.

The **Church of the Incarnation** (689-6350) on Madison Avenue at East 35th is modest on the outside, but its art collection—Tiffany stained glass window, Saint-Gaudens and Daniel French sculptures, and so on—is anything but modest. More obvious, perhaps, is the gold-leaf dome atop **St. Vartan Cathedral** on Second Avenue between East 34th and East 35th, but then it is the seat of the Armenian Orthodox Church in the United States. The Byzantine **St. Bartholomew's** on Park at East 50th is truly byzantine: part James Renwick, part Stanford White. St. Patrick's is the Gothic giant, but **St. Thomas'** just up the street at Fifth and 53rd is stubborn as a little David (757-7013).

The **New York Daily News Building** on 42nd and Second Avenue was used as the scene for the *Daily Planet* in the successful *Superman* movies, and there's an inside joke to that: The building has its own "planet," a huge revolving globe, in the lobby. Across the street is **Tudor City,** Henry VIII–style apartments, restaurants, shops, and services built in the 1920s as a sort of early urban renewal project.

The **Japan Society** on East 42nd between First and Second Avenues (832-155) offers changing exhibits of antique scroll paintings, textiles, ceramics, arms, and antiques as well as lectures and exhibitions; it also has a traditional Japanese garden.

This wasn't really "good" territory until well into the twentieth century. From Fourth Avenue (before it was called Park) east to the river lay stockyards and slums; there were railroad yards between Lexington and Madison, where Grand Central is now, and the gashouse, glue factories, prisons, workhouses, and asylums were all on what is now Roosevelt Island in the East River. In fact, what seems to be a pretty series of gardens down the center of Park Avenue actually covers the remnants of the railroad tracks.

Consequently, there aren't a lot of old neighborhood names attached to this part of the island; even so, there are still stretches of fine brownstones between Third and Second and even some particularly fine old apartment buildings nearer the East River. **Sutton Place,** the southernmost section of York Avenue that runs between East 54th and 59th, was yet another, though later, London-style development aimed at the first families, and various of the Morgans and Vanderbilts in their turn lived here (the residence of the U.N. Secretary-General is there now).

You may also see references to **Murray Hill,** the prosperous residential area (and now the site of many luxury hotels and apartment buildings as well) from about East 34th to about 41st between Third and Madison Avenues. (Some guides place Murray Hill as far south as the mid-20s.) Legend has it that Mary Murray invited General Howe to tea in 1776, knowing he would be far too polite to refuse, and thus bought Washington time to escape up the island to Fort Tryon. Just on the east side of Third Avenue is **Sniffen Court,** a beautifully preserved mews of ten Romanesque Revival houses, built about 1850, at 150–160 East 36th Street.

On the other hand, Fifth Avenue along the 40s and 50s was the site of huge palaces during the Gilded Age, half a dozen belonging to the Vanderbilts alone and nearly as many to the Astors. (See the history section earlier in this chapter.) One of the greatest of those old mansions is now a fine museum: the magnificent **J. Pierpont Morgan Library** at 36th and Madison (685-0008), which houses an unparalleled collection of illuminated medieval manuscripts, rare books, etchings, musical scores, and prints. Fifth Avenue may not be "Millionaire's Mile" anymore (unless you're paying the American Express bill after a shopping tour of the 50s), but looking up toward Central Park and the avenue's climax at Grand Army Plaza, with its fountain and equestrian statue of Sherman, you can stroll up the avenue feeling like a million.

■ Zone 10: The West Side ■

The West Side above the Theater District had never had much identity of its own until fairly recently. There was some port trade—the big cruise ships and liners still use piers in the lower 50s—and some hotel and theater spillover, but not of the better sort. In the early part of the twentieth century it was a respectable if not particularly fashionable district, populated first by Jewish immigrants who gradually prospered and moved out of the Lower East Side and later by middle-class blacks, who began to be pushed out again by Puerto Rican immigrants and blue-collar white families from Hell's Kitchen. But with the creation of **Lincoln Center for the Performing Arts**—which involved the demolition of San Juan Hill, the Hispanic neighborhood in the West 60s, and the degenerating middle-class houses around it, exactly the area portrayed in *West Side Story*—businesses began to return. (For more on Lincoln Center, see Part 6, "Entertainment and Nightlife.")

The southwest corner of the zone is **Columbus Circle,** where Broadway, Eighth Avenue, and West 59th/Central Park South come together. The lumpish Coliseum-looking thing is, in fact, the **Coliseum,** a convention and sometimes exhibit hall. Columbus Circle in general, which should be a natural showplace, has been the site of repeated redevelopment schemes, debates, and abortive designs for many years now. The massively renovated **Trump International Hotel** (née the Paramount Building, née Gulf & Western), with its mini-mall and chic eateries, is the latest and so far most successful attempt to revitalize the circle and is now a tourist attraction in itself.

Lincoln Center and its associated plazas and annexes pretty much take up the area from Columbus Avenue (the extension of Ninth Avenue, remember, not Eighth) and very nearly Broadway to Tenth Avenue between West 62nd and West 66th Streets. The campus of **Fordham University** is just to its south, and the **School of American Ballet** and **Juilliard School of Music** are associated with the Lincoln Center complex, so the neighborhood is spotted with small cafes and shops that attract students and culturelovers, as well as several health clubs and gymnasiums.

The main branch of the **Museum of American Folk Art** (977-7170) is in what is called Lincoln Square, within the Lincoln Center confines on Columbus Avenue between West 65th and 66th. It specializes in textiles, furniture, and decorative arts from the eighteenth century, with particularly nice quilts and frequent lectures and demonstrations.

And if you ever wondered who or what "Tammany" really was, it, or rather he, was actually Tamanend, an Indian chief who supposedly befriended William Penn. The New York society, incorporated in 1789, was originally a Masonic-style social organization with a Native American twist: 13 "tribes"—to salute the 13 colonies—and pseudo-Indian ceremonies and titles. If you look up at the weathervane in the museum atrium, you will see old Tamanend, looking sadly into the future, which would only associate his name with corruption.

The **Hotel des Artistes** on West 67th Street at Central Park West was actually constructed as artists' studios, with its two-story spaces designed to take advantage of the daylight (and exterior sculptures for inspiration), but now these are highly prized apartments. Noel Coward, Rudolph Valentino, Alexander Woollcott, Norman Rockwell, Isadora Duncan, and Howard Chandler Christy all lived there; Christy, fortunately, rather than Rockwell, did the murals of romantic nudes in the popular **Café des Artistes** (877-3500) in the lobby.

There are a few buildings in the neighborhood that will catch your eye. The towered apartment buildings along Central Park West mostly date to the 1920s, when building regulations allowed greater height in return for at least partial light (which is why so many New York skyscrapers have those angled or pointed tops).

The pretty Art Nouveau building at West 64th and Central Park West is the home of the **New York Society for Ethical Culture** (874-5210). The apartment on Central Park West at the southern corner of **West 66th** is the one transformed by the proto-Zoroastrian evil spirit in *Ghostbusters*. The **Spanish and Portuguese Synagogue** on the corner of West 70th Street at Central Park West, though built (with Tiffany windows) only in 1897, is home to the oldest Jewish congregation in the city, dating to the arrival in 1654 of fugitives from the Inquisition; it still adheres rigorously to Sephardic ritual (by appointment; 873-0300).

■ Zone 11: The East Side ■

This is arguably the most beautiful area of Manhattan, fashionable and prosperous almost from the very beginning and, like the dowager of a good family, remarkably well-preserved. It is an area of apartment houses open only to true millionaires (and not always open to them, either); of the most expensive of boutiques, art and antiques houses, elegant hotels, private clubs, and old-line restaurants, churches, and educational institutions.

The riverfront was the original draw; it was an in-town "beach" and resort area in the early nineteenth century before bridges made travel to the outer boroughs common. The wealthy (who still lived firmly downtown) built summer homes all the way up the East River to what is now Harlem, boating up- and downtown, taking carriages along the Boston Post Road (Third Avenue) and later the El. A huge entertainment complex called Jones's Wood filled the whole stretch east of the Post Road from near what is now the **Rockefeller University/Cornell University Medical Center** neighborhood in the 60s north to John Jay Park at East 76th; it offered genteel bathing facilities, theatrical entertainments, a beer garden, and parade grounds.

The apartment buildings on the East Side broke ground in several ways;

they were so large that even families with whole staffs of servants might share them. (And nowadays, several families can fit within the various subdivisions of one formerly palatial apartment.) The new luxury townhouses had elaborate bathrooms, not just water closets. They were fully electrified, not just refitted. And of course they had the immense swath of Central Park for their front yard. Those that had to settle for views of Madison Avenue or Park Avenue offered elaborate lobbies and exterior detail instead: look at the outside of the building on the corner of **East 66th Street and Madison.**

Once Caroline Schermerhorn Astor—the same Mrs. William Astor whose feuding with her nephew remarkably produced the Waldorf-Astoria Hotel—actually moved all the way up Fifth Avenue as far as 65th Street, the last great millionaires' migration began. Several of their mansions are still visible, including the **Frick Collection,** home of steel boss Henry Clay Frick, on Fifth at East 70th Street; the extravagant Second Empire **Lotos Club** on East 66th just off Fifth Avenue, former home of pharmaceutical tycoon and civil rights activist William Schieffelin; and the onetime **George T. Bliss House** on East 68th just off Fifth Avenue, which has four giant columns for just one little overlook. No wonder Fifth Avenue became the semi-official parade route, with its blocks of balconies like reviewing stands along one side and the peoples' part on the other.

The Beaux Arts home of banker Henri Wertheim on East 67th just off Fifth is now the **Japanese Consul General's residence.** The side-by-side 1890s French Renaissance homes of Oliver Gould Jennings and Henry T. Sloane are now the **Lycée Français** on East 72nd Street between Fifth and Madison Avenues. What is now the **Explorer's Club** on East 70th between Madison and Park was built for Stephen Clark, owner of the Singer Sewing Machine Company, patron of the Metropolitan Museum of Art, and founder of the Baseball Hall of Fame in Cooperstown. The Venetian Revival home of Edwin Berwin, who had the coal monopoly for American warships, is now an apartment building at **Fifth and East 64th.** And the neo-Tudor **Lenox School** on East 70th between Lexington and Third Avenues was originally the home of Stephen Brown, head of the New York Stock Exchange. Astor's own home was torn down to make room for the partially Romanesque, partially Byzantine, and Astorially opulent **Temple Emanu-El.**

Hunter College has one of the most enviable locations in town, around Park Avenue between East 68th and 69th Streets. Hunter's community center is the **Sarah Delano Roosevelt Memorial House**—or, rather, houses— on East 65th between Park and Madison; FDR's mother famously commissioned these twin townhouses, one for herself and one for the newly married Franklin and Eleanor, with a single entrance and various connecting doors.

It was in the fourth-floor front bedroom that FDR endured his long bout with polio, and Eleanor the almost equally paralyzing domination of her mother-in-law.

Among smaller museums of note in this area are the **Abigail Adams Smith Museum** on East 61st Street between York and First Avenues, named for—but never occupied by—the daughter of John Quincy Adams. She and her husband were the landowners, at least; they originally planned to built a country estate there called Mount Vernon in honor of George Washington, under whom William Smith had been a colonel. But they had to sell the land in 1799 without getting much farther than building the stone stable (later an inn) that is now the museum. It has been furnished in the Federal style, given a period garden, and stocked with antiques; and especially for children, the tour (by costumed members of the Colonial Dames of America, which maintains the house) is pretty interesting.

The **Asia Society,** housing the collection of John D. Rockefeller III, is on Park Avenue at East 70th Street. If you enjoy more commercial art, the **Society of Illustrators** at 128 East 63rd east of Park Avenue exhibits graphic arts, illustrations, classic and modern award-winning book jackets, and so on. The **New York Women's Exchange** on Third Avenue above East 64th is more than a century old, one of those cooperatives designed to help women make money from their handicrafts, and it's still an interesting source of crafts and gifts.

The **Seventh Regiment Armory** on Park between East 66th and 67th, where many of the city's major art and antiques exhibits are held, looks like a oversized sand castle, but the inside, if you can see past the wares of the fairs, was furnished by Louis Comfort Tiffany.

Among other buildings with strange histories is the one at **131 East 71st Street** between Park and Lexington; it was built during the Civil War, but designer Elsie de Wolfe redid the facade in 1910 as a sort of silent advertisement of her own style. The **Knickerbocker Club** building on East 62nd at Fifth Avenue used to have a twin next door; it was famous as the home of Mrs. Marcellus Hartley Dodge, a Rockefeller cousin, who rather sadly filled her five-story mansion with all the stray dogs she could rescue. Next to it is the **810 Fifth Avenue** building, onetime home to William Randolph Hearst, Richard Nixon, and Nelson Rockefeller—penthouse, bomb shelter, and all.

Madison Avenue is now more commercial than residential, but oh, what commercialism! (For more on the shopping opportunities on Madison Avenue, see the "Great Neighborhoods for Shopping" section in Part 9.)

The **Queensboro Bridge** is the one referred to by the groovy-feelin' Paul Simon, and many New Yorkers, as "the 59th Street Bridge." Incidentally, though **Roosevelt Island,** a few football fields offshore in the East River, is now a residential community, it once held a rather exciting assortment of institutions—lunatic asylums, smallpox hospitals, workhouses, poorhouses, and prisons; it was almost the dark reflection of the wealth of the East Side. (It was once called Welfare Island, as a matter of fact, but of course that word isn't P.C. anymore.) There are a few historical buildings left, including a lighthouse; and the **Roosevelt Island Aerial Tramway,** a 250-foot-high sky ride, crosses over from Second Avenue and 60th Street about every 15 minutes (832-4543).

■ Zone 12: The Upper West Side ■

As suggested in the "Very Short History" section of Part 1, development of the West Side was the stepchild of the Gilded Age. It required the daring of a few developers and the construction of the El up Ninth Avenue to persuade middle-class and professional Manhattanites that it was worth living above Midtown. On the other hand, because the land was a better bargain, many of the apartment buildings and brownstones were more gracious and seemed to have more elbow room. Broadway, in particular, has a European boulevardlike spaciousness in this area. Nowadays, it is a popular area for relatively affluent professionals, studded with restaurants, especially along Columbus Avenue.

In its heyday, Riverside Drive was the Fifth Avenue of the West Side, with mansions gazing out over their own Frederick Olmsted greenery, Riverside Park, instead of Central Park and with the Hudson River beyond that. Only a few of the old buildings remain, although Riverside Drive itself is still residential; look for the turn-of-the-century **Yeshiva Chofetz Chaim,** the former Isaac Rice home, at West 89th for an example.

It was the construction of the **Dakota** on Central Park West at 72nd Street, the first luxury apartment building on the Upper West Side, in the 1880s that sparked a development boom. Designed by Plaza Hotel architect Henry Hardenberg and commissioned by Singer Company heir Edward Clark (see Zone 11), it is still probably the most famous apartment building the city, used as the movie setting of *Rosemary's Baby* (Boris Karloff is said to haunt the building) and now, unfortunately, best known as the home and assassination spot of John Lennon.

Once the Dakota was in place, other developers hastened to get in on the act, and this resulted in such other extravagances as the Beaux Arts **Dorilton** at West 71st and Broadway; the **Alexandria** on West 70th, with its hieroglyphic detailing, monsters, and rooftop pharaohs; and the Belle Epoque **Ansonia Hotel** on Broadway at West 74th, which attracted such musical eminences as Toscanini, Caruso, and Stokowski. William Randolph Hearst was originally satisfied with the view of the top three floors of the 12-story **Clarendon** on Riverside Drive and West 86th, but after a few years he decided he needed the whole thing and bought it out. He kept it for 25 years.

The block of West End Avenue between West 76th and 77th Streets is an intact group of Victorian townhouses from 1891; another intriguing group is the red and white townhomes on West 78th Street between Columbus and Amsterdam Avenue built in 1886 by Grand Central Oyster Bar mason Raphael Gustavino.

The stretch of **Central Park West** between West 75th and West 77th is a historical district, dating from the turn of the century. The double-towered **St. Remo** between 74th and 75th is a little younger, finished in 1930, but it has its pride; this is the co-op that turned down Madonna, though several other famous actors and musicians do live here. The same architect, Emery Roth, topped himself by giving the **Beresford** at West 81st Street three turrets a few years later.

One of the oddest corners is a little gated mews off West 94th Street near West End Avenue known as **Pomander Walk;** though built in 1921, it looks just like a movie set of old London or maybe Stratford-on-Avon — and in fact, it was modeled after the stage set of a popular play of the time called *Pomander Walk.* So it sentimentally attracted such tenants as Lillian and Dorothy Gish and Humphrey Bogart.

Although the Upper West Side can't rival the East Side's "Museum Mile," it does have some popular attractions. The **New-York Historical Society** building on Central Park West between West 76th and West 77th houses an eclectic collection ranging from American-made fine silver and decorative arts to original prints for John J. Audubon's *Birds of America,* Hudson River School painters, furniture that marches through the building in chronological order, and Gilbert Stuart's portrait of Washington. (The society was founded in 1804, and in its youth, "New-York" apparently sported a hyphen.)

The **Museum of Natural History,** newly refurbished and riding the crest of dinosaur fever, faces Central Park from West 77th Street to 79th. **The Hayden Planetarium** at 81st Street is undergoing a renovation of its own that will keep it closed until at least 1998. The **Children's Museum of Manhattan,** one of the city's first institutions to go heavily into interactive exhibits, is on West 83rd Street between Broadway and Amsterdam Avenue.

Symphony Space, which is a cult location both for its Bloomsday marathon readings of *Ulysses* every June 16 and its 12-hour free spring musical marathon of classical and American music, is on Broadway at West 94th Street.

■ Zone 13: The Upper East Side ■

This is the heart of "Museum Mile," that fantastic array of museums and collections ranging 20 blocks, from the **Metropolitan Museum of Art** at 82nd Street (535-7710) past the **Guggenheim** (423-3500), the **Museum of the City of New York** (534-1672), the **National Academy Museum** (369-4880), and the **Cooper-Hewitt National Museum of Design** (860-6868), among others.

Like the rest of the East Side, it didn't really hit its stride until about a century ago, when the Fourth Avenue railroad became Park Avenue and the Met, as the Metropolitan Museum is almost universally known, had acquired a reputation rivaling the great collections of Europe (and when conditions in Midtown, increasingly crowded, middle-class, and noisy, made these "inner suburbs" more desirable). Like the area to the south, it is studded with the onetime homes of the wealthy; the French Renaissance **Jewish Museum** on Fifth Avenue at East 92nd (423-3200) was once the home of financier Felix Warburg, and the **Cooper-Hewitt** on East 91st at Fifth Avenue was originally Andrew Carnegie's home (he asked for something "modest and plain"). The National Academy Museum at 89th was Archer Huntingdon's home. (Many of the facilities along Museum Mile are detailed in Part 11.)

The shortest of strolls will be enough to show you what real wealth bought 80 or 90 years ago. The current headquarters of the **Commonwealth Fund** at East 75th and Fifth was built for an heir to a Standard Oil fortune; the Renaissance Revival mansion at **25 East 78th Street** and Madison Avenue was built for a railroad president. New York University's **Institute of Fine Arts,** down the block on 78th at Fifth, is housed in what was once the home of American Tobacco founder James Duke and was copied from a chateau in Bordeaux. And around the corner on Fifth Avenue between 78th and 79th Streets is the **French Embassy,** once the home of finance icon Payne Whitney.

Consider the single block of East 91st Street between Fifth and Madison Avenues. Facing the Cooper-Hewitt at No. 1 East 91st is the **last palace of "Millionaire's Row,"** built for banker Otto Kahn and now a convent school; at No. 7 is the **Burden House,** the home of a Vanderbilt shipping heiress who married a Burden steel scion and a prominent society rental site (the spiral staircase, centered under a stained-glass dome, was known as "the stairway to heaven." And next to that, at **No. 9,** is the house where jazz record producer John Hammond was "set up" by his wife's old-society family.

One of the ex–Mrs. Vanderbilts commissioned the French Revival mansion at **60 East 93rd Street** between Park and Madison. Flashy Broadway figure and party boy **Billy Rose** was a millionaire of a lesser sort, perhaps, but he lived well enough to build a great Scottish-romantic mansion of his own across the street at No. 56 (now an alcoholism treatment facility). Even the **Synod of Bishops of the Russian Orthodox Church outside Russia** across the street was once a private home, the mansion of banker George Baker; its collection of icons is a must-see for devotes of Byzantine and Eastern Orthodox art (by appointment only; 289-4645).

The **block of East 80th Street** between Lexington and Park also has three mansions lined up one after another, built for a Whitney (No. 120), a Dillon (No. 124), and another Astor (No. 130).

If these mansions start to overwhelm you, go east. **Gracie Mansion** (570-4751), the official residence of the major of New York and original home of the Museum of the City of New York, is in **Carl Schurz Park** overlooking the East River toward (what else?) Astoria at East 88th Street. Its name salutes Scottish immigrant Archibald Gracie, who built a summer home here back in 1799, although an earlier house is known to have been destroyed during the Revolutionary War. It has only been the mayor's residence since the days of Fiorello La Guardia—like Lincoln Center, it was the brainstorm of Parks Commissioner Robert Moses. And compared to the competitive glories of the Upper East Side's millionaires' mansions, it still has a summery, relaxed beauty.

There are other famous cultural sites on the Upper East Side not shoe-horned in along "Museum Mile." The **92nd Street Y** (427-6000), as the Young Men and Women's Hebrew Association there is commonly known, is famous for its concerts, readings, and lectures by national and international as well as local artists and writers. The original **Playhouse 91,** home of the Jewish Repertory Theater, is on East 91st between First and Second (831-2000).

And there's a little less familiar architecture as well. The newly repolished **Whitney Museum of American Art** (570-3600), too aggressively modern for Museum Mile, juts out in an inverse pyramid over Madison Avenue at East 75th Street. The **Russian Orthodox Cathedral of St. Nicholas** at East 97th and Fifth is like the whole Kremlin squashed together, with five onion domes and multicolored tile detailing—Moscow on, if not the Hudson, at least the East River (by appointment only; 289-1915). The **Islamic Center of New York** on Third at East 96th Street is the spiritual home to the city's Moslems (there may be as many as half a million); it was computer-measured to ensure that it faces directly toward Mecca.

A few old-time neighborhood nicknames persist. **Yorkville** is what used to be New York's Germantown but is now just as much black and Hispanic as European, running nearly the length of the Upper East Side from Lexington Avenue over to the river. Carl Schurz, for whom the park surrounding Gracie Mansion is named, was a German immigrant who became editor of the *New York Post* and *Harper's Weekly* and, after the Civil War, secretary of the interior. **Hell Gate** was not a gang hangout but the spot where the Harlem River and Long Island Sound converge into New York Harbor—perhaps a hellish spot for river pilots. **Carnegie Hill,** which ranges from the Cooper-Hewitt (formerly the Carnegie mansion) at 91st Street north atop off the boutique and cafe area of Madison Avenue, is a rapidly upscaling residential neighborhood.

■ Zone 14: Columbia University and Harlem ■

If one were an artist, especially an Afrocentric one, a new "profile" of the island of Manhattan might suggest itself—rough, to be sure, but as plausible as most poster art—as an Egyptian pharaoh. The main part of the island would be his head (they didn't advertise themselves as having much nose, anyway), the lower third would be one of those false beards they wore, and Zones 14 and 15, the Heights and Harlem, would be the high, curveaway crown.

The Heights, though often overlooked by tourists, are filled with important educational institutions, historical sites, and beautiful churches and museums and nineteenth-century houses. And Harlem, of course, is both New York's proudest and poorest black neighborhood: onetime center of a cultural renaissance and on the verge of becoming one again, but also the area with the highest death rate among young black men in the nation. East Harlem runs with an almost official harshness into the Upper East Side at 97th Street, despite the extension of "Museum Mile" up to **El Museo del Barrio** on 104th. Whole rooms from John D. Rockefeller's onetime mansion at Fifth and 51st Street have been moved to the **Museum of the City of New York** on Fifth at 103rd; and three of that in-town home's formal gardens are now the **Conservatory Garden** facing the City Museum in Central Park. (The namesake greenhouses have been taken down, but there is still a famous "Secret Garden" there.) But walk across 103rd to the east, and you'll find yourself in an area Rockefeller wouldn't have stabled horses in.

There are real "heights," or at least ranges of hills, that stand between the Upper West Side and such western neighborhoods as Morningside Heights (between about West 110th and Martin Luther King Boulevard); Hamilton Heights, also known as Harlem Heights, centered on City College of New York and running up to around Trinity Cemetery at West 155th Street; and Washington Heights above that (see Zone 15). The Heights run about four blocks west from the long green of Riverside Park;

Harlem (and East Harlem, as the area beyond Fifth Avenue is called) runs to the East River and up alongside the Harlem River, an area of nearly six square miles.

Morningside Park, a sort of comma between Central Park and Riverside Park, opened in the late nineteenth century and almost immediately became an enclave of scholars and theologians. **Columbia University,** whose campus ranges from about 116th Street to 124th from Morningside to Riverside Drive, is the heart of this neighborhood, with **Barnard College,** the **Union Theological Seminary,** and massive **Riverside Church** on its western flank and the extraordinary and still-growing **Cathedral of St. John the Divine** to the south. Strolling the Columbia campus in particular is restful, with its long lawns, the neoclassical Low Library building, the vaulted St. Paul's Chapel, and so on. (Tours are conducted irregularly from the library; call 854-4900.)

Riverside Church, at 122nd Street, was another of John D. Rockefeller Jr.'s gifts to the city, a 21-story Gothic beauty inspired by the cathedral at Chartres; its carillon of 74 bells is the largest in the world (one weighs 20 tons by itself), and the 22,000-pipe organ is one of the largest. The art inside salutes a more modern selection of "saints" than usual, among them Florence Nightingale and Booker T. Washington. It even has its own little theater. It also offers a spectacular view of the river and the city from the observation deck off the bell tower, nearly 400 feet high. Free tours are offered following Sunday services, about 12:30 p.m. (222-5900).

And if you want to know who's buried in **Grant's Tomb,** walk through Riverside Park to that mausoleum on the hill. (The answer, incidentally, is both Grant and his wife.)

Washington National Cathedral has been completed at long last—after nearly 90 years—but the **Cathedral Church of St. John the Divine** on Amsterdam Avenue at 112th Street (316-7540), begun in 1892, is still only two-thirds complete.

A block up Morningside Drive at West 114th Street is a more intimate chapel, the **Eglise de Notre Dame.** It contains a replica of the grotto of Lourdes where young girls saw visions of the Virgin Mary; a woman who believed her son was healed there had the replica constructed in thanks.

If you drew a line extending Central Park West (Eighth Avenue) past Cathedral Parkway, which runs along the northern border of Central Park, and on up into the Heights where Eighth Avenue is called Frederick Douglass Boulevard, it would be a very rough estimate of the western edge of **Harlem.** In fact, **Hamilton Heights,** which has several beautiful blocks of row houses along Convent Avenue between about 141st and 145th Streets, was a highly desirable neighborhood for both turn-of-the-century white and early-twentieth-century black residents, when it was nicknamed **Sugar Hill** and housed such jazz celebrities as Cab Calloway, Duke Ellington, and Count Basie. The current **Hamilton Heights Historic District**—so named because the area was once the country estate of Alexander Hamilton—is centered on four blocks of finely preserved row houses, many of them now residences of City College (CCNY) faculty and administrators. (Hamilton's 1802 house, which has been moved to 287 Convent Avenue, is currently closed for historic renovation.) The **watchtower** just south of CCNY on Amsterdam at 135th Street and the gatehouses at 113th and 119th Streets are remnants of the old aqueduct system.

And speaking of remnants: **Our Lady of Lourdes Church** at 142nd Street and Amsterdam is a true miracle of salvage, having been put together in 1904 from bits of the old National Academy of Design at Park and East 23rd Street, the A. T. Stewart department store on the old Ladies' Mile, and the former Madison Avenue apse of St. Patrick's Cathedral, removed to make room for what is now the Lady Chapel.

At the top of Hamilton Heights are **Trinity Cemetery** and **Audubon Terrace,** which face each other across Broadway between West 153rd and 155th Streets. This whole area was once part of the estate of John James Audubon, and the naturalist himself, along with many of those whose names appear repeatedly in these pages—Astors, Schermerhorns, Van Burens, and Clement Clarke Moore—are buried at Trinity Cemetery. (Audubon's gravestone is, appropriately, carved with birds.)

Several institutions of more specialized interest are gathered at Audubon Terrace, including the **American Numismatic Society** (234-3130), with its internationally famous collection of stamps and coins, and the **Hispanic Society of America** (926-2234), a little-known museum with a fantastic collection of Spanish art by Goya, El Greco, Velázquez, and so on, as well as ceramics and antiques; the equestrian figure atop the bronze memorial in the Terrace is the medieval Spanish hero El Cid. And the **American Academy of Arts and Letters,** which mounts periodic exhibitions featuring the works of the members, is also here (368-5900). This might be a good place for groups with different interests; the pretty little **Church of Our Lady of Esperanza** is another attraction. Audubon Terrace is a sort of family affair itself; Architect Charles Pratt Huntington designed the buildings, his philanthropist cousin Archer Huntington donated most of the money and the bulk of the Spanish art collection, and Charles's wife, Anna Hyatt Huntington, sculpted the Cid. (The Museum of the American Indian used to be here too, until it moved into the Custom House downtown.) This isn't even the only Huntington museum. Archer Huntington donated his private home on Fifth Avenue for the National Academy Museum and School of

Fine Arts (see Zone 13), and Anna created a sculpture of Diana that still stands in the foyer there.

Although Harlem is generally thought of as a black area, it is actually a mix of African American, Caribbean, and Hispanic (particularly Puerto Rican) families. East Harlem is often referred to as **El Barrio,** Spanish for "the neighborhood," or **Spanish Harlem.** However, in recent years, a growing Cuban/Caribbean community has flourished along Broadway north of Hamilton Heights as well.

In any case, Harlem certainly began as a black neighborhood; it was the first African slaves, in fact, imported by the Dutch, who blazed the original Broadway by moving up the island to Nieuw Haarlem in 1658. And while most of the area was taken up by the large farms and country estates, the East and Harlem riverfronts were an inevitable ramshackle assortment of immigrants and watermen. It was a popular upper-middle-class suburb for most of the nineteenth century, with its own commuter rail system, the New York and Harlem Railroad, to carry businessmen back downtown; but around the turn of the century, things began to go sour. Businesses went bankrupt, buildings emptied, and the continual northward press of development from the wealthier sections of Manhattan drove black and immigrant families into many of the poorer areas.

By the early twentieth century, Harlem was the major community for blacks with all levels of income. The famous Harlem Renaissance of literature, music, and philosophy had a powerful effect on both high art and popular culture, raising Harlem's profile and giving greater force to the growing civil rights debate. Yet in turning the area into a sort of tourist attraction for white Manhattanites, the great jazz halls and speakeasies such as the Cotton Club and Sugar Cane Club may have fostered the very sense of separateness the Renaissance had hoped to overcome.

Despite the predations of time, poverty, and unimaginative urban renewal, many old brownstones are still visible in such areas as the **Mount Morris Park Historical District,** a Victorian enclave that was dominated by German-Jewish families "moving up" from the Lower East Side. It covers about five blocks between Lenox Avenue and Marcus Garvey Park (formerly Mount Morris Park) between West 119th and 124th Streets. The fire tower in the park dates from 1856. **St. Martin's Episcopal Church** at Lenox and 122nd has a fine carillon of its own, about 40 bells strong.

A couple of blocks northwest of the park are the **Studio Museum of Harlem,** west of Lenox Avenue on 125th Street (864-4500), a small but select collection of African, African American, and Caribbean fine arts that also offers lectures and educational programs; and the famed **Apollo Theater** on West 125th between Adam Clayton Powell and Frederick Douglass

Boulevards (864-4500), founded as a vaudeville house in 1914 and the major showcase of black talent well into the 1960s. It has been revived, and the Wednesday Amateur Night tradition is as strong and lively as ever.

From here it's only a block's walk to **Sylvia's,** a soul food restaurant so famous that its gospel brunch is on many Harlem tours; it's located on Lenox between West 126th and 127th Streets (996-0660). Then head straight up Lenox to West 135th and the **Schomburg Center for Research in Black Culture,** the largest library of African and African American cultural and sociological materials in this country (491-2200).

On West 138th Street between Lenox and Adam Clayton Powell Avenue is the **Abyssinian Baptist Church,** equally famous as the onetime pastoral seat of Powell himself and for its gospel choir; its Sunday services draw busloads of tourists from all around the world (862-7474). The blocks of West 138th and 139th from Adam Clayton Powell Avenue over to Frederick Douglass constitute the **St. Nicholas Historic District,** another group of late-nineteenth-century homes designed by several different prominent architects of the day. The neighborhood is also known as **Striver's Row** because it drew a pre-yuppie-era group of ambitious young professionals.

At the top of St. Nicholas Park at West 141st Street is the famous **Harlem School of the Arts,** which has come to rival the New York High School for the Performing Arts (the model for the school in *Fame)* for the quality of its music, dance, and theater classes (926-4100).

If you like walking, you can fairly easily follow the path we've laid out from Marcus Garvey Park back to Harlem Heights. Sadly, although conditions are improving, we still cannot recommend that you wander other parts of Harlem by yourself, especially after dark; it's best to stick to the most famous sites, take cabs, or hook up with a tour group.

If you are particularly interested in contemporary black theater, you may also wish to contact the **Frank Silvera Writers' Workshop** at West 125th and St. Nicholas (662-8463) and the small but prestigious **National Black Theater** at Fifth and East 125th Street (722-3800).

■ Zone 15: The Heights ■

The area north of Trinity Cemetery and Audubon Terrace, called Washington Heights, was the area to which Washington's troops retreated—the Morris-Jumel Mansion served as his headquarters—during the early battles of the Revolutionary War, and it centers on Fort Tryon Park. While the park's official highlights are the remaining defiant bulwark and its overlook, the 62-acre park offers a far finer overview of Manhattan's original beauty, the Hudson River and the fine woods and animal life; and it serves as a natural approach to the stunning Cloisters collection of the Met. And even if you don't consider Washington's survival a miracle, as many historians do, there is another miracle associated with this zone—that of the St. Frances Cabrini Chapel.

The **Morris-Jumel Mansion** at West 160th Street and Edgecrombe (923-8008), which dates from 1765, is one of the very few colonial buildings still standing in New York. It was a summer estate—its grounds stretched from Harlem to the Hudson—belonging to Roger Morris, a prominent Loyalist who had served as aide to General Braddock. Morris refused to act against his former colleague (and rumored rival for the hand of the wealthy Mrs. Morris), but even so, his estates were confiscated by the revolutionary state government, and the Morrises returned to England. Washington did in fact sleep here and briefly used it as a headquarters; so, ironically, did Sir Henry Clinton, the British commander. The "Jumel" part is equally intriguing: French-Caribbean Creole merchant Stephen Jumel bought it in 1810 and lavishly remodeled it with the help of his socially ambitious wife, Eliza; she allegedly slept her way through much of New York society, let her husband bleed to death so as to make her a very rich widow, and then married the ruined, aging Aaron Burr—only to divorce him on his deathbed. Among her furniture is a "dolphin" chair said to have been purchased from Napoleon.

Fort Tryon Park, which runs from Broadway to Riverside Drive between West 192nd and Dykeman Streets, is only part of the original Billings estate; the massive series of arches on Riverside Drive was the "driveway." It was landscaped, like most of New York's great parks, by Frederick Law Olmsted, and it has an incredible assortment of views and gardens. The effect is immediately visible and almost shocking as you get off the A Train at 190th Street; although they have not yet been fully restored, the stone terraces down the hillside and the arched entrance to the park seem to bound a different world, a medieval one; it couldn't be a better setting for the Cloisters. Its various paths and roadways (watch out for buses) are popular with joggers and exercise walkers but rarely crowded. There is a marker, a bit of remaining battlement, on the hilltop of the park that recalls the defense of Fort Washington from the British. (A little gatehouse, down the slope from the marker, has been turned into a nice little cafe, good for a break.)

The Cloisters (923-3700) is actually the medieval-collection arm of the Metropolitan Museum of Art (you can use the same admission badge to enter both on a single day), and it is actually constructed of several medieval French and Spanish cloisters. This is one of New York's premier attractions, gloriously evocative and frequently nearly deserted. Astonishingly, the estate that is now Fort Tryon Park, the Cloisters buildings—painstakingly transported from Europe and reassembled here—as well as the Palisades across the Hudson River and the art and manuscripts of the collection itself were all gifts of the blessedly philanthropic John D. Rockefeller Jr.

Almost at the other end of the spectrum is the **Shrine of St. Frances X. Cabrini** on Fort Washington Avenue at 190th. Mother Cabrini, as she is usually called, is the patron saint of immigrants, and her remains (with the exception of her head, which is actually in Rome) are encased within the altar. The miraculous story here is that shortly after her death in 1917, a blind child was touched with a lock of her hair and received sight; naturally, he entered the priesthood. Mother Cabrini was the first American citizen to be canonized, but since she was Italian by birth, Mother Elizabeth Seton can honestly claim to be the first American-born saint (see Zone 1).

A few blocks from the Cloisters at Broadway and West 204th Street (304-9422) is the **Dyckman House,** the only surviving eighteenth-century Dutch farmhouse (ca. 1783) on the island, authentically fitted out and surrounded by a smokehouse and garden.

Other sites of interest in Washington Heights include **Yeshiva University,** the oldest Jewish seminary in the country, founded in 1886 (at West 186th Street and Amsterdam Avenue); and the **High Bridge,** the oldest footbridge (and sometime aqueduct) between Manhattan and the mainland. Begun in 1839, it stretches across the Harlem River from Highbridge Park at West 174th Street to West 170th in the Bronx. And if your children have read *The Little Red Lighthouse and the Great Gray Bridge,* head to Fort Washington Park at about West 178th Street and you'll see the **lighthouse** just below the eastern tower of the George Washington Bridge.

■ Zone 16: Brooklyn ■

Brooklynites have good reason to resent all those jokes about accents and Coney Island culture. Even if it seceded from the rest of New York City, Brooklyn would be the nation's fourth largest city, with enough famous landmarks, museums, and resorts to make it a long weekend's destination of its own.

Start by walking across the Brooklyn Bridge itself, which offers one of New York's best viewpoints in all directions. Fulton Ferry Landing is the site of Bargemusic (see Part 6, "Entertainment and Nightlife"), and beyond that is the **Brooklyn Heights Historic District.** Ranging from the riverfront Expressway to about Atlantic Avenue, this area is an amazing pre–Civil War enclave of more than 600 churches and homes (including those of Walt Whitman, Arthur Miller, W. H. Auden, Thomas Wolfe, and Truman

Capote). **The Promenade,** along the East River, has a spectacular view of Manhattan and a marker for Four Chimneys, where Washington billeted during the War of Long Island. The **Brooklyn Historical Society,** which spotlights local heroes ranging from the Brooklyn Dodgers to *The Honeymooners,* is in the historic district at Pierrepont and Clinton Streets (call (718) 624-0890).

Brooklyn's population has always been a vital ethnic mix, but these days it has replaced Manhattan as the real melting pot: Its many distinct communities include Caribbean (especially Jamaican and Haitian), Middle Eastern and Arabic, Scandinavian, Russian, Polish, Orthodox Jewish, and Italian. Many famous neighborhoods and destinations—not just Coney Island but also Brighton Beach and Rockaway Beach, Flatbush, Brooklyn Heights, Prospect Park, and Jamaica Bay—are in this 75-square mile borough. (Incidentally, be careful not to confuse the Broadway in Brooklyn with the Broadway in Manhattan; Brooklyn's runs southeast from the Williamsburg Bridge.)

The most important neighborhood for first-time visitors is the area around **Prospect Park,** at the junction of Eastern Parkway and Flatbush Avenue (call (718) 965-8900). This, the Central Park of Brooklyn—designed by the same men, Frederick Olmsted and Calvert Vaux, and with similar facilities and features—includes a children's zoo, officially the **Prospect Park Wildlife Conservation Center** (call (718) 965-8999), that is even larger than the more famous Bronx facility; an **antique carousel** as fine as Central Park's and rescued from Coney Island; a mid-nineteenth-century Italianate villa; and a skating rink and croquet shed designed by Stanford White. It even has its own cemetery, a Friends (Quaker) burial ground where Montgomery Clift is interred.

The northern boundary of the park adjoins the **Brooklyn Botanic Garden** grounds, which then lead over to the **Brooklyn Museum of Art,** a collection nearly as comprehensive as the Metropolitan's but far more comprehensible. On weekends and holidays, a free trolley links these three major attractions. And serving as a grand foyer to it all is **Grand Army Plaza** at Plaza Street and Flatbush Avenue: Olmsted and Vaux's grand oval, with its triumphal Soldier's and Sailor's Arch and a monument bust of JFK.

In addition to these sites, Brooklyn has several other attractions of particular interest to families. At the closer end are the **Brooklyn Children's Museum** (call (718) 735-4322), actually only another few blocks away from the parks we just discussed; and the **New York Transit Museum** (call (718) 330-3060), a little east of the Brooklyn Heights Historic District, a former subway station that now houses a fine collection of vintage cars, signal equipment, old photos, drawings, and subway mosaics that served as directions for the illiterate and non-English-speaking immigrants.

At the southern end of the borough is the famous **Coney Island** amusement park, somewhat less lustrous than in its heyday as "the world's largest playground" but still good for a stroll along the boardwalk, a ride on the teeth-rattling wooden Cyclone roller coaster, and an original Nathan's hot dog; and the **New York Aquarium** (call (718) 265-3400), with its shark tank, Sea World–style whale and dolphin "theater," and hands-on Discovery Cove. And even farther east is **Jamaica Bay Wildlife Refuge Center,** a ten-mile stretch of beach near Rockaway that is a migratory marker for more than 300 species of birds. Park rangers lead hikes on weekends (call (718) 318-4340). The park even has its own subway stop at Broad Channel.

The **Brooklyn Academy of Music** (BAM) on Lafayette near Fulton Street (call (718) 636-4100), as mentioned in Part 6, is not only a respected concert venue and home of the Brooklyn Philharmonic but also has its own opera house, the restored and aptly named Majestic Theater a block down Fulton Street, and several smaller performance spaces. As the BAM boosters like to point out, its history is every bit as lustrous as Broadway's: Bernhardt, Booth, Pavlova, Rachmaninoff, Sandburg, Churchill, and Caruso all performed here. Its October Next Wave Festival is extremely popular.

■ Zone 17: Queens ■

Queens offers another example of a fine day's sight-seeing, since most of what a visitor is likely to want to see is at **Flushing Meadows–Corona Park,** especially if you figure in the Mets' **Shea Stadium,** also used as a concert venue, and the **U.S. Tennis Association**'s complex, where the U.S. Open is held. Here is Queens's main public park, with its own rowboat lake, ice rink, bike rentals, and so on, and frequent special events (call (718) 760-6600); it was the site of two World's Fairs (1939–40 and 1964–65) and is still home of the New York Hall of Science, the **Queens Wildlife Center** (call (718) 271-7761), and the Queens Museum of Art. It's a world unto itself—that is, the 350-ton Unisphere globe, created for the 1964 World's Fair, still stands at the entrance. And this world, too, we owe to Robert Moses, who dredged out what had been a notorious swamp and rubbish pile to make a place worthy of an international exhibition.

The **New York Hall of Science** (call (718) 699-0005) was originally constructed as the science pavilion for the 1964 World's Fair but is scrupulously and often astonishingly up-to-date; it has interactive video stations that store outer-space transmissions, super-TV-sized microscope displays, and scores of hands-on demonstrations of light, music, color, and physical properties.

If Brooklyn's Museum of Art is like a miniature Metropolitan, the **Queens Museum of Art** (call (718) 592-9700) is like a miniature New

York. It houses a huge and detailed scale model (1 inch to 100 feet) of New York called the Panorama that was also constructed for the 1964 World's Fair and updated in the early 1990s. It has almost 900,000 individual buildings, and airplanes that actually "take off" from La Guardia.

Astoria, the northwest part of Queens (the part that faces the Upper East Side across the East River), is home to the **American Museum of the Moving Image** at 35th Avenue and 36th Street (call (718) 392-5600) and the **Isamu Noguchi Garden Museum** on 22nd Street near 43rd Avenue (call (718) 784-3390). The Noguchi museum, one of the few collections in the world devoted to one man's work, fills 12 galleries with his celebrated lamps and theatrical sets, and a gorgeous sculpture garden displays his larger pieces.

Astoria's famous Greek ethnic community is second in size only to that in Athens itself; it is packed with restaurants, delicatessens, bakeries, and gift shops. Just stroll Broadway in the 30s and follow your nose.

■ Zone 18: The Bronx ■

There was a time when this was rich woodlands, then farmland (it was the estate of Dutch farmer Jonas Bronck); it was genteel country estate territory in the nineteenth century; and even into the early twentieth century it was a prestigious address. Sadly, at this point in history those northward waves and ripples of alternating prosperity and decay have left it in a slough. However, there is revived interest in the area, and some philanthropic and government funding is coming in for restoration.

Its most famous attractions, of course, are the **Bronx Zoo** (formally, the International Wildlife Conservation Park), the **New York Botanical Garden,** and **Yankee Stadium,** the House that Ruth Built—and when you come out of the subway at 161st Street, you'll see why the old Yankees-Dodgers contests were called "subway series": You can see right into the stands from the tracks.

The Grand Concourse, which is the great boulevard of the Bronx, runs right up toward the botanical garden. The garden and the Bronx Zoo are neighbors, more or less, although there is a bit of a walk between the respective entrances. Both are near the campus of **Fordham University.**

The **Edgar Allan Poe Cottage** (call (718) 881-8900) at Grand Concourse and East Kingsbridge Road is where Poe and the dying Virginia lived from 1846 to 1848, and it houses many of his manuscripts and memorabilia.

Toward the northern edge of the Bronx (and of the subway lines) are several historical estates, most notably the **Van Cortlandt House Museum** in Van Cortlandt Park (call (718) 543-3344), a restored mid-eighteenth-century mansion used by Washington as one of his headquarters (there was skirmish fire in the yard) and furnished with authentic period Dutch and American pieces as well as Delft ceramics. On the east side, Van Cortlandt Park adjoins **Woodlawn Cemetery** (call (718) 920-0500), where the wealthy (Woolworths, Macys, Goulds, Belmonts, Armours, etc.) built eternal homes as elaborate as their temporal ones; get a map at the Webster Street entrance.

A few blocks west of Van Cortlandt Park is **Wave Hill,** the former estate of financier/conservationist George Perkins and at various points home to Theodore Roosevelt, Mark Twain, Arturo Toscanini, and so on. Take one glimpse of its view, over the Hudson River toward the Palisades, and you'll see why. The mansion itself is now used for concerts (in the vaulted Armor Hall), art exhibits ranging from sculpture to topiary, and demonstrations; the gardens and grounds are also open.

Although it requires a little more logistical forethought, those interested in sailing and whaling might want to visit **City Island** just off the northeast shore of the Bronx, a community of sailing vessels, boatyards (including the manufacturers of several America's Cup champs), and marinas. It is also home to the small but intriguing **North Wind Undersea Institute Museum** (call (718) 885-0701), which has a whale jaw for an entry arch and tanks where the police seals—real underwater animal officers, not navy divers—rehearse their rescue and retrieval skills.

▪ Zone 19: Staten Island ▪

"I'll take Manhattan / The Bronx and Staten Island, too . . ." Staten Islanders could be forgiven for sometimes feeling as if they were an afterthought, famous primarily as the turnaround point for the Staten Island Ferry. In fact, Staten Island would still be part of New Jersey if the Duke of York hadn't put it up as a prize in a sailing contest in 1687. It wasn't even connected to any other borough until 1964, when the Verrazano Narrows Bridge between Staten Island and Brooklyn opened; it's the world's longest suspension bridge and still the only actual point of contact. And Staten Islanders have repeatedly voiced enthusiasm for breaking away from the rest of New York; a 1993 referendum on secession passed by a 2-to-1 vote.

Despite this apparent sense of independence, or perhaps because of it (too much progress can be a short-sighted thing), Staten Island is the site of several very old structures that might be worth an excursion, especially for families interested in American history. (For information on the ferry, see the section on Zone 1.) And while it's a little farther south than most tourists usually get, the **Greenbelt** (call (718) 667-2165), or more formally High Rock Park, is nearly three times the size of Central Park—an outdoor paradise one could scarcely envision from the rusty environs of the ferry terminal.

The 28-building **Snug Harbor Cultural Center** at Richmond Terrace and Tysons Street (call (718) 448-2500) was founded in 1801 as a home for aging sailors and served as one, at least in part, for nearly 150 years. Now converted to an arts center (the visitors center has listing of current exhibitions), it still has several fine Greek Revival structures dating to the 1830s. The oldest, Main Hall, with its seafaring-themed stained glass, is now the **Newhouse Center for Contemporary Art** (call (718) 273-2060). Snug Harbor is also the site of the **Staten Island Children's Museum** (call (718) 273-2060), which emphasizes performances as well as science, and the **Staten Island Botanical Garden,** with its lush orchid greenhouse and the brand-new traditional Chinese scholar's garden, built by local contractors with the assistance of 40 craftsmen from Suzhou (call (718) 273-8200).

Overlooking the Narrows a little north of the Verrazano Bridge is the **Alice Austen House** on Hylan Boulevard at the Bay (call (718) 816-4506), a long, low, gracious cottage built in 1710 and named for the prominent nineteenth-century photographer who lived most of her life here. Her more than 3,500 photographs of the evolution of New York life went almost unnoticed, and at the age of 84, having lost everything in the stock market crash, she had to move into the poorhouse. But only a year later, she and her work were "discovered" by *Life* magazine, and she was able to spend her last years in a nursing home. Her photos are exhibited in the house on a rotating basis.

Historic Richmond Town (call (718) 351-1611) on Clarke Avenue south of the Staten Island Expressway is even older, at least in part. It includes 29 buildings, about half of them open to the public, in a restored "village" something like a Williamsburg of the north. Among the open structures is the 1695 Voorlezer House, the oldest elementary school in the country; the 1839 Bennet House, now called the Museum of Childhood (see the toy room); and the 1840 General Store–cum–post office. Like Williamsburg, it is populated by costumed craftsmen and artisans who give demonstrations and sell reproductions as souvenirs in the Historical Museum gift store.

Thanks to a recent spate of movies and celebrity campaigns, there is increasing interest in Tibetan culture, and one of the few museums of Tibetan art is the **Jacques Marchais Center** ((718) 987-3500) at 388 Lighthouse Avenue, not far from Historic Richmond Town. "Marchais" was actually Asian art dealer Mrs. Harry Klauber, who built this replica of a Himalayan temple to house her private collection of Buddhas, religious artifacts, and other contemplative figurines. There are even life-sized stone Buddhas in the garden.

Central Park and Other Green Spaces

$\mathbf{A}$s great cities go, New York is still young: brash, mercurial, simultaneously bursting out of its seams and shooting its cuffs. But that it early on considered itself the equal of any European capital is evident from its sweeping avenues and the long rise of Central Park, a project whose design and construction fascinated and eventually captured the imagination of people from every social class in the city. In fact, an early proposal to put it on the old Jones's Wood site (see the section on Zone 11) was furiously shouted down as being too niggardly and peripheral.

Ultimately, the construction of the park—the original construction, setting aside later additions—took 16 years. It covered almost 850 acres and required 5 million tons of fill dirt and rock (not counting the glacial rocks and schist that already stick up all over the park) and another 5 million trees, increasing the number of hardwood species from about 40 to more than 600, and more than 800 kinds of shrubs and bushes.

Its recreational facilities are particularly rich, including 22 separate playgrounds as well as the famous skating rink, and so on (for more information, see Part 8, "Exercise and Recreation"). It has concessions stands and real restaurants, but there is an almost inexhaustible supply of other family attractions, plus long stretches of theme gardens, performance venues, and many miniparks, within the overall park. And that doesn't even count people-watching, picnicking, or sun-bathing.

When Central Park was begun, or rather, when the first attempts to clear the squatters and renderers out of the rather fetid area were begun, Frederick Law Olmsted wasn't even a landscape designer; he was a journalist. But he was fascinated by the concept of a European-style commons, or "Greensward," as he called it, and backed by fellow writers Horace Greeley, William Cullen Bryant (who had been one of the first to inveigle against consuming development), and Washington Irving, he successfully applied to become superintendent of the park. A year later, in partnership with his friend Calvert Vaux, who was an architect and landscape professional, he secured the designer's position as well.

They did not always agree. Olmsted wanted no reservoirs or museums or structures of any sort beyond arches and bridges; Vaux himself designed most of the bridges, as well as the original Metropolitan Museum of Art building. Olmsted was far more exercised about blocking the construction of the Sheepfold, a haven for the flock that grazed what is still called the Sheep Meadow, but it was pushed through by Tammany Hall's Boss Tweed (it's now the Tavern on the Green restaurant). Nor did Olmsted and Vaux like the idea of monuments, though the park now has close to 100 busts, plaques, statues, and memorial gardens. What he would have said about the World War I–era proposal to put an airfield in, one can only imagine.

■ "New York's Backyard" ■

Central Park ranges nearly 50 blocks, from Central Park South (59th Street) to Central Park North (110th), and fills three avenues, from Fifth to Eighth. It is crossed from east to west in only five places, at roughly 65th, 72nd, 79th, 85th, and 99th Streets—"roughly" both because most of the transverse roads have pleasant curves rather than gridlike rigidity and because vehicular traffic is prohibited during the middle of the day and all weekend.

Several of the most famous children's attractions are in the southernmost segment of the park, including **Wollman skating rink,** the **Zoo** (officially the Central Park Wildlife Conservation Center), and the **Carousel.** The Carousel (879-0244), a 1908 model with 58 hand-carved horses, is just south of the 65th Street transverse and about midway across. It was moved to Central Park from Coney Island in 1951, replacing a far less attractive merry-go-round. Back in the nineteenth century, real horses, on a treadmill beneath the carousel gazebo, pulled little carriages around.

Looking north, the **Dairy** is to the right of the Carousel, closer to Fifth Avenue. The twin-peaked shed is now the main visitors center (360-1333), though when the park opened it was a real milking operation, with sweetly costumed milkmaids and its own pet herd. Urban Park Rangers (427-4040) sometimes lead tours of the park from here. The **Chess and Checkers House,** a gift of financier Bernard Baruch, is on a rock just southwest of the Dairy. And beyond that, across Center Drive, are **Heckscher Playground** and the **softball fields,** which pretty much fill up the southeast part of this section to Columbus Circle.

The Pond, a reed-edged sanctuary filled with ducks and other wildlife, is curled up near Grand Army Plaza in the literal shadow of the St. Moritz and Helmsley Park Lane hotels. You can sometimes see the Plaza Hotel reflected in the water, which is only fair, since it was onetime Plaza owner

Donald Trump who became impatient with the city's long and cantankerous campaign to restore Wollman Rink and did it himself. On the other hand, before Wollman Rink was built at all, the pond was twice the size it is now; that may be appropriate for a Trump development, too.

The frontispiece of the zoo, near where East 64th Street runs into Fifth Avenue, is the **Arsenal** building (360-8141), which originally earned its cannon, but in the years since it was built in 1851, it has been a weather station, a police station, a menagerie, the original Museum of Natural History, and finally, fittingly, the Manhattan headquarters of the Parks and Recreation Department. The original Olmsted-Vaux plans for the park are exhibited here. The **Zoo** itself (861-6030) is only ten years old; it was built when the parks department found new homes for the animals that were too large for such a crowded facility and constructed more contemporary, eco-sensitive settings for the animals it did keep. The monkey house is now a real jungle gym, the bats have an eternally nocturnal home, and the reptiles have a swamp that is almost a pre-Olmsted joke. Free tours daily at 2:30 p.m. and weekends at 10:30 a.m. as well.

(Don't just check your watch; check out the **Delacorte Clock** by the zoo entrance. Every 30 minutes, a bronze menagerie of musical animals appears to peal out nursery rhymes.)

Just above the 65th Street Transverse, almost to Central Park West, is the elaborate **Tavern on the Green** restaurant, with its famous conservatory-style Crystal Room and the quainter upstairs dining rooms and lounge, still reminiscent of a sheepfold's loft. The **Sheep Meadow** is the 15-acre green alongside the Tavern, and nearby is the **Bowling Green,** where top-ranked competitive collegiate and professional croquet teams still play (360-8133).

Just to the right of the Sheep Meadow and Bowling Green, running just about down the middle of this second rung of the park's ladder, is a popular **roller-skating strip.** And on the other side of that is **the Mall,** an unusually formal section of the park designed by planter Ignaz Anton Pilat, who worked under Olmsted and Vaux; it features a promenade of elms, which formed a sight line of 10 blocks all the way up to Belvedere Castle atop Vista Rock. Unfortunately, the bandshell there, the second on the site, is no longer used; summer concerts are now held on the adjoining playground, **Rumsey Field,** which, in case you need a good meeting point, is the one with the statue of Mother Goose.

Facing the old bandshell across Terrace Drive (the 72nd Street transverse) is **Bethesda Terrace,** a fountain setting at the edge of the lake that offers a grand view of the Ramble on the other side. The statue atop the fountain represents "The Angel of the Waters," from a story in the Gospel of John that says the touch of an angel gave healing powers to Bethesda pool in Jerusalem. **The Lake,** which is about one-third of the way up the park, is the second largest body of water in the park, pinched together in the middle and crossed by Vaux's 60-foot-high cast-iron **Bow Bridge.** (Vaux meant that it tied the lake up like a bow, but it also tends to suggest a rather lopsided bow tie.)

In the northeast corner of the Lake is **Loeb Boathouse** (517-2233), with its Venetian gondola and rowboat rentals and indoor-outdoor **cafe.** A little beyond Loeb toward Fifth Avenue is an unconnected, smaller lake called **Conservatory Water,** where the Kerbs Model Boathouse houses the miniature yachts that race every Saturday afternoon in summer. Nearby are the statues of the **Mad Tea Party** from "Alice's Adventures in Wonderland" and **Hans Christian Andersen;** Andersen's only permanent audience is a bronze bird, but his memorial is the gathering place for storytime on Saturdays at 11 a.m.

To the west of Bethesda Terrace is the **Cherry Hill** overlook, which offers a view of the Mall, the Lake, and the Ramble; beyond that, between the southernmost little finger of the Lake and the West 72nd Street entrance, is **Strawberry Fields,** Yoko Ono's simple but beloved memorial to John Lennon; it looks across to the Dakota apartments, where he was assassinated. The mosaic pathway, reading "Imagine," was a gift from the city of Naples, Italy; and the "peace garden" includes plants from 161 nations.

North of the Lake is **the Ramble,** still one of the nicest and quietest parts of the park and a haven for birds and bird-watchers alike; more than 250 species have been spotted here, many of which migrate along the Atlantic flyway. The Ramble is 37 acres of woods and wildflower gardens, stretching pretty much from the Lake up to the 79th Street transverse, with a small brook tumbling down tiny waterfalls. On the western shore of the lake at about 77th Street is the Ladies Pavilion.

Across from the Ramble, in the middle of the 79th Street transverse, is **Vista Rock** and its crowning glory, **Belvedere Castle,** a somewhat smaller but impressive replica of a Scottish stone castle—turrets, terraces, and all— that was just meant to be part of the decor back in Olmsted and Vaux's day. Today it houses the **Central Park Learning Center** (772-0210), a branch of the National Weather Service that has information on wildlife and whose roof offers a splendid view of the park. West of the castle near Winter Drive are the **Swedish Cottage** (988-9093), a marionette theater originally built for the Philadelphia Exposition of 1876, and the **Shakespeare Garden,** a sort of Bard-lover's botanical Bartlett's; all the trees and flowers planted around the pools are mentioned in his works.

Visible across Belvedere Lake to the northwest is the **Delacorte Theater,** the 2,000-seat site of the popular summer Shakespeare in the Park shows, named for publisher George Delacorte, who also donated the animal-fair clock at the zoo and the Mad Tea Party sculpture. In fact, he is said to have been the model, somewhat exaggerated, for the Mad Hatter himself.

Visible to the northeast is **Cleopatra's Needle,** actually built by Thutmos III in 1600 B.C.E., despite its popular nickname. The obelisk and its twin were presented by the Khedive of Egypt to the city of New York and to Queen Victoria in 1881. Translations of the hieroglyphs, which have been nearly eradicated by twentieth-century pollution, are engraved on plaques donated by that Cleopatra lover, moviemaker Cecil B. DeMille. Beyond Cleopatra's needle, along Fifth Avenue from East 81st to 84th, is the **Metropolitan Museum of Art.** And the great green oval in the center of the park from Belvedere Lake nearly to the 85th Street transverse is the **Great Lawn.**

At least, now it's a lawn. It started out as a reservoir; it was the site of Central Park's Hooverville, as the Depression-era shantytowns were called, and later was used as an athletic field. Most recently, resodded and regraded, it has been the venue for several famous concerts, including Simon and Garfunkle's 1981 concert, which drew a crowd of half a million; the even larger "No Nukes" show a year later; and Pavarotti's recital in 1993. It is also where the Metropolitan Opera and the New York Philharmonic stage their summer concerts.

The 85th Street transverse is geographically the waistline of the park. Above it is the 106-acre **reservoir,** by far the largest of the park's half-dozen bodies of water, which takes up most of the area between the 85th and 97th Street transverses. It dates back to the original Croton reservoir system of 1862 and was in active use until only a couple of years ago. The remaining corner of this section, northwest of the reservoir, is where the tennis courts are.

North of the 97th Street transverse are the large **North Meadow** and smaller **East Meadow,** which even for some city dwellers seems to be the end of the park. However, there are more gardens and even some historic sites above about 105th Street. The **Conservatory Garden,** actually three formal gardens (and no conservatory building) that were once part of the Rockefeller Mansion in Midtown, includes a "Secret Garden," with an appropriate statue of Dickon and Mary; the entrance gate, also from the Rockefeller estate, is on Fifth Avenue at 103rd. (Even stranger, it lies almost at the foot of the Museum of the City of New York, at the top of which are rooms from the same Rockefeller home.)

Behind the Conservatory Garden is **the Mount,** which is now bare but once held a tavern (later a convent!) from which Washington's men held off the British. It looks down on **McGowan's Pass** at East 106th Street and beyond the pass to the former site of a pair of 1812 forts (now identified by markers only). Look for the blockhouse below East Drive (about West 109th Street) south or the Adam Clayton Powell Boulevard entrance.

At the opposite end of the park from Wollman Rink is **Lasker Rink,** another ice-skating rink—a wading pool in summer. Unlike Wollman, this one's free (534-7639).

Finally, at the top of the park beyond the **Harlem Meer** lake is **Charles A. Dana Discovery Center** (860-1370), once the boathouse and now the newest outpost of the Urban Park Rangers, particularly dedicated to environmental issues.

■ Other Green Corners of the City ■

Perhaps only cities with elbow-crunching crowds really value open spaces. Like the most densely populated capitals of Europe and Asia, New York has, with revived resolution, maintained its squares and even established newer parks to give its residents and visitors respite from the noise and strife.

Among the most popular Manhattan hideaways is **Bryant Park,** behind the New York Public Library between Fifth and Sixth Avenues and 40th and 42nd Streets (that's poet and *Evening Sun* publisher William Cullen Bryant in bronze and Gertrude Stein in stone). It has its own restaurant, the Bryant Park Grill; public rest rooms; and a half-price/same-day Music and Dance Tickets booth.

Washington Square Park at the foot of Fifth Avenue in Greenwich Village is street theater (and dog society central) even when the summer troupes aren't out in force. Some of those game boards are for chess, and some are for go. There are **community gardens** behind the Jefferson Market Library in Greenwich Village (see Zone 4) and on the West Side between Amsterdam and Columbus Avenues from 89th to 90th Streets.

There are very urban sculpture gardens such as the **Abby Aldrich Rockefeller Sculpture Garden** at the rear of the Museum of Modern Art and the **Iris and G. Gerald Cantor Roof Garden** atop the Metropolitan Museum of Art.

The city also has several pass-throughs, such as **Fisher Park,** a precisely arranged connection of 54th and 55th Streets between Sixth and Seventh Avenues. It has a fountain, kitelike awnings, and benchlike pedestals around its trees.

Such mansion-turned-museums as the **J. Pierpont Morgan Library** and the **Frick Collection** have internal gardens.

When in doubt, however, head for the water. You could walk the entire western periphery of Lower Manhattan from Hudson River Park at the south end of TriBeCa down along the 1.2-mile-long waterfront promenade of Battery Park City to Battery Park and around to the Staten Island Ferry terminal. East Side Park runs from the Lower East Side up through the East Village to Gramercy Park; the United Nations gardens on First Avenue range from 42nd to 48th Streets.

Riverside Park is the anchor of a green swatch that goes up the Hudson riverfront from West 72nd Street with little interruption all the way to the Spuyten-Duyvil Creek.

And lest we seem to neglect the outer boroughs, as so many people do, we suggest you look up at the descriptions of Zones 16–19; no borough in New York is without a substantial public park and/or botanical garden, several of which rival Central Park in beauty and wealth of facilities.

PART EIGHT

Exercise and Recreation

Double Your Pleasure, Double Your Fun

A few years ago, it would have seemed silly to put a chapter on exercise in a vacation guide—particularly a guide to a city as famed for self-indulgence as New York. But most of us at the *Unofficial Guides* are into some form of aerobic exercise, if only as a matter of self-preservation. It reduces stress, helps offset those expense account and diet-holiday meals (no, it's not true that food eaten on vacation has no calories), and even ameliorates some of the effects of jet lag. Even more remarkably, we have discovered that jogging, biking, and just plain walking are among the nicest ways to experience a city on its own turf, so to speak; and we're happy to see that more and more travelers feel as we do.

Even more intriguingly, New York is a paradise for workout buffs, since the gyms and exercise clubs in this town are often on the front lines of alternative routines. If you've read about kickboxing aerobics or some other new style but you haven't seen a lesson offered in your hometown yet, this is the place.

One good thing about indoor workout gear is that is takes up relatively little room and, at least until that step class, may double as walking-about wear. Also, if you are staying in one of the ritzier hotels, such as the New York Palace, the fitness center may have T-shirts and even shoes you can borrow for your workout, thus lightening your load even more. And if you're caught short, there are certainly T-shirts and shorts to be had on the street, if not at the gym.

If you are an outdoor type, however, consider the seasonal weather that time of year when you're packing. In the summer months, when it can be not only hot but extremely humid, it's really a good idea to schedule exercise early in the day or in the first cool of the evening; those late-afternoon showers can make a nice difference. (On the other hand, insects prefer the cooler hours, too, so pack some bug spray—better yet, double up and get some of that sunscreen with repellent built in.) Holiday decorations can make for wonderful jogging in cold weather, if the sidewalks aren't slick; but again, it may be damp, so pack a weather-resistant layer. And remember that first-aid kit: We go nowhere without sports-style adhesive strips (get the flexible ones), ibuprofen or some other analgesic, petroleum jelly, and a small tube of antiseptic. And consider doubling your socks.

Chelsea Piers and Central Park

The redevelopment of the old Hudson River pier area between 17th and 23rd Streets into the **Chelsea Piers Sports and Entertainment Complex** may have cost millions, but it's sure bringing it back in now. Among its attractions are one of those Japanese multilevel golf driving ranges with 52 stalls and a 200-foot fairway—which, considering how crowded the courses are in the neighboring boroughs, is likely to be your best shot (336-6400); two outdoor roller rinks (336-6200) and two indoor ice rinks (336-6100); a huge field house with basketball, batting cages, gymnastics bars, and the like (336-6500); and a mega–workout club, the **Sports Center at Chelsea Piers,** with track, boxing ring, pool, 10,000-square-foot rock-climbing wall, and weight training areas (336-6000). Sports club passes are $31 a day; individual facilities such as the skating rinks charge about the same as Central Park ($4 adults, $3 kids, and $7.50 for skates). Spend the whole day: There's an Origins spa right next door for post-workout massages, sports manicures, and so on (336-6780), and a brewpub for rewards (336-6440).

Central Park is where all outdoor sports meet—and meet up with Frisbee football, softball, pick-up flag football, and the like. It can get so crowded, especially on weekends, that you'll welcome a little organizational support. For information on other areas to play, call the Manhattan Department of Parks and Recreation (360-8133). Look at the listings for the individual sports later in this chapter for associated clubs and phone numbers. Also read the description of Central Park in Part 7, "New York's Neighborhoods."

Within Central Park, just for starters, there are rowboats at Loeb Boathouse (517-2233), which is also where the bikes are; rock-climbing classes around 97th Street; a half-dozen baseball diamonds and four soccer fields; tennis courts; regulation croquet (the competitive game, not the backyard version) and lawn bowling near West 69th (360-8133); the Wollmer ice-skating/roller-skating rink; and a front nine of miniature golf, thanks to Donald Trump, near the Wollmer rink in summer.

There is even a bird-watching hotline that keeps up with unusual sightings and nestings (979-3070), and with more than 100 species hanging around, that can be a lot. We once thought we had caught a young man yelling obscure obscenities at a playground full of kids in the park; eventually we realized he was practicing bird calls.

Working Out

■ **Workout Clubs and Gyms** ■

As we've said, New York has such a body-conscious culture that you can try out almost anything—and since that world overlaps with the competitive business world, there are even 24-hour clubs where the most obsessive of networkers can go in the wee hours.

Among the hottest workout clubs—the ones always written up in fitness magazines—and some of their unusual classes are **The Sports Center at Chelsea Piers** (see above), which offers Michael Olajide's "Aerojump" interval training with jump ropes and kickboxing; the 24-hour **Crunch Fitness** clubs (404 Lafayette, 620-7867, and 54 East 13th Street, 475-2018), which offer the Brazilian martial arts/acrobatics/dance discipline called *capoeira* and funkaerobics, among other change-up routines, for $20 a day; **Equinox Fitness** clubs (344 Amsterdam Avenue, 721-4200, or 897 Broadway, 780-9300), whose menu includes E-Sculpt, a combination dance/yoga/body sculpting routine developed by star trainer Molly Fox, and spinning and aerojump classes for a $26 pass. There's even an ad-lib outdoor workout—part hike, part climb, part push-up. The **IP PowerStrike Studios** (496-1254), founded by aerobics pro Patricia Merno and black belt Ilaria Montagnani, also offers kickboxing classes. Somewhat more self-conscious trendies head for the **Reebok Sports Club** (160 Columbus Avenue; 362-6800).

Both Crunch and Equinox have developed their own lines of shampoos, moisturizers, and skin treatments, incidentally, designed to offset the special skin and scalp problems sweating and chafing can produce, so if you forget your own, you're in good hands.

Buffing is a particularly strong draw for gay New Yorkers, and the most gay-friendly gyms are toward the Village and Chelsea, among them the **YMCA** branch at 224 East 47th Street (756-9600), **McBurn** (215 West 23rd Street; 471-9210), **Better Bodies** (22 West 19th Street; 929-6789), and the **Chelsea Gym** (267 West 17th Street; 255-1150).

For more traditional swimming, racquetball, track, and so on, the big **West Side YMWCA** is the largest of the 19 branches, with two pools, basketball and volleyball, racquetball and squash, massage rooms, free weights, and so on for a $15 daily pass (5 West 63rd Street; 875-4105). Other popular branches are the **Midtown YWCA** (610 Lexington; 775-4500) and the **Vanderbilt YMCA** (224 East 47th; 756-9600), both also $15. Also check out the 92nd Street YMHA (1395 Lexington; 427-6000).

■ Walking ■

Considering how strongly we've urged you to do your touring on foot, you may have already guessed that we find not agony but ecstasy in the feet. We frequently walk 100 blocks a day in Manhattan (for pleasure as well professional scouting) and almost never choose even the subway over a distance of fewer than 20 blocks. It's almost impossible not to enjoy the sidewalks of New York, and it's unfortunate that many of its most beautiful sections, particularly downtown, have been so reduced to the tour-stop circuit that most tourists never ever experience it. If you go out a little early, say 7:30 or 8 p.m., before the sidewalks get so crowded, you can walk Fifth Avenue or Madison Avenue at a fairly brisk pace, too; but you'll have to deal with the traffic signals.

Of course, we walk pretty briskly. Many visitors will want to stroll more slowly, because they're busy looking, and keep their power-walking for another time. The most obvious walking area, of course, is **Central Park,** where you can either stick to the 7-mile Outer Loop or the 4-mile Middle Loop (from 72nd Street south) or the 1½-mile reservoir track; but it's even more fun to just take whatever asphalt trails attract you. You can't really get lost—some part of the outer world's skyline is almost always visible, and you'll come back across the main road several times—but there is always something new to discover that way: statues (have you found the Mad Tea Party yet?), lakes, ornate old bridges, gingerbread-trimmed buildings, the carousel, flower beds, dancing dogs, tiny transmitter-driven sailboats reminiscent of *Stuart Little,* chess players, stages, and so on. (For more on the layout, see Part 1 and the "Central Park" section of Part 7.)

You can even use the park as an "incidental" bit of exercise if you're going to any of the big museums along Fifth Avenue or Central Park West. Even the sidewalk alongside the park, which is flagstone, conveys an exhilarating sense of freedom.

Another popular park for walkers is **Riverside Park** on the Upper West Side between West 72nd and 145th Streets, so if you're really interested in seeing the natural sights, you can turn out of Central Park along the main crossroads at West 86th, 97th, or even at the top of park, 110th Street/Cathedral Parkway, and go four blocks to the Hudson and Riverside Park, which is another four miles long.

■ Running and Jogging ■

If you hadn't already guessed that Central Park was also runners' central, a quick glance will convince you. Central Park Drive, which has a dedicated lane, is about seven miles long, or you can come in halfway at 72nd Street and do the southern part of the loop for about four miles; the famous track around the Reservoir is just over a mile and a half. The road is closed to traffic from 10 a.m. to 3 p.m. every weekday (except, please note, during the holidays, when the traffic crush is too heavy), and all weekend, starting at 7 p.m. Friday. There are runners there at most any (daylight) hour, especially on weekends; feel free to join the pack. For group therapy, call the **New York Road Runners Club** (860-4455), or hook up with their regular runs: about 6:30 and 7:15 p.m. weekdays and 10 a.m. Saturdays and Sundays. Meet at the club at East 89th Street or catch up at the starting point, just inside the park at Fifth and 90th. Handicapped joggers can hook up with the **Achilles Track Club** for safe runs through Central Park (921-4495).

Another popular stretch for runners, as for walkers, is Riverside Park by the Hudson River, discussed in the preceding section. There is another two-mile stretch along the **Hudson Promenade** in the Village near the piers at the foot of Christopher Street; there's a track along the East River between the **Queensboro Bridge** and Gracie Mansion; and if you'd like a short but sharp and visually stunning interval run, take the mile-long **Brooklyn Bridge** over and back, and consider the view of the Manhattan skyline a reward for chugging that high curve.

■ Biking and Blading ■

New York has some of the most elaborate bike stores in the country, including **Metro Bicycle,** which will rent some of its models out for the day (360 West 47th and other locations; 581-4500), and **Pedal Pushers** (1306 Second Avenue, between 58th and 69th; 288-5592). If you're sticking with Central Park (a good idea, especially for newcomers), you can rent bikes right at the **Loeb Boathouse,** which is near East 74th Street. A few of the bike-tour organizers, such as **Bite of the Big Apple Tours** (603-9750), which lead two-hour rides through the lower part of Central Park, include bike rental in the $25 fee. Really experienced riders who prefer longer tours or races should contact the **New York Cycle Club** (242-3900).

Central Park is the place for recreational biking not only for its beauty but also because it has a designated biking/jogging lane that stretches for about seven miles. (See the preceding section, "Running and Jogging," for auto-free hours.) You must stick to the road, however; no impromptu mountain or trail riding allowed.

If you're more into blades, either ice or in-line, **Blades** has a half-dozen locations that teach, rent, and sell ice skates and rollers (they also equip you with protective gear). Among the most convenient locations are those at Columbus and Broadway at 72nd (787-3911); in the Village at Bleecker and Third (477-7350); at the Chelsea Piers development (336-6299); and at the Sky Rink itself at the Piers (336-6199). Blades also sponsors free clinics at the 72nd Street entrances, both East and West, weekend afternoons from April to October. The Achilles Track Club, mentioned in the "Running and Jogging" section, also escorts roller bladers through the park.

Central Park's **Wollman Rink** is open for in-lining in summer and, more famously, ice-skating in winter (517-4800); you can hear the music almost any time. You can rent skates for the rink ($6.50) or for the rest of the park ($15). Even more famous, of course, is the **Rockefeller Plaza** rink, also seasonal (757-5730), although you can't just take off into the city from there. For group skates and lessons, contact the **New York Road Skaters Association** (534-7858). **Sky Rink** at Chelsea Piers also offers lessons (336-6100) and a little pickup hockey as well.

If you are a serious blader, into the semiguerilla sorts of expeditions, contact the **Night Skates,** who meet at various sites around town, including Columbus Circle, Union Square, or skate shops (ask for information), and pick a route for the night. Also look over the biking and running routes mentioned in the preceding sections.

Other Recreational Sports

This is not a city where every hotel has its own **swimming** pool. In fact, only a handful do; so if lapping is your thing, check into Chelsea Piers, of course, or Asphalt Green, another of those we-do-it-bigger sports facilities. They have an Olympic-sized lap pool at York Avenue at 91st Street (369-8890; $15). Several of the national health club chains have reciprocal arrangements with Manhattan clubs, so ask your home club manager what he might have listed.

There are 30 Hard-Tru **tennis courts** in Central Park that you can get for $5 an hour, though you need a permit (280-0201) and you have to sign up on a first-come, first-served basis. Sheets go up on the half-hour for the next hour's slot. Riverside Park's clay courts are volunteer-maintained (do your part) and first-come, first-served. If you don't mind paying for your time, call Crosstown Tennis (114 West 31st Street; 947-5780) or the Tennis Club, which sort of overlooks Grand Central (15 Vanderbilt Venue; 687-3841). The Midtown Tennis Club has four courts inside and four outside (on the roof, which is a lot of fun); they range from $25 to $60 an hour (341 Eighth Avenue; 989-8572).

Horseback riding through the park is legendary, and so is the Claremont Riding Academy on West 89th, a couple of blocks from the park (724-5100). Rental is $35 an hour; the same amount buys you a 30-minute private lesson or one-hour group lesson.

You'll see **rock climbing** in Central Park—they call it Rat Rock, and it's near Fifth Avenue around 62nd Street—but if you want something tougher, drop $10 at the City Climbers Club (533 West 59th Street; 974-2250); ExtraVertical Climbing Center (61 West 62nd Street; 586-5718) or the Reebok and Crunch gyms mentioned above.

Pick-up softball, basketball, and **volleyball** are visible all over town, but the competition is really tough, especially when it comes to B-ball: Just watch a few minutes outside the cages at West Fourth and Sixth Avenue near Washington Square, famous as the original stomping grounds of Dr. J.

For more opportunities to join in, pick up the weekly sports handout in gyms and sports stores around town.

Virtual Sports

These aren't really "exercise" clubs at all, but playrooms; and a surprising number of adults as well as kids are addicts of these simulated, virtual, and all-season skip-the-exertion versions. (Okay, okay, some are pretty exciting.) In any case, they are important rainy-day or kids' options.

Lazer Park is right in Times Square (entrance at 163 West 46th; 395-3060) and offers some fairly lively games of Laser Tag (in a 5,000-foot arena maze) and Battletech, along with a flight-ride simulator, virtual reality sports and space-pilot decks, interactive arcade games, and up-to-date video games.

Xs New York is also in Times Square on Broadway between 41st and 42nd (888-XS2-PLAY), but it puts more emphasis on virtual and interactive play than on physical competition; it also has a 32-station cyber cafe for on-line addicts in danger of withdrawal; food; and very palpable stereo equipment. If jet lag or adrenaline has you going late, Xs is open until midnight, and until 2 a.m. weekends.

Hackers, Hitters, and Hoops (123 18th Street; 929-7482) is a little less relentlessly high-tech. It does have some virtual reality games, but it also offers hands-on padded play areas, batting cages, billiards tables, miniature golf, ski machines, and so on. And it has a large traditional sports bar with big-screen TVs for the old folks. Late hours, too.

Also see the description of the Empire State Building in Part 11, "New York's Attractions," for more simulated excitement.

Spectator Sports

New York's pro sports teams are legendary and seemingly legion. However, this is one time when "New York" means all five boroughs, and a little more. Both NFL teams, the **New York Giants** and the **New York Jets,** play "at home" at Giants Stadium in the Meadowlands of New Jersey—and frankly, tickets are almost impossible to get, unless you're visiting friends with connections (or you're willing to pay a high price to a scalper). Besides, unless your friends are also driving, you'll have to catch a bus from the Port Authority to the stadium. However, if you feel like making a stab at it, you can call the Meadowlands box office at (201) 935-3900. You can also see if there are any odd seats left with TicketMaster at (212) 307-7171 or check the newspaper classified ads for tickets or ticket resale packagers.

The more frankly named **New York/New Jersey MetroStars** also play their soccer matches at the Meadowlands, but tickets may be easier to come by. Ditto another NBA team, the **New Jersey Nets,** and the second area NHL team, the **New Jersey Devils;** call the box office or TicketMaster. The third NHL team, the **New York Islanders,** is actually in New York—Long Island's Nassau Coliseum—but farther out in Uniondale, and it takes both the Long Island Railroad (to Uniondale) and then a bus (N70, 71, or 72) to get there, so only fanatics need apply.

But you don't have to leave town to score. If you aren't lucky enough to live in an area where you can see baseball live, you have never seen base-ball. (And you'll never see baseball fans the way you'll see them in New York, for good or evil.) **Yankees Stadium**—the House that Ruth Built—is in the Bronx, though at the end of so easy a subway ride that going to a game there is on our list of recommended things to do. If you're stay-ing on the West Side, catch the C or D line; if you're on the East Side, get the No. 4 train. Both deliver you right to the 161st Street/Yankee Stadium station. Do not take a taxi; it's not only about 20 times more expensive, it might also take you five times longer to get there. Besides, you'd miss an essential part of the experience: joining the fan crowd. Call the box office at (718) 293-6000 or TicketMaster at (212) 307-7171. Get there early enough to wander around and check out the plaques beyond the outfield saluting Mickey Mantle, Babe Ruth, Lou Gehrig, Joe DiMaggio, and others. They used to be actually in play, flat in the turf, but cooler heads prevailed.

The **New York Mets'** Shea Stadium is in Queens—in Flushing Meadow, alongside the U.S. Tennis Association complex, where the U.S. Open is held. That stadium is also easily reached by subway. (Perhaps we betray an American League bias—okay, going to *any* baseball game is highly recommended.) To get to Shea, take the 7 line from the big 42nd Street station (Times Square) right to the Willett Street/Shea Stadium stop. You can quite possibly walk up and get tickets, but it might be better to call the stadium box office at (718) 507-8499 or TicketMaster at (212) 307-7171.

However, both the NHL **New York Rangers** and the NBA **New York Knicks** call Madison Square Garden home. Unfortunately, they have a pretty regular following, so tickets are problematic. Call (212) 308-NYRS for Rangers info, (212) 465-JUMP for the Knicks, or, you guessed it, Ticket-Master at (212) 307-7171. Hey, what's a monopoly for?

Even hotter these days is women's pro basketball, and the **WNBA New York Liberty** also tend the Garden; call TicketMaster.

Also at the Garden: the **Golden Gloves** boxing cards in January and February; the **National Invitational Tournament** college basketball championships in March; and the **Women's Tennis Association Tour championships** (what used to be known as the Virginia Slims Championship) every November. For any of these events, try the same numbers for the box office and TicketMaster.

The **U.S. Open** is held in the weeks leading up to Labor Day weekend at the U.S. Tennis Center in Flushing Meadow, and even with its new Arthur Ashe grandstand court, it's frequently a sell-out. (See the Mets listing for subway directions.) Unless you're already in the loop for finals tickets, they'll cost you a very close haircut, but earlier tickets may be around. Call the office at (718) 563-8957 for more information or check in with our friends at TicketMaster.

Horse racing has a long and aristocratic tradition in New York, and though the crowds may be more democratic these days, the thoroughbred bloodlines are as blue as ever. You can take the subway (Far Rockaway A) to **Aqueduct Stadium** in Queens from mid-October to May (for information call (718) 641-4700) or the Long Island Rail Road's Belmont Special from Penn Station to **Belmont Park** (call (718) 641-4700) from May to July and again from Labor Day to mid-October. (In between, the very old-style racing circuit moves upstate to hallowed Saratoga Springs.) The Belmont Stakes, the third jewel of the Triple Crown, is the first or second Saturday in June.

If you prefer harness racing, the standardbreds wheel around **Yonkers Raceway** Mondays, Tuesdays, Fridays, and Saturdays year-round; for race information call (718) 562-9500. For that, you'll have to catch the Liberty Line's BXM4C bus from Madison Avenue at 39th Street (for schedule information call (914) 682-2020).

PART NINE

Shopping in New York

Keeping Your Eyes on the Prize
(and the Price)

It may seem almost redundant to talk about a shopping guide to Manhattan. In fact, it's almost impossible *not* to shop in a city whose souvenirs—miniature Statues of Liberty, Empire State Buildings, (little) Big Apples—are so instantly familiar. There are Fifth Avenues in a million cities, but no dedicated follower of fashion will mistake that address for any other. Nearly every toney hotel lobby now comes complete with a fancy gift shop, if not a couple of name-brand boutiques. And then there are the street vendors, the shopping marts, the jewelry malls, the flea markets . . .

In fact, if you're not careful—even if it's exactly what you have in mind—you could find yourself spending your whole visit, and more than your budget, haphazardly acquiring things. That seems like a waste in more ways than one. When every city you visit seems to have the same designer shopping malls filled with the same stores and labels, New York is a treasure trove of specialty items, one-of-a-kind gifts, and real connoisseur's delights. We can't list them all (have you hefted a Manhattan Yellow Pages lately?), but we have picked out some we particularly like.

And as usual, we have tried to pick out ways that you can combine your shopping expeditions with explorations of neighborhoods, which have much nicer views than all those prepackaged malls and dispense with some of the hype in favor of the rich variety of New York. Sure, this is prime window-shopping territory, and you can see, and buy, a little of almost everything just by wandering around; but intriguingly, communities of merchants seem to have evolved that coincide with great walking opportunities, so if you know what sort of purchases you want to make, you can look them over for hours and see history at the same time.

For example, are you longing to personalize your suburban townhome with unusual furniture and home accessories? Head to SoHo. Love gazing at art galleries? You could spend a whole visit in SoHo and its sibling rival, Chelsea. Designer couture? Fifth Avenue, of course, but also the newly hot upper Madison Avenue. You can get discounts on clothes at a factory-shop mall, but why not wander the Lower East Side, the neighborhood that made discount shopping famous? New York is famous for gourmet foods, and super-markets such as Dean & Deluca and Zabar's are classics, but what about noshing on real pickles or fresh-from-the-oven matzo? And if you're looking for a real ethnic experience, skip the markets in Little Italy in favor of Arthur Avenue in the Bronx and see the neighborhood groceries out there.

For those collectors who are more single-minded, we have included a selection of stores and purveyors of specific goods. Rare books, black ties, vintage rock and roll—you want it, we got it. And if all this fails, you can shop as the rich and famous do: Contact the **Intrepid New Yorker** folks (534-5071) and hire a personal shopping guide.

All Together Now: Department Stores, "Malls," and Flea Markets

We're not by any means suggesting that you settle for department-store shopping in New York, but sometimes traveling is a matter of so many gifts, so little time. In that case, you need a lot of options at one address. Besides which, there are some stores in New York so famous in and of themselves that they almost qualify as tourist attractions. (And there are a couple, perhaps not so well-known, that might change your vision of department stores.) Or you may like the spontaneity and treasure-hunt aspect of flea markets. Or, especially if you want to get that souvenir stuff out of the way in a hurry, you might just want to hustle through the company-logo superstores that are the gift shop equivalents of amusement parks.

Probably the best-known names in department-store shopping in Manhattan are **Barney's, Bergdorf Goodman, Bloomingdale's, Macy's,** and **Saks.**

Barney's original Chelsea store is on Seventh Avenue at 17th Street, and there's a branch at the World Financial Center downtown; but nowadays *the* Barney's is the $100 million Midtown megastore on Madison Avenue at East 61st (826-8900). It is really more of a clothing store than a true all-purpose emporium, but it's a landmark.

The B&G logo of Bergdorf Goodman (753-7300) has been at the cornerstones of Fifth and 57th, both literally and metaphorically, for generations; and maybe that's exactly the reason it recently embarked on a very modern retooling. The seventh-floor housewares department, already a magnet for forward-thinking brides and newly promoted partners, is now 3,000 square feet larger and arranges its own exhibitions. Famed chef Daniel Boulud helped set up the new tea salon, and while so many stores are cutting back on either prices or service, Bergdorf is booming: It now has a whole men's store, called simply Bergdorf Goodman Men, on the opposite side of the street. Bergdorf is so dependable that should you suddenly discover that the dinner you're invited to is black-tie, you can call the gender-appropriate store to dispatch a personal shopper to your hotel with an armful of outfits for you to try on.

Bloomingdale's is the designer version of a department store, and it looks it. Everything is name-brand—you could hang your clothes out in the living room and never worry about feeling label-challenged—from Polo to Petrossian (yup, a caviar stand). It even has an American Express office (on Third Avenue at East 59th Street; 785-2000).

Macy's is the most moderate-priced of the bunch, and perhaps its merchandise isn't as cutting-edge as some; but it covers nearly all the bases—from kitchen goods (and carry-out) in the basement to antiques on the ninth floor, and from haircuts to pedicures. And its rather stubborn nostalgia is fairly represented by that famous Thanksgiving Day Parade (Broadway between West 34th and 35th; 695-4400).

Sak's Fifth Avenue (753-4000) is just where you'd expect it to be, on Fifth between 49th and 50th Streets next to St. Patrick's Cathedral. This is an old-money outlet with an old-money outlook on fashion, jewelry, fine foods, jewelry, and even lunch; the Cafe SFA on the eighth floor has views of the cathedral and Rockefeller Center across the street.

Our personal favorite is much less famous, far more limited in stock, and on the expensive side, but it is so beautifully appointed—even the store hardware is gorgeous—that it's worth a look. **Takashimaya** (Fifth Avenue between East 54th and 55th; 350-0115), in a fine six-story townhouse, begins with a tea shop in the basement and rises through a flower shop and spa and art galleries to its men's, women's, and home furnishings floors. One visit, and you'll have a whole new respect for interior design.

■ Mile-High Malls ■

Even less do we suggest you look for a shopping mall in Manhattan (especially as the streets are already full of Gaps, etc.) If you must run off a quick list, however, there are a couple of shopping towers ("malls" in the city are more likely to be vertical than horizontal) that won't be far off your path.

The **Manhattan Mall** at Sixth Avenue and 33rd Street has nine levels of shops, a typical food court, and a useful brochure-heavy visitors center on the seventh floor (465-0500). The fourth and fifth floors of **Trump Tower** (plus the big names at street level) form a mini-mall; and the pink marble atrium, with its astonishing waterfall, is something of a tourist attraction in itself (on Fifth Avenue between 56th and 57th Streets). **Rockefeller Center** also has a mini-mall that you can tour while admiring the Plaza display of the moment, the skating rink, the Deco buildings, and so on (just off Fifth between 49th and 50th). And the renovated **South Street Seaport,** part of the built-up Lower Manhattan area near the Fulton Fishmarket at

Water Street, is now an attractive, if somewhat predictable, mall of shops, restaurants, and marine-history souvenir stores.

■ Flea Markets ■

We do recommend this very characteristic diversion. What would shopping in Manhattan be without a visit to the flea markets? Semi-pro shopping, that is—not the sort of amateur souveniring you can do anywhere, but spot, dash, and bargain stuff. Frequently there are serious antiques dealers as well (see more on antique centers later in this section), but with flea markets, you need to be a little more careful about derivations and aging.

Some flea markets are regularly scheduled, some are more impromptu (especially in good weather), and a few are more like block parties with vendors involved, especially downtown. A few general rules apply to all, however. Don't expect dealers to accept credit cards, although a few whose merchandise is particularly expensive (antique furniture and so on) might. In most cases, expect to pay cash and carry your prize off with you. If you want to skim off the cream of the crop, go early; if you're hoping to score a real bargain, wait till the afternoon, when some dealers may be willing to shave the price so they don't have to pack everything up. Some markets may charge a nominal entrance fee of a dollar or two.

These are the most dependable spots to shop, but the Weekend section of the *New York Times* may mention some special fairs; also check the classified ads.

The most famous, the original, is the **Annex Antiques Fair and Flea Market**—popularly known as the "26th Street flea market"—which brings more than 500 vendors together every weekend in a trio of parking lots that stretch along Sixth Avenue from West 24th toward West 27th. The antiques area, around 26th, is open both Saturdays and Sundays, from 9 a.m. to 5 p.m., but the general market at the southern end is open only on Sundays—and that's the one to see if you're hoping to celebrity-hunt while you're trying to distinguish the Tiffany from the trash. (This is also a good place to learn more about such merchandise, as many of the dealers are extremely professional.) From there it's a short walk to the **Chelsea Antiques Annex,** a.k.a. "The Garage," at 122 West 25th Street, which is run by the same people and opens and closes in tandem with the outdoor market.

But unless you are a flea market veteran, you may find it easier to grasp the opportunities at the somewhat smaller **SoHo Antiques Fair and Flea Market,** which sets up Saturdays and Sundays from 9 a.m. to 5 p.m. at the corner of Broadway and Grand Street. Another good smaller flea market is the **Greenwich Village Flea Market** at P.S. 41 on Greenwich Avenue near Seventh; it is open Saturdays only from noon to 7 p.m.

If you have the stamina, you can do the East Side/West Side two-step over the weekend by swinging through the upscale flea markets at **P.S. 183** on East 66th Street between First and York Avenues (Saturday only, 6 a.m. to 6 p.m.) and the **Intermediate School 44** on Columbus Avenue at West 76th (Sunday only, 10 a.m. to 5:30 p.m.).

One-Stop Shopping: Museum Shops and Theme Stores

■ Art-ifacts: The Museum Shops ■

If you're sick of the cookie-cutter gift list, treat yourself to a mall of the mind, so to speak. Along two straight lines, one in Midtown and the other on the East Side, are clusters of the smartest—meaning chic *and* brainy—shops, all a little different and all, so to speak, of museum quality.

The first line, of course, is along Museum Mile, that stretch of Fifth Avenue between 82nd and 104th Streets along which nine major collections are assembled. All have some sort of gift shop, but it's fair to say that the **Metropolitan Museum of Art** at 82nd Street (535-7710) has one of the most stunning collections anywhere, filled with not only merchandise relating to current and hit exhibits—replica jewelry, Egyptiana, art-design scarves, notepaper, and the like—but also classic reproduction posters, decorative glass, books, T-shirts, desk accessories, card cases, calendars, vases, reproduction statuary, Impressionist umbrellas, Munch and Dali wristwatches, and even rugs. It has its own bridal registry, too. Check out some of the art being sold on consignment upstairs.

The **Jewish Museum** on Fifth at 92nd (423-3200) has a small but striking collection of jewelry, menorahs, and scarves, many with designs adapted from religious or historical works.

The **Cooper-Hewitt National Museum of Design** at 91st (860-6868) is design central for those whose taste in silver, platters, and small personal and office items such as pens, bath luxuries, salt-and-peppers, and coasters tends to an earlier, more sensual age than the sleek modernity of MoMA's collection (this is, after all, the former Carnegie mansion). But if you do like that smart postmodern look, step into the shop at the **Guggenheim** at 89th Street (423-3615) and peruse their selections. And the **International Center for Photography** at 94th (860-1777) is the only museum anywhere that collects and exhibits only photographs; its calendars, prints, and coffee-table books are first-rate.

A short stroll away, though not literally in "the Mile," are the **Frick Collection** (Fifth and 70th), which has lovely notepaper, calendars, postcards, and notebooks; the Whitney Museum's **Store Next Door** (Madison Avenue between 74th and 75th; 606-0200), with its sometimes elegantly spare (Shaker-influenced), sometimes witty assortment of ties, toys, and other home and closet whimsy; and the **Asia Society** bookstore (Park Avenue between 70th and 71st), which stocks not only adult and children's books on Asian culture, cooking, language, and design but also toys, jewelry, teapots and chopsticks, Indonesian carvings, and unusual paper goods.

Along a somewhat more imaginary aisle in Midtown Manhattan, on a line that cuts from West 53rd to West 49th Streets between Fifth and Sixth Avenues (though closer to Fifth), you'll find half a dozen more museum shops within easy reach.

The **American Craft Museum** is both an exhibit space and one of the finest art-gift shops in town (40 West 53rd; 956-6047). Though the selection is not large, the jewelry is particularly attractive, sometimes spectacular, and there are often some glassworks as well as paperweights and other decorative items.

The **MoMA Design Store** (44 West 53rd Street; 767-1050) has for good reason inspired one of the great mail catalogues of our box-stuffing era. Every one of these products—glassware, writing pens, kids' flatware, vases, photo frames, even watches and ties—have passed such muster with the museum's design mavens that they have become part of the permanent collection. And smart as they are, they are frequently great bargains: Among our personal favorite acquisitions have been spiral-twist stretch bracelets, something like Slinkees for the wrist, for $10. And **MoMA's bookstore** (across the street in the lobby at 11 West 53rd; 708-9700), which stocks more than 6,000 coffee-table books, catalogues, and quality paperbacks, is also packed with educational videos, CD-ROMS, art posters, calendars, and so on.

Just around the corner (straight through the block, if you could do it) on 52nd Street is the new **Museum of Television and Radio** (621-6800), which has a small store but one ideally suited to those whose kids (or spouses) still have crushes on Mary Tyler Moore or Captain Kirk. It stocks videos, T-shirts, posters, vintage radio shows, and stocking stuffers with character, so to speak.

A short stroll away is the **Museum of American Folk Art** store at 62 West 50th, also straight through between Fifth and Sixth Avenues (247-5611), plumb full of the sort of urbane-country decor—a purely American oxymoron, surely—that wows well-heeled sophisticates addicted to quilts, clever pillow appliqués, stencils, and artisanal Christmas tree ornaments. And if you don't make it up to Museum Mile, the Met has a two-story branch in Rockefeller Center at 15 West 49th Street (332-1360), where you can find a full selection of its merchandise, rugs and all.

Among other attractive stops are the trio of stores at the **Metropolitan Opera House** in Lincoln Center: the Met shop on the main floor (580-4090); the broader Performing Arts shop on the lower level (580-4356); and the Poster Gallery (580-4673), which stocks not only great records and biographies but also diva (and danseur) T-shirts, mugs, and the sort of unabashed art lover's accessories that fill PBS catalogues. The shop at the **National Museum of the American Indian** (835-8093) in the old Customs House at 1 Bowling Green downtown near Battery Park has native American music and meditational tapes, beadwork kits, and turquoise jewelry of the sort that is once again popular with young people, plus T-shirts, arrowheads, and reproductions of famous paintings of the West. And if you're headed down that way, you might want to check out the maps, model ships, and other old-salt stuff at the **South Street Seaport Museum Shops** (669-9400).

■ Brand Loyalty: Theme Stores ■

The '90s have given birth to a whole new boom in merchandising: stores specializing in movie and television tie-ins, corporate brand names, celebrity properties, and so on. They are virtually theme parks disguised as stores, and the Disney Store in Times Square, with its connection to the restored Amsterdam Theater, is just the most obvious example. If your kids are determined to have these sorts of souvenirs, there are several along almost any major tour route.

On Fifth Avenue near the foot of Central Park are the **Coca-Cola Store** and the **Warner Bros. Studio Store;** the **Disney Studio Store** is a block away at 55th. (Both Disney and Warner Bros. have stores in Times Square as well.) The multistory **Nike Town** is on 57th just around the corner toward Madison Avenue, as is the **Original Levi's Store.**

The **Radio City Avenue Store** is right next to the Radio City Music Hall box office on Sixth Avenue between 50th and 51st and, naturally, sells logo apparel and such souvenirs as the Rockette Doll. The **NBC Studio Store,** right around the corner in Rockefeller Center, is stocked with T-shirts, coffee mugs, and caps from *Seinfeld, Frasier, Friends, The Tonight Show, Saturday Night Live,* and so on. (You don't need tickets to impress your friends anymore, just T-shirts.)

And since more and more restaurants have their own in-house merchandise stores, check out the **Official All-Star Cafe** in Times Square (Broadway and 45th; 840-8326), basking in the reflected (two-story) glory of athlete celebs Andre Agassi, Tiger Woods, Wayne Gretsky, Joe Montana, Ken Griffey Jr., Shaquille O'Neal, and Monica Seles; or the **Fashion Cafe,** brainchild of supermodels Claudia Schiffer, Christy Turlington, Naomi Campbell, and Elle MacPherson (Rockefeller Plaza at 51st Street). Or how about the **Harley-Davidson Cafe** (Sixth Avenue and West 56th; 245-6000), the **Jekyll & Hyde Club** (Sixth and 57th; 541-9505), **Planet Hollywood** (333-7827) and the **Motown Cafe** (489-0097; both between West 57th between Sixth and Seventh), and the **Hard Rock Cafe** (West 57th between Seventh and Broadway; 459-9320)? These last five are all close enough to serve as an instant playground pub tour.

Of course, if your particular brand loyalty lies with a famous designer, you're headed uptown, so see the following sections on Fifth Avenue and Madison Avenue.

Great Neighborhoods for Shopping

■ **Windows on the World: Fifth Avenue** ■

There are a few streets whose stores and window displays are so famous that they don't even need city names attached. Rodeo Drive. Champs d'Elysée. Via Venneto. And Fifth Avenue.

Fifth Avenue was nicknamed "Millionaire's Row" at the turn of the century, when the Vanderbilts, Astors, and Goulds all built palaces for themselves along the road, and it's never quite given up that expensive spirit. A few of the nineteenth-century mansions are still standing, and the churches of the area give you an idea of the luxury such tycoons expected even in their houses of worship. (Remember that Fifth Avenue is the east/west dividing line, and don't let addresses on the numbered streets confuse you. Cartier at East 52nd Street faces B. Dalton at West 52nd.)

To get a serious sense of both the retail and historical beauties of Midtown, start at the corner of 49th Street and head north toward Central Park. On your left: **Rockefeller Center,** which fills the blocks between Fifth and Sixth Avenues and West 48th and 51st Streets and incorporates Radio City Music Hall and the NBC Studios (look around the corner onto West 49th and you'll see that famous window into the *Today* show). There are also many shops in the lower levels of the complex, and the famous ice rink/outdoor cafe (a Jekyll and Hyde trick that follows the seasons) and gardens, as well as many seasonal displays on the plaza. There is actually a minimuseum of the complex on the concourse level at 30 Rockefeller Plaza, with photos and video, and a walking tour guide is available free at the information desk in the lobby. Notice the gilded gods of industry on the front, the carvings, the bas relief, and the fine Art Deco detailing.

Across the street are **Saks Fifth Avenue,** one of the city's finest department stores, and St. Patrick's Cathedral, which was built by James Renwick Jr. in the 1880s. Just above that is the elaborate facade of the famous jeweler **Cartier** at the corner of East 52nd, which is one of those few turn-of-the-century mansions that are still intact. Legend has it that the original owner traded the house to Pierre Cartier for a string of pearls.

The French Gothic St. Thomas Church at the corner of Fifth and 53rd was built in 1914; the University Club at 54th was built in 1899 by Charles

McKim (a partner of Stanford White) in imitation of the Italian palazzos. McKim also designed what is now the Banco di Napoli across the street. The Fifth Avenue Presbyterian Church, built in 1875, was where the Roosevelts, Auchinclosses, and Walcotts worshiped, helping give it the reputation of being the city's most influential congregation.

Now the credit-card boutiques begin to thicken: **Christian Dior** at Fifth Avenue and East 55th; **Takashimaya** (discussed earlier) and **Elizabeth Arden** between East 54th and 55th; **Façonnable** and **Gucci** at East 54th; **Henri Bendel** between West 55th and 56th; and **Harry Winston,** megajeweler to the rich and famous, at West 56th.

The Trump Tower at East 56th and Fifth Avenue houses **Ferragamo** and O.J. favorite **Bruno Magli.** Between West 56th and 57th, look for **Steuben,** the art-glass company; **Tiffany & Co.; Burberry's; Chanel; Fendi;** and **Van Cleef & Arpel's. Norma Kamali** is just around the corner on 56th. The building that houses **Bulgari** at 730 Fifth was the first home of the Museum of Modern Art.

Bergdorf Goodman (discussed earlier) and **Bergdorf Goodman Men** fill the blocks from West 57th to 58th. And as you get to the bottom of the park, where Fifth meets 58th Street, you'll see **FAO Schwarz,** one of the most famous toy stores in the world.

■ **Clothing on the High Side: The East Side** ■

If you love that Italian-label look but don't have time to fly to Rome, relax. These days, the signs along Madison Avenue in the '60s and '70s read like satellite transmissions from the Via Venetto, with just enough American and international designer boutiques to keep you grounded.

Some of the big-name stores have set up along the numbered streets between Madison and Fifth Avenues, so that the old couture row, the new Madison, and the museum district are beginning to merge. As an example, start east along 57th Street from Fifth (discussed earlier) toward the intersection of Madison and you can see the signs for **Chanel, Charivari, Burberry's, Hermes, Coach, Prada, Louis Vuitton,** and **Gurkha;** turn the corner onto Madison for **Tourneau,** the watch temple. **Emporio Armani** is on Madison at 59th, at East 60th. **Emilio Pucci** is just around the corner on 64th Street between Madison and Fifth.

But the real name-label parade begins at the northwest corner of West 65th and Madison with the **Giorgio Armani** boutique, a stunning white four-story showplace that resembles the National Gallery's East Building—not to mention Armani couture itself. It gazes serenely across at the **Kenar, Kriza,** and **Valentino** boutiques and shelters the **BCBG/May Azria** shop on its left.

Across 66th are the new **Bulgari** showroom, **Charles Jourdan, Cerutti** children's clothing, **David Berk Cashmere,** and **Nicole Miller,** who is to ties as the *New Yorker* is to cartoons. **Emmanuel Ungaro** holds down the corner of Madison and 67th. Cross 67th to **Kenzo, Moschino,** and **Davide Cenci,** and peek around the corner to 21 East 67th for the classic English country tweeds, cufflinks, and other gentry goods at the boutique of the 150-year-old **House of Dormeuil.**

Above 67th you'll find **Frette** Italian linens and **Joseph Tricot** London sweater chic (570-0077). Above 68th Street are the complete ready-to-wear collections of **Gianni Versace** (in a negative-image Roman temple with black capitals and silver-gilded capitals); **MaxMara; Malo,** the European cashmere king; **Jaeger** sportswear; **Joan and David; Bogner** ski couture; and **TSE Cashmere.** The new **Dolce Gabbana** store at the corner of Madison and 69th is 7,000 square feet of retro-rococo chic, and around the corner on 69th Street are the banners announcing **Prada.**

Cross 69th to **Missoni, Cashmere-Cashmere, Maraolo** Italian shoes, **Romeo Gigli, Fila,** and **Andrea Carrano.** If you're crazy for natural fibers or custom-woven linens, it's dueling designer labels: the Italian **Pratesi** vs. the French **D. Porthault.**

Yves Saint Laurent's couture store and his Rive Gauche boutique are side by side on Madison between 70th and 71st Streets, along with **Gianfranco Ferre, Sonia Rykel,** and **Santoni's** handmade Italian footwear.

Ralph Lauren has four floors of Polo clothing, accessories, and home luxuries on the west side of Madison between 71st and 72nd Streets and a whole second building full of Polo Sport casualwear and his trademark weathered look on the east side. And even though you can't wear them, you couldn't display your couture on any more astonishing art furniture than the chairs of **Pierre Deux.**

Givenchy's haute couture store is on Madison at East 75th; jewelry designer **Mish** shares the third floor of a townhouse at 22 East 77th with **Stubbs & Wootton,** who made those embroidered velvet slippers that demand a smoking jacket, or at least a butler.

Even some of the downtown stalwarts have doubled up uptown, including **Liliana Ordas,** whose Morgane Le Fay collection of sleek gowns looks like a whole store designed around Stevie Nicks, between 64th and 65th; jewelry designer Susan Reinstein of **Reinstein/Ross** just off to the west on 73rd Street; **Eileen Fisher** at 79th; and **Betsey Johnson** and **agnes b.,** both between 80th and 81st Streets.

■ Clothing on the Hip Side: SoHo ■

Fashion- and/or bargain-conscious visitors have a great reason to wander the SoHo area—aside from the fun of the street theater, that is.

Retro, nouveau, haute, and so-so, SoHo is big boutique territory, so unless you want to have an Armani T-shirt just like everybody else's, you can get more in-circle designerwear at places such as **Scoop** (532 Broadway; 925-2886), which plays runway videos behind the racks of Calvins and Isaaks; **Morgane Le Fay,** Liliana Ordas's splendidly mysterious cave of dresses and capes (151 Spring Street; 925-0144); Laura Whittcomb's **Label** (263 Lafayette Street; 966-7736); and Rei Kawakubo's **Comme des Garcons** (116 Wooster Street; 219-0661).

You'll recognize the eponymous works of **Todd Oldham**—who could miss them?—at his store at 123 Wooster (219-3531); of **Kate Spade** (59 Thompson Street; 965-0301); of the lower-case upper-class **agnes b.** (116 Prince; 925-4649); of the pricey but irresistibly distinctive **Yohji Yamamoto** (103 Grand; 966-9066); and of Miuccia Prada at **Miu Miu** (100 Prince Street; 334-5156). One of **Betsey Johnson**'s several New York locations is 130 Thompson (420-0169). Also look into **Stevan Allen** (Wooster Street), whose sharp-eyed owner is famous for picking future hot designers on the less expensive upswing; **Product** (71 Mercer Street; 274-1630); **Palma** (521 Broome Street; 966-1722); **Alpana Bawa** (41 Grand Street; 965-0559); **X-Large** (Lafayette Street; 334-4480); **Yoshi** (461 West Broadway; 979-0569); and the frankly named **Il Boutique** (474 West Broadway; 533-8660).

The first name in vintage chic, of course, is **Harriet Love,** author of the best-selling guide to the stuff and maven of the store that outfitted onetime-employee-turned-pop-singer Cyndi Lauper (126 Prince Street; 996-2280). **Opal White** specializes in serious vintage—Edwardian and Victorian fashions, including formalwear and wedding dresses (by appointment only: 131 Thompson Street; 677-8215). Also check out the twin tongue-in-cheek-twisters **Smylonylon** (222 Lafayette Street; 431-0342) and **Arkle & Sparkle** (216 Lafayette; 925-9699). For the traditional Japanese look, as opposed to Tokyo modern couture, try **Kimono House** (120 Thompson Street).

As with home furnishings, art, and hip in general, the neighborhood is filling out through Little Italy, making Mott and Elizabeth Streets a trendy transition to the bargain-minded Lower East Side. Imelda Marcos wannabes must make a beeline for **Sigerson Morrison** (242 Mott; 219-3893), unless you already have kid leather pumps the color of a swashbuckler's wine and velvet loafers for your dinner jacket. Milliner **Kelly Christy** makes hats to order from a set of designs with names Ben & Jerry would love (though not at ice cream prices), such as the Jackie Kennedy–style pillbox called O and the fruit-topped Cherry Swirl (235 Elizabeth Street; 965-0686). Traditional ethnic prints and sari scarves are put together in untraditional ways at **Calypso** (280 Mott; 965-0990).

■ Clothing on the Bargain Side: ■ The Lower East Side

The Lower East Side has been famous for years as the place bargains were best; serious shoppers flew in to gawk along Orchard Street, where last season's department store and even designerwear could be had for, well, if not a song, then a chorus or two. These days, with sales so much more common and outlet malls thriving, the trek is a little lower on some visitors' itineraries, but the merchants of the neighborhood, now being more aggressively promoted as the Historic Orchard Street Bargain District, have banded together to raise their profile again. So if you do have that bargain bug—and, after all, how many of your office mates can tell last year's classics from this year's?—head east from SoHo into this evocative old section.

More than 300 businesses in this neighborhood are still family-owned, and with just a little imagination (and maybe a stop in the Lower East Side Tenement Museum or other historic landmark), you'll be able to see it as it was when the pushcart and peddler era was melding into the wholesale world—especially if you go on a Sunday, when a lot of the area streets are blocked off for pedestrian traffic and turned into open-air vendor markets. And you'll definitely still hear the rhythms of the Yiddish millions of East European Jews stamped on the bargaining patter of the vendors, even though the community's ethnicity now ranges from South American to Southeast Asian. You may find nineteenth-century echoes in some stores' cash-only, or at least no credit card, policies and the haggling over prices you may get into every once in a while. But there are a few entirely modern things you should remember as well. The first is that many of those sidewalk vendors are hawking bootleg or counterfeit goods. And maybe you shouldn't flash your cash too carelessly. But if you like the hurly-burly of contact sport shopping, this is the place, and you might get a real bargain if you work at it.

To keep from getting disoriented in all this retail abundance, stop by the offices of the Historic Orchard Street Shopping District at 261 Broome Street (226-9010) and pick up a brochure/map of the neighborhood; or if you drop by Katz's Deli at the corner of Ludlow Street and East Houston (254-2246) any Sunday at 11 a.m. from April through December, you can hook up to a free hour-long shopping tour. (If Katz's looks particularly familiar to you, it's probably because the most famous scene in *When Harry*

Met Sally—the, uh, loud one—was shot here.) Meanwhile, here's just a few spots to get you started.

Feet first: Check into the likes of **Orchard Bootery** (179 Orchard; 996-0688), which has lots of wider-sized fashion footwear; **Giselle Sportswear** (143 Orchard; 673-1900); cashmere at **Fishkin Knitwear** (around the corner at 314 Grand; 226-6538); and the really big-name double-breasteds at **Jodamo International** menswear (321 Grand Street; 219-1039). **Kenar** has a discount outlet at 196 Orchard (254-8899) that sells the uptown store's leftovers for 20 to 50 percent off; and lingerie-lovers linger at **A. W. Kaufman** (73 Orchard; 226-1629) and **Louis Chock** across the street (73 Orchard; 473-1929); try on leather coats at **Carl & Sons** (172 Orchard; 674-8470) and **Bridge Leather** (98 Orchard; 477-5813). Actually, you can't escape leather shops on Orchard Street, any more than you will run out of any other kind of clothing; walk around a little before you buy, or at least try to bargain a little.

Do a hat trick at **Stetson's** (101–7 Delancey; 473-13434). For designer handbags, look to **Fine & Klein** (119 Orchard; 674-6720), **Ber-Sel Handbags** (75 Orchard; 966-5517), and **Sole of Italy** (125 Orchard; 674-2662). If you really just want another Samsonite or American Tourister rollalong, there's plenty of that stuff to be found as well. On the other hand, there's just one place for umbrellas, **Salwen's** (43 Orchard; 226-1693), because if you don't hear Irving Salwen play Yiddish folks songs on the guitar, you haven't really gotten the Lower East Side experience.

Marcesa hangs up imported evening gowns from French and Italian designers (108 Orchard Street; 674-6344), and that SoHo chic-boutique thang is headed east, so keep your eyes peeled for iconoclastic designers setting up shop. The fabric stores are clustered along Hester and Orchard Streets, and the tailoring shops are clustered north of Delancey toward East Houston along Rivington Street, Allen Street, and Stanton; get something custom-made. If you sew yourself, or even if you don't, take a gander at the incredible variety of zippers at **A. Feibusch,** from doll-sized to double-length (33 Allen Street; 226-3964).

Thanks to chic creep, so to speak, the strip of Orchard Street between Houston and Delancey is on the verge of becoming another youth-oriented bar-and-boutique area—O-Ho, perhaps. Many of these are retro-hip spots, with overtones of funk and psychedelia as well as hip-hop. If the shopping expedition covers two generations, this could be the answer.

■ Art Galleries: Chelsea and SoHo ■

It's almost a battle between these old villages for the city's art scene crown. In the last two or three years, both have seen the number of galleries and exhibit spaces increase several times.

SoHo is estimated to house 250 art galleries; its art scene has grown so rapidly that its annual September arts festival boomed from 60 events in 1965 to 200 in 1996 and spread out to 11 days of visual arts exhibits, performances, and dance in 1997. Festival director Simon Watson puts out a monthly newsletter called "Simon Says" (available at neighborhood galleries) listing 40 recommendations for art-gazing, and he also organizes Saturday afternoon museum/gallery walks led by area dealers. It is so firmly established that the Guggenheim Museum has a SoHo branch on Broadway, which has become the center aisle of the arts walk of the neighborhood. Each week the exhibits here are listed in the front of the *New Yorker* magazine under "Galleries: Downtown."

Chelsea, meanwhile, has benefited from some defections by prominent arts dealers either from farther uptown or, ironically, from SoHo, where space is getting tight and pricey again. But there are so many that the *New Yorker* has added a separate "Galleries: Chelsea" listing.

However, unless you have several days to devote solely to the pursuit of fine art, you probably need to focus your attention on certain sections of either neighborhood. Note that most SoHo galleries are open on Saturday and closed on Sunday and Monday; Chelsea galleries used to be open on Sunday, but many are now shifting to Saturday hours instead. Be sure to check ahead if you had weekend wandering in mind.

If you prefer to stick to Midtown, you can spend a lot of time amid the old, fine, and famous cluster of galleries in the area bounded by West 56 and 57th Streets and Fifth and Sixth Avenues just below Central Park; though most of these are also closed on Sundays, a fair number are open on Mondays. These are listed in the *New Yorker* under "Galleries: Uptown."

Chelsea. The easiest way to take in some of Chelsea's major galleries is to stroll back and forth along the streets from West 20th to West 26th Streets between Tenth and Eleventh Avenues.

In the 500 block of West 20th Street, for example, some of the reputable dealers include the **Stefan Stux Gallery** (535 West 20th) and **Bill Maynes** (529 West 20th), both formerly in SoHo. **Paolo Baldacci Gallery** has relocated from uptown to 521 West 21st Street near **Paula Cooper** (534 West 21st Street). Former Cooper Gallery directors **Christopher D'Amelio and Lucien Terras** now have their own eponymous gallery around the corner at 525 West 22nd Street, which is also the address of **303 Gallery.** And the four-story **Dia Center for the Arts,** which arguably sparked the neighborhood movement when it expanded here from SoHo, is at 548 West 22nd.

Among the many other addresses to look for are 515 West 24th, a triple-gallery space housing **Metro Pictures, Barbara Gladstone,** and **Matthew Marks. Jose Freire's Team Gallery** (527 West 26th Street) faces **Clementine** (526 West 26th Street).

The stunning Art Deco building across 11th Avenue stretching from 26th to 27th is the Starrett-Lehigh Building, originally constructed over the Lehigh Valley Railroad yards and with elevators that hauled whole freight cars, fully loaded, into the warehouse. It is now a multigallery complex that includes not only visual arts spaces such as **Pamela Auchincloss** but also **Jan van der Donk** rare books and the even more fantastic **Bound and Unbound** conceptual art bookstore.

SoHo. Almost any SoHo block has an art, photography, or print shop mixed in with the boutiques, if you just want to trust to chance (or skim the gallery listings in one of the local publications and see what appeals to you). The two buildings at 415 and 420 West Broadway by themselves house well over a dozen galleries, including the famed **Leo Castelli Gallery** (420 West Broadway), and one of the branches of the **Dia Center for the Contemporary Arts** is a few doors down at 393 West Broadway.

But a stroll down Broadway between Prince and Houston offers more than a full day's worth of art-gazing and architectural interest. The **Guggenheim Museum SoHo** at 575 Broadway, one of the city's most important collections of modern art, has 30,000 square feet of exhibit space in a six-story nineteenth-century loft originally designed for owner John Jacob Astor II as a garment manufacturing and retailing complex. The cast-iron "storefronts" and the iron columns inside are all original. (In contrast, the teapot chandeliers inside the museum's "T" room are very modern.) The **New Museum of Contemporary Art** at 583 Broadway is not so establishment (in the prestige sense) but serves as almost a preview space for cutting-edge artists. The **Alternative Museum** is only one of several galleries inside 594 Broadway, but it sometimes mixes poetry readings and music with the visuals.

Although the cast-iron facade of the **Museum for African Art** at 593 Broadway, which moved from its smaller Upper East Side space in 1993, is original, the interior spaces were designed by Maya Lin, architect of the Vietnam Veterans Memorial (the "black wall") in Washington. It is the only museum other than the Smithsonian's Museum of African Art that focuses on sub-Saharan cultural artifacts: life-sized carvings, masks, weavings, jewelry, and so on.

Many other fine old buildings along that stretch have been transformed into multigallery spaces. Among the dealers at 560 Broadway, for example, are **Max Protetch, Bridgewater/Lustberg, Salvatore Ala, Nancy Margolis,** and **Katharina Rich Perlow,** plus a Dean & DeLuca gourmet shop. There are similar multistudio offerings at 568 Broadway, which houses **Castelli Graphics,** the print (Jasper Johns, Roy Lichtenstein, etc.) and photography arm of Leo Castelli Gallery, and 580 Broadway. You'll also see

Denise Bibro (584 Broadway); the **June Kelly Gallery** (591 Broadway); **Wooster Gardens** (558 Broadway); **P. P. O. W.** (532 Broadway); **Elizabeth Harris Gallery** (524 Broadway); the **Thread Waxing Space** (476 Broadway) . . . well, you get the idea.

■ Home Furnishings and Interiors: SoHo ■

The lower end of SoHo around Greene and Broome Streets sweeps the market in cool furniture and home design, a number of them partial boutiques from the artisans who own them, including **Moss** (146 Greene Street; 226-2190); **Troy** (138 Greene; 941-4777); **Aero Studios** (132 Spring Street; 966-1500); and **Todd Hase** (51 Wooster Street; 334-3568). A little more commercial but still intriguing are the multi-culti **Coconut Co.** (131 Greene; 539-1940); **Anthropologie** (375 West Broadway, 343-7070), which mixes clothing for the urban frontierfolk with artistically weathered furniture; **Portico Home** (379 West Broadway; 941-7800) and **Dialogica** (484 Broome; 966-1934).

Zona is a classic of the urban-country look, particularly in the southwestern and neo-Italian styles (97 Greene Street; 925-6750); so is Zona's obvious admirer **Distant Origin** (153 Mercer; 941-0025). Italy is the spiritual home, and often the actual one as well, of the ceramic designs and linens at **Ceramica** (59 Thompson Street; 941-1307). Those with super-sensitive skins, or simply with ecological concerns, would be grateful for gifts from **Ad Hoc Softwares,** which has nothing to do with computers and everything to do with unbleached and chemical-free bed linens, natural body products, and the exquisitely designed Global Japanese knives (410 West Broadway; 925-2652).

Don't miss the programmable "lighting machines," with their full, remote-controlled palettes of color, at **Artemide** (46 Greene Street; 925-1588); it's big bucks, but a big bang, too. At **Tansuya,** you can custom-order cabinets, trays, and other furniture lacquered in the traditional Japanese fashion (159 Mercer Street; 966-1782). Furnishings, folk art, and just odd je ne sais quois conversation items abound at **0 to 60s** (75 Thompson Street; 925-0932). And oversized items—art along the Claes Oldenburg lines—is the theme at **Think Big** (390 West Broadway; 925-7300).

But the home furnishings neighborhood is expanding—don't they always?—and in the single block of Lafayette Street between East Houston and Prince (which was once considered Little Italy but is rather rapidly shifting toward the city's hip pocket), you can find astonishing antique etched-glass doors, Deco lighting fixtures, huge marble tubs, wrought-iron gates, ritzy toilet paper holders, and even the occasional elevator box at the

50,000-square-foot **Urban Archaeology** (285 Lafayette; 431-6969); custom retro at **Salon Modern** (281 Lafayette; 219-3439); Tuscan-rustic tidbits for the meditation garden at **Rooms & Gardens** (290 Lafayette; 431-1297); late-nineteenth- and twentieth-century antiques at **Secondhand Rose** (270 Lafayette; 431-7673); funkier fringe is-it-old-or-is-it-just-camp Americana at **Coming to America** (276 Lafayette; 343-2968); a one-stop shop for every little thing for the Hamptons at **Brian Windsor Art, Antiques and Garden Furniture** (272 Lafayette; 274-0411); and one-of-a-kind Howdy-Doody-meets-the-Mad-Hatter-in-Manhattan accessories and furniture at **Lost City Arts** (275 Lafayette; 941-8025).

For smaller accessories, check out the desktop toy-techs at **Dom USA** (382 West Broadway; 334-5580). If you wander beyond Lafayette toward the Lower East Side, look for the mod-minimalist housewares at **Shi** (233 Elizabeth Street; 334-4330) or glassware at **Orio Trio** (248 Elizabeth; 219-1501). **Just Shades** (21 Spring Street; 966-2757) stocks exactly what it says, but here you can dress your windows with rice paper, silk, burlap, parchment, and a host of custom designs.

If there is any possibility that you have not found what you want in the SoHo neighborhood, there are also a large number of home furnishing shops in the East Village, especially along East 9th Street.

Specialty Shopping

If you're already a collector, or are shopping for someone who is, you can almost certainly find whatever it is in New York. In fact, you can probably find too many or get waylaid by all the other goodies in town. There are whole volumes devoted to shopping in Manhattan, and we ain't just talking the phone book; but unless shopping is your life, or you plan to move to town permanently, this list should help you get started.

Antiques. It would be impossible to pick the finest antiques dealers in a city like this, so we've only mentioned a few and their specialties. (Also look through the "Specialty Shopping" section for specific items.) Don't overlook the auction houses, especially **Christie's,** which has a 24-hour hotline for auction information (Park Avenue and 59th Street; hotline 371-5438 or 546-1000); its somewhat lower-scale—relatively speaking—branch, **Christie's East** at 219 East 67th (606-0400); and **Sotheby Parke Bernet** (York Avenue at East 72nd Street; hotline 606-7245 or 606-7000) and its junior gallery, **Sotheby's Arcade** (606-7409). All of these and several other reputable firms advertise previews and auctions in the *New York Times.* Also be sure to refer to the "Flea Markets" section, since one woman's flea is often another woman's find.

If you like just to walk in and out of shops to see what catches your eye, the area around East 60th Street between Second and Third Avenues is treasure alley. If you like to ground yourself in a single building and see as many dealers as possible, head for the **Chelsea Building** at 10 West 25th Street (929-0909), which has 150 dealers spread over 12 floors; or the **Manhattan Art and Antiques Center,** with 100 galleries of Asian, African, American, and European works (1050 Second Avenue; 355-4400). **Antiques at the Showplace** houses 100 dealers on two huge floors (40 West 25th Street; 633-6063), but like its neighboring flea markets, it's open only on weekends.

Down in SoHo, one of the big names in designer circles is **Niall Smith,** who specializes in late-eighteenth- and early-nineteenth-century European neoclassical furniture (96 Grand Street; 941-7354). Also in SoHo are **Michael Carey American Arts & Crafts** (77 Mercer Street; 226-3710), whose airy display room is elegant with Gustav Stickley and furniture and accessories from other period designers, and the similar-minded **Peter-Roberts Antiques** (134 Spring; 226-4777). **Eileen Lane** refurbishes deco for redecoration (150 Thompson; 475-2988). For something your neighbors will never be able to get from Pier 1, look into the **Claiborne Gallery,** which specializes in nineteenth-century Mexican pieces and iron furniture by Omer Claiborne, whose daughter Leslie Cozart now runs the gallery (452 West Broadway; 475-3072).

Architectural Remnants. In addition to SoHo's **Urban Archeology,** mentioned earlier, Brooklyn's **Architectural Salvage Warehouse** in the Williamsburg area (487-6800 or (718) 388-4527) was established by the New York Landmarks Preservation Commission to supply historically minded New Yorkers (you don't have to show ID) with doors, mantels, wrought iron, chandeliers, and so on. The trick here is, you'll have to arrange your own shipping.

Art Supplies. The **Art Store** may have a minimalist name, but it takes artist's supplies to the max, with more than 3,000 varieties of brushes alone and everything from the least expensive colored pencils to the rarest prestige-label oils, not to mention more colors than you knew they could invent names for. It fills two floors of a classic cast-iron building at 5 Bond Street (533-2444).

Asian Art and Antiques. For Japanese woodblocks, contact **Ronin Gallery** (605 Madison Avenue; 688-0188); **Things Japanese** (127 East 60th Street, upstairs; 371-4661); or the very fine **Joan B. Mirviss, Ltd.** by appointment; 799-4021. **Art of the Past** (1242 Madison Avenue; 860-7070) specializes in East Asian art and antiques, while those in high gear may want to head to **Tiber West** (1109 Lexington Avenue; 255-3416).

For chinoiserie, try **Ralph M. Chait Galleries** (12 East 56th Street; 758-0937), **Chinese Art and Antiques** (825 Broadway; 505-0549), and **J. J. Lally** (41 East 57th; 371-3380), or step into **Imperial Fine Oriental Art** (790 Madison Avenue; 717-5383). For Korean bedding and fine linens, try **Seoul Handicrafts** (284 Fifth Avenue; 564-5740).

Autographs. Forget those mall stores, with their preframed sports photos and replicated signatures. Head to the East Side to **James Lowe** (30 East 60th; 759-0775), **Kenneth Rendell** (989 Madison Avenue; 717-1776), or **Tollett & Harman** (by appointment, 175 West 76th; 877-1566) for authenticated signed letters, manuscripts, photographs, and other documents. Inquire about their searching for specific persons' autographs or professional evaluations if you have such items to insure or sell.

Baby and Children's Clothing. Bebe Thompson's timeless designer wear in SoHo (98 Thompson Street; 925-1122) and the artist-made cotton kid's stuff at **Just Kidding** in TriBeCa (180 Franklin Street; 219-0035) make those Gap kids look old hat. If you coo over pictures of babies in medieval lace, head for **La Layette et Plus** (170 East 61st Street; 688-7072). Modern-day French designs are the only sweets at **Tatine et Chocolat** (760 Madison Avenue; 744-0975), and the **Utility Kids** store at 69th and Madison is a rainbow palette of primary-bright play pieces. **Once upon a Time** may be considered a used-clothing store for kids, but many items have never been worn, and the others are in impeccable condition (171 East 92nd Street; 831-7619).

Bakelite. Fans of early-twentieth-century art-plastic should look into the collection at **Julie's Artisanal Gallery** at 687 Madison Avenue (688-2345); just the window display will make you grin.

Bones. Since the auctioning of Sue, the *T. rex* at Sotheby's, bones have become big business. Actually, they already were starting to be, but for most tourists, the skeletons, teeth, fossils, and anatomical charts at **Maxilla & Mandible** will be a revelation (451–55 Columbus Avenue; 724-6193). It's just around the corner from the American Museum of Natural History, where dinosaurs are truly king, Rex or no; so this is a natural for kid's day. M&M owner Harry Galiano used to work at the American Museum of Natural History, in fact, and his museum-quality merchandise is impeccably treated.

If you're down in SoHo, look into **Evolution,** which also has a fascinating assortment of bugs, skulls, horns, feathers, shells, and fossils—plus T-shirts to match (120 Spring Street; 343-1144).

Books. If you have the title, they have the book, or at least they can get it for you (and maybe wholesale). Manhattan is crammed with general-interest bookstores, of course, including the original **Barnes & Noble, B. Dalton,** and **Doubleday** stores; and most neighborhoods have at least one hangout that caters to nightowls. **Rizzoli** (31 West 57th; 759-2424) must be one of the prettiest stores in town, especially now that the big megastores have pretty much dispensed with decor.

But not surprisingly, the capital of American publishing is also a haven for fine antique, rare, used, and specialty books, several of them on the East Side. Contact **Imperial Fine Books** (790 Madison Avenue, 2nd floor; 861-6620); **Ursus Books** (981 Madison; 226-7858); **Martayan Lan** (48 East 57th Street; 308-0018); **Ximenes Rare Books** (19 East 69th Street; 744-0226); or **James Cummins** (699 Madison Avenue, 2nd floor; 688-6441).

The most famous secondhand bookstore in New York is the **Strand** (828 Broadway; 473-1452), which has an estimated eight miles of shelves at rock-bottom prices, plus some first editions, autographed copies, and serious rare books for those on lavish budgets. The **Gotham Book Market,** though not as huge, is a prestigious shop of the old literary-salon sort (41 West 47th Street; 719-4448). **Argosy Books** is six floors of maps, posters, antiquarian books, and autographs.

Hacker Art Books has a huge inventory of books on fine and decorative arts, architecture, techniques, and you-name-it (45 West 57th Street; 688-7600). **Biography Bookshop** in Greenwich Village is just what it sounds like, incorporating not only straight biographies but also diaries, children's versions, and biographical fiction (400 Bleecker Street; 897-8655).

Books of Wonder in Chelsea is the sort of children's bookstore you never grow out of, one where authors and illustrators pop in for pleasure as well as for autographings (132 Seventh Avenue; 989-3270). **Different Light Books,** now relocated from its famous Greenwich Village location to Chelsea, is still the premiere gay bookstore in the city (151 West 19th Street; 989-4850), but the **Oscar Wilde Memorial Bookshop** still keeps the Village supplied (Christopher and Gay Streets; 255-8097).

Printed Matter Bookstore, which is inside the wonderful old six-story Gay '90s building-turned-studio-space at the corner of Wooster and Broome Streets in SoHo, is a nonprofit outlet for books designed and produced by artists, often by hand; but most of the thousands of volumes are astonishingly inexpensive, about the cost of a vintage glass of wine around the corner at the SoHo Kitchen & Bar (59 Wooster; 925-0325).

With home-style fare back on the trend menus (and container gardening a Martha Stewart–style craze), you may be furrowing your brow for just that particular zucchini casserole recipe. **Joanne Hendricks Cookbooks** is heaven for culinary wannabes, including those who remember their moms working out of treasures that have long been out of print (488 Greenwich Street; 925-4697 for appointments). An even larger selection, more than 7,000 titles both in and out of print, is available at **Kitchen Arts and Letters,** the love child of former Harper & Row editor Nachum Waxman (1435 Lexington Avenue; 876-5550).

Kinokuniya is a shop in Rockefeller Plaza that sells books on Japanese food, culture, art, martial arts, and fine literature in both English and Japanese; it's a branch of the Japanese Barnes & Noble, so to speak (10 West 49th Street; 765-7766). Across the plaza is the **Traveler's Bookstore,** which has both guides to and journals from (22 West 52nd Street; 664-0995). And in the Rockefeller Center Promenade is the Librarie de France/Libreria Hispanica, a.k.a. **the Dictionary Store,** which has thousands of French- and Spanish-language records, books, magazines, and newspapers (581-8810).

Liberation Books specializes in African American history and literature (421 Lenox Avenue; 281-4615). And **University Place Books** has titles in and about more than three dozen African and West Indies dialects (821 Broadway; 254-5998).

The two **Murder Ink** shops at 2486 Broadway (362-8905) and 1465-B Second Avenue (742-7023) are so full of mystery choices it's a crime to miss them—unless you're a Sherlockian, in which case you should head to the **Mysterious Bookshop** of Baker Street Irregular Otto Penzler (129 West 56th Street; 765-0900). Science fiction fans head to the **Forbidden Planet** (821 Broadway; 473-1576). For comic books (admittedly a paperback of a different color) head down to **Village Comics** (163 Bleecker Street, 2nd floor; 777-2770) or **St. Mark's Comics,** which carries underground, limited-edition, and other hard-to-find copies (11 St. Mark's Place; 598-9439).

And if you happen to need a Bible in some language other than English, try the **International Bible Society** at 172 Lexington Avenue; they stock good books in umpteen languages (213-5454).

Bridal Gowns. Here the first, and second, name in wedding designs is **Vera Wang** (by appointment only, 991 Madison Avenue; 628-3499). For more downtown tastes, try **Jane Wilson-Marquis** in SoHo (155 Prince Street; 477-4408) or nineteenth-century romanticist **Opal White** (by appointment only, 131 Thompson Street; 677-8215). But if you expect to have to try on hundreds and hundreds of dresses to find the right one, you'll have to spin over to Brooklyn for the designer-label parade at **I. Kleinfeld & Son** (8202 Fifth Avenue, Brooklyn; (718) 833-1100). Make an appointment; they welcome as many as 100 brides-to-be every day.

Caviar. Petrossian is the most famous name in mail-order caviar, and for good reason, but their headquarters are proof that good taste goes both ways. Whether you're buying beluga by the tin or just dropping by for a snack, this beautiful marble room, something like an ice cream parlor for sophisticates, is a great stop-off. There's a whole menu as well, and it's a fine one (West 58th Street at Seventh Avenue; 245-2214).

Classic Records. For the widest selection in vintage vinyl, particularly rock and roll, try **Strider Records** (22 Jones Street; 675-3040) in Greenwich Village; or head to **St. Marks Sounds** (20 St. Marks Place; 677-3444). If it's Broadway cast recordings or early jazz you want, try **Footlight Records** in the East Village (113 East 12th; 533-1572). **Adult Crash** specializes in

Japanese imports (66 Avenue A; 387-0558). For 45 rpms, try **Downstairs Records** at 35 West 43rd Street (354-4684).

Consignment Clothing. This is one town where resale is still high-fashion, so you can really come back from a New York trip wearing designer clothing at department-store prices. Big-name evening dresses are the hottest items at **Designer Resale** (324 East 81st Street; 734-3639) and **Encore** (1132 Madison Avenue upstairs; 879-2850). In the same general neighborhood, though a little less chi-chi, are **Michael's** (1041 Madison Avenue; 737-7273) and the just-as-chic men's designer boutique called **Gentlemen's Resale** (303 East 81st Street; 734-2739). If you'd like to double your savings by making a contribution to the Rain Forest Foundation, head to **Transfer** (220 East 50th Street; 355-4230), which turns 10 percent of its proceeds over to the fund.

Cookware and Kitchen Goods. The hottest styles in stoves, namely the porcelain-coated restaurant-quality Garland stoves that the chefs, chef's critics, and celebrities with private chefs now buy for home use, are sold with a smile at **Mazer Store Equipment** in the Lower East Side (207 Bowery; 674-3450). Designer cookware, flatware, and even antique cupboards are the goods at **Platypus** in SoHo (126 Spring Street; 219-3919), while **Broadway Panhandler** (477 Broome; 966-3434) gives "baker's dozen" a whole new meaning: It stocks not just dozens but hundreds of kinds of cake pans. For serious cookware in the French style try **Lamalle** (36 West 25th Street, 6th floor; 242-0750).

Cosmetics and Skin Care. Nobody cares more about facial products and cosmetics than Big Apple women (and men); none are more into earth-friendly brands than those around the Village. Try **M.A.C. SoHo** (113 Spring Street; 334-4641) for new looks and counseling (ask for a discount if you're in the modeling or theatrical biz) or **Face Stockholm,** with its palette of 140 eye shadows (110 Prince Street; 334-3900). For all-natural herbal cosmetics and body products, try **Erbe** (Prince and Spring Streets; 966-1445) or the Estée Lauder–owned but honorable **Origins** (402 West Broadway; 219-9764). For deeper treatments—facials, peels, aromatherapies, and the like—book some time in **Bliss** (568 West Broadway; 219-8970) or the **Aveda Esthetique** (456 West Broadway; 473-0280). And if you're tired of trying to find that perfect lipstick, check out **Three Custom Color** (447 W. 45th Street; 262-7714). They can custom-blend lipsticks to your specification (two for $45) or let you choose from their own ready-to-wears ($15 apiece). Not sure? Try three samples for $5.

Kiehl's (109 Third Avenue; 667-3171) has been a Manhattan byword for nearly a century and a half, still owned and operated by the same family and still making its body treatments, shampoos, and skin care items by hand from all natural ingredients.

Decorative Arts. With all the revived interest in imperial Russia, Fabergé, and so on, it's fascinating to step into **A La Vielle Russie** (781 Fifth Avenue; 752-1727), which has been selling Russian enamels, jewelry, and, yes, Fabergé since the Romanovs were in power.

If it's early-twentieth-century style you seek, you can indulge your craving for Art Deco at **DeLorenzo** (958 Madison Avenue, 55 E. 65th; 772-1080) or **Barry Friedman** (1117 Madison, 32 E. 67th; 794-8950), while **20th Century Antiques** favors Art Nouveau (878 Madison, 568 Broadway; 925-1192). Tiffany classics are the house specialty at **Macklowe Gallery & Modernism** (667 Madison Avenue; 644-6400).

Susan P. Meisel specializes in twentieth-century pieces, too, but within that phrase is included Clarice Cliff pottery from between the wars, vintage Mexican silver, and so on (133 Prince Street; 254-0137).

Furs. The center of the retail fur trade in Manhattan is on Seventh Avenue between 28th and 29th Streets in Chelsea, a neighborhood often called (a little grandly) the Fur District. Among the most reliable names here are **G. Michael Hennessy** (695-7991) and **Gus Goodman** (244-7422), both in the 333 Seventh Avenue building, though on different floors. But the greatest bargain, especially for the nonrich and unknown, is the **Ritz Thrift Shop** at 107 West 57th Street (265-4559), which buys, refits, and reconditions estate-sale furs, turns antique coats into linings or novelty coats, and sometimes just offers nice but not premium new coats at half-price or even lower. They'll buy their own coats back, too, although at a very much lower price and so long as they're still in very good condition; so you can keep trading up.

Gourmet Foods. In search of the perfect pickle or real old-fashioned sauerkraut? Where else but the Lower East Side, where **Guss Pickle Products,** the city's oldest, is still dishing 'em out (35 Essex Street; 254-4477). With that get the matzo to go at **Streit's Matzo Company** (150 Rivington Street; 475-7000). From dried fruit to nuts, go nuts at **A. L. Bazzini's** in TriBeCa, which smells like honey-roasted heaven and sells a real PB&J sandwich that would have given Proust fits (339 Greenwich Street; 334-1280).

Aux Delices des Bois in TriBeCa is one of the foremost importers of rare and wild mushrooms, Italian, French, and Asian (4 Leonard Street; 334-1230). Nearby is **Cheese of All Nations,** which has just about what it sounds like, and more than a thousand of them (153 Chambers Street; 732-0752). Olives, all colors, sizes, and brines of them, are the hot items at the **Gourmet Garage** in SoHo (453 Broome Street; 941-5850). Imported coffees are easy enough to come by these days, but **McNulty's Tea and Coffee Co.** in Greenwich Village also stocks a few hundred types of tea leaves (109 Christopher Street; 242-5351); **Aphrodisia** has a few hundred leaves to choose from, too—in this case herbs, spices, and herbal remedies (264 Bleecker Street; 989-6440).

Of course, if you like all your temptations under one roof, there are New York's three most famous names in food: **Zabar's, Balducci's,** and **Dean & DeLuca.** Zabar's, on the West Side, just goes to show you what a serious Jewish deli can be (2245 Broadway; 787-2000). Balducci's may not be the Village veggie stand any more, but it's still run by the same folks (424 Sixth Avenue; 673-2600). D&D, the Bloomingdale's of food, is located at 560 Broadway (431-1691).

With Little Italy shrinking, it's harder to get the classic deli-shopping experience. But if you happen to be planning a visit to either the Bronx Zoo or the New York Botanical Gardens, you can combine the excursion with a trip to Arthur Avenue only a few blocks away, market heart of an Italian American community. The **Arthur Avenue Retail Market** at 2344 Arthur, an old-fashioned covered market opened in 1940 by then-Major Fiorello La Guardia, is about in the middle of a whole block of meat markets, bakeries, cheese stores, gift shops, cafes, seafood markets, and of course Italian restaurants. (For details on visiting the zoo and gardens, see Part 11, "New York's Attractions.")

If you're looking for fresh fruit, the sidewalk stand is alive and well all over the town, but if you want an open-air farmers' market, visit the **Union Square Market** Wednesdays, Fridays, and Saturdays, where you can get vegetables, fruits, eggs, honey, and so on (at the north end of the square on 17th Street between Broadway and Park Avenue South).

Interior Design. If you don't make it farther south than the Gramercy Park neighborhood, see the modular display and storage options in **Alu** (138 West 25th Street; 924-8713), or take your best shot—at photography and at personalizing your own interiors—by having **Duggal** transfer the image digitally to drapes, vinyl, paper, silk, ceramic tile, even black velvet (9 West 20th Street; 242-7000).

Jewelry. If you want diamonds, you have to cruise the **Diamond District,** a continuous wall of glittering store windows and mini-malls along 47th Street between Fifth and Sixth Avenues, traditionally operated by Orthodox Jewish and (increasingly) Middle Eastern dealers. The most eye-bulging pieces already set with precious and semiprecious stones are in an even more glittery row along Fifth Avenue between 56th and 57th, including **Tiffany & Co.** (755-8000); **Harry Winston** (245-2000); **Bulgari** (315-9000); and **Van Cleef & Arpels** (644-9500).

But if you want the one-of-a-kind look without the Indian-curse pedigree or the Shah of Iran price tag, visit **Reinstein/Ross,** Susan Reinstein's boutique, in SoHo (122 Prince Street; 226-4513) or **Pedro Boregaard** in Midtown (18 East 53rd Street, 15th floor; 826-3660). For custom-made pieces, go to **Stuart Moore** just down the street (128 Prince; 941-1023) or **Eurocraft Custom Jewelry** in the clothing district (42 West 48th Street; 221-7553)

Sanko Cultured Pearls (45 West 47th Street; 819-0585) has a fine reputation, though you have to make an appointment.

Jukeboxes. Refurbished Wurlitzers, slot machines, and soft drink dispensers are among the nostalgia for sale at **Back Pages Antiques** in SoHo (125 Greene Street; 460-5998).

Neon. If you've discovered the artsy side of neon (and argon, and all the other colors of the electrified rainbow), head for **Let There Be Neon** in TriBeCa (38 White Street; 226-4883), studio-store of artist Rudi Stern.

Photography. Cindy Sherman is just one of the big names whose work can be found at **Metro Pictures** in SoHo (150 Greene Street; 925-8335), while hours of browsing won't begin to exhaust the fine options at **Laurence Miller Gallery** (138 Spring Street, upstairs; 226-1220).

For photographic books and antiques as well as prints, try **A Photographer's Place** at 133 Mercer Street (431-9358) or **Jaap Rietman** (134 Spring Street, upstairs; 966-7044), both in SoHo. And although it's really a little farther south in TriBeCa, the **SoHo Photo Gallery** is the oldest and most comprehensive co-op in the country (15 White Street; 226-8571).

Snakes. The latest living fashion accessories/low-maintenance pets are available in more than 100 varieties at **Village Rainforest** on Eighth Avenue (529-4487).

Sports Souvenirs. Baseball card collectors collect at **Card Collectors** (105 West 77th Street; 873-6999) or the **Collector's Stadium** (214 Sullivan Street; 353-1531). Athletic logo clothing is in every shopping mall these days, but "official" T-shirts, warm-up jackets, and such can be scooped up at the **Yankees Clubhouse** stores (110 East 59th Street, 758-7844; and 393 Fifth Avenue, 685-4693) or the **Mets Clubhouse** (575 Fifth Avenue; 986-4887). Or, of course, you could go to a real game . . .

Spy Stuff. Cold war or no, the **Counter Spy Shop** (or Shoppe: it's a Bonded branch of a Mayfair, London, operation) has all the mini-minicams, bulletproof vests, night-vision binoculars, scramblers, and lie detectors you could ever need. One location is in the lobby of the Waldorf-Astoria at 301 Park Avenue (750-6645), so for heaven's sake, try not to look too shady. There's also a branch at 444 Madison Avenue (688-8500).

Typewriters. Some of us still love the old-fashioned bang-'em-out keyboards; others, who can't afford computers equipped with foreign language software, might trade their elderly relatives for some of the international beauties. **Tytell Typewriter Co.** (116 Fulton Street upstairs; 233-5333) has hundreds of unusual typefaces for custom keyboards as well as parts for repairing even ancient manual jobs.

Vintage Posters and Cartoons. The best collection of Toulouse-Lautrec and the like—in fact, the only complete collection of Lautrec's "advertising" posters—belongs to Wine Spectator/Cigar Aficionado tycoon Marvin Shenken. Unfortunately, unless you're invited to his offices, you probably won't be able to see them, but you can pick up a few items almost as rare at **La Belle Epoque** on the Upper West Side (282 Columbus Avenue; 362-1770) and SoHo (827 Broadway; 254-6436). **Poster America** specializes in twentieth-century posters, but it's equally famous for its home in the old stables that once served—literally—the carriage trade of the 1880s (138 West 18th Street; 206-0499). Movie buffs can try **Triton Gallery** (323 West 45th Street; 765-2472) or **Jerry Ohlinger's Movie Materials** (242 West 14th Street; 989-0869).

If it's animation cels you want, head for **Animazing Gallery** in SoHo (415 West Broadway; 226-7374), the only authorized Disney and Warner Bros. art gallery in the city.

Watches. Counterfeit Rolexes, Piagets, and Movados are all over town, and for $25 or $30 bucks they can be a fun souvenir, although whether they'll run for 24 hours or 24 months is a matter of pure chance. So is whether the hands work, incidentally. A better bet is **Twelve o'Clock High** (255-2649), which began as a weekend vendor's stand at Spring and Greene Streets in the Village and now has a cart in Union Station; the owner scouts out intriguing watches from Japan and elsewhere that also cost only $25 or $30 but that really work. I have several. Or try **Mostly Watches** (200 West 57th Street; 265-7100).

For guaranteed models of those luxury names—the ones that shout platinum! titanium! white gold! and so on—visit **Tourneau,** whose double-page ads in the *New York Times* and luxury-class magazines are whole catalogues in themselves (Fifth at 54th; 758-3265 and 57th and Madison; 768-6098). For more unusual vintage timepieces and clocks, try **Fanelli**

Antique Timepieces (790 Madison Avenue;), **Time Will Tell** (962 Madison Avenue; 861-2663), or **Aaron Faber** (666 Fifth Avenue; 586-8411).

Wines. Sherry Lehman's inventory is famous, and not by accident; it's probably the largest in the world. The catalogues, which come out every couple of months, make great souvenirs and gifts as well (Madison Avenue at East 61st Street; 838-7500).

Manhattan is also home to a new kind of wine store, **Best Cellars,** where the less label-conscious can find help and hope. Here wines are arranged not simply by varietals (since having drunk a lot of California chardonnay will not necessarily give you a fair concept of French or Australian chardonnay) but by "taste"—that is, "fresh" (light-bodied), "luscious" (round, richly flavored), and so on. So you just go after the sort of wine you like. And most of them are bargain-priced, to boot (Lexington at 87th; 426-4200).

PART TEN

Sight-Seeing and Tours

Let Your Fingers Do the Walking . . . First

The nice thing about sight-seeing is that you can do it at your own pace, looking closely at what intrigues you, gazing appreciatively at what only pleases you, and pushing right on past what stirs not a flicker of interest. In New York, you can tour by land, sea, air, or, at least in some places, horse-drawn carriage. You can see historic spots or literary haunts, cathedrals or courts, authentic remnants or virtual realities. (And you can pay nothing or, well, something.)

You can see them all best if you get right down to street level. New York is particularly well suited to walking tours, and that's what we recommend. (Skylines are lovely, but you have to be at a distance to see them.) We want you to get up close and personal here. Keep your eyes open and your schedule a little loose: Several office buildings around town have minimuseums and free galleries on the street level; some technology firms have informal try-out rooms.

But it's a little smarter to consider your preferences before you start off—before you leave home, if you have time, or maybe on the plane. New York offers so much that it can be confusing if not downright intimidating. So we've outlined some "categories" of special interest, suggested some specialized tours you might be interested in, and even (modestly) mentioned some personal favorites. We recommend some neighborhoods over others for strolling, and have sketched out a few starting points and highlights in Part 7, "New York's Neighborhoods."

In Part 9, "Shopping in New York," we've combined souveniring with introductory walks around the most important neighborhoods (to visitors, at least), with a little background flavor and a few landmarks for orientation. Some of the more important museums, historic houses, and buildings are described in more detail in Part 11, "New York's Attractions."

And as soon as you can, sit down with that list and a subway map; you'll be surprised what unusual tours you can devise for yourself beyond the more obvious such as Museum Mile or even a single neighborhood walk. For example, using the 1/9 and A trains, which connect at the Washington Heights Station, you can launch a family-friendly history outing combing the Dyckman House, High Bridge, Fort Tryon, and even the Little Red Firehouse (see the second on Zone 15 in Part 7.) You could even make it to Yankee Stadium—or let one parent bliss out over the medieval art of the Cloisters.

Devout visitors might want to work their way up the island from saint to saint, from the Shrine of Mother Elizabeth Seton (Zone 1) to the Shrine of St. Frances Cabrini (Zone 15); or from St. Patrick's Cathedral (Zone 9) up to Riverside Church and the heart-stopping Cathedral of St. John the Divine (Zone 14).

Some tourists might want to pick areas that offer the most attractions in the smallest, concentrated space: for instance, the several museums of Audubon Terrace (Zone 15) or Midtown around MoMA (Zone 9). The more progressive clustering of attractions in Brooklyn, from Grand Army Plaza to the zoo in Prospect Park, the Botanic Gardens, and Brooklyn Museum of Art, makes that borough a perfect subway jaunt—if you could possibly accomplish it all in one day. (The trolley helps; see Zone 16 in Part 7.) And the Bronx Zoo and nearby New York Botanical Gardens are, for families, a five-star expedition pair.

On the other hand, we know that not everybody prefers do-it-yourself tours. Some people find it distracting to try to read directions and anecdotes while walking, and others use packaged tours as a way of getting a mental map of the area. So we've also listed some of the most reputable guided tours available. (These are almost surely not all of them: Tourism is a boom industry in New York, and you'll see flyers for new tours every month. If you do want to take a guided tour, check through the material at the information desks and visitors centers or even your hotel lobby; you may find a discount coupon lurking.)

We also realize that New York is not one-size-fits-all. Walking is wonderful if you're young and fit, but if your party includes children or seniors, make sure to pace yourself. Build in a timely stop in a park; split the touring day into "shifts" so that, if necessary, those with less stamina can head back to the hotel for a rest while the others continue; or lay out the schedule on the democratic scheme—that is, put the attractions everyone wants to see first, the could-be-missed intermediate ones later, and the only-for-fanatics excursions last. That way, whoever wants to drop out can.

If each member of the party has his own must-sees, then set a particular hour to split up and a clearly understood place to regroup. If you're worried about a teenager getting completely wound up in whatever museum or exhibit he's into and losing track of the time, schedule this separate tour session just before lunch; there are few things that can override a kid's stomach alarm, even a *T. rex* skeleton.

Finally, because the food and beverage lures are everywhere, especially around major tourist attractions, avoid stomach overload or whining children by carrying a supply of snacks in plastic bags. And don't forget water or soda: It's easy to become dehydrated when you're doing a lot of walking.

■ Categories and Recommendations ■

Best Children's Fare

Abigail Adams Smith Museum (Zone 11)
American Museum of Natural History (Zone 12)
Bronx Zoo (Zone 18)
Brooklyn Children's Museum (Zone 16)
Central Park
Children's Museum of Manhattan (Zone 12)
Forbes Magazine Galleries (Zone 4)
Hayden Planetarium (Zone 12) (under reconstruction)
Intrepid Sea-Air-Space Museum (Zone 8)
Museum of Television and Radio (Zone 9)
Museum of the City of New York (Zone 13)
New York City Fire Museum (Zone 2)
New York Hall of Science (Zone 17)
New York Transit Museum (Zone 16)
Roosevelt Island Aerial Tramway (Zone 11)

Best Views

Brooklyn Bridge (Zone 1/3)
Empire State Building (Zone 7)
Marriott-Marquis View Restaurant (Zone 8)
Riverside Church (Zone 14)
Rockefeller Center's Rainbow Room (Zone 9)
Statue of Liberty (Zone 1)
World Trade Center (Zone 1)

Ethnic and "Roots" Exhibits

Ellis Island Immigration Museum (Zone 1)
Japan Society (Zone 9)
The Jewish Museum (Zone 13)
Lower East Side Tenement Museum (Zone 3)
El Museo del Barrio (Zone 14)
The Museum for African Art (Zone 2)
The Museum of Jewish Heritage/Holocaust (Zone 1)
Museum of Chinese in the Americas (Zone 3)
National Museum of the American Indian (Zone 1)
Schomberg Center for Research in Black Culture (Zone 14)

Smaller, Less Crowded Museums of Note

The Asia Society (Zone 11)
The Cloisters (Zone 15)
The Frick Collection (Zone 11)
Hispanic Society of America (Zone 14)
Isamu Noguchi Garden Museum (Zone 17)
Jacques Marchais Center of Tibetan Art (Zone 19)
Museum of the City of New York (Zone 13)
New-York Historical Society (Zone 12)
Pierpont Morgan Library (Zone 9)

Photography Collections

Alice Austen House (Zone 19)
International Center for Photography (Zones 8 and 14)
Museum of Modern Art

Free Museum Hours

Asia Society, Tuesday 6–8 p.m.
Bronx Museum of the Arts, Wednesday 3–9 p.m.
Bronx Zoo, Wednesday 10 a.m.–4:30 p.m.
Cooper-Hewitt National Design Museum, Tuesday 5–9 p.m.
Solomon R. Guggenheim Museum, Friday 6–8 p.m. (pay what you
    wish)
International Center of Photography, Tuesday 6–8 p.m. (pay what
    you wish)
Jewish Museum, Tuesday 5–8 p.m.
Museum of Modern Art, Thursday and Friday 5:30–8:30 p.m. (pay
    what you wish)

New Museum of Contemporary Art, Saturday 6–8 p.m.
New York Botanical Garden, Wednesday 10 a.m.–4 p.m.; Saturday
   10 a.m.–noon
New York Hall of Science, Wednesday and Thursday 2–5 p.m.
Whitney Museum of American Art, Thursday 6–8 p.m.

■ Personal Favorites ■

Everybody has favorite things to do or must-sees to recommend to New
York visitors, but mine may be a little different than some. A few are pretty
well-known, but frankly, a lot of superhyped tourist attractions aren't all
that attractive—and some might as well be in another city. If you're going
to see New York, at least make it a unique experience. You don't need to
relive my favorite things, but they may help you understand what I mean
by seeing through to the real city and getting away from the stereotype.

1. Visiting the Frick Collection. Pure and simple. I only wish the pipe
   organ still played.

2. Visiting the Cloisters. A medievalist's fantasy come true. One perfect weekend trip would encompass the Cloisters, the medieval area
   at the main Metropolitan Museum of Art building, and the illuminated manuscripts at the Pierpont Morgan Library. And to top
   it off, a pipe organ concert at one of the cathedrals. Talk about an
   antidote to modern life!

3. Walking through Central Park. I routinely walk 50 or more blocks
   at a time (luckily, I really enjoy walking), and even if I have to make
   a detour, I nearly always manage to use the park as part of the route.
   And at that, I don't think I've ever walked exactly the same way. Nor
   do I think I've ever not seen something new: another nook of a
   pond, another fine rock formation, another statue. I've made friends
   with dogs, horses (and their humans), bird-watchers, bird callers,
   lost balls, kids seeking lost balls, nannies seeking lost children, bik-
   ers, bladers, joggers, aspiring skaters, model boat enthusiasts, concert roadies, food vendors, street artists, locals, tourists, tourists in
   need of photographic assistance—and dozens more. And once or
   twice I've been absolutely alone, no small feat in this city.

4. Living the Park Avenue lush life on the cheap. Nothing is more fun
   than catching a fine art or estate sale auction at Sotheby's or
   Christie's. Not only will you learn a surprising amount about the

art of selling art, but it's also pure theater. There are professional bidders, dozens of them, on the phone to their bosses or patrons all over the world; bids are flashed up in half a dozen currencies and the delicate art of actually placing a bid—a crooked finger, a nod, a raised eyebrow—is the commercial equivalent of a southern belle's fan language. (Do keep still, though, or you may discover you've made a really major purchase.) Occasionally you may have to buy an auction catalogue, but frequently you can just go in and sit unless the room is full of active buyers, and previews, usually held for several days before the sales themselves, are open to the public. I once lucked into a Christie's auction of the sort of jewelry one only sees in museum paintings and laser-guarded cases, usually with royal credentials and curses to go along, and it was wonderful fun. That was just the beginning: Christie's is on the second floor, and downstairs is Caviarteria (Park Avenue at 59th Street; 759-7410), where you can have champagne by the glass, caviar, and chocolate before strolling back toward Central Park a block away. Now that's the good life.

5. Making personal "touchstone stops." I have never visited the city without having a drink at the Oak Bar in the Plaza Hotel. I stayed there as a child (in full Eloise regalia and stringy long hair), and even now I think the two great nocturne paintings of winter in New York among the most evocative ever. One of them, which portrays what looks like a huge French chateau, actually represents the extravagant home (one of them, at least) of Cornelius Vanderbilt, which once filled the block of Fifth Avenue coming up next to the Plaza; it's what you would have seen walking out the lobby door 100 years ago. A close second cocktail favorite is the Rainbow Bar atop Rockefeller Plaza. I prefer this view to some of the even higher ones because I like being amid the city's lights rather than above them.

6. Eating out. That needs no elaboration, either. There is nearly every type of ethnic cuisine here somewhere, and a lot of times an even better version, thanks to the wonders of modern refrigeration and prime-quality ingredients, than you could get in the country itself. (I don't worry about making myself understood; one way or another, I've never gone hungry.)

7. Getting theater tickets. I tend to prefer nonmusicals, and frequently I head for off- or even off-off-Broadway, but you shouldn't miss seeing some show or other.

Packaged Tours

There are well over a thousand licensed tour guides in New York, and many times as many unlicensed ones. And no wonder: The city draws 30 million visitors every year, and the numbers keep going up. That's good news and bad—good because you as a tourist have a huge number of tours and guides to choose from, and bad because it can be difficult to differentiate between the worthwhile and the time-consuming.

Frankly, we're not so enthusiastic about most packaged mass tours. We think it's more rewarding to select the attractions you're truly interested in and go on your own or with a more intimate group. After all, most of the "sights" on those sight-seeing tours are so famous you already know what the outside looks like, and a lot of the time that's all you see out the window, anyway. And you're a lot more likely to end the day feeling, just as you did in the morning, that Manhattan is a large, crowded, and loud place.

Besides, there are several drawbacks to taking these overview tours. For one thing, simply loading and off-loading passengers at every stop—not to mention dealing with traffic—takes up a substantial portion of the time you are supposedly sight-seeing. And a more recent twist is that more and more of the neighborhoods, from SoHo to Harlem, are complaining about tour bus traffic and the noise and pollution created by idling vehicles. Commercial traffic is banned around some important historical areas, most notably Washington Square.

On the favorable side, you are apt to be swept around enough to get an idea of the island's layout, and if you plan to return frequently, that might be an advantage. Many of the longer tours have lunch or dinner and even a little entertainment scheduled right along with the ride, which may be a relief for those with sticker or map shock. Those with limited walking power might prefer to stay on the bus, in any case. Those shy of sidewalk adventures may find security in numbers. And you can hear a lot of history and humor in a single dose, if that's what you like.

Note that prices frequently change; you might want to ask whether the tour company has discounts for members of AARP, AAA, and such.

Gray Line Tours, which has buses, double-decker buses, and trolleys, remains one of the most reliable packaged tour operators. You can spend from two hours to the whole day in its care; see the whole island or just a district or two; and get picked up from many major hotels as well as its headquarters at the side entrance to the Port Authority Bus Terminal on 42nd Street near Eighth Avenue (397-2600). A nice feature is that hop-on, hop-off tickets are good for two days, so you can spread it out if you don't want to make the whole circuit at once. Gray Line has tour guides who speak French, German, Italian, Spanish, and Portuguese as well as English. If you want to be picked up from the airport as well, call 315-3006.

Other top companies include **New York Apple Tours,** which has a 46-stop itinerary "from Harlem to the Statue of Liberty" that also allows passengers to get on and off as they please (944-9700 or (800) 876-9868); and **New York Double Decker** tours, which runs something like a shuttle service that leaves from various hotels every half-hour between 9 a.m. and 5 p.m. Their two-day on-off pass is $19 for adults and $10 for children, available either at its hub at the Empire State Building (967-6008 or (800) 692-2870) or right on board. Tours are offered in German, French, and Spanish as well as English.

Harbor cruises lasting about 90 minutes and offering views of the Statue of Liberty and the downtown skyline with the World Trade Center and other notable buildings are offered by **NY Waterways** (call (800) 533-3779); there's free bus pickup from various sites around town. **Seaport Liberty Cruises** swing around the Statue of Liberty and Ellis Island from the South Street Seaport in about an hour; they also offer two-hour jazz cruises on Thursday evenings and blues cruises on Wednesdays (630-8888). The same group offers a four-hour "sea-land-sky" package in conjunction with Heritage Trails and the World Trade Center; call (888) 4-TRAILS. For an even higher view than the Trade Center, take a helicopter tour: The Gray Line office sells no-reservation tickets for flights leaving continually from 9 a.m. to 6 p.m. weekdays (683-4575).

More fun than a simple harbor cruise is the **Circle Line** tour, a surprisingly entertaining three-hour circumnavigation of Manhattan entirely by water. The ships, all former coast guard cutters or navy landing craft, head down the Hudson past the Statue of Liberty, back up the East River along the old Upper East Side, and through Spuyten-Duyvil Creek. The headquarters are at Pier 83 at West 42nd Street; three tours leave daily April through mid-December (563-3200).

Guided Walking Tours

As we've said, we think walking tours, either independent or guided, are the way to really see New York. Just use a little common sense when planning your visit.

Many walking tours are weather-dependent, so be sure to ask how to confirm whether the tour is on if the skies darken. The big tour companies are full-time, but many of the smaller tour groups (or personal guides) have more limited schedules. Most walking tours offered through museums or other groups are on weekends; so are most of the specialty tours, though you can often arrange for a weekday tour if you get in touch with the company in advance. Tips are appreciated by some but declined by others, particularly those arranged by nonprofit agencies; you can ask when you call.

Some of the best things really are free, even in New York. The **Urban Park Rangers** offer weekend walking tours through Central Park and other green areas in all five boroughs, and the guides are as family-friendly as the price. Call 427-4040 or (800) 201-7275. The **Times Square Tours** have great guides, too—professional actors, in fact. They start at noon on Fridays, rain or shine, at the Times Square Visitors Center at 226 West 42nd Street. And the Friday "Weekend" section of the *New York Times* often mentions special-interest tours arranged through nonprofit organizations or museums.

But if you want to set up a more personalized tour, or one with a specialized focus, contact **Big Apple Greeters,** who can put you in contact with an expert in your field if you give them a few days' notice (669-8159). The tour guides are volunteers, and the buddy-system tour, arranged though the Manhattan borough president's office, is free (though it would be nice if you offered to buy lunch or something). Who says New York isn't friendly?

Of course, most tour guides are trying to make a paid living at this. Especially if you're interested in authentic flavor (as opposed to memorized brochure stuff), the neighborhood walking tours are the way to go.

Among the very best such tours are the **Big Onion Walking Tours** ("Long before it was dubbed the Big Apple, those who knew New York City called it The Big Onion," announces the brochure). Most of the Big Onion tours cover the historically polyglot region of Little Italy, Chinatown, Bowery, and the Lower East Side, but they have expanded their staff to cover Gramercy Park and Union Square, Historic Harlem, the East Village, Brooklyn Heights and the Brooklyn Bridge, "Revolutionary New York," TriBeCa, and so forth.

Big Onion is the brainchild of two history scholars, Seth Kamil and Ed O'Donnell, and they and a staff of graduate students from NYU and Columbia University bring to life the eras of Tammany Hall, tenement life, sweatshops and flophouses, and ethnic gang struggles. You can either take a sort of two-hour overview tour that covers the waterfront, so to speak, or sign up for the more in-depth walks titled "Jewish Lower East Side," "Irish New York," "Immigrant Experiences," or "The Bowery." And speaking of authentic flavors, you can even sign up for the "Multiethnic Eating Tours," in which you nosh a pickle, swipe a dumpling, and savor fresh mozzarella as you go. Tours range from $9 to $15 for adults (depending on whether food or museum admissions are involved) and from $7 to $13 for students and seniors; call 439-1090 (or e-mail bowtnyc@aol.com) for a schedule of tours or reservations.

Similarly evocative tours are the specialty of the **Adventure on a Shoe-string** folks, who put together itineraries such as "The World of Edith Wharton" and "Hell's Kitchen Hike" ($5; 265-2663).

If you're interested in historical sites in Harlem, African American culture, particularly jazz, gospel, and soul (as in food), contact **Harlem Spirituals** ($30–$75; 391-0900), which offers tours in a half-dozen languages— hey, gospel is hot!—or **Harlem Your Way** ($32 and up; 690-1687).

If architecture and design are of interest, try the **Municipal Art Society,** which offers a variety of tours around town that cost between $10 and $15 (439-1049); or **NYC Cultural Walking Tours** (979-2388).

NYU/New School for Society Research professor **Joyce Gold** has been leading her walking tours of Manhattan neighborhoods for more than 20 years; the group tours are $12, but you can also arrange a private tour (242-5762). Queens College history professor **Harriet Davis-Kramm** offers a theme tour related to labor called "Manhattan Memories" (628-9517). Former high school teacher (academics are big in the tour biz these days!) **Ruth Alscher-Green** can lead you "River to River" downtown ($35 for one person or $50 for two; 321-2823). Self-described "radical historian" **Bruce Kayton** arranges his tours off the beaten track on the beaten tracks. That is, his Greenwich Village tour points out sites of murder, riots, and general mayhem, and his Harlem tour is as much about the Black Panthers as it is the black arts scene ($6; (718) 492-0069).

Other highly regarded walking tours include **Citywalks** by John Wilson ($12; 989-2456); the **New York City Cultural Tours,** either the Sunday public ones ($10) or customized private ones ($15 an hour; 989-2456); **A La Carte New York** (410-2698); and **Bravo New York** ((718) 834-8655).

Rock and Roll Tours of New York offers customized nostalgia tours, including a Beatlemania tour that shows you where the Fab Four (and other stars) stayed, ate, and sang in town (807-7625). **Sidewalks of New York** has tours pointing out the former haunts and homes of famous writers and artists (like the White Horse Tavern, where Dylan Thomas did the inventory and his liver so much damage), and also one showing off the taverns themselves ($10; 517-0201).

Some tours are, unfortunately, available only in warm weather (i.e., high tourist season). **The New-York Historical Society** sponsors summer walking tours through Central Park highlighting its history and evolution; tours are at 2 p.m. Fridays, Saturdays, and Sundays (673-3400). The occasional but fascinating tours offered by the **Museum of the City of New York** cover "Historic Harlem" and arts-oriented tours (but again, these are mostly good-weather options) every other Sunday from April to October ($10; 534-1672, ext. 206). You might also check in with the **Cooper-Hewitt National Design Museum** (860-6321) to see what they have coming up.

Self-Guided Walking Tours

There are several books in print with in-depth walking tours of New York, but frankly, we're confident that what we've pointed out in the zone profiles of Part 7, "New York's Neighborhoods," will tell you most of what you want to know. However, in some neighborhoods, you can easily pick up additional guides as you go. Some of the very best are the **Heritage Trails/New York** maps of downtown prepared by a nonprofit state foundation and full of first-class historical information. If you are mostly interested in directions, there is a free map with highlights marked, but for $4 you can get a brochure with quite a lot of information.

The Heritage Tours Visitor Information Center is inside the Federal Hall National Memorial on Wall Street at Broad (a cooperative gesture by the National Park Service), and in good weather there is a kiosk on the plaza outside the building as well. There are four "trails," color-coded and so organized that each one not only treats a particular subject but also concentrates the distance required. You can combine them as you wish, of course.

Heritage Tours also offers guided tours of from two to four hours, including a mixed waterfront cruise/walking tour, and occasional special interest tours highlighting George Washington's experiences in New York, downtown architecture, the African American experience, and so on. For information and tour reservations call 269-1500 or (888) 4-TRAILS.

Many other neighborhoods can supply do-it-yourself walking tour guides for a few dollars at most; **the Chinatown History Project** at 70 Mulberry Street has one for $4 (619-4785) and also offers occasional guided tours of the neighborhood.

Backstage and Behind the Scenes

There are actually four separate tours of facilities at Lincoln Center, but the two finest—which are also two of the finest in town—are the backstage tours of the **Metropolitan Opera House,** led by members of the Opera Guild ($8 and reservations required; 769-7020), and a general **Lincoln Center** tour that explores at least three theaters in the complex and comes with enthusiastic background info and the nicest kind of gossip ($8.50; tours usually from 10 a.m. to 4:30 p.m.). Venues toured depend on rehearsal, matinee, and set-construction schedules, so call ahead if you want to know which theaters are going to be included (875-5351).

Tours of **Carnegie Hall** are free, offered at 11:30 a.m. and 2 and 3 p.m. Mondays, Tuesdays, Thursdays, and Fridays; for more information call 247-7800. Members of the Municipal Arts Society lead free tours of Grand Central Terminal every Wednesday at 12:30 p.m. (935-3960). Tours of the **New York Public Library,** like its neighbor Grand Central a gem of Beaux Arts design, are also free at 11 a.m. and 2 p.m. (869-8089).

The **Radio City Music Hall** tour lasts about an hour, shows off the theater's wonderful art deco interior, and usually includes an up-close-and-personal appearance by at least one Rockette. Tours are weekdays from 10 a.m. to 5 p.m. and Sundays 11 a.m. to 5 p.m.; adult admission $12.50, children ages 12 and under $9. For information call 632-4041. While you're in the neighborhood, ask about the **NBC Studio Tour** (664-4000; no children under 6). You can even get a behind-the-scenes tour of **Madison Square Garden** if you're a total sports nerd (465-5800).

The **United Nations** tour, which also lasts about an hour, includes the Security Council chamber, the General Assembly room, and exhibits of historical importance as well as international art contributions (963-7713).

Several of the museums, especially the larger ones, offer highlights tours that give you an overview of the exhibits. The **American Museum of Natural History** (769-5100) offers highlights tours at 10:15 and 11:15 a.m. and 1:15, 2:15, and 3:15 p.m.; meet on the second floor in the Hall of African Mammals. The **Metropolitan Museum of Art** highlight tours are conducted in Italian, Spanish, and German as well as English at 10:15 and 11:15 a.m. and 1, 2, and 3:15 p.m.; tours leave from the center desk in the great front hall.

PART ELEVEN

New York's Attractions

■ An Abundance of Riches ■

Okay, you've at least skimmed the neighborhood profiles in Part 7 and the lists of sight-seeing recommendations in Part 10, and hopefully you've settled on a few areas of special interest to you or your group. The following are more in-depth descriptions of a few of the most important attractions in each zone, to add to your enjoyment of each or perhaps help you winnow down the selection even further. After all, if you're faced with only a few hours, choosing among the museums in Zone 13 alone might come down to whether you prefer Asian, European, or American art—or even ancient, medieval, or modern.

We try to estimate how long it will take to see, in any reasonable sense, the extent of the collection or building, although of course you must factor in both the extent of your own interest and your stamina when sketching out your schedule. We've also tried to convey the degree to which a particular museum or church might interest visitors of different ages and backgrounds so that you might be able to set up a tag-team plan allowing members of your group to divide up within a neighborhood and see things to their particular liking, then reunite. In that case, however, be sure to calculate not only the time involved in seeing an attraction but also the possible extra time required to stand in line. Again, if a particular teenager is boat- or book-crazy, she may score an otherwise two-star attraction a four.

In a few cases, we have suggested free tours of attractions; for information on other tours, see Part 10, "Sight-Seeing and Tours."

Zone 1: Lower Manhattan, Wall Street, and the Battery

The good thing about riding the **Staten Island Ferry** (806-6970) is that you can do it anytime, whenever your schedule is open for about an hour (or a little more, if you have to wait in line). You can choose to see Manhattan by dawn or sunset or even moonlight. It's a very cooling trip in summer and picturesque in the snow. And astonishingly, it's now free. On the other hand, once the thrill of the view of the Statue of Liberty and Lower Manhattan has paled, some children may be restless; there isn't anything else to do on board but wait for the other end. Ferries leave every 20–30 minutes during the day, more like every 45 minutes at night.

Incidentally, note that the Staten Island Ferry terminal is just a little east of Battery Park at the foot of Whitehall Street; the Circle Line/Statue of Liberty ferries leave from a little farther beside Castle Clinton.

If, under the constant press of stock-market news and inflation/recession stories, you'd like to see the **New York Stock Exchange** in action, get in line at 9 a.m. for a free but limited ticket, pick up a brochure at the main desk (20 Broad Street at Wall Street; 656-5165), and then head directly to the glass-walled observation deck, where you can look down on the frantic hand-signals and such. The rest of the "exhibits" are a quick walk. If, on the other hand, you prefer your assets in a more tangible form, you can tour the vaults of gold at the **Federal Reserve Bank,** but you'll have to get a reservation at least a week in advance (720-6130).

The famous view from the **World Trade Center** can be enjoyed in various ways, probably depending on what ages the members of your party are. You can pay for a ticket ($6 for adults, $3 for children) to the 107th-floor observation deck of tower No. 2 (the more southerly) and take the escalator up to the rooftop if you don't mind the occasional quiver of the building in the wind. You can even tell your kids this is a thrill ride, especially if you also ride the express elevator—a quarter-mile in less than one minute. Look out, look down, and look over at Tower 1: Philippe Petit walked a tightrope between the two towers in 1974 (don't tell your kids *that).* Tickets are sold on the mezzanine level (435-7377).

Or you could go over to Tower No. 1 and ride up just as far to one of the restaurants and bars there and see the city over your glass and through theirs. Even the bar tab at what is now called the Greatest Bar on Earth won't cost much more than $6. (However, it must be said that the renovations following the infamous 1993 bombing aversely affected the view from some angles.)

Ellis Island National Monument

Type of attraction: Recreation of immigrants' first contact with America

Location: New York Harbor

Nearest subway station: Bowling Green or South Ferry

Admission: $7 for adults; $5 for seniors; children $4, ages 2 and under free (combination ticket covers ferry transport and admission to Liberty Island)

Hours: Daily, 9:30 a.m.–5 p.m.; until 6 p.m. July and August. Closed Christmas.

Phone: 363-7620; ticket and ferry information, 269-5755

When to go: Weekdays

Special comments: The museum is wheelchair-accessible and offers other handicap assistance.

Overall appeal by age group:

Pre-school	Grade School	Teens	Young Adults	Over 30	Senior Citizens
½	★★★	★★★	★★★★★	★★★★★	★★★★

Author's rating: ★★★★★

How much time to allow: 1½ to 2 hours

Description and comments: Few museums can have an association for as many Americans as this one; by some estimates, half of the nation's population has roots here. From 1892 to 1954, when the processing center was abandoned, as many as 10,000 immigrants per day, a total of more than 17 million, stumbled off often wretched boats into the waiting lines of Ellis Island, where they were examined, cross-examined (whether or not they could speak English), quarantined, frequently rechristened, and just as frequently turned away. And that total would be higher if the station hadn't been used to house German POWs during World War II. Many of the arrivals were children or orphans; the very first immigrant to set foot on the island, on New Year's Day, was 15-year-old Annie Moore.

Visitors follow the immigrants' route, entering through the main baggage room and up to the high-vaulted and intentionally intimidating

Registry and then the bluntly named Staircase of Separation. Exhibits include the stark dormitories and baggage, dozens of rooms full of poignant photos and oral histories, video clips and dramatic presentations, and a thousand individual remembrances of home—crucifixes, jewelry, clothing, family heirlooms—donated by the families of those who passed through. The 1898 main building has been magnificently restored at a cost of more than $150 million, from the copper roofing to the rail-station-like glass and wrought-iron entranceway; plans for the other buildings are uncertain. The Immigrant Wall of Fame lists half a million names, including the grandfathers of presidents from Washington to Kennedy, whose descendants contributed to the restoration. Except for the very youngest, who may get tired in the long lines, almost everyone will be taken with this experience—not only the older visitors, who remember the melting-pot era best but also those school-age visitors for whom multiculturalism is a daily affair. First- and second-generation Americans will be especially affected.

Touring tip: Try to get there as early as possible, or waiting in line may add another hour to your time. Ferries leave every 30–45 minutes.

Fraunces Tavern Museum

Type of attraction: Historic replica of Revolutionary site

Location: 54 Pearl Street (at Broad Street)

Nearest subway station: Bowling Green or South Ferry

Admission: $2.50 for adults; $1 for seniors and children

Hours: Museum open Monday through Friday, 10 a.m. to 4:45 p.m.; Saturday and Sunday, noon to 4 p.m.

Phone: Museum, 425-1778; restaurant, 269-0144

When to go: Anytime

Special comments: Convenient but not important

Overall appeal by age group:

Pre-school	Grade School	Teens	Young Adults	Over 30	Senior Citizens
★★	★★	★★★	★★	★★½	★★

Author's rating: This seems most useful as an atmospheric warm-up to other historical locations. ★½

How much time to allow: 45 minutes

Description and comments: This replica of the 1719 original, which was destroyed by British cannon from the harbor, is a little too clean for real history, sort of the Williamsburg effect, and the restaurant fare is a little cute; but the four buildings connected to it are really old, and the twin chimneys, late room, and careful brickwork are accurate, if not authentic. (Actually, it's developing some age of its own; the building was bought and restored back in 1907.) In the late eighteenth century, when New York was still the national capital, this single complex housed the Departments of Foreign Affairs (now State), War (now Defense), and the Treasury—as well as the tavern. The upstairs is the museum, with colonial artifacts, paintings, and prints, as well as the reproduced Long Room, where Washington said farewell to his troops after the Revolutionary War ended (December 4, 1783) and he was, as he thought, retiring to the life of a private gentleman farmer. Washington's likeness hangs from the signboard, and conceivably it did back then, too; Fraunces, the man who turned the Georgian structure into a tavern in 1763, had been Washington's steward.

Touring tip: Plan this stop as a lunch break, but don't be too casual; it gets a lot of local business-suit business.

Museum of Jewish Heritage

Type of attraction: Re-creation of Jewish culture over the last century—that is, before, during, and after the Holocaust

Location: Battery Park City

Nearest subway station: Bowling Green or South Ferry

Admission: $7 for adults; $5 for seniors and students; children ages 5 and under free

Hours: Sunday through Wednesday, 9 a.m.–5 p.m.; Thursday, 9 a.m.–8 p.m.; Friday, 9 a.m.–2 p.m. Closed Saturdays and Jewish holidays (museum closes at 2 p.m. the afternoon before major holidays) and Thanksgiving.

Phone: 968-1800 for information; for tickets call TicketMaster at 307-4007

When to go: Anytime; tickets are timed and numbers restricted

Special comments: The museum is wheelchair-accessible. The third-floor reception room, with its panoramic view of the harbor, is available for rental.

Overall appeal by age group:

Pre-school	Grade School	Teens	Young Adults	Over 30	Senior Citizens
½	★★★	★★★	★★★★	★★★★	★★★★★

Author's rating: This seems to hit seniors (who remember the bad times) and teenagers (who may not previously have really understood the Holocaust) the hardest. ★★★★

How much time to allow: 2 to 3½ hours

Description and comments: This carefully orchestrated collection, which begins in a subtle key, crashes into the Holocaust, and climaxes in a visual paean to the future and specifically to the United States, is subtitled "A Living Memorial to the Holocaust," with emphasis on the "Living," and it has a gentler, more affirmative, and in some ways more objective tone than the larger U.S. Holocaust Memorial Museum in Washington. Instead of placing visitors in the character of victims, as the Washington site does with its "passports," the New York museum tries to make all visitors, Jewish and not, feel included in the story by emphasizing the importance of tradition and faith. And while the Washington memorial is almost entirely focused on the Holocaust itself, this collection also speaks to the recovery of Judaism, the state of Israel—a happier present and future. "They tried to exterminate us," says the Washington memorial, which is designed to resemble a ghastly furnace; "we have survived," says this six-sided temple-like structure. The key to its mission is in the dual message carved in the wall of the foyer: "Remember . . . NEVER FORGET." And right next to it, "There is hope for the future."

The lower floor (one moves from the bottom up) spotlights the richness of Jewish family life in the late nineteenth and early twentieth centuries, with clothing and artifacts from holidays and special occasions, such as a gorgeous silver and silk bride's headdress and belt, as well as simpler reminders of Sabbath and toys. (Wherever possible, the photograph of the item's owner—victim or survivor—is shown with it.) One of the most spectacular items is a handpainted Sukkah mural, almost Byzantine in its elaborate panels and portraits, showing life in Budapest in the 1920s and 1930s, along with biblical scenes, family portraits, and rituals, created by an untrained kosher butcher.

The second story tells the story of the Holocaust itself, with thousands of photos of the executed (posted on the stall-like wooden slabs that symbolize the boxcars that carried Jews to the concentration camps); toys and mementos of both escapees and victims; and a salute to those who, like Raoul Wallenberg and the now famous Oskar Schindler, helped Jews escape the Nazis. (Notice how many of the smaller interior gallery spaces are six-sided, like the building itself.) The third floor, which spotlights the post-Holocaust era, is a bit of a letdown until one reaches the last gallery, a glass-walled expanse, almost blinding after all that granite darkness, that looks directly out upon the icons of Jewish freedom: the Statue of Liberty, Ellis

Island, and the lesser-known but equally important railroad terminal on the Jersey shore, from which many immigrants began their new lives.

There are two dozen videos in the museum (many of the witnesses are part of Steven Spielberg's *Shoah* project). Intriguingly, the bulk of the museum's thousands of photographs and personal items are in storage so secret that most staff members don't know its location.

Touring tip: There is no cafeteria in the museum, but just outside its parking lot is the new and understated Robert Wagner Park, a two-story brick structure that offers a fine view of the harbor and has clean public rest rooms as well as (from about April to mid-December) a nice little cafe.

National Museum of the American Indian

Type of attraction: Part art collection, part anthropology lesson
Location: Old U.S. Custom House, 1 Bowling Green (near State and Whitehall Streets)
Nearest subway station: Bowling Green or South Ferry
Admission: Free
Hours: Daily, 10 a.m.–5 p.m.
Phone: 668-6624
When to go: Anytime

Overall appeal by age group:

Pre-school	Grade School	Teens	Young Adults	Over 30	Senior Citizens
★½	★★★	★★★	★★½	★★★	★★½

Author's rating: There is beautiful work here, and surprising (to many Americans) diversity, but it may run into a generational guilt gap; for whatever reason, it captures many children's attention faster than their parents'. ★★★
How much time to allow: 1 to 1½ hours

Description and comments: This is a branch of the Smithsonian Institution, and not surprisingly, its captions and clarity of information are first-rate. It includes artifacts not only from the more familiar (from TV and movies) Plains Indians but also from the Aztec, Olmec, Mayan, northwestern, and even Siberian tribes. Unfortunately, it seems to lack emotional power. It was only moved to the Custom House a few years ago, and it doesn't quite seem to have grown into the space yet. Or perhaps a Beaux Arts rotunda seems too formal for these intensely personal effects.

In any case, there's a bit of the Ken Burns approach here, with lots of voice-over narratives and mini–oral histories running into and over one another as you pass through various exhibits. And the rooms, which lead into one another but only rarely back to the center, can be confusing. There are often demonstrations of weaving or music in the center area, which children will enjoy.

Touring tip: Don't overlook the building itself, with its exterior sculptures of metaphoric goddesses by Daniel Chester French representing Asia (the meditative one), America (the optimistic one), Europe (with the vestiges of her empire), and Africa (unawakened). Well, it was pre-PC. Also, good and reasonable items are available in the gift shop.

St. Paul's Chapel

Type of attraction: Small, remarkably peaceful pre-Revolutionary church
Location: Broadway at Fulton Street
Nearest subway station: Cortlandt or Fulton Street
Admission: Free; donations requested for concerts
Hours: Monday through Friday, 9 a.m.–3 p.m.; Sunday, 7 a.m.–3 p.m.
   Closed Saturday.
Phone: 602-0874
When to go: Anytime
Special comments: George Washington's private pew and a few artifacts are
   preserved here.

Overall appeal by age group:

Pre-school	Grade School	Teens	Young Adults	Over 30	Senior Citizens
½	★★	★★	★★★	★★★	★★★

Author's rating: ★★★★
How much time to allow: 30 minutes

Description and comments: You might almost walk right by this little church without noticing it, it seems so beleaguered by development; even Trinity Church (see description below) has some bulk to protect it from the surrounding skyscrapers. But it's a blessing in its own right—warmly though simply painted, the wood lit by Waterford crystal chandeliers, and with President Washington's box unobtrusively roped off. It dates from the mid-1760s, and in one of those ironies of history, is purely Georgian—the style named for the kings New Yorkers would shortly renounce. More specifically, it is modeled on St.-Martin's-in-the-Field in London's Trafalgar Square and, like St. Martin's, is renowned for the quality of its concerts (noon, usually Monday and Thursday). It's one of the very few buildings to have survived the great fire of 1776.

Touring tip: Don't enter, as most people do, right off Broadway; that's actually the altar end. Walk around the yard (the cemetery once reached all the way to the river, providing a much grander setting) and come in at the "rear"; the effect is much more dramatic.

Also, from here go north a block to the Gothic Woolworth Building at 233 Broadway and walk into the elaborate and often hysterically funny interior; kids will go wild over the gargoyles, including the caricatures of architect Cass Gilbert clutching a model of the building and F. W. Woolworth himself counting out coins—"fives and dimes," in fact.

South Street Seaport and Museum

Type of attraction: Combination historic district, shopping mall, and maritime museum
Location: Water Street between John Street and Peck Slip
Nearest subway station: Fulton Street
Admission: Museum, $6 for adults; $5 seniors; $3 children
Hours: Monday through Saturday, 10 a.m.–7 p.m.; Sunday, 10 a.m.–6 p.m.
Phone: General information, 669-9400; museum, 748-8600; web site at www.southstreet.com
When to go: Anytime
Special comments: The hours given above are retail area hours; restaurants may be open later.

Overall appeal by age group:

Pre-school	Grade School	Teens	Young Adults	Over 30	Senior Citizens
—	★★	★★	★★★	★★★	★★

Author's rating: ★★
How much time to allow: 1½ to 4 hours

Description and comments: This is sort of a miniature theme park, covering 11 square blocks (some of them cobblestone) of real and reproduced seafaring New York. (It's a Rouse development, like Boston's Faneuil Hall and Baltimore's Harborplace.) In its heyday, the first half of the nineteenth century, it was so busy that South Street was nicknamed the "street of sails." But once steamships took over, the deeper-water piers on the Hudson River side gradually drew ship traffic away from this area. It wasn't until the early 1980s that its commercial potential was understood. From the visitors center in the former Pilothouse, where you pick up the free guide maps, you look right to the main food stand and shopping mall of Pier 17 and beyond that to the very real, 150-year-old Fulton Fish Market. One of the nicest stretches, in terms of architectural preservation, is Schermerhorn Row, warehouses on the south side of Fulton Street between Front and South Streets dating from the very early nineteenth century (that's how far back the Schermerhorn money goes); they were later used as hotels and shops and are now boutiques and restaurants.

Quite frankly, most of the good stuff here is free: the view from Pier 17 (one of the most evocative and least publicized views of the harbor); craftsmen building and restoring small boats; and the view of the Brooklyn Bridge, which took 16 years to build and the lives of 20 of the 600 workers—many from the bends because they emerged too quickly from underwater assignments. (John Roebling, who designed it, had his foot crushed in a freak accident on the pier just before construction was to begin in 1869 and died three weeks later. His son took over, but repeated bouts of the bends left him partially paralyzed, and finally Roebling's widow took over as supervisor.) The best reason to buy the museum ticket is to tour the tall ships anchored there: the 1991 *Peking,* the second largest sailing ship ever built, and the three-masted *Wavertree* of 1885. If you want to take a harbor tour from here, on the schooner *Pioneer* (March to November only), you can either make reservations up to two weeks in advance (669-9400) or take a chance on unreserved tickets at 10 a.m. Other commercial cruises also leave from here.

Touring tip: Walk past Fulton Fish Market to the corner of Peck Slip and Front Street and look at the mural on the ConEd substation; it's a trompe d'oeil painting of the Brooklyn Bridge (which in reality rises just beyond it), designed to make the station less obtrusive. Also look for the lighthouse at the intersection of Fulton and Water Streets. A memorial to the 1,500 passengers of the *Titanic* who perished in the 1912 catastrophe, it originally overlooked the harbor from the Seamen's Church near the current Vietnam Veterans Memorial but was moved here in 1976.

Statue of Liberty/Liberty Island

Type of attraction: America's premier symbol of freedom
Location: New York Harbor

Nearest subway station: Bowling Green or South Ferry

Admission: $7 for adults; $5 for seniors; children $4; children under age 3 free (combination ticket covers ferry transport and admission to Liberty Island)

Hours: Daily, 9:30 a.m.–5:30 p.m.; until 6 p.m. July and August. Closed Christmas.

Phone: 363-3200; ticket and ferry information, 269-5755

When to go: Weekdays

Special comments: Wheelchair access extends only to the observation deck at pedestal height; only stairs ascend to the crown.

Overall appeal by age group:

Pre-school	Grade School	Teens	Young Adults	Over 30	Senior Citizens
½	★★	★★½	★★★	★★★	★★½

Author's rating: For all its very real emotional appeal, the actual impact of this attraction close-up may depend on the length of time you have to stand in line, making it problematic for small children. Also, it may be hard on older visitors, as the view from the observation deck is neither here nor there, so to speak; nice of New York, but too close to the statue to be effective. ★★★

How much time to allow: 1½ to 4 hours

Description and comments: This most famous symbol of liberty is also a reminder of the revolutionary fervor often required to obtain it. It was a gift from the republic of France, which first supported our Revolution and then (albeit crudely) imitated it. It was a massive feat of both art (sculpted by visionary Frederic-Auguste Bartholdi, who used his mother as the model for that stern and yet tirelessly merciful face) and engineering (erected by Gustave Eiffel, whose own eventual monument would be the landmark tower in Paris). It was formally unveiled on October 28, 1896, and restored for its centennial at a cost of $70 million (plus $2 million more for the fireworks). However, the torch had corroded so badly that a replica, covered in 24-carat gold, was put in its place and the original moved to the lobby.

There are four stations, so to speak: the outside of the base, engraved with Emma Lazarus's "New Prometheus" ("Give me your tired, your poor / Your huddled masses . . ."); the exhibit hall inside the base, with its record of Bartholdi's 17-year struggle and the many patriotic and commercial uses his figure has been used for; the observation decks at the top of the pedestal; and the view from the crown—the crowning touch, so to speak. The crown is also the symbol of Liberty's "Enlightening the World," which was Bartholdi's title for the massive sculpture. The seven rays represent the seven continents and the seven seas.

While you're waiting, you can ponder the numbers: The statue itself is a little over 150 feet tall, twice that counting the pedestal and base; and it weighs 225 tons—100 tons of which represents the copper sheeting that covers the frame. There are 354 steps from the pedestal up into the crown, the equivalent of 22 stories. And don't feel bad about your own nose; hers is 4½ feet long.

Touring tip: As with the Ellis Island ferry, it's best to get an early start, or you may wind up spending half a day here. And if the lines are very long, the staff may close them off early. Note also that the last ferries leave Lower Manhattan in midafternoon; call for exact times. (The only consolation for having to wait till late is that in winter you'll see the Manhattan skyline begin to light up.)

Trinity Church

Type of attraction: Fine Gothic Revival church from the mid–nineteenth century

Location: Broadway at Wall Street

Nearest subway station: Wall Street (4, 5) or Rector Street (N, R)

Admission: Free

Hours: Monday through Friday, 7 a.m.–6 p.m.; Saturday and Sunday, 7 a.m.–4 p.m.

Phone: 602-0800

When to go: Midafternoon

Special comments: Hearing-impaired services at 2 p.m.

Overall appeal by age group:

Pre-school	Grade School	Teens	Young Adults	Over 30	Senior Citizens
½	★	★★	★★½	★★★	★★★

Author's rating: ★★★

How much time to allow: 30 minutes

Description and comments: This church, as much as any other single edifice, is responsible for the Gothic Revival craze of the nineteenth century; its balance of interior extravagance (carved wood, stained glass, and ornate stone) and exterior restraint (itself a metaphor for religious faith) is striking. Actually, this is the third church on this site: The first one was built in 1698 and burned in the conflagration of 1776; the second was razed in 1839. There's a small museum behind the altar with records of the congregation's homes. The brass doors are a tribute to Ghiberti's *Doors of Paradise* at the Duomo in Florence. Thanks to painstaking efforts by restorationists, who removed a supposedly protective layer of paraffin, the sandstone's original cherry tone is back. The 280-foot steeple pointed unrivaled to heaven until the late nineteenth century, and even surrounded by the towers of international finance, it has a certain obdurate confidence.

Romantics take note: This is where Founding Federalist and dueling victim Alexander Hamilton is buried.

Touring tip: This is a wonderful place to hear music, either choral or concert. Come Sundays or check local listings for special events.

Zone 3: Chinatown, Little Italy, and the Lower East Side

Lower East Side Tenement Museum

Type of attraction: Reconstructed early-twentieth-century slum
Location: 90 Orchard Street (the actual tenement building is 97 Orchard)
Nearest subway station: Delancey or Grand Street
Admission: $8 for adults; $5 for seniors and students
Hours: Gallery 90, the office/shop, is open Tuesday through Friday, noon–5 p.m.; Saturday and Sunday, 11 a.m.–5 p.m. Tours weekdays at 1, 2, and 3 p.m., weekends every 45 minutes. Closed Monday.
Phone: 431-0233; web site at www.wnet.org/tenement!
When to go: Weekdays
Special comments: Only guided tours are available; reserve in advance if possible.

Overall appeal by age group:

Pre-school	Grade School	Teens	Young Adults	Over 30	Senior Citizens
½	★½	★★	★★★	★★★	★★★

Author's rating: The only way to understand 12 people living in one room is to see it. ★★★
How much time to allow: 1 to 1½ hours

Description and comments: In 1903, city officials reported that there were at least 2,200 people, most of them immigrants, packed into the single block bounded by Orchard, Delancey, Broome, and Allen Streets, in buildings like this 1863 tenement, restored in the main to turn-of-the-century conditions (it had no water, heat, or toilets until 1905). One apartment was left just as it was found in 1988, having been abandoned for about 50 years; another was restored to the (relatively) comfortable state it was in when the Gumpertz family lived there in 1878. The museum puts together changing exhibits portraying life of the neighborhood. Incidentally, this is not, as some people may think, a "Jewish museum"—it's a very hybrid one.

Touring tip: The museum also offers hour-long neighborhood heritage tours weekends at 1:30 and 2:30 p.m., which leave from Gallery 90; you can buy either tickets for tours alone (also $8 and $6) or a combination ticket for a tenement tour and walking tour ($12 for adults and $10 for seniors and students).

A block north at 89 Rivington Street is the **Roumanian Shul,** a continuously active 1881 Romanesque structure with handsome windows that, like the Eldridge Street Synagogue, is undergoing a thorough facelift.

Zone 4: Greenwich Village

Forbes Magazine Galleries

Type of attraction: Fantastic collection of toys, both children's (tin soldiers, model boats) and adults (Fabergé) collected by Malcolm Forbes Sr.

Location: 62 Fifth Avenue (at 12th Street)

Nearest subway station: 14th Street–Union Square

Admission: Free, but limited numbers admitted per day

Hours: Tuesday through Saturday, 10 a.m.–4 p.m. Closed Sunday and Monday.

Phone: 206-5548

When to go: Before lunch if there are children in the party, after if not

Special comments: Children ages 15 and under must be accompanied by an adult, and no more than four children per adult are allowed.

Overall appeal by age group:

Pre-school	Grade School	Teens	Young Adults	Over 30	Senior Citizens
★★★	★★★★	★★★	★★★	★★★	★★½

Author's rating: This says something about how some adults, particularly unrealistically wealthy ones (meaning both Forbes and the Romanovs), never have to outgrow childhood. Quite the escape even now. ★★★½

How much time to allow: 1 to 1½ hours

Description and comments: If you think you've seen toy soldiers before, think again. The more than 12,000 flat and 3-D tin figures arranged in dioramas here—not just soldiers of every historical period and nation, but cowboys and Indians, Aztecs and Spaniards, knights and ladies, and so on—are only about one-tenth of Forbes's collection. The room built to match the famous "counterpane" illustration from Robert Louis Stevenson's *Child's Garden of Verse* has a glass bubble above the dummy figure allowing visitors to become the "child" in the picture. This labyrinth of galleries begins with a series of cases holding more than 500 vintage toy boats (not model boats, an interesting distinction) arranged in flotillas against a background of etched-glass art deco panels from the *Normandie;* it continues with a collection of period and special-edition Monopoly sets, trophies, and sporting awards (with a plaque of dubious moral portent suggesting that these are intended to remind viewers of the brevity of worldly success!) and rotating exhibits of presidential memorabilia, including Nixon's letter of resignation and models of Washington's headquarters at Yorktown and Jefferson's bedroom at Monticello.

The grand finale is a collection of 300-plus Fabergé eggs, personal accessories, jewelry, and household items formerly belonging to the Romanovs of Russia, including the Imperial Diadem of diamonds, platinum, gold, and cobalt enamel. Forbes's collection of the famous eggs, 12 of the surviving 43, includes such spectacular examples as the Coronation Egg, presented by Nicholas II to Alexandria in 1899, which opens to reveal a tiny replica of the coronation coach. Finally, there is a gallery with changing selections of the paintings, prints, and autographs from the collection.

Touring tip: This can be so exhilarating for kids that they get a little loud, and the space is very small. Older adults may want to go at lunchtime to avoid the competition. The tight space and highly focused lighting can make this tiring for some older visitors. Also note that the galleries are occasionally closed on regular viewing days; it wouldn't hurt to call ahead.

Zone 7: Gramercy Park and Madison Square

Empire State Building

Type of attraction: Landmark tower with famous view and
commercialized amusement

Location: 350 Fifth Avenue (at 34th Street)

Nearest subway station: 34th Street

Admission: $6 for adults; $3 for seniors and children; free for children
ages 4 and under

Hours: Daily, 9:30 a.m.–midnight

Phone: 736-3100

When to go: After dark

Special comments: Some small children may find this rather scary.

Overall appeal by age group:

Pre-school	Grade School	Teens	Young Adults	Over 30	Senior Citizens
★	★★½	★★★	★★★	★★½	★★½

Author's rating: A nice view, but not the only choice. And since this is
squarely on many bus tour routes, it can be very crowded. ★

How much time to allow: 30–45 minutes

Description and comments: There are two observation decks: one on the
86th floor, which is a glass-enclosed viewing area surrounded on all sides by
open-air decks (from which, promoters say, you can see ships 40 miles out
at sea); and an entirely enclosed one on the 102nd level, near the top of the
spire, whose range, on the legendary clear day, is supposed to be 80 miles.
The decks are open until midnight, when the view is even nicer and, oddly,
less vertiginous. Its pride of reputation is shown in the lobby paintings,
which picture the seven wonders of the ancient world and the "Eighth
Wonder of the Modern World"—the Empire State Building. It's 1,454 feet
tall (counting the transmitters and all; the 102nd-floor observatory is 1,250
feet up), and it took six months to build, required 10 million bricks, and

weighs 360,000 tons. There are 1,860 steps, as veterans of the annual race up can attest, and 73 elevators. King Kong wasn't really here, of course; but the tower was struck by a fog-bound bomber back in 1945 just above the 78th floor, and it's still struck by lightning as many as 500 times a year. It hasn't served as many as McDonald's, but it has hosted more than 90 million visitors in its time, over 3.5 million every year. The exterior lights— always on, to avoid a second plane crash—are color-coded on holidays and special occasions: red, white, and blue on Independence Day; green for St. Patrick's; pink for Gay Liberation Day, and so on. Once it was lit blue to honor Frank "Ol' Blue Eyes" Sinatra.

The building now includes some more commercial tourist attractions as well. On the concourse, where the ticket booth is located, there's a Guinness World Records Exhibit Hall with dioramas and photos of some strange human endeavors. On the second floor is the New York Skyride, a Disney World–ish simulated flight that soars over, under, and sometimes through the Brooklyn Bridge, World Trade Center towers, Coney Island, and the like in only seven minutes ($11.50 for adults, $9.50 for children; 279-9777). There are several other smaller simulated adventures, something like IMAX movies with motion, opening in the building as well.

Touring tip: There's a snack bar at the 86th-floor level. Tickets are sold on the concourse level below the main lobby; you don't have to use the tickets on the same day you buy them. Note that the ticket office closes at 11:30 p.m.

Zone 8: Midtown West and the Theater District

As we've mentioned elsewhere, the *Times Square* corporations and theaters have figured out that a booming tourist attraction requires a tour; if you'd like to find out how much there is here (some really historical, some purely commercial), head for the Times Square Visitors Center at 226 West 42nd Street, Fridays at noon.

Intrepid Sea-Air-Space Museum

Type of attraction: Minifleet of retired Navy and Coast Guard vessels, including the World War II aircraft carrier *Intrepid*

Location: Pier 86, West 76th Street at 12th Avenue

Nearest subway station: 42nd Street or 50th Street

Admission: $10 for adults; $7.50 for seniors and veterans; $5 for children ages 6 to 12; free for children ages 5 and under and members of the armed forces with ID

Hours: Every day, 10 a.m.–5 p.m.; Labor Day to Memorial Day, Wednesday through Sunday only.

Phone: 245-2533

When to go: Early or immediately after lunch

Special comments: Only limited areas of some of the 6 vessels, and the exhibit halls, are wheelchair-accessible, and other areas (particularly staircases) may be difficult for older visitors, small children, or the claustrophobic. In addition, these are not generally air-conditioned or heated facilities; dress accordingly. Note that the ticket office closes at 4 p.m.

Overall appeal by age group:

Pre-school	Grade School	Teens	Young Adults	Over 30	Senior Citizens
★½	★★★	★★½	★★½	★★★	★★★

Author's rating: This is really a sort of amusement-park-cum-elephant-graveyard, and for those with a real interest (or experience) in naval history, it's a four- or even five-star attraction. But don't underestimate this. If you add up the time recommended for touring the various vessels, it totals nearly five hours, and there are two exhibit halls as well. And there can be waiting lines for the guided tours. Better pick your spots. ★★★

How much time to allow: 2 to 5 hours

Description and comments: This complex includes half a dozen vessels and a mix of guided and self-guided tours. The centerpiece is, of course, the *Intrepid,* which has a 900-foot flight deck on which sit 40 real planes dating from the 1940s to the 1990s (including an A12 Blackbird spy plane). Visitors can wander through the bridge and most of the corridors and may well spend, as staffers estimate, three hours on the carrier alone. Only guided tours of specific areas are offered of the guided-missile submarine *Growler* (17 minutes), the Vietnam-era destroyer escort *Slater* (22 minutes), the Coast Guard lightship *Nantucket* (10 minutes), and the *S.S. Elizabeth* research ship; both (partial) guided and self-guided tours cross the fleet destroyer *Edson* (40 minutes). Pioneers Hall uses antique equipment, mock-ups, and some video to trace the history of flight; Technologies Hall show-cases modern and futuristic methods of space and underwater exploration, including rockets, robots, and even some weapons.

Touring tip: As noted, this is almost a whole day's outing; it's best to pack snacks and water, particularly if there are children in your party.

Zone 9: Midtown East

As noted in Part 7, "New York's Neighborhoods," this area is rich in attractions, many of them architectural.

You don't need permission to stroll around **Grand Central Terminal** at East 42nd and Park Avenue, but if you'd like to know more about the classical sculptures and so on, contact the Municipal Arts Society, which leads free tours Wednesdays at 12:30 p.m. (Notice anything about the constellations on the newly cleaned ceiling? They're reversed—"As God would see it," the artist said.) The same is true of the **New York Public Library** on Fifth Avenue at 42nd, another civic treasure, with its signature lions (representing Patience and Fortitude) at the entrance, twin fountains (Beauty and Truth, which would please Keats), interior murals, paintings, documents (Jefferson's copy of the Declaration of Independence), and so on. The ceiling of the Guttesman Exhibition Hall sometimes outshines the exhibits. But if you like, free tours leave from the front desk every day at 11 a.m. and 2 p.m.

Museum of Modern Art

Type of attraction: Premier collection of modern and contemporary art and design

Location: 11 East 53rd Street

Nearest subway station: Fifth Avenue–53rd Street

Admission: $8.50 for adults; $5.50 for seniors and students; children ages 15 and under free

Hours: Saturday through Tuesday, 11 a.m.–6 p.m.; Thursday and Friday, noon to 8:30 p.m. Closed Wednesday.

Phone: 708-9480

When to go: Weekdays; Friday afternoons

Special comments: Thursday and Friday after 5:30 p.m., admission is "pay what you please."

Overall appeal by age group:

Pre-school	Grade School	Teens	Young Adults	Over 30	Senior Citizens
½	★★	★★	★★★	★★★★	★★★

Author's rating: Challenging and often difficult, but fascinating—clearly the world's leading modern art collection, just as advertised. As at many really first-rate museums, you can't really see it all in a few hours, but you can only take so much in at a time, anyway. ★★★★★

How much time to allow: 2 to 4 hours

Description and comments: First-timers may be surprised at how many of these great paintings and prints they already "know," because so many of the most famous and frequently reproduced twentieth-century works hang here, from those by the Impressionists to those by the Cubists to the Pop Artists and so on. (Stop by the main desk and ask for the self-guided tour; it points up many of these "greatest hits," including Van Gogh's *Starry Night*, Monet's *Water Lilies*, and Picasso's *Demoiselles d'Avignon*.) Not only two-dimensional but three-dimensional pieces are featured; late-nineteenth- and early-twentieth-century painting and sculpture is on the second floor, postwar on the third. MoMA is also famous for its vetting of industrial and commercial design, from automobile bodies to typewriters, architectural models to appliances, even watches; one of Movado's most famous faces, the one with a single dot at the 12, is called "the Museum Watch" because MoMA approved of it so highly. The shop also has many disabled-friendly utensils.

Touring tip: Every Friday is Jazz Night in the Garden Cafe, and in good weather it's out in the Sculpture Garden. Also call and ask about film screenings, or check the local press; the museum's collection of films tops 10,000. The museum's Italian restaurant, Sette MoMA, serves until 10:30 p.m. Monday, Tuesday, and Thursday through Saturday.

Museum of Television and Radio

Type of attraction: A combination archives and rerun haven

Location: 25 West 52nd Street

Nearest subway station: 47th–50th Street/Rockefeller Center or Fifth Avenue–53rd Street

Admission: $6 for adults; $4 for seniors and students; $3 for children ages 12 and under

Hours: Open Tuesday through Sunday, noon–6 p.m.; theaters only open Thursday till 8 p.m. and Friday till 9 p.m. Closed Monday.

Phone: 621-6600 for general information; 621-6800 for daily schedule

When to go: Early, at least to check schedule

Special comments: If you want to use the archives, add at least another hour, but the kids will be happy parked in one of the theaters. Note that the age group appeal may vary depending on the day's screenings.

Overall appeal by age group:

Pre-school	Grade School	Teens	Young Adults	Over 30	Senior Citizens
★½	★★★	★★★	★★★	★★★½	★★½

Author's rating: Although the computerized files are still being organized, meaning that it can be laborious to look some topics or subjects up, it's fascinating; and the rare films shown are a delight. ★★★

How much time to allow: 1 to 2½ hours

Description and comments: A handsome if simple building, with five floors of exhibits, various-sized screening theaters, and radio listening room, all fully wheelchair-accessible and with listening-assist devices at the front counter and closed-captioning decoders in the library. The museum shop is good for gifts and souvenirs, too, mixing T-shirts and posters with industry coffee-table books.

Not as famous as most of New York's older museums, this is nevertheless a fine attraction, and one with strong interest for all ages. In fact, with its ongoing screenings on various floors, through which visitors are welcome to sit for as long or as short a time as they like, this is channel surfing to the max. In a single afternoon, for example, you might be able to see rare footage of Sinatra's "Rat Pack" in action, a segment of *The George Burns and Gracie Allen Show,* Jackie Kennedy taking CBS for a tour of the White House, a full-length Wallace and Gromit claymation adventure, bits of *Sesame Street* and *Fraggle Rock,* some Beakman science, a semiserious documentary on the evolution of sci-fi TV, and so on. The hallways are filled with changing photographic exhibits on such topics as journalists and special-effects makeup. The museum also produces salutes and series featuring the works of specific actors or directors, and many of these are shown in the evenings, making this an all-day bargain. Screenings begin at noon each day, and the full schedules are available at the counter, along with six months' advance schedules of the special exhibitions and series. There are special screenings of children's programming on weekends, but there is plenty of kid-vid all week long, too.

You can take a guided tour of the museum if you're curious about its history and collection (offered only a couple of times a day), but it's easily negotiated alone. The real treasure trove is the library, for which you need time-specific tickets (available at the front counter). You cruise the museum's library on computer, picking segments from 75,000 radio and TV programs and even TV and radio advertising, and then are sent to a private booth to screen (or hear) your selections. If you're not sure what you'd like to see, skim the category of 400 highlights, which are the segments most frequently requested by visitors—the final episode of *The Mary Tyler Moore Show,* for example.

Touring tip: Stop by the museum lobby as close to noon as possible, particularly if you want to use the library, and get that time set aside; this will also give you time to figure out which screenings you'd like to see. Or you can check the museum's Internet site at www.mtr.org. Note that there is no cafeteria on site and no eating or drinking allowed inside, although you can step outside onto the sidewalk.

Pierpont Morgan Library

Type of attraction: World-class collection of medieval and Renaissance illuminated manuscripts, rare books, and master drawings

Location: 29 East 36th Street (at Madison Avenue)

Nearest subway station: 33rd Street

Admission: $5 for adults; $3 for seniors; children ages 11 and under free

Hours: Tuesday through Friday, 10:30 a.m.–5 p.m.; Saturday, 10:30 a.m.–6 p.m.; Sunday, noon to 6 p.m. Closed Monday.

Phone: 685-0008

When to go: Weekdays; late afternoon

Special comments: There are child-friendly areas, but some special exhibits, say of children's books and illustrations, might have even higher appeal for young visitors.

Overall appeal by age group:

Pre-school	Grade School	Teens	Young Adults	Over 30	Senior Citizens
★	★★	★★½	★★★	★★★★	★★★

Author's rating: As admitted medieval history freaks and bibliophiles to boot, we think this is an incredible collection, and usually not very crowded. ★★★★

How much time to allow: 1½ to 3½ hours

Description and comments: Legendary financier J. P. Morgan may have been giving himself aristocratic airs when he built this Renaissance palace of a home, but he and his collection must have been a perfect fit for this warm, otherworldly complex. Gold and full-color manuscripts, the most delicate of red-chalk sketches, the almost illegibly tiny handwriting of the Brontë children, Mozart's own scores, Gutenberg's Bible, Voltaire's briefcase,

Dickens's cigar case—the rotating pleasures of this museum are perhaps specialized, but they are certainly superior. The sheer number of books will fill you with envy, and the glorious murals, woodwork, plaster detailing—well, it's a multimillionaire's mansion. What can you say? Just let yourself be transported back in time. A three-story glass-domed garden serves as the walkway between the original home and the library.

Touring tip: There is a pretty little cafe on site that serves breakfast, lunch, and even, appropriately, tea, so true book-lovers can make quite a day of it.

St. Patrick's Cathedral

Type of attraction: The largest Catholic cathedral in the country

Location: Fifth Avenue between 50th and 51st Streets

Nearest subway station: 47th–50th Street/Rockefeller Center or 51st Street

Admission: Free

Hours: Sunday through Friday, 7 a.m.–8:30 p.m.; Saturday, 8 a.m.–8:30 p.m.

Phone: 753-2261

When to go: Late morning or midafternoon to avoid interrupting services

Overall appeal by age group:

Pre-school	Grade School	Teens	Young Adults	Over 30	Senior Citizens
½	★★	★★	★★½	★★★	★★★

Author's rating: Although this clearly has greater resonance for Catholic visitors, it is quite beautiful and well worth a visit, if only as a rest between other attractions. ★★

How much time to allow: 30–45 minutes

Description and comments: This looks almost as much like a fairy-tale castle as a cathedral, it's so busy with spires and arches and stained glass. Among the highlights are its huge and transporting organ (more than 7,000 pipes) and the 26-foot Rose Window, both right over the main Fifth Avenue entrance; the pietà in the rear near the Lady Chapel, which has its own set of gorgeous stained glass windows; and the all-bronze baldachin that protects the high altar. Altogether there are 70 stained glass windows, more than half from Chartres and Nantes. The figures on the bronze front doors represent the saints of New York.

Touring tip: So much of the cathedral's power comes from the windows that sunlight (or reflected snow) really makes a difference; try to avoid a rainy day.

United Nations

Type of attraction: Part monument, part office building of the international council

Location: First Avenue from 42nd to 48th Streets (main entrance at 46th Street)

Nearest subway station: 42nd Street–Grand Central Terminal

Admission: Grounds and lobby admission free; tours $6.50 for adults; $4.50 for seniors and students; $3.50 for children

Hours: March through December, daily, 9:15 a.m.–4:15 p.m.; January and February, open weekdays only

Phone: 963-7713

When to go: Anytime

Special comments: Children ages 4 and under are not permitted. Tours are conducted in 20 languages.

Overall appeal by age group:

Pre-school	Grade School	Teens	Young Adults	Over 30	Senior Citizens
—	★★	★★½	★★★	★★★	★★★

Author's rating: Impressive, but if you follow the news closely, it looks a lot like it does on TV. ★★½

How much time to allow: 1 to 1½ hours

Description and comments: You don't have to sign up for the tour if the Chagall stained glass lobby, the exterior promenade of flags, the architecture (Le Corbusier, et al.), and the gardens are enough for you. However, if you want to see the General Assembly in action, the Security Council chamber, the various committee rooms, and the shops, do take the tours, conducted by students from all over the world. Tours take about an hour and leave about every half hour.

Whether or not you take the tour, don't forget to circle the grounds. Most of the sculptures are antiviolence metaphors, such as the pistol with its barrel tied in a knot, a gift from Luxembourg; and the hammering of swords into plowshares. The most intriguing is the post–Cold War version of St. George and the dragon, called *Good Defeats Evil,* wherein the dragon is a construction of a Russian ballistic missile and an American Pershing missile. It's especially fascinating because it was a gift from the former Soviet Union.

Touring tip: There's a nice gift shop here, especially if you know someone who collects international flags; even more impressively, the on-site post office has U.N. stamps that can be bought and used only here. The Delegates Dining Toom overlooking the East River is open to the public for lunch only (963-7625).

Zone 11: East Side

The Frick Collection

Type of attraction: Fine collection of eighteenth- and nineteenth-century art in gracious mansion

Location: 1 East 70th Street (at Fifth Avenue)

Nearest subway station: 68th Street–Hunter College

Admission: $5 for adults; $3 for seniors and students

Hours: Tuesday through Saturday, 10 a.m.–6 p.m.; Sunday, 1 to 6 p.m.

Phone: 288-0700

When to go: Weekdays

Special comments: Children under 10 are not admitted.

Overall appeal by age group:

Pre-school	Grade School	Teens	Young Adults	Over 30	Senior Citizens
—	★½	★★	★★★½	★★★★	★★★★

Author's rating: A personal favorite, glorious in both setting and collection. ★★★★★

How much time to allow: 1½ to 3 hours

Description and comments: Maybe this betrays a Western romantic or even DWM-nostalgic mindset, but this is to our taste the perfect philanthopic collection, small by Met standards but studded with exquisite portraits (Whistler, Goya, El Greco, Titian, Vermeer, Sargeant, Holbein, Rembrandt), landscapes (Turner, Constable), allegories (Fragonard and an entire boudoir's worth of Boucher panels painted for Madame de Pompadour). Then there's the enamel Limoges miniatures, the garden court with its lily pond, the ghost of the pipe organ (the pipes are still there, in the hallway, though the works are gone), all those Oriental rugs (you are looking down, aren't you?), and just a smattering of fine furniture left from the days when steel magnate Henry Clay Frick and his family lived here.

Touring tip: This is only two blocks from the **Asia Society** collection at 70th and Park, which is a fine match in terms of temperament and pacing even if it is a world, or half a world, away in art.

Zone 12: Upper West Side

American Museum of Natural History

Type of attraction: Popular and wide-ranging scientific and research collection

Location: Central Park West at 79th Street

Nearest subway station: 81st Street–Museum of Natural History or 79th Street

Admission: $8 for adults; $6 for seniors and students; $4.50 for children ages 12 and under; additional charge for some special exhibits. IMAX $3 for adults; $2 for seniors; and $1.50 for children.

Hours: Sunday through Thursday, 10 a.m.–5:45 p.m.; Friday and Saturday, 10 a.m.–8:45 p.m.

Phone: 769-5100; IMAX, 769-5050

When to go: Weekdays

Special comments: Hayden Planetarium is closed for reconstruction.

Overall appeal by age group:

Pre-school	Grade School	Teens	Young Adults	Over 30	Senior Citizens
★★	★★★	★★★	★★★★	★★★	★★½

Author's rating: Thanks to the museum's careful combination of adult and family-style exhibits, this will keep a whole group occupied really as long as you want. ★★★★

How much time to allow: 2 to 4 hours

Description and comments: This is a museum that inspires affection and frequently a kind of nostalgia; its dioramas of Africa and the evolutionary progress of man and its gemstones (worth an estimated $50 million and including the famous Star of India sapphire) are perennial favorites, and they're the sort of exhibits we all seem to remember. The famous dinosaur skeletons are far more convincing since their cleaning and reconfiguration; the new exhibit halls are airy and the captioning first-rate. The museum's special exhibits have been headline-chasers, perhaps, focusing on the newly renovated dinosaur floor (and plugging into *Jurassic Park* fever) and the endless fascination of oversized diamonds, but they have certainly been blockbuster successes. There are several new hands-on and interactive exhibits, and a children's Discovery Room opens on weekends from noon to 4 p.m. It has a couple of gift shops, but the one in the midst of the big cats is the most fun.

The four statues atop the columns outside on Central Park West represent Lewis and Clark, Daniel Boone, and John J. Audubon. Walk around to the West 77th Street Side or Columbus Avenue to try to see the museum as it looked at the turn of the century, with its Romanesque Revival structure already once expanded.

Touring tip: The museum offers highlights tours at 10:15 and 11:15 a.m. and 1:15, 2:15, and 3:15 p.m.; meet on the second floor in the Hall of African Mammals. On Friday and Saturday nights, the museum offers a combination IMAX/dinner admission ticket. The museum has a cafeteria, cocktail bar, and restaurant.

Children's Museum of Manhattan

Type of attraction: Engaging, TV-generation-savvy educational playhouse
Location: West 83rd Street between Amsterdam Avenue and Broadway
Nearest subway station: 86th Street
Admission: $5 for adults; $2.50 for seniors and children
Hours: Tuesday through Sunday, 10 a.m.–5 p.m. Closed Monday.
Phone: 721-1223
When to go: Anytime

Overall appeal by age group:

Pre-school	Grade School	Teens	Young Adults	Over 30	Senior Citizens
★★	★★★½	—	—	—	—

Author's rating: This is for kids younger than 11, but if we were . . . ★★★
How much time to allow: 1½ to 4 hours

Description and comments: This is an MTV-era museum, and somehow you can tell. The Time Warner Center for Media is a combination TV studio, film stage, and newscast set where kids write and produce their own shows (with the help, if needed, of "entertainers" already on the set). There are multimedia and multisensory exhibits about the human brain and the insect viewpoint; paper-making classes; and workshops on things such as

making music on computer. Weekend theatrical performances include pup-
pet shows, storytelling, dance, and concerts. The "SoundsFun" installation
is a 14-foot "ear" with a trampoline for an eardrum. The "urban treehouse"
is pretty cool, too.

Touring tip: If your child seems more interested in the fine arts than modern media, check out the *Children's Museum of the Arts* in SoHo (941-
9198), really more of an educational playsite, where there are workshops in
puppet-making, clay, drawing, and acting.

Zone 13: Upper East Side

Cooper-Hewitt National Design Museum

Type of attraction: Collection of international design and design art

Location: East 91st Street and Fifth Avenue

Nearest subway station: 96th Street or 86th Street

Admission: $3 for adults; $1.50 for seniors and students; children ages 11 and under free

Hours: Tuesday, 10 a.m.–9 p.m.; Wednesday through Saturday, 10 a.m.–5 p.m.; Sunday, noon–5 p.m. Closed Monday.

Phone: 860-6868

When to go: Midafternoon

Special comments: This is a branch of the Smithsonian Institution; members get in free. Everyone gets in free Tuesday from 5 to 9 p.m.

Overall appeal by age group:

Pre-school	Grade School	Teens	Young Adults	Over 30	Senior Citizens
½	★★	★★	★★★	★★★	★★

Author's rating: The strength of the museum's appeal to younger visitors depends heavily on the special exhibits on view at the time, but adults will probably always find something to like. ★★★

How much time to allow: 1–1½ hour

Description and comments: This was originally the "modest" home of Andrew Carnegie (the first private establishment with an elevator, incidentally); the two families whose names are linked in the title collected textiles, jewelry, glassware, silver, furniture, and artisan paper from all over the world. Although the museum's collection as a whole is quite large, only a small fraction is on view at one time, but there may be several different exhibits coexisting; for example, most of one whole room may be given over to a lineup of six or eight intriguing chairs, while the library and the hallway may serve as a "rogue's gallery" of lettering styles. (Additional gallery space was created in the mid-1990s.)

Incidentally, this has one of the most intriguing museum shops in the city, with a lot of clever, attractive, and convenient writing implements, clocks and calculators, and other utensils.

Touring tip: The museum is surrounded by fine homes from the early twentieth century; see the section on Zone 13 in Part 7, "New York's Neighborhoods." It is one block from the Jewish Museum at 92nd Street (see description below). It is also very near the **National Academy of Design,** which despite its name is less design-specific and more generally "artistic" than the Cooper-Hewitt, at Fifth and 89th (860-6868).

Solomon R. Guggenheim Museum

Type of attraction: Fine collection of twentieth-century European art
Location: Fifth Avenue at 88th Street
Nearest subway station: 86th Street
Admission: $10 for adults; $7 for seniors and students; children ages 11 and under free
Hours: Sunday through Wednesday, 10 a.m.–6 p.m.; Friday and Saturday, 10 a.m.–8 p.m. Closed Thursday.
Phone: 423-3500
When to go: Anytime
Special comments: On Friday, 6–8 p.m., pay what you wish. Although the great spiral ramp seems good for wheelchairs and keeping kids interested, it can be hard on the legs.

Overall appeal by age group:

Pre-school	Grade School	Teens	Young Adults	Over 30	Senior Citizens
½	★★	★★	★★★	★★★	★★★

Author's rating: ★★★½
How much time to allow: 1½ to 3 hours

Description and comments: This is one of those museums more famous for its architecture than for its collection. Frank Lloyd Wright's upwardly expanding six-floor spiral, like a squared-off chambered nautilus (it's been called ruder things), frames the Great Rotunda and looks up to a often brilliantly lit glass dome; the exhibits fill the walls of the long ramp and lead off into the chambers. Among the permanent exhibits are major pieces by Klee, Picasso, Kandinsky, Chagall, and Modigliani; the museum also has a fine selection of French Impressionists, including Monet, Renoir, and Van Gogh.

Though in the shadow of the giant Museum of Modern Art collection, the Guggenheim, which has more European works, forms a strong duet with the Whitney Museum of American Art. (Also, it reaches back a little farther into the nineteenth century.) Guggenheim himself was aggressive in collecting avant-garde and new talent, and that was the reputation the museum was supposed to have, although it has been criticized for "maturing." Its new SoHo branch (and the vast branch that is soon to open in Bilbao, Spain) may give it new vitality.

Touring tip: Those interested in very up-to-date or cutting-edge art will want to visit the Guggenheim SoHo (423-3600); that usually costs $8 for adults, but an $11 combination ticket provides admission to both in a single day.

Jewish Museum

Type of attraction: Surprisingly rich collection of ancient Judaica and Jewish art

Location: Fifth Avenue at 92nd Street

Nearest subway station: 96th Street

Admission: $7 for adults; $5 for seniors and students; children ages 11 and under free

Hours: Sunday through Thursday, 11 a.m.–5:45 p.m.; Tuesday, 11 a.m.–8 p.m. Closed Monday.

Phone: 423-3200

When to go: Anytime

Special comments: Free on Tuesday, 5–8 p.m.

Overall appeal by age group:

Pre-school	Grade School	Teens	Young Adults	Over 30	Senior Citizens
½	★★	★★★	★★★½	★★★½	★★★★

Author's rating: One becomes so accustomed to seeing Christian relics and even Asian religious art that the age and variety of these ruins and sacred objects are startling. ★★★½

How much time to allow: 1 to 2 hours

Description and comments: This fine collection, now moving toward its centennial, centers around a permanent exhibition on the Jewish experience—religious and secular—that ranges back 4,000 years. Among its works are temple facades from Sumeria, wall paintings of biblical battles, Torah covers and crowns, fine art and sculpture, candelabras, flatware, manuscripts, ceremonial cups, and a gripping three-dimensional installation by Eleanor Antin and George Segal. The collection also includes many fine portraits of Jewish Americans and a computer/video library. Downstairs is a gallery used for special exhibitions.

Like many of the fine specialized museums in the city, this was originally a mansion, and the two-level wood-paneled library, which is filled with fine arks and altars and ceremonial items and holds an almost pulpitlike spiral staircase, is a beauty. There is also a family exhibit area designed for children and parents to visit together. Incidentally, the stonework in the rear extension was done by the same masons who are working on the **Cathedral of St. John the Divine** (see description in Zone 14).

Touring tip: This museum is extremely accessible for wheelchair users; but if you can use the stairs, be sure to come down stairwell No. 1, a glass-brick turret with a plaintively beautiful audio installation. There is a cafe in the basement.

Metropolitan Museum of Art

Type of attraction: One of the greatest museum collections in the world

Location: Fifth Avenue between 80th and 84th Streets (entrance at 82nd)

Nearest subway station: 86th Street

Admission: $8 for adults; $4 for seniors and students; children ages 11 and under free

Hours: Sunday and Tuesday through Thursday, 9:30 a.m.–5:30 p.m.; Friday and Saturday, 9:30 a.m.–9 p.m. Closed Monday.

Phone: 870-5500

When to go: Friday and Saturday evenings for dining and music; call for special events schedule (570-3949)

Special comments: No strollers allowed on Sundays.

Overall appeal by age group:

Pre-school	Grade School	Teens	Young Adults	Over 30	Senior Citizens
★	★★	★★½	★★★★	★★★★	★★★★

Author's rating: We could visit this every time we were in New York and never feel as if we had seen it all. ★★★★★

How much time to allow: 1½ to 5 hours

Description and comments: The figures are almost unbelievable: 3.5 million pieces of art, some dating back more than 5,000 years, and representing every culture in the world; 32 acres of exhibit space; 5 million visitors a year. It was founded in 1870 by New York's leading philanthropists and city boosters, who intended it to rival the great museums of Europe and prove New York the equal of any Old World center—and they were willing to pony up to make it happen. It worked, too. This is one place where even experienced museumgoers can usefully sign up for a highlights tour (570-3930).

You can't see it all, so pick a century, a style, or a special exhibit and start there. Or pick a centerpiece. For example, the American wing gently spirals down past Tiffany glass and Arts and Crafts pieces to the neoclassical sculpture in the garden court; the Temple of Dendur, which was erected by Augustus, has been reconstructed in a chamber of glass at the end of the Egyptian wing (a thank-you from the nation of Egypt for the United States' help in rescuing monuments threatened by the Aswan Dam); and the Astor Court, a replica of a Ming Dynasty–era scholar's garden created by artisans from Souzhou, China, using traditional techniques, is the jewel at the heart of the Asian art department on the second floor. Or you could luxuriate in medieval art, including ornately carved altarpieces and icons; all-American painting; or entirely reinstalled rooms—art, furniture, and all—from the Lehman townhouse on West 54th Street. And these are just the permanent exhibits. The Metropolitan continually hosts or initiates special collections of blockbuster art from other countries or by great masters. Another possibility, especially for first-timers, is the hour-long highlights tours at 10:15 and 11:15 a.m. and 1, 2, and 3:15 p.m., leaving from the front hall.

Despite the museum's seeming austerity, there are several areas that even small children seem to like: the classical statues, the Egyptian mummies, and the reconstructed Temple of Dendur; the armor; the musical instruments; the furnished rooms, and so on. Depending on the exhibit, they may also get a kick out of the Costume Institute downstairs, which owns 45,000 pieces of clothing dating back to the seventeenth century. And there's a playground just outside, to the south, for emergencies.

Touring tips: There are several places to eat in the museum: the classical-looking but often loud full-service restaurant on the ground floor (570-3964); the sponsors' dining room on the second floor, open to the public on weekends; and the good-weather wine bar on the roof in the sculpture garden. The gift shop is famous. The Metropolitan also administers the **Cloisters** in the Heights (see description below); admission to one includes admission to the other on the same day. Across the street on Fifth between 83rd and 84th Streets is the small and specialized **Goethe House German Cultural Center** (439-8700), which often has exhibits of contemporary German art, films, and concerts.

Whitney Museum of American Art

Type of attraction: World-class collection of twentieth-century American art

Location: Madison Avenue at 75th Street

Nearest subway station: 77th Street

Admission: $8 for adults; $6 for seniors and students; children ages 11 and under free

Hours: Wednesday and Friday through Sunday, 11 a.m.–6 p.m.; Thursday, 1 to 8 p.m.

Phone: 570-3676

When to go: Anytime

Special comments: Free admission Thursday from 6 to 8 p.m.

Overall appeal by age group:

Pre-school	Grade School	Teens	Young Adults	Over 30	Senior Citizens
½	★★½	★★★	★★★	★★★½	★★★½

Author's rating: ★★★★

How much time to allow: 1½ to 3 hours

Description and comments: There is much to be said for an insider's eye, and since the Whitney was founded (originally in SoHo) by sculptor Gertrude Vanderbilt Whitney, its collection of modern American art in many opinions rivals the international collection of the Museum of Modern Art. (She founded a new museum when the prestigious and no doubt somewhat pompous Metropolitan turned down her offer to donate the whole collection.)

Since its recent expansion and extensive exterior cleaning, this inverted concrete pyramid (almost a joke on Frank Lloyd Wright's elaborately geometrical Guggenheim) seems less forbidding and more quirky, though still mysterious; instead of seeming to lower, it seems to be playing at reticence, hiding its goods behind the drawbridge like a castle. It's a collection with a great deal of humor; and though it has many serious and dark pieces as well, it may surprise you how interested younger patrons may be in the cartoon-like Lichtensteins or robust Thomas Hart Bentons, the boxing art of George Bellows, Warhol's post-advertising art and other familiar elements of Pop Art, O'Keeffe's flowers, or the super-realistic Hopper paintings—or even many of the brilliantly colored abstracts. The famous Calder assemblage called "Circus" that used to be mounted just inside the main entrance has been moved upstairs; it is still the only piece on permanent display. The Whitney's most famous exhibit is probably the notorious Biennial, which is an invitation-only selection of work from American artists over a two-year span. Its film selections are almost as quirky; call for schedule.

Touring tip: There is a cafe in the museum, a branch of the Upper East Side home-style restaurants called Sarabeth's (570-3670).

Zone 14: Columbia University and Harlem

Cathedral Church of St. John the Divine

Type of attraction: Vast though unfinished Episcopal cathedral

Location: Amsterdam Avenue at 112th Street

Nearest subway station: Cathedral Parkway (110th Street)

Admission: Suggested donation, $3

Hours: Daily, 7 a.m.–6 p.m.

Phone: 316-7540

When to go: Weekdays midmorning or afternoon to avoid disrupting services

Special comments: Try to hook up with one of the tours; there's so much going on.

Overall appeal by age group:

Pre-school	Grade School	Teens	Young Adults	Over 30	Senior Citizens
★	★★	★★	★★★	★★★	★★★

Author's rating: The continued ambitions (or is that aspirations?) of the builders are somehow moving, the adherence to traditional building methods even more so. ★★★

How much time to allow: 1½ to 2 hours

Description and comments: After more than a century, this almost symbolically style-embracing cathedral is still only two-thirds complete, and it may take most of a second century and half a billion dollars to finish it. But already it is a wonder, part Romanesque and part Gothic; a little Spanish, a little French, a little Italian. When finished, it will be the largest cathedral in the world—as large as Notre Dame and Chartres put together, with 300-foot towers and a 600-foot nave. There's a scale model in the gift shop that shows how at least the front half, from tower to tower, will look. Builders are trying to stick to real medieval methods. Up until recently, the stone blocks were being carved out just as they had been centuries ago (some

Harlem students apprenticed under imported British master masons), and there are no steel supports. The portals were cast by the man who cast the Statue of Liberty; the so-called temporary dome has lasted nearly 90 years. Be sure to look closely at the stone carvings atop the columns and friezes. They're not all solemn; some feature famous New York landmarks and creatures.

Inside, the "melting pot" philosophy has been extended to religion: The various chapels salute other major religions and ethnic groups, and the justly famous concerts and lectures are as often secular as sacred.

Touring tip: Tours are offered Tuesday through Saturday at 11 a.m. and 12:30 p.m.

Grant's Tomb/General Grant National Memorial

Type of attraction: Monumental memorial to Civil War hero and president

Location: 122nd Street and Riverside Drive

Nearest subway station: 125th Street (1, 9) or 116th Street/Columbia University

Admission: Free

Hours: Daily, 9 a.m.–5 p.m.

Phone: 666-1640

When to go: Anytime

Overall appeal by age group:

Pre-school	Grade School	Teens	Young Adults	Over 30	Senior Citizens
½	★★	★★	★★½	★★½	★★

Author's rating: The 1990s revival of interest in Civil War heroes has given new life to this often belittled attraction, but it still seems a little extravagant. ★½

How much time to allow: 30–45 minutes

Description and comments: It was modeled on the original mausoleum—the tomb of Mausoleus, one of the Seven Wonders of the World. Busts, marble, bronze, columns, and all, it's a fantastic salute to an often maligned figure. Perhaps after he died in terrible pain from jaw cancer, his critics felt a little guilty. Belated or not, it was a show of public support; more than 90,000 Americans chipped in the $600,000 needed for the memorial. The inside was inspired by Napoleon's tomb in Paris—a subtle compliment to

Grant's martial career—with marble sarcophagi and mosaics showing Grant shaking hands with Lee, etc. There is a minimuseum of his presidential and military campaigns as well. The mosaic-topped benches outside are far more modern and in some cases relatively P.C.; they were designed by Brooklyn's Pedro Silva and put together by volunteers, and they show American historical vignettes from taxis and subways to Indians.

Touring tip: Riverside Church, one of the area's most impressive churches, is just across the park; if you hear bells, it's Riverside's world-class carillon. The carillon deck offers a spectacular view; see Part 7, "New York's Neighborhoods," for details.

El Museo del Barrio

Type of attraction: Smallish but distinguished collection of pan-American Hispanic art and culture

Location: Fifth Avenue at 104th Street

Nearest subway station: 103rd Street

Admission: $4 for adults; $2 for seniors and students; children ages 11 and under free

Hours: Wednesday through Sunday, 11 a.m.–5 p.m. Closed Monday and Tuesday.

Phone: 831-7272

When to go: Midafternoon

Overall appeal by age group:

Pre-school	Grade School	Teens	Young Adults	Over 30	Senior Citizens
★	★★	★★★	★★★½	★★★★	★★★½

Author's rating: Its cultural message is pointed without being at all preachy. ★★★

How much time to allow: 1 to 1½ hours

Description and comments: This is not an especially large facility, and it shares its space with a training center, but its exhibits are well-considered and well-displayed, and the hands-on children's room, while small, is a good place to park the youngest members of the group. The collection includes religious carvings, textiles, prints, paintings, vintage photographs, pre-Columbian artifacts, and contemporary art; the exhibits often focus on thematic issues such as dream symbols or regional developments.

Touring tip: When you come up from the subway, you may be startled; this is the area where the Upper East Side vanishes and East Harlem appears. However, the walk—through a small playground and under the old railroad bridge—is perfectly safe and perhaps educational. The **Museum of the City of New York** is right next door.

Museum of the City of New York

Type of attraction: Historical collection that shines specific and often unusual lights on city history

Location: Fifth Avenue at 103rd Street

Nearest subway station: 103rd Street

Admission: $5 for adults; $4 for seniors and children

Hours: Wednesday through Saturday, 10 a.m.–5 p.m.; Sunday, 1–5 p.m.

Phone: 534-1672

When to go: Anytime

Overall appeal by age group:

Pre-school	Grade School	Teens	Young Adults	Over 30	Senior Citizens
★★½	★★★	★★	★★★	★★★	★★★

Author's rating: ★★★

How much time to allow: 1½ to 2 hours

Description and comments: This might be the sort of museum in which families could split up to see different wings and then regroup—say, at the huge mezzanine-level model of what the museum will look like once its vast wing-addition is built in the twenty-first century. The rotating exhibits are often quirky and fascinating, focusing on such topics as the long tradition of circuses in New York (the theme music included a snatch from *Washington Week in Review,* perhaps a joke on media circuses!); the building of the Empire State Building and some of the art it has inspired; the Broadway tradition with posters and recordings. And there are some fine examples of native craftsmanship, furniture, household items, and the like. In the basement is a mini–fire museum and a selection of antique city maps. But the two best exhibits are the toys—including novelty banks, fire trucks and trains, tin soldiers and animals, and a series of dollhouses from the eighteenth, nineteenth, and even early twentieth centuries—and the reconstructed Moorish-fantasy bedroom and dressing room from John D. Rockefeller's demolished mansion at Fifth and 51st. (You'll spot a matching room in the Brooklyn Museum of Art.) Just look at the stenciled canvas ceiling over the sleigh bed; or the woodwork in the dressing room, decorated with appropriate implements such as scissors and combs and mirrors worked in mother-of-pearl. There are other restored rooms and a display of custom Spode, Royal Doulton, Crown Derby, and Minton porcelain belonging to another prominent household. These rooms are up on the fifth floor and are quite frequently overlooked.

Touring tip: The Conservatory Garden section of Central Park, transplanted from the same Rockefeller mansion as the bedroom, is just across the street; imagine looking out from one onto the other. Also, see tips for **El Museo del Barrio.**

Zone 15: The Heights

The Cloisters

Type of attraction: Premier medieval art collection in evocative
historical setting

Location: Fort Tryon Park

Nearest subway station: 190th Street

Admission: $8 for adults; $4 for seniors and students; children ages
11 and under (with adult) free

Hours: Tuesday through Sunday, 9:30 a.m.–5:15 p.m. (9:30 to 4:15
November though February). Closed Monday.

Phone: 923-3700

When to go: Weekdays

Special comments: One ticket covers both the Metropolitan Museum of
Art and the Cloisters on the same day.

Overall appeal by age group:

Pre-school	Grade School	Teens	Young Adults	Over 30	Senior Citizens
★	★★	★★½	★★★	★★★	★★½

Author's rating: It was a stroke of genius (and immeasurable philan-
thropy) to build a period home for part of the Metropolitan's
medieval art collection. ★★★★★

How much time to allow: 1½ to 2 hours

Description and comments: This fantastic assemblage of stone, with its
serenely beautiful and stylistically otherworldly saints, stained glass, prayer-
eroded stone, and entombed crusaders, is like a dream. You're not even surprised to find, hanging on one wall, the frequently reproduced pictures of
the hunting of the Unicorn. Or the almost-as-familiar illuminated *Belles
Heures* of the Duc de Berry. The cloisters of the title—five of them, taken
from the ruins of French monasteries dating from the twelfth through the
fifteenth centuries, plus a twelfth-century Spanish apse and a Romanesque
chapel—have been fitted together on two levels, so that you can actually

stroll through them as the residents did. (They are actually organized chronologically, so you sort of circle from the Romanesque period, about 1000, to the Gothic era, ca. 1500.) The stone block benches of the chapter house are curved with the long erosion of centuries of use. One of the cloister gardens has been planted to match the courtyard garden seen in one of the huge tapestries, another with the herbs and medicinal plants of the Middle Ages. There is an air- and light-conditioned room of jewels, enamels, reliquaries, and manuscripts (this is one of those museums where a penlight might be helpful). There are also sculptures and altarpieces and a rare and extremely fine early fifteenth-century triptych of the Annunciation by Robert Campin of Tournai.

The Cloisters frequently offers lectures, some of them aimed at students, and wonderfully atmospheric concerts; call for schedules.

Touring tip: The museum itself is at least in part wheelchair-accessible (there is an elevator down by the security desk), but handicapped patrons would be well advised to spring for a cab, at least from the 175th Street subway station, which is accessible. Or take the M4 bus, which, though notoriously slow, stops right at the museum entrance.

Zone 16: Brooklyn

Brooklyn Botanic Garden

Type of attraction: Landscaped park with Japanese garden and greenhouse complex

Location: Washington Avenue at Eastern Parkway

Nearest subway station: Prospect Park or Eastern Parkway–Brooklyn Museum

Admission: $3 for adults, $1.50 for seniors and students with ID; 50 cents for children ages 6 to 16; ages 5 and under free

Hours: Tuesday through Friday, 8 a.m.–4:30 p.m.; Saturday, Sunday, and holidays, 10 a.m.–4:30 p.m. Closed Monday.

Phone: (718) 622-4433

When to go: Anytime

Overall appeal by age group:

Pre-school	Grade School	Teens	Young Adults	Over 30	Senior Citizens
½	★★	★★	★★	★★★	★★★

Author's rating: ★★★

How much time to allow: 1 to 1½ hours

Description and comments: Even if you only walk through the grounds on your way from Prospect Park or the subway to the Brooklyn Museum of Art, it's worth a few minutes to look into the greenhouses, particularly the lily-pond room, the mini–rain forest (which includes several promising medicinal trees), and the bonsai garden; and it's absolutely essential to see the Japanese Tea Garden, with its many small pleasures and twists. If possible, see this in late April or May, when the thousands of Japanese cherry trees blossom (as they do more famously in Washington, D.C.), along with nearly 80 magnolias. Among other popular areas is the fragrance garden, which is heavily perfumed and has Braille labeling.

Touring tip: On weekends and holidays, a free trolley circles among the Botanic Garden, the Brooklyn Museum of Art, and the Prospect Park zoo; call (718) 965-8967.

Brooklyn Children's Museum

Type of attraction: Interactive underground playground
Location: Brooklyn Avenue at St. Mark's Place
Nearest subway station: Kingston
Admission: $3
Hours: Wednesday through Friday, 2–5 p.m.; Saturday, Sunday, and holidays, noon–5 p.m. Closed Monday and Tuesday.
Phone: (718) 735-4403
When to go: Anytime

Overall appeal by age group:

Pre-school	Grade School	Teens	Young Adults	Over 30	Senior Citizens
★★★	★★★	★★	★★	★★	★★

Author's rating: ★★
How much time to allow: 1 to 1½ hours

Description and comments: The first thing to understand is that this is designed to be run almost amok in; the building is a warren, and the various areas are connected to a main tunnel called the "people tube." Almost everything here is hands-on or even body-on; musical computers, ecological exhibits, role play, and so on. The museum also offers storytelling, field trips, and workshops; call for schedule.

Touring tip: This is a fine facility, but unless you have reason to head out this far, you can probably keep the kids happy elsewhere.

Brooklyn Museum of Art

Type of attraction: World-class collection of cultural artifacts and fine art
Location: Eastern Parkway at Washington Avenue
Nearest subway station: Eastern Parkway
Admission: $4 for adults; $2 for students; $1.50 for seniors (some special exhibits extra)
Hours: Wednesday through Friday, 10 a.m.–5 p.m.; Saturday, 11 a.m.–9 p.m.; Sunday, 11 a.m.–6 p.m. Closed Monday and Tuesday.
Phone: (718) 638-5000; web site at www.brooklynart.org
When to go: Anytime
Special comments: Strollers are permitted in only a few areas on weekends.

Overall appeal by age group:

Pre-school	Grade School	Teens	Young Adults	Over 30	Senior Citizens
½	★★	★★½	★★★★	★★★★	★★★

Author's rating: In some ways, a more user-friendly mirror of the Met. ★★★★½

How much time to allow: 2 to 4 hours

Description and comments: Probably only in a city that already boasted the Metropolitan Museum of Art could the Brooklyn Museum be so often overlooked. (And if Brooklyn hadn't been absorbed into New York City, the original plans for the museum, which would have made it the largest in the world, might have been fulfilled.) Its collections may be a little smaller, but they're no less well-exhibited; in fact, the Met can be so overwhelming that the Brooklyn Museum is almost nicer (and it's certainly less crowded). Its Egyptian and African holdings and the nineteenth-century American and European (particularly French) collections are world-renowned, and it has its own complex of 28 reconstructed rooms from the New York area going back to the seventeenth century and up to the Gilded Age (more Rockefeller Moorish-ness); but it has particular strengths in less familiar areas as well, including the art of Native American peoples, spectacular Persian paintings, and a smallish but exquisite gallery of Korean art. BMA's definition of "prints" should set a new dictionary standard: from Dürer woodblocks to Whistler lithographs, from Toulouse-Lautrec posters to Cassatt portraits, Winslow Homer engravings, and Picasso line drawings. In the past few years, the museum has also hosted several blockbuster exhibits, including "Monet in the Mediterranean" and "In the Light of Italy: Corot and Early Open-Air Painting."

Touring tip: There is a nice little cafe on the ground floor. Also, check the schedule of the **Brooklyn Academy of Music** (call (718) 636-4100), which is only a pleasant walk or a couple of subway stops back toward Manhattan; you might be able to top off your day with a concert.

Zone 17: Queens

American Museum of the Moving Image

Type of attraction: Entertainment history as entertainment

Location: 35th Avenue and 36th Street

Nearest subway station: Steinway Street

Admission: $8 for adults; $5 for seniors and college students with ID; $4 for children; children ages 4 and under free

Hours: Tuesday through Friday, noon–5 p.m.; Saturday and Sunday, 11 a.m.–6 p.m. Closed Monday.

Phone: (718) 784-0077

When to go: Weekends for film programs

Special comments: Admission includes screenings

Overall appeal by age group:

Pre-school	Grade School	Teens	Young Adults	Over 30	Senior Citizens
★½	★★	★★★½	★★★★	★★★½	★★★

Author's rating: Intriguing look at not only cinematic techniques but also the integration of "science" and "art," and the selling of both. ★★★½

How much time to allow: 1½ to 4 hours

Description and comments: The museum is actually part of a larger movie-making complex—the restored historic Astoria Studios, where Valentino, the Marx Brothers, and Gloria Swanson worked in the 1920s and Woody Allen and Martin Scorsese have worked in the 1990s. In between it was used for army training films. Only the museum building is open to the public. It's a combination of memorabilia, costumes, props, posters, oddities (à la Planet Hollywood), reconstructed sets, and screening rooms. Smaller kids will get a kick out of exhibits that let them "enter" the set—speak through actors' mouths, put their heads on other bodies, and so on. The major exhibit, "Behind the Scenes," is an interactive explanation of the technology and history of the music biz, which allows visitors to make computer-animated shorts, step into the set of *The Glass Menagerie*, compare the tedious manual film-splicing process of yesteryear with no-hands computer editing, and the like. Screenings range from vintage rarities (silents are shown with music) to cutting-edge art films, and lectures are often lively and celebrity-studded; call for schedule.

Touring tip: Astoria's Greek community, second in size only to that of Athens itself, is worth a visit; 31st Street and Broadway are among local streets lined with restaurants, delis, gift shops, and pretty churches.

Zone 18: The Bronx

Bronx Zoo/International Wildlife Conservation Park

Type of attraction: Famous old-fashioned zoo in transformation to
modern times

Location: Bronx River Parkway at Fordham Road

Nearest subway station: Pelham Parkway

Admission: $3 for adults; $1.50 for seniors and children ages 2–12;
infants free

Hours: Daily, 10 a.m.–4:30 p.m.; April through October, until 5:30 p.m.

Phone: (718) 367-1010; web site at www.bronxzoo.com

When to go: Wednesday; weekdays

Special comments: Wednesday free

Overall appeal by age group:

Pre-school	Grade School	Teens	Young Adults	Over 30	Senior Citizens
★★★	★★★★	★★★½	★★★	★★★	★★

Author's rating: Although several of the older facilities badly need
upgrading (particularly the monkey house), the endangered snow
leopards and Mexican wolves alone are worth the visit. ★★★½

How much time to allow: 1½ to 4 hours

Description and comments: The main buildings date from the turn of the
century and for that reason are both wonderful (the monkey house has play-
ful animals around the roof edge, the former big-cat house has lions and
tigers around the frieze, etc.) and in some places looking a little sad. However, the zoo is moving quickly toward replacing all the old-fashioned cage-
type enclosures with naturalistic ones, divided up by "continent," and some
of these, including the wildlife marsh and savannah areas, are quite fine.
The Wild Asia minizoo (with its glass-enclosed tropical rain forest, elephant
plain, tiger hillside, and encircling monorail), the bat house, and the hands-
on petting zoo are extremely popular. There are more than 4,300 creatures
living here, representing 775 species.

Like the nearby Botanical Gardens, the zoo goes all-out for kids from Thanksgiving past New Year's, staying open until 9 p.m. and filling the park with animal-shaped light "trees" and sculptures, with a special focus on reindeer and other seasonal topics.

Touring tip: Frankly, the zoo is not a whole lot closer to the subway than the botanical gardens are (see "Touring tips" in the description just below), and for out-of-towners, the route is a little confusing. It would be easier to use Metro North to the Botanic Garden stop and do a combination day (and perhaps even if you aren't stopping by the gardens, although you really should). The grounds adjoin, but the entrances don't; there's about a half-mile walk from the garden's main gate to the zoo, but at least it's a fairly straight shot. Or take a Liberty Line bus for about $4; call (718) 652-8400 for information.

There is a full-service cafe, plus seasonal outdoor concessions, stalls, and smaller cafes.

New York Botanical Garden

Type of attraction: Half "natural," half formal array of gardens with dazzling greenhouse complex

Location: 200th Street and Southern Boulevard

Nearest subway station: Bedford Park Boulevard

Admission: Grounds $3 for adults; $1 for seniors and students; children ages 5 and under free; greenhouse and tram tours additional

Hours: Tuesday through Sunday, 10 a.m.–4 p.m. Closed Monday.

Phone: (718) 817-8700

When to go: Midweek

Special comments: Free admission on Wednesday and Saturday, 10 a.m. to noon

Overall appeal by age group:

Pre-school	Grade School	Teens	Young Adults	Over 30	Senior Citizens
★★★	★★★★	★★½	★★★	★★★	★★★★

Author's rating: Restful and restorative, and particularly family-friendly; four-star attraction for gardeners. ★★★½

How much time to allow: 1½ to 4 hours

Description and comments: Within this 250-acre spread are family gardens; a 40-acre forest with a variety of shortish but pretty hiking trails (conveniently timed for pressed visitors) through the sorts of hardwoods New York state had in abundance back in the last days of the Mohicans; and more than two dozen specialty gardens: a seasonal rose garden, a cherry valley, a picnic area, a giant water lily pond, a rock garden, orchid houses, a mini-maze, an herb garden, and so on. The real star is the Enid A. Haupt Conservatory, the glorious Crystal Exposition–style greenhouse complex, which recently completed a four-year, $25 million restoration and now encloses both upland and lowland rain forests (with mezzanine-level walkway), deserts from the Americas and Africa, and special collections. The garden's children's fare is first-rate, with special "treasure map" guides to the conservatory gardens, a hands-on adventure garden, family plant-your-own areas, and the like, plus a wide variety of special programs, children's walking tours, and demonstrations.

Incidentally, the gardens make a surprisingly buoyant addition to a holiday trip. The plants inside the conservatory are covered in lights, along with many outdoor trees; a huge model train exhibition winds through both imaginary and real miniature New York landscapes; special family concerts and performances are scheduled, and so on.

Touring tips: The garden is actually about eight blocks from the Bedford Park subway stop, and while it's downhill on your way there, it's a hard uphill return. However, Metro North commuter trains (532-4900) run from Grand Central right to a Botanic Garden stop a stone's throw from the side entrance in about 20 minutes. Also, during summer months, a shuttle operates among the American Museum of Natural History, the Metropolitan Museum of Art, and the botanical garden; call the garden's main number for information.

There is a full-service cafe between the conservatory and the train-side gate.

PART TWELVE

Dining and Restaurants

■ Introduction ■

The New York restaurant scene—considered by some the best in the world or, more modestly, the best in the United States—is booming, blooming, reveling in the refinements of the hautest of haute cuisine and the redolence of exotic flavors from every part of the globe. You can spend a king's ransom, find bargain-basement beaneries, or choose moderation somewhere in between. Eating out in New York is a major attraction not just for tourists but for natives as well. Trying the new, vying for reservations at the trendy, or simply sharing a meal with friends at a neighborhood favorite is recreation, sport, and entertainment for thousands of New Yorkers.

And the star performers in this gourmet grand prix are the chefs and the superchefs, often doubling as owners and managers, who have emerged from their steamy, pot-bound posts to become celebrities themselves. Even the renowned *New York Times* takes note of every move they make in the gastronomic game of musical kitchens. The opening of a new establishment overseen by a chef/owner/celeb can generate as much excitement as a Broadway premiere. The recent debuts of Le Cirque 2000 (Sirio Maccioni), Jean-Georges (Jean-Georges Vongerichten), Balthazar (Keith McNally), and Bouley Bakery (David Bouley) were gala events, attracting New York nabobs and the media.

The number of restaurants is daunting—over 4,000 in Manhattan alone—and the variety exhilarating. The array of ethnic kitchens, from Afghan to Vietnamese, with culinary contributions from Ethiopia, Hungary, Jamaica, Lebanon, Peru, Ukraine, Tibet, and many more seems inexhaustible; you could easily sample a different cuisine every week for well over a year with no repeats. This survey of over 100 of New York's niftiest nosheries covers a wide spectrum of price categories, global origins and New York neighborhoods, tried and true oldies, popular trendies, off-beat ethnics, and local favorites. We have tried to give an overall impression of food and mood and what it will cost. Don't be surprised if some of our menu recommendations are not available. Many New York restaurants change their menus often to take advantage of ultra-fresh seasonal offerings, and sometimes the chefs de cuisine change as often as the menus.

Keeping abreast of what's "in" and what's "out" is more than a passing pastime. Foodies, local and otherwise, have to stay on their toes because things can change in a "New York minute." Right now, if you're sipping a mega-martini, eating sushi, and puffing on a fine cigar and the noise level is in the killer decibels, you're in with the "in-crowd." This town is still awash in coffee, caff, de-caff, frothy, and plain; there are, at last reckoning, 28 Starbucks, 23 New World Coffees, 10 Dalton Coffee Limiteds, and too many individual java joints to count. Microbreweries have had a malt-down, but sake bars are on the rise.

If food of the Asian persuasion turns your taste buds on, New York is the place. Restaurants that serve the complex cuisines of China, India, and Japan—in their many regional variations—are so numerous that an entire guide could easily be devoted to them. The "sushi situation" alone would fill a small book—it's a wonder that there's a sufficient supply of creatures swimming in the seas to satisfy New Yorkers' growing sushi lust. Thai and Vietnamese restaurants, once hard to find, have sprung up all over the city with a range of prices and decor (Le Colonial, 149 East 57th Street, 752-0808, with the sexy chic of prewar Saigon, is a Southeast Asian power scene with prices to match, while in Chinatown, the decor-less Nha Trang, 87 Baxter Street, 233-5948, serves an excellent dinner for under $20). And the lesser-known dishes of Burma, Sri Lanka, the Philippines, Indonesia, Korea, Cambodia, and Malaysia are well represented.

■ Looking for Luxury in All the Right Places ■

For many, a trip to the Big Apple isn't complete without a visit to one or more of the grand dames of "La-Le Land," those bastions of classic French elegance and classic French cooking. La Caravelle (33 West 55th Street; 585-4252); La Cote Basque (60 West 55th Street; 688-6525); La Grenouille (3 East 52nd Street; 752-1495); Le Chantilly (106 East 57th Street; 751-2931); Le Perigord (405 East 52nd Street; 755-6244); and Lutèce (249 East 50th Street; 752-2225) remain among New York's finest. The decor, service (the traditional sangfroid has warmed up), and food are of the highest order, and so are the prices. Do expect to see the rich and famous, but not necessarily the trendy; don't expect to get a quick reservation or a fabulous table. And do expect to pay $65 or more per person for dinner without a sip of wine or designer water.

In addition to the grandes dames, there are the "golden oldies," the legendary landmarks that continue to reign high in the pantheon of destination dining spots. The Four Seasons (99 East 52nd Street; 754-9494) has kept its glitter, glamour, great food, and power scene rep, as has the quintessentially clubby "21" (21 West 52nd Street; 582-7200), expected to get even better under its new owners. Howard Chandler Christy's lissome "nouveau" nymphs still loll on the walls of the Café des Artistes (1 West 67th Street; 877-3550), and celebrities, knowing natives, and visitors still flock to this 80-year-old West Side enchantress; and Windows on the World (1 World Trade Center; 524-7000), the ultimate "room with a view," perched on the 107th floor of the World Trade Center, is breathtaking again after a multi-million-dollar facelift. You can have lunch or dinner at Windows, sip a drink at The Greatest Bar on Earth, or try the $125 prix fixe (six courses, five wines) at the ultra-elegant Cellar in the Sky. The Rainbow Room (30 Rockefeller Plaza; 632-5000), sublimely romantic, ravishingly theatrical, ranks as New York's premiere special occasion restaurant. You get a romantic rush just walking down the stairs or stepping onto the dance floor, and chef Waldy Malouf is a master at mixing the classic with the new on his multi-starred menu. Bear in mind that big-time glitz comes at a cost—all these restaurants are expensive and often hard to book.

■ Hotel Hoopla ■

The dazzle—at dazzling prices—is back in New York hotel dining, not only in the polished, posh decor but also in the excellence of their tables. Lespinasse, in the St. Regis (2 East 55th Street; 339-6719), is often considered New York's numero uno for its visual beauty and for chef Gray Kunz's culinary artistry. Les Célébrités (Essex House, 155 West 58th Street; 484-5113) offers Christian Delouvrier's sumptuous, classic French menu in sumptuous surroundings. Le Régence in the Plaza Athénée (37 East 64th Street; 606-4647) serves regal French food in a veritable Versailles of a dining room. Master-chef Daniel Boulud's superb, innovative French food has earned Restaurant Daniel (20 East 76th Street; 288-0033) one of New York's very few four-star ratings and the number one spot in this year's "Top Table" ratings in *Gourmet* magazine. It's in, but not really of, the Hotel Surrey, and rumor has it that Daniel will move to fancier digs later this year. I. M. Pei's soaring ceilings and marble walls in the Four Seasons Hotel (57 East 57th Street; 758-5757) showcase the super-sophisticated Fifty Seven Fifty Seven, where executive chef Susan Weaver's sensational seasonal offerings are served. The refurbished Royalton Hotel (44 West 44th Street;

944-8844) is home to the chic Cafe 44, which in turn is home to a chic, heady power-lunch scene. The food, if anyone notices, is innovative American and good. The movers, shakers, and deal-makers eat their power breakfasts in baronial elegance at the Regency (Hotel Regency, 540 Park Avenue; 339-4050) or in stately style in the ever classic Edwardian Room at The Plaza Hotel (768 Fifth Avenue at 59th Street; 546-5310).

■ Where's the Beef? ■

New York may not be the carnivore capital of the world, but it sure has its share of prime steak houses. If you're on a tear for rare meat and costly cholesterol, you won't be disappointed. Peter Luger in Brooklyn, now over a century old, still tops most lists (see our profile) and sets the standard for dry aged steak. The Palm (837 Second Avenue; 687-2953), renowned for its caricature-covered walls, New York–gruff service, and more than substantial portions is always a winner for sirloin, large lobsters, and fabulous cottage-fried potatoes. Its younger clone, Palm Too (840 Second Avenue; 697-5198), is across the street. Sparks (210 East 46th Street; 687-4855) is the epitome of Midtown macho con mucho—both steak and seafood. The Post House (28 East 63rd Street; 935-2888) serves its surf and turf, fine wines, and cigars in subdued, upscale surroundings. Smith & Wollensky (797 Third Avenue; 753-1530), another New York institution, bustles with beef-eating power brokers and has one of the best red wine lists in town. Maloney & Porcelli (37 East 50th Street; 750-2233) is prime example of the "new" New York steak house, casual, softer, woman-friendly, but with a 24-ounce rib eye that will leave strong men murmuring, "Awesome."

■ What to Wear, Where ■

Rigid dress codes, for the most part, have succumbed to the comfort principle; even the uptight stock market has instituted "dress-down Fridays." Casual clothes will take you to most places that fall into the inexpensive and moderate categories, but if you're headed for Gotham's tonier tables, you might find that you'll be better suited and better served by suiting up (we've noted the establishments that require jackets). Some general rules of thumb: If you are lunching in Midtown, where business brahmins browse, wear a suit; if you're dining at Daniel, Chanterelle, or the like, dress; if you're dancing at the Rainbow Room, make Fred and Ginger proud; if you've just produced your first movie or written your first best-seller, wear whatever you want, all-black Armani preferred; in trendy TriBeCa or SoHo, wear all black anything. Put on a tie (or the equivalent thereof) for a power breakfast, and take it off for brunch.

▪ **Where to Find a Deal for a Meal** ▪

Good restaurants with reasonable prices are yours for the choosing, but if you want to eat at some of the more expensive spots for less-than-à-la-carte cost, there are ways. Check our restaurant profiles for prix fixe prices— lunch, pretheater dinner, and dinner. When they're offered, you can often get quite a deal on a multicourse meal. For example, the pretheater dinner at Alison on Dominick is $19.97 prix fixe, when normally it would average $51; the buffet lunch at Dawat (210 East 58th Street; 355-7555), a super-classy Indian eatery with a classy clientele, is $12.95, while dinner would be triple that; prix fixe dinner in the Grill Room of the Four Seasons is $29.50, and you could double that on the regular menu. If you happen to be in New York between the end of June and Labor Day, you can take advantage of the $19.98 special lunches served by an impressive array of the best and the beautiful. Check the big ads in the New York newspapers just before the feeding frenzy begins and make your reservations posthaste. They go faster than frequent flyer seats, and some restaurants make this grand gesture for one week only, usually the last in June. The 1997 list included Aureole, Aquavit, Chanterelle, Patria, Le Perigord, Café des Artistes, Felidia, and many more.

— S. H.

The Restaurants

We have developed detailed profiles for the best and most interesting restaurants (in our opinion) in town. Each profile features an easily scanned heading that allows you, in just a second, to check out the restaurant's name, cuisine, star rating, cost, quality rating, and value rating.

Cuisine. This is actually less straightforward than it sounds. A couple of years ago, for example, "pan-Asian" restaurants in Washington, D.C. were serving what was then generally described as "fusion" food—Asian ingredients with European techniques, or vice versa. Since then, there has been a pan-Asian explosion, but nearly all specialize in what would be street food back home: noodles, skewers, dumplings, and soups. Once-general categories have become subdivided—French into bistro fare and even Provençal, "new continental" into regional American and "eclectic"—while others have broadened and fused: Middle Eastern and Provençal into Mediterranean, Spanish and South American into nuevo Latino, and so on. In some cases, we have used the broader terms (i.e., "French") but added descriptions to give a clearer idea of the fare. Again, though, experimentation and "fusion" is ever more common, so don't hold us, or the chefs, to too strict a style.

Star Rating. The star rating is a rating that encompasses the entire dining experience, including style, service, and ambience in addition to the taste, presentation, and quality of the food. Five stars is the highest rating possible and connotes the best of everything. Four-star restaurants are exceptional and three-star restaurants are well above average. Two-star restaurants are good. One star is used to indicate an average restaurant that demonstrates an unusual capability in some area of specialization—for example, an otherwise unmemorable place that has great barbecued chicken.

Cost. To the right of the star rating is an expense description that provides a comparative sense of how much a complete meal will cost. A complete meal for our purposes consists of an entrée with vegetable or side dish and choice of soup or salad. Appetizers, desserts, drinks, and tips are excluded.

Inexpensive	$14 and less per person
Moderate	$15–30 per person
Expensive	Over $30 per person

Quality Rating. On the far right of each heading appear a number and a letter. The number rates the food quality on a scale of 0 to 100; 100 is the best rating attainable. It is based expressly on the taste, freshness of ingredients, preparation, presentation, and creativity of food served. There is no consideration of price. If you are a person who wants the best food available, and cost is not an issue, you need look no further than the quality ratings.

Value Rating. If, on the other hand, you are looking for both quality and value, then you should check the value rating, expressed in letters. The value ratings are defined as follows:

A   Exceptional value; a real bargain

B   Good value

C   Fair value; you get exactly what you pay for

D   Somewhat overpriced

F   Significantly overpriced

■ Locating the Restaurant ■

Just below the heading is a designation for geographic zone. This zone description will give you a general idea of where the restaurant described is located. We've divided New York into the following 19 geographic zones (see pages 12–18 for detailed zone maps):

Zone 1	Lower Manhattan, Wall Street, and the Battery
Zone 2	SoHo and TriBeCa
Zone 3	Chinatown, Little Italy, and the Lower East Side
Zone 4	Greenwich Village
Zone 5	The East Village
Zone 6	Chelsea
Zone 7	Gramercy Park and Madison Square
Zone 8	Midtown West and the Theater District

Zone 9	Midtown East
Zone 10	West Side
Zone 11	East Side
Zone 12	Upper West Side
Zone 13	Upper East Side
Zone 14	Columbia University and Harlem
Zone 15	The Heights
Zone 16	Brooklyn
Zone 17	Queens
Zone 18	The Bronx
Zone 19	Staten Island

Payment. We've listed the type of payment accepted at each restaurant using the following code: AMEX equals American Express (Optima), CB equals Carte Blanche, D equals Discover, DC equals Diners Club, MC equals MasterCard, and VISA is self-explanatory.

Who's Included. Restaurants in New York open and close at an alarming rate. In a "Big Apple Blink," Bouley (top of the tops for years) and the legendary Russian Tea Room were history, and many don't make it through their first year. So, for the most part, we have tried to confine our list to establishments with a proven track record over a fairly long period of time. The exceptions here are the newer offspring of the demigods of the culinary world—these places are destined to last, at least until our next update. Newer restaurants (and older restaurants under new management) are listed but not profiled. Newer or changed establishments that demonstrate staying power and consistency will be profiled in subsequent editions. Also, the list is highly selective. Noninclusion of a particular place does not necessarily indicate that the restaurant is not good, only that it was not ranked among the best in its genre. Detailed profiles of individual restaurants follow in alphabetical order at the end of this chapter.

The Best New York Restaurants

Name	Star Rating	Price Rating	Quality Rating	Value Rating	Zone
Afghani					
Caravan	★★★½	Moderate	89	A	8
American					
Aureole	★★★★	Expensive	93	B	11
Grange Hall	★★★★	Moderate	93	A	4
Gramercy Tavern	★★★½	Expensive	89	B	7
Patroon	★★★½	Expensive	86	C	9
Seagrill	★★★½	Expensive	89	C	9
Sign of the Dove	★★★½	Expensive	87	B	11
Blue Ribbon	★★★	Moderate	82	B	2
Tavern on the Green	★★★	Mod/Exp	83	B	10
EJ's Lunchonette	★★½	Inexpensive	79	B	12, 13, 4
Mike's American Bar & Grill	★★	Moderate	74	C	8
American *(Southwest)*					
Mesa Grill	★★★	Expensive	81	C	7
Santa Fe	★★½	Moderate	79	B	10
Argentinean					
Old San Juan	★★★	Inexpensive	86	B	8
Asian					
Cendrillon	★★★	Moderate	84	B	2
Zen Palate	★★½	Inexpensive	78	B	12, 8, 7
Asian fusion					
Rain	★★★	Moderate	85	C	12
Republic	★★½	Inexpensive	79	B	7, 12
Barbecue					
Virgil's Barbecue	★★½	Moderate	74	C	8
Belgian					
Petite Abeille	★★½	Inexpensive	86	A	6

	Star Rating	Price Rating	Quality Rating	Value Rating	Zone
The Best New York Restaurants (continued)					
Name					
Bistro					
Sanzin	★★★	Expensive	84	C	2
Florent	★★½	Moderate	79	B	4
Tartine	★★½	Inexpensive	77	C	4
Brazilian					
Churrascaria Plataforma	★★★	Moderate	88	C	8
Cabana Carioca	★★½	Inexpensive	84	A	8
Cantonese					
The Nice Restaurant	★★★½	Moderate	91	B	3
Tindo	★★★	Moderate	82	B	3
Chinese (see also Dim Sum)					
Joe's Shanghai	★★★½	Moderate	91	A	3, 17
Shun Lee, Shun Lee Cafe	★★★½	Exp/Mod	85	C	10
Cuban					
Margon Restaurant	★★½	Inexpensive	84	A	8
Dim Sum (see also Chinese)					
The Nice Restaurant	★★★½	Moderate	91	B	3
French					
Chanterelle	★★★★	Very Exp	95	B	2
Il Bucco	★★★★	Expensive	94	C	5
Jean-Georges	★★★★	Expensive	95	B	10
Le Bernadin	★★★★	Very Exp	96	B	8
Le Cirque 2000	★★★★	Very Exp	95	B	9
Vong	★★★½	Expensive	87	B	9
Alison on Dominick	★★★	Expensive	83	C	2
Balthazar	★★★	Mod/Exp	83	C	2
Cité	★★★	Expensive	85	B	8
Trois Jean	★★★	Expensive	82	C	13
Demarchelier	★★½	Expensive	77	C	13

The Best New York Restaurants (continued)

Name	Star Rating	Price Rating	Quality Rating	Value Rating	Zone
La Boite en Bois	★★½	Moderate	78	B	10
Greek					
Molyvos	★★★	Expensive	84	B	8
Indian					
Jackson Diner	★★★½	Moderate	87	A	17
Mavalli Palace	★★★½	Moderate	87	A	7
Shaan	★★★	Mod/Exp	84	B	8
International					
Man Ray	★★½	Moderate	79	C	6
Irish					
Molly's	★★★	Moderate	88	B	7
Italian					
Il Bucco	★★★★	Expensive	94	C	5
La Pizza Fresca	★★★★	Moderate	95	A	7
Il Mulino	★★★½	Expensive	90	B	4
Pó	★★★½	Moderate	87	B	4
Coco Opera	★★★	Expensive	82	C	10
Osteria Del Circo	★★★	Expensive	83	C	8
Piccolo Angelo	★★★	Moderate	84	B	4
Remi	★★★	Expensive	84	C	8
Rosario's	★★★	Inexpensive	87	A	1
Becco	★★½	Moderate	79	A	8
Iammo Bello	★★½	Inexpensive	83	A	11
Italian (Northern)					
Orso	★★★	Moderate	82	C	8
Paola's	★★★	Mod/Exp	85	B	13
Remi	★★★	Expensive	84	C	8
Italian (Tuscan)					
Coco Pazzo Teatro	★★★	Expensive	82	C	8
Bar Pitti	★★½	Moderate	78	C	4

	Star	Price	Quality	Value	
Name	Rating	Rating	Rating	Rating	Zone
Japanese (see also Sushi)					
Nobu	★★★★	Expensive	95	B	2
Honmura An	★★★½	Expensive	89	B	2
Sushisay	★★★½	Expensive	87	B	9
Tomoe	★★★½	Mod/Inexp	88	B	4
Seryna	★★★	Expensive	84	B	9
Jewish Deli					
Second Avenue Deli	★★½	Moderate	79	C	5
Mr. Broadway Kosher Deli	★★★	Moderate	84	A	7
Korean					
Woo Chon	★★★	Moderate	82	C	9
Kosher					
Chick Chack Chicken	★★★	Inexpensive	90	A	5
Kosher Yemenite					
Bissaleh Classic	★★★	Moderate	87	B	13
Latin American					
Patria	★★★	Expensive	84	B	7
Cafe con Leche	★★½	Inexpensive	79	B	12
Malaysian					
Penang	★★★	Moderate	83	C	12, 2
Mediterranean					
Picholine	★★★½	Expensive	89	C	10
Delphini	★★★	Moderate	82	B	12
Mexican					
Gabriela's	★★★	Moderate	86	A	12
Rosa Mexicano	★★★	Moderate	84	B	9

The Best New York Restaurants (continued)

The Best New York Restaurants (continued)					
Name	Star Rating	Price Rating	Quality Rating	Value Rating	Zone
Middle Eastern					
Sahara East	★★½	Moderate	84	B	5
Moroccan					
Cafe Mogador	★★½	Moderate	84	A	5
Lotfi's	★★½	Moderate	79	C	8
New American					
Union Square Cafe	★★★★	Expensive	92	B	7
Gotham Bar & Grill	★★★½	Expensive	89	C	4
Pasta					
Tre Pomodori	★★½	Moderate	85	A	7
Pizza					
Patsy's Pizza	★★★	Inexpensive	93	A	14
Portuguese					
Cabana Carioca	★★½	Inexpensive	84	A	8
Puerto Rican					
Old San Juan	★★★	Inexpensive	86	B	8
Russian					
Firebird	★★★	Mod/Exp	88	B	8
Petrossian	★★★	Expensive	83	C	8
Scandinavian					
Aquavit	★★★	Expensive	85	B	9
Seafood					
Le Bernadin	★★★★	Very Exp	96	B	8
Oceana	★★★½	Expensive	90	C	9
Seagrill	★★★½	Expensive	89	C	9
Soul Food					
Jezebel	★★★	Expensive	83	C	8

The Best New York Restaurants (continued)					
Name	Star Rating	Price Rating	Quality Rating	Value Rating	Zone

Soul Food *(continued)*

Soul Fixin's	★★★	Inexpensive	88	A	6

Soup Take-out

Soup Kitchen International	★★★½	Inexpensive	94	A	8

Spanish

Il Bucco	★★★★	Expensive	94	C	5
Xunta	★★★	Moderate	87	B	5

Steak

Cité	★★★	Expensive	85	B	8
Peter Luger	★★★	Expensive	84	B	16

Sushi *(see also Japanese)*

Tomoe	★★★½	Inexp/Mod	88	B	4

Tearoom

Lady Mendl's Tea Salon	★★★	Moderate	88	C	7

Thai

Sripraphai Thai Bakery	★★★½	Inexpensive	92	A	17
Vong	★★★½	Expensive	87	B	9

Vegetarian

Mavalli Palace	★★★½	Moderate	87	A	7
Kate's Joint	★★★	Moderate	86	B	5
Zen Palate	★★½	Inexpensive	78	B	12, 8, 7

Vietnamese

New Pasteur	★★★½	Inexpensive	88	A	3
Saigon Grill	★★★	Inexpensive	90	A	12
Monsoon	★★½	Moderate	78	B	12

■ More Recommendations ■

The Best Brunch

Anglers and Writers   420 Hudson Street 675-0810

Cafe Botanica   Essex House, 160 Central Park South 484-5120

Café des Artistes   1 West 67th Street 877-3500

Good Enough to Eat   485 Amsterdam Avenue 410-7335

Le Zoo   314 West 11th Street 620-0390

Peacock Alley   Waldorf-Astoria, 301 Park Avenue 872-4895

Sign of the Dove   (see profile)

Zoe   90 Prince Street 966-6722

The Best Burgers

Corner Bistro   331 West 4th Street 242-9502

Cozy Soup & Burger   739 Broadway 477-5566

Gotham Bar & Grill   (see profile)

Joe Allen   326 West 46th Street 581-6464

Molly's   (see profile)

P. J. Clarke's   915 Third Avenue 759-1650

Paul's Palace   131 Second Avenue 529-3033

The Best Burgers (continued)

Riviera Cafe   225 West 4th Street 929-3250

Steak Frites   9 East 16th Street 463-7101

21 Club   21 West 52nd Street 582-7200

The Best Restaurants in Chinatown

Excellent Dumpling House   111 Lafayette Street 219-0212

Grand Sichuan   125 Canal Street 334-3323

Joe's Shanghai   (see profile)

Kam Chueh   40 Bowery 791-6868

The Best Restaurants in Chinatown (continued)

Mandarin Court   61 Mott Street 608-3838

New Pasteur   (see profile)

New York Noodletown   28½ Bower   349-0923

Nha Trang   87 Baxter 233-5948

The Nice Restaurant   (see profile)

Sweet and Tart Cafe   76 Mott Street 334-8088

Tindo   (see profile)

The Best Delis

Barney Greengrass   541 Amsterdam Avenue 724-4707

Ben's Best   96–40 Queens Blvd., Rego Park, Queens (718) 897-1700

Carnegie Deli   854 Seventh Avenue at 54th Street 757-2245

Fine and Schapiro   138 West 72nd 877-2874

Katz's Deli   205 East Houston 254-2246

Mr. Broadway Kosher Deli   (see profile)

Pastrami King   124–24 Queens Blvd., Kew Gardens, Queens, (718) 263-1717

Second Avenue Deli   (see profile)

The Best Kosher

Bissaleh Classic   (see profile)

Chick Chack Chicken   (see profile)

Haikara Grill   1016 Second Avenue 355-7000

Jasmine's   11 East 30th Street 251-8884

Le Marais   150 West 46th Street 869-0900

Levana   141 West 69th Street 877-8457

Mr. Broadway Kosher Deli   (see profile)

Second Avenue Deli   (see profile)

The Best Romantic Dining

Box Tree   250 East 49th Street 758-8320

Cafe Nicholson   323 East 58th Street 355-6769

King's Carriage House   251 East 82nd Street 734-5490

March   405 East 58th Street 754-6772

One if by Land, Two if by Sea   17 Barrow Street 228-0822

The Screening Room   54 Varick 334-2338

Sonia Rose   132 Lexington Avenue 545-1777

The Best Family Dining

Bissaleh Classic   (see profile)

Chick Chack Chicken   (see profile)

City Crab   235 Park Avenue 529-3800

Popover Cafe   551 Amsterdam Avenue 595-8555

Ratners   138 Delancey 677-5588

Royal Canadian Pancake House   2286 Broadway 873-6052;
    1004 Second Avenue 980-4131; 180 Third Avenue 777-9288

Two Boots   37 Avenue A 505-2276

Virgil's   (see profile)

The Best Fireplaces

The Black Sheep   344 West 11th Street 242-1010

Christer's   145 West 55th Street 974-7224

I Trulli   122 East 27th Street 481-7372

La Ripaille   605 Hudson Street 255-4406

Molly's   (see profile)

Vivolo   140 East 74th Street 737-3533

The Best Gardens

Barbetta   321 West 46th Street 246-9171

The Best Gardens (continued)

Barolo 398 West Broadway 226-1102

Boathouse Cafe Central Park Lake, East Park Drive
 at 72nd Street 517-2233

La Refuge 166 East 82nd Street 861-4505

Sahara East (see profile)

Verbena 54 Irving Place 260-5454

The Best Night-Owl Prowls

Blue Ribbon (see Profile) (Closes 4 a.m.)

Corner Bistro 331 West 4th Street 242-9502 (Closes 3:30 a.m.)

Granville 40 East 20th Street 253-9088 (Closes 4 a.m.)

Hole in One (see profile in Part 6) (Closes 2:30 a.m.)

Hot Tomato 676 Sixth Avenue 691-3535 (Closes 4 a.m.)

Kiev 117 Second Avenue 674-4040 (Open 24 hours)

Le Bar Bat (see profile in Part 6) (Closes 2 a.m.)

Lucky Strike 59 Grand Street 941-0479 (Closes 4 a.m.)

Odean 145 Broadway 233-0507 (Closes 3 a.m.)

Sahara East (see profile) (Closes 2 a.m.)

Saka Gura (see profile in Part 6) (Closes 3 a.m.)

Tindo (see profile) (Closes 3 a.m.)

Woo Chon (see profile) (Open 24 hours)

The Best Pizza

Arturo's Pizza 106 West Houston 677-3820

John's Pizza 278 Bleecker Street 243-1680

Lombardi's 32 Spring Street 941-7994

Nova Grill 2330 Broadway 579-5100

Patsy's Pizza (see profile)

Pizza Fresca (see profile)

Sal and Carmine's Pizza   2671 Broadway 663-7651

Sofia Fabulous Pizza   1022 Madison at 79th 734-2676

Two Boots   42 Avenue A 254-1919; 74 Bleecker 777-1033;
   75 Greenwich Avenue 633-9096

V & T Pizza   1024 Amsterdam Avenue 663-1708

The Best Raw Bars

Aquagrill   210 Spring Street 274-0505

Blue Ribbon   (see profile)

Blue Water Grill   31 Union Square West 675-9500

Docks   633 Third Avenue 986-8080; 2427 Broadway 724-5588

Oyster Bar   Grand Central Station, Lower Level 490-6650

Redeye Grill   890 Seventh Avenue 541-9000

The Best Noisy Bar Scenes

Bar Six   502 Sixth Avenue 691-1363

Bubble Lounge   228 West Broadway 431-3433

Cub Room   131 Sullivan Street 677-4100

Mesa City   1059 Third Avenue 207-1919

Monkey Bar   Hotel Elysee, 60 East 54th Street 838-2600

The Best Noisy Bar Scenes (continued)

Pravda   281 Lafayette Street 226-4696

The Best Steak Houses

Churrascaria Plataforma   (see profile)

Frank's Restaurant   85 Tenth Avenue 243-1349

Palm   837 Second Avenue 687-2953

Palm Too   840 Second Avenue 697-5198

Pampa   768 Amsterdam Avenue, near 98th Street 865-2929

Peter Luger   (see profile)

Sparks Steak House   210 East 46th Street 687-4855

The Best Ultracheap Restaurants (under $6)

Cabana Carioca   (see profile)

Chick Chack Chicken   (see profile)

Excellent Dumpling House   111 Lafayette Street 219-0212

Iammo Bello   (see profile)

Moncks Corner   644 Ninth Avenue 397-1117

Rosario's   (see profile)

Soul Fixin's   (see profile)

Teresa's   103 First Avenue 228-0604

So You Won't Drop While You Shop

The Cafe   Trump Tower, 725 Fifth Avenue 754-4450
(near Bergdorf Goodman, Henri Bendel, Tiffany, and more)

Cafe S.F.A.   Sak's Fifth Avenue, 611 Fifth Ave., 8th floor 940-4080

Contrapunto   200 East 60th St., upstairs 751-8616 (near Bloomie's)

Fred's at Barney's   Lower level, Madison Ave. at 61st St. 833-2200

Le Train Blue   Bloomingdale's, 1000 Third Avenue, 6th floor
705-2100

The Tea Box   Takashimaya, 693 Fifth Avenue 350-0180

Yellowfingers   200 East 60th Street 751-8615 (near Bloomie's)

The Best Legends and Landmarks

Algonquin Hotel   59 West 44th St. 840-6800 (stick to the lobby bar)

Grand Ticino   228 Thompson Street 777-5922 (*Moonstruck* set)

Landmark Tavern   626 Eleventh Avenue 757-7859

Oyster Bar   Grand Central Station, Lower Level 490-6650

Pete's Tavern   129 East 18th Street 473-7676

Rao's   455 East 114th Street 722-6709

White Horse Tavern   567 Hudson Street 989-3956

ALISON ON DOMINICK

			QUALITY
French-Country	★★★	Expensive	83
			VALUE
			C

38 Dominick Street (between Hudson and Varick Streets)
 727-1888   Zone 2 TriBeCa/SoHo

Customers: Local
Reservations: Necessary
When to go: Anytime
Entrée range: $25–33
Payment: All major credit cards
Service rating: ★★★

Friendliness rating: ★★★
Wine selection: Extensive, with some
 low prices and some whoppers
Dress: Casual to dressy
Disabled access: Yes, but not for
 bathrooms

Dinner: Monday–Saturday, 5:30–10:30 p.m.; Sunday, 5:30–9:30 p.m.

Atmosphere & setting: On a small, out-of-the-way west SoHo street (rather deserted in the late evening), this intimate space is simply dressed in white and black—white enamel walls, soft black velvet banquettes, black-and-white photos, and slim mirrors that skim the tops of the banquettes. A wavy canopy of white muslin floats overhead, and a heavy black curtain covers the back wall. The very closely set tables each sport a single candle.

House specialties: Herbed goat cheese and potato Napoleon; seared foie gras; sautéed arctic char in Rhône wine sauce; juniper-and-chartreuse-marinated roast duck breast and leg confit.

Other recommendations: House-cured salmon infused with Pernod; pan-roasted cod with savoy cabbage, potatoes, and chorizo; pan-seared filet mignon with foie gras and black truffle butter; warm chocolate timbale.

Summary & comments: If books and critics didn't tell you that this is one of the "coziest" of New York's "romantics," you might think it just another of the underdone chic spots that dot SoHo. The food, on the other hand, is very good and well-deserving of the accolades it has garnered over the years; the same can be said of the wine list. The unfailingly warm, friendly, and informed service adds to the overall appeal.

AQUAVIT

			QUALITY
Scandinavian	★★★	Expensive	85
			VALUE
			B

13 West 54th Street (close to Fifth Avenue)
307-7311   Zone 9 Midtown East

Customers: Business, local
Reservations: Recommended
When to go: Anytime
Entrée range: Dinner, $58 prix fixe
  only; upstairs cafe, $18–23 à la
  carte
Payment: All major credit cards

Service rating: ★★★
Friendliness rating: ★★★
Bar: Full service, with a great array of
  aquavit
Wine selection: Fair
Dress: Business; casual upstairs
Disabled access: No

Brunch: Sunday, noon–2:30 p.m.
Lunch: Monday–Friday, 12–2:30 p.m.; Monday–Saturday,
  noon–3 p.m. in the cafe
Dinner: Every day, 5:30–10:30 p.m.

Atmosphere & setting: This is a Wow!, but a cool Nordic one. Once the Rockefeller townhouse, it now has an eight-story glass atrium, with a copper waterfall descending into the downstairs courtyard room (where the more serious dining occurs) and clean modern lines all around. There's a bar and cafe upstairs that serves lighter fare and where a "flight of aquavit," guaranteed to produce liftoff, can be sampled.

House specialties: Herring plate; smorgasbord plate; roasted arctic venison chop with pumpkin gnocchi; black-pepper-smoked char; tea-cured Muscovy duck; warm chocolate cake.

Other recommendations: Gravlax; seared foie gras with parsnip puree; honey-mustard-glazed salmon; halibut wrapped in Swedish ham.

Summary & comments: This is Scandinavian food at its best in a dramatic setting that only adds to the pleasure. The prices, like the decor, soar, but for fine food in Gotham City, it's not outrageous. Lunch downstairs is a la carte or $29 prix fixe; dinner is $58 prix fixe only; or for $75 you can splurge and get the five-course tasting menu. The cafe upstairs is somewhat less expensive.

AUREOLE

American	★★★★	Expensive	QUALITY
			93
			VALUE
			B

34 East 61st Street (between Madison and Park Avenues)
  319-1660   Zone 11   East Side

Customers: Well-heeled, well-dressed	Friendliness rating: ★★★
Reservations: Required	Bar: Full service
When to go: Anytime	Wine selection: Excellent and
Entrée range: Dinner, prix fixe only,	interesting
$63; tasting menu, $85	Dress: Dressy, business
Payment: All major credit cards	Disabled access: No
Service rating: ★★★★	

Lunch: Monday–Friday, noon–2:30 p.m.
Dinner: Monday–Thursday, 5:30–11 p.m.; Friday and Saturday,
  5:30–11:30 p.m.

Atmosphere & setting: The two lower floors of a narrow East Side townhouse have been transformed into a discreetly opulent space with subtle lighting, charming barnyard bas-relief on the beige walls, and grand florals that add brilliant touches of color. The small garden, open in summer, is a New York gem.

House specialties: Hand-cut bluefin tuna tartare; caramelized Clarke Farm chicken with sweet corn risotto; roasted halibut with lemon thyme brown butter; wood-grilled lamb mignons with lentil cakes; any of the fabulous desserts.

Other recommendations: Pan-seared "foie gras steak"; Chesapeake crab and avocado timbale; fricassee of lobster with provençal artichokes; crisp red snapper with Manila clams.

Summary & comments: Always a contender, and often a winner, for the number one spot on New York's top ten lists, Aureole is elegant in every way, expensive and well worth it. Chef/owner Charlie Palmer, doyen of New American cooking—if it's old enough to have a doyen—oversees the fabulous fare, and the desserts are so wonderfully sculpted that they could be exhibited at MoMA or the Guggenheim. The service is impeccable and without a soupçon of snobbism.

BALTHAZAR

			QUALITY
French	★★★ Moderately expensive		83
			VALUE
			C

80 Spring Street
  965-1414   Zone 2 TriBeCa/SoHo

Customers: The "trendetti,"
  celebrities, local
Reservations: Necessary
When to go: Anytime
Entrée range: $14–25
Payment: All major credit cards
Service rating: ★★★

Friendliness rating: ★★★
Bar: Full service and usually full
Wine selection: Good and not
  overpriced; house wine by the
  carafe is drinkable and inexpensive
Dress: Chic—upscale or down
Disabled access: Yes

Brunch: Saturday and Sunday, 11:30 a.m.–4 p.m.
Lunch: Monday–Friday, noon–5 p.m.
Dinner: Sunday–Thursday, 6 p.m.–12:30 a.m., with a late-night
  menu to 2 a.m.; Friday and Saturday, 6 p.m.–3 a.m.

Atmosphere & setting: Keith McNally, his advisers, and a fortune in francs (or dollars) turned what had been a leather store into a fabulous facsimile of a timeworn Paris brasserie that looks as though it has nestled on this East SoHo street for years. Outside, red awnings mark the spot; inside, uneven old-gold-ocher walls, slightly scuffed and stained, peeling mirrors, a tiled floor, an old bar with a pewter top, and paper-covered wooden bistro tables set the trendy stage.

House specialties: Balthazar salad; goat cheese flan; steak au poivre; steak frites; beef short ribs; seared salmon with polenta; whole roast chicken.

Other recommendations: Artichoke soup with morels; brandade; duck shepherd's pie; fettucine with broccoli rabe and sun-dried tomatoes; cassoulet.

Summary & comments: Balthazar, Keith McNally's latest SoHo venture, is so hot that it sizzles and swarms with celebs of every variety (knowing who's who can be a test of your New York savvy). So it's no surprise that reservations are at a premium, and the noise level, when the bar is overpopulated, is almost unbearable for older ears. The celebs in the power seats on "power alley" may not care about the food, but if you do, you won't be disappointed. Bistro classics are very well prepared, as are the lighter dishes, and the prices are surprisingly reasonable. The adjacent Balthazar Bakery offers bread, pastry, and sandwiches—and more celebrities.

BAR PITTI

Italian-Tuscan	★★½	Moderate	QUALITY
			78

VALUE
C

268 Ave. of the Americas (between Houston and Bleecker Streets)
982-3300   Zone 4   Greenwich Village

Customers: Local
Reservations: Only for parties of
4 or more
When to go: Anytime
Entrée range: $9.50–14
Payment: Cash only

Service rating: ★★
Friendliness rating: ★★
Bar: Full selection
Wine selection: Very limited
Dress: Greenwich Village casual
Disabled access: Yes

Lunch: Every day, noon– 4 p.m.
Dinner: Every day, 6 p.m.–midnight

Atmosphere & setting: As the name suggests, this could be a small trattoria near the Pitti Palace, and there's a black-and-white blowup of Florence on the warm rosy walls to underscore that feeling. In warm weather, the tightly packed tables spill out onto the sidewalk; when it's colder, they're confined to two smallish, usually crowded rooms.

House specialties: Check the daily specials: fettunta, garlicky grilled country bread, a Tuscan trademark rare in New York; penne rustica; panino Toscano, a sizable roast pork sandwich.

Other recommendations: Rigatoni Pitti; osso buco; pappardelle alla Fiesolana; panna cotta.

Summary & comments: A good neighborhood trattoria with reasonable prices, and that's enough to attract the locals in droves. The people-watching here on the southern edge of Greenwich Village is an attraction in itself, and your neighbors' conversations, unavoidable in the sardine-packed quarters, can be better than the soaps.

BECCO

Italian	★★½	Moderate	QUALITY
			79

VALUE
A

355 West 46th Street (between Eighth and Ninth Avenues)
397-7597   Zone 8   Midtown West/Theater District

Customers: Pre- and post-theater,
tourists, locals
Reservations: Recommended; a must
before theater

When to go: Anytime
Entrée range: $16.95–29.95
Payment: All major credit cards
Service rating: ★★★

(Becco)

Friendliness rating: ★★★
Bar: Full service
Wine selection: Good; there's a sizable
  list for only $18

Dress: Casual, theater
Disabled access: No

Lunch: Monday–Sunday, noon–3 p.m.
Dinner: Monday–Saturday, 5 p.m.–midnight; Sunday, 3–10 p.m.

Atmosphere & setting: This thriving Restaurant Row-er is thronged with theatergoers. The narrow dining area in the front, with its beamed ceilings, has a few touches that suggest a country inn, but tables are so close together that the happy din can become daunting. The lights are dimmed, and so is the noise, in the upstairs dining room; the back room, with its large skylight, takes you away from the madding crowd.

House specialties: Sinfonia di pasta, unlimited servings of three pastas that change daily; antipasto of grilled, marinated veggies and fish; homemade fruit sorbets; ricotta tart with orange caramel sauce.

Other recommendations: Osso buco with barley risotto; grilled swordfish with balsamic sauce; Italian stuffed peppers; rack of lamb.

Summary & comments: You get a lot for your lire at this popular Theater District trattoria run by the Bastianich family, who also run the famed Felidia. And if you're not careful, you can eat yourself into blissful pretheater oblivion and sleep through the first act. The portions are generous, especially the pasta trio, which can include gnocchi and risotti; the service is exceptionally friendly and fast considering the constant crush; and the price is right.

BISSALEH CLASSIC			
Kosher Yemenite	★★★	Moderate	**QUALITY** 87
			VALUE B

1435 Second Avenue
  717-2333   Zone 13 Upper East Side

Customers: Families
Reservations: Only for parties of
  6 or more
When to go: Anytime
Entrée range: $6.50–18
Payment: VISA, MC

Service rating: ★★★
Friendliness rating: ★★★★
Bar: Full
Wine selection: Extensive kosher
Dress: Casual
Disabled access: Good

(Bissaleh Classic)

Breakfast, Lunch, & Dinner: Sunday–Thursday, 10 a.m.–1 a.m.; Saturday, half hour past sundown to 2 a.m.

Atmosphere & setting: Nicer ambience than you'd expect from the fast-food-style a la carte menu and low prices: high ceilings, wood floors, and walls painted in desert/earth colors with framed pictures of Middle Eastern scenes. Long tables, great for families.

House specialties: Eggplant or Turkish salads, hummous (chickpea spread), borekas (savory pies in flaky pastry), bissaleh (long pastry pies, like calzones) with potato, malawahs (dense buttery multilayered flatbreads), cheese blintzes, fish dishes, smoothies (unsweetened, milkless mixed fruit shakes), mint tea.

Other recommendations: Middle Eastern breakfasts are served all day: foul madamas (here spelled "full"), a garlicky fava bean stew; various blintzes, and omelets—including "Israeli Breakfast," an omelet with chopped cucumbers, tomatoes, and sour cream. The freebie rolls (with garlic butter on the side) are almost worth the trip, as is the excellent tomato puree condiment dosed with shrug, a fiery green spice blend.

Summary & comments: When most people think of Jewish food, they think of Ashkenazi staples like knishes, bagels, and chicken soup. Bissaleh serves the *other* Jewish cuisine, the Yemenite recipes found in Israeli cafes. This cooking recalls Lebanon and Morocco more than Poland or Germany; you'll find lots of Mediterranean ingredients like lemon, olives, fava beans, eggplant, honey, and sesame. The menu features delicious flaky pastries (bissaleh, malawah, boreka, and ftut) in various forms, alternately stuffed or topped with things like feta cheese, spinach, potato, or mushrooms. "Pizza" is the topping/filling to avoid, but most everything else will please, and this meatless dairy kitchen is a dream come true for vegetarians.

BLUE RIBBON

Eclectic American	★★★	Moderate	QUALITY 82
			VALUE B

97 Sullivan Street (near Spring Street)
274-0404   Zone 2 TriBeCa/SoHo

Customers: Local, trendies, night owls	**Entrée range:** $9.50–27
Reservations: Only for parties of 5 or more	**Payment:** All major credit cards
	Service rating: ★★★
When to go: Dinner only	**Friendliness rating:** ★★★

(Blue Ribbon)

Bar: Full service
Wine selection: Interesting
Dress: Anything goes

Disabled access: Yes, but very crowded

Dinner: Tuesday–Sunday, 4 p.m.– 4 a.m. Closed Monday.

Atmosphere & setting: A smallish, square, very dark room that seems to be a magnet for young and not-so-young trendies. It's not the decor that does it. If you can see through the throng at the bar, you'll find a wall of painted dark red brick, dark red plush banquettes, and one large semicircular enclosure seating five or more, with a few interestingly odd paintings above and closely spaced tables. It's noisy.

House specialties: Pu-pu platter; grilled shrimp remoulade; chicken wings; striped bass with artichoke, red pepper, and roasted garlic in red wine sauce; paella Basquez; duck breast with wild rice; chocolate Bruno; banana split.

Other recommendations: Barbecue ribs; spicy fish soup; sweetbreads with arugula, wild mushrooms, and carrot; roast chicken with sweet potatoes; rack of lamb with potato cake and thyme; strawberry sundae.

Summary & comments: This is the happening place in the happening SoHo scene. Open until 4 a.m., it attracts a late-night crowd, local chefs included, but it's jammed from 8 p.m. on. Expect to wait at least one hour, and very possibly more, to sample chef Eric Bomberg's eclectic menu. Hanging out here is fun; the crowd is anything but dowdy. But if the waiting game is not for you, go north up Sullivan Street and see if you can get into Blue Ribbon Sushi (119 Sullivan Street), Blue Ribbon's hip Japanese sibling restaurant. Or keep on going to Jean Claude (137 Sullivan Street), another perfect Parisian transplant from St. Germain or Montparnasse— noisy, smoky, good bistro food, and not too expensive (cash only).

LA BOITE EN BOIS			
French	★★½	Moderate	**QUALITY** 78
75 West 68th St. (between Central Park West and Columbus Ave.) 874-2705 Zone 10 Upper West Side			**VALUE** B

Customers: Loyal locals, Lincoln
  Center attendees
Reservations: Recommended
When to go: Anytime

Entrée range: $17–22
Payment: Cash and personal check
Service rating: ★★★
Friendliness rating: ★★★

(La Boite en Bois)

Bar: Full service
Wine selection: Good range, good prices

Dress: Casual
Disabled access: No

Brunch: Sunday, 11:30 a.m.–2:30 p.m.
Lunch: Monday–Saturday, noon–2:30 p.m.
Dinner: Monday–Saturday, 5:30–10:30 p.m.; Sunday, 4–10 p.m.

Atmosphere & setting: This simple, cozy, hole-in-the-wall bistro takes you from the sidewalks of Manhattan right into the French countryside. And it's so close to Lincoln Center that you'll make the curtain easily.

House specialties: Rack of lamb au jus; French string bean with wild mushroom salad; breast of duck with wild rice; tiny quail with lentils; seafood crêpe with tomato coulis; praline mousse.

Other recommendations: Pan-roasted chicken with herbs; pot-au-feu de poisson; côte de veau grillée au calvados; crème brûlée.

Summary & comments: Popular with concertgoers-in-the-know, this small space can get quite crowded, but by 7:45 p.m. it clears out and quiets down. The service is personal and attentive. There's a special pretheater dinner menu at $29. An even better dinner deal is three courses of your choice for $32 and no time constraints.

CABANA CARIOCA

Brazilian/Portuguese	★★½	Inexpensive	QUALITY 84
			VALUE A

123 West 45th Street
581-8088   Zone 8 Midtown West/Theater District

Customers: Businessmen at lunch; tourists, theater workers, ethnic at dinner
Reservations: None accepted for lunch; dinner only for 4 or more
When to go: Lunch for buffet, dinner for bar specials
Entrée range: $4.99–18.95

Payment: VISA, MC, AMEX, D, DC, JCB; cash only at the bar
Service rating: ★★★
Friendliness rating: ★★
Bar: Full service
Wine selection: Small
Dress: Casual
Disabled access: Fair

Lunch: Every day, 11:30 a.m.–3 p.m. (first floor); Monday–Friday, 11:30 a.m.–2:30 p.m. (third floor)
Dinner: Monday–Thursday, 3–11 p.m.; Friday and Saturday, 3 p.m.–midnight; Sunday, 3–10 p.m.

(Cabana Carioca)

Atmosphere & setting: Service is offered on three levels, connected by steep steps (painted in garish Happy Colors). With tables close together and sound levels high, this is not the place for lingering or romance. Management tries for a fun, colorful, tropical look, but it's been a while since the last makeover, and things are starting to get just a tad seedy at the edges. Don't look too closely; just enjoy.

House specialties: Roast chicken, shrimp gumbo, pot roast, shell steak, caipirinhas.

Other recommendations: Caldo verdhe (potato soup with kale and chorizo sausage) is satisfying, almost a meal in itself for $1.90. Ask for some homemade hot sauce—vinegary and terrific (shake the bottle!)—and don't forget to spoon farofa (toasted yucca flour) over the beans.

Summary & comments: The buffet lunch is an astounding bargain: $9.95 ($6.45 on the third floor) buys you unlimited access to a large array of meat, salad, and vegetable dishes, as well as desserts (come early; the steam tables are less frequently replenished later on). But there's an even better deal: dinner specials, available only at the bars—and the tables near them—on all three levels, such as a crunchy, garlicky half roast chicken; homey pot roast; a huge mound of garlicky/spicy baby shrimp gumbo (not really gumbo, but tasty); or a pretty serviceable garlic-marinated steak. Each includes a heap of rice, excellent black beans, and lots of homemade thick-cut potato chips, plus unlimited access to the salad bar, all for well under $10. Amazing. But if you're here for a bargain, be wary of drinks; ordering beer or cocktails will almost double your tab (but they make good caipirinhas—Brazilian cocktails of distilled sugar cane and tons of limes). The spotty regular menu is not particularly recommended, nor is the feijoada (Brazilian black bean stew); stick with the bar and the buffet.

Numerological oddity: An address you'll never forget: *1-2-3* West *4-5* Street between *6 and 7* Avenues.

CAFE CON LECHE

			QUALITY
Latin American	★★½	Inexpensive	**79**

<table>
<tr><td></td><td></td><td></td><td>VALUE</td></tr>
<tr><td></td><td></td><td></td><td>B</td></tr>
</table>

424 Amsterdam Avenue (between 80th and 81st Streets)
595-7000   Zone 12 Upper West Side
726 Amsterdam Avenue (between 94th and 95th Streets)
678-7000   Zone 12 Upper West Side

Customers: Ethnic, local	**Service rating:** ★★
Reservations: Only for parties of	**Friendliness rating:** ★★★
5 or more	**Bar:** Full service
When to go: Anytime	**Wine selection:** Very limited
Entrée range: $6.50–13.95	**Dress:** Very casual
Payment: Major credit cards	**Disabled access:** All on one level

Brunch: Saturday and Sunday, 8 a.m.– 4 p.m.
Lunch & Dinner: Monday–Sunday, 8 a.m.–midnight

Setting & atmosphere: There's a constant stream of take-out customers and knowing neighborhood denizens who need their morning fix of strong Cuban coffee mixed with steaming milk at the counter in the first of these two bright, narrow rooms, and more small tables set close together are in the second. A little cramped, but cheery and fun. The recently opened sibling, 15 blocks north, is newer and brighter and equally appealing.

House specialties: The eponymous cafe con leche, at $1 a pop, is fabulous; picadillo or ropa vieja (both Cuban specialties) with rice and beans; grilled Cuban sandwich with ham, cheese, pork, and pickles; sweet plantains, a deep-fried Cuban improvement on candied sweet potatoes that's positively addictive.

Other recommendations: Paella that comes with the works; huevos rancheros; calamares caribe; batidos, smooth shakes made with tropical fruits; a white garlic sauce that's great on everything except dessert; and an equally good homemade hot sauce.

Summary & comments: Authentic, inexpensive Cuban and Dominican food served with a smile, though it can take awhile to get the check. The lunch specials are a deal for the dinero ($5.95–6.50), and brunch on weekends offers interesting island alternatives.

CAFE MOGADOR

Moroccan	★★½	Moderate	QUALITY
			84
			VALUE
			A

101 St. Marks Place
   677-2226   Zone 5   East Village

Customers: Local
Reservations: Accepted (necessary
   Wednesdays)
When to go: Anytime (arrive by
   8 p.m. for the Wednesday night
   belly dancing)
Entrée range: $4.95–11.95

Payment: Cash only
Service rating: ★★★
Friendliness rating: ★★
Bar: Beer and wine only
Wine selection: House
Dress: Casual
Disabled access: Very poor

Brunch: Saturday and Sunday, 11 a.m.–4 p.m.
Lunch & Dinner: Every day, 8:30 a.m.–12:30 a.m.

Atmosphere & setting: Mogador looks less Moroccan than a standard-issue East Village bohemian cafe. It's a casual space below street level with tiny tables, faux oil lamps, and ceiling fans.

House specialties: Several flavors of tagine (a thick, complex stew made with chicken or lamb, served over rice or couscous), bastilla (an exotic dish of sweet and savory chopped chicken in flaky pastry) containing real saffron, homemade baklava (very sweet and cinnamony), and great fresh-squeezed pulpy lemonade, served with a mint leaf.

Entertainment & amenities: Wednesdays only: good live Arabic music at 8 p.m., belly dancing at 9 p.m. It's not just tourist shlock; the dancer's very good, and the musicians are some of the best in town. $3 music charge; arrive by 8 p.m. for best seating.

Summary & comments: If you're a fan of Moroccan cooking—or are looking for an authentic experience, stay away. This leisurely East Village cafe doesn't purport to serve the Real Deal. But it's not fake tourist fodder, either—they do honest Moroccan American food, as if made from hand-me-down recipes from someone's great-grandmother. The little appetizer plates (you'll be shown a trayful of selections) are tempting simple things like spicy sliced carrots, peppery garlic potatoes, and long-stewed chicken livers. As with the rest of the menu, all are pleasing but none attention-grabbing; this is more everyday food than a special occasion eat. The cafe's relaxing (the busboys are too relaxed; you must beg and whimper for water), a rare Manhattan place where you can eat an exotic (but not *too* exotic) bite, look out the window, sigh, and daydream.

CARAVAN

Afghani	★★★½	Moderate	QUALITY 89
			VALUE A

741 Eighth Avenue
262-2021   Zone 8 Midtown West/Theater District

Customers: Local; pretheater	Service rating: ★★½
Reservations: Only for pretheater dining (6–8 p.m.)	Friendliness rating: ★★
	Bar: Beer and wine
When to go: Anytime	Wine selection: Decent
Entrée range: $7.50–13.50	Dress: Casual
Payment: VISA, MC, AMEX, DC	Disabled access: Good

Lunch & Dinner: Every day, noon–11:30 p.m.

Atmosphere & setting: An airy quiet space with creamy peach walls and blonde wood, hanging carpets, Islamic prints, and oil lanterns with phony red bulbs. Track lighting and fresh flowers on tables. Except for the pretheater rush (starts at 6 p.m. on show nights), the place is rarely crowded.

House specialties: Pumpkin or potato turnovers, steamed scallion dumplings with yogurt mint sauce, kabuli or shireen palows (rice dishes similar to pilafs), homemade noodles topped with yogurt/butter/garlic sauce (with or without meat).

Other recommendations: Dough (an unsweetened yogurt/mint beverage) is the national drink.

Summary & comments: It's located in the heart of Broadway, but Caravan has neither the glitz nor the hard edge of that area. This quiet oasis serves Afghani comfort food. The unbelievably satisfying noodle dishes taste like home, even if you're not from Kabul; the turnovers are as dainty and appealing as if they were made by your aunt. Pulaws, like rice pilaf, are downright grandmotherly. Nothing bowls you over with its culinary splendor, but as you eat, you find yourself growing happier and happier. Prices are great, service—though not as friendly as the food—is courteous, and they'll get you out in time for your show. The only thing to avoid is the grilled meat kebabs; they're actually pretty good, but you want more intricately cooked things here.

CENDRILLON

			QUALITY
Filipino/Asian	★★★	Moderate	84
			VALUE
			B

45 Mercer Street (between Broome and Grand Streets)
343-9012   Zone 2 TriBeCa/SoHo

Customers: Ethnic, local
Reservations: Recommended
When to go: Anytime
Entrée range: $11.50–18.50
Payment: All major credit cards
Service rating: ★★★

Friendliness rating: ★★★
Wine selection: Good, and good range of prices
Dress: Casual
Disabled access: Yes

Brunch: Saturday and Sunday, 11:30 a.m.–4:30 p.m.
Lunch: Tuesday–Friday, 11:30 a.m.–4:30 p.m.
Dinner: Tuesday–Sunday, 5:30–11 p.m.

Atmosphere & setting: A few twinkling lights on a relatively quiet street mark the entry to this unusually shaped but inviting SoHo establishment. Comfortable booths with carved wooden tables front the open kitchen and lead to an airy high-ceilinged back dining room. Exposed brick walls throughout, accented with touches of carved wood, hold changing exhibits of contemporary paintings.

House specialties: Amy's spring roll; grilled octopus salad with eggplant fritter; chicken in adobo; Romy's spareribs; black rice paella with crab, shrimp, and Manila clams; banana crêpe with banana, rum, and cashew ice cream; mango tart with fresh mango ice cream.

Other recommendations: Grilled foxtail kare-kare; Balinese lamb shank with tomatillo and mango chutney; salt-roasted duck with cellophane noodles; warm chocolate cake with passion fruit sorbet.

Summary & comments: Chef/owner Romy Doroton offers fine Filipino fare and enhances his menu with a few "fusion" features that showcase his flare with Asian ingredients. Mr. Doroton and his staff are wonderfully helpful and friendly and make this an excellent place to try a new cuisine—still of the Asian persuasion, but different enough to make it fun and intriguing. Remember to leave room for one of the desserts; they are truly worth the calorie expenditure.

CHANTERELLE

			QUALITY
French	★★★★	Very Expensive	**95**
			VALUE
2 Harrison Street (at Hudson Street)			**B**

966-6960   Zone 2   TriBeCa/SoHo

Customers: Local	Service rating: ★★★★
Reservations: A must	Friendliness rating: ★★★
When to go: Anytime	Bar: Full service
Entrée range: Prix fixe dinner, $75 and $89	Wine selection: Excellent
	Dress: Dressy
Payment: All major credit cards	Disabled access: Yes

Lunch: Tuesday–Saturday, noon–2:30 p.m.
Dinner: Monday–Saturday, 5:30–11 p.m.

Atmosphere & setting: Elegance prevails: peachy, sort of chanterelle-colored walls are punctuated with dark, carved wood panels. Polished brass chandeliers light the room warmly, and the tables are spaced to make intimate dining more than a possibility.

House specialties: Grilled seafood sausage; quenelles of chicken with chanterelles; squab with star anise and vegetable rolls; soft-shell crabs with a coulis of garlic chives and young ginger; chocolate Savarin.

Other recommendations: Foie gras sautéed with nectarines; saddle of rabbit filled with spinach and summer truffles; roasted tuna with pistou; millefeuille of plums and cinnamon mousse.

Summary & comments: One of the finest New York restaurants, Chanterelle has maintained its ambrosial aura for 18 years, and if anything, the quality has only gone up. But so have prices. Though it is well worth every penny and is a grand place to celebrate a special occasion, you might try it for lunch (the set lunch is a mere $35), if your pennies are otherwise allocated.

CHICK CHACK CHICKEN

			QUALITY
Kosher Roast Chicken	★★★	Inexpensive	**90**
			VALUE
121 University Place			**A**

228-3100 or 228-3102   Zone 5   East Village

Customers: Locals, businessmen, families	When to go: Crowded for lunch, deserted after
Reservations: Not accepted	Entrée range: $3.29–6.99

(Chick Chack Chicken)

Payment: All major credit cards
Service rating: ★★★
Friendliness rating: ★★★
Bar: None

Wine selection: None
Dress: Casual
Disabled access: Good

Lunch & Dinner: Sunday–Thursday, 11 a.m.–10 p.m.; Friday, 11 a.m.–2 hours before sundown. Closed Saturday.

Atmosphere & setting: A tidy storefront with a few tables and a standing-only counter. The atmosphere—punctuated by crackling hot coals and permeated with the scent of spinning roasting chickens—easily compensates for the functional decor.

House specialties: Rotisserie chicken, mashed potatoes, kasha varnichkes (oniony buckwheat groats with bow-tie pasta), potato pancakes—all glatt kosher.

Entertainment & amenities: They deliver.

Summary & comments: This place turns out some of the best charcoal-fired marinated chicken in town, and their mashed potatoes (Jewish style, with chicken fat added) are tops as well. Kasha varnichkes are properly soulful. Eating in is a pleasant but utilitarian experience; much of the business is takeout. This kid-friendly establishment is also the only great quick meal in the area.

CHURRASCARIA PLATAFORMA

Brazilian	★★★	Moderate	QUALITY 88
			VALUE C

316 West 49th Street
245-0505   Zone 8 Midtown West/Theater District

Customers: Tourists, businessmen (at lunch), pretheater
Reservations: Recommended
When to go: Avoid weekend dinner crush; probably too heavy for lunch
Entrée range: Prix fixe $27.50 ($25 for lunch); children under 5 years, free; ages 5–10 years, half-price

Payment: VISA, MC, AMEX, DC
Service rating: ★
Friendliness rating: ★★
Bar: Full
Wine selection: Decent selection
Dress: Casual
Disabled access: Rest rooms not accessible

(Churrascaria Plataforma)

Lunch: Every day, noon–4 p.m.
Dinner: Every day, 4 p.m.–midnight

Atmosphere & setting: Enormous space, dominated by a monster salad bar at center. Desserts and cocktails are dispensed by beautiful young waitresses wheeling carts. The place is brightly lit, with refined, understated decor, but amid all the swirling meat and trips to the salad bar, who's paying attention? Sound level is high at peak times.

House specialties: All-you-can-eat meat, with all the trimmings (including gigunda Brazilian salad bar and good fried stuff).

Other recommendations: Caipirinhas are the traditional accompaniment; they're a cocktail of cachaça (a spirit similar to rum) and lots of fresh lime. Here, they also make them with passion fruit for an extra-tropical flavor.

Entertainment & amenities: Live Brazilian music Wednesday–Sunday nights.

Summary & comments: Rodizio is a Brazilian tradition where all-you-can-eat roast meats are brought to your table by skewer-bearing waiters. It's all very ritualized in Brazil, and this is the only one of a rash of local rodizios that observes all the rituals (it's also the only one that's Brazilian-owned and -run). You're served the traditional plates of fried yucca, french fries, batter-fried bananas, and particularly good fried polenta. Management hopes you'll fill up on this cheap stuff, as well as the extensive salad bar (vegetarians will be more than sated: tons of salads, vegetables, and even a few entrées in their own rights, like the good shrimp moqueca, a peppery stew with coconut milk), but savvy diners hold out for the meat. Pace yourself carefully as more than a dozen cuts come around. The best thing of all doesn't come unless you ask for it, though: unbelievably delicious black beans, made from specially imported small and silky beans. Spoon farofa (garlicky toasted yucca flour) over them. If all the meat doesn't give you a coronary, the service will; confused and incompetent waiters take their cue from the managers, who pompously stroll through in suit and ties, scanning the room for trouble spots and summarily ignoring your desperate pleas for service, dessert, or the check. Bad service also extends to the reservations line; call three times and you'll get three different answers regarding table availability.

CITÉ

			QUALITY
French/Steak	★★★	Expensive	85

	VALUE
	B

120 West 52st Street (between Sixth and Seventh Avenues)
 956-7100   Zone 8 Midtown West/Theater District

Customers: Business, local,
 oenophiliacs
Reservations: Recommended
When to go: Anytime
Entrée range: $19.75–29; prix fixe
 wine dinner, $49.50
Payment: All major credit cards

Service rating: ★★★
Friendliness rating: ★★★
Bar: Full service
Wine selection: Very good
Dress: Business, at least a jacket
Disabled access: Yes

Lunch: Monday–Friday, noon–3 p.m.
Dinner: Every day, 5–11:30 p.m.

Atmosphere & setting: Billed as a French steak house, this large, high-ceilinged, comely space is edged with art deco grillwork galore from Au Bon Marché, the venerated Paris department store, and lit with crystal chandeliers. The feeling is festive, dressed up but not stuffy, a little noisy when crowded, but not overwhelmingly so.

House specialties: Dill-cured salmon gravlax; grilled tuna niçoise; veal chop; filet au poivre; filet mignon and frites.

Other recommendations: Shrimp cocktail; baby rack of lamb with polenta; roast prime rib; bittersweet chocolate terrine; crème brûlée rice pudding.

Summary & comments: To be honest, the draw here is not the fine steaks or the equally fine service and ambience, it's the "Taste of the Grape"—the $49.50 prix fixe dinner, a Bacchanalian bonanza that's served after 8 p.m. and constitutes one of New York's great bargains. It includes three courses chosen from the full menu and all the wine and champagne you can sip, sample, or slurp. The only problem may be walking a straight line afterward.

COCO OPERA

			QUALITY
Italian	★★★	Expensive	82

	VALUE
	C

58 West 65th Street (Columbus Avenue)
 873-3700   Zone 10 West Side

Customers: Lincoln Center, business,
 local
Reservations: Recommended

When to go: Anytime
Entrée range: $17–28
Payment: All major credit cards

(Coco Opera)

Service rating: ★★★
Friendliness rating: ★★★
Bar: Full service

Wine selection: All Italian, strong on
    Tuscan and Piemontese reds
Dress: Business, dressy
Disabled access: Yes

Lunch: Monday–Saturday, 11:30 a.m.–3 p.m.; Sunday, 11 a.m.–
    3:30 p.m.
Dinner: Monday–Wednesday, 5–11:30 p.m.; Thursday–Saturday,
    5 p.m.–midnight; Sunday, 5–11 p.m.

Atmosphere & setting: Two-tone wicker armchairs at the tables on the
street-level dining area lend it a verandalike aspect, heightened by large windows that give onto the busy street. Take the few steps to the upper level and
the feeling reverts to New York stylish—sponged pale yellow walls with a
bold blue column and blue hanging lights for accent, white Mission-esque
chairs with blue-tipped feet, chives plants instead of the usual flowers on
every table. The tables are well-spaced, and it's restfully quiet.

House specialties: Farrotto (an ancient, nutty-flavored Italian grain that's
suddenly trendy) or risotto of the day; pizza ai frutti di mare; spaghetti alle
vongole; Florentine-style grilled steak (for two); veal paillard; campari-
orange soda.

Other recommendations: Porcini mushrooms with polenta; grilled calamari; ricotta-spinach ravioli; oven-seared salmon; biscotti and vin santo.

Summary & comments: This is the newest Pino Luongo entry in the
restaurant sweepstakes, and it has every reason to be a winner. Just across the
street from Lincoln Center in the space vacated by Sfuzzi, it's got location,
authentically flavorful Tuscan fare, a large comfortable bar that serves pizza
between mealtimes, and pleasing service.

COCO PAZZO TEATRO

Italian-Tuscan	★★★	Expensive	QUALITY 82
			VALUE C

243 West 46th Street (between Broadway and Eighth Avenues)
    827-4222   Zone 8 Midtown West/Theater District

Customers: Theater, business
Reservations: Recommended
When to go: Anytime
Entrée range: $21.50–34

Payment: All major credit cards
Service rating: ★★★
Friendliness rating: ★★★
Bar: Full service

(Coco Pazza Teatro)

Wine selection: Good, strong on
   Italian vintages

Dress: Casual, business, theater
Disabled access: Yes

Lunch: Every day, noon–3 p.m.
Dinner: Sunday–Monday, 5–10 p.m.; Tuesday–Saturday, 5 p.m.–midnight

Atmosphere & setting: Cooly attractive, this Theater District Coco sports blond wood; blue, green, and faux marble columns with clever box lights; and a still-life wall painting. The well-spaced tables are adorned with a pretty blue bottle topped by a potato holding an orchid sprig—*pazzo*, no?

House specialties: Cacciucco alla Toscana, spicy seafood stew; oversized lobster and crabmeat ravioli; fettucine ai funghi.

Other recommendations: House-cured salmon with fennel and orange salad; "vegetali alla Morandi," seasonal vegetables in mushroom broth; grilled squab with wild mushrooms.

Summary & comments: Just a year older than Coco Opera, this Pino Luongo operation is a smash hit. Prices here are lower than those at the established, celebrity-strewn Coco Pazzo on the Upper East Side (23 East 74th Street), but the food is just as good, and there's less pretension all around. Good choice before the curtain goes up or after it comes down. Coco Pazzo in a jar? Indeed, the popular pasta sauces are now available for easy transport and instant nostalgia. The fourth in the cast of Cocos, Coco Marina, has recently opened in the World Financial Center.

DELPHINI			
			QUALITY
Mediterranean	★★★	Moderate	82
			VALUE
			B

519 Columbus Avenue (corner of 85th Street)
   579-1145   Zone 12 Upper West Side

Customers: Local
Reservations: Recommended
When to go: Anytime
Entrée range: $15–22
Payment: AMEX only
Service rating: ★★★

Friendliness rating: ★★★
Bar: Full service
Wine selection: Good
Dress: Casual
Disabled access: Yes

Brunch: Sunday, 11 a.m.–3:30 p.m.
Dinner: Sunday–Tuesday, 5–11 p.m.; Wednesday–Thursday, 5 p.m.–midnight; Friday and Saturday, 5 p.m.–1 a.m.

(Delphini)

Atmosphere & setting: Romance, in a Mediterranean milieu, has come to the Upper West Side. Lit with candles only (no electric bulbs in sight), Delphini is heavy on atmosphere and the promise of intimate encounters. The tables are strewn with rose petals, the ceiling hung with ornate Spanish chandeliers, the walls adorned with mirrors that glow in the dark. A sidewalk cafe springs up when the weather permits.

House specialties: Bastilla, spiced Moroccan puff pastry with squab; ancas de rana, crispy Portuguese frog's legs; spicy Caesar salad; paella Valenciana; almond-crusted salmon; lamb sausage risotto.

Other recommendations: Wild mushroom polenta cakes; crab and roasted corn cakes; warm octopus salad; striped bass with salsa verde; North African lamb with apricot tagine.

Summary & comments: The menu offers a good mélange of Mediterranean food—Greek, Moroccan, Italian, Spanish, and more—and that, coupled with attractive interior, has made it a favorite with the local crowd. In other words, it can get quite crowded and a bit noisy. The small pretty bar, decked with a large bowl of sangría, encourages cigar smoking, so beware if puffers and their effluvium are not your preference. The service is accommodating and the portions ample.

DEMARCHELIER

French	★★½	Expensive	QUALITY
			77
			VALUE
			C

50 East 86th Street (just off Madison Avenue)
249-6300   Zone 13   Upper East Side

Customers: Local, the ladies who lunch	**Service rating:** ★★
Reservations: Recommended for dinner	**Friendliness rating:** ★★
	Bar: Full service, smoking
When to go: Anytime	**Wine selection:** Good, big on Bordeaux
Entrée range: $16.75–27.50	**Dress:** Casual
Payment: All major credit cards	**Disabled access:** No

Brunch: Sunday, noon– 4 p.m.
Lunch & Dinner: Every day, noon–midnight

Atmosphere & setting: The distinctly French charm of this neighborhood bistro — crocheted half-curtains in the front windows, a blackboard with specials on the sidewalk — is achieved with little fuss. The walls are a warm ocher, and wall sconces add to the glow.

(Demarchelier)

House specialties: Daily specials; onion soup; salade Demarchelier, chef's salad with an unusual veggie combo; steak tartare; grilled salmon; frites.

Other recommendations: Warm goat cheese salad; Veal paillard; mussels marinière; tarte tatin; crème caramel.

Summary & comments: Solid bistro food—not fab, not drab—lures the locals for lunch and dinner. Tables for two are very close together, and when it's packed you may find yourself involved in your neighbor's conversation. Close to Upper East Side centers of culture, it's a good place to revive the spirits after a hike up Museum Mile.

EJ'S LUNCHEONETTE

American	★★½	Inexpensive	QUALITY 79
			VALUE B

477 Amsterdam Avenue (between 81st and 82nd Streets)
    873-3444   Zone 12 Upper West Side

1271 Third Avenue (at 73rd Street)
    472-0600   Zone 13 Upper East Side

432 Sixth Avenue (9th and 10th Streets)
    473-5555   Zone 4 Greenwich Village

Customers: Locals and local children
Reservations: Not accepted
When to go: Anytime
Entrée range: $9.95–14.95
Payment: No credit cards
Service rating: ★★★

Friendliness rating: ★★★
Wine selection: Limited; 3 house wines
Dress: Casual
Disabled access: All on one level

Breakfast, Lunch, & Dinner: Monday–Thursday, 8:30 a.m.–10:30 p.m.; Friday and Saturday, 8:30 a.m.–11 p.m.; Sunday, 8:30 a.m.–10 p.m.

Atmosphere & setting: This luncheonette could just as well be on Main Street in Small Town, U.S.A. It's kitsch, cute, comfortable "Dinersville" all the way from the blue-and-white vinyl booths to the Formica tables and the counter and blue-topped stools. The separate locations differ in detail only.

House specialties: Buttermilk or multigrain flapjacks with a dozen different toppings; ditto for the buttermilk or bran Belgian waffles; Caesar salad (highly recommended by two seven-year-olds); EJ's club sandwich; salami and eggs, pancake-style; great home fries; Stewart's root beer float.

(EJ's Luncheonette)

Other recommendations: Macaroni and cheese; grilled tuna club with wasabi; veggie wrap with basil mayo; EJ's chicken Reuben. Check the daily specials and the special kid's menu.

Summary & comments: The portions in this no-frills, child-friendly neighborhood hangout are more than ample, and the food is good. Kids can tear around or cry their little eyes out and no one seems to mind—and if you do, this is not for you. Great place for breakfast (watch out for the crowds on weekends) or for some sustenance before or after doing the dinosaurs at the Museum of Natural History.

FIREBIRD			
Russian	★★★ Moderately expensive	**QUALITY** 88	
		VALUE B	

365 West 46th Street (between Eighth and Ninth Avenues)
586-0244   Zone 8 Midtown West/Theater District

Customers: Theatergoers, local, tourists
Reservations: Recommended
When to go: Anytime
Entrée range: $17.25–24.75
Payment: All major credit cards
Service rating: ★★★
Friendliness rating: ★★★

Bar: Full service, with a selection of 14 vodkas
Wine selection: Good, with some surprisingly low-priced choices
Dress: Upscale casual, Theater District dressy
Disabled access: Yes

Lunch: Tuesday–Saturday, 11:15 a.m.–2:15 p.m.
Dinner: Sunday–Thursday, 5–10:30 p.m.;
  Friday and Saturday, 5–11:15 p.m.

Atmosphere & setting: Two spruced-up brownstones stand behind gilt-edged gates manned by a Cossack costumed sentry. No, you're not really in Imperial St. Petersburg, but you're close. The fabulously overdone, charmingly ornate interior, with eight rooms and two pretty bars, is decorated with chandeliers, lushly patterned carpets, Fabergé-ish objects, Russian wall hangings, ballet costumes, and ancient books. Despite the pomp, the greeting is gracious and the atmosphere not at all forbidding.

House specialties: Wild mushroom and three-grain soup; buckwheat blini with sour cream; lightly smoked salmon with cucumber salad and five-grain bread; crab and rice croquettes with mâche; grilled marinated sturgeon; Uzbek skewered quail; pelmeni Siberian.

(Firebird)

Other recommendations: Kasha and wild mushroom salad; roasted eggplant caviar; Karsky shashlik; roast chicken with bulgar-okra salad; Armenian yogurt-spiced lamb.

Summary & comments: Firebird prides itself on detail—the china was specially designed, the wait staff garbed by Oleg Cassini—and on serving the authentic cuisine of Czarist Russia in the ambience of equal authenticity. Best of all, it's fun; you actually hear people say "Wow!" when they walk in. At $19.95, the pretheater prix fixe is an excellent bargain—soup, five items from the daily offerings of "Zakuska" (Russian appetizers), and blini. It's a wonderfully theatrical addition to Theater District dining.

FLORENT				
			QUALITY	
Diner/Bistro	★★½	Moderate	79	
			VALUE	
			B	

69 Gansevoort Street (between Washington and Hudson Streets)
989-5779 Zone 4 Greenwich Village West

Customers: Anything goes	**Friendliness rating:** ★★★
Reservations: Not accepted	**Bar:** Full service
When to go: Anytime	**Wine selection:** Minimal
Entrée range: $7.95–17.95	**Dress:** Anything goes
Payment: Cash	**Disabled access:** Yes
Service rating: ★★★	

Brunch: Saturday and Sunday, 11 a.m.–4 p.m.
Lunch: Monday–Friday, 11 a.m.–3:30 p.m.
Breakfast & Dinner: Monday–Thursday, 9 a.m.–5 a.m.;
Friday–Sunday, open 24 hours

Atmosphere & setting: Turn the corner of Hudson Street and you leave the bistro-fied West Village for Manhattan's wholesale meat market. Florent, an elongated ur-diner, sits in the middle of the block and fits in perfectly. There's not a frill in sight, unless you count the late-night/early-morning clientele and the occasional paper streamers and strings of pearls festooning the interior. (Or as a charming waiter put it, "We're always decorating with something tacky.") The atmosphere is set by the crowd that ranges from debs and celebs to ordinary and extraordinary New Yorkers of every hue and persuasion.

House specialties: Check daily specials; dry aged New York sirloin au poivre; meat loaf with mashed potatoes; boudin noir with apples and onions; omelet with smoked salmon and arugula (brunch); crème caramel.

Other recommendations: Homemade rillettes with roasted garlic; moules frites; steak (aged rib eye) frites; chicken breast stuffed with wild mushrooms.

Summary & comments: This is a great after-hours spot—supper and breakfast are served from midnight on—and it's just as good at other times. The food, a balance of bistro and diner dishes, is hearty and plentiful, and the people-watching may not be hearty, but it sure is plentiful. The wait staff, young and ebullient, seems to be having as good a time as the customers. A bit hard to find at night; be sure to check a street map before setting out.

GABRIELA'S

Mexican	★★★	Moderate	QUALITY
			86
			VALUE
			A

685 Amsterdam Avenue
961-0574   Zone 12 Upper West Side

Customers: Locals	**Friendliness rating:** ★★★
Reservations: For parties of 6 or more	**Bar:** Beer, tequila
When to go: Anytime	**Wine selection:** Small
Entrée range: $6.95–12.95	**Dress:** Casual
Payment: VISA, MC, AMEX	**Disabled access:** Rest rooms not
Service rating: ★★½	accessible

Brunch: Saturday and Sunday, 11:30 a.m.–3 p.m.
Lunch & Dinner: Monday–Thursday, 11:30 a.m.–11 p.m.; Friday and Saturday, 11:30 a.m.–midnight; Sunday, 11:30 a.m.–10 p.m.

Atmosphere & setting: The room, like the food, is brighter and slicker than standard-issue Mexican restaurants; decor is cheerful/colorful, with cactus murals on the walls and mini-candelabras over each table. It's comfortable without pandering (a la Benny's Burritos and other chains).

House specialties: Rotisserie chicken, posole (an ultra-satisfying huge bowl of pork and hominy corn soup), crema de elote y poblano (spicy/creamy corn soup), tamales, panucho yucateco (Yucatán-style stuffed tortillas), cochinita pibil (roast pork marinated in orange juice and numerous spices), tinga poblana (crispy tortillas topped with shredded pork), garnachas (tortillas filled with cheese, scallions, and hot peppers), licuados (fruit shakes), and aguas frescas (fresh fruit drinks).

Summary & comments: This is a relatively upscale, gringo-friendly establishment that cooks some unusual dishes with uncommon panache. It's the only place for rare Yucatán-style specialties like panuchos yucatecos (thick stuffed tortillas with black bean paste) and Yucatán roast chicken (there are also some touches from Oaxaca and Veracruz). Stick with more complex specialties, from the "platter" part of the menu, rather than simpler stuff like tortas, tacos, quesadillas, and enchiladas. Such antojitos (snacks) can be good here, but the kitchen's more consistent with ambitious items like cochinita pibil and crema de elote y poblano. Don't miss the five terrific varieties of tamales (one—made with mushrooms—is tucked under the "Vegetarian Platters" menu heading).

GOTHAM BAR & GRILL

New American	★★★½	Expensive	QUALITY
			89

	VALUE
	C

12 East 12th Street (between University Place and Fifth Avenue)
620-4020   Zone 4 Greenwich Village

Customers: Business, local
Reservations: Recommended
When to go: Anytime
Entrée range: $26.50–34
Payment: All major credit cards
Service rating: ★★★

Friendliness rating: ★★
Bar: Full service
Wine selection: Very good
Dress: Business, dressy, casual chic
Disabled access: No

Lunch: Monday–Friday, noon–2 p.m.
Dinner: Sunday–Thursday, 5:30–10 p.m.;
  Friday and Saturday, 5:30–11 p.m.

Atmosphere & setting: This heroic, lofty space has been tamed by sophisticated alterations—grand, fabric-draped overhead lighting fixtures, tables on varying levels, ocher columns, teal trim, bountiful bouquets of flowers on pedestals and on the imposing bar. All is dimly lit and austerely opulent.

House specialties: Chicken, foie gras and black trumpet terrine; seared skate salad; roast quail and wild mushroom risotto; grilled saddle of rabbit; rack of lamb with garlic mashed potatoes; caramelized banana cake filled with bitter chocolate custard.

Other recommendations: Goat cheese ravioli; Chinese spiced duck breast with seared foie gras; red snapper in shellfish broth; lemon tart with warm blueberry compote.

Summary & comments: Chef Alfred Portale, a major influence on New American cuisine and mentor to many of its now successful practitioners, maintains his culinary edge, his creative energy, and his dedication to superb dining. His soaring, structured presentations seem perfectly suited to the impressive room they are served in. Though the service could be a tad more impressive, the Gotham keeps its standing as a perennial favorite, a fine place for a special occasion. One of the few fine restaurants that serves a special "$19.98" lunch throughout the year.

GRAMERCY TAVERN

American	★★★½	Expensive	QUALITY
			89

	VALUE
	B

42 East 20th Street (between Broadway and Park Avenue South)
  477-0777   Zone 7 Gramercy Park, Madison Square

Customers: Business, local, celebs
Reservations: Essential in the main
  dining room
When to go: Anytime
Entrée range: $56 prix fixe dinner
Payment: All major credit cards
Service rating: ★★★

Friendliness rating: ★★
Bar: Full service
Wine selection: Excellent, many
  available by the glass or a 3 oz.
  tasting glass
Dress: Anything goes
Disabled access: Yes

Lunch: Monday–Friday, noon–2 p.m.; Tavern Menu, daily, noon–closing
Dinner: Monday–Thursday and Sunday, 5:30–10 p.m.;
  Friday and Saturday, 5:30–11 p.m.

Atmosphere & setting: Lovely and inviting—flowers in profusion deck the entry, spill over a table near the open grill, ornament the dining spaces, even bloom in the rest rooms. Floor-to-ceiling windows front the tavern room, with its big, black-topped bar, and boldly colored paintings of fruits and vegetables brighten the upper walls. The lighting in the more formal, cathedral-ceilinged dining rooms goes from early American to trendy glass buckets; the decorations follow suit with a few American primitive portraits, a quilt, and large metal starfish. Somehow it all works well together.

House specialties: Ricotta ravioli with morels; lobster and artichoke salad; tuna tartare; whole roasted dourade with fava beans; loin of lamb with lemon confit, maple crème brûlée.

Other recommendations: Marinated hamachi with roasted beets; roasted cod with brandade. On the Tavern Menu: grilled portobello mushroom salad, grilled baby octopus, wood-grilled vegetable "Dagwood."

(Gramercy Tavern)

Summary & comments: Danny Meyer, the wonderful man who brought you Union Square Cafe, teams up here with chef Tom Colicchio, whose lyric interpretation of American cuisine virtually sings with succulent freshness. Together, this dynamic duo has created another big-time winner with an appropriately big-time following. The staff is agreeable, attentive, and attractive, the three A's that aid and abet memorable dining. The Tavern Room, less formal and less expensive than the dining room, has its own menu and thereby affords a simpler approach to sampling the fabulous fare.

GRANGE HALL

American	★★★★	Moderate	QUALITY 93
			VALUE A

50 Commerce Street
924-5246   Zone 4 Greenwich Village

Customers: Locals, couples	**Friendliness rating:** ★★★★
Reservations: Recommended	**Bar:** Full service
When to go: Anytime	**Wine selection:** Decent range of
Entrée range: Small dishes, $3.75–7;	Americans
main dishes, $10.25–16.75	**Dress:** Nice casual or better
Payment: AMEX	**Disabled access:** Good (use
Service rating: ★★★★	Commerce Street entrance)

Brunch: Saturday, 11 a.m.–3 p.m.; Sunday, 10:30 a.m.– 4 p.m.
Lunch: Monday–Friday, noon–3 p.m.
Dinner: Monday, 5:30–11 p.m.; Tuesday–Saturday, 5:30–11:30 p.m.; Sunday, 6–11 p.m.

Atmosphere & setting: Situated on a twisty picture-postcard block in the most beautiful part of Greenwich Village, the exterior is inviting, and the interior even more so: smart and hiply elegant, warmly lit and well-appointed, but not at all pretentious. The retro decor ('40s sophistication with a twist) doesn't intrude, and the jazz soundtrack wafts romantically; this is low-key urbane dining. There's a striking mural by young artist David Joel.

House specialties: Acorn squash, freshly made sausage, potato pancakes, Yukon Gold scalloped potatoes, oven-roasted organic chicken, cranberry-glazed pork chops, farm vegetable platter, soups, salads.

Other recommendations: Those potato pancakes are an ideal bar snack if you just stop by for drinks.

(Grange Hall)

Summary & comments: Grange Hall started out as the latest offering from a group known for their stable of theme eateries. This one was designed to be "Upscale Retro Blue Plate," but the restaurant has become loved on its own terms rather than as a contrived novelty. They've stocked the place with smart, funny young waiters and a great bar (good for solo dining and quite popular for martinis late into the night) and serve a seasonal menu of savvily cooked American dishes. The dishes use simple ingredients, but the chef's far too sophisticated to let his food devolve into clichéd comfort food; everything's cooked with flare, and simplicity never lapses into dullness. This is the perfect spot for carnivores to bring vegetarians; in addition to well-cooked meat dishes, there are numerous vegetable small plates that can accumulate into a meal. (Also, larger plates can be shared; it's all very mix-and-match.) If you've been dipping deep into New York's unparalleled ethnic food scene and want to relax with a more familiar—but still exciting—menu, this is the place.

HONMURA AN

Japanese (Soba)	★★★½	Expensive	QUALITY
			89
			VALUE
170 Mercer Street			B

334-5253   Zone 2   TriBeCa/SoHo

Customers: Ethnic, local, SoHo celebs
Reservations: Recommended for dinner
When to go: Anytime
Entrée range: $9–21.75
Payment: All major credit cards

Service rating: ★★★
Friendliness rating: ★★★
Bar: Wine, beer, and sake
Wine selection: Fair
Dress: Casual
Disabled access: No

Lunch: Wednesday–Saturday, noon–2:30 p.m.
Dinner: Tuesday–Thursday, 6–10 p.m.; Friday and Saturday, 6–10:30 p.m.; Sunday, 6–9:30 p.m.

Atmosphere & setting: Plain wooden stairs with a few distinctly Japanese flower arrangements lead to a serene second-floor space that's the epitome of elegant understatement. Large pieces of plain white rice paper hang on the high brick walls, and polished wooden tables and dark green banquettes circle the room. A glass-enclosed corner is dedicated to the in-house production of the soba (buckwheat) noodles used in most of the main dishes.

(Honmura An)

House specialties: Hot soba with sliced duck; anything soba; tempura, with rice in a lacquer box—and giant prawns specially shipped from a fish market in Tokyo; soba sushi, a sushi thick roll made of soba (what else!) with mashed prawns that must be ordered in advance.

Other recommendations: Any of the small tasting dishes; cold soba seiro, plain noodles with dipping sauce served on a lacquer tray.

Summary & comments: The soba specialties, uncommon and superb, plus the tranquil setting and unobtrusive service make this an extremely popular SoHo spot. This is a subtle cuisine that could fast become a miraculously healthy addiction. The $17 prix fixe lunch makes a great intro, as does the pricier $43, four-course prix fixe soba dinner.

IAMMO BELLO

Italian Cafeteria	★★½	Inexpensive	QUALITY
			83
			VALUE
			A

39 East 60th Street
935-9418   Zone 11 East Side

Customers: Local, business	**Service rating:** ★★★½
Reservations: Not accepted	**Friendliness rating:** ★★★
When to go: Early or late to miss the crowds, but queues move quickly even at peak hours	**Bar:** None
	Wine selection: None
	Dress: Casual
Entrée range: $4–7.50	**Disabled access:** No
Payment: Cash	

Lunch: Monday–Friday, 11:30 a.m.–4 p.m.; Saturday, 10 a.m.–3 p.m. Closed Sunday.

Atmosphere & setting: A quick-moving queue snakes through this subterranean cafeteria, past myriad steam tables manned by hyperkinetic servers. All remaining space is crammed with long tables full of harried, ravenous eaters, forks and jaws working at a prodigious pace. It's all so fast-paced that you feel as if a request to pass the salt might elicit a hail of shakers flung at you from all directions.

House specialties: Wonderful heros like chicken, veal, eggplant, or meatball parmigiana (with good, funky Parmesan cheese rather than the usual clots of bad mozzarella); zesty chicken francese (hot only on Thursdays, other days available cold at the antipasto bar); delicious homey lasagna; soups; well-fried calamari (Fridays only). Skip the deftly flavored pastas if

(Iammo Bello)

you demand al dente (impossible to achieve in a steam table), but you'll be missing a pretty good alfredo sauce.

Other recommendations: There are various fancy pizzas (including one with nicely grilled vegetables) as well as regular slices (intriguingly different from the usual Gotham slice) available from a separate concession in the back. Up front, the abundantly stocked self-service antipasto bar costs $5.75/pound (don't miss the rice with vegetables).

Summary & comments: Iammo Bello means "come here, handsome," in Italian, but this no-frills bustling cafeteria depends more on its cooking than its looks to attract. Chicken francese is downright scrumptious, and even rough, unsubtle dishes like lasagna taste soulful. There's a certain satisfaction that comes from having eaten a really good $6 meal in a neighborhood filled with mediocre $30 lunches. As Italian cafeterias go, this isn't quite as good as Rosario's (see profile), but it's much more centrally located, and the food is certainly worlds above the heros, pastas, and salads served in local pizzerias.

IL BUCCO				
French/Spanish/Italian	★★★★	Expensive	**QUALITY**	**94**
			VALUE	**C**

47 Bond Street
    533-1932   Zone 5 East Village

Customers: Local
Reservations: A must
When to go: Anytime
Entrée range: $12–24
Payment: Cash only
Service rating: ★★★
Friendliness rating: ★★

Bar: Full service
Wine selection: Carefully selected collection of unusual (but savvy) choices
Dress: Expensive informal
Disabled access: Good

Dinner: Tuesday–Thursday, 6 p.m.–midnight; Friday and Saturday, 6 p.m.–1 a.m.; Sunday, 5–11 p.m. Closed Monday.

Atmosphere & setting: Antique store by day, restaurant by night, woody, atmospheric Il Buco has an old European farmhouse feeling quite unlike that of any other spot in the city. You eat at rough candlelit tables surrounded by old furnishings and knickknacks, all for sale. It's tremendously romantic in its rustic way.

House specialties: Changing seasonal menu, but risottos, grilled octopus, homemade sausages, pastas, flourless chocolate cake, and plum cake are delicious fixtures.

(Il Bucco)

Entertainment & amenities: The wine cellar allegedly was the inspiration for Edgar Allen Poe's story "A Cask of Amontillado," and it's got atmosphere galore; have a peek.

Summary & comments: Il Buco's cooking incorporates French, Italian, and Spanish influences, and the chef shows considerable command in all three culinary languages; the risotto is creamy, peasanty, and completely unpretentious; the octopus tastes like firsthand Mediterranean rather than a cooking school grad working from a recipe. This rogue kitchen has its own distinctive style; it follows no trends. Though not widely known, Il Buco is much loved by a discerning few, and the smallish place fills up most nights. This is an especially good locale for special occasions—long tables can be reserved either in the middle of the main room or in a rear alcove.

IL MULINO

Italian	★★★½	Expensive	QUALITY 90
			VALUE B

86 West Third Street (between Sullivan and Thompson)
673-3783   Zone 4 Greenwich Village

Customers: Business, local
Reservations: Highly recommended
When to go: Anytime
Entrée range: $21.75–30
Payment: All major credit cards
Service rating: ★★★

Friendliness rating: ★★★
Bar: Full service
Wine selection: Good
Dress: Upscale, business suits
Disabled access: Yes

Lunch: Monday–Friday, noon–2:30 p.m.
Dinner: Monday–Saturday, 5–11:30 p.m.

Atmosphere & setting: There's no mistaking this for a Village trattoria; low-key elegance and low-key lighting prevail from the small, pretty bar in the front to the single perfect rose and heavy white cloths on the each table. Tall potted plants separate the dining room from the entrance; the ceiling is mercifully soundproofed, though this is hardly the place for a raucous crowd; and the walls that are not exposed brick are covered in soft, feathery wallpaper. The service is unobtrusively attentive.

House specialties: Check the daily specials; carpaccio; spaghettini carbonara; filet of beef with caper sauce; rolled veal braised in wine, cream, and wild mushrooms.

Other recommendations: Spaghettini with clams; spicy veal with anchovies, capers, and mushrooms; chicken and sausage in white wine.

(Il Mulino)

Summary & comments: Ranked high among New York's estimable eateries and often designated "Il Primo" of the Italians, this is a good choice for fabulous food at fabulous prices. Start slowly; it's all too easy to overeat. Complimentary appetizers, fried zucchini, superb salami, a hunk of excellent Parmesan, and more arrive at the table along with irresistible breads. The pastas and main courses are copious, and at the end, there'll be a glass of grappa with plump white raisins. Even with reservations, there is often a wait in the evening; lunch is far more relaxed.

JACKSON DINER

			QUALITY
Indian	★★★½	Moderate	**87**
			VALUE
			A

37– 03 74th Street
  (718) 672-1232   Zone 17 Queens

Customers: Locals, ethnic, foodies
Reservations: Helpful (not accepted weekends after 7 p.m.)
When to go: Saturdays are crowded
Entrée range: $6.75–8.95
Payment: Cash only

Service rating: ★★★
Friendliness rating: ★★★
Bar: None
Wine selection: None
Dress: Casual
Disabled access: Good

Lunch: Every day, 11:30 a.m.–4 p.m.
Dinner: Monday–Friday, 4–10 p.m.; Saturday and Sunday, 4–10:30 p.m.

Atmosphere & setting: This used to be a plain old diner, and it still looks like it, despite attempts at decorative touch-ups (track lighting, peach-colored walls). Long tables are covered with sticky red checkerboard plastic tablecloths, and each comes with its own worn plastic water pitcher.

House specialties: Samosas (fried potato/pea turnovers), masala dosa (huge crunchy lentil crêpe stuffed with potatoes, peas, and cashews), murgh tikka palakwala (chunks of tandoori chicken in a sauce of creamed spinach, ginger, cumin, and tomato), goat or lamb biryani (rice pilaf), tandoori chicken.

Other recommendations: The chutneys (sauces) and dal (beans) that accompany most dishes are good enough to eat by themselves. Skip the temptingly cheap lunch buffet and order from the menu.

Summary & comments: This is the best Indian restaurant in New York. It's in an old-fashioned diner taken over by Indians some years ago, but ambience is not the thing—*food* is. They have shmancy sister restaurants in Manhattan and Long Island (both called Diwan), but even at four times the price, neither comes close to the soulful cooking at Jackson Diner. Both northern and southern Indian dishes are offered, and there are winners on both sides of the menu. Jackson Diner's located in the heart of Little India, and you'll find myriad shops and spice stores nearby.

JEAN-GEORGES

French	★★★★	Expensive	QUALITY
			95
			VALUE
			B

1 Central Park West (at 60th Street)
299-3900   Zone 10   West Side

Customers: Local
Reservations: Required
When to go: Anytime
Entrée range: Dinner, prix fixe, $78; tasting menu, $105; Mistral Terrace, $15–20
Payment: All major credit cards
Service rating: ★★★★

Friendliness rating: ★★★
Bar: Full service
Wine selection: Excellent, good range of prices from $22 to $1,000
Dress: Jacket required for men; dressy
Disabled access: Yes

Lunch: Monday–Friday, noon–3 p.m. Cafe, Monday–Saturday, noon–3 p.m.; Sunday, 10 a.m.–3 p.m.

Dinner: Monday–Saturday, 5:30–11:30 p.m. Cafe, Monday–Saturday, 5:30–11:30 p.m.; Sunday, 5:30–10 p.m. Mistral Terrace, daily, 11 a.m.–11 p.m.

Atmosphere & setting: Restaurant designer Adam Tihany has kept this large dining room simple and spare with subdued tones of beige and gray melting into a graceful greige. The huge windows let in sun and sky and views of Central Park during the day; at night the lights of Columbus Circle and Central Park South twinkle in the distance, and the gargantuan globe that sits outside the Trump International Tower takes on extra prominence. The overall feeling is more cool than cozy, but definitely elegant.

House specialties: Foie gras and duck prosciutto roulade; asparagus with morel mushrooms; lobster tartine; baked artic char; chocolate soufflé with warm raspberries and vanilla ice cream.

Other recommendations: Sea scallops in caper-raisin emulsion with caramelized cauliflower; broiled squab with corn pancake and foie gras; turbot uba Chateau Chalon sauce; rhubarb tart with rhubarb crème glacée.

(Jean-Georges)

Summary & comments: Jean-Georges, given four stars by the *New York Times* (only six restaurants in New York have that honor), is the eponymous jewel in Jean-Georges Vongerichten's culinary crown—he also owns JoJo, Vong, and the Lipstick Cafe. This is where Vongerichten concentrates on his signature French cuisine, the innovative, intensely flavored dishes that made his Restaurant Lafayette, now closed, a four-star hit. The food is superb, as is the service; each dish is finished at your table, and this kind of attention is rare indeed. Jean-Georges was a New York sensation from the moment it opened, and reservations are hard to come by, but try. Breakfast, lunch, and dinner are served in the Nougatine Cafe, the front room and bar of the restaurant. Entrées are less expensive there, and the atmosphere is somewhat less formal. The outdoor Mistral Terrace is open seasonally.

JEZEBEL

Soul Food	★★★	Expensive	QUALITY
			83
			VALUE
			C

630 Ninth Avenue (corner of 45th Street, entrance on 45th)
582-1045   Zone 8 Midtown West/Theater District

Customers: Local, tourists
Reservations: Recommended
When to go: Anytime
Entrée range: $17.75–29.75
Payment: AMEX only
Service rating: ★★★

Friendliness rating: ★★★
Bar: Full service
Wine selection: Not extensive
Dress: Casual to dressy
Disabled access: Yes

Lunch: Monday–Friday, noon–3 p.m.
Dinner: Every day, 5:30 p.m.–midnight

Atmosphere & setting: It's easy to miss the low-key entrance, but open the door and it's the Vieux Carré, sultry and seductive all the way. Fringed shawls hang from the ceiling like Spanish moss; large potted palms, camellias, and vases of lilies bloom all around the room; oriental carpets accent the polished floors; and the walls are covered in posters—authentic French Art Nouveau, authentic American Andy Warhol, and a few Josephine Baker biggies. Mirrored columns, white wooden swings, crystal chandeliers, glass-topped tables with lace-bottomed clothes, wicker screens, and wrought-iron chairs all add to the lushly romantic effect.

House specialties: She-crab soup; Gula curried goat; smothered pork chops; shrimp Creole; barbecue spareribs.

(Jezebel)

Other recommendations: Smothered garlic shrimp; Jezebel's green pea soup; coconut sweet potato pie; pecan pie.

Summary & comments: "Down-home" goes upscale here, and all is over-seen by Alberta Wright—the sophisticated yet soothingly savory soul food that comes out of the kitchen and the fabulous festoonery of the dimly lit dining room. This is an unexpected wow of a Theater District restaurant, a performance in itself, and worth the trip even if a show is not on the evening's schedule.

JOE'S SHANGHAI				
Chinese	★★★½	Moderate	**QUALITY**	**91**
			VALUE	**A**

9 Pell Street (between Mott and Bowery)
233-8894   Zone 3 Chinatown

136–21 37th Avenue, Flushing
(718) 539-4429   Zone 17 Queens

Customers: Locals, foodies
Reservations: Only for parties of 10 or more
When to go: Off hours (between 2:30 and 5:30 p.m., or after 9:30 p.m.), to avoid wait
Entrée range: $6.25–19.95
Payment: Cash only

Service rating: ★★★
Friendliness rating: ★★★½
Bar: Beer only, and a limited variety
Wine selection: BYOB
Dress: Casual
Disabled access: Queens good, Manhattan fair (one step to dining room)

Lunch & Dinner: *Manhattan*, every day, 11 a.m.–11:15 p.m.; *Queens*, every day, 11 a.m.–10:30 p.m.

Atmosphere & setting: Several notches up from a Chinatown-style no-frills cafe, almost always busy but comfortable. The big tables are shared, but that's part of the ritual.

House specialties: Crabmeat steamed buns, stewed pork balls, shredded pork with pickled cabbage soup, anything with mushrooms, shrimp-fried rice cake, hot and sour soup, pork shoulder (with honey glaze), Shanghai fried flat noodles, shredded turnip shortcakes, soya (mock) duck.

Summary & comments: By all means, start with the crabmeat steamed buns, amazing soup-filled dumplings that New Yorkers have been going wild over. Wait for them to cool a bit, then delicately (don't puncture—you'll lose the soup!) transfer a dumpling to a spoon into which you've pooled a bit of soy/ginger sauce and a dab of hot sauce. Nibble a hole in the skin, suck the soup, then down the dumpling. The shiitake mushrooms are great here, and the stewed pork balls are the lightest meatballs you've ever tasted, in a succulent sauce. Don't order typical Chinese restaurant fare, though— try to stick with the Shanghai specialties. Ask the harried but affable waiters for tips, or ask about good-looking dishes passing by.

KATE'S JOINT

Vegetarian	★★★	Moderate	QUALITY
			86
			VALUE
			B

58 Avenue B
777-7059   Zone 5 East Village

Customers: Locals	Service rating: ★★
Reservations: Only for parties of	Friendliness rating: ★★
6 or more	Bar: Beer and wine
When to go: Anytime	Wine selection: Small
Entrée range: $8–10	Dress: Casual
Payment: VISA, MC, AMEX, D,	Disabled access: Good
DC, JCB	

Brunch: Saturday and Sunday, 10 a.m.–4:30 p.m.

Lunch & Dinner: Monday–Friday, 9 a.m.–11 p.m.; Saturday and Sunday, 10 a.m.–11 p.m.

Atmosphere & setting: Informal, mellow bohemian cafe with broodingly dark-colored walls and a good view of the East Village sidewalk parade.

House specialties: Grilled vegetable hero, soups, hummous (chickpea spread) with roasted garlic, mock-meat dishes (especially chile-con-tofu-carne).

Summary & comments: There are few vegetarian restaurants of merit in New York, but this is a notable exception. Chef/owner Kate Halpern cooks with a deft, knowing touch; her grilled vegetable hero is a knockout, her hummous assertively pungent and garlicky, and her mock meat dishes (made from carefully marinated tofu) both delicious and convincingly meat-like. While the regular menu is reliable, daily specials are more hit-and-miss. Expect the usual spacy vegetarian restaurant service (it must be the meat deprivation). Kate's was a pioneer in the new restaurant row that's cropped up on formerly scary Avenue B; while the neighborhood's still borderline, it's no longer dangerous.

LADY MENDL'S TEA SALON

			QUALITY
Tearoom	★★★	Moderate	**88**

<table>
<tr><td></td><td></td><td></td><td>VALUE</td></tr>
<tr><td></td><td></td><td></td><td>C</td></tr>
</table>

56 Irving Place
  533-4466   Zone 7 Gramercy Park, Madison Square

Customers: Hotel guests, locals
Reservations: Accepted
When to go: Anytime
Entrée range: $25 prix fixe
Payment: VISA, MC, AMEX, D, DC
Service rating: ★★

Friendliness rating: ★★★½
Bar: Beer, wine, champagne, port, sherry
Wine selection: Very small
Dress: Nice casual
Disabled access: No

Hours: Wednesday–Sunday, seatings at 3 p.m. and 4:30 p.m.

Atmosphere & setting: This tearoom, located in the pricey Inn at Irving Place, aims for an upscale English boardinghouse look. Unlike some of the Midtown hotel teas, this room—equipped with a working fireplace—is whisper-quiet.

House specialties: A five-course tea, with all the usual fixtures: crustless sandwiches of cucumber and smoked salmon; pâtés; warm scones; clotted cream; jams; tarts; and chocolate mousse cake, all served with a pot of tea per guest.

Entertainment & amenities: People-watching; The Inn at Irving Place is an exclusive hotel, so high-powered and celebrity guests are common.

Summary & comments: The food is nearly irreproachable; sandwiches are properly fussy, scones (perhaps the best item) taste homemade, and chocolate mousse cake is far better than the usual. There is a wide selection of teas and herbal infusions—all fancier than on-the-shelf brands—and each guest is served from one of the handsome antique pots collected by the owners. As you'd expect at a proper tea, everything's served on bone china. The problem is service: it's attention to detail and comfort that makes tea "Tea," and while the staff's friendly enough, attention to detail is not their forte. You're not given a little strainer for your tea, so bits of stuff make their way into your cup; additional hot water is not brought, so the tea turns irredeemably tepid by the end; plates are left empty for longer than you'd like; and one must ask for seconds. If you're looking for pampering and meticulous service, look elsewhere; otherwise, this is a relaxing and satisfying way to pass a late afternoon.

LA PIZZA FRESCA

Italian	★★★★	Moderate	QUALITY
			95
			VALUE
			A

31 East 20th Street
598-0141   Zone 7 Gramercy Park

Customers: Local, businessmen, foodies
Reservations: Only for parties of 4 or more
When to go: Anytime
Entrée range: $7.95–14.95
Payment: VISA, MC, AMEX

Service rating: ★★★½
Friendliness rating: ★★★
Bar: Beer and wine only
Wine selection: Wide and interesting range of Italians
Dress: Nice casual
Disabled access: Good

Lunch: Monday–Friday, noon–3:30 p.m.; Saturday, noon–4 p.m.; no lunch Sunday
Dinner: Monday–Saturday, 5:30–11 p.m.; Sunday, 5–10:30 p.m.

Atmosphere & setting: Stylishly modern and sleek, with white stucco walls and the wood-burning oven on proud display.

House specialties: Neapolitan pizzas, such as cime di rapa (with broccoli rabe, sausage, and buffalo mozzarella) and margherita (tomato, buffalo mozzarella, Parmigiano-Reggiano, olive oil, and basil); genuinely home-style Italian pastas such as goncchetti al pesto genovese (handmade potato gnocchi with pesto) and penne all' arrabbiata (with red pepper and garlic-spiced tomato sauce); all of the salads; espresso and cappuccino made from Illy brand coffee.

Summary & comments: This is immaculately authentic, beautifully prepared wood-burning oven pizza Neapolitan style (by far the best pizza of its type in the city) topped with imported buffalo mozzarella that's incredibly buttery and subtle (other ingredients are equally heavenly). The pastas are equally stunning, made just like Over There. This kitchen can do no wrong, but skip dessert—only the tiramisu is made in-house, and the chef's heart isn't in it. The espresso's primo.

LE BERNADIN

			QUALITY
Fish/French	★★★★	Very expensive	**96**
			VALUE
			B

155 West 51st Street (between Sixth and Seventh Avenues)
489-1515   Zone 8 Midtown West/Theater District

Customers: Business, local
Reservations: Required
When to go: Anytime
Entrée range: Dinner is prix fixe only,
$68; $120 for the seven-course
tasting menu
Payment: All major credit cards

Service rating: ★★★★
Friendliness rating: ★★★
Bar: Full service
Wine selection: Excellent
Dress: Dressy; jackets required
for men
Disabled access: Yes

Lunch: Monday–Friday, noon–2:30 p.m.
Dinner: Monday–Thursday, 5:45–10:30 p.m.; Friday and Saturday,
5:45–11 p.m.

Atmosphere & setting: Formal elegance, without arrogance, suffuses this
grand space, and the clientele dress and act accordingly—this is, unmistakably, a setting for serious dining. Blue-gray walls, adorned with fine classic
maritime paintings in ornate frames, rise to a teak ceiling. Small roses top
tables, handsomely set and graciously spaced.

House specialties: Truffled lobster and celeriac "cappuccino" (soup); yellowfin tuna carpaccio; roasted monkfish with savory cabbage; poached skate
in brown butter; millefeuille of chocolate.

Other recommendations: Herbed crabmeat in saffron ravioli; crispy
Chinese-spiced red snapper with cèpes; poached halibut in warm vinaigrette; spice-crusted swordfish, duck sauce, and sauté of cavaillon melon;
frozen coffee parfait with hazelnut meringue.

Summary & comments: Flawless fish, flawless service. Another New York
candidate for number one—whether restaurant, fish restaurant, or French
restaurant. Only the very finest fish and celestial shellfish are accorded the
honor of appearing at table here, and these stars of the sea are prepared with
panache and perfection by Eric Ripert, who has reached the same glorious
gastronomic heights as Gilbert Le Coze, his renowned predecessor. Dining
at Le Bernadin is a privilege, one that you pay a hefty, privileged price for.
Deep pockets are de rigueur.

LE CIRQUE 2000

			QUALITY
French	★★★★	Very expensive	95

	VALUE
	B

455 Madison Avenue (in the New York Palace Hotel)
794-9292   Zone 9 Midtown East

Customers: Local, celebs, New York's social elite
Reservations: Recommended
When to go: Anytime
Entrée range: $26–38
Payment: All major credit cards
Service rating: ★★★★

Friendliness rating: ★★★
Bar: Full service
Wine selection: Very good, and a wide range of prices
Dress: Dress-up time
Disabled access: Yes

Lunch: Monday–Saturday, 11:30 a.m.–3 p.m.; Sunday, 11:30 a.m.–2:30 p.m.
Dinner: Monday–Saturday, 5:30–11 p.m.; Sunday; 5:30–10:30 p.m.

Atmosphere & setting: Any restraint Adam Tihany demonstrated in the low-key decoration of Jean-Georges he's made up for in spades (Technicolor spades, that is) here. The grand, stately, turn-of-the-century rooms of the Villard Houses that make up part of the Palace Hotel have been left in all their Gilded Age, chandeliered, marbled splendor. But Mr. Tihany has cleverly inserted a circus into the heart of these baronial walls: looping steel tubing with neon accents over the futuristic bar, high-backed purple chairs with multicolored clown buttons in the main dining room, red and white light columns in the grill room that complement the red and yellow banquettes and red high-backed, yellow-clown-buttoned chairs. The effect of these whimsical juxtapositions is giddy, over the top, but fabulous.

House specialties: Sautéed foie gras; fish soup; cassolette of vegetables in black truffle broth; sweetbreads with fava beans and morels; sea bass in crispy potatoes with red wine sauce; veal with fresh morels; crème brûlée.

Other recommendations: Tuna tartare; potato gnocchi with crabmeat and broccoli rabe; crab salad; seared duck with curried duck leg; risotto with lobster; broiled salmon with lemon grass crust; oeuf a la niège; chocolate torchière.

Summary & comments: If there were any doubts that Sirio Maccioni could bring all the posh pizzazz and superlative food of his original Le Cirque to this new location, they have vanished. If a restaurant, like love, can be better the second time around, this is it. Maccioni, the magical master of this three-ring culinary circus, has truly done it again. Chef Sottha Khunn's creations are sensational, and pastry chef Jacques Torres is no slouch. The service is superb, and the well-known faces that frequented the 65th Street establishment are back in force. It's usually quite difficult to get a reservation—keep trying.

LOTFI'S

			QUALITY
Moroccan	★★½	Moderate	**79**
			VALUE
			C

358 West 46th Street (between Eighth and Ninth Avenues)
582-5850   Zone 8 Midtown West/Theater District

Customers: Pretheater, local
Reservations: For pretheater
When to go: Anytime
Entrée range: $12.95–16.95
Payment: All major credit cards
Service rating: ★★★

Friendliness rating: ★★★
Bar: No
Wine selection: Limited
Dress: Casual
Disabled access: Fair

Dinner: Monday–Saturday, 4:30 p.m.–midnight

Atmosphere & setting: Tucked away on Restaurant Row, Lotfi's could just as easily be on a small street in Casablanca or Marrakesh. Traditionally tiled walls, blue-and-white pottery dishes and couscousières, art deco mirrors, a few brass lamps, and menus in soft, gold-tooled leather folders enhance the authentic Moroccan feel, as do the spicy aromas coming from the kitchen.

House specialties: Couscous, the national dish of Morocco, in its many variations; lemon chicken tagine; fish tagine Safi-style (the hometown of the chef/owner); homemade "merguez" lamb sausage.

Other recommendations: B'stilla with chicken or the more traditional squab; breewats, a flaky pastry with many different stuffings; "deluxe" salad offers six Moroccan mainstays.

Summary & comments: Moroccan food is interesting and fun, and it's a great change of pace, especially in the Theater District and especially in this warm, family-run establishment. It can be spicy or sweet (fruit and meat and nuts mix together in unusual harmony) or both, and the owners, husband and wife, are more than willing to tell you about the specialties.

MAN RAY

			QUALITY
International	★★½	Moderate	**79**
			VALUE
			C

169 Eighth Avenue (18th and 19th Streets)
627-4220   Zone 6 Chelsea

Customers: Local, Joyce Theater
   attendees
Reservations: Only for pretheater
When to go: Anytime

Entrée range: $8.95–11.95
Payment: All major credit cards
Service rating: ★★
Friendliness rating: ★★

(Man Ray)

Bar: Full service	Dress: Casual
Wine selection: Limited	Disabled access: In bar area only

Brunch: Saturday and Sunday, 11 a.m.–3:30 p.m.
Lunch: Monday–Friday, noon–3 p.m.
Dinner: Monday–Thursday and Sunday, 5:30–11 p.m.; Friday and Saturday, 5:30 p.m.–midnight

Atmosphere & setting: Cool, dark, decorated with a few large blowups of the famous eponymous photographer's work and a reproduction of one of his paintings. A long bar hosts a lively Chelsea scene; an equally long banquette, topped with photo exhibits by contemporary artists, offers seating if you don't want to belly up. The raised dining area in the rear, with back-lit art deco designs and a glass brick wall, is pleasant and not too noisy.

House specialties: Black pepper linguine with seafood; Caribbean fried chicken with black bean salsa; fried calamari with ginger sauce; Caesar salad with smoked trout.

Other recommendations: Maryland crab cakes; farfalle with grilled salmon in vodka tomato cream sauce; fried goat cheese "cigars" with aioli (at brunch).

Summary & comments: This longtime Chelsea stalwart is right next to the Joyce Theater, New York's mecca of modern dance, and there's not much reason to go any farther pre- or post-performance if a well-prepared, not overly trendy nor overly priced dinner is your object. The pizzas (one will do for two) or any of the appetizers or sandwiches make a good snack after watching those lithe bodies in constant motion.

MARGON RESTAURANT

Cuban Cafeteria	★★½	Inexpensive	QUALITY 84
			VALUE A

136 West 46th Street
   354-5013   Zone 8 Midtown West/Theater District

Customers: Local, businessmen	Service rating: ★★½
Reservations: Not accepted	Friendliness rating: ★★★
When to go: Quick lunch	Bar: None
Entrée range: $5.25–7.25	Wine selection: None
(breakfast, $2)	Dress: Casual
Payment: Cash only	Disabled access: No

Breakfast: Monday–Friday, 6–10:30 a.m.; Saturday, 6:30–10:30 a.m.

(Margon Restaurant)

Lunch: Monday–Friday, 10:30 a.m.–4 p.m.; Saturday, 10:30 a.m.–
2:30 p.m. Closed Sunday.

Atmosphere & setting: A harshly lit, bare-bones hustle-your-tray-through-
the-line basement cafeteria.

House specialties: Roast chicken, octopus salad, rice and beans, fried plantains; all the standard-issue Latino luncheonette fare, but good!

Summary & comments: If you need to catch a quick lunch in Midtown,
this place will get you in and out in a jiffy (don't sweat long lines; they move
quickly), but patrons' fast-shoveling forks belie the high quality of the food.
Everything's very fresh and made with care. There are precious few Latin
lunch counters left in this part of town, and friendly, efficient Margon is a
proud bastion.

MAVALLI PALACE

			QUALITY
Indian Vegetarian	★★★½	Moderate	**87**
			VALUE
46 East 29th Street			**A**

679-5535   Zone 7 Gramercy Park, Madison Square

Customers: Indian businessmen and
families, local aficionados
Reservations: For parties of 3 or more
When to go: Anytime (especially good
for a light lunch or business bite)
Entrée range: $6.75–14.95
Payment: VISA, MC, AMEX, DC

Service rating: ★★★
Friendliness rating: ★★★½
Bar: Full
Wine selection: Decent
Dress: Nice casual
Disabled access: Good, but rest rooms
not accessible

Lunch: Tuesday–Sunday, noon–3 p.m.
Dinner: Tuesday–Sunday, 5–10 p.m. Closed Monday.

Atmosphere & setting: Quiet, relaxing, surprisingly elegant—perfect for
a date—considering the reasonable price. Wood floors and uncommonly
well-spaced tables (and commensurately low noise level).

House specialties: Sukka alu (mildly spicy potatoes with green curry
leaves), chanamasala (chickpeas with pomegranate), alu gobhi (cauliflower
and potatoes sautéed with tomatoes and spices), onion rava masala (rice
crêpe filled with potatoes, peas, and onions), masala dosa (similar, with lentil
crêpe), kancheepuram iddly (fluffy spiced lentil cakes), uttappam (a
spongy/crunchy pancake with various toppings), thalis (decorative metal
pans bearing tastes of many items).

(Mavalli Palace)

Other recommendations: A couple of items that elsewhere are mere after-thoughts are particularly good here: masala cashew nuts (fried and spicy) and pappadum (the ubiquitous spicy lentil crackers—here baked, not fried).

Summary & comments: You won't miss the meat, promise. South Indians have cooked vegetarian for countless centuries, and they've got it figured out. Most offerings here are light and easy to like; if you've got a meat-and-potatoes appetite, there are several combination plates and thalis to choose from. Mavalli's concerned service, stylishly low-key ambience, and subtle refined cooking combine to make this a worthy choice. Spudophiles take note: this kitchen excels at anything with potatoes.

MESA GRILL

American/Southwest	★★★	Expensive	QUALITY
			81
			VALUE
			C

102 Fifth Avenue (15th and 16th Streets)
807-7400   Zone 7 Gramercy Park, Madison Square

Customers: Local, business
Reservations: Recommended
When to go: Anytime
Entrée range: $18−27
Payment: All major credit cards
Service rating: ★★★
Friendliness rating: ★★

Bar: Full service, with 20 different kinds of tequila
Wine selection: Good
Dress: Casual; some business at lunch
Disabled access: Yes, downstairs

Lunch: Monday–Friday, noon–2:30 p.m.
Brunch: Saturday and Sunday, 11:30 a.m.–3 p.m.
Dinner: Monday–Sunday, 5:30–10:30 p.m.

Atmosphere & setting: Substantial columns, painted with bands of south-western colors, hold up the two-story high ceiling. The lime green and yellow walls sprout tin lighting fixtures, and the banquettes are covered in a kitsch-cute "Hi-ho Silver" design. All this to let you know that you're in for spicy southwestern fare. The tables are close, and the noise level can rear up and buck like a bronco. Quieter late in the evening and at brunch.

House specialties: Shrimp and roasted garlic corn tamale; spicy salmon tartare with plantain chips; roasted ancho chicken; Black Angus steak with Mesa steak sauce and horseradish potatoes.

Other recommendations: Grilled Yucatán tuna with fresh oregano spoon-bread; wild mushroom, roasted garlic, and goat cheese quesadilla; chocolate custard corn pone with whisky butterscotch sauce.

(Mesa Grill)

Summary & comments: Celebrity-chef Bobby Flay has pizzazz aplenty, and this smart venue is the perfect place for him to strut his southwestern stuff. Every dish has a spicy regional accent—even the romaine salad has red chile croutons, the red snapper is crusted with blue corn tortillas, and there's blue corn again in the biscotti. The appetizers are especially interesting and pretty on their Fiesta-ware plates, and the main courses are large enough to satisfy the hungry cowboys in the cookhouse, though some of the combos can be a little over the top. The clientele is trendy, the atmosphere animated.

MIKE'S AMERICAN BAR & GRILL

American	★★	Moderate	QUALITY
			74
			VALUE
			C

650 Tenth Avenue (between 45th and 46th Streets)
246-4115   Zone 8 Midtown West/Theater District

Customers: Local
Reservations: Optional
When to go: Anytime
Entrée range: $9–14
Payment: All major credit cards
Service rating: ★★★

Friendliness rating: ★★★
Bar: Full service
Wine selection: Very limited
Dress: Truly casual
Disabled access: Yes

Lunch: Every day, noon–4 p.m.
Dinner: Every day, 5 p.m.–midnight

Atmosphere & setting: Take equal measures of funky, kooky, and loopy; shake; pour into an old, unrefurbished longshoreman's "gin mill"; garnish with quirky decor-of-the-month (in honor of a new movie, an old movie, or the time of year) that changes at whim; add red-and-white checked plastic tablecloths, a solid bar in the front, and a few mirrors; and voilà, it's Mike's.

House specialties: Pan-fried quesadillas with goat cheese, spinach, and red pepper; "killer" hot chili; double enchilada plate; grilled marinated leg of lamb with carrot puree.

Other recommendations: Deep-fried spicy calamari; Caesar salad with roasted garlic dressing; grilled marinated pork chop with corn salad and chutney.

Summary & comments: Not exactly on the beaten path, but only a block off, this Hell's Kitchen "dive" is fun and an inexpensive Theater District alternative. The food is reliable and the portions ample, and smoking is permitted. The crowd is a casual New York mix where one's choice of partner is never a problem. Mike's junior menu is available at lunch for those under 12, with a soda and a scoop of ice cream to go with the PB&J.

MOLLY'S			

			QUALITY
Irish Pub Food	★★★	Moderate	**88**
			VALUE
287 Third Avenue			**B**
889-3361 Zone 7 Gramercy Park			

Customers: Locals
Reservations: Limited
When to go: Anytime
Entrée range: $10.50–18.95
Payment: VISA, MC, AMEX, D,
   DC, JCB

Service rating: ★★½
Friendliness rating: ★★
Bar: Full
Wine selection: Small selection
Dress: Casual
Disabled access: Fair

Lunch: Every day, 11 a.m.–4 p.m.
Dinner: Every day, 5 p.m.–midnight

Atmosphere & setting: Classic Irish pub; woody and snug, complete with fireplace. Lots of booths and tables (the largest, a round table seating eight, is handy for after-work get-togethers).

House specialties: Cheeseburgers, shepherd's pie and chicken pot pie, respectable steak, mashed potatoes, and most fried items.

Other recommendations: Avoid specials; stick with the main menu. Ask for fried onions on your cheeseburger (they're sensational), and request the special walnut dressing on your salad.

Summary & comments: The area has plenty of anonymous Irish bar/restaurants to choose from, but this is the standout. Typical pub food is grand (best cheeseburgers and shepherd's pie in Manhattan), and they transcend type with touches like a surprisingly worthy bread basket and fresh (gasp!), not overcooked vegetable sides. Guinness stout, properly creamy and not overchilled, is among the best in town.

MOLYVOS

			QUALITY
Greek	★★★	Expensive	84
			VALUE
			B

871 Seventh Avenue (between 55th and 56th Streets)
582-7500   Zone 8 Midtown West/Theater District

Customers: Business, local
Reservations: Recommended
When to go: Anytime
Entrée range: $17.50–23.50
Payment: All major credit cards
Service rating: ★★★
Friendliness rating: ★★★

Bar: Full service; excellent ouzo selection
Wine selection: Good; especially interesting Greek selections
Dress: Business, casual
Disabled access: Fair; two steps to the dining room

Lunch: Every day, noon–3 p.m.
Dinner: Monday–Thursday, 5:30 p.m.–midnight; Friday and Saturday, 5:30 p.m.–1 a.m.; Sunday, 5:30–11 p.m.

Atmosphere & setting: An airy, comfortable Greek taverna with a bright front room and substantial bar that leads into large, somewhat dimmer main dining room. Greek key panels top stenciled planks, the terra-cotta sponged walls are dotted with black-and-white photos of Molyvos, and all is accented with Hellenic objects, plates, amphorae, glass bottles, and the capital of a marble column.

House specialties: Marinated lamb shanks; moussaka; pastitsio; wood-grilled whole fish; baklava.

Other recommendations: Rabbit stifado; steamed salmon wrapped in grape leaves; stuffed baby eggplants; cod dolmades; loukoumades (dessert fritters with honey sauce).

Summary & comments: Don't gorge on the tasty tasting plate of tara-masalata and tzatziki; you'll need lots of room for the large portions of won-derfully, authentically prepared Greek dishes. The mezedes (appetizers) alone can make a meal, but then you'd miss the delights of the main courses. John Livanos, who with his partner Rick Moonen also run the very upscale Oceana, pays real homage to Molyvos, his native town on the island of Lesvos, and to the real glory of Greek cooking. Great place before or after a concert at Carnegie Hall.

MONSOON

Vietnamese	★★½	Moderate	QUALITY
			78

			VALUE
435 Amsterdam Avenue (corner of 81st Street)			**B**
580-8686 Zone 12 Upper West Side			

Customers: Ethnic, local	**Friendliness rating:** ★★
Reservations: For parties of 7 or more	**Wine selection:** Limited to house red
When to go: Anytime	and white; beer is better
Entrée range: $ 6.50–14.95	**Dress:** Casual
Payment: All major credit cards	**Disabled access:** Yes, but crowded and
Service rating: ★★	narrow entry

Lunch & Dinner: Sunday–Thursday, 11:30 a.m.–11 p.m.; Friday and
Saturday, 11:30 a.m.–midnight

Atmosphere & setting: Typical one-size-fits-all New York oriental (in other
words, not much attention is paid to decor), with a few paper lanterns and
bamboo awnings.

House specialties: Vietnamese seafood bouillabaisse, a good assortment of
sea creatures in hot and sour stock served in a casserole; steamed lady finger,
shrimp dumplings in red miso sauce; stir-fry chicken with lemon grass and
red chili sauce; banh hoi, angel hair noodles; banana pudding.

Other recommendations: Sugar-cane shrimp; red curry with beef, served
with a pancake; pho, the traditional, hearty ox-tail soup with rice noodles
and filet of beef; summer rolls.

Summary & comments: This bustling neighborhood favorite gets very
crowded in the evening, and the waiting line often flows onto the street, but
the food is good and worth the wait. Lunch is a far calmer affair, and it's a
good place to take the kids after an excursion to the nearby Museum of Natural History.

MR. BROADWAY KOSHER DELI

Jewish Deli	★★★	Moderate	QUALITY
			84

			VALUE
1372 Broadway			**A**
921-2152 Zone 7 Midtown West			

Customers: Locals, businessmen	**Entrée range:** $4.25–21.75
Reservations: Accepted	**Payment:** VISA, MC, AMEX, D, DC
When to go: Anytime	**Service rating:** ★★★

(Mr. Broadway Kosher Deli)

Friendliness rating: ★★★
Bar: Beer and wine
Wine selection: Small (kosher)

Dress: Casual
Disabled access: Fair

Lunch & Dinner: Monday–Thursday, 9 a.m.–9 p.m.; Friday, 9 a.m.–
3 p.m.; Sunday, 11 a.m.–9 p.m. Closed Saturday.

Atmosphere & setting: From the front, this looks like just another of the area's many kosher fast food spots, but the rear is classic Jewish deli, a bustling cavern with darting waiters, tables crammed with pickles and cole slaw, and regulars who look like they eat *a lot* of pastrami trying to squeeze their way through the tight floor plan.

House specialties: Outstanding garlicky baba ganoush (eggplant salad); potato knishes; couscous; kasha varnichkes (oniony buckwheat with bow-tie noodles); potato pancakes (deep fried, but good); homemade french fries; chicken soup with matzo balls; falafel; derma (rich spicy stuffing in sausage casing); fried "Moroccan cigars" (pastry flutes stuffed with finely minced meat); homemade gefilte fish.

Other recommendations: There's a terrific self-service Middle Eastern salad bar up front, for take-out (at $3.99/pound) or to accompany falafel and shwarma sandwiches.

Summary & comments: Mr. Broadway Kosher Deli & Restaurant is known by many names: it's also Me Tsu Yan Kosher Chinese Restaurant and Chez Lanu, serving North African dishes. The confluence of cuisines makes for some strange culinary juxtapositions, from customers smearing hummous on their hot dogs to the Moroccan couscous served with a homely piece of Eastern European roast chicken riding on top. For both Middle Eastern and deli specialties, Mr. Broadway is a winner. The kitchen somehow manages to turn out perfectly balanced baba ganoush and flaky potato knishes without watering down the soulfulness of chicken soup or tender gefilte fish. Corned beef is, of course, of paramount importance in a Jewish deli; theirs is good and well-cut but perhaps a bit too lean (everything's a tad lighter than usual here; perhaps it's the Sephardic influence). Chinese dishes—glatt kosher, like everything else—are handily available for those for whom real Chinese isn't an option. This place is only five years old and unpedigreed in NYC deli history, but the more venerated delis seem grimily past their primes, while Mr. Broadway thrives.

NEW PASTEUR

			QUALITY
Vietnamese	★★★½	Inexpensive	**88**
			VALUE
			A

85 Baxter Street
608-3656 or 608-4838   Zone 3 Chinatown

Customers: Ethnic, locals, foodies
Reservations: Suggested
When to go: Avoid the peak hours of
  8–10 p.m.
Entrée range: $3.75–9
Payment: Cash only

Service rating: ★★★
Friendliness rating: ★★½
Bar: Beer and wine
Wine selection: House
Dress: Casual
Disabled access: Fair

Lunch & Dinner: Every day, 11 a.m.–10 p.m.

Atmosphere & setting: Spare storefront with little decoration to detract from the memorable cooking. Be prepared to share tables.

House specialties: Any of the phos (elemental beef-based soups), barbecued beef (with vermicelli or on its own), shrimp rolls, fried spring rolls, barbecued shrimp roll on sugarcane, iced coffee.

Summary & comments: Vietnamese food is "hot" in New York, and chi-chi startups are opening all over town. Yet year in and year out, homely New Pasteur (formerly Pho Pasteur) outclasses them all with no-nonsense first-class cooking. The barbecued beef is a marvel of gastronomic engineering, an entire beefy symphony compressed into each small nugget (wrap them in lettuce leaves, along with mint, cucumber slices, sprouts, and carroty fish sauce; the Vietnamese eat almost everything this way). If New Pasteur is full, as it often is, head up the block to larger and more upscale Nha Trang, whose food is nearly as good.

THE NICE RESTAURANT

			QUALITY
Cantonese and Dim Sum	★★★½	Moderate	**91**
			VALUE
			B

35 East Broadway
406-9510   Zone 3 Chinatown

Customers: Business, families
Reservations: Suggested
When to go: As early as possible for
  dim sum

Entrée range: $7.25–14 (up to
  $24 for specials); dim sum:
  $1.80–3.50
Payment: AMEX

(The Nice Restaurant)

Service rating: ★★★★
Friendliness rating: ★★½
Bar: Beer only
Wine selection: None

Dress: Nice casual
Disabled access: Upstairs room not
  accessible; downstairs (closed
  Monday and Friday), one step up

Dim sum: Every day, 8 a.m.–noon
Lunch: Every day, 11 a.m.–4 p.m.
Dinner: Every day, 4–10 p.m.

Atmosphere & setting: Not as over-the-top as some of the more garish Hong Kong–style pavilions, the Nice is done up mostly in burgundy red (imagine a Chinese version of an upscale suburban catering hall). Noise levels run high, but it's an excited buzz, emanating from avid eaters.

House specialties: Minced conch and seafood with coconut curry sauce in conch shell; crispy seafood roll, minced squab with pine nuts in lettuce leaf; baby veal chops hot pot; tofu, minced chicken, and salted fish casserole; sautéed snow pea shoots with shredded dried scallops; stewed abalone in oyster sauce; crispy shrimp with walnuts.

Other recommendations: Dim sum: garlic har gow (garlic shrimp dumplings).

Summary & comments: The top end of Cantonese cuisine recalls that of France, what with the complexities of flavor, intricate presentation, attention to aroma and aftertaste, and strikingly unusual juxtapositions. The Nice Restaurant consistently attains these lofty heights; order well and you'll taste fancy Cantonese/Hong Kong banquet cooking at its best. Any of the above list of sensational—and largely off-menu—specialties will leave you forever convinced that Chinese food is much more than General Tso or shrimp in lobster sauce. The Nice puts on one of Chinatown's better dim sums, too, but arrive early, avoid fried things, and don't forget to special-order the amazing garlic shrimp dumplings from a manager.

NOBU			
			QUALITY
Japanese	★★★★	Expensive	95
			VALUE
			B

105 Hudson Street (at Franklin Street)
  219-0500   Zone 2 TriBeCa/SoHo

Customers: Local, business, celebs,
  ethnic
Reservations: Absolutely necessary
When to go: Anytime

Entrée range: $21–26; multicourse
  "Omakase," chef's choice, $60;
  sushi and sashimi a la carte,
  $2.75–7

(Nobu)

Payment: All major credit cards
Service rating: ★★★
Friendliness rating: ★★★
Bar: Full service
Wine selection: OK, but sipping sake

might be better
Dress: Business, casual
Disabled access: Fair; call in advance
to arrange

Lunch: Monday–Friday, 11:45 a.m.–2 p.m.
Dinner: Every day, 5:45–10 p.m.

Atmosphere & setting: Birch tree columns, blond wood, high copper-leafed ceiling, plush banquettes, a wall of black river stones, and a large sushi counter are all part of David Rockwell's stunningly original million-dollar decor. Just as stunning are the number of well-known faces to be seen.

House specialties: The "Omakase" tasting dinner; toro tartar with caviar; black cod with miso; sea urchin in spinach; Matsushisa shrimp and caviar; yellowfin sashimi with jalapeño; squid "pasta" with garlic sauce.

Other recommendations: Broiled toro with spicy miso; shrimp and lobster with spicy lemon sauce; salmon tartar with caviar; sea urchin tempura; toro "to-ban" yaki.

Summary & comments: No doubt, Nobu is one of the most exciting eateries in New York. Chef Nobu Matsushisa's brilliant, innovative menu is as stunningly original as the decor and considered by some to be the city's best Japanese food, by others to be just the city's best food. The menu is huge, with over a hundred small and medium-size dishes—a grazer's paradise for out-of-this-world sushi and beyond. Reservations are very hard to get (sometimes it's hard to get anything but a busy signal); book way, way in advance if you can.

OCEANA				
			QUALITY	
Fish	★★★½	Expensive	90	
			VALUE	
55 East 54th Street (between Madison and Park Avenues)			C	
759-5941 Zone 9 Midtown East				

Customers: Business, local
Reservations: Recommended
When to go: Anytime
Entrée range: Prix fixe only; lunch
$35, dinner $55
Payment: All major credit cards
Service rating: ★★★

Friendliness rating: ★★★
Parking: Garage, complimentary after
4 p.m.
Bar: Full service
Wine selection: Excellent
Dress: Jacket and tie
Disabled access: No

(Oceana)

Lunch: Monday–Friday, noon–2:30 p.m.
Dinner: Monday–Saturday, 5:30–10:30 p.m.

Atmosphere & setting: This Midtown townhouse has been transformed into a luxury yacht, the kind captains of industry—and otherwise—and their wealthy pals ply the seas in. Downstairs, diners look out of faux windows on what might be Capri, maybe Antibes, or at a vintage ocean liner sailing by. The elegant, high-ceilinged upstairs bar serves oysters and the like and welcomes cigar smokers.

House specialties: Salmon tartare wrapped with smoked salmon; lobster ravioli; pan-seared Bay of Fundy salmon; Oceana East Coast bouillabaisse; chocolate mousse cake with praline ice cream.

Other recommendations: Tuna carpaccio; soft-shell crabs (in season); seared red snapper with pale green mashed potatoes; jumbo lump crab cakes; blood orange soufflé glacé.

Summary & comments: Everything is fishy here, and it's fabulous—chef Rick Moonen may serve some of the best seafood in New York. The presentations are as exquisite to look at as the dishes are to eat, and the desserts created by David Carmichael tend toward the ambrosial. Tables are rather close together, and when it's crowded, an occasional high-level business discussion can be overheard, but that's all part of the scene, as is the impeccable service. Don't look for a la carte bargains here; everything is prix fixe—expensive and well worth it. The catch of the day is culinary cachet.

OLD SAN JUAN

Puerto Rican/Argentinean	★★★	Inexpensive	QUALITY
			86
			VALUE
			B

765 Ninth Avenue (51st and 52nd Streets)
    Zone 8 Midtown West/Theater District

Customers: Pretheater, ethnic, locals
Reservations: Not accepted
When to go: Anytime
Entrée range: $6.50–15.95
Payment: Major credit cards
Service rating: ★★★
Friendliness rating: ★★★

Bar: Full service
Wine selection: Limited, heavy on the Argentinean
Dress: Pretheater, casual
Disabled access: Everything on street level

Lunch & Dinner: Sunday–Thursday, 11 a.m.–11 p.m.; Friday and Saturday, 11 a.m.–2 a.m.

(Old San Juan)

Atmosphere & setting: This recent addition to Ninth Avenue's growing restaurant roster is not big on decor. There's a luncheonette-like counter to handle the take-out crowd, plus a very small bar and a larger, low-ceilinged dining room with random Puerto Rican objects on the walls. But when you're welcomed by the owner, who says, with all sincerity, "I want you to be happy," who needs designer decor?

House specialties: Cazuela de mariscos, seafood in a casserole served over yellow rice; asopaos, soupy Puerto Rican rice stews, in various flavors; mofongo, a garlicky mound of mashed plantains and pork cracklings, with crab or roast pork; churrasco Argentino, a grilled skirt steak.

Other recommendations: Pasteles puertoriquenos, a comforting tamalelike concoction steamed in a banana leaf; clams in garlic sauce; Argentinean empanadas; stewed goat; caramel-crusted bread pudding.

Summary & comments: Old San Juan is a new entry in Manhattan's ethnic restaurant array and a needed one. With its huge Puerto Rican population, the city should have more places, accessible to non-natives, that feature the island's hearty, savory dishes. It's crowded, but that doesn't diminish the service, which would be more than reputable in a far more expensive establishment. The daily lunch specials, at $5.50, are truly hard to beat.

ORSO

Northern Italian	★★★	Moderate	QUALITY
			82
			VALUE
			C

322 West 46th Street
489-7212   Zone 8 Midtown West/Theater District

Customers: Theatergoers, theater people, local	**Friendliness rating:** ★★★
Reservations: Necessary	**Bar:** Full service
When to go: Anytime	**Wine selection:** Italian only; house wine by the carafe is serviceable and well-priced.
Entrée range: $18–22	
Payment: VISA, MC only	**Dress:** Casual
Service rating: ★★★	**Disabled access:** No

Lunch & Dinner: Every day, noon–11:45 p.m.

Atmosphere & setting: This star of Restaurant Row occupies a narrow space with a low-ceilinged bar area that leads to a vaulted back room where an active, open kitchen is fronted by a counter topped with large flower pots heaped with bread and lemons. Modesty prevails, the lights are low,

(Orso)

adornment is limited to framed black-and-white photos, and, *grazie Dio*, there is soundproofing so that you can hear your dining companions and gather snatches of theatrical gossip from your neighbors. ·

House specialties: This menu changes daily, but there are always wonderful thin-crusted pizzas; pasta with porcini mushrooms; grilled vegetable plate; calf's liver with onions.

Other recommendations: Ultra-thin pizza bread with oil and rosemary; arugula salad with prosciutto; bruschetta; panzanella; gelato.

Summary & comments: Orso has been a winner for over 15 years, and it's still hard to get a reservation—so if this is your pretheater destination, book well in advance. The northern Italian dishes are expertly and authentically prepared, the waiters are cordial, the setting is relaxed, theater folk actually eat here, and the prices are fair.

OSTERIA DEL CIRCO

Italian	★★★	Expensive	QUALITY 83
			VALUE C

120 West 55th Street (between Sixth and Seventh Avenues)
265-3636   Zone 8 Midtown West/Theater District

Customers: Business, local, tourist	Bar: Full service; serves a top-notch
Reservations: Recommended	"Negroni"
When to go: Anytime	Wine selection: Very good
Entrée range: $19–29	Dress: Midtown melange of business
Payment: All major credit cards	and casual
Service rating: ★★★	Disabled: Yes
Friendliness rating: ★★	

Lunch: Every day, 11:30 a.m.–3 p.m.
Dinner: Every day, 5:30–11 p.m.

Atmosphere & setting: Relentlessly cheerful, the big-top ceiling sports billowing red and yellow tenting, clown figures revolve between bar and dining room, and the bright blue balloon-patterned banquettes face chairs with harlequin seats. Even the waiters are decked out in striped shirts that match the striped menu covers.

House specialties: Egi's ravioli; cacciucco, Tuscan fish soup with lobster and prawns; grilled rare yellowfin tuna; breast of duck from the rotisserie; bomboloncini, light, custard-filled Tuscan doughnuts.

(Osteria del Circo)

Other recommendations: Risotto with asparagus; roasted leg of lamb with tomato confit and garlic sauce; bollito misto; lemon mascarpone pyramid; check the daily specials.

Summary & comments: Sirio "Le Cirque" Maccioni's three sons run this popular trattoria, and their culinary lineage shows in the quality of the kitchen, which features their mother Egidiana's family recipes. This is not the place for quiet, intimate dining; the circus atmosphere extends beyond designer Adam Tihany's multi-million-dollar decor, and the open, airy dining area attracts tourists as well as celebs. The large, angled bar, with a trapeze ladder overhead, and its small surrounding tables are inviting, and a light bar menu is available. Circo Take Out, with a separate entrance in Fisher Park, has great stuff that comes directly from Circo's kitchen, plus daily soup and panini (sandwich) specials, that you can eat right there or take back to your room.

PAOLA'S			
			QUALITY
Northern Italian	★★★	Moderately expensive	85
			VALUE
347 East 85th Street (between First and Second Avenues)			B
794-1890 Zone 13 Upper East Side			

Customers: Local	**Service rating:** ★★★
Reservations: Recommended	**Friendliness rating:** ★★★
When to go: Dinner only	**Wine selection:** Good; a bit pricey
Entrée range: $16.95–26.95	**Dress:** Casual
Payment: All major credit cards	**Disabled access:** Fair

Dinner: Sunday and Monday, 5–10 p.m.; Tuesday–Saturday, 5–11 p.m.

Atmosphere & setting: Lovely and low-key; you could be sitting in a side-street establishment in Florence or Sienna. The two rooms are small, the tables subtly lit with candles, the walls dark red with gilt-edged mirrors in a repeated pattern. When it fills up, the noise level can rise, *ma non troppo,* and in the warmer months, the noise spills out the windowed doors to the umbrella-topped tables of the sidewalk cafe.

House specialties: Pan-seared baby artichokes; homemade "malfatti," dumplings made of swiss chard and ricotta; chicken and sweet sausage in wine sauce; ricotta cheesecake.

Other recommendations: Ravioli stuffed with beets and ricotta; pappardelle with duck sauce; risotto (changes daily); filet mignon with barolo wine and mushrooms; tiramisu.

(Paola's)

Summary & comments: A cut or two above a neighborhood trattoria, this intimate Upper East Side Italian is worth the trip. The service is very solicitous, with a constant chorus of *buon appetito*s and *grazie*s, and the food is authentic, homey, and very comforting—just like eating in Mama's own kitchen.

PATRIA				
				QUALITY
Latin American	★★★		Expensive	**84**
				VALUE
				B

250 Park Avenue South (corner of 20th Street)
777-6211   Zone 7 Gramercy Park, Madison Square

Customers: Local, business	**Friendliness rating:** ★★★
Reservations: Recommended	**Bar:** Full service
When to go: Anytime	**Wine selection:** Very good
Entrée range: $20–29	**Dress:** Casual, business
Payment: All major credit cards	**Disabled access:** Fair; bathroom not
Service rating: ★★★	accessible to wheelchairs

Lunch: Monday–Friday, noon–2:45 p.m.
Dinner: Monday–Thursday, 6–10:45 p.m.; Friday and Saturday,
  5:30–11:45 p.m.; Sunday, 5:30–10 p.m.

Atmosphere & setting: Bold and bright, animated with gold-ocher columns, colorful mosaics on the floors and walls, big windows, big paintings, and a big bar in the center of the action. There are comfortable booths and banquettes on the lower dining tier and well-spaced tables on the two upper tiers.

House specialties: Ecuadoran ceviche; black lobster empanada; whole red snapper with coconut conch rice; "the original," plantain-coated mahi mahi with fufu and grilled lily salad; "chocolate cigar."

Other recommendations: Oysters Rodriguez; Honduran "fire & ice," ceviche of tuna, chilies, ginger, and coconut milk; Patria pork; churrasco nica, beef tenderloin with chimichurri; Guatemalan chicken in mole sauce.

Summary & comments: Douglas Rodriguez's eclectic, exotic take on Latin American cuisine is truly different and exciting. The dishes are as novel in their presentation (plantains, for example, virtually take wing) as they are unusual in the combinations and juxtapositions of ingredients. Patria has deservedly become a very popular place with an interesting crowd at lunch and dinner. It takes a pile of pesos to pay the bill, but you'll have an *experiencia muy rica*.

PETROSSIAN

			QUALITY
Russian	★★★	Expensive	**83**

<table>
<tr><td></td><td></td><td></td><td>VALUE</td></tr>
<tr><td></td><td></td><td></td><td>C</td></tr>
</table>

182 West 58th Street (at Seventh Avenue)
245-2214   Zone 8 Midtown West/Theater District

Customers: Business, the ladies who lunch, caviar cravers
Reservations: Recommended
When to go: Anytime
Entrée range: $25–34
Payment: All major credit cards
Service rating: ★★★

Friendliness rating: ★★★
Bar: Full service
Wine selection: Very good, especially the champagne by the glass
Dress: Upscale; jackets and ties
Disabled access: No

Brunch: Saturday and Sunday, 11:30 a.m.–3 p.m.
Lunch: Monday–Friday, 11:30 a.m.–3 p.m.
Dinner: Monday–Saturday, 5:30–11:30 p.m.; Sunday, 5:30–10:30 p.m.

Atmosphere & setting: Only one block from Carnegie Hall, this dimly lit caviar cave is nestled in a corner of the Alwyn Court (a.k.a. *Rosemary's Baby's* building). Art Nouveau lovelies grace the mirrors behind the polished granite bar. The dining area, mirrored, small, and darkly elegant, is appointed in rose, black, and well-buffed wood.

House specialties: Caviar! Beluga, Sevruga and Ossetra, and so on, served with toast or blini and crème fraîche; "teasers," an assortment of a smoked fish appetizers with a touch of foie gras; sautéed loin of arctic venison; sea scallop soufflé with truffles.

Other recommendations: Borscht with piroshki; foie gras salad; steamed lobster; tropical fruit, vodka sorbets; Valrhona chocolate soufflé; lemon tart.

Summary & comments: You can blow a big budget on the caviar, but don't be intimidated—you can also dine surprisingly well on the $22 prix fixe lunch that includes a glass of fine champagne or the $35 prix fixe dinner, graciously served throughout the evening. Brunch, too, is excellent. The Boutique offers caviar and foie gras to go.

PATROON

			QUALITY
American	★★★½	Expensive	**86**
			VALUE
			C

160 East 46th Street (between Lexington and Third Avenues)
883-7373   Zone 9 Midtown East

Customers: Business, local
Reservations: Recommended
When to go: Anytime
Entrée range: $26–75 (porterhouse steak for 2)
Payment: All major credit cards
Service rating: ★★★

Friendliness rating: ★★
Bar: Full service
Wine selection: Very good and quite expensive
Dress: Business
Disabled access: Yes

Lunch: Monday–Friday, noon–2:30 p.m.
Dinner: Monday–Saturday, 5:30–11 p.m.

Atmosphere & setting: The line of limos parked outside lets you know that this is a hot spot and watering hole. Inside, the atmosphere is unabashedly clubby, solid and solidly American with a masculine slant, though the plush banquettes often hold as many "power femmes" as hommes. Upstairs holds the extremely popular cigar lounge, where the sweet smell of success is overwhelming.

House specialties: Risotto with asparagus and fava beans; lobster and cod cake with snow pea shoots; spitfire-roasted duck; wood-grilled filet mignon with roasted shallot mashed potatoes.

Other recommendations: Seared foie gras with rhubarb compote; wood-grilled porterhouse steak (for two); braised rabbit with black trumpet ravioli; roasted lamb chops with eggplant; and goat cheese flan.

Summary & comments: This is New York's newest "tycoonery," a place where "power" is the appropriate prefix for every meal. The portions are as substantial as the prices, but price is not a problem for this keen-to-be-seen crowd of business big wheels, media moguls, politicians, celebs, and the wannabes in all those categories. Aside from the "scene," the food is interesting and goes well beyond steak house fare.

PATSY'S PIZZA

			QUALITY
Pizzeria	★★★	Inexpensive	**93**

	VALUE
2287 First Avenue	**A**

534-9783   Zone 14 Harlem

Customers: Locals, foodies
Reservations: Not necessary
When to go: Anytime
Entrée range: Whole pizzas, $9–12
Payment: Cash only
Service rating: ★★

Friendliness rating: ★★
Bar: None
Wine selection: None
Dress: Casual
Disabled access: Good

Hours: Monday–Thursday, 11:30 a.m.–midnight; Friday, 11:30 a.m.–1 a.m.; Saturday, 11:30 a.m.–midnight; Sunday 1–11 p.m.

Atmosphere & setting: Though it's been in dire need of renovation for decades, the new owner of Patsy's stubbornly refuses to fix the place up. The room with the oven (where you order) is extremely dingy and harshly lit but permeated with the collective spirit of a century of great pizza, so it might be a pity to lose that atmosphere (I hope they never eliminate the pile of coal in front of the oven). Next door there's a room with tables and friendly but amateurish waiter service.

House specialties: Fantastic unpretentious brick oven pizza by the slice from an ancient coal-burning oven.

Entertainment & amenities: A semi-broken black-and-white television blasting Spanish programs (ordering area only).

Summary & comments: While this is the only top-notch brick oven pizzeria that will serve slices, you should really get a whole pie in order to experience the full grandeur (order slices—from pies that have been sitting—and you may face less crusty crust, though the taste is still tops). The nabe is Spanish Harlem, so taxi in after dark and remain on full alert. Across the street, open during warm weather only, Rex's is an eccentric spot serving some of the city's best Italian ices (avoid strawberry, though!). Important note: the other Patsy's Pizzas in Manhattan have merely licensed the name; they're unrelated and not recommended.

Malaysian	★★★	Moderate	QUALITY
			83
			VALUE
			C

240 Columbus Avenue (71st Street)
769-3988   Zone 12 Upper West Side
109 Spring Street (between Greene and Mercer Streets)
274-8883   Zone 2 TriBeCa/SoHo

Customers: Local, ethnic
Reservations: Only for parties of
6 or more
When to go: Anytime
Entrée range: $7.95–19.95
Payment: All major credit cards
Service rating: ★★★
Friendliness rating: ★★★

Bar: Full service
Wine selection: Limited, but the
beers on tap seem to be the
beverage of choice.
Dress: Casual
Disabled access: Upper West Side,
fair, no access to bathrooms;
SoHo, none

Lunch: *West Side,* noon–4:40 p.m.; *SoHo,* 11:30 a.m. till closing. Express
lunch menu served noon–5 p.m. at both locations.

Dinner: *West Side,* Monday–Friday, 4:30 p.m.–midnight; Saturday,
4:30 p.m.–1 a.m.; Sunday, noon–11 p.m.; *SoHo,* Monday–Thursday,
4:30 p.m.–1 a.m.; Friday till 1 a.m.; Saturday till 1:30 a.m.; Sunday,
1–11:30 p.m.

Atmosphere & setting: Downtown, it's rain forest funk with a waterfall, no
less. On the West Side, it's wood paneling, wooden tables, windows, and
bamboo with a few non–rain forest potted plants. The subterranean "lounge"
is low on lights and high on decibels and smoke. There's more decoration
outside—a large relief of plowing water buffalo—than in.

House specialties: Pasembur, a salad with jicama, squid, and jellyfish; roti
canei, Indian flat bread with curry dipping sauce; chicken with shredded
mango and peppers served in a mango shell; spiced, deep-fried whole red
snapper with a spicy sauce.

Other recommendations: Penang clay pot noodles with seafood; Malaysian
nasi goreng; fired taro stuffed with seafood; beef rendang.

Summary & comments: It's the gen-Xers, not the flying fish, who play on
this "road to Mandalay." Both locations can jam up on weekends, and beep-
ers are handed out to locate waiting customers who stray down the block.
Malaysian cooking, which reflects the Indian, Chinese, and Malayan popu-
lations, was "Asian fusion" centuries before the term was coined by trendy
chefs, and what is served here is authentic, exotic, and spicy—though the
clay pot dishes and soups tend to be blander. The service, despite the full
house, is amazingly quick and attentive to detail.

PETER LUGER

			QUALITY
Steak House	★★★	Expensive	84

			VALUE
			B

178 Broadway (corner of Driggs Avenue), Brooklyn (Williamsburg)
  (718) 387-7400   Zone 16 Brooklyn

Customers: Local, business, tourists
Reservations: Required for dinner
When to go: Anytime
Entrée range: $18.95–28.95
Payment: Cash only
Service rating: ★★★

Friendliness rating: ★★★
Bar: Full service, proud of its
  "oversized drinks"
Wine selection: Fair
Dress: Casual
Disabled access: Yes

Lunch & Dinner: Monday–Friday, 11:45 a.m.–9:45 p.m.; Saturday,
  11:45 a.m.–10:45 p.m.; Sunday, 1–9:45 p.m.

Atmosphere & setting: Just over the bridge in the Williamsburg section of
Brooklyn—fascinating in itself—this 110-year-old landmark steak house is
as plain as its menu. Scrubbed wooden tables, scrubbed wooden floors, a few
beer steins, half-timbered walls, waiters with the requisite gruff manner who
are really helpful and fun.

House specialties: USDA prime dry aged steak; creamed spinach; Luger's
German fried potatoes; apple strudel with lots of whipped cream.

Other recommendations: Double thick loin lamb chops; steak sandwich;
chopped steak (at lunch); pecan pie.

Summary & comments: Where's the beef? It's here, it's porterhouse, and it's
memorable. This is a magnet for carnivores who are willing to throw cholesterol cares to the wind (at least for a night). The long bar gets so crowded
with steak-seekers—Wall Street wunderkinder, tourists from all the world,
and steadfast habitués—that the stools have long since disappeared. Well
worth the trek into Brooklyn, and actually quite easy to get to.

PETITE ABEILLE

			QUALITY
Belgian Luncheonette	★★½	Inexpensive	86

			VALUE
			A

107 West 18th Street
  367-9062   Zone 6 Chelsea

Customers: Local, business, ex-pat
  Belgians
Reservations: Not accepted
When to go: Anytime

Entrée range: $5.75–$8.75
Payment: AMEX, D
Service rating: ★★
Friendliness rating: ★★★

(Petite Abeille)

Bar: None
Wine selection: None
Dress: Casual

Disabled access: Good; staff helps with step

Brunch: Saturday and Sunday, 9 a.m.–4 p.m.
Breakfast, Lunch, & Dinner: Monday–Friday, 7 a.m.–7 p.m.; Saturday and Sunday, 9 a.m.–6 p.m.

Atmosphere & setting: Boxy but pleasant, with a distinctly European flair. There's a counter for take-out and drinks.

House specialties: Waffles (unadorned, as per Belgian tradition), carbonade (hearty sweet/savory beef stew), steump de carrot (ultra-homey carrot-flecked mashed potatoes), various sausage dishes, quiches, salads, and sandwiches.

Other recommendations: Do not miss your chance to buy prized Belgian Côte d'Or chocolate—it's not officially imported here (shhhh), and this is probably the only place that sells it.

Entertainment & amenities: They deliver.

Summary & comments: It's hard to decide whether you're eating in a Really Good Restaurant masquerading as a cheap lunchroom or if this is simply a super-high-quality lunchroom. Don't expect gastronomic miracles, just skillfully cooked Belgian comfort food, unusual but accessible, easy to enjoy, and you can't beat the price. They offer a primitive variety of waiter service, but you'll do best by pitching in with trips to the counter to select things. There's a more full-service Petite Abeille in Greenwich Village (466 Hudson; 741-6479), with longer hours, a different menu, and particularly good pommes frites—though service can be peevish.

PICCOLO ANGELO

Italian	★★★	Moderate	QUALITY
			84
			VALUE
			B

621 Hudson Street (Jane Street)
229-9177   Zone 4 Greenwich Village

Customers: Local
Reservations: Recommended
When to go: Dinner only
Entrée range: $11.50–15.95; pastas, $7.95–10.95
Payment: VISA, MC
Service rating: ★★★

Friendliness rating: ★★★
Wine selection: Limited, mostly Italian; hold out for the inexpensive homemade "house" wine
Dress: Casual
Disabled access: No

(Piccolo Angelo)

Dinner: Tuesday–Thursday, 4–11 p.m.; Friday and Saturday, 4–11:30 p.m.; Sunday, 4–10 p.m.

Atmosphere & setting: This storefront West Village classic is piccolo indeed. The decor is limited to exposed brick with a few black-and-white prints. The tables are on top of each other and the noise level is high, but that doesn't stop regulars and a steady stream of newcomers from huddling in the doorway while they wait to be seated.

House specialties: Listen to the list of daily specials; fettucine with porcini mushrooms; linguine with white clam sauce; lobster ravioli; rack of lamb with marsala.

Other recommendations: Hot seafood antipasto; shrimp Fra'Diavolo; grilled portobello mushrooms; eggplant rolitini; ricotta cheesecake.

Summary & comments: This place is family-run in the best sense. Renato Migliorini and his son, Peter, welcome customers and worry over the pint-sized kitchen, which somehow manages to turn out enough traditional, "home-cooked" Italian food to satisfy the full house expecting to be fed. When Papa lists the ample array of daily specials, it sounds more like a fast recitative from a Verdi opera. Listen closely; he's loathe to repeat, and these are the dishes to eat. Try to resist the irresistible garlic bread—you'll need room for the large, very reasonably priced portions.

PICHOLINE

Mediterranean	★★★½	Expensive	QUALITY
			89

VALUE
C

35 West 64th Street (between Columbus and Central Park West)
724-8585   Zone 10 West Side

Customers: Local, business, Lincoln Center
Reservations: Recommended
When to go: Anytime
Entrée range: $25.50–32; pretheater prix fixe, $45 and $53; tasting menus, $62 and $75
Payment: All major credit cards

Service rating: ★★★
Friendliness rating: ★★★
Bar: Full service
Wine selection: Interesting selections in a good range of prices
Dress: Business, dressy, upscale casual
Disabled access: Yes

Lunch: Tuesday–Saturday, 11:30 a.m.–2 p.m.
Dinner: Monday–Saturday, 5:30–11:45 p.m.; Sunday, 5–10 p.m.

(Picholine)

Atmosphere & setting: East Side elegance on the West Side, with tapestries on the walls, lavishly framed paintings, ornate ceilings, shaded chandeliers, brocade banquettes, and some well-placed French country touches. The "picholine" (a small green olive) theme appears on the pretty plates and the warm olive green of the lower walls.

House specialties: Spiced barbecued quail; tuna carpaccio; wild mushroom and duck risotto; organic chicken "under brick," with white bean brandade; turbot en papillote; bouillabaisse; warm chocolate tart with coconut sorbet and hazelnut sauce.

Other recommendations: Grilled octopus; warm corn and chanterelle salad; shellfish paella; Moroccan spiced loin of lamb with vegetable couscous; tournados of salmon with horseradish crust; lemon curd "cannoli" with Bing cherry compote.

Summary & comments: The imaginative, inventive Mediterranean menu created by chef-proprietor Terrance Brennan is reason enough to come to here, but its proximity to Lincoln Center is an added plus. The attentive and informed staff and the gracious setting help make Picholine one of the area's very best. The well-appointed "wine room" is ideal for a small private party.

PÓ			
Italian	★★★½	Moderate	**QUALITY** 87
			VALUE B

31 Cornelia Street (between Bleecker and West 4th Streets)
645-2189   Zone 4 Greenwich Village

Customers: Local, aficionados from the boroughs and the burbs	**Service rating:** ★★★
	Friendliness rating: ★★★
Reservations: A must	**Wine selection:** Limited, but good
When to go: Dinner only	and fairly priced
Entrée range: $13–15	**Dress:** Casual
Payment: AMEX only	**Disabled access:** Fair

Lunch: Wednesday–Sunday, 11:30 a.m.–2:30 p.m.
Dinner: Tuesday–Thursday, 5:30–11 p.m.; Friday and Saturday, 5:30–11:30 p.m.; Sunday, 5–10 p.m.

Atmosphere & setting: A thimbleful of space (with hardly more than a dozen tables), creamy buff walls, and the patterned tin ceiling so characteristic of old Village buildings. Mirrors above the simple banquettes and discreet lighting are the sole decoration, but the feeling is warm, informal, and inviting.

House specialties: Check daily specials; grappa-cured salmon; black pepper tagliatelle with three mushrooms; grilled rabbit with caponata; marinated quail with plums and pomegranate molasses.

Other recommendations: Braised fennel salad with barley tabbouleh; linguine with clams, pancetta, and hot chilies; grilled baby octopus with barbecued onions and sun-dried tomatoes; terrine of dark chocolate.

Summary & comments: The decor is not the draw here—it's the very well-prepared, often inventive Italian food. Excellent white bean bruschetta, good bread, and olive oil come to the table to whet your appetite, but don't over-nibble; you'll need the room for what follows. If choosing is too taxing, try the six-course tasting menu for $35. The prices are as unpretentious as the setting; ditto for the service, helpful and friendly without fuss. Perhaps not as well kept a West Village secret as many of its repeat patrons would like: Reservations can be hard to come by, so plan ahead for this one.

RAIN			
			QUALITY
Asian fusion	★★★	Moderate	85
			VALUE
100 West 82nd Street (Columbus Avenue)			C
501-0776 Zone 12 Upper West Side			

Customers: Local
Reservations: Recommended
When to go: Anytime
Entrée range: $11–22
Payment: All major credit cards
Service rating: ★★★

Friendliness rating: ★★★
Bar: Full service
Wine selection: Good
Dress: Informal, casual
Disabled access: No

Brunch: Saturday and Sunday, 11 a.m.–3 p.m.
Lunch: Monday–Friday, noon–3 p.m.
Dinner: Every day, 5:30–10 p.m.

Atmosphere & setting: With a few simple strokes, the ground floor of this Upper West Side brownstone has taken on the sultry feel of Rangoon in the rainy season. Rattan settees with boldly flowered cushions cluster around low bamboo tables in the always crowded bar area, and the large dining area is simple and comfortable—tables covered with no-nonsense white paper; plain, polished wood floors; and slowly circling ceiling fans.

House specialties: Crispy Vietnamese spring rolls stuffed with shrimp, vegetables, and glass noodles; Thai-style fajitas, a cross-cultural knockout that

(Rain)

combines roast duck and Asian vegetables wrapped in moo-shu pancakes; a delicate salmon fillet roasted in a banana leaf and spiced with pepper and garlic.

Other recommendations: Daily specials; Malaysian chicken satay, with the traditional cucumber salad and peanut sauce; pad thai, rice noodles with chicken, shrimp, bean sprouts, and egg; crispy whole fish served with tangy "three-flavor" sauce. And if your sweet tooth needs satisfying, the fried coconut ice cream is a must. Asian eggs Benedict (with Malaysian sausage and a gingery hollandaise) on the brunch menu will spice up any lazy Sunday morning.

Summary & comments: Chef Taweewat Hurapan handles this combo of Southeast Asian cuisines—Thai, Vietnamese, and the lesser-known Malaysian—with ease and elegance. Traditional dishes alternate with innovative adaptations, and the presentations have a stylish pizzazz not often found in Asian restaurants. This is a very popular spot with the trendy and the non-, so book well in advance for weekend dinners. Only half the tables can be reserved; the rest are held for walk-ins, and that can leave you lifting libations in the bar for quite a while.

REMI			
			QUALITY
Northern Italian	★★★	Expensive	84
			VALUE
145 West 53rd Street (between Sixth and Seventh Avenues)			C
581-4242 Zone 8 Midtown West/Theater District			

Customers: Business, local
Reservations: Recommended
When to go: Anytime
Entrée range: $19.50–26
Payment: All major credit cards
Service rating: ★★★

Friendliness rating: ★★★
Bar: Full service, with an amazing selection of grappas
Wine selection: Very good
Dress: Business
Disabled access: Yes

Lunch: Monday–Friday, noon–2:30 p.m.
Dinner: Monday–Saturday, 5:30–11:15 p.m.; Sunday, 5:30–10 p.m.

Atmosphere & setting: Chalk up another dramatic dining domain for designer Adam Tihany. Here he's created a grand view of Venice, with a huge fantasy mural of the fabled city that sweeps across one wall; flying buttress arches connect it to the large-paned windows that form the opposite wall and look out onto a glass-roofed atrium set with tables when weather per-

(Remi)

mits. Inside, the bold blue and white stripes of the banquettes are echoed in the striping on the waiters' shirts and parquet floors.

House specialties: Shrimp cakes with warm mushroom salad and baby greens; homemade cannelloni filled with veal and spinach; risotto of the day; braised veal shank with seasoned vegetables; cioccolatissima (warm chocolate soufflé).

Other recommendations: Quail wrapped in bacon with grilled polenta; homemade agnelloti with beef in red wine sauce; sautéed halibut with potato and black truffle sauce; zabaglione.

Summary & comments: This sophisticated restaurant offers a sophisticated menu that draws a matching crowd, especially at lunch, when local corporate and publishing types conduct a bit of business over their antipasti. Chef and co-owner Francesco Antonucci serves up interesting Venetian and northern Italian dishes that obviously please the dedicated clientele. Check out the risotto of the day—it's always *delicioso,* and the salads are large enough for two. Consider this for a pretheater dinner when it's not quite so crowded.

REPUBLIC

Asian fusion	★★½	Inexpensive	QUALITY 79
			VALUE B

37 Union Square West (East 17th Street)
  627-7172   Zone 7 Gramercy Park, Madison Square

2290 Broadway (between 82nd and 83rd Streets)
  579-5960   Zone 12 Upper West Side

Customers: Local, ethnic
Reservations: Not their style
When to go: Anytime
Entrée range: $6–9
Payment: All major credit cards
Service rating: ★★★

Friendliness rating: ★★★
Wine selection: Four reds, five whites; sakes, hot and cold; tap and bottled beer
Dress: Casual
Disabled access: All on one level

Lunch & Dinner: Monday–Wednesday, noon–11 p.m.; Thursday–Sunday, noon–midnight

Atmosphere & setting: The red stars placed here and there seem to proclaim this as "the People's Republic of Noodles," and the proletarian-plain pale wooden tables with backless benches that stripe the room in even rows reinforce the feeling. The chic, spare Union Square space is cavernous, with

(Republic)

huge black-and-white photo blowups of models engaged in eating or wearing noodles. A long, slate-topped counter and bar stretch in front of a white-brick, mirrored wall. The newer, West Side establishment is a smaller carbon copy sans bar and brick.

House specialties: Spicy seafood salad; grilled Japanese eggplant; spicy coconut chicken; glass noodles; chicken udon.

Other recommendations: Salmon sashimi salad; barbecued pork with cold vermicelli; seared marinated salmon with curried rice.

Summary & comments: This stylish "noodlerium" also offers "small dishes"—seaweed salad, grilled calamari, sashimi salad—and a few good rice options. The noodles, with and without broth, are well-prepared, incredibly cheap, and healthy to boot— crunchy vegetables punctuate many choices. The service by the black-clad staff is speedy but with a smile. This is not a place to linger or lounge, and if it's crowded at these communal tables, be prepared to "love thy neighbor."

ROSA MEXICANO			
Mexican	★★★	Moderate	**QUALITY** 84
			VALUE B

1063 First Avenue (58th Street)
753-7407   Zone 9 Midtown East

Customers: Local, ethnic, tourist
Reservations: Recommended
When to go: Dinner only
Entrée range: $16–26
Payment: All major credit cards
Service rating: ★★
Friendliness rating: ★★★

Bar: Full service; emphasis on margaritas, especially the pomegranate variation
Wine selection: Limited
Dress: Casual
Disabled access: Yes

Dinner: Every day, 5–11:30 p.m.

Atmosphere & setting: It's always fiesta time here, with a boisterous bar scene in the front. Colorful cutout banners flutter from the dark rose ceilings over dusty rose adobe walls, star lighting fixtures twinkle, potted ferns add a little greenery, and traditional copper plates add a little elegance to the table settings. The smaller part of the L-shaped dining room is a tad quieter.

House specialties: Guacamole; crepas de cuitlacoche (Mexican corn fungus—a real delicacy); enchiladas de mole poblano; posole (a stew with pork, chicken, and hominy); alambres de camarones (grilled, skewered marinated shrimp).

Other recommendations: Ceviche of bay scallops; menudo (tripe stew); enchiladas de pato (duck with a green mole sauce); crepas camarones (crêpes filled with shrimp in a chile pasilla sauce).

Summary & comments: Above and beyond the usual Tex-Mex fare, this is as close to authentic, classic Mexican cuisine as you will find in New York. Be sure to order the made-to-order-at-your-table guacamole; it has become a renowned signature dish. The color and dash of the food and the setting are guaranteed to lift your spirits, even before you down a few divine margaritas.

ROSARIO'S

Italian	★★★	Inexpensive	QUALITY
			87
			VALUE
			A

38 Pearl Street
514-5763   Zone I Lower Manhattan

Customers: Businessmen	Friendliness rating: ★★½
Reservations: Not accepted	Bar: Beer and wine
When to go: Anytime	Wine selection: Three reds
Entrée range: $4.75–7	Dress: Casual
Payment: VISA, MC, AMEX, D	Disabled access: Fair
Service rating: ★★★½	

Breakfast & Lunch: Monday–Friday, 8 a.m.–3 p.m. Closed Saturday and Sunday.

Atmosphere & setting: Bustling no-nonsense cafeteria.

House specialties: Menu changes daily; familiar dishes like lasagna, veal/chicken/eggplant parmigiana (dish or hero), escarole, penne ala vodka, minestrone, and so on.

Summary & comments: Rosario's makes their own mozzarella and their own pasta, and the food is extremely tasty, if inelegant. Prices are almost insanely low; they make their profit from volume, processing dozens of customers per minute with miraculous efficiency. Steam-table service doesn't permit al dente pasta; if that bothers you, stick with soups, heroes, and entrées. Why can't every neighborhood have a place like this?

SAHARA EAST

			QUALITY
Middle Eastern	★★½	Moderate	84

VALUE
B

184 First Avenue
  353-9000   Zone 5 East Village

Customers: Locals, ethnic
Reservations: Accepted
When to go: Warm weather
Entrée range: $8.95–14.95
Payment: Cash only
Service rating: ★½

Friendliness rating: ★★★★
Bar: Beer and wine
Wine selection: Small
Dress: Casual
Disabled access: Poor (big step at front door)

Lunch: Every day, 10 a.m.–5 p.m.
Dinner: Every day, 5 p.m.–2 a.m.

Atmosphere & setting: A narrow little cafe, but pass through to the large garden in back decorated with lights and hanging knickknacks.

House specialties: Falafel, grape leaves, fattoush (salad with pita croutons), lamb or chicken shish kebab, lamb or chicken couscous.

Other recommendations: Shisha (aromatic tobacco, optionally flavored with apple), smoked from ornate water pipes fueled by glowing coals; bargain lunch specials.

Entertainment & amenities: Live music on Friday and Saturday, 9–11:30 p.m.

Summary & comments: Sahara can turn out some high-quality food, but the tiny kitchen gets overwhelmed when things are busy. The dilemma is that the place is most fun when crowded, so one must weigh food against ambience when choosing a time to eat here (busy nights are Thursday through Sunday). On nice clear evenings, the garden fills up, and the perfumed shisha smoke wafts as snakily as the music. Older Middle Eastern guys and East Village hipsters blend effortlessly into the scene, and it feels wonderful to be a part of it all. On these busy kitchen nights, stick with the dishes we've listed and you'll do fine. If, however, food is more important to you than setting, go on off nights and ask the friendly chef about the day's specials. In any case, service is very friendly but maddeningly slack. Put yourself on the same slow track, puff an apple shisha (try it—it's much mellower than cigarettes; this is the place that made shisha chic), and relax into the Egyptian groove.

SAIGON GRILL

			QUALITY
Vietnamese	★★★	Inexpensive	**90**

	VALUE
	A

2381 Broadway
   875-9072   Zone 12 Upper West Side

Customers: Local
Reservations: Only for 5 or more
   (none accepted on weekends)
When to go: Avoid peak hours,
   especially on weekends
Entrée range: $6.50–14 (much less
   at lunch)

Payment: All major credit cards
Service rating: ★★½
Friendliness rating: ★★
Bar: Beer only
Wine selection: None
Dress: Casual
Disabled access: No

Lunch & Dinner: Every day, 11 a.m.–midnight

Atmosphere & setting: Clean, bright (but no-frills) bustling storefront. Good for kids.

House specialties: Barbecued spare ribs, barbecued pork chop, barbecued chicken, crispy whole sea bass, grilled boneless chicken, summer rolls, coconut sticky rice, pickled vegetable salad.

Summary & comments: "Grill" is right: This place turns out some of the best grilled dishes around. Most Vietnamese restaurants in New York are run by Vietnamese of Chinese ethnicity, but here the two traditions run together. The wonderful barbecue spare ribs with peanut/plum sauce, for example, taste pretty Chinese. Hybrid or no, this is a real find, especially in a nabe where good Asian food is rare. Great as the grilled meats are, perhaps the best dish of all is the crispy whole sea bass (sweetly subtle sauce, ultra-flaky, and very fresh). Kids and adults will both like the wonderful coconut sticky rice (strewn with ground peanuts).

SANTA FE

			QUALITY
American/Southwest	★★½	Moderate	**79**

	VALUE
	B

72 West 69th St. (between Columbus Ave. and Central Park West)
   724-0822   Zone 10 West Side

Customers: Local, Lincoln Center
Reservations: Recommended
When to go: Anytime
Entrée range: $12.75–18.75
Payment: All major credit cards
Service rating: ★★★

Friendliness rating: ★★★
Bar: Full service
Wine selection: Limited
Dress: Casual
Disabled access: No

(Santa Fe)

Lunch: Monday–Friday, noon–4 p.m.; Saturday–Sunday, 11 a.m.–4 p.m.
Dinner: Tuesday–Saturday, 4 p.m.–midnight; Sunday–Monday, 4–11 p.m.

Atmosphere & setting: The bottom floor of this Upper West Side townhouse has been washed in soft southwestern colors, coral walls, golden sand ceilings, white on the trim and on the candle-strewn, mirror-topped fireplaces. Acoma pots, decorated wooden bowls, handwoven Oaxacan rugs, and a few typical Santa Fe oil paintings foster the feeling that you're nestled below the Sangre de Cristo mountains.

House specialties: Southwestern shrimp jambalaya; Yucatán chicken; black bean and sweet potato burrito; chipotle chicken Santa Fe.

Other recommendations: Grilled cumin and chipotle pork chop; southwestern grilled vegetable pizza; scallop ceviche.

Summary & comments: One of the first around town to offer southwestern fare, this tranquil, pretty place has been going strong for 15 years. The upscale approach to both the traditional and the trendy cooking of the region, without any backsliding into Tex-Mex, margaritas that are mighty good and *muy fuerte,* and young, friendly waitpersons are reason enough to encourage a visit. And if Lincoln Center is your ultimate destination, this a fine choice, pre- or post-performance.

SEAGRILL

American/Seafood	★★★½	Expensive	QUALITY
			84
19 West 49th Street (at Rockefeller Plaza)			VALUE
332-7610 Zone 9 Midtown East			**C**

Customers: Business, local, tourists
Reservations: Recommended
When to go: Anytime
Entrée range: $26–30
Payment: All major credit cards
Service rating: ★★★
Friendliness rating: ★★★

Bar: Full service
Wine selection: Very good list and very good by-the-glass selections
Dress: Jackets required for men; most of the women wear them too.
Disabled access: Yes

Lunch: Monday–Friday, 11:45 a.m.–2:45 p.m.
Dinner: Monday–Saturday, 5–9:45 p.m. Closed Sunday.

Atmosphere & setting: An elevator at street level brings you down from Midtown madness to a sleekly modern, spacious dining room with much glass and polished brass. In winter, you look out on the famed Rockefeller

(Seagrill)

Plaza skating rink, and in summer, you can sit outside under large striped umbrellas or gaze at the lush potted greenery.

House specialties: Tuna and black truffle tartare; Baltimore crab cakes with stone-ground mustard sauce; steamed mussels in Thai red curry; Chilean sea bass with wilted spinach and Chinese black bean broth; warm chocolate steamed pudding; Key lime pie with black current coulis. Check the daily specials.

Other recommendations: Grilled lobster with homemade fettucine; coriander-crusted swordfish; barbecued squab with foie gras.

Summary & comments: Chef Ed Brown has brought new pizzazz to this classy Midtown seafood establishment. Prices are high here, but so is the quality and service, and you can't beat the location. Weekdays, there's always a sizable business lunch crowd (expense accounts do help) seated on the comfortably upholstered chairs at the comfortably spaced tables.

SECOND AVENUE DELI

Jewish Deli	★★½	Moderate	QUALITY 89
			VALUE C

156 Second Avenue
677-0606   Zone 5 East Village

Customers: Locals, tourists
Reservations: Not accepted
When to go: Anytime
Entrée range: $11.95–21.95
Payment: VISA, MC, AMEX
Service rating: ★★★

Friendliness rating: ★★★
Bar: Wine and beer
Wine selection: Limited kosher
Dress: Casual
Disabled access: Good

Breakfast, Lunch, & Dinner: Sunday–Thursday, 7 a.m.–midnight; Friday and Saturday, 7 a.m.–2 a.m.

Atmosphere & setting: Classic deli, with wisecracking, kvetching meat slicers working up front and booths and pickle-filled little tables crammed in wherever they'll fit. Lots of action; feels just like the old days.

House specialties: Freebie pungent health salad; great smooth chopped liver; authentic matzo ball soup; knishes; derma (rich stuffing—here with globs of paprika—in sausage casing); cholent (an ultra-slow-cooked meat and potato stew); sweet/orangy stuffed cabbage; homemade applesauce. There's much debate over the corned beef; theirs is very lightly "corned," but this allows more beefy flavors to emerge.

(Second Avenue Deli)

Other recommendations: Skip dessert; the deli may be open Friday nights and Saturdays, but they're kosher nonetheless, and desserts made with dairy substitutes aren't worth the calories.

Entertainment & amenities: They'll ship food anywhere via mail order.

Summary & comments: When people think of New York City restaurants, they think of delis. Ha. It's actually easier to find good corned beef in Montreal or Los Angeles than here. While Second Avenue Deli's offerings are spotty, it's the only remaining old-time deli that consistently makes a few dishes very well. Don't stray from our suggestions and you'll have the Authentic New York Deli Experience, if not a fantastic taste experience. You'll find better consistency at Mr. Broadway Kosher Deli (see profile), but they have none of the history and little of the soul of this somewhat sloppy but very traditional place.

SERYNA			
			QUALITY
Japanese	★★★	Expensive	79
			VALUE
			C

11 East 53rd Street (between Fifth and Madison Avenues)
980-9393 or 980-9394   Zone 9 Midtown East

Customers: Business, local, ethnic
Reservations: Recommended
When to go: Anytime
Entrée range: $19.50–135
Payment: All major credit cards
Service rating: ★★

Friendliness rating: ★★, but ★★★ in tatami rooms
Bar: Full service
Wine selection: Limited
Dress: Business, casual
Disabled access: Not easy

Lunch: Monday–Friday, noon–2 p.m.
Dinner: Monday–Friday, 5:30–10 p.m.; Saturday, 6–10 p.m.

Atmosphere & setting: A rock garden and waterfall lead to the recessed entrance, away from the hubbub of the street. From the calm beige-carpeted bar, it's a few steps down to the wood-paneled dining room with bare wooden tables. The traditionally clad waitresses and the dark red lamp shades add touches of color to the simple surroundings. Crowded at lunch, more serene at dinner. Private tatami rooms, at $40 a pop, are available upstairs.

House specialties: Beef, both ishiyaki and shabu-shabu; lobster sashimi; eel teriyaki.

Other recommendations: Tuna and yellowtail sushi; poached Norway salmon; seaweed salad.

(Seryna)

Summary & comments: If you want to beef it up and you have a yen (and the yen) for the real stuff—wagyu/Kobe beef from Japan—it's here, it's excellent, and it's expensive. Steaks, cooked ishiyaki-style on hot rocks at your table, or shabu-shabu, dipped for seconds only into a copper pot of hot broth, are the stars, but other offerings are interesting and uniformly well prepared and presented. The service is attentive and courteous.

SHAAN			
Indian	★★★	Moderate/Expensive	**QUALITY** 84
			VALUE B

57 West 48th Street (between Fifth and Sixth Avenues)
977-8400   Zone 8 Midtown West/Theater District

Customers: Business, publishing types at lunch
Reservations: Recommended for dinner
When to go: Anytime
Entrée range: $10.95–$29.95
Payment: All major credit cards
Service rating: ★★★
Friendliness rating: ★★★

Parking: Validated garage parking at dinner
Bar: Full service
Wine selection: Small; Indian beer is a better choice here
Dress: Business, casual
Disabled access: Fair; bathrooms downstairs

Brunch: Saturday and Sunday, 11 a.m.–3 p.m.
Lunch: Monday–Friday, noon–3 p.m.
Dinner: Every day, 5:30–11 p.m.

Atmosphere & setting: An island of subcontinental serenity in a spacious, well-appointed, marble-floored dining room with decorative weavings on the walls. The attractive bar area, done in soft green, has a lovely, noteworthy chandelier made from 37,000 gemstone beads. A buffet lunch is served downstairs in a slightly lower-ceilinged room that also serves for private parties. A cool but comfortable quietude prevails.

House specialties: Dali batata poori, stuffed flaky pastry topped with tangy tamarind sauce, is a fine opener; lobster krahi is a worthwhile splurge; shrimp Goa, a south Indian curry; pudina chaap, lamb chops tossed in a spicy mint sauce, a Parsi speciality.

Other recommendations: Chicken, lamb, and goat from the tandoor oven; gobhi alu matar, cauliflower, potatoes, and peas with onions, ginger, and spices; alu baigon dahiwala, potatoes and eggplant cooked in yogurt, for veggie-only folks. The poori bread is a puffy delight.

(Shaan)

Summary & comments: This large, handsome room has gone through many incarnations over the years, starting as the Forum of the Twelve Caesars. It's still elegant, with tables far enough apart for private tête-à-têtes and confidential business discussions. The classy, interesting Indian cuisine is top-notch, as is the service. The $13.95 prix fixe lunch buffet (eight different main dishes) is a super buy, and there's an ample pretheater prix fixe dinner for $21.95 served until 7 p.m.

SHUN LEE, SHUN LEE CAFE

Chinese	★★★½	Exp/Mod	QUALITY 84
			VALUE B

43 West 65th Street
595-8895, 769-3888 (Cafe)   Zone 10 West Side

Customers: Local, business, Lincoln Center
Reservations: Recommended
When to go: Anytime
Entrée range: $12.50–32.50; in the cafe, most entrées are $10.95
Payment: All major credit cards

Service rating: ★★
Friendliness rating: ★★
Bar: Full bar
Wine selection: Good
Dress: Dressy, business; casual in the cafe
Disabled access: Yes

Lunch: Every day, noon–4 p.m.
Dinner: Monday–Saturday, 4 p.m.–midnight; Sunday, 4–10:30 p.m.

Atmosphere & setting: Dark and dramatic: Large silver-white dragons with little red eyes chase each other across black walls above luxurious black banquettes and black floors, and soft halogen lighting flatters the complexion. Silver-white monkeys swing over the small bar in the entrance where you are greeted by tuxedoed maitre d's. This is a snazzy take on the Chinese scene, and the clientele seems to revel in it.

House specialties: Szechuan wonton; steamed dumplings; beggar's chicken (order 24 hours in advance); Grand Marnier prawns; Cantonese sausage with Szechuan sausage; dim sum (cafe only).

Other recommendations: Sliced duckling with young ginger root; lobster in black bean sauce; rack of lamb, Szechuan-style.

Summary & comments: High-style chinoiserie, with high-style Chinese cooking to match, make this an upscale Lincoln Center favorite. Both food and mood are elegant, and both are reflected in the prices. Some of the same excellent food is available in the more casual cafe, which has its own entrance, for a lot less. The cafe, black and white checked from floor to ceiling, also offers very good dim sum from wandering carts and abrupt but rapid service.

SIGN OF THE DOVE

American	★★★½	Expensive	QUALITY
			85

			VALUE
			C

324–342 Park Avenue South
861-8080   Zone 7 Gramercy Park, Madison Square

Customers: Local, tourist
Reservations: Recommended
When to go: Anytime
Entrée range: $22–38
Payment: All major credit cards
Service rating: ★★★

Friendliness rating: ★★★
Bar: Full service
Wine selection: Top-notch
Dress: Dressy, upscale casual
Disabled access: Fair; no wheelchair
  access to bathrooms

Brunch: Sunday, 11 a.m.–2:30 p.m.
Lunch: Tuesday–Saturday, noon–2:30 p.m.
Dinner: Monday–Saturday, 5:30–11 p.m.; Sunday, 5:30–10 p.m.

Atmosphere & setting: Enchantingly elegant, all warm, rosy brick, vaulted glass ceilings, graceful mirrored arches, ornate grillwork, soaring potted palms, charming pedestaled angels, white sheers floating against long windows, brocade-backed chairs, and fabulous florals. There are three adjoining dining rooms down a small set of stairs, and the muted, pastel-hued, wicker-furnished "Music Room" up another. The cafe, with a long bar and little round tables, has its own space and offers a lighter menu at dinner. Sidewalk sipping when the weather is warm.

House specialties: Lobster salad with lemon crème fraîche; seared Hudson Valley foie gras with corn crêpes; roast loin of venison with soft polenta; pepper-crusted tuna in hot and sour bouillon; oyster pan roast (brunch); plum brown butter cake; wonderful bread.

Other recommendations: Skate wings browned in butter; mushroom consomme with mascarpone and potato dumplings; roast Atlantic cod; grilled veal T-bone; crisp apple upside-down tart with caramel ice cream.

Summary & comments: Even the most jaded New Yorkers hear strains of "Isn't It Romantic" when they enter this lovely setting. For over 30 years the Sign of the Dove has been the sign of romance, fine food, and gracious service, and it hasn't lost any of its cachet over time. If anything, chef Andrew

(Sign of the Dove)

D'Amico's unique slant on New American cuisine has upped the standards. Weekend brunch here is a tradition, a great place to show visitors the classy, subdued, sophisticated side of the brassy Big Apple.

(A moveable feast: Sign of the Dove is relocating to the address listed above. The romance and glamour will remain; the space will be a bit bigger. Be sure to call before going.)

SOUL FIXIN'S

Southern/Soul Food	★★★	Inexpensive	QUALITY 87
			VALUE B

371 West 34th Street
736-1345   Zone 6 Chelsea

Customers: Local	**Service rating:** ★★
Reservations: Not accepted	**Friendliness rating:** ★★½
When to go: Anytime	**Bar:** None
Entrée range: Lunch, $5–7;	**Wine selection:** None
dinner, $6–8	**Dress:** Casual
Payment: Cash only	**Disabled access:** Good

Lunch: Monday–Friday, 11 a.m.–5 p.m.
Dinner: Monday–Friday, 5–10 p.m.; closed Saturday and Sunday

Atmosphere & setting: Minimal—this is mostly a take-out joint, but there are a bunch of self-service tables and chairs both inside and out on the sidewalk.

House specialties: Chicken in all forms—particularly barbecued; candied yams, collard greens, macaroni and cheese, cornbread, lemonade.

Summary & comments: It almost defies the imagination to realize that plates of truly soulful victuals can be had within a couple blocks of the Empire State Building (a nabe considered bereft of good eats) for five bucks. Soul Fixin's makes soul food as good or better than nearly any served Uptown for a loyal and largely African American clientele of Midtown workers. Everything's cooked with deft aplomb: chicken and pork chops are reliably tender and flavorful, collard greens have lots of smoke and are not at all mushy. Candied yams are individual halves of spuds neither overspiced nor oversweet, done to the perfect texture (no mean feat when you're cooking ahead for steam-table service). Homemade lemonade and iced tea are just right: smooth, not too sweet, and refreshing. Even the cornbread—often a throwaway in soul food take-outs—is very good. The kitchen takes a relatively healthy approach, using a minimum of pork and fat.

Soup Take-out	★★★½	Inexpensive	QUALITY
			94
			VALUE
			A

259A West 55th Street
757-7730   Zone 8 Midtown West/Theater District

Customers: Local regulars, tourists
Reservations: Not accepted
When to go: Go late (after 3 p.m.) to avoid the worst crowds
Entrée range: $6–10
Payment: Cash only

Service rating: ★★★½
Friendliness rating: ★
Bar: None
Wine selection: None
Dress: Casual
Disabled access: Good

Hours: Monday–Friday, noon–6 p.m. (sometimes later). Closed Friday, Saturday, and all summer.

Atmosphere & setting: You wait in line, inching ever so slowly toward the venerated take-out window. Once at the head of the line, you peer in and glimpse a nervous high-pitched buzz like a Broadway backstage; assistants go about their souply tasks at full tilt, braced for the inevitable calamitous repercussions should they err in even the most trifling detail. A variety of signs—including an LED zipper—clearly state The Rules. At the center of this hurricane, a model of calm haughty efficiency, stands the Soup Man.

House specialties: There's always a chicken-based soup (either chicken vegetable or chicken broccoli), comparatively light and simple, with plenty of meat and carefully cut vegetables. The chef's personal favorites are the bisques—either seafood, lobster, or crab. These are the richest and most expensive choices, of an almost diabolical complexity. You'll find a not-very-spicy medium-thick chili (turkey, vegetable, chicken, or beef), and often Indian mulligatawny (extremely complex and sweetish). The remainders are seafood chowders, various peasanty soups, and delicious oddballs like mussels and spinach or bacon, lettuce, and tomato.

Other recommendations: In hot weather, there are cold soups like vichyssoise and gazpacho.

Entertainment & amenities: Watching newcomers fret and rehearse their order while in line.

Summary & comments: In spite of Jerry Seinfeld's famous sobriquet, owner/chef Al Yeganeh is *not* a Nazi. He's a very conscientious man who has a few irrefutably logical rules: Know what you want by the time you reach the window after your 45-minute wait (duh), have your money ready, and move to the left so the next person can step forward and order. Al—regulars refer to him as Al, though none would dare call him that to his face—

feels sorry for those waiting (he keeps raising prices to discourage crowds, to no avail), so those who ignore his prominently posted rules—thus delaying service—receive no bread. Soup comes in small, large, or extra-large containers. If you order an extra-large, you'll be interrogated as to your intentions: Food shouldn't go unrefrigerated for long periods, so if you order a big one you'd best be prepared to convince Al that you and several friends intend to ingest forthwith. This isn't the most expensive soup in town; these ultra-nourishing concoctions (which come with bread, fruit, and a chocolate), are actually the cheapest four-star lunch in town. What's more, the price allows him to use the choicest ingredients: real saffron, the finest lobster, and so on. The hallmark of Al's soups is the incredible spectrum of textures: huge chunks down to microscopic in-suspension particles; dozens of ingredients collaborating in a soupy symphony, each arranged in perfect balance. Eat on benches one block north at the northeast corner of 56th Street and Eighth Avenue. You won't notice even the coldest winds while huddled with your take-out container of steaming soupy magnificence.

SRIPRAPHAI THAI BAKERY

Thai	★★★½	Inexpensive	QUALITY
			92
			VALUE
			A

64–13 39th Avenue
(718) 899-9599   Zone 17 Queens

Customers: Ethnic, local
Reservations: Not accepted
When to go: Anytime
Entrée range: $4.50–10.50
Payment: Cash only
Service rating: ★★★

Friendliness rating: ★★
Bar: None
Wine selection: None
Dress: Casual
Disabled access: Good

Hours: Every day, 11 a.m.–10 p.m.

Atmosphere & setting: A clean, pleasant, well-lit white box. The ambience, like their name, is more bakery than restaurant.

House specialties: Chinese broccoli with crispy pork; sautéed noodles with meat, chili, and basil leaves; pan-fried egg with ground pork; sticky rice; Thai spaghetti with curry sauce; rice with mixed vegetables; banana sticky rice.

Summary & comments: This is much more than a bakery, though it's no elegant restaurant by any means. Sripraphai is nothing less than the best—and only authentic—Thai eatery in New York. The people who run this place are very serious; they must be to steadfastly remain the city's sole bastion of genuine Thai cooking. If you want gringo-friendly Thai, eat anywhere else; if you want the uncompromisingly real thing, raw and unadorned, eat here. As a single concession to novices, there's a photo album with snapshots of most dishes. One caution: Beware of the catfish. This ain't crunchy/fluffy cornbread-battered catfish a la New Orleans; this stuff is quite different, and not recommended for beginners. Don't miss the impressive collection of freshly prepared cookies, crackers, and little Thai munchies near the cash register, available for in-store or take-out consumption. Best dessert of all (maybe in all of New York): luscious sticky rice, stuffed with banana, steamed inside a banana leaf.

SUSHISAY

Japanese	★★★½	Expensive	QUALITY
			87
			VALUE
			B

38 East 51st Street (between Madison and Park Avenues)
755-1780   Zone 9 Midtown East

Customers: Ethnic, business, local	Service rating: ★★
Reservations: Recommended	Friendliness rating: ★★★
When to go: Anytime	Wine selection: Minimal
Entrée range: $13–33; sushi available	Dress: Casual, business
a la carte	Disabled access: No
Payment: All major credit cards	

Lunch: Monday–Friday, noon–2:15 p.m.
Dinner: Monday–Friday, 5:30–10 p.m.; Saturday, 5–9 p.m.

Atmosphere & setting: Startlingly simple, sharp-angled, and bright with off-white and light wood walls, and light wood tables. Understated Japanese floral arrangements add spots of vibrant color here and there, and a large, 20-seat sushi bar, manned by six sushi chefs and jammed with Japanese businessmen at lunch, forms the centerpiece.

House specialties: Special deluxe bento (appetizers, sushi, and sashimi served in an elegant lacquer box); special makimoto (three kinds of rolled sushi); sea urchin hand roll, spicy codfish sushi, Japanese mackerel sushi, and anything else that appeals on the a la carte sushi list.

Other recommendations: Cooked sushi assortment (good for sushi beginners); chirashi (assorted fish fillets on vinegar-seasoned rice); sushi deluxe (an assortment of fresh and cooked items).

(Sushisay)

Summary & comments: Celestial sushi and sashimi draws praise and crowds. An excellent Midtown choice for the freshest of fresh fish. Order the preselected assortments, or make individual selections from the extensive à la carte list of sushi and hand rolls. The ambience and service are friendly; the high prices reflect the location.

TARTINE				
			QUALITY	
French bistro	★★½	Inexpensive	77	
			VALUE	
			C	

253 West 11th Street (corner of West 4th Street)
  229-2611   Zone 4 Greenwich Village

Customer: Local
Reservations: Not accepted
When to go: Anytime
Entrée range: $7.75–11.95
Payment: Cash only
Service rating: ★★

Friendliness rating: ★★
Wine selection: Bring your own wine
  or beer.
Dress: Casual
Disabled access: For outside tables

Brunch: Saturday and Sunday, 10:30 a.m.–4 p.m.
Lunch: Tuesday–Friday, 11:30 a.m.–4 p.m.
Dinner: Tuesday–Saturday, 5:30–10:30 p.m.; Sunday, 5:30–10 p.m.

Atmosphere & setting: This cute corner bistro on a pretty West Village street attracts lots of locals. There's usually a line waiting for the ten Formica-topped tables squeezed into the small exposed brick interior or for space in the outside cafe (weather permitting).

House specialties: Desserts—dacquoise, tarte tatin a la mode, custard-filled fruit tarts—are all made on the premises and are top-notch; salade basquaise; grilled salmon with citrus vinaigrette; croque monsieur made with brioche.

Other recommendations: Check the daily specials.

Summary & comments: Basic bistro fare at very fair prices, the added savings of BYOB, and the cozy setting make this a very popular place. The service can be a little gruff, but there are few serving many, and they do seem to try. Saturday and Sunday brunch at $9.50 is a bargain bet, especially inviting on warm summer's day.

TAVERN ON THE GREEN

			QUALITY
American	★★★　　Moderate/Expensive		**83**

	VALUE
Central Park West and 67th Street	**B**

873-3200　　Zone 10　West Side

Customers: Locals, tourists	Friendliness rating: ★★★
Reservations: Recommended	Parking: Discounted at adjacent lot
When to go: Anytime	Bar: Full service
Entrée range: $18–32	Wine selection: Very good
Payment: All major credit cards	Dress: Dress-up to casual
Service rating: ★★★	Disabled access: Yes

Brunch: Saturday and Sunday, 10:30 a.m.–3:30 p.m.
Lunch: Monday–Friday, 11:30 a.m.–3:30 p.m.
Dinner: Every day, 5:30–11 p.m.

Atmosphere & setting: Warner Leroy's legendary, flamboyant fantasy of an eatery sits on the edge of Central Park and sparkles year-round. A trillion tiny white lights transform trees and terrace in winter, replaced by the glow of 1,000 Japanese lanterns in spring and summer. There's decor galore— mirrored halls, stained glass, five-tiered chandeliers, faux Tiffany lamps, and gilded horse heads. The glassed-in Crystal Room is a little noisy, but prettier than the half-timbered, heavier Chestnut Room.

House specialties: Caesar salad with Parmesan crisps; sautéed crab cakes; fennel-crusted Norwegian salmon; roast rack of venison with chestnut puree; a knockout New York cheesecake; pineapple and tangerine strudel with banana sorbet.

Other recommendations: Rotisserie roast chicken with rosemary roast potatoes; lobster risotto; apple-stuffed brioche French toast for brunch.

Summary & comments: Always among the highest-grossing restaurants in the country, Tavern's bright lights shine on, attracting—surprise, surprise— jaded New York natives as well as busloads of out-of-towners. Always fun for a family fete—book in advance and get there on time. Chef Patrick Clark has spruced up the New American menu and changes it seasonally. Portions are generous, and the service, despite the many mouths waiting to be fed, is attentive and friendly. The three-course, pretheater (served 5– 6:30 p.m.), prix fixe dinner, price depending on the entrée chosen, is a very good deal.

TINDO

		QUALITY
Cantonese/Chinese ★★★	Moderate	82
		VALUE
		B

1–3 Eldrige Street (near East Broadway)
966-5684   Zone 3   Chinatown

Customers: Ethnic	Service rating: ★★
Reservations: No	Friendliness rating: ★
When to go: Anytime	Wine selection: Beer only
Entrée range: $4.95–16.95	Dress: Very casual
Payment: Cash only	Disabled access: No

Lunch & Dinner: Thursday–Tuesday, 11:30–3 a.m. Closed Wednesday.

Atmosphere & setting: There's an offbeat charm to this storefront, wedge-shaped, nine-table hole-in-the-wall set so close to the Manhattan Bridge that you can hear the crossing subways rattle. The windows are festooned with blinking Christmas lights and garlands of plastic fruit, and two large drawings share wall space with the daily specials, written in Chinese only. That's the extent of the "decor," but decor is not what this place is about. The upstairs auxiliary dining room (accessible through an unmarked entrance around the corner) seats larger groups but has considerably less charm—though it does sport a picturesque view of subways ascending the Manhattan Bridge.

House specialties: Anything on the little green specials menu, especially boiling-at-your-table hot pots like baby beef and black pepper, baby eggplant with squid and ground pork, and clams in Thailand sauce. Also: steamed oyster in shell in cognac sauce, scrambled egg and shrimp (served atop velvety chow fun noodles), and scallops with black pepper sauce. The salt and pepper squid is probably the best fried calamari in Manhattan, and the fried prawns with homemade mayonnaise and honey walnuts (one of the few banquet-style offerings) are simply awesome. Some dishes (especially noodles and soups) on the regular menu are merely very good; stick with the specials menu or ask the owner (a bespectacled woman who's usually downstairs) for advice.

Other recommendations: Less to the Western palate: salted thousand-year-old egg with dried octopus and minced pork (a real homestyle Hong Kong dish that's not on the English menu; a dead ringer for corned beef hash with fried egg), chives with salt fish, ground pork with salt fish, stuffed goose intestine.

Summary & comments: Although almost everyone in here is Chinese and the service is a bit brusque, you won't feel uncomfortable; Tindo is an

(Tindo)

authentic, nontouristy Chinatown restaurant and the top choice in China-town for home-style Cantonese. Shrimp with scrambled egg—dotted with scallions and served atop tender rice noodles—is the very essence of Cantonese comfort food, and the chef imbues it with love as well as scrumptiousness.

TOMOE				
Japanese/Sushi	★★★½	Mod/Inexp	**QUALITY**	88
172 Thompson Street (between Houston and Bleecker Streets) 777-9346 Zone 4 Greenwich Village			**VALUE**	B

Customers: Ethnic, local
Reservations: Not accepted
When to go: Anytime
Entrée range: $8.50–20
Payment: AMEX only
Service rating: ★★

Friendliness rating: ★★★
Bar: Beer and sake
Wine selection: Stick to sake and beer
Dress: Very casual
Disabled access: No

Lunch: Every day, 1–3 p.m.
Dinner: Tuesday–Sunday, 5–11 p.m.

Atmosphere & setting: The quintessential Village hole-in-the-wall storefront with a few Japanese touches—lantern lights, prints on the wall—and a mini–sushi bar. A dozen plain, worn wooden tables are squeezed so close together that you can easily become part of another party without being invited. The whole small thing could use a bit of a face lift, but that's not what matters here.

House specialties: You can't go wrong with the main events—sushi, sashimi, and maki—the raw fish used here is wonderfully fresh, tender, and succulent.

Other recommendations: Shumai, little boiled dumplings; korokke, a Japanese take on the potato latke.

Summary & comments: No one comes here for the decor or the ambience, but dedicated "sushiphiliacs" come in droves and are willing to line up on the often frigid or sweltering sidewalk for a chance to indulge in very well priced, very well prepared sushi and the like. Lunch is a great way to avoid the crowds, and the "Tomoe lunch special," at $13.50, offers a healthy sample of all the goodies.

TRE POMODORI

Pasta	★★½	Moderate	QUALITY
			85
			VALUE
			A

210 East 34th Street
545-7266   Zone 7 Gramercy Park, Madison Square

Customers: Locals, businessmen
Reservations: Recommended for large
   parties or at peak hours
When to go: Anytime
Entrée range: $6.95–15.95
Payment: Cash only
Service rating: ★★½

Friendliness rating: ★★★½
Bar: Beer and wine
Wine selection: Small; South
   Americans best
Dress: Casual
Disabled access: Fair

Dinner: Monday–Friday, 5–11 p.m.; Saturday and Sunday,
  5 p.m.–midnight

Atmosphere & setting: A very narrow, cozy parlor with tiled floor, framed
pictures dotting the walls, and candles flickering on tables.

House specialties: All pastas, especially linguine vongole (baby clams, oil,
garlic), agnolotti al porcini (ultra-mushroomy pasta pockets), and linguine
fra diavolo (black linguine with calamari and spicy tomato sauce); risotto;
apple tart.

Summary & comments: This is *not* a great restaurant, but it is a useful one.
If you're looking for a low-key place to get surprisingly tasty plates of pasta
at bargain prices without getting gussied up (but you don't feel like a no-frills
hole-in-the-wall either), this is a top choice, particularly when you're in East
Midtown—where restaurants fitting that bill are hard to come by. The waiters will serve fast for those rushing back to work (or out to shows), but lingering is never discouraged. Avoid the spotty appetizers (specials are often
better, and salads are always OK) and pricier entrées and cut straight to what
they cook best: pasta. The linguine with baby clams is a splendid, classic version, very satisfying, and there's a broad range of other choices—18 in all.
Risotto, sometimes a special, is also very good, as are the gratis crunchy
toasts with tomato and basil. Desserts are only fair (best: apple tart). Service
can be slightly confused but is always good-natured.

TROIS JEAN

			QUALITY
French	★★★	Expensive	82

	VALUE
	C

154 East 79th Street (between Lexington and Third Avenues)
   988-4858   Zone 13 Upper East Side

Customers: Local
Reservations: Recommended
When to go: Anytime
Entrée range: $21–29.50; 3-course prix fixe, $39.50; 6-course tasting menu, $55
Payment: All major credit cards
Service rating: ★★

Friendliness rating: ★★★
Bar: Full service
Wine selection: Well-chosen, well-priced, extensive by-the-glass selections
Dress: Casual
Disabled access: Downstairs only

Lunch: Monday–Saturday, noon–2:30 p.m.
Tea: Every day, 2:30–5:30 p.m.
Dinner: Every day, 5:30–10:30 p.m.

Atmosphere & setting: A very Gallic red door proclaims that this is a very Gallic bistro—a few blinks and it's a side street in Paris, not the Upper East Side. Arched windows front the narrow downstairs dining room and its dark wood bar, lit with Mucha-esque lamps. The upstairs area is brighter and lighter, with the requisite lace half-curtains on the high windows. Tables are close together, but that's part of eating in a bistro.

House specialties: Cassoulet "Jean Dumonet"; grilled hangar steak with shallot sauce; foie gras terrine; pan-seared skate; pyramide au chocolat. Menu changes seasonally.

Other recommendations: Roast chicken; grilled yellowfin tuna with aïoli; risotto with black truffles; steak tartare; warm apple tart.

Summary & comments: An easy walk from the Metropolitan Museum, Trois Jean, under chef Jean-Louis Dumonet, provides some of the best bistro food, classic and creative, in New York. A good choice for lunch or high tea; at dinner the crowds collect and the noise level rises as the service level sometimes declines, though recent criticism seems to have rectified that problem. The three-course pretheater—or, better, "postmuseum"—dinner is a winner at $25 (cash only).

UNION SQUARE CAFE

			QUALITY
New American	★★★★	Expensive	**92**

<table>
<tr><td colspan="3"></td><td>VALUE</td></tr>
<tr><td colspan="3"></td><td>B</td></tr>
</table>

21 East 16th Street (between Union Square West and Fifth Ave.)
243-2040   Zone 7 Gramercy Park, Madison Square

Customers: Local, business	**Friendliness rating:** ★★★★
Reservations: Recommended	**Bar:** Full service
When to go: Anytime	**Wine selection:** Excellent, both by the
Entrée range: $18–27	bottle and by the glass
Payment: All major credit cards	**Dress:** Casual, business
Service rating: ★★★★	**Disabled access:** Fair

Lunch: Monday–Saturday, noon–2:30 p.m.
Dinner: Monday–Thursday, 6–10:15 p.m.; Friday and Saturday,
6–11:15 p.m.; Sunday, 5:30–9:45 p.m.

Atmosphere & setting: Airy dining spaces—a few steps down, a small flight up—with creamy beige walls, dark green chair rails, vibrant modern paintings, a mural of many merry maidens ("The Women of USC"), and bright bunches of fresh flowers. The cherry-wood floors and a long, dark wood bar add to the warm, welcoming ambience. All is stylish without trying too hard.

House specialties: Be sure to check the daily specials; hot garlic potato chips; house-smoked Atlantic salmon with spicy bean cake; black bean soup; grilled filet mignon of tuna; flourless chocolate torte with peanut butter and chocolate ganache.

Other recommendations: Sautéed salmon with sorrel crème fraîche; roasted lemon-pepper duck. For lunch: yellowfin tuna burger with creamy cabbage slaw and the USC hamburger; warm banana tart with honey-vanilla ice cream.

Summary & comments: This is one of the most desired dining destinations for New Yorkers, and the raves are well-deserved. Owner Danny Meyer and chef Michael Romano have set the standard for flawless, informed, amiable service and exciting, eclectic, inventive New American cooking. Amazingly, you won't have to mortgage the family home to pay the bill, and you'll have a great meal. If you're rushed or dining alone, you can eat very comfortably at the bar.

VIRGIL'S BARBECUE

Barbecue	★★½	Moderate	QUALITY
			74

			VALUE
			C

152 West 44th Street
921-9494   Zone 8   Theater District

Customers: Businessmen, tourists	Friendliness rating: ★★★½
Reservations: Recommended	Bar: Full
When to go: Anytime	Wine selection: Small
Entrée range: $12–24	Dress: Casual
Payment: VISA, MC, AMEX, DC	Disabled access: No
Service rating: ★★★	

Lunch: Monday, 11:30 a.m.–4:30 p.m.; Tuesday–Thursday,
11:30 a.m.–4:30 p.m.; Sunday, 11:30 a.m.–4:30 p.m.
Dinner: Monday, 4:30–11 p.m.; Tuesday–Thursday, 4:30 p.m.–
midnight; Sunday, 4:30–10 p.m.

Atmosphere & setting: Studied hillbilly, very Disney-esque—you expect
the Country Bear Jamboree to strike up an Animatronic tune at any
moment. Two levels: The top is for serious dining, while the ground level
has tables, booths, and an inviting (and quite popular) long bar.

House specialties: Lamb barbecue sandwich, hamburgers, Brunswick stew,
barbecue salad, hush puppies, onion rings, lemonade, Zap's potato chips.

Other recommendations: The cornbread comes with really good maple
butter; for a transcendent experience, ask your server to bring you some as
a dip for the hushpuppies.

Summary & comments: This restaurant is a great place for families, and
you can't beat the convenient location, but foodwise, it's recommended only
for a few certain things. The menu's unreliable, so rather than hunker down
for an elaborate meal, head to the bar—or one of the informal tables downstairs—and grab a hamburger (redolent of hickory smoke) or lamb barbecue sandwich (very respectable, and much better than the ho-hum brisket
or pulled pork), fabulous oniony hushpuppies (or merely good
garlicky/funky onion rings), maybe a dish of Brunswick stew, and one of the
impressive range of beers (lemonade's top-notch, too). If you don't stray too
far from these tips and don't expect to make a Dining Experience of it all,
you'll leave content—and without having emptied your wallet (this is one
of those restaurants where prices look reasonable on the menu but the bill
comes with smelling salts). Skip the chili and the barbecue plates (as
opposed to sandwiches); forego the ribs and desserts. Don't get fancy. Oh,
and Virgil's bar (a happening nightspot, good for solo or group drinking)
has friendly bartenders and is one of the only places in New York where
you'll find wondrous Zap's potato chips from New Orleans.

VONG			
		QUALITY	
Thai/French	★★★½	Expensive	**87**
		VALUE	
		B	

200 East 54th Street (just east of Third Avenue)
486-9592   Zone 9 Midtown East

Customers: Business, local
Reservations: Recommended
When to go: Anytime
Entrée range: $19–32; pretheater prix fixe dinner, $35; the $25, 3-course prix fixe lunch is a very good deal.

Payment: All major credit cards
Service rating: ★★★
Friendliness rating: ★★★
Bar: Full service
Wine selection: Very good
Dress: Business, upscale casual
Disabled access: Yes

Lunch: Monday–Friday, noon–2:15 p.m.
Dinner: Monday–Thursday, 6–10:45 p.m.; Friday, 5:30–10:45 p.m.; Saturday, 5:30–11:15 p.m.; Sunday, 5:30–9:45 p.m.

Atmosphere & setting: Restaurant designer David Rockwell's sensuous, dreamy take on the saffron-robed splendors of the East is splendid indeed, with gold-leafed, floor-to-ceiling wall montages, burnished metallic ceilings, unique custom lighting, and a red-rubbed wooden wall that undulates from the very inviting Orchid Bar to the main dining room. Sprays of orchids and birds of paradise on each table, a rainbow of raw silk cushions, screens, potted palms, and several semi-enclosed nooks that offer an unusual allotment of Midtown privacy add to the lush Asian ambience.

House specialties: Crab spring roll with tamarind dipping sauce; prawn satay with oyster sauce; crisp squab with egg-noodle pancake; veal chop dusted with spices with kumquat chutney; kiwi tart with "confiture de lait" and lime-yogurt ice cream.

Other recommendations: Scallops and squid in a curry sauce, raw tuna with vegetables wrapped in rice paper; Muscovy duck breast, with a spicy tamarind sauce and duck egg rolls; crispy rice crêpes with raspberries and coconut cream; sticky rice with mango and coconut milk.

Summary & comments: "Vongderful!" is the appropriate accolade for Jean-Georges Vongerichten's fabulous fusion fare. More Thai than French, his constantly changing, inventive menu delights the palate in a palatial setting, from the delicate rice cakes with peanut sauce that arrive at the table before you order to the divinely inspired desserts. This is upscale orientalia all the way, and that includes the elegant presentation, the attentive service, and the price. If a splurge with an Asian accent is what you're looking for, this is it.

WOO CHON

			QUALITY
Korean	★★★	Moderate	**82**
			VALUE
			C

8–10 West 36th Street (between Fifth and Sixth Avenues)
695-0676   Zone 9 Midtown East

Customers: Ethnic, local
Reservations: Accepted
When to go: Anytime
Entrée range: $12.95–59.95 (a huge assortment of beef, intestines, and tongue—in fact, most of a female cow—that can serve quite a few folks)

Payment: All major credit cards
Service rating: ★★★
Friendliness rating: ★★★
Bar: Limited; try the soju (Korean vodka), sake, and beer
Wine selection: Very limited
Dress: Casual
Disabled access: Yes, downstairs

Open: 24 hours

Atmosphere & setting: A bright, two-level space with traditional wooden tables equipped with a barbecue apparatus in the center. The walls, covered with pages from old Korean books, add interest to the simple surroundings.

House specialties: Dumplings, japchae (rice noodles), pajun (seafood and scallion pancake), galbi gui (marinated prime ribs), bulgogi (thin slices of rib eye), sogogi gooksoo jungol (beef with white noodles cooked in a hot pot); assorted bibimbap ryu (veggies, etc., with rice in a stone dish—a favorite of Korean monks).

Other recommendations: Three varieties of kimchee (spicy); jangau gui (broiled eel with special sauce); saewoo gui (shrimp barbecue); dak gui (marinated chicken filet barbecue).

Summary & comments: One of the more accessible of the authentic Korean eateries in town, this one has helpful waitpersons and an extravagant menu filled with color photos to aid the uninitiated. The barbecues broiled at the table and the hot pot dishes cooked at the table are best bets for first-time tasters of this fascinating cuisine. Try some of the appetizers too, but beware—some of the spicy dishes can really burn!

XUNTA

			QUALITY
Spanish/Tapas	★★★	Moderate	87

	VALUE
	B

174 First Avenue
  614-0620   Zone 5   East Village

Customers: Young locals	**Service rating:** ★★½
Reservations: Only for 4 or more	**Friendliness rating:** ★★½
When to go: Before 7 p.m. to avoid	**Bar:** Full
crowds (Tuesdays are also light)	**Wine selection:** Good, Spanish
Entrée range: $5.25–16.25	**Dress:** Nice casual
Payment: VISA, MC, AMEX, D, DC	**Disabled access:** Very poor (3 steps)

Dinner: Sunday–Thursday, 4 p.m.–midnight; Friday and Saturday,
4 p.m.–2 a.m.

Atmosphere & setting: Funky basement with Iberian touches and a young
clientele. This seems more like a hangout than a restaurant; you'd certainly
never expect to find good food here. This small space gets crowded on weekends.

House specialties: Pulpo a feira (octopus with paprika), tortilla española
con cebolla (Spanish potato omelet with onion), lulas rechaeas (stuffed calamari), gazpacho, sardines, gambas ala plancha (grilled shrimp), cheeses,
hard-to-find Galician white wines (Albariños).

Entertainment & amenities: Live flamenco musicians and dancers Mondays and Thursdays at 8:30 p.m. (call to confirm day and time).

Summary & comments: The tapas craze has hit New York in a big way, but
this Galician bar is the only place that makes the Real Stuff. Holy grail tapas
like octopus and potato omelet are closer to true Spanish style than at any
other tapas bar in town. And the Albariños (young, tart white wines) are
sipped the authentic way, out of white ceramic bowls. Items can be ordered
either as small dishes *(tapas)* or larger *raciones*. Bear in mind that genuine
tapas are unpretentious lusty accompaniments to drink, not haute cuisine,
so the rollicking bar scene and crude seating are part and parcel of the experience.

ZEN PALATE

			QUALITY
Vegetarian/Asian	★★½	Inexpensive	78

VALUE
B

2170 Broadway (between 76th and 77th Streets)
   501-7768   Zone 12 Upper West Side

663 Ninth Avenue (Corner of 46th Street)
   582-1669   Zone 8 Midtown West/Theater District

Union Square East (16th Street)
   614-9291   Zone 7 Gramercy Park, Madison Square

Customers: Ethnic, local
Reservations: Not accepted
When to go: Anytime
Entrée range: $7–8; $4–6 for pastas and soups
Payment: All major credit cards
Service rating: ★★★

Friendliness rating: ★★
Wine selection: No liquor license; BYOB
Dress: Casual
Disabled access: Upper West Side, yes; Midtown, yes; Downtown, no

Lunch & Dinner: *Upper West Side,* Sunday–Thursday, noon–10:30 p.m.; Friday and Saturday, noon–11:30 p.m. *Midtown,* daily, 11:30 a.m.–11 p.m. *Downtown,* lunch daily, 11 a.m.–3:30 p.m.; dinner, 5:30–11 p.m.

Atmosphere & setting: This laid-back trio offers pockets of peace, with soft ocher walls, clouds on the ceiling in Midtown, patterned latticework Uptown, and dramatic architecture in the Union Square branch.

House specialties: Vegetable dumplings; spinach linguine salad with sesame peanut dressing; Zen lasagna; eggplant in garlic sauce; tofu honey pie.

Other recommendations: Basil moo-shu rolls; stir-fried fettuccine; Zen ravioli with special sauce; fresh-squeezed vegetable juice.

Summary & comments: An inexpensive oasis for noncarnivores, but you don't have to be a vegetarian to get the good karma and good vibes that come with the more than soul-satisfying cuisine here. The veggie variations are flavorfully inventive, and some are surprising in their intensity. The T-shirts worn by the waiters say "harmony," and somehow there is more in these small spaces than is usually found in Gotham City.

Hotel Information Chart

■ **How to Use This Chart** ■

The following 20 pages contain the information necessary to evaluate the suitability of a given hotel or motel. The chart is ordered alphabetically, with the entry for any specific hotel appearing in the same position on the page for four consecutive pages as follows:

In general the listings are self-explanatory and are designed to allow you to access desired information quickly. For example, does the hotel you are considering have a bar? A quick scan of the "Bar" column will provide the answer. A checkmark is an affirmative. If the hotel you are considering has a checkmark under "Meeting Facilities," then meeting facilities are available. Conversely, a blank space indicates that the feature or service is unavailable.

Star Ratings apply to the quality of a property's standard rooms, as discussed on page 86. The more stars, the better the rooms.

The Rack Rate is how much the hotel charges for a nondiscounted standard guest room. Each dollar sign ($) equals $80. For example, $$$ indicates an average rack rate of $240 per night. The charge may be somewhat less on weekdays and somewhat more on weekends.

The Room Rating gives a numerical value to the quality of the standard guest rooms and allows for a meaningful comparison between hotels with the same Star Rating. Once again, 100 is the best, and 0 is the worst. Room Ratings are explained in detail on page 86.

"On-site Dining" tells you how many restaurants or food-service operations are managed by a particular hotel, and what the culinary specialty of each restaurant is. For example:

③ Italian, Mexican, Steak

means that the hotel offers three nice restaurants: an Italian restaurant, a Mexican restaurant, and a steakhouse.

Under the headings for "Pool/Sauna" and "Exercise Facilities" a checkmark indicates that the service is available. In some instances only some services are available and those services are indicated in the column by name. The word *privileges* means that the hotel has contracted with a local facility to provide these services free of charge to hotel guests.

Hotel	Room Rating	Room Quality	Zone	Street Address
The Algonquin Hotel	★★★★	84	9	59 W. 44th Street New York , NY 10036
Ameritania Hotel	★★★½	82	8	1701 Broadway New York, NY 10019
The Barbizon	★★★★	85	11	140 E. 63rd Street New York, NY 10021
Beekman Tower Hotel	★★★★	86	9	3 Mitchell Place New York, NY 10017
Best Western Seaport Inn	★★★½	79	3	33 Peck Slip New York, NY 10038
The Box Tree	★★★★	88	9	250 E. 49th Street New York, NY 10017
The Carlyle	★★★★★	96	13	35 E. 76th Street New York, NY 10021
Chelsea Savoy	★★★½	77	6	204 W. 23rd Street New York, NY 10011
Crowne Plaza	★★★★	83	8	1605 Broadway New York, NY 10019
Crowne Plaza at the United Nations	★★★★½	93	9	304 E. 42nd Street New York, NY 10017
Crowne Plaza LaGuardia	★★★½	75	17	104-04 Ditmars Boulevard East Elmhurst, NY 11369
Days Hotel New York City	★★★	73	8	790 8th Avenue New York, NY 10019
Doral Court	★★★★½	90	9	130 E. 39th Street New York, NY 10016
Doral Inn	★★★★	85	9	541 Lexington Avenue New York, NY 10022
Doral Park Avenue Hotel	★★★★½	92	9	70 Park Avenue New York, NY 10016
Doral Tuscany	★★★★½	93	9	120 E. 39th Street New York, NY 10016
Doubletree Hotel Guest Suites	★★★★	87	8	1568 Broadway New York, NY 10036
The Drake Swissotel	★★★★½	92	9	440 Park Avenue New York , NY 10022
Essex House Hotel Nikko New York	★★★★★	97	8	160 Central Park South New York, NY 10019

Local Phone	Guest Fax	Toll-Free Res. Line	Discounts Available	No. of Rooms	Rm. Sq. Footage	Rack Rate
(212) 840-6800	(212) 944-1419	(800) 548-0345		165	170	$$$$–
(212) 247-5000	(212) 247-3316	(800) 922-0330	Govt.	206	210	$$$–
(212) 838-5700	(212) 888-4271	(800) 223-1020		300	230	$$$+
(212) 355-7300	(212) 756-9366	(800) 637-8483		172	250	$$$–
(212) 766-6600	(212) 766-6615	(800) HOTEL-NY	AAA, AARP, Govt.	72	240	$$+
(212) 758-8320	(212) 308-3899			13	n/a	$$$$–
(212) 744-1600	(212) 717-4682	(800) 227-5737		192	180	$$$$$+
(212) 929-9353	(212) 741-6309			90	n/a	$$+
(212) 977-4000	(212) 333-7393	(800) 243-NYNY	AAA, AARP, Govt., Mil.	770	320	$$$$–
(212) 986-8800	(212) 986-1758	(800) 879-8836	AAA, AARP	300	248	$$$–
(718) 457-6300	(718) 899-9798	(800) TO-CROWNE	AAA, AARP	358	600	$$+
(212) 581-7000	(212) 974-0291	(800) 325-2525	AAA, AARP, Govt.	367	210	$$+
(212) 685-1100	(212) 889-0287	(800) 223-6725	AAA, AARP, Govt., Mil.	199	235	$$$$–
(212) 755-1200	(212) 421-3876	(800) 223-6725	AAA, AARP, Govt., Mil.	700	180	$$$–
(212) 687-7050	(212) 808-9029	(800) 22-DORAL		188	270	$$$$–
(212) 686-1600	(212) 779-7822	(800) 223-6725	AAA, AARP, Govt., Mil.	121	300	$$$$+
(212) 719-1600	(212) 921-5212	(800) 325-9033	AAA, AARP, Govt.	460	440	$$$+
(212) 421-0900	(212) 371-4190	(800) 372-5369	AAA, Govt.	495	300	$$$$$–
(212) 247-0300	(212) 315-1839	(800) 645-5687	AAA, AARP, Govt.	597	170	$$$$$–

Hotel	Meeting Facilities	Pool/ Sauna	Exercise Facilities	Window Glaze	Parking Per Day	Nearest Subway
The Algonquin Hotel	✓		✓	Dbl	n/a	1 block
Ameritania Hotel	✓		✓	Dbl	$12	3 blocks
The Barbizon		Pool	Privileges	Dbl	$29	1 block
Beekman Tower Hotel	✓	Whirlpool	✓	Tpl and Dbl	$23	5 blocks
Best Western Seaport Inn			Privileges	Dbl	$20	5 blocks
The Box Tree	✓			Sgl	$20	5 blocks
The Carlyle	✓	Sauna, Steam room	✓	Dbl	$39	2 blocks
Chelsea Savoy				Dbl	$16	1 block
Crowne Plaza	✓	Pool, Sauna, Steam room	✓	Dbl	$34	1 block
Crowne Plaza at the United Nations	✓	Whirlpool	✓	Sgl and Tpl	$23	2 blocks
Crowne Plaza LaGuardia	✓	Pool, Sauna, Whirlpool	✓	Tpl	$5	17 blocks
Days Hotel New York City	✓		Privileges	Dbl	$11	2 blocks
Doral Court	✓	Privileges	Privileges	Dbl	n/a	2 blocks
Doral Inn		Sauna	✓	Dbl	n/a	1 block
Doral Park Avenue Hotel		Whirlpool	Privileges	Dbl	$25	3 blocks
Doral Tuscany	✓	Privileges	Privileges	Dbl	n/a	2 blocks
Doubletree Hotel Guest Suites	✓		✓	Dbl	$30	1 block
The Drake Swissotel	✓	Sauna	✓	Dbl	$36	1 block
Essex House Hotel Nikko New York	✓	Sauna, Steam room	✓	Dbl	$35	1 block

* C = Corporate, F = Franchise, I = Independent, P = Proprietary, SC = Small Chain

Bar	On-site Dining	Extra Amenities	Business Amenities	Ownership*
✓	③ Dinner show, Pub fare, Continental	Free breakfast	Dataport	C
✓	① Italian		Dataport	I
	① Breakfast only	CD players in rooms, Hair salon	Dataport, 2 phone lines	I
✓	② American	All-suite property	Dataport, 2 phone lines	SC
		Free breakfast		F
✓	① French Continental	Free breakfast		I
✓	③ Dinner club, American/ French, Tea room	Live piano in lounge, Massages	Dataport, 2 phone lines, Fax machine	I
✓	① Cafe			I
✓	③ Cafe, Italian/ Continental, Continental	Spa	2 phone lines	C
✓	① Bistro		Dataport, 2 phone lines	C
✓	① Continental		Dataport	F
✓	① Deli		Dataport	F
✓	① not available at press time	Excercise equipment in room	Dataport, 2 phone lines	C
✓	① not available at press time		Dataport	C
✓	① New American		Dataport	C
✓	① not available at press time		Dataport, 2 phone lines	C
✓	① American	Children's play room	Dataport, 2 phone lines	C
✓	① American/Eclectic		Dataport, 2 phone lines, Fax machine	C
✓	③ French, Nouveau, American	Spa	Dataport, 2 phone lines, Fax machine	C

Hotel	Room Rating	Room Quality	Zone	Street Address
Fitzpatrick Manhattan Hotel	★★★★	87	9	687 Lexington Avenue New York, NY 10022
Flatotel International	★★★★½	93	9	135 W. 52nd Street New York, NY 10019
Four Seasons Hotel	★★★★★	98	9	57 E. 57th Street New York, NY 10022
The Franklin	★★★★	89	13	164 E. 87th Street New York, NY 10128
The Gorham	★★★★	89	8	136 W. 55th Street New York, NY 10019
Grand Hyatt	★★★★	88	9	150 E. 42nd Street New York, NY 10017
Holiday Inn JFK Airport	★★★½	81	17	144-02 135th Avenue Jamaica, NY 11456
Hotel Beacon	★★★	73	12	2130 Broadway New York, NY 10023
Hotel Bedford	★★★½	77	9	118 E. 40th Street New York , NY 10016
Hotel Casablanca	★★★½	79	8	147 W. 43rd Street New York, NY 10036
Hotel Delmonico	★★★★½	90	9	502 Park Avenue New York, NY 10022
Hotel Elysee	★★★★★	96	9	60 E. 54th Street New York, NY 10022
Hotel Inter-Continental New York	★★★★½	94	9	111 E. 48th Street New York, NY 10017
Hotel Metro	★★★½	78	7	45 W. 35th Street New York, NY 10001
Hotel Plaza Athenee	★★★★½	90	11	37 E. 64th Street New York, NY 10021
Hotel San Carlos	★★★★	86	9	150 E. 50th Street New York, NY 10022
Hotel Wales	★★★★	84	13	1295 Madison Avenue New York, NY 10128
The Inn at Irving Place	★★★★½	93	7	56 Irving Place New York, NY 10003
JFK Airport Hilton	★★★½	75	17	138-10 135th Avenue Jamaica, NY 11436

Local Phone	Guest Fax	Toll-Free Res. Line	Discounts Available	No. of Rooms	Rm. Sq. Footage	Rack Rate
(212) 355-0100	(212) 355-1371	(800) 367-7701	AAA, AARP	92	450	$$$$-
(212) 887-9400	(212) 887-9795	(800) FLATOTEL		168	n/a	$$$$+
(212) 758-5700	(212) 758-5711	(800) 332-3442		370	600	$$$$$$$$-
(212) 369-1000	(212) 369-8000	(800) 600-8787	Govt.	47	150	$$$-
(212) 245-1800	(212) 582-8332	(800) 735-0710		116	360	$$$$$-
(212) 883-1234	(212) 697-3772	(800) 233-1234	AAA, Senior Citizen	1,347	350	$$$$-
(718) 656-6357	(718) 322-2533	(800) 692-5359	AAA, AARP, Govt.	360	320	$$$+
(212) 787-1100	(212) 724-0839	(800) 572-4969	AAA, Govt.	200	320	$$-
(212) 697-4800	(212) 697-1093	(800) 221-6881		136	300	$$
(212) 869-1212	(212) 391-7585	(888) 922-7225		48	270	$$$+
(212) 355-2500	(212) 755-3779	(800) 821-3842	AAA, AARP	150	800	$$+
(212) 753-1066	(212) 980-9278	(800) 535-9733		99	300	$$$+
(212) 755-5900	(212) 644-0079	(800) 327-0200		682	350	$$$$-
(212) 947-2500	(212) 279-1310	(800) 356-3870		174	150	$$+
(212) 734-9100	(212) 753-1468	(800) 447-8800		152	300	$$$+
(212) 755-1800	(212) 688-9778	(800) 722-2012		146	240	$$+
(212) 876-6000	(212) 860-7000	(800) 428-5252	AAA, AARP	86	150	$$$-
(212) 533-4600	(212) 533-4611	(800) 685-1447		12	360	$$$$+
(718) 322-8700	(718) 529-0749	(800) HILTONS	AAA, AARP, Govt.	330	200	$$-

Hotel	Meeting Facilities	Pool/ Sauna	Exercise Facilities	Window Glaze	Parking Per Day	Nearest Subway
Fitzpatrick Manhattan Hotel		Pool, Privileges	Privileges	Dbl	$35	2 blocks
Flatotel International	✓		✓	Dbl	$20	2 blocks
Four Seasons Hotel		Whirlpool	✓	Tpl	$37	4 blocks
The Franklin			Privileges	Dbl	Free	1 block
The Gorham			✓	Dbl	$20	1 block
Grand Hyatt	✓		✓	Dbl	$34	Beneath hotel
Holiday Inn JFK Airport	✓	Pool, Sauna, Whirlpool	✓	Dbl	Free	None
Hotel Beacon	✓			Dbl	$15	3 blocks
Hotel Bedford				Sgl and Dbl	$20	1 block
Hotel Casablanca		Privileges	Privileges	Tpl	$18	One-half block
Hotel Delmonico		Privileges	Privileges	Sgl, Dbl, and Tpl	$29	1 block
Hotel Elysee			Privileges	Dbl	$24	1 block
Hotel Inter-Continental New York	✓	Whirlpool	✓	Dbl	$42	2 blocks
Hotel Metro	✓		✓	Dbl	$20	1 block
Hotel Plaza Athenee	✓		✓	Dbl	$38	7 blocks
Hotel San Carlos				Dbl	$25	3 blocks
Hotel Wales		Privileges	Privileges	Dbl	$28	5 blocks
The Inn at Irving Place	✓		Privileges	n/a	$20	3 blocks
JFK Airport Hilton	✓		✓	Dbl	Free	None

* C = Corporate, F = Franchise, I = Independent, P = Proprietary, SC = Small Chain

Bar	On-site Dining	Extra Amenities	Business Amenities	Ownership*
✓	① Continental	Irish theme	Dataport, Fax machine	C
✓	① Breakfast only	Kitchenettes, Free breakfast		C
✓	① Contemporary American	Spa	2 phone lines	C
		Free breakfast		P
✓	② Breakfast Room, Northern Italian	Whirlpools in suites, Nintendo	Dataport, 2 phone lines, Fax machine	I
✓	③ Continental, Pub fare, American			C
✓	① American	Free airport shuttle		F
	① Coffee shop	Kitchenettes		I
✓	① American/Italian	Kitchenettes, Free breakfast	Dataport	I
✓		Free breakfast	Dataport, 2 phone lines	I
✓	① Lunch only	Kitchenettes	Dataport, Fax machine	I
✓	① Continental	Wine/hors d'oeuvres weeknights, Free breakfast	Dataport	I
✓	① American Grill	Live entertainment in bar	Dataport, 2 phone lines	C
✓	① Tuscan	Free breakfast	Dataport	I
✓	① French		Dataport, 2 phone lines	I
		Free breakfast	Dataport	I
	② American	Harp music in lobby, Free breakfast		C
✓	② Tea room, Pub fare		Dataport, 2 phone lines	P
✓	① American		Dataport	C

Hotel	Room Rating	Room Quality	Zone	Street Address
Jolly Madison Towers Hotel	★★★½	79	9	22 E. 38th Street New York, NY 10016
Kimberly	★★★½	81	9	145 E. 50th Street New York, NY 10022
The Kitano New York	★★★★½	92	9	66 Park Avenue New York, NY 10016
LaGuardia Marriott	★★★½	79	17	102-05 Ditmars Boulevard East Elmhurst, NY 11369
Le Parker Meridien New York	★★★★½	95	8	118 W. 57th Street New York, NY 10019
Loews New York Hotel	★★★	72	9	569 Lexington Avenue New York, NY 10022
The Lombardy	★★★★½	90	9	111 E. 56th Street New York, NY 10022
The Lowell	★★★★★	96	11	28 E. 63rd Street New York, NY 10021-8088
Lyden Gardens	★★★★	88	11	215 E. 64th Street New York, NY 10021
The Mansfield	★★★★½	90	9	12 W. 44th Street New York, NY 10036
The Mark	★★★★★	96	13	Madison Ave. at E. 77th Street New York, NY 10021
The Mayflower Hotel	★★★	68	10	15 Central Park West New York, NY 10023
The Michaelangelo	★★★★½	94	8	152 W. 51st Street New York , NY 10019
The Millennium Hilton	★★★★½	91	1	55 Church Street New York, NY 10007
Millennium Broadway	★★★★½	93	8	145 W. 44th Street New York, NY 10036
Morgans	★★★★½	94	9	237 Madison Avenue New York, NY 10016
Murray Hill East Suites	★★★½	78	9	149 E. 39th Street New York, NY 10016
The New York Hilton and Towers	★★★★½	92	8	1335 6th Avenue New York, NY 10019
New York Marriott East Side	★★★★	83	9	525 Lexington Avenue New York, NY 10017

Local Phone	Guest Fax	Toll-Free Res. Line	Discounts Available	No. of Rooms	Rm. Sq. Footage	Rack Rate
(212) 802-0600	(212) 486-6915	(800) 225-4340	AARP	225	n/a	$$$–
(212) 755-0400	(212) 486-6915	(800) 683-0400	AAA	186	600	$$$+
(212) 885-7000	(212) 885-7100	(800) 548-2666		150	320	$$$$$–
(718) 565-8900	(718) 898-4955	(800) 228-9290	AAA, AARP, Govt., Mil.	436	230	$$$–
(212) 245-5000	(212) 307-1776	(800) 543-4300		698	312	$$$$+
(212) 752-7000	(212) 758-6311	(800) 836-6471	AAA, AARP, Govt.	722	265	$$+
(212) 753-8600	(212) 832-3170	(800) 223-5254		101	470	$$$+
(212) 838-1400	(212) 319-4330	(800) 221-4444		65	350	$$$$$+
(212) 355-1230	(212) 758-7858	(800) ME-SUITE	AAA, AARP, Govt.	74	550	$$$+
(212) 944-6050	(212) 764-4477	(800) 255-5167		123	150	$$$–
(212) 744-4300	(212) 744-2749	(800) 843-6275		180	400	$$$$$+
(212) 265-0060	(212) 265-2026	(800) 223-4164	AAA, AARP	365	150	$$$–
(212) 765-1900	(212) 541-6604	(800) 237-0990		178	325	$$$$–
(212) 693-2001	(212) 571-2316	(800) 835-2220	AAA, AARP	561	500	$$$$+
(212) 768-4400	(212) 768-0847	(800) 622-5569	Govt.	627	150	$$$+
(212) 686-0300	(212) 779-8352	(800) 334-3408		113	240	$$$$–
(212) 661-2100	(212) 818-0724	(800) 248-9999		120	300	$$$–
(212) 586-7000	(212) 315-1374	(800) 445-8667	AAA, AARP	2,041	320	$$$–
(212) 755-4000	(212) 980-6175	(800) 228-9290		643	275	$$$–

Hotel	Meeting Facilities	Pool/ Sauna	Exercise Facilities	Window Glaze	Parking Per Day	Nearest Subway
Jolly Madison Towers Hotel	✓			Dbl	n/a	4 blocks
Kimberly		Privileges	Privileges	Dbl	$23	One-half block
The Kitano New York	✓	Privileges	Privileges	Dbl	$31	4 blocks
LaGuardia Marriott	✓	Pool, Sauna, Whirlpool	✓	Dbl	Free	None
Le Parker Meridien New York	✓	Pool	✓	Dbl	$32	One-half block
Loews New York Hotel	✓	Sauna	✓	Dbl	$30	One-half block
The Lombardy	✓		✓	Dbl	$18	3 blocks
The Lowell			✓	Dbl	$45	2 blocks
Lyden Gardens			Privileges	Dbl	$27	7 blocks
The Mansfield			Privileges	Dbl	n/a	2 blocks
The Mark	✓	Sauna, Steam room	✓	Dbl	$35	3 blocks
The Mayflower Hotel	✓		✓	Dbl	$28	1 block
The Michaelangelo	✓		✓	Dbl	$28	2 blocks
The Millennium Hilton		Pool, Sauna	✓	Tpl	$35	1 block
Millennium Broadway	✓	Steam room	✓	Dbl	$35	2 blocks
Morgans	✓	Whirlpool	✓	Dbl	$32	4 blocks
Murray Hill East Suites	✓		Privileges	Dbl	$20	3 blocks
The New York Hilton and Towers	✓	Sauna	✓	Dbl	$35	3 blocks
New York Marriott East Side	✓		✓	Dbl	$28	3 blocks

* C = Corporate, F = Franchise, I = Independent, P = Proprietary, SC = Small Chain

Bar	On-site Dining	Extra Amenities	Business Amenities	Ownership*
✓	① Italian	Spa	Dataport	C
✓	② Continental, American	Spa privileges	Dataport, 2 phone lines, Fax machine	I
✓	② American, Japanese		Dataport, 2 phone lines, Fax machine	C
✓	① American			C
✓	② American/Continenetal, Pub fare	Jog track, CD players, VCRs, health club	Dataport, 2 phone lines, Fax machine	F
✓	① International		Dataport	C
✓	① French	Kitchens		I
✓	② Tea room, Steakhouse		Dataport, 2 phone lines	I
		Kitchens	Dataport	C
		Free breakfast		I
✓	① French-American		Dataport, 2 phone lines, Fax machine	P
✓	① Continental			I
✓	① Italian	Free breakfast	Dataport, 2 phone lines, Fax machine	I
✓	② New American, American	Live piano in lobby	Dataport, 2 phone lines, Fax machine	C
✓	① Continental		Dataport, 2 phone lines	I
✓	① Japanese-Latino	Free breakfast	Dataport, 2 phone lines	I
		Kitchens		I
✓	② American		Dataport, 2 phone lines	C
✓	① American		Dataport	C

Hotel	Room Rating	Room Quality	Zone	Street Address
New York Marriott Financial Center	★★★★	89	1	85 West Street New York, NY 10006
New York Marriott Marquis	★★★★	88	8	1535 Broadway New York, NY 10036
New York Marriott World Trade Center	★★★★	89	1	3 World Trade Center New York, NY 10048
The New York Palace	★★★★★	96	9	455 Madison Avenue New York, NY 10022
Newark Airport Hilton		78	n/a	1170 Spring Street Elizabeth, NJ 07201
Newark International Airport Marriott	★★★★	83	n/a	Newark International Airport Newark, NJ 07114
Novotel New York	★★★★	87	8	226 W. 52nd Street New York, NY 10019
Omni Berkshire Place	★★★★★	96	9	21 E. 52nd Street New York, NY 10022
Paramount	★★★★½	93	8	235 W. 46th Street New York, NY 10036
The Pierre	★★★★★	96	11	2 E. 61st Street New York, NY 10021
The Plaza	★★★★½	91	9	Fifth Avenue at Central Park South New York, NY 10019
Quality Hotel by Journey's End	★★★½	81	8	3 E. 40th Street New York, NY 10016
Radisson Empire Hotel	★★★★	84	10	44 W. 63rd Street New York, NY 10023
Regal U.N. Plaza	★★★★½	94	9	1 United Nations Plaza New York, NY 10017
The Regency Hotel	★★★★½	95	11	540 Park Avenue New York, NY 10021
Renaissance New York Hotel	★★★★½	91	8	714 Seventh Avenue New York, NY 10036
Rihga Royal Hotel	★★★★½	95	8	151 W. 54th Street New York, NY 10019
Roger Williams	★★★★½	90	9	131 Madison Avenue New York, NY 10016
Roosevelt Hotel	★★★½	78	9	45 E. 45th Street New York, NY 10017

Local Phone	Guest Fax	Toll-Free Res. Line	Discounts Available	No. of Rooms	Rm. Sq. Footage	Rack Rate
(212) 385-4900	(212) 227-8136	(800) 228-9290	AARP	504	380	$$$$+
(212) 398-1900	(212) 704-8930	(800) 228-9290	Govt., Mil.	1,911	570	$$+
(212) 938-9100	(212) 938-1948	(800) 228-9290	AARP	817	380	$$$+
(212) 888-7000	(212) 355-0820	(800) 697-2522		900	320	$$$$$
(908) 351-9557	(908) 351-9557	(800) HILTONS	AAA, AARP	375	400	$$$–
(973) 623-0006	(973) 623-7618	(800) 228-9290	AAA	590	300	$$$–
(212) 315-0100	(212) 765-5369	(800) 221-3185		474	276	$$$–
(212) 753-5800	(212) 355-7646	(800) 843-6664		396	300	$$$$+
(212) 764-5500	(212) 354-5237	(800) 225-7474		601	150	$$$+
(212) 838-8000	(212) 758-1615	(800) 743-7734		202	455	$$$$$$–
(212) 759-3000	(212) 759-3167	(800) 759-3000		805	380	$$$$$$–
(212) 447-1500	(212) 213-0972	(800) 668-4200	AAA, AARP	189	260	$$$–
(212) 265-7400	(212) 245-3382	(800) 333-3333		376	160	$$$–
(212) 758-1234	(212) 702-5051	(800) 233-1234	AAA	427	240	$$$$+
(212) 759-4100	(212) 826-5674	(800) 233-2356		362	220	$$$$–
(212) 765-7676	(212) 765-1962	(800) 628-5222	AAA, AARP	305	340	$$$+
(212) 307-5000	(212) 765-6530	(800) 937-5454		500	460	$$$$$
(212) 448-7000	(212) 448-7007	(888) 448-7788		200	300	$$$$$$–
(212) 661-9600	(212) 885-6161	(800) 223-0888		1,033	200	$$$$–

484 Hotel Information Chart

Hotel	Meeting Facilities	Pool/ Sauna	Exercise Facilities	Window Glaze	Parking Per Day	Nearest Subway
New York Marriott Financial Center	✓	Pool, Sauna	✓	Dbl	$25	2 blocks
New York Marriott Marquis	✓	Sauna, Whirlpool	✓	Dbl	$30	3 blocks
New York Marriott World Trade Center	✓	Pool, Sauna	✓	Dbl	$25	Beneath hotel
The New York Palace	✓		✓	Dbl	$46	2 blocks
Newark Airport Hilton	✓	Pool, Whirlpool	✓	Tpl	Free	None
Newark International Airport Marriott	✓	Pool, Sauna	✓	Tpl	Free	None
Novotel New York	✓			Dbl	$16	1 block
Omni Berkshire Place	✓		✓	Tpl	$32	1 block
Paramount	✓		✓	Dbl	n/a	2 blocks
The Pierre	✓		✓	Dbl	$33	One-half block
The Plaza	✓		✓	Dbl	$35	Beneath hotel
Quality Hotel by Journey's End			Privileges	Dbl	$18	2 blocks
Radisson Empire Hotel	✓		Privileges	Dbl	$25	One-half block
Regal U.N. Plaza	✓	Pool, Sauna, Whirlpool	✓	Dbl	$27	4 blocks
The Regency Hotel	✓	Sauna, Whirlpool	✓	Dbl	$35	2 blocks
Renaissance New York Hotel	✓		✓	Dbl	$29	Beneath hotel
Rihga Royal Hotel		Whirlpool	✓	Dbl	$38	2 blocks
Roger Williams				Sgl	Free	2 blocks
Roosevelt Hotel	✓			Dbl	$20	1 block

* C = Corporate, F = Franchise, I = Independent, P = Proprietary, SC = Small Chain

Bar	On-site Dining	Extra Amenities	Business Amenities	Ownership*
✓	② American, Tavern		Dataport	C
✓	④ Continental, Steakhouse, American, Deli	Hair salon, Barber		C
✓	② American, Continental	Running track, Massages	Dataport, 2 phone lines	C
✓	② Mediterranean, French	Spa services	Dataport, 2 phone lines, Fax machine	I
✓	① American	Free airport shuttle	Dataport	C
✓	② American, Continental	Located inside airport		C
✓	① French	Live music in lobby weeknights		P
✓	① Oriental-Mediterranean	Sundeck	Dataport, 2 phone lines	C
✓	① Continental			I
✓	② Continental, Tea room	Nightly piano music, Hair salon	Dataport, 2 phone lines	C
✓	④ Continental, American, Steak, Seafood	Live music in lobby, Hair salon	2 phone lines	C
	① Breakfast only		Dataport	F
✓	② Steakhouse, American	CD library	Dataport, 2 phone lines	F
✓	① New American	Harpist in lobby	Dataport, 2 phone lines, Fax machine	C
✓	② Lounge, French-American	Hair salon	2 phone lines	I
✓	① American	Live music in lobby	Dataport, 2 phone lines	C
✓	① New American	Live music in lounge	Dataport, 2 phone lines, Fax machine	C
		Free continental breakfast, Free dessert buffet	Dataport, 2 phone lines	C
✓	② American		2 phone lines	I

Hotel	Room Rating	Room Quality	Zone	Street Address
The Royalton	★★★★½	93	9	44 W. 44th Street New York, NY 10036
Sheraton LaGuardia East Hotel	★★★½	82	17	135-20 39th Avenue Flushing, NY 11354
Sheraton Manhattan Hotel	★★★★½	94	8	790 7th Avenue New York, NY 10019
Sheraton New York Hotel and Towers	★★★★	89	8	811 7th Avenue New York, NY 10019
Sheraton Newark	★★★½	81	n/a	128 Frontage Road Newark, NJ 07114
Sheraton Russell Hotel	★★★★½	91	9	45 Park Avenue New York, NY 10016
The Sherry-Netherland	★★★★½	91	9	781 Fifth Avenue New York, NY 10022
The Shoreham	★★★★½	92	9	33 W. 55th Street New York, NY 10019
SoHo Grand	★★★½	84	2	310 W. Broadway New York, NY 10013
The St. Regis	★★★★★	98	9	2 E. 55th Street New York, NY 10022
The Stanhope	★★★★½	94	13	995 5th Avenue New York, NY 10028
Surrey Hotel	★★★★½	94	13	20 E. 76th Street New York, NY 10021
Trump International Hotel and Tower	★★★★★	98	10	1 Central Park West New York, NY 10023
The Waldorf Towers	★★★★★	97	9	100 E. 50th Street New York, NY 10022
The Waldorf-Astoria	★★★★½	95	9	301 Park Avenue New York, NY 10022
The Warwick Hotel	★★★★	87	8	65 W. 54th Street New York, NY 10019
Washington Square Hotel	★★★½	78	4	103 Waverly Place New York, NY 10011
Westin Central Park South	★★★★★	96	8	112 Central Park South New York, NY 10019
The Wyndham	★★★½	79	9	42 W. 58th Street New York, NY 10019

Local Phone	Guest Fax	Toll-Free Res. Line	Discounts Available	No. of Rooms	Rm. Sq. Footage	Rack Rate
(212) 869-4400	(212) 869-8965	(800) 635-9013		168	250	$$$$+
(718) 460-6666	(718) 445-2655	(800) 325-3535		173	360	$$$–
(212) 581-3300	(212) 841-6730	(800) 325-3535	AAA, AARP, Govt.	650	180	$$$+
(212) 581-1000	(212) 841-6730	(800) 325-3535	AAA, AARP, Govt.	1,750	180	$$$$–
(973) 690-5500	(973) 690-5076	(800) 325-3535	AAA, AARP, Govt.	502	340	$$+
(212) 685-7676	(212) 889-3193	(800) 325-3535	Govt.	150	230	$$$$–
(212) 355-2800	(212) 319-4306	(800) 247-4377		120	375	$$$$–
(212) 247-6700	(212) 765-9741	(800) 553-3347	AAA, AARP, Govt.	84	250	$$$+
(212) 965-3000	(212) 965-3200	(800) 965-3000		367	275	$$$$$–
(212) 753-4500	(212) 541-4736	(800) 759-7550	AAA, AARP	313	425	$$$$$$$–
(212) 288-5800	(212) 517-0088	(800) 828-1123		157	400	$$$$$–
(212) 288-3700	(212) 628-1549	(800) 637-8483	AAA, AARP	130	320	$$$$–
(212) 299-1000	(212) 299-1058	(888) 44-TRUMP		168	800	$$$$$$$$–
(212) 355-3100	(212) 872-4799	(800) 925-3673		242	n/a	$$$$$$–
(212) 355-3000	(212) 872-7272	(800) WALDORF		1,138	n/a	$$$$$–
(212) 247-2700	(212) 957-8915	(800) 223-4099	AAA, Govt.	422	240	$$$+
(212) 777-9515	(212) 979-8373	(800) 222-0418		180	120	$$–
(212) 757-1900	(212) 757-9620	(800) 937-8461		208	310	$$$$$+
(212) 753-3500	(212) 754-5638	(800) 257-1111		204	180	$$–

Hotel	Meeting Facilities	Pool/ Sauna	Exercise Facilities	Window Glaze	Parking Per Day	Nearest Subway
The Royalton			✓	Dbl	$30	4 blocks
Sheraton LaGuardia East Hotel	✓		✓	Dbl	$7	1 block
Sheraton Manhattan Hotel	✓	Pool, Sauna	✓	Dbl	$25	2 blocks
Sheraton New York Hotel and Towers	✓	Privileges	✓	Sgl	$30	Beneath hotel
Sheraton Newark	✓	Pool	✓	Dbl	$10	None
Sheraton Russell Hotel	✓	Privileges	Privileges	Dbl	$25	5 blocks
The Sherry-Netherland			✓	Dbl	$40	1 block
The Shoreham		Privileges	Privileges	Sgl	$18	1 block
SoHo Grand	✓		✓	Tpl	$25	1 block
The St. Regis	✓	Pool privileges, Sauna, Steam room	✓	Dbl	$38	2 blocks
The Stanhope	✓	Sauna	✓	Dbl	$35	7 blocks
Surrey Hotel	✓		✓	Dbl	$35	4 blocks
Trump International Hotel and Tower		Pool, Sauna, Steam room	✓	Dbl	$45	One-half block
The Waldorf Towers	✓	Whirlpool	✓	Dbl	$37	7 blocks
The Waldorf-Astoria	✓	Whirlpool	✓	Dbl	$37	1 block
The Warwick Hotel	✓		✓	Dbl	$26	2 blocks
Washington Square Hotel	✓		✓	Sgl	n/a	1 block
Westin Central Park South	✓	Sauna	✓	Dbl	$35	2 blocks
The Wyndham				Dbl	n/a	1 block

* C = Corporate, F = Franchise, I = Independent, P = Proprietary, SC = Small Chain

Bar	On-site Dining	Extra Amenities	Business Amenities	Ownership*
✓	① American		Dataport, 2 phone lines	I
✓	① American/Chinese	Shopping arcade	Dataport, 2 phone lines	C
✓	① Bistro	Convention center	Dataport, 2 phone lines, Fax machine	C
✓	② Cafe, American	Convention center		C
✓	② Steakhouse, American			C
✓	① American		Dataport, 2 phone lines, Fax & Printer	C
✓	① Italian		Dataport, 2 phone lines, Fax machine	I
✓	① French	Free breakfast & dessert buffets	Dataport	I
✓	① New England	Goldfish in room by request	Dataport, 2 phone lines	I
✓	② American, French	Live piano and harp in salon	Dataport, 2 phone lines	C
✓	① French Provincial			I
✓	① French	Kitchens	Dataport, 2 phone lines	C
✓	① French	All-Suite property, Kitchens	Dataport, 2 phone lines, Fax machine	I
✓	③ French, American, Japanese	Spa	Dataport, 2 phone lines, Fax machine	C
✓	③ French, American, Japanese	Cocktail terrace with live pianist, Hair salon	Dataport, 2 phone lines, Fax machine	C
✓	① Italian Cafe		2 phone lines	I
✓	① American			I
✓	① International		Dataport, 2 phone lines	C
				F

INDEX

1998 *Unofficial Guide* **Reader Survey**

If you would like to express your opinion about New York or this guide-book, complete the following survey and mail it to:

> 1998 *Unofficial Guide* Reader Survey
> PO Box 43059
> Birmingham AL 35243

Inclusive dates of your visit: _____

Members of your party:

	Person 1	Person 2	Person 3	Person 4	Person 5
Gender:	M F	M F	M F	M F	M F
Age:					

How many times have you been to New York? _____
On your most recent trip, where did you stay? _____

Concerning your accommodations, on a scale of 100 as best and 0 as worst, how would you rate:

The quality of your room?	_____	The value of your room?	_____
The quietness of your room?	_____	Check-in/check-out efficiency?	_____
Shuttle service to the parks?	_____	Swimming pool facilities?	_____

Did you rent a car? _____ From whom? _____

Concerning your rental car, on a scale of 100 as best and 0 as worst, how would you rate:

Pick-up processing efficiency?	_____	Return processing efficiency?	_____
Condition of the car?	_____	Cleanliness of the car?	_____
Airport shuttle efficiency?	_____		

Concerning your dining experiences:

Including fast-food, estimate your meals in restaurants per day? _____
Approximately how much did your party spend on meals per day? _____
Favorite restaurants in New York: _____

_____

Did you buy this guide before leaving? ☐   while on your trip? ☐

How did you hear about this guide? (check all that apply)

Loaned or recommended by a friend ☐   Radio or TV ☐
Newspaper or magazine ☐   Bookstore salesperson ☐
Just picked it out on my own ☐   Library ☐
Internet ☐

What other guidebooks did you use on this trip? _____

_____

_____

On a scale of 100 as best and 0 as worst, how would you rate them?

_____

_____

Using the same scale, how would you rate *The Unofficial Guide(s)?*

_____

Are *Unofficial Guides* readily available at bookstores in your area? _____

Have you used other *Unofficial Guides?* _____

Which one(s)? _____

_____

_____

_____

_____

Comments about your New York trip or *The Unofficial Guide(s):*

_____

_____

_____

_____

_____

_____

_____

_____

_____

_____

_____

_____